Lecture Notes in Computer Science 2908

Edited by G. Goos, J. Hartmanis, and J. van Leeuwen

Springer
Berlin
Heidelberg
New York
Hong Kong
London
Milan
Paris
Tokyo

Kijoon Chae   Moti Yung (Eds.)

Information Security Applications

4th International Workshop, WISA 2003
Jeju Island, Korea, August 25-27, 2003
Revised Papers

 Springer

Series Editors

Gerhard Goos, Karlsruhe University, Germany
Juris Hartmanis, Cornell University, NY, USA
Jan van Leeuwen, Utrecht University, The Netherlands

Volume Editors

Kijoon Chae
Ewha Womans University, Department of Computer Science and Engineering
11-1, Daehyun-Dong, Seodaemun-Gu, Seoul 120-750, Korea
E-mail: kjchae@ewha.ac.kr

Moti Yung
Columbia University, Department of Computer Science
New York, NY 10027-7003, USA
E-mail: moti@cs.columbia.edu

Cataloging-in-Publication Data applied for

A catalog record for this book is available from the Library of Congress.

Bibliographic information published by Die Deutsche Bibliothek
Die Deutsche Bibliothek lists this publication in the Deutsche Nationalbibliografie;
detailed bibliographic data is available in the Internet at <http://dnb.ddb.de>.

CR Subject Classification (1998): E.3, D.4.6, F.2.1, C.2, J.1, C.3, K.6.5

ISSN 0302-9743
ISBN 3-540-20827-5 Springer-Verlag Berlin Heidelberg New York

Springer-Verlag is a part of Springer Science+Business Media

springeronline.com

© Springer-Verlag Berlin Heidelberg 2004
Printed in Germany

Typesetting: Camera-ready by author, data conversion by PTP-Berlin, Protago-TeX-Production GmbH
Printed on acid-free paper   SPIN: 10981382   06/3142   5 4 3 2 1 0

Preface

The 4th Workshop on Information Security Applications (WISA 2003) was sponsored by the following Korean organizations and government bodies: the Korea Institute of Information Security and Cryptology (KIISC), the Electronics and Telecommunications Research Institute (ETRI), and the Ministry of Information and Communication (MIC). The workshop was held in Jeju Island, Korea during August 25–27, 2003. This international workshop provided ample technical sessions covering a large spectrum of information security applications. Subjects covered included network/mobile security, electronic commerce security, digital rights management, intrusion detection, secure systems and applications, biometrics and human interfaces, public key cryptography, and applied cryptography.

The program committee received 200 papers from 23 countries (representing most geographic areas where security and applied cryptography research is conducted throughout the world). Each submitted paper was peer-reviewed by three program committee members. This year, we had two tracks: long and short presentation tracks. We selected 36 papers for the long presentation track and 34 papers for the short presentation tracks. This volume contains revised versions of papers accepted for the long presentation track. We would like to note that getting accepted to both tracks was an achievement to be proud of, given the competitive nature of WISA this year. Papers in the short presentation track were only published in the WISA preproceedings as preliminary notes; extended versions of these notes may be published by future conferences or workshops.

Many people worked very hard to produce a successful WISA 2003 workshop and its technical program. We are grateful to the organizing committee, the steering committee and the workshop general chairs for their support. We thank Springer-Verlag editors for their careful scrutiny and guidance in preparing the workshop proceedings. We are extremely thankful to the program committee members for spending their time on and devoting their efforts to reviewing the submitted papers and selecting the technical program. We also acknowledge the help of the external reviewers: Ahto Buldas and Markku-Juhani Saarinenl. We note that the program committee had members from numerous areas of research relevant to the workshop's subject and from many geographic areas, a fact that assured the breadth and the international nature of WISA. Finally, we would like to express our sincere thanks to all the authors of all the submitted papers, without whom this workshop would not have been possible.

October 2003

Kijoon Chae
Moti Yung

Organization

Advisory Committee

Man Young Rhee, Seoul National Univ., Korea
Hideki Imai, Tokyo Univ., Japan
Bart Preneel, Katholieke Universiteit Leuven, Belgium
Thomas A. Berson, Anagram Laboratories, USA
Gil Rok Oh, ETRI, Korea

General Co-chairs

Sehun Kim, KAIST, Korea
Chee Hang Park, ETRI, Korea

Steering Committee

Kil-Hyun Nam, Korea National Defense Univ., Korea
Sang Jae Moon, Kyungpook National Univ., Korea
Dong Ho Won, Sungkyunkwan Univ., Korea
Hyun Sook Cho, ETRI, Korea
Sung Won Sohn, ETRI, Korea

Organization Committee Chair

Jae Kwang Lee, Hannam Univ., Korea

Organization Committee

Finance	Kyo Il Chung, ETRI, Korea
	Hong Geun Kim, Korea Information Security Agency, Korea
Publication	Gwangsoo Rhee, Sookmyung Women's Univ., Korea
	Ji Young Lim, Korean Bible Univ., Korea
Publicity	Hyung Woo Lee, Hanshin Univ., Korea
	Dong Chun Lee, Howon Univ., Korea
Registration	Jae Cheol Ha, Korea Nazarene Univ., Korea
Treasurer	Jae Hoon Nah, ETRI, Korea
Local Arrangements	Byoung Joon Min, Incheon Univ., Korea
	Wang-Cheol Song, Cheju National Univ., Korea

Program Co-chairs

Kijoon Chae, Ewha Womans Univ., Korea
Moti Yung, Columbia Univ., USA

Program Committee

William Arbaugh, Univ. of Maryland, USA
Feng Bao, Institute for Infocomm Research, Singapore
Chin-Chen Chang, National Chungcheng Univ., Taiwan
Jean Sebastien Coron, Gemplus, France
Ed Dawson, QUT, Australia
Carl Ellison, Intel, USA
Marc Fischlin, Fraunhofer Gesellschaft SIT, Germany
Pierre-Alain Fouque, DCSSI, France
James Hughes, StorageTek, USA
Jong Soo Jang, ETRI, Korea
Aggelos Kiayias, Univ. of Connecticut, USA
Kwangjo Kim, ICU, Korea
Seungjoo Kim, KISA, Korea
Yongdae Kim, Univ. of Minnesota, USA
Kazukuni Kobara, Tokyo Univ., Japan
Pil Joong Lee, POSTECH, Korea
Dongdai Lin, SKLOIS, China
Helger Lipmaa, Helsinki Univ. of Technology, Finland
Fabian Monrose, Johns Hopkins Univ., USA
Shiho Moriai, Sony Computer Entertainment, Japan
Giuseppe Persiano, Univ. of Salerno, Italy
Bart Preneel, Katholieke Universiteit Leuven, Belgium
Pankaj Rohatgi, IBM, USA
Jae-Cheol Ryou, Chungnam National Univ., Korea
Kouichi Sakurai, Kyushu Univ., Japan
Tomas Sander, HP, USA
Serge Vaudenay, Federal Institute of Technology, Switzerland
Sung-Ming Yen, National Central Univ., Taiwan
Okyeon Yi, Kookmin Univ., Korea

Table of Contents

Network Security

Mobile Security

Intrusion Detection

Internet Security

Secure Software, Hardware, and Systems I

Secure Software, Hardware, and Systems II

E-commerce Security

Digital Rights Management

Biometrics and Human Interfaces I

Biometrics and Human Interfaces II

Public Key Cryptography / Key Management

Applied Cryptography

Model Checking of Security Protocols with Pre-configuration

Kyoil Kim[1], Jacob A. Abraham[1], and Jayanta Bhadra[2]

[1] Computer Engineering Research Center,
The University of Texas at Austin
{kikim,jaa}@cerc.utexas.edu
[2] Motorola Inc.
jayanta.bhadra@motorola.com

Abstract. Security protocols are very vulnerable to design errors. Thus many techniques have been proposed for validating the correctness of security protocols. Among these, general model checking is one of the preferred methods. Using tools such as Murφ, model checking can be performed automatically. Thus protocol designers can use it even if they are not proficient in formal techniques. Although this is an attractive approach, state space explosion prohibits model checkers from validating secure protocols with a significant number of communicating participants. In this paper, we propose *"model checking with pre-configuration"* which is a "divide-and-conquer" approach that reduces the amount of memory needed for verification. The verification time is also reduced since the method permits the use of symmetry more effectively in model checking. The performance of the method is shown by checking the Needham-Schroeder-Lowe Public-Key protocol using Murφ.

1 Introduction

1.1 Security Protocols and an Intruder

With the growing role of e-commerce in commercial transactions, the role of security (authentication) protocols has become more important. Ironically, security protocols are very prone to errors and are very vulnerable to attacks [1]. It is, therefore, important to develop methods for ensuring that security protocols have minimal vulnerabilities.

The most famous example of flaws in authentication protocols is the *Needham-Schroeder Public-Key Protocol* (NSPKP) [2]. The simple version of NSPKP is described below.

1. $A \to B : \{N_a A\}_{K_b}$
2. $B \to A : \{N_a N_b\}_{K_a}$
3. $A \to B : \{N_b\}_{K_b}$

K. Chae and M. Yung (Eds.): WISA 2003, LNCS 2908, pp. 1–15, 2004.

where N_a and N_b are nonces - generally, random numbers - and K_a and K_b are A's and B's public keys respectively. Each line of the above description has the following format.

$$MsgSer \quad SndID \rightarrow RcvID : Message$$

where $MsgSer$ is the serial number of the message, $SndID$ is the sender's name and $RcvID$ is the receiver's name. Figure 1 shows an exchange of messages using

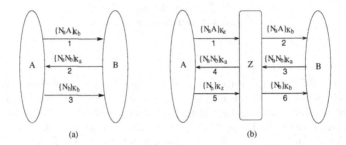

Fig. 1. (a) Message exchanges in NSPKP (b) The attack scenario

NSPKP and a possible attack scenario. The number under each arrow represents the order of the message. It is generally assumed that an intruder controls the communication network and thus is able of intercepting, blocking and generating a message using its own knowledge [3,4,5,6,7]. Therefore, an intruder, Z, can break this protocol using two of its transactions (one with A and the other with B) as described in figure 1(b). In this scenario, B believes it is communicating with A while A does not have the corresponding protocol run. Thus, we can say the NSPKP lacks the property of authentication correctness.

1.2   Protocol Validation by Model Checking and Its Limitation

Since Lowe found the flaw in NSPKP using the FDR (Failures Divergence Refinement) [3], many general model checkers such as Murφ [5] have been used successfully for the validation of security protocols. Model checking is considered one of the preferred methods by protocol designers because of the potential for full automation. However, general model checking suffers from the state space explosion problem in which the state space grows exponentially with the number of protocol sessions.

There are several papers aimed at reducing the size of the state space for validation of security protocols [6,7]. Symmetry properties and partial order reductions are generally used for reducing the state space. These techniques successfully reduced the size of the state space to some extent, but it still remains that the size of the state space increases exponentially with the number of protocol sessions.

Proposed in this paper is *"model checking with pre-configuration"* which is an effective divide-and-conquer method for the verification of security protocols using general model checkers. This method not only reduces the amount of memory required by the model checkers but it also reduces the CPU time. Murφ is used to show the performance of this method.

2 Protocols as State Graphs in Model Checking

2.1 Principals and Instances

A *principal* is an entity who communicates with other principals via a security protocol and what is authenticated via a security protocol is the identity of the principals. *Principal names* are used in protocol messages for referring to the principals. For NSPKP in section 1.1, A and B are the names of the principals. There are two kinds of principals. One kind is the honest principals who always obey the rules of the protocol while communicating. The set of all honest principal names is **P**. The other kind of principal is the intruder, who is assumed to have full control of the communication network.

A principal may execute the protocol many times to communicate with other principals. In this model, an honest principal instantiates an *instance* of a proper role (i.e. initiator, responder, etc) for each protocol run. Thus, each honest instance has only one protocol run. In model checking, a determination is needed of the number of honest instances allowed for each role to bound the space for the verification. We use positive integers as instance names for convenience and 0 (zero) is reserved for the intruder's instance. The set of all honest instance names is **I**. So, each instance has two names - the *instance name* for identifying the instance from other instances and the *principal name* for the authentication identity in communication using a security protocol.

2.2 States

The global state of the system is represented by a vector:

$$S = [s_1, s_2, ..., s_N, z]$$

where N is the total number of honest instances, s_i is the local state of an honest instance i, and z is the state of the intruder. When we say just "state," it means the global state.

The local state of i is determined by the vector of current values of i's local state variables which include the serial number of the next message to be received and protocol variables. The local state of an initiator instance i of NSPKP is represented as follows.

$$s_i = [number_i, name_i, partner_i, partner\_nonce_i]$$

where $number_i$, $name_i$, $partner_i$ and $partner\_nonce_i$ are respectively the next message number, i's principal name, the partner's principal name and the partner's nonce. The instance i's nonce is considered as a constant and is omitted since each instance runs the protocol only once. Responder instances have the same form of local states, too.

The state of the intruder is the set of messages that the intruder has intercepted so far including its initial knowledge. The initial knowledge of the intruder includes his private key, his shared keys with other principals and the names and the public keys of principals.

2.3   Effective States and Protocol Invariants

An *active* instance is an instance which has already started the communication using the protocol. *Inactive* instances are before sending or receiving the first message of the protocol. Instances don't have to have even a principal name as long as they are inactive. We think the value of the principal name is *null* before the instance has a specific principal name assigned. So, we add *null* to **P**.

Protocol invariants are logic expressions which are evaluated in each state for checking if the desired properties are satisfied. The logic values of protocol invariants are determined by the states of active instances and the intruder. It is because inactive instances are not actually involved in the communication in that state. In other words, the values of protocol invariants are determined by the effective state that is defined as follows.

$$E = [e_1, e_2, ..., e_N, z]$$

where e_i is same to s_i if the instance i is active. Otherwise, e_i is *null*. N and z are same to those in the definition of the state S. The effective state of the state S_l is noted by E_l.

2.4   State Graph

The finite state machine associated with the protocol is described as a direct graph $\mathbf{G} = \{\mathbf{S}, \mathbf{T}, S_0, \mathbf{Q}\}$ in [7]. $\mathbf{S}$ is the set of all the vertices in the graph which represent all possible states of the protocol. $\mathbf{T}$ is the set of all the directed edges in the graph which represent binary relations on pairs of states labeled by transition rules. A transition rule is triggered by a message event which is explained in the section 2.5. $S_0 \in \mathbf{S}$ is the start state of the protocol. $\mathbf{Q}$ is the set of protocol invariants.

2.5   Message Event

A message event *me* is represented by a vector:

$$me = [sn, rn, m]$$

where sn and rn represent the sender's and the receiver's instance names respectively, and m is the message that is sent to the receiver from the sender. $\mathbf{M}$ is the set of all message events.

There are two kinds of messages. *Regular messages* are generated by instances according to the protocol. If m is a regular message, the message event is called a regular message event and noted by re. *Special messages*, which are sent to honest instances from the verification system, are used for modifying the configuration, which is explained in section 3. A special message event se is the message event whose m is a special message.

In a message event, either of the sender or the receiver of a message is an honest instance. For the regular messages, if an honest instance is the sender, the intruder must be the receiver because our intruder always intercepts [7]. Reversely, the receiver must be an honest instance when the intruder is sending a message because the intruder sends messages always to honest instances. For special messages, it is obvious that the receivers are always honest instances. A function $Honest(\cdot)$ is defined as follows:

- "$Honest : \mathbf{M} \to \mathbf{I}$" is a function which takes a message event me as its argument and returns the name of the honest instance of me.

2.6   Special Message and Virtual State

Since there may be multiple possible transition rules triggered in a state, the system is nondeterministic. Traditional model checking generally traverses all possible transitions from a state in "*single run*" of a model checker. However in our method, since we want to traverse just a part of the possible transitions from a state in single run, we need some control on transitions to restrict them. The concept of special messages is a model of this control to explain our method in the frame of the state graph. Since special messages are not actual messages and a special message event se does not change any local state, there is no change of the state. This contradicts the model of our system where a message event causes a transition to a new state. To solve this problem, we introduce the concept of *virtual states*.

A virtual state $S_{l'}$ of a state S_l is a state whose local states and the intruder state are same to those of S_l, but is differently indexed by adding the prime symbol to the index of S_l. Thus, model checkers do not need to evaluate the protocol invariants over virtual states.

2.7   Transition

For the simplicity's sake, we use '*transition*' rather than '*transition rule*.' A *transition* consists of a pair of states and a message event which triggers the transition between the two states. ($S_l \xrightarrow{me} S_m$) represents a transition from S_l to S_m as a message event me occurs in S_l. $\mathbf{M}_l$ is the set of all possible message events in a state S_l.

2.8   Concatenated Transitions

The set of all concatenated transitions $\mathbf{CT}$ of a state graph $\mathbf{G} = \{\mathbf{S}, \mathbf{T}, S_0, \mathbf{Q}\}$ is defined as follows.

- For $t_l \in \mathbf{T}$, $t_l \in \mathbf{CT}$
- For $ct_l, ct_m \in \mathbf{CT}$, if the last state of ct_l and the first state of ct_m are same, ct_l and ct_m can be concatenated by sharing the same state. The concatenation of ct_l and ct_m is noted by $ct_l \cdot ct_m$ and $ct_l \cdot ct_m \in \mathbf{CT}$.
- $ct_l \cdot ct_m$ is represented by $(S_l \xrightarrow{me_l} S_m \xrightarrow{me_n} S_n)$ when $ct_l = (S_l \xrightarrow{me_l} S_m)$ and $ct_m = (S_m \xrightarrow{me_n} S_n)$.

2.9 Trace and History

A *trace* is a concatenated transition which has the start state S_0 as the first state. $trace = (S_0 \xrightarrow{me_1} S_1 \xrightarrow{me_2} ... \xrightarrow{me_n} S_n)$ denotes a trace from S_0 to S_n. On a trace, we name the states with subscripts of serial numbers from the start state to the last state.

The *message history* of a concatenated transition ct_l is the list of all regular message events in ct_l in the same order as they appear in ct_l. For example, the message history of ct_1 is (re_1, re_2) when $ct_1 = (S_1 \xrightarrow{re_1} S_2 \xrightarrow{se_1} S_3 \xrightarrow{re_2} S_4)$. The message history of a trace gives an attack scenario when any invariant is evaluated as false in the last state of the trace.

3 Configuration

Configuration is introduced for explaining our method in which some of the state variables are allowed to have only the pre-determined values on a trace. That is, for variables whose values are assigned in the configuration, messages must have the same values to those in configuration. However, we restrict the state variables of the configuration to the principal names in this section for a clear and simple explanation. Configurations including other variables are explained in section 4.2.

3.1 Definition

The *configuration* of a state is used to pre-determine the values of some or all state variables and restrict the future transitions which occur after that state. So, the configuration is a guide for transitions. In this section, the configuration is assumed to have only principal names as its components. *Configuration* of principal names is represented by a vector:

$$C = [c_1, c_2, ..., c_N]$$

where N is the total number of instances and c_i is the principal name of instance i. $\mathbf{C}$ denotes the set of all possible configurations.

In the start state S_0, the configuration is a vector of all *nulls*. A special message is sent to the corresponding honest instance whenever it is needed to pre-determine the principal name of the instance. When an honest instance receives a special message in a state S_l, the state is changed to $S_{l'}$, a virtual state of

S_l as explained in section 2.6. When the state is S_l and i receives the special message that pre-assigns i's principal name as A, the value of c_i, which is *null* in the configuration of S_l, must be changed to A, i.e. the c_i in the configuration of $S_{l'}$ is A. Figure 2 shows this situation. The state $S_{l'}$ is circled with a dotted line to show that it is a virtual state. After any c_i has changed to some principal name from *null*, it can not change its value again on the trace. It is because each instance runs the protocol only once on a trace. When all c_is are assigned

Fig. 2. State transition due to a special message event

non-null values, we call it a *complete configuration*. In this paper, C_i denotes the configuration of the state S_i.

3.2 Properties of Configuration

A function $Name(\cdot)$ is defined as:

- "*Name* : $\mathbf{I} \times \mathbf{C} \to \mathbf{P}$" is a function which takes an honest instance i and a configuration C as its arguments and returns the *i-th* element of C (i.e. the principal name of i).

A binary relation $\triangleright$ between two different configurations C_m and C_n is defined as:

- $C_m \triangleright C_n$ means that $Name(i, C_n) = Name(i, C_m)$ if $Name(i, C_m) \neq null$.

Then, we can easily derive following properties.

Property 1. If $C_l \triangleright C_m$ and $C_m \triangleright C_n$, $C_l \triangleright C_n$.

Property 2. For a trace $(S_0 \xrightarrow{me_0} S_1 \xrightarrow{me_1} ... \xrightarrow{me_{(n-1)}} S_n)$, $C_k \triangleright C_n$ for $0 \leq k \leq n$.

3.3 Pre-configuration and In-Configuration

In model checking with *pre-configuration*, each instance receives a special message in S_0. As a result, the configuration becomes complete before starting the actual communication. On a trace, after making the configuration complete, there is no more special message and the configurations of all the states are identical. *In-configuration* is another strategy in which a special message is sent to each instance just before the instance sends or receives the first message of the protocol.

Figure 3 shows the two methods. Assume that (1) there are two honest instances 1 and 2, (2) in S_j, the instance 1 is about to send a message to the instance 2, and (3) the instance 2 may have either A or B as his principal name and there are two possible choices of $\{N_1\}_{K_a}$ and $\{N_1\}_{K_b}$ for the message. In the figure, (a) shows the original state graph of general model checking in this situation. We just display only the messages on the transition edges for simplicity. (b) shows the same situation with in-configuration. First, c_2 is assigned a proper principal name, so we have two virtual states, $S_{j'1}$ and $S_{j'2}$, in the state graph. Note that the state graph of in-configuration just adds virtual states maintaining the states and the structure of the original state graph. For pre-configuration, we give just one case of the traces, where c_2 is assigned B. Since c_2 is assigned B, we have only one possible transition with $\{N_1\}_{K_b}$ from S_j.

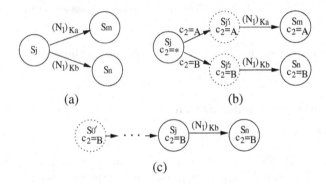

(a)   (b)

(c)

Fig. 3. (a)Original State Graph (b)In-configuration (c)Pre-configuration

In this paper, we call model checking with pre-configuration "pre-configuration" and use "in-configuration" for that with in-configuration for the sake of simplicity if there is no confusion. $\mathbf{G}^{pre}$ and $\mathbf{G}^{in}$ represents the state graphs of the pre-configuration and the in-configuration respectively. Any state, transition or trace with a superscript of 'pre' or 'in' is in $\mathbf{G}^{pre}$ or $\mathbf{G}^{in}$ respectively.

3.4 Equivalence

Two concatenated transitions ct_a and ct_b are *equivalent*, $ct_a \equiv ct_b$, if and only if the evaluations of invariants over ct_a and ct_b give the same result, and the message histories of ct_a and ct_b are same to each other.

For example, two transitions $t_l^{pre} = (S_l \xrightarrow{me} S_{l+1})$ and $t_m^{in} = (S_m \xrightarrow{me'} S_{m+1})$ are equivalent if $E_l = E_m$ and $me = me'$. Since $E_l = E_m$ and $me = me'$, $E_{l+1} = E_{m+1}$. Thus, two transitions generate the same verification result because the effective state determines the values of the invariants and the message histories of t_l^{pre} and t_m^{in} are same to each other as me.

Lemma 1. *For all $me \in M_l$, if i is active in S_l and $E_l = E_m$, then $me \in M_m$ where $i = Honest(me)$.*

Proof. Since i is active, me is determined by s_i and z. Both of s_i and z are included in the effective state. So, if $E_l = E_m$, then $me \in M_m$.   ∎

Lemma 2. *For $me \in M_l$, if i is inactive in S_l, $E_l = E_m$ and $Name(i, C_l) = Name(i, C_m)$, then $me \in M_m$ where $i = Honest(me)$.*

Proof. Since i is inactive, me is determined by c_i and z. So, if $Name(i, C_l) = Name(i, C_m)$ and $E_l = E_m$, then $me \in M_j$.   ∎

3.5   Equivalence between Pre-configuration and In-Configuration

Now, we show that $\mathbf{G}^{pre}$ and $\mathbf{G}^{in}$ are equivalent by showing there is an equivalent trace in $\mathbf{G}^{in}$ for each trace in $\mathbf{G}^{pre}$ and vice versa.

In both of the two start states, S_0^{pre} and S_0^{in}, all values of the states and the configurations are initialized with nulls. However, when we just consider a trace in $\mathbf{G}^{pre}$, we may take $S_{0'}^{pre}$ as the start state instead of S_0^{pre} where $S_{0'}^{pre}$ is the virtual state of S_0^{pre} with the complete configuration of that trace. It is because S_0^{pre} and $S_{0'}^{pre}$ has the same state and there is no regular message event between S_0^{pre} and $S_{0'}^{pre}$.

Theorem 1. *For every $trace^{pre}$, there exists a $trace^{in}$ and $trace^{in} \equiv trace^{pre}$.*

Proof. The proof is given by the technique of the mathematical induction.

1. For $S_{0'}^{pre}$ and S_0^{in}, $E_{0'}^{pre} = E_0^{in}$ and $C_0^{in} \rhd C_{0'}^{pre}$.

2. Assume that $E_l^{pre} = E_l^{in}$ and $C_l^{in} \rhd C_l^{pre}$ for S_l^{pre} and S_l^{in}. If there is $t_l^{pre} = S_l^{pre} \xrightarrow{me_l} S_{l+1}^{pre}$, there exists ct_l^{in} from S_l^{in} to S_{l+1}^{in} such that $E_{l+1}^{pre} = E_{l+1}^{in}$ and $C_{l+1}^{in} \rhd C_{l+1}^{pre}$. Moreover, the message histories of ct_l^{in} and t_l^{pre} are same to each other.

The proof of 2 is given as follows. me_l must be a regular message event since $C_{0'}^{pre}$ is a complete configuration. We divide it into two cases where $i = Honest(me_l)$.

Case 1. (i is active in S_l^{pre}) There is $t_l^{in} = (S_l^{in} \xrightarrow{me_l} S_{l+1}^{in})$ since $E_l^{pre} = E_l^{in}$ (by lemma 1). $E_{l+1}^{pre} = E_{l+1}^{in}$ because $E_l^{pre} = E_l^{in}$ and the message events of t_l^{pre} and t_l^{in} are same. Because i is active, $C_{l+1}^{in} = C_l^{in}$. Thus, $C_{l+1}^{in} \rhd C_{l+1}^{pre}$. Note that $C_{l+1}^{pre} = C_l^{pre}$ since $C_{0'}^{pre}$ is complete.

Case 2. (i is inactive in S_l^{pre}) There exists $t_l^{in} = (S_l^{in} \xrightarrow{se_l} S_{l'}^{in})$ which makes $Name(i, C_{l'}^{in}) = Name(i, C_l^{pre})$. Since a special message does not affect the current value of the state, $E_{l'}^{in} = E_l^{in} = E_l^{pre}$. Thus, there exists a concatenated transition $t_l^{in} \cdot t_{l'}^{in} = (S_l^{in} \xrightarrow{se_l} S_{l'}^{in} \xrightarrow{me_l} S_{l+1}^{in})$ which is equivalent to t_l^{pre} (by lemma 2). It is obvious that $E_{l+1}^{pre} = E_{l+1}^{in}$. Because i's is the only different principal name between C_l^{in} and C_{l+1}^{in} and $Name(i, C_{l+1}^{in}) = Name(i, C_{l+1}^{pre})$, $C_{l+1}^{in} \rhd C_{l+1}^{pre} = C_l^{pre}$.   ∎

Theorem 2. *For every $trace^{in}$, there exists a $trace^{pre}$ and $trace^{pre} \equiv trace^{in}$.*

Proof. Assume that the last state of $trace^{in}$ is S_n^{in}. Then there must be $trace^{pre}$ which satisfies that $C_n^{in} \rhd C_{0'}^{pre}$.

   1. For S_0^{in} and $S_{0'}^{pre}$, $E_0^{in} = E_0^{pre}$ and $C_0^{in} \rhd C_{0'}^{pre}$.

   2. Assume that $E_l^{in} = E_l^{pre}$ and $C_l^{pre} \rhd C_l^{in}$ for S_l^{in} and S_l^{pre}. If there is $t_l^{in} = S_l^{in} \xrightarrow{me_l} S_{l+1}^{in}$, then there exists t_l^{pre} from S_l^{pre} to S_{l+1}^{pre} such that $E_{l+1}^{in} = E_{l+1}^{pre}$ and $C_{l+1}^{in} \rhd C_{l+1}^{pre}$. Moreover, the message histories of t_l^{pre} and t_l^{in} are same to each other.

   The proof of 2 is given as follows. We assume that me_l is a regular message event since special message events do not change the values of the state and do not affect the message history. i is the honest instance of me_l.

Case 1. (i is active in S_l^{in}) There is $t_l^{pre} = (S_l^{pre} \xrightarrow{me_l} S_{l+1}^{pre})$ since $E_l^{pre} = E_l^{in}$ (by lemma 1). $E_{l+1}^{pre} = E_{l+1}^{in}$ because $E_l^{pre} = E_l^{in}$ and the message histories of t_l^{pre} and t_l^{in} are same to each other. $C_{l+1}^{in} \rhd C_{l+1}^{pre}$ because $C_n^{in} \rhd C_{0'}^{pre}$.

Case 2. (i is inactive in S_l^{in}) Since me_l occurs in S_l^{in}, $Name(i, C_l^{in})$ is not null. So, $Name(i, C_l^{pre}) = Name(i, C_l^{in})$ since $C_l^{in} \rhd C_l^{pre} = C_{0'}^{pre}$. Now, $t_l^{pre} = (S_l^{pre} \xrightarrow{me_l} S_{l+1}^{pre})$ is possible since $E_l^{in} = E_l^{pre}$ and $Name(i, C_l^{pre}) = Name(i, C_l^{in})$ (by lemma 2). It is obvious that $E_{l+1}^{pre} = E_{l+1}^{in}$ and $C_{l+1}^{in} \rhd C_{l+1}^{pre}$.   ∎

Theorem 3. *Model checking of a security protocol over $\mathbf{G}^{pre}$ makes the same verification result to that over $\mathbf{G}^{in}$.*

Proof. If a flaw is found in $\mathbf{G}^{pre}$, then the same flaw and the same attack scenario are found in $\mathbf{G}^{in}$. It is because there is $trace^{in}$ that is equivalent to $trace^{pre}$ (by theorem 1). Since equivalent traces generate the same result in evaluating the protocol invariants, the flaw must be found in $trace^{in}$. Moreover the two traces generate the same attack scenario since the message histories of equivalent traces are same to each other. Furthermore, if a flaw is found in $\mathbf{G}^{in}$, then the same flaw and the same attack scenario are found in $\mathbf{G}^{pre}$. This can be easily proved in the same way of the above.   ∎

Since the state graph of in-configuration just adds virtual states to the state graph of traditional model checking, we conclude that model checking with pre-configuration and traditional model checking generate the same verification result.

4   Model Checking with Pre-configuration

4.1   Divide and Conquer

To deal with the very large number of states, we may divide the state graph into many subgraphs and model checking the subgraphs one by one. For a subgraph

$\mathbf{G'} = \{\mathbf{S'}, \mathbf{T'}, S_0', \mathbf{Q}\}$ of $\mathbf{G} = \{\mathbf{S}, \mathbf{T}, S_0, \mathbf{Q}\}$, S_0' is a state of $\mathbf{G}$, i.e. $S_0' \in \mathbf{S}$. $\mathbf{S'}$ is the set of all reachable states in $\mathbf{G}$ from S_0'. Definitely, $\mathbf{S'} \subset \mathbf{S}$. $\mathbf{T'}$ is the set of transition rules between any two states in $\mathbf{S'}$. Also, $\mathbf{T'} \subset \mathbf{T}$. $\mathbf{Q}$ of $\mathbf{G'}$ must be same to that of $\mathbf{G}$.

To do model checking on $\mathbf{G}$ using the divide and conquer technique, the union of all subgraphs must be equal to $\mathbf{G}$. So,

$$\mathbf{G} = \mathbf{G'_1} \cup \mathbf{G'_2} \cup ... \cup \mathbf{G'_K}$$

where $\mathbf{G'_1}, ..., \mathbf{G'_K}$ are the subgraphs of $\mathbf{G}$.

However, we cannot divide $\mathbf{G}$ into any arbitrary subgraphs. Each subgraph must be verifiable independently by a model checker. If S_0' of a subgraph is other than S_0 or any virtual state of S_0, it is hard to run a model checker on the subgraph independently. It is because there must be some regular message events occurred before S_0' and it is impossible to know the intruder's state without the information about the previous regular message events. Even if we know the intruder's state and find a flaw by model checking, it is hard to generate a suitable attack scenario since we don't know the message history before S_0'. A subgraph whose start state is S_0 or any virtual state of S_0, is called an *independent subgraph* since we can run a model checker on it independently without knowing other information than what the subgraph has.

Pre-configuration is inherently suitable for divide and conquer. In a state graph $\mathbf{G}$ with pre-configuration, first we must make a virtual state of the start state to generate any trace. Assume that there are K virtual start states and $\mathbf{G'_1}$, $\mathbf{G'_2}$, ..., $\mathbf{G'_K}$ are the subgraphs with the virtual states as their start states respectively. Thus, $\mathbf{G'_1}$, $\mathbf{G'_2}$, ..., $\mathbf{G'_K}$ are independent subgraphs and $\mathbf{G} = \mathbf{G'_1} \cup \mathbf{G'_2} \cup ... \cup \mathbf{G'_K}$. Moreover, since the virtual states of $\mathbf{G}$'s start state have different complete configurations, there cannot be a transition between any two subgraphs.

4.2   Extended Configuration

We may extend the configuration by adding some more state variables of honest instances to the definition of the configuration. For example, we may add the principal names of the communicating partners to the configuration. In this case, the configuration must be defined as follows.

$$C = [(c_1, p_1), (c_2, p_2), ..., (c_N, p_N)]$$

where N is the total number of instances, c_i is the principal name of instance i and p_i is the principal name of the communicating partner of i.

The property of the principal names for the configuration to work is that an honest instance can have only one principal name and cannot change it on a trace. Since most of the variables of protocols found in [1] have the same property, they also can be added to the configuration. When some other variables are added to the configuration, we can show the equivalence between the pre-configuration and the in-configuration in the very similar way. We must use the concept of *active/inactive variables* which are defined in a very similar way of *active/inactive instance* for the proof.

For NSPKP, there are three possible templates for the configuration:

1. $C_\alpha = [c_1, c_2, ..., c_N]$
2. $C_\beta = [(c_1, p_1), (c_2, p_2), ..., (c_N, p_N)]$
3. $C_\gamma = [(c_1, p_1, n_1), (c_2, p_2, n_2), ..., (c_N, p_N, n_N)]$

where c_k, p_k and n_k are the principal name, the partner's principal name and the partner's nonce of an instance k respectively. Note that these configuration templates can also be used for many other security protocols found in [1].

While the pre-configuration is a model of our technique for explaining it in the frame of the state graph, the in-configuration is suitable for modeling the current general model checking of security protocols.

5   Symmetry

In model checking of a security protocol, an honest principal name does not have any special meaning but is just a label to differentiate the principal from other principals. That is, honest principal names are equivalent and we may swap the principle names assigned to honest instances without changing the behaviors of the verification system. This is the symmetry property which has been mentioned in several researches [6,8].

To show an example, we assume that there are two honest instances, an initiator and a responder. Since we have two instances, two different principal names are enough to name the instances. So, there are four possible cases for the pair of principal names of two instances, which are $[A, A], [A, B], [B, A]$ and $[B, B]$. However, A and B are swappable, $[A, A]$ and $[B, B]$ are equivalent to each other and so are $[A, B]$ and $[B, A]$. The former two cases are equivalent since an honest principal instantiates one initiator instance and one responder instance in both of them. Similarly, we know the latter two cases are equivalent. Thus, we need to run a model checker on only two cases, $[A, A]$ and $[A, B]$ for example. They have the form of C_α in the section 4.2 and this means that the symmetry property reduces the number of the configurations. This is basically an application of *principal symmetry* found in [6]. To find if the two cases of C_α are equivalent by the principal symmetry, we just need to swap the principal names of a case and see if the result is same to the other case.

We can reduce more number of the configurations when we use C_β. Assume that there are five instances and the instance 1 through 4 are initiators and the instance 5 is a responder. First we can reduce the number of configurations as mentioned above. For example, $[(A, *), (A, *), (B, *), (B, *), | (C, *)], [(A, *), (A, *), (C, *), (C, *), | (B, *)]$ and $[(B, *), (B, *), (C, *), (C, *), | (A, *)]$ are all equivalent where $*$ represents any principal name but the name of the instance itself. '|'s are inserted intentionally just as a delimiter between the initiators and the responder. So, we maintain only the first configuration and remove the latter two. Now, it is time for a further reduction. We also explain the additional reduction by examples. In $[(A, B), (A, B), (B, A), (B, A), | (C, B)]$ and $[(A, B), (A, B), (B, A), (B, A), | (C, A)]$, two principals A and B are equivalent by symmetry. Both of them have two initiator instances and each instance has the other as its partner. Thus, the two configurations are equivalent.

6   Verification Results

6.1   System for the Verification

Figure 4 shows our verification system. With a configuration template which was specified by the user, the configuration generator makes all the possible configurations and feed them one by one to a model checker. The machine used

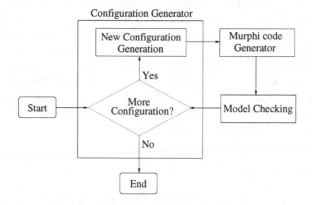

Fig. 4. Verification System with Pre-configuration

for the verification was a PC with dual 1GHz Athlon CPUs and 3Gbyte memory. We verified the Needham-Schroeder-Lowe Public-Key Protocol (NSLPKP), the fixed version of the NSPKP by Lowe [3]. Three configuration templates in the section 4.2 are used for the pre-configuration. To show the performance of our method, we compare the verification results with the traditional model checking (TMC) using Murφ without pre-configuration.

6.2   Memory Usage

Table 1 shows the amount of memory required. The numbers are the size of the memory required for the hash table and the state queue of Murφ, and we need to add approximately 1Mbyte memory to get the total required memory for model checking. The symmetry property was used for reducing the number of configurations for all pre-configuration cases if possible. When we use Murφ for the verification without pre-configuration, the size of memory needed grows exponentially with the increase of the numbers of initiators and responders. Murφ

Table 1. Memory usage (Mbytes)

# of Initiators: # of Responders	1:1	1:2	2:2	2:3
TMC	0.9	97	Aborted	Aborted
C_α	0.4	22	1,403	Aborted
C_β	0.04	0.6	18	653
C_γ	0.02	0.08	0.4	1.7^a

Note: a. Estimated value

was aborted due to lack of memory when run with more than one initiators and two responders. With the pre-configurations of C_α, the size of memory required is reduced to less than half of that of TMC, but cannot verifies the (2:3) case where (2:3) means two initiators and three responders. C_β uses much less amount of memory to verify the same cases compared with C_α and successfully verified the (2:3) case. However, it still shows the tendency of state space explosion. C_γ needs very little amount of memory for all cases. We do not expect the space explosion problem with C_γ since the rates of increase of memory size is almost constant. However, we did not run Murφ with all configurations for the case of two initiators and three responders in C_γ. We just did model checking with randomly sampled configurations because its total run time is too long. More detailed explanation is given in the next section.

6.3   Execution Times

Table 2 shows the execution times. Though C_γ shows the best result in memory usage, it has an explosion problem in the run time and the time for the (2:3) case was recorded with an estimated value from randomly selected 20,000 configurations. The results show C_β is much faster than other methods. The differences between C_β and other methods become larger as the number of instances grows, but C_β also shows an explosion problem in the run time. However, with C_β, we are able to handle much larger designs with practically decent amount of run time and much smaller memory requirements.

Table 2. Execution times (CPU seconds)

# of Initiators: # of Responders	1:1	1:2	2:2	2:3
TMC	0.17	75.3	Aborted	Aborted
C_α	0.15	47.8	44,225	Aborted
C_β	0.03	3.2	635	563,549
C_γ	0.21	28.7	8138	$3,391,588^a$

Note: a. Estimated value

7   Discussion and Conclusion

In this paper, We propose the pre-configuration technique which is a simple and effective divide-and-conquer method to address the state space explosion problem of the security protocol verification using general model checkers. The proposed method has been proved to be equivalent to the traditional model checking without pre-configuration.

Based on the verification result with NSLPKP, we found that there are a trade-off between the size of memory needed and the execution time. The best configuration template is C_β which consists of the principal name and the partner name of each instance. Though C_γ shows the best result in memory usage, too fine division makes so long run time for verification. One possible reason for this is that we had to initiate a new Murφ run for every configuration and Murφ is not optimized for running such finely divided many cases. The results show the reduction of the number of configurations using the partner symmetry is very effective in the case of C_β. We conclude that C_β is the best configuration when consider the both of the memory usage and the run time.

Though we can verify larger designs with C_β than TMC, C_β still has an explosion problems in space and time. Further research will be focused on developing an optimized model checker for verifying security protocols with fine pre-configurations like C_γ.

References

1. J. Clark and J. Jacob, "A Survey of Authentication Protocol Literature: Version 1.0," Online: http://www.cs.york.ac.uk/jac/papers/drareview.ps.gz, 1997.
2. R. Needham and M. Schroeder, "Using Encryption for Authentication in Large Networks of Computers," *Communications of the ACM*, Vol. 21, No. 12, pp. 993–999, 1978.
3. G. Lowe, "Breaking and fixing the Needham-Schroeder public-key protocol using FDR," *Proc. 2nd International Workshop on TACAS*, Vol. 1055 of LNCS, pp. 147–166, Springer-Verlag, 1996.
4. A. W. Roscoe and M. H. Goldsmith, "The perfect "spy" for modelchecking cryptoprotocols," *Proc. of the DIMACS Workshop on Design and Formal Verification of Security Protocols*, Online: http://dimacs.rutgers.edu/Workshops/Security/program2/program.html, 1997.
5. J. C. Mitchell, M. Mitchell and U. Stern, "Automated Analysis of Cryptographic Protocols Using Murφ," *Proc. of IEEE Symposium on Security and Privacy*, pp. 141–151, 1997.
6. E. M. Clarke, S. Jha and W. Marrero, "Verifying Security Protocols with Brutus," *ACM Transactions on Software Engineering and Methodology*, Vol. 9, No. 4, pp. 443–487, October 2000.
7. V. Shmatikov and U. Stern, "Efficient Finite-State Analysis for Large Security Protocols," *Proc. of the 11th IEEE Computer Security Foundations Workshop*, pp. 106–115, 1998.
8. "Murφ: User manual," Online: http://sprout.stanford.edu/dill/Murphi/Murphi3.1.tar.Z.

Remote Access VPN with Port Protection Function by Mobile Codes

Yoshiaki Shiraishi[1], Youji Fukuta[2], and Masakatu Morii[2]

[1] Department of Informatics, Kinki University,
3-4-1 Kowakae, Higashi-Osaka, 577-8502 JAPAN
zenmei@info.kindai.ac.jp
[2] Department of Information Science and Intelligent Systems,
The University of Tokushima, Tokushima, 770-8506 JAPAN
{youji,morii}@is.tokushima-u.ac.jp

Abstract. Concern about SSL VPN technology as a class of VPNs has been growing recently because a key advantage of SSL VPN is that it requires no specialized client software. When a user requests access to a server, the SSL client module, a Java applet code, is downloaded into the host first. However, it is quite likely that not all applications run well because a client can not connect with a server through an HTTPS tunnel in some applications. This study proposes a remote access VPN architecture that allows any application to use the VPN. The proposed VPN uses the same Java applet as existing SSL VPNs, but the function of the applet, which we call mobile code, is changed dynamically by Java Remote Method Invocation (RMI). The VPN client applet can cooperate with a VPN server and a firewall in server side. As a result, the proposed VPN has strength against Denial of Service (DoS) attacks.

1 Introduction

The Internet is evolving at an extremely high rate. One requirement for providing not only advanced, but also classical, network services is seamless access with high security of the server for service providers irrespective of enterprise or consumer service level. Main security threats under the environment are interruption of service as a result of intrusion into service provision network, and interception, modification, and fabrication of data between clients and the server. The above are attacks on availability, confidentiality, integrity, and authenticity [1]. Firewall [2] and intrusion detection systems are generally used to maintain availability of service; various security protocols are used to protect data from interception, modification, and fabrication. Particularly in security protocols, virtual private network (VPN) technology has been brought to public attention. IPsec [3] and PPTP [4] are known as network layer-type VPN, whereas SOCKS V5 [5], SSL [6]/TLS [7] and SSH [8] are known as transport/application layer-type VPN. The network/datalink layer-type VPNs are used mainly to establish a secure virtual path for providing network-to-network or network-to-host access, but some disadvantages in the VPN client side are that the process of the

K. Chae and M. Yung (Eds.): WISA 2003, LNCS 2908, pp. 16–26, 2004.
© Springer-Verlag Berlin Heidelberg 2004

protocol is heavy and it is necessary to install the VPN appliance in network-to-network VPNs or VPN client software under the network layer in network-to-host VPNs. Transport/application layer-type VPNs are used mainly for providing network-to-host or host-to-host access, but this process also has disadvantages: client applications of network services must be ready to use its correspondent security protocol; also, the server must be ready to receive a request.

If we seek to reduce the necessary effort to use the security protocol in the client side, it is better to use a transport/application layer-type VPN protocols, in general. Concern with SSL VPN technology as a class of VPNs which act on the transport/application layer has been growing recently [9,10]. That is the reason why a key advantage of SSL VPN is that no specialized client software as that explained above, is required. In most SSL VPNs, VPN client software is installed as a Java applet, then client application communicates with the server via the applet in the localhost. When a user requests to use the service through VPN connections, the user connects with an applet download server first; then the downloaded applet starts and is executed statically. If the function of such an applet is changed dynamically, we can realize various intelligent services with high security. For instance, there are services to realize load balancing of the server and traffic with security.

This paper proposes a remote access VPN that uses the same Java applet as existing SSL VPNs use, but the function of the applet, which we call mobile code, is changed dynamically by Java Remote Method Invocation (RMI) [11]. By calling and controlling methods in the client side from the server side, the VPN client applet can cooperate easily with a VPN server and a firewall in the server side. Thereby, the proposed VPN offers strength against Denial of Service (DoS) attacks.

2   Remote Access VPN

There are two types of remote access VPNs when a client communicates with a service server and uses an application; one is a network-to-host VPN and another is a host-to-host VPN.

Figure 1 shows the general form of the network-to-host VPN. A VPN gateway is set in a server side network and a VPN client module is installed in a client host. A VPN connection is established between the VPN client module and the VPN gateway; application data flows in the VPN connection. This type is used in cases where there are some application servers: for example, where a user connects with the intranet of the user's company. IPsec, PPTP, SOCKS V5, etc. are generally used for network-to-host VPN.

Figure 2 shows the general form of the host-to-host VPN. A VPN server module is set in a server host; a VPN client module is included in an application software or installed in a client host. IPsec, SSL/TLS, SSH, etc. are generally used for host-to-host VPN.

Figures 1 and 2 show that any conventional protocol requires a certain VPN client module or application software that supports the protocol. However, such installation or support is troublesome for many users. On the other hand, a new technology, SSL VPN, has been proposed and brought to attention, recently. SSL VPN realizes a clientless VPN access to applications with no pre-installation of a VPN client. When a user requests access to a server, the SSL client module, which is a Java applet code, is downloaded into the host at first, as shown in Fig. 3. However, it is quite likely that not all applications run well because a client can not connect with a server through an HTTPS tunnel in some applications. This paper is intended as a development of a light VPN such that any application can use the VPN.

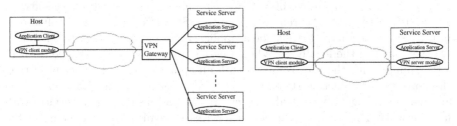

Fig. 2. Host-to-Host VPN

Fig. 1. Network-to-Host VPN

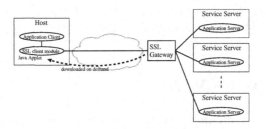

Fig. 3. SSL VPN

3   VPN Using Mobile Codes

This section presents the architecture of the proposed VPN with mobile codes and its sequence flow.

3.1   Architecture

Figure 4 shows the architecture of a remote access VPN using mobile codes. The proposed system comprises Request Receiver (RR), User Manager (UM), Access

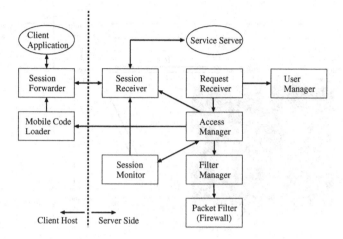

Fig. 4. Architecture

Manager (AM), Filter Manager (FM), Packet Filter (PF), Mobile Code Loader (MCL), Session Forwarder (SF), Session Receiver (SR), and Session Monitor (SM).

Request Receiver (RR): RR executes a user authentication process when it receives a request to connect with a service from the user. The RR queries whether the service is available to the user, using a received user's information. If authentication succeeds, then the RR sends the request message to open a connection to AM, otherwise the RR sends the message 'access denied' to the user.

User Manager (UM): UM processes an authentication request, then the UM replies that a service is 'available' or 'unavailable' to the user.

Access Manager (AM): AM receives a message to open a connection; then, it creates SR, requests to create SF to MCL, requests to open a service port to FM, and requests to monitor a state of established connection to SM. When the AM receives a notification of the session end, it requests closure of the service port to FM, requests to destruction of SF, and destroys SR.

Filter Manager (FM): FM opens a channel by the change of a packet filter configuration in PF when it receives the request message from AM. If the FM receives the closing message of a connection from the AM, it closes the channel.

Packet Filter (PF): PF follows a FM instructions, and passes or discards data packets.

Mobile Code Loader (MCL): MCL creates SF when it receives a creation message from AM. If the MCL receives a destruction message from AM, it destroys SF.

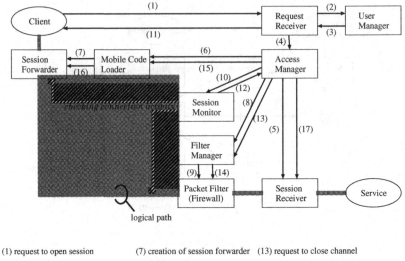

Fig. 5. Mechanism

(1) request to open session	(7) creation of session forwarder	(13) request to close channel
(2) verificating user	(8) request to open channel	(14) setting to close channel
(3) notification of acceptance	(9) setting to open channel	(15) request to destroy session forwarder
(4) request to open service	(10) request to monitor	(16) destruction of session forwarder
(5) creation of session receiver	(11) permission to use service	(17) destruction of session receiver
(6) request to create session forwarder	(12) notification session end	

Session Forwarder (SF): SF forwards data packets from a client to SR. A certain encryption method is included in the SF. It provides an encryption function.

Session Receiver (SR): SR receives data packets forwarded from SF. A certain encryption method is included in the SR. The SR decrypts the received data, then forwards the decrypted data to an application server.

Session Monitor (SM): SM monitors whether a connection is active.

3.2 Sequence Flow

Figure 5 is a flow of the proposed VPN.

(1)   A client requests a service use to RR. The user sends the user information, i.e. a user ID and password, at this time.

(2)   The RR sends that user information to UM.

(3)   The UM sends the user verification result to the RR.

(4)   If the user is authorized to use the service, the RR requests opening of the service to AM.

(5)   The AM creates an SR.

(6)   The AM sends MCL to the client host.

(7) The MCL gets SF module from the AM and creates the SF in the client host.
(8) The AM requests opening of the channel to FM.
(9) The FM sets the packet filtering rule so as to pass the allowed data packets.
(10) The AM requests monitoring of whether the connection between the SF and the SR is alive; then the SM starts to monitor the session.
(11) The RR sends the message allowing use of the service to the client. The connection between the client and the server is established at this time. Thereafter, the user can use the service.
(12) When the SM detects the session end, the SM sends the closing request to the AM.
(13) The AM requests closing of the service port to the FM.
(14) The FM re-sets the packet filtering rule so as to discard the data packets of the closed connection.
(15) The AM requests destruction of the SF to the MCL.
(16) The MCL destroys the SF.
(17) The AM destroys the SR.

Let A be a port number of a client in an application, B a port number of a service, C a receiving port number of client side in SF, X a sending port number in SF, Y a receiving port number in SR, and Z a sending port number to a service in SR as shown in Fig. 6. Port number C is set to the same number B by SF so that the application client can connect with the server without a change of client software. Although we can set specified numbers to A and Z, any number is assigned to A and Z automatically at the kernel level in the OS, here. X and Y are set by AM because the numbers must be known to set a packet filtering rule in PF.

An encrypted communication is realized by introducing certain encryption/ decryption functions into SF and SR. For purposes of this paper, it is not necessary to discuss the encryption flow in detail.

4 Implementation

This section presents an implementation of the proposed remote access system. MCL is distributed as a Java applet code from a Web server identically to some

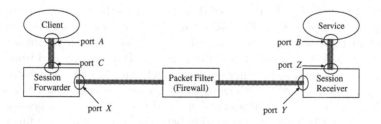

Fig. 6. Forwarding and filtering

```
public class MobileCodeLoader extends Applet implements Remote {

    private Object object;

    public void init () {
        try {
            object = (Object) new SessionForwarder ();
            UnicastRemoteObject.exportObject (object);
            bind (object);
        }
        catch (RemoteException e) {
        }
    }

    public void destroy () {
        super.destroy ();
        unbind (object);
    }

    private void bind (Object object) {
        // cleate RMI registry in this Applet and
        // register object to RMI registry.
    }

    private void unbind (Object object) {
        // erase object from RMI registry.
    }

        ⋮

}
```

Fig. 7. Outline of MCL applet code

existing SSL VPN schemes after a user is authenticated. The authentication process is executed in the Web server. The MCL and AM include Java RMI [11] codes. We can consider the MCL and the AM as an RMI server and an RMI client, respectively. By RMI technology, the AM can call a remote object such as SF in the client host via the MCL.

The applet consists of MobileCodeLoader (MCL) class and SessionForwarder (SF) class; the servlet consists of the AccessManager (AM) class, SessionManager (SM) class, FilterManager (FM) class, and SessionReceiver (SR) class. The MCL class has an RMI registry and registers an instance of the SF class to the RMI registry by a bind() method, as shown in Fig. 7. The RMI client, a function of the servlet, can refer an instance of class in RMI server, a function of the applet from the class name by RMI registry. A declaration of the remote interface is needed so that an object of AM class shown in Fig. 8 can invoke methods in the SF class, as in Fig. 9. The class file of the remote interface is placed in the same directories of the applet and the servlet. Then, AM can invoke the runSessionForwarder() and the stopSessionForwarder() methods in the SF class similarly to local methods.

Figures 10, 11 and 12 show outlines of the SF, SR and SM class, respectively. The SF class includes the runSessionForwarder() method, which forwards data from port C to port Y in SR and from port X to port A in the client, and some other necessary methods. The SR class includes the runSessionReceiver() method which forwards data from port Y to port B in a server and from port Z to port X in SF, and some other necessary methods. The SM class includes the checkConnection() method, which observes the session established between SF and SR, and the sessionEndHandler() method which sends a notification of the session end to AM when the connection between SF and SR is not functional.

We employ iptables-1.2.7a [12] as a packet filter in PF. The FM class includes openFilter() and closeFilter() methods, as shown in Fig. 13. The methods change

```
public class AccessManager extends HttpServlet {

     public void AccessManager () {
     }

     public void runSessionReceiver (int portY, int portB, String hostService) {
(5)     // get instance of SessionReceiver class and
        // execute SessionReceiver.runSessionReceiver (portY, portB, hostService).
     }

     public void runSessionForwarder (int portC, int portY, String hostSessionReceiver) {
(6), (7)  // get instance of SessionForwarder class from RMI registry and
          // execute SessionForwarder.runSessionForwarder (portC, portY, hostSessionReceiver).
     }

     public void allowSession (int portX, String hostSessionForwarder, int portY, String hostSessionReceiver) {
(8), (9)  // get instance of FilterManager class and
          // execute FilterManager.openFilter (portX, hostSessionForwarder, portY, hostSessionReceiver).
     }

     public void runSessionMonitor (Socket socket) {
(10), (12)  // get instance of SessionMonitor class and
            // execute SessionMonitor.checkConnection (socket).
     }

     public void denySession (int portX, String hostSessionForwarder, int portY, String hostSessionReceiver) {
(13), (14)  // get instance of FilterManager class and
            // execute FilterManager.closeFilter (portX, hostSessionForwarder, portY, hostSessionReceiver).
     }

     public void stopSessionForwarder () {
(15), (16)  // get instance of SessionForwarder class from RMI registry and
            // execute SessionForwarder.stopSessionForwarder ().
     }

     public void stopSessionReceiver () {
(17)    // get instance of SessionReceiver class and
        // execute SessionReceiver.stopSessionReceiver ().
     }
        ⋮
}
```

Fig. 8. Outline of AM servlet code

```
public interface RemoteInterface extends Remote {
    public void runSessionForwarder (int portC, int portY, String hostSessionReceiver)
        throws RemoteException;
    public void stopSessionForwarder () throws RemoteException;
}
```

Fig. 9. Remote interfaces code used by an applet and a servlet

```
public class SessionForwarder implements RemoteInterface {

    public void SessionForwarder () {
    }

    public void runSessionForwarder (int portC, int portY, String hostSessionReceiver) {
        // run forwarding session from portC to portY on hostSessionReceiver.
    }

    public void stopSessionForwarder () {
        // stop forwarding session.
    }
}
```

Fig. 10. Outline of SF class included in an applet and invoked from servlet

a filtering rule for input packets in PF by executing the iptables command. We set the rule that all output packets are accepted and all input and forwarded packets are dropped, as the policy. When AM requests to open the channel to FM, the openFilter() method is called so that the packets can pass from port X to port Y. When the session forwarding ends, the closeFilter() method is called so that the allowed packets can not pass.

Next, we show experimental results of the above implemented system. After sending a request of service use from a client, some processes are carried out until the client can connect with a service. Data between the client and the service are exchanged through SF and SR. We measure the starting up time which is until the service is available and the throughput of the connection between the client and the service. Table 1 shows specifications of computers in the experimental system. These computers are connected to a 100Base-TX hub. Table 2 shows the average start up time, where the size of an applet is 15.1 Kbytes. Table 3

```
public class SessionReceiver {

    public void SessionReceiver () {
    }

    public void runSessionReceiver (int portY, int portB, String hostService) {
        // run receiving session from portY to portB on hostService.
    }

    public void stopSessionReceiver () {
        // stop receiving session.
    }

}
```

```
public class SessionMonitor {

    public void SessionMonitor () {
    }

    public void checkConnection (Socket socket) {
        // start checking connection alive of the socket.
        // if the session end is notificated, then stop the check and call sessionEndHandler ().
    }

    public void sessionEndHandler () {
        // send notification of the session end to AccessManager.
    }

}
```

Fig. 11. Outline of SR class included in a servlet

Fig. 12. Outline of SM class included in a servlet

```
public class FilterManager {

    public void FilterManager () {
    }

    public void openFilter (int portX, String hostSessionForwarder, int portY, String hostSessionReceiver) {
        String command = "/sbin/iptables -A INPUT -p tcp"
                        + " -s " + hostSessionForwarder + " --sport " + Integer.toString (portX)
                        + " -d " + hostSessionReceiver + " --dport " + Integer.toString (portY)
                        + " -j ACCEPT";
        exec (command);
    }

    public void closeFilter (int portX, String hostSessionForwarder, int portY, String hostSessionReceiver) {
        String command = "/sbin/iptables -D INPUT -p tcp"
                        + " -s " + hostSessionForwarder + " --sport " + Integer.toString (portX)
                        + " -d " + hostSessionReceiver + " --dport " + Integer.toString (portY)
                        + " -j ACCEPT";
        exec (command);
    }

    private void exec (String command) {
        // execute the specified command.
    }

}
```

Fig. 13. Outline of FM class included in a servlet

Table 1. Specifications of computers

Servlet, service server and firewall	CPU	Pentium 4 2.4 GHz
	Memory	512 Mbytes
	NIC	Intel PRO/100 S Server
	OS	Vine Linux 2.6CR
	Web Server	Apache-2.0.45
	Servlet Container	Tomcat-4.1.24
Client host	CPU	Pentium III 733 MHz
	Memory	320 Mbytes
	NIC	Intel PRO/100
	OS	Vine Linux 2.6CR
	Web Browser	Mozilla 1.1
	Java Plug-In	Java2 Plug-in 1.4.0_03

shows the average throughputs of a down-link and up-link when a file of 12.1 Mbytes are exchanged by FTP. From the Tables 2 and 3, it is possible to use the system based on the proposed architecture, in practical.

Table 2. Average time

Table 3. Average throughput

Process	Time
Time of reading and starting an applet	1.4 s
Time of starting of a servlet	2.2 s
Total start up time	3.6 s

Direction	Throughput
Service → Client	64.0 Mbps
Client → Service	61.0 Mbps

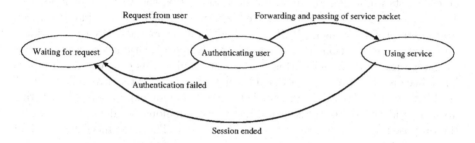

Fig. 14. State transition

5 Consideration

We will discuss the security of the proposed VPN. Figure 14 shows a state transition of the proposed architecture. We can describe the service using flow by "Waiting for request", "Authenticating user", and "Using service" phases. In the waiting for request phase, RR waits for an access request from a user. When the RR receives the request, the state moves to the phase of authenticating the user. In the phase of authenticating the user, the RR authenticates the user. If the user is authorized, the state moves to the phase of using service; otherwise the state returns to the phase of waiting for the request. When the phase moves from authenticating the user to using a service, SF and SR start and data packets of the connection between the SF and SR are allowed to pass in PF. The conditions to reach the service port in the server are success in user authentication and in connection with the SF, as stated above. The state does not move to the phase of authenticating the user at all if a user's information is not known by an attacker. If access to SF is limited only in the connection from a client application, other access to SF is denied. In addition, if a packet filtering rule is set correctly by using the source IP address, attacks to the service can not succeed to any great extent.

If an attacker uses IP address spoofing, we have only to apply a certain message authentication code (MAC) to the packets between SF and SR. Thereby, the proposed VPN architecture has strength against the above active attacks.

In the proposed VPN, port numbers of SF and SR can be changed easily and dynamically. That is the reason why an object such as SF can call from AM in a server side by RMI technology. We can defend data from traffic analysis [1] which is a passive attack. By changing port numbers dynamically, the proposed VPN has strength against DoS attacks because attack packets can not reach the server where the open port in PF is not known.

6   Conclusion

This paper proposed a remote access VPN architecture using mobile codes, and described its implementation. In the proposed VPN, the VPN client module, a Java applet, is downloaded from a Web server, and the client module is invoked from a server side by using RMI technology. The proposed VPN can provide a port protection function to a server and a client application because it is easy to change the port number. Moreover, most applications can use the proposed VPN because the proposed VPN does not use complicated protocols such as HTTPS, but port forwarding technology. We also made experiments about start up time and throughput. Experimental results demonstrated that we can use the proposed VPN as a practical solution of VPN. The introduced light-weight encryption function and its consideration remain for further studies.

References

1. W. Stallings, Cryptography and Network Security: Principles and Practice, 2nd edition, Prentice Hall, New Jersey, 1998.
2. W.R. Cheswick and S.M. Bellovin, Firewalls and Internet Security, Addison-Wesley, Boston, MA, 1994.
3. S. Kent and R. Atkinson, "Security Architecture for the Internet Protocol", RFC 2401, Nov. 1998.
4. K. Hamzeh, G. Pall, W. Verthein, J. Taarud, W. Little, and G. Zorn, "Point-to-Point Tunneling Protocol (PPTP)", RFC 2637, July 1999.
5. M. Leech, M. Ganes, Y. Lee, R. Kuris, D. Koblas, and L. Jones, "SOCKS Protocol Version 5", RFC 1928, Mar. 1996.
6. A. Freier, P. Karlton, and P. Kocher, "The SSL 3.0 Protocol," Netscape Communications Corp., Nov. 18, 1996.
7. T. Dierks and C. Allen, "The TLS Protocol Version 1.0", RFC 2246, Jan. 1999.
8. T. Ylonen, T. Kivinen, M. Saarinen, T. Rinne, and S. Lehtinen, "SSH Protocol Architecture", draft-ietf-secsh-architecture-14.txt, IETF, July 2003.
9. Aventail Corp., http://www.aventail.com/ .
10. ArrayNetworks Inc., https://www.arraynetworks.net/ .
11. Sun Microsystems, Inc., Java Remote Method Invocation, http://java.sun.com/products/jdk/rmi/ .
12. netfilter/iptables, http://www.netfilter.org/ .

A Role of DEVS Simulation for Information Assurance

Sung-Do Chi, Jong Sou Park, and Jang-Se Lee

Department of Computer Engineering
Hangkong University, Seoul, KOREA
{sdchi,jspark,jslee2}@mail.hangkong.ac.kr

Abstract. Information assurance protects against a violation of information and its technologies that construct, operate and control information infrastructures, and assure the reliability and the availability of those. One of the efforts for information assurance is to build model of each computer and network system and perform the simulation to evaluate various threats to that model so that the vulnerability is estimated and optimal security policy can be generated. We argue about the need and difficulties of simulation in information assurance and suggest information assurance method using DEVS formalism, hierarchical & modular modeling and simulation environment, to solve the difficulties. The application and validity of suggested methodology will be proven through the vulnerability analysis method based on simulation and SECUSIM, which is a tool of training cyber-attack.

1 Introduction

As information technologies progress, whole social infrastructures are getting automatic using the technologies so that we increasingly come to rely on information systems and information and communication networks. These infrastructures are enormously affecting economy and security of a nation. As network components that composes main information and communication infrastructures use incomplete system products, the infrastructures are vulnerable to external attacks and thereby hacking is on the rise for years [1,2]. To deal with this, information assurance protects against a violation of information and its technologies that construct, operate and control information infrastructures, and assure the reliability and the availability of those. One of methods that assure information is modeling and simulation of information and communication infrastructures. Not only can various threats to them be evaluated through this but also this is recognized as an effective method to evaluate current security measure and produce alternatives [3,4].

Cohen [5], who was a pioneer in the field of network security modeling and simulation, interestingly suggested a simple network security model composed of network model represented by node and link, cause-effect model, characteristic functions, and pseudo-random number generator. However, cyber attack and defense representation based on cause-effect model is so simple that practical difficulty in application comes about. Amoroso suggested that the intrusion model [6] should be represented by se

K. Chae and M. Yung (Eds.): WISA 2003, LNCS 2908, pp. 27–41, 2004.
© Springer-Verlag Berlin Heidelberg 2004

quence of actions, however, the computer simulation approach was not considered clearly. Wadlow [7] suggested an intrusion model, but it failed to go beyond the conceptual modeling level. Finally, Nong Ye [2,8] noticeably proposed a layer-based approach to complex security system, but failed to provide a practical modeling and simulation techniques of the relevant layers. To overcome these limitations and difficulties, we argue about approach using DEVS (Discrete Event System Specification) formalism, which is advanced modeling and simulation environment. DEVS provides the hierarchical and modular modeling and simulation environment based on the object-oriented concept. Thus, (i) the event-based nature of cyber-attack behavior can be expressed effectively. And (ii) complicated and various structural modeling of information infrastructure can be accomplished. Also (iii) evaluation of generation of attack scenarios, the consequence of cyber-attack, the effect of defense, vulnerability and survivability is convenient. Finally, (iv) hierarchical modeling of network components and packet-oriented event-based dynamic characteristic can be properly described.

This paper is constructed as follows. First of all, we argue about the need of simulation and its difficulties in information assurance. And to overcome these, we introduce in short DEVS formalism - hierarchical & modular modeling and simulation environment. Then, we propose the methodology of DEVS-based information assurance and explain this step by step. Finally, as an application example, we introduce SECUSIM, a tool for training cyber-attack, and describe about simulation-based vulnerability analysis method.

2 Simulation Concept for Information Assurance

Generally, the simulation for model, not for real system, has no time and space limitations and is easy for application and flexible so that this is inexpensive relatively. Also, there are little risks to real system because of the experimentation for model. Of course, although the accuracy of model should be premised in order for the simulation result to have meaning, above things are big attractiveness only simulation can give us. The good points that we can gain through simulation in information assurance are as follows [9].

- Deep analysis through generating of detailed attack behavior
- The network vulnerability analysis related to path selection
- Analysis of new attack method that hasn't been classified so far
- Prediction of the damage and riffle effect due to successful attack
- Verification of the effectiveness of defense strategy
- Analysis of damages and suggestion of the method endures breakdown when key
   components operate wrong (information survivability)

With these good points, it is possible to have many application related to information assurance from hacking training system to vulnerability analysis system. Meanwhile, multi-disciplinary co-work is essential to the simulation approach needed for information assurance. That is, coherent and integrated research in largely three sectors including Information security, Simulation, and Computer network is required. The core issues of each field are as follows:

(1) Information Security
- The definition of metrics for information assurance (Vulnerability, survivability, dependability, etc.)
- The definition and classification of cyber-attack scenario
- The definition and classification of defense strategy
- Mechanism of Intrusion detection system, firewall and so on

(2) Computer Network
- Features and classification according to network devices (Router, Gateway, Server, etc.)
- Features and classification according to network topology (CSMA/CD, Token-ring, etc.)
- Features according to network components (O/S, H/W, Application S/W, File system, etc.)
- Features and classification according to packets
- The method and feature of Communication

(3) Simulation
- Discrete event system modeling
- Simulation engine design
- Network configuration and modeling
- Attacker modeling (human psychological modeling)
- Analyzing technique

We can reach the ultimate information assurance through only systematic and integrated study of these various fields. Even though many researchers have done their best, there is no conclusion to deserve close attention. Especially, Cohen's study has been known for unique in security modeling possible for practical simulation test. Cohen suggested the cause-and-effect model of cyber-attack and defense, and tried simple modeling based on statistics. But it means only the first attempt of simulation and has limitations in practical use [5]. Meanwhile, Amoroso and Nong Ye studied security modeling not for the model that can be immediately applied to simulation test but for theological one. Amoroso stressed out that one completed attack have to be expressed by time track of a series of actions suggesting intrusion model according to time track [6]. NongYe suggested the layer-based approach that is made step by step for modeling and stressed out the modeling in functional phase is essential among these phases [2,8].

Although their researches suggest the conclusions of their own in network security modeling, there are some problems. Cohen's approach expresses the cyber-attack and defense based on the cause-result model so simply that it has limitations in practical application. Whereas the consecutive behaviors to the intrusion model Amoroso suggested have good points in responding to the model, computer simulation approach is not clear due to the security mechanism based expression. In NongYe's case, abstraction approach to complicated systems is good, but it does not give concrete examples in modeling and simulation method that applied these phases. That is, there are no implementation and test based on the approach. Cohen summarized the difficulties of simulation approach as follows.

"Since we are modeling very complex phenomena involving mixes of human behavior and interactions of complex interdependent systems with time bases ranging from nanoseconds to years. There is no widely accepted information physics that would allow us to make an accurate model, and the sizes of the things we are modeling are so large and complex that we cannot describe them with any reasonable degree of accuracy. Also there are no consensus on how to describe a network security system, and no set of commonly accepted metrics upon which to base a set of measurements to be used for simulation [5]."

Above all, effective use of advanced modeling and simulation method is essential to overcome these difficulties. So we argue about the methodology for information assurance through DEVS formalism, which provides advanced simulation environment.

3 DEVS Formalism

3.1 Concept

We now review the basic concepts of the Discrete Event System Specification (DEVS) formalism and its associated simulation methodology. In the conceptual framework underlying the DEVS formalism [10,11], the modeling and simulation enterprise concerns four basic objects:
- Real system, in existence or proposed, which is regarded as fundamentally a source of data.
- Model, which is a set of instructions for generating data comparable to that observable in the real system. The structure of the model is its set of instructions. The behavior of the model is the set of all possible data that can be generated by faithfully executing the model instructions:
- Simulator, which exercises the model's instructions to actually generate its behavior.
- Experimental frames capture how the modeler's objectives impact model construction, experimentation and validation. Experimental frames are formulated as model objects in the same manner as the models of primary interest. In this way, model/experimental frame pairs form coupled model objects which can be simulated to observe model behavior of interest.

The basic objects are related by two relations :
- Modeling relation, linking real system and model, defines how well the model represents the system or entity being modeled. In general terms a model can be considered valid if the data generated by the model agrees with the data produced by the real system in an experimental frame of interest.
- Simulation relation, linking model and simulator, represents how faithfully the simulator is able to carry out the instructions of the model.

The basic items of data produced by a system or model are time segments. These time segments are mappings from intervals defined over a specified time base to values in the ranges of one or more variables. The variables can either be observed of measured. The structure of a model may be expressed in a mathematical language called a formalism. The discrete event formalism focuses on the changes of variable values and generates time segments that are piecewise constant. Thus an event is a change in a variable value which occurs instantaneously. In essence the formalism defines how to generate new values for variables and the times the new values should take effect.

3.2 SES

A System Entity Structure(SES) provides the means to represent a family of models as a labeled tree [10,11,12]. Two of its key features are support for decomposition and specialization. The former allows decomposing a large system into smaller systems. The latter supports representation of alternative choices. Specialization enables representing a generic model (e.g., a O/S type) as one of its specialized variations (e.g., Linux or Window2000, etc.) Based on SES axiomatic specifications, a family of models (design-space) can be represented and further automatically pruned to generate a simulation model. Such models can be systematically studied and experimented with based on alternative design choices. An important, salient feature of SES is its ability to represent models not only in terms of their decomposition and specialization, but also their aspects (SES represents alternative decompositions via aspects.)

3.3 Experimental Frame

A related concept that is essential for modeling and simulation is the experimental frame - a specification of the conditions under which a system is to be observed or experimented with [10,11,12]. It is the operational formulation of the objectives motivating a modeling and simulation project. A typical experimental frame consists of a generator and a transducer, each of which can be either a federate or a live entity. The generator stimulates the system under investigation in a known setting. The transducer observes and analyzes a desired set of federates (and therefore federation) outputs as well as monitors and controls an experiment under some defined conditions.

3.4 DEVS Models

The DEVS model represents a component's dynamic behavior and has a well-defined mathematical structure as follow [10,11]:

$$M = < X, S, Y, \delta_{int}, \delta_{ext}, \lambda, ta >$$

Where X is the set of input event types, S is the sequential state set, Y is the set of external event types generated as output, δ_{int} (δ_{ext}) is the internal (external) transition function dictating state transitions due to internal (external input) events, λ is the output function generating external events as the output, and ta is the time advanced function. The DEVS environment supports building models in a hierarchical and modular manner, in which the term "modular" means the description of a model in such a way that is has recognized input and output ports through which all interaction with the external world is mediated [10,11,12]. This property enables hierarchical construction of models so that the complex network security models can be easily developed.

4   DEVS-Based Information Assurance

4.1   Approach

We approach the problem of information assurance by drawing DEVS formalism offers systematic modeling and simulation framework based on object-oriented, hierarchical and modular environment. The good points of drawing DEVS are as follows. By this, difficulties Cohen said can be easily solved.

- Event-based nature of Cyber-attack behaviors can be expressed effectively.
- Complicated structural modeling of Information infrastructure by using SES can be easily accomplished.
- Evaluation of generation of attack scenarios, the consequence of cyber-attack, the effect of defense, vulnerability and survivability is convenient through experimental frame concept.
- Hierarchical modeling of network components and packet-oriented event-based dynamic characteristic can be described properly.

Fig. 1 shows the relationship between state transition diagram of component models can be expressed by DEVS and cyber-attack behavior.

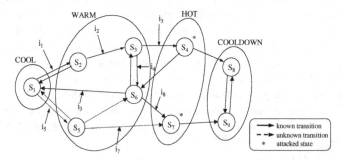

Fig. 1. State transition diagram and Cyber-attack scenario

In Fig. 1, S_i means the total state set consisted of state values of target host and arrows means transition of states. (Solid line represents known transition and dotted line represents unknown transition.) Transition of states is performed by execution of the input command in the packet inputted from the outside (i.e., attackers). Through these serial state transitions, sometimes, it reaches attacked state, accordingly, the set of commands that make initial state to arrive at attacked state (i.e., HOT level) can be defined as attack scenario. Therefore, known attack scenarios in this case are $\{i_1, i_2, i_3\}$ and $\{i_1, i_2, i_4, i_8\}$.

In the meantime, unknown attack scenario $\{i_5, i_7\}$ can be obtained from deep modeling and simulation analysis [13,14,15]. COOL, WARM, HOT, and COOLDOWN in Fig. 1 represent four levels of the attack suggested by Wadlow [7]. COOL means normal level that threats aren't detected, WARM means the level that an attack is in progress but there is no evidence, HOT means the level that attack is successful and confirmed, and COOLDOWN means the level that major security incident has occurred.

4.2 Overall Methodology

Fig. 2 shows the overall methodology for information assurance using DEVS formalism.

Phase I is concept-stipulating stage and specifies overall structure of network based on information and communications by using SES that provides means to express structural knowledge considering objectives, requirements, and constraints.

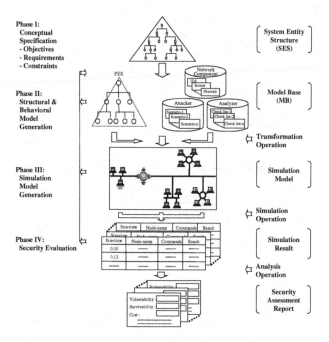

Fig. 2. Overall Methodology

Phase II generates PES, which is network structure for test, by applying pruning opion to the network structure based on information and communications expressed by

SES. Also behavioral models about the network component, the attacker, and the analyzer can be built through DEVS formalism and saved into MB. Especially, based on this basic behavior model for network component, command-level modeling using pre/post-condition can be accomplished by grouping and characterizing of commands that are used in various services. Phase III generates ultimate simulation model for a cyber attack simulation by combining dynamic models of MB with the network structure of PES applying a transformation operation and performs various simulations on generated simulation models. Finally, Phase IV can analyze detailed behaviors of cyber attack on each node through simulation trajectory. And vulnerabilities characteristics as well as defense policies of each component and/or network may be efficiently evaluated by applying vulnerability metric about node, link and network to simulation results [16].

As the Phase I of proposed methodology, Fig. 3 shows SES of the network security model for information infrastructure.

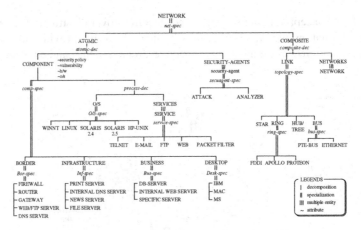

Fig. 3. SES representation of network systems

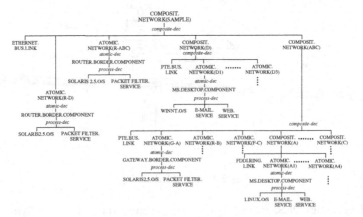

Fig. 4. A PES example

NETWORK, which is the root entity, can be classified into ATOMIC with single network and COMPOSITE with multiple networks. ATOMIC is divided into COMPONENT for security factors consideration and SECURITY-AGENTS for multiple entities. COMPONENT is again divided into O/S and several SERVICES. Besides, it can be divided into more detailed subsystems such as BORDER, INFRASTRUCTURE, BUSINESS, DESKTOP. In parallel, SECURITY-AGENTS can be divided into ATTACKER which generates attack scenario and ANALYZER which analyzes the simulation results. COMPOSITE is divided into more detailed levels such as NETWORKS, a multiple entity, which can link multiple network groups and LINK which links them all. Fig. 4 shows a pruned entity structure (PES) obtained by applying the pruning operation into the SES and also Fig. 5 depicts the conceptual diagram of the PES in Fig. 4. A final simulation model in each entity of the PES can be established by attaching the dynamics models discussed next.

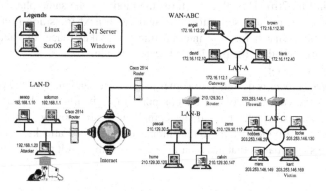

Fig. 5. Conceptual network configuration of a PES in Fig. 4

As Phase II, The command-level component modeling can be constructed on the basis of the experimental frame concept. Although a network model can be tested in a stand-alone fashion, it really does not "come to life" until it is coupled with modules capable of providing it input and observing its output. Thus, the experimental frame concept may be suitably utilized to couple with a given model (network model), generates input external events (cyber attack commands), monitor its running (consequences), and process its output (vulnerability). Fig. 6 depicts the modeling approach with the experimental frame module underlying SES/MB framework. In Fig. 6, Attacker inputs planned commands one by one into Network as well as Analyzer. Simulation proceeds by Network's responding to Attacker as well as Analyzer. If enough data are collected for analysis, Analyzer terminate simulation by sending stop commend to Network and Attacker. Then it analyzes each component's vulnerability through statistical procedure on the collected commands and attack results. A detailed modeling method can be illustrated as follows:

(1) Network Component Modeling

As described in the preceding section, Network component model comprises various services such as Telnet, E-mail, Ftp, Web, and Packet Filtering. Dynamics of these component models can be represented in various ways according to their respective state variables such as service type, H/W type, and O/S type, etc. Fig. 7(a) is a typical example of DEVS representation of component model. In Fig. 7(a), the external transition function processes the external input through the 'in port by applying command-table represented in pre/post-condition when phase is passive. During the procedure, it remains in busy state. On the other hand, the internal transition function, when phase is busy, is converted to passive and the output function delivers processed results in packet through 'out port. Based on this basic behavior model, command-level modeling can be accomplished by grouping and characterizing of commands that are used in various services.

(2) Attacker Modeling

The attacker model outputs a sequence of attacking commands according to its attacking scenario. The basic mechanism that produces this behavior is the "extract next command" and "hold-in active attacking-time" phrase in the internal transition function shown in Fig. 7(b). This phrase returns the model to the same phase, active after each internal transition and schedules it to undergo a next transition in a time given by attacking-time. Just before the internal transition takes place, the output of next command is proceeded by the pre-defined scenario table.

(3) Analyzer Modeling

The analyzer model is designed to gather the statistics and analyze the performance index such as the vulnerability of each component on given network. For the simulation convenience, we have defined the component vulnerability as the number of successful attacks divided by the total number of attempted attacks. To do this, the analyzer stores commands that arrive at its 'in port on the result table as shown in Fig. 7(c).

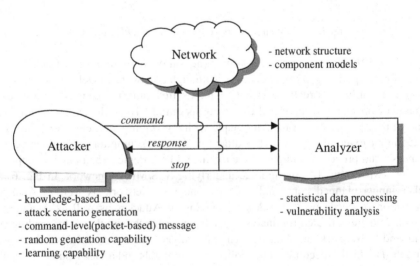

Fig. 6. Network security modeling approach using the experimental frame concept

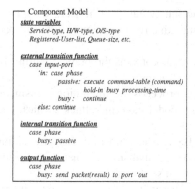

(a) Network component model

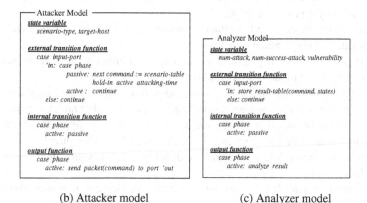

(b) Attacker model   (c) Analyzer model

Fig. 7. DEVS representation of network security models

5 Applications

5.1 Application I: Security Training Systems

As a concrete application example, we have been successfully developed and tested the network security simulation tool, SECUSIM, that is able to specify attack mechanisms, verify defense mechanisms, and evaluate their consequences. The conceptual diagram of SECUSIM is depicted in Fig. 8. SECUSIM is currently implemented on the basis of Visual C++ and enables a simulation of twenty attack patterns against hundreds network components. The software architecture of SECUSIM consists of the following five modules [17];

- GUI: It contains the functionality of network component attribute initialization, attribute value change due to simulation results and packet level graphic animation
- Network Configurator: It contains the graphic editing functionality that supports building up network structure.
- Simulation Engine: It proceeds the simulation by using a database which contains network component model base and attack scenario. Also it produces results to GUI.
- Component Model Base: It is a model base that contains behavior characteristics represented by DEVS formalism. It consists of various servers, routers, gateways, firewalls, and links.
- Attack Scenario Database: It is a database that contains instruction-level cyber attack scenario in order to analyze cyber attack behavior.

The SECUSIM contains five modes, from entry-level education purpose to actual network security analysis purpose.

(1) Basic Mode: By using cyber attack scenario database, it can provide various kinds of information about attack mechanism.
(2) Intermediate Mode: It performs cyber attack simulation for a given network by selecting attacker model and target host.
(3) Advanced Mode: It provides the verification function for cyber attack mechanism by applying direct tests to instructions that is a part of cyber attack scenario.
(4) Professional Mode: It provides various vulnerability analysis functions for network link and node by cyber attack simulation. This cyber attack simulation first set up many target nodes, attackers and defense mechanism, then the simulation proceeds.
(5) Application Mode: It provides some graphic editing functions that allow users to create his/her own network structure.

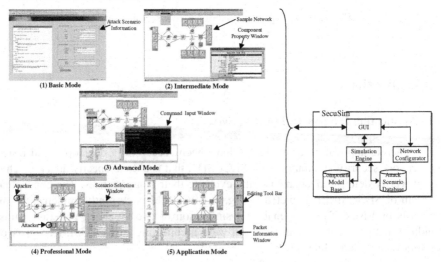

Fig. 8. A conceptual diagram of SECUSIM

5.2 Application II: Vulnerability Analysis Systems

As another application example, we have defined the vulnerability metrics of node, link, and network respectively so that proposed the simulation-based vulnerability analysis methodology [9].
(1) Node vulnerability

Node vulnerability represents comprehensive vulnerability value of vulnerability items network components have. We defined the value range of vulnerability items from 0 to 1 respectively and this value can be obtained through simulation evaluation. And node vulnerability can be obtained ultimately by getting arithmetic average considering impact level on each item when attacking is successful. That is, vulnerability item can be broken down fixed vulnerability that is dependent on O/S type and changeable vulnerability that could be caused on system configuration such as password. Impact level represents the extent of damage when the attack uses appropriate vulnerability is successful and the value is defined ranging from 0 to 1.

For example, password vulnerability item, $Vul_{password}$, which is the item of reading availability of password set by authorized users, has a characteristic of 'changeable' by users changing password, and impact level is mediate or 0.5.

Every node component on network has partial set for all vulnerability items according to configuration of themselves. So node vulnerability can be obtained by the arithmetic average of multiplying impact level of each vulnerability item by vulnerability value. Namely the node vulnerability of ith component, NV_i, is defined as follows;

$$NV_i = \sum (w_j \times vul_j) / \sum w_j . \tag{1}$$

Where the w_j and vul_j represent the impact level and evaluated value of jth vulnerability item, respectively.
(2) Link vulnerability

Because of diversified access path according to increased access points due to worldwide internet construction, link vulnerability analysis is essential. So, we defines metric, LV_i, of link vulnerability that has the value of 0 to 1 like node vulnerability as follows.

$$LV_i = n_{success} / n_{trial} . \tag{2}$$

Here, LV_i is obtained in direct measure through simulation unlike the node vulnerability using indirect measure. In the formula (2), the $n_{success}$ represents the number of successful attack scenarios and the n_{trial} denotes the number of attack scenarios injected into the target components from the attacker model. Namely, after generating attack scenarios according to uniform distribution, link vulnerability analysis progresses simulation and counts whether it makes the attack on targeted node or not. And again it resets the initial values and generates next attack scenario and simulates. Through this method it does the same processing repeatedly until satisfactory statistics are obtained. The vulnerability and countermeasure on access path can be analyzed effectively by evaluating various vulnerabilities of every link that attack is attempted through the method like this.

(3) Network vulnerability

Network vulnerability is a combined vulnerability metric grouped by network unit and this can be used as a means for synthetic evaluation about global vulnerability of network. The network vulnerability may be simply obtained by taking the arithmetic means of vulnerabilities of corresponding nodes and links. But in this case, it is more reasonable that synthetic evaluation is made giving weight to not so much calculation by simple arithmetic average as the importance according to the role of each node. Therefore we propose i^{th} network vulnerability, $NetV_i$, as follows.

$$NetV_i = \sum (W_j \times NV_j) / \sum W_j. \tag{3}$$

Where, the W_j represents the weight of importance of jth node about appropriate network.

The proposed simulation-based vulnerability metrics has been successfully developed and tested by using the DEVS formalism [9]. As vulnerability characteristics are systematically organized, understood, evaluated, and captured in our simulation approach, information assurance mechanisms may be designed more efficiently to cover attacks at various levels and scales of the system for layered, complimentary defense mechanisms.

6 Conclusions

This study has discussed the role of the simulation methodology for the information assurance that require to classify threats, to specify attack mechanisms, to verify protection mechanisms, and to evaluate consequences. To deal with this, we have employed the advanced modeling and simulation concepts, DEVS formalism, underlying the object-oriented S/W environment. Thus, the event-based nature of cyber-attack behavior can be expressed effectively. And complicated and various structural modeling of information infrastructure can be accomplished. Also evaluation of generation of attack scenarios, the consequence of cyber-attack, the effect of defense, vulnerability and survivability is convenient. Finally, hierarchical modeling of network components and packet-oriented event-based dynamic characteristic can be properly described.

As the applications of proposed methodology, first, we have been successfully developed the network security simulation tool, SECUSIM, that is able to specify attack mechanisms, verify defense mechanisms, and evaluate their consequences, and second, the simulation-based vulnerability metrics has been successfully established so that, i) it can analyze not only fixed components vulnerability that is dependent on O/S type but also changeable components vulnerability that could be caused on system configuration. ii) Besides, it can analyze the link vulnerability on access routes and iii) abstraction-related network vulnerability suitable for the hierarchical characteristic of network. As information assurance characteristics are systematically organized, understood, evaluated, and captured in our simulation approach, information assurance mechanisms may be designed more efficiently to cover attacks at various levels and scales of the system for layered, complimentary defense mechanisms. We leave here future further studies for intelligent attacker model, distributed simulation, and other metrics for information assurance such as survivability, etc.

Acknowledgement. This research was supported in part by the Ministry of Information & Communication of Korea, under the "Support Project of University IT Research Center(ITRC)" and supported by IRC (Internet Information Retrieval Research Center) in Hankuk Aviation University. IRC is a Kyounggi-Province Regional Research Center designated by Korea Science and Engineering Foundation and Ministry of Science & Technology

References

1. T. A. Longstaff, Clyde Chittister, Rich Pethia, Yacov Y. Haimes. Are We Forgetting the Risks of Information Technology. IEEE Computer 2000:43–51.
2. Nong Ye, C. Hosmer, J. Giordano, J. Feldman. Critical Information Infrastructure Protection through Process Modeling and Model-based Information Fusion. In: Proc the Information Survivability Workshop, 1998.
3. A. Jones. The challenge of building survivable information-intensive systems. IEEE Computer 2000: 39–43.
4. DoD. Defensive Information Operations. Technical Report #6510.01B, 1997.
5. F. Cohen. Simulating Cyber Attacks, Defenses, and Consequences. In Proc IEEE Symposium on Security and Privacy Special 20th Anniversary Program. Berkeley, CA, 1999.
6. E. Amoroso. Intrusion Detection. AT&T Laboratory: Intrusion Net Books, 1999.
7. T. A. Wadlow. The Process of Network Security. Addison-Wesley, 2000.
8. N. Ye and J. Giordano. CACS - A Process Control Approach to Cyber Attack Detection. Communications of the ACM.
9. Jang-Se Lee, Jeong-Rye Jeong, Sung-Do Chi, and Jong Sou Park. Simulation-based Vulnerability Analysis. Computer Systems Science & Engineering (submitted).
10. B. P. Zeigler. Object-oriented Simulation with Hierarchical, Modular Models: Intelligent Agents and Endomorphic systems. Academic Press, 1990.
11. Zeigler, B.P., H. Praehofer, and T.G. Kim. Theory of Modeling and Simulation 2ed. Academic Press, 1999.
12. B.P. Zeigler. Multifacetted Modeling and Discrete Event Simulation. Academic Press, 1984.
13. S.D. Chi. Model-Based Reasoning Methodology Using the Symbolic DEVS Simulation. Trans. of the Society for Computer Simulation International 1996;14(3):141–151.
14. Zeigler, B.P. and S.D. Chi. Symbolic Discrete Event System Specification. IEEE Trans. on System, Man, and Cybernetics 1992;22(6):1428–1443.
15. S.D. Chi, et al. Automated Cyber-Attack Scenario Generation Using the Symbolic Simulation. Trans. of the Society for Computer Simulation International (submitted).
16. S.D. Chi, et al. Network Security Modeling and Cyber-attack Simulation Methodology. In Proc 6th Australian Conf. on Information Security and Privacy, LNCS 2119. Sydney, 2001.
17. S.D. Chi, et al. SECUSIM: A Tool for the Cyber-Attack Simulation. In Proc ICICS 2001 Third International Conference on Information and communications Security, LNCS 2229. Xian, China, 2001.

Enhancing Grid Security Infrastructure to Support Mobile Computing Nodes

Kwok-Yan Lam[1], Xi-Bin Zhao[2], Siu-Leung Chung[3], Ming Gu[1], and Jia-Guang Sun[1]

[1] School of Software, Tsinghua University, Beijing, PR China
{lamky,guming,sunjg}@tsinghua.edu.cn
[2] School of Software, Tsinghua University, Beijing, PR China[†]
zxb@ujs.edu.cn
[3] School of Business Administration, The Open University of Hong Kong
slchung@ouhk.edu.hk

Abstract. With the rapid development of the global information infrastructure, the use of virtual organization (VO) is gaining increasing importance as a model for studying business and organizational structures. The notion of VO is significant in that it could serve as a basic framework for implementing geographically distributed, cross-organizational application systems in a highly flexible manner. To further enhance the pervasiveness of VO, it is of great importance that participation of mobile computing nodes be supported. Thus, security is a critical issue due to the open nature of the wireless channels that provide connectivity to mobile devices. This paper discusses, from an application angle, the importance of supporting mobile devices in VO. It also discusses the design of security infrastructures that support mobile nodes in mission-specific applications. A simple grid security infrastructure that supports participation of mobile computing nodes is also proposed to illustrate the implementation feasibility of the infrastructure.

Keywords: Secure Systems and Applications, Mobile security, Grid Computing

1 Introduction

Grid computing system has emerged as a special form of distributed computing and is distinguished from conventional distributed computing systems by its focus on larger-scale resource sharing. The early form of Grid computing was shaped by the application scenarios at which scientific computing involving a massive number of geographically distributed computing nodes were implemented. As the Grid approach was widely discussed and experimented, the objectives of the Grid computing has been generalized to refer to large-scale

---

[†] Usual address: School of Computer Science & Telecommunications Engineering, Jiangsu University, Zhenjiang, PR China

K. Chae and M. Yung (Eds.): WISA 2003, LNCS 2908, pp. 42–54, 2004.

sharing of resource, be it CPU or storage or other expensive equipments, over a wide geographical distribution [1].

A Grid computing system is defined as a platform that supports distributed system applications which require fast access to a large quantity of distributed resources in a coordinated manner. In particular, resources are often distributed in a wide-area network with components administered locally and independently. Conventional distributed computing systems may be viewed as operating system platforms with system services, such as files and CPU cycles, implemented and administered as distributed user-level processes. Thus allowing expensive mainframe computers to be replaced by low-cost computing components. Whereas a Grid computing system may be viewed as a sophisticated distributed computing system with high-level abstractions and services to facilitate large-scale sharing of resources.

Grid computing is therefore more complex than conventional distributed computing in that computations may involve distributed processes that must be able to acquire resource dynamically and communicate efficiently.

Resource sharing under the Grid computing system is built on the Virtual Organization (VO) model [1]. The objectives of the Grid are to facilitate coordinated resource sharing and problem solving in dynamic, multi-institutional virtual organizations. The key requirement of VO is the ability to negotiate resource-sharing arrangements among a set of participating parties and then use the resulting resource pool for achieving some application objectives. Analogous to the Client-Server computing model of the 80s, VO is an abstraction for designing distributed systems. Unlike the Client-Server model which supported a simple inter-process communication paradigm within the system, VO provides a more flexible abstraction for implementing distributed systems with more complex inter-process relationships. Therefore, the key issue in Grid computing is the provision of services and protocols that facilitate implementation of VO over a widely distributed environment.

The notion of VO has enabled Grid computing systems to support a wide variety of applications beyond scientific computing. In particular, recent development in e-commerce has made the concept of VO especially suitable for organizing and implementing distributed commercial applications. For example, e-commerce applications in the healthcare industry typically require large-scale sharing of resources (medical records, laboratory test results and expensive equipments) by participating organizations. The sharing is usually specific to certain tasks originated from business objectives that require close cooperation and coordination of a number of medical information systems and computing components. A Grid computing system with support for VO will help simplify the design and implementation of such applications. In addition, security is a critical requirement in such applications and is a major issue in VO design.

To further encourage the adoption of Grid computing as a platform for commercial applications, it is desirable to support participation of mobile computing nodes as resource sharing parties. Due to the high penetration of mobile computing devices, most e-commerce models have been extended to include mobile devices as transacting parties. Electronic transactions conducted over the mobile platform are gaining popularity due to the convenience and portability of low-cost handheld devices. In order to promote the adoption of e-commerce, system designers have been actively exploring approaches that may attain higher penetration than the wired Internet. With the explosive growth of mobile phone population and the fast adoption of wireless network technology, support for e-commerce transactions over the mobile platform has become an attractive option [2,3].

As a pervasive platform for supporting commercial computing applications, Grid computing systems should be designed to allow mobile users to initiate or participate in Grid computing without compromising security and performance. In a typical mobile computing environment, one or more of the transacting parties are based on some wireless computing devices. However, security over the mobile platform is more critical due to the open nature of wireless networks.

Furthermore, security is more difficult to implement on a mobile platform because of the resource limitation of mobile handheld devices. In practice, handheld devices such as palm top or pocket PC are the most commonly embraced platforms as end user devices for mobile computing [4]. Nevertheless, computing operations on handheld devices are subjected to resource constraints such as smaller memory, slower CPU and smaller display. These constraints pose serious limitations to security mechanisms for mobile computing.

Therefore, a Grid security infrastructure that supports the participation of mobile nodes will play a significant role in the development of Grid computing. The increasing popularity and importance of Grid computing have motivated a lot of research and development initiatives in Grid computing systems. The Globus project is one of the important efforts in the Grid community to develop infrastructure and toolkits for facilitating development of Grid applications [5]. The Globus Security Infrastructure (GSI) is based on public key cryptography and the Secure Socket Layer mechanism, and is designed to address Grid security problems such as delegation and single sign-on.

This paper discusses the importance of supporting mobile devices in Grid applications and the design of the security infrastructure in order for mobile nodes to be supported by the Grid. The organization of this paper is as follows. Section 2 motivates the discussion by illustrating the role of mobile nodes in Grid computing. This section presents as an example a commercial application that may be implemented over the Grid and with the need for mobile nodes. Section 3 briefly describes the Globus security infrastructure and explains the difficulties of supporting mobile devices on this infrastructure. Section 4 proposes a system architecture and security mechanism for extending the Grid Security Infrastructure to support mobile nodes. Section 5 concludes the discussion of this paper.

2   A Grid Application with Mobile Nodes

The concept of Grid computing has been generalized to include large-scale sharing of resources over a geographically distributed environment. A Grid computing system is a system platform that provides protocols and services to facilitate coordinated resource sharing. The notion of VO was introduced as an abstraction for organizing and implementing distributed components of Grid applications. It provides a framework for developing certain important commercial applications arisen from e-commerce.

There is a growing trend in deploying e-commerce in traditional organizations to improve operational efficiency and service quality. Through the provision of e-commerce services, traditional organizations have been working aggressively to adopt the Internet to improve efficiency of internal work flows as well as to enhance the interactions with their customers. For example, e-government in the public sector and e-banking in the financial industry are increasingly popular in many countries nowadays.

However, the potential of the Internet will be better exploited if e-commerce is considered at a macroscopic level i.e. to support commercial applications that require closer cooperation and interactions among business partners [6]. In it's simplest form of deployment, most organizations use the Internet simply as a channel for delivering services to customers or for improving internal communications. Recent development in e-commerce has led a lot of commercial organizations to adopt the Internet as a platform for conducting business.

Therefore, distributed applications involving multiple organizations are commonplaces for sophisticated e-commerce system. The establishment and management of dynamic and cross-institutional virtual organization sharing relationships require new architecture model and system infrastructure. In general, resource sharing in a distributed computing system is implemented by interprocess communication primitives. Thus issues related to Grid computing is more complex than conventional distributed computing because of the requirements of coordinated resource sharing in a flexible and dynamic manner within the virtual organization.

From practical experiences, the VO abstraction is especially suitable for implementing mission-specific applications initiated by special operations such as disease control, crisis management or law enforcement. The accomplishment of such mission-specific operations typically requires close cooperation of multiple organizations. These organizations may or may not have prior working relationship and may not trust each other. The cooperation is driven by events and is established dynamically in response to the occurrence of the events. In general, sharing of resources in such circumstances is subjected to stringent control of the resource owner. These characteristics fit the profile of VO applications and the problem is preferably addressed using the VO abstraction.

To illustrate, we consider a commercial application scenario in which Grid computing is a suitable approach. In this example, an epidemiological surveillance and control taskforce is established in response to the outbreak of Dengue Fever in Asia, a fatal disease transmitted by mosquitoes which can leads to clinical shock and death within 24 hours [7]. In order to monitor and control the spreading of the fever effectively, there are a number of key areas to be monitored closely. Among others, for example, it is important to keep track of hospitals' reports of suspicious cases for the Dengue symptoms, to retrieve immigration records of patients in recent weeks to determine the source of infection (whether the source is local or from overseas), to access to oversea data such as the DengueNet which is a global surveillance system for Dengue fever, to identify the residential and work addresses of patients with the Dengue symptoms and to study inspection reports from the environment authority on the hygienic conditions of the surrounding community of possible source of the disease. Information available through the monitoring of key human behaviors in the surrounding community, such as inappropriate disposal of discarded household items that contribute to the availability of mosquito larval habitats, can help environment authority to take proper measures against the spreading of the disease.

It is obvious from this example that, in order to combat the disease more effectively and efficiently, close cooperation among a number of otherwise independent institutions is necessary. In this case, the immigration authority, the environment authority and the health authority, etc. Typically, some form of cross-institutional taskforce will be established for the special mission. The participating institutions are geographically distributed and independent of one another. Some of these institutions, for example the immigration authority and the environment authority, will have to conduct some parts of their operation in field conditions.

The operation of the taskforce will require access to computer systems and data across the participating organizations. These organizations need to provide interconnectivity to facilitate the operation of the taskforce. For operations undertaken in field conditions, support for mobile devices is needed. For legislative reasons, these systems normally do not share information except for special situations in which authorization by top officials from the government administration is granted. Note that cross-institutional cooperation of this nature is common in law-enforcement operations. However, due to the sensitive nature of such operations, this paper uses the healthcare scenario as an example for illustration.

Therefore, a task involving cross-institutional cooperation and sharing of distributed resources is created. Furthermore, the sharing is not without restriction. In general, each of the autonomous participants continues to have full ownership and control of their own system and data. As a result, the operation of the taskforce conforms to a scenario typically modeled the VO abstraction. The creation and management of the VO is somehow dynamic. Sharing of resources among VO participants requires sophisticated access control mechanisms.

The Grid computing system is therefore identified as a suitable framework for commercial cross-institutional applications of this nature. The Grid architecture is defined in accordance with the needs of creating and managing virtual organizations. It identifies fundamental system components, specifies the purpose and function of these components, and indicates how these components interact with one another. Existing Grid computing systems may be adopted to support implementation of such application systems.

However, as mentioned, in most of the real commercial applications, some part of the operations may be undertaken in field conditions, thus requiring support for mobile devices. Therefore, the Grid infrastructure should be designed to allow participation of mobile users in order to enhance the pervasiveness of Grid computing. In this connection, the design of Grid security infrastructure is especially important due to the criticalness of security issues in commercial applications and the constraints of mobile devices in implementing security mechanisms. Consequently, existing Grid computing systems may need to be extended in face of such commercial computing applications. For example, the sophisticated security mechanisms offered by Globus cannot be efficiently implemented on mobile handheld devices.

3   The Grid Security Infrastructure

Built on the platform offered by distributed computing systems, Grid computing systems need to address additional services to allow creation and management of relationships among participants in the virtual organization in a flexible manner. The complexities of Grid problems are aggravated by

1. The characteristics of typical Grid applications in which Grid participants are multi-institutional, and inter-participant relationships are highly dynamic.
2. The open nature of the Internet where strong security protection for inter-process communications is essential.

The need to support complex communication structures in an open network environment leads to demand for more sophisticated security solutions for Grid applications. Therefore, authentication protocols and access control required for Grid applications are core issues in Grid computing systems. The focus is on the secure communication among Grid nodes and enforcement of access control policy at each node in face of the Grid problems.

Due to the dynamic nature of sharing relationships in VO, security solutions for Grid computing systems must allow applications to coordinate diverse access control policies and to operate securely in heterogeneous environments. VO may grow and shrink dynamically, acquiring resources when required to solve a problem and releasing them when they are no longer needed. Grid security solutions need to provide mutual authentication that allows a user, the processes that comprise a user's computation, and the resources used by those processes, to verify each other's identity.

Each time a process obtains a resource, it does so on behalf of a particular user. However, it is frequently impractical for that user to interact directly with each such resource for the purposes of authentication. Thus Grid security solutions should have the following characteristics:

1. Strong authentication of users.
2. Single sign-on.
3. Delegation.
4. Interoperable with various local security solutions.

The Globus Security Infrastructure (GSI) provides an implementation of security infrastructure that aims to meet the abovementioned requirements [8]. GSI provides a number of services for Grid applications, including mutual authentication and single sign-on. In this connection, the GSI introduced the concept of user proxy in order to eliminate the needs for user intervention. A user proxy is defined to be a session manager process and is given permission to act on behalf of a user for a limited period of time.

The GSI uses public key cryptography as the basis for its functionality and is based on the Secure Sockets Layer (SSL) for its mutual authentication protocol. Extensions to these standards have been added for single sign-on and delegation. The Globus Toolkit's implementation of the GSI adheres to the Generic Security Service API (GSS-API), which is a standard API for security systems promoted by the Internet Engineering Task Force (IETF).

GSI is based on public key infrastructure, X.509 certificates, and the Secure Socket Layer (SSL) communication protocol. Every user and service on the Grid is identified via a certificate, which contains information vital to identifying and authenticating the user or service. A trusted third party (a CA) is used to certify the link between the public key and the subject in the certificate. The link between the CA and its certificate must be established via some non-cryptographic means, or else the system is not trustworthy. GSI certificates are encoded in the X.509 certificate format.

In order for Grid participants to achieve mutual authentication, each Grid participants need to perform digital signature using their private keys and go through the SSL authentication protocol. The GSI software provided by the Globus Toolkit expects the user's private key to be stored in a file in the local computer's storage. To prevent other users of the computer from stealing the private key, the file that contains the key is encrypted via a password (also known as a "pass phrase"). To use the GSI, the user must enter the pass phrase required to decrypt the file containing their private key.

The GSI provides a delegation capability, by extending the standard SSL protocol, to simplify the security interface to the Grid user. The objective of the delegation function is to reduce the number of times the user must enter his pass phrase. If a Grid process requires that several distributed resources be used (each requiring mutual authentication), the need to re-enter the user's pass phrase can be avoided by means of the delegation function.

The delegation function is implemented using a new entity called "proxy". A proxy is created to represent the user, within a time limit, in a Grid application. It consists of a new certificate (with a new public key in it) and a new private key. The new certificate contains the owner's identity, modified slightly to indicate that it is a proxy. The new certificate is signed by the owner, rather than a CA.

The certificate also includes a time notation after which the proxy should no longer be accepted by others.

The proxy's private key is a short-term key, thus has a less stringent security requirement as the owner's private key. It is thus possible to store the proxy's private key in a local storage system in clear form and with its protection rely on the access control of the file system. Once a proxy is created and stored, the user can use the proxy certificate and private key for mutual authentication without entering a password. The use of short-term digital certificate for implementing security that aims to balance risk and efficiency is discussed in [9].

The proxy also serves as the basis of the single sign-on implemented by Globus which provides a mechanism by which a process can authenticate to its user proxy or another process. This authentication identifies the user that created the process. When proxies are used, the mutual authentication process differs slightly. The remote party receives not only the proxy's certificate (signed by the owner), but also the owner's certificate. During mutual authentication, the owner's public key (obtained from her certificate) is used to validate the signature on the proxy certificate. The CA's public key is then used to validate the signature on the owner's certificate. This establishes a chain of trust from the CA to the proxy through the owner.

While the GSI offers a sophisticated security solution for implementing security in Grid applications, the existing approach needs to be enhanced in order to support mobile Grid participants efficiently. The use of the extended SSL approach in GSI makes it not suitable for low-cost mobile computing devices. In order to support the GSI, a mobile device needs to implement the extended SSL protocol which is computation-intensive and connection-oriented. Such operations cannot be efficiently implemented on mobile devices in practice. In this paper, we extend the GSI by introducing a wireless protocol gateway for representing mobile nodes. A lightweight security mechanism is provided to minimize computation overhead on mobile devices.

4   Security Framework for Mobile Nodes

In this section, we discuss the security architecture and mechanism for supporting mobile devices in the Grid security infrastructure. A new security mechanism is needed for supporting mobile nodes because of the limitations and constraints of such devices. Regardless of the attractive features of handheld devices, there are non-trivial challenges to be addressed in order for handheld computing devices to be adopted as a practical platform for running the GSI which requires implementation of computation-intensive operations.

In this connection, the concept of wireless protocol gateway, which serves as a fixed-line agent for the handheld devices, is introduced. In order to support mobile nodes but with minimal impact on the existing GSI, a mobile user connects to a wireless protocol gateway which in turn authenticates to the user proxy on behalf of the user. The user has an established trust relationship with the wireless protocol gateway. With the wireless protocol gateway, handheld

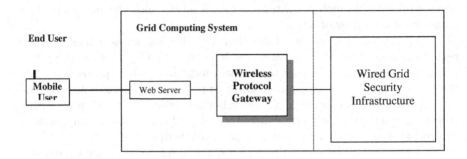

Fig. 1. System Architecture of Mobile Grid Nodes

devices are connected to the proxy server indirectly i.e. through the gateway server. To minimize computational overhead on the mobile device, the end user is authenticated to the wireless protocol gateway through some simple strong authentication scheme, and the gateway server in turn executes the complex protocol on behalf of the handheld devices.

In this architecture, the mobile user authenticates to a wireless protocol gateway instead of connecting to a proxy directly. This design aims to avoid changing the existing GSI so as to help minimize impact on existing Grid applications. Furthermore, from industry experiences, a new design can be adopted more smoothly if it does not require changes to existing infrastructure and applications. In this paper, the system architecture in Figure 1 is adopted for extending the GSI:

In addition to the proposed security architecture, a security mechanism is included to protect the connection between the mobile device and the wireless protocol gateway. Due to resource constraints of mobile platforms, the use of SSL protocol (which is also known as the TLS protocol [10]) for mutual authentication is not suitable for mobile devices. For example, the WTLS protocol was developed by the WAP Forum [11] as a variant of the TLS protocol to cater for the resource limitations of wireless devices. In this setting, a protocol gateway called WAP Gateway was developed to provide connectivity between a WAP-based handheld device and the application web server.

In its simplest form, wireless handheld devices such as mobile phones may adopt the WAP technology and securing electronic commerce transactions using WTLS. With the use of WTLS, the security architecture is as shown in Figure 2 below.

The architecture illustrated in Figure 2 leads to a major security concern. The WAP Gateway which translates WTLS-protected data to TLS-protected creates a security gap at the WAP gateway. As a protocol gateway, the WAP gateway receives WTLS traffic from mobile handheld devices, decrypts the WTLS data

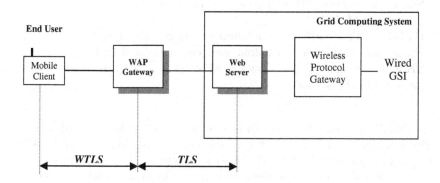

Fig. 2. WAP-Based System Architecture of Mobile Grid Nodes

and re-encrypt them by sending the data to the TLS traffic. Therefore, mobile user data is exposed at the WAP gateway. The situation is worsened by the fact that the WAP gateway is typically hosted outside of the perimeter of the GSI. The existence of the security gap will undermine the security of the GSI. Though future version of the WAP protocol suite is believed to provide TLS at handheld devices, the computation overhead of TLS on mobile devices remain a serious hurdle.

In face of the difficulties of implementing security mechanisms on mobile devices, a simple security mechanism is devised for use by mobile Grid nodes. The mobile Grid user may connect to the wireless protocol gateway securely through this mechanism, and the wireless protocol gateway will in turn logon to the proxy server on behalf of the mobile user. This way, single sign-on provided by the existing GSI may be used by the mobile user. The security mechanisms suitable for deployment on a mobile platform needs to satisfy the following requirements:

- Secure.
- Easy to implement.
- Low computation needs.
- Achieve entity authentication at the end as one of the protocol objectives.
- Achieve key exchange at the end as one of the protocol objectives.

The security mechanism presented in this paper is based on the ISO/IEC 9798 Entity Authentication protocol [12]. In the description of the mechanism, we use the following denotation:

- **S** denotes the server side of the authentication.
- **C** denotes the client side of the authentication.
- $EK_A[X]$ denotes the public key encryption operation on data **X** controlled by the public key of **A**.

- **SGN$_A$[X]** denotes the signature operation on data **X** controlled by the private key of **A**.
- **R$_a$** is a nonce identifier (a random number) generated by **S**.
- **R$_b$** are nonce identifiers (random numbers) generated by **C**.
- **SK** is the symmetric session key shared by **S** and **C** for protecting transaction messages in the session.

In this discussion, 1024-bit RSA is used as the public key algorithm used by **S**. **SK** is a 128-bit binary value for some symmetric algorithms such as AES or 3DES. All nonce identifiers are 128-bit binary values.

A mobile user wishing to participate in the Grid application initiates the security mechanism from his/her mobile handheld device. The mechanism is implemented as an authentication protocol [13] between the handheld device and the wireless protocol gateway. The mechanism starts with the client **C** sending an authentication request to the server **S**. In response to the request, the following protocol messages are exchanged between **S** and **C**. Upon successful completion of the protocol run, the two parties are mutually authenticated and share a secret key for protecting subsequent messages in the same session.

Authentication Protocol $\wp$:

M1.	S → C :	Ra
M2.	C → S :	**SGN$_C$[Ra, R$_b$, S], EK$_S$[R$_a$, R$_b$, SK]**
M3.	S → C :	**SGN$_S$[C, R$_b$]**

An informal description of the protocol $\wp$ is as follows. The protocol mechanism is based on the ISO/IEC 9798-3 standard and the logic of the protocol is straightforward. Thus an informal treatment is more effective in describing the protocol. Analysis of the mechanism using formal logic is outside of the scope of this paper.

M1: The server **S** starts the authentication by sending a random challenge **R$_a$** to **C**. The purpose of **R$_a$** is to allow the server to assure the freshness of messages involved in this protocol run [14].

M2: The client **C** returns a response to **S** which consists of two message tokens: the entity authentication token and the key exchange token. The entity authentication token enables **S** to verify that it is communicating with the genuine **C**. When verifying the entity authentication token, **S** checks the value of **R$_a$** so as to ensure that **M2** is not a replay of some previous protocol message. The nonce identifier **R$_b$** introduces additional randomness to avoid signing on a random strong chosen by another party. **R$_b$** also serves as a random challenge for **S** to authenticate itself to **C**. The key exchange token in **M2** is a structure similar to the authentication token. In this token,

SK is the session key generated by **C** and is available only to **S** because the decryption operation **DK$_S$[X]** is known only to **S**.

M3: The server **S** authenticates to **C** by signing on the nonce value **R$_b$**.

Therefore, the mechanism $\wp$ has the following characteristics that allow it to satisfy the abovementioned security requirements of mobile commerce:

- $\wp$ provides security by achieving authentication and key exchange.
- **C** authenticates to **S** by proving knowledge of private key of **C** and vice versa.
- At the end of the protocol, **S** and **C** share a session key **SK** such that **SK** is chosen by the genuine **C** and is readable by the entity that knows the private key of **S**.
- **C** performs one public key encryption, one digital signature operation and one signature verification function. Note that encryption and verification operations typically have lower computing overhead than decryption and signature operations.
- Achieve entity authentication and key exchange at the end as one of the protocol objectives.

To summarize, the proposed scheme $\wp$ is a computation-economical security mechanism that meets the security requirements of mobile Grid nodes and is suitable for implementation on resource-scarce devices. This scheme was designed to meet the security needs of security-sensitive mobile applications including electronic financial services and electronic government services initiated over mobile handheld devices.

5 Conclusion

This paper discussed the importance of supporting mobile nodes in VO. The notion of VO is significant in that it could serve as a basic framework for implementing geographically distributed, cross-organizational application systems in a highly flexible manner. To further enhance the pervasiveness of VO, it is of great importance that participation of mobile computing nodes be supported. In this paper, we discussed, from an application angle, the importance of supporting mobile devices in VO. Security for such applications is a critical issue due to the open nature of the wireless channels that provide connectivity to mobile devices. The paper also discussed the design of security infrastructures that support mobile nodes in mission-specific applications. A simple grid security infrastructure that supports participation of mobile computing nodes is also proposed to illustrate the implementation feasibility of the infrastructure. For illustration, we proposed an enhancement to the GSI and a simple security mechanism for connecting mobile nodes to the enhanced GSI. A wireless protocol gateway as an extension of the GSI was explained.

With the enhanced GSI, mobile users securely connect to the wireless protocol gateway through the mechanism $\wp$. Upon successful completion of mutual authentication, the wireless protocol gateway executes complex GSI protocols with the proxy server in order to participate in VO operations with delegation and single sign-on capabilities. This is a pragmatic approach in that it aims to support Grid nodes in GSI without creating impact on existing GSI and Grid computing applications.

This research is part of our effort in designing security infrastructure for commercial Grid applications which extend from the wired to the wireless Internet. The security mechanism presented in this paper has been implemented and in use successfully by some e-commerce and e-government applications.

References

1. I. Foster, C. Kesselman, S. Tuecke, "The anatomy of the grid: enabling scalable virtual organizations", *Int. J. Supercomputer Applications*, Vol. 15, Issue 3, 2001, pp. 200–222.
2. B. Anckar, D. D'Incau, "Value creation in mobile commerce: Findings from a consumer survey", *Journal of Information Technology Theory & Application*, Vol. 4, Issue 1, 2002.
3. K. Parson, J. Schaeffler, "U.S. wireless phone penetration climbs", *Wireless Insider*, October 2001.
4. G. Sean, "Networking in the palm of your hand", *Network Computing*, Vol. 13, Issue 16, August 2002.
5. I. Foster, C. Kesselman, "Globus: A Metacomputing Infrastructure Toolkit", *International Journal of Supercomputer Applications*, Vol. 11, No. 2, 1997.
6. D. Tapscott, D. Ticoll, A. Lowy, "The rise of business web", *Ubiquity*, Vol. 1, Issue 3, March 2000.
7. "Dengue fever prevention and control", *Weekly Epidemiological Record*, Vol. 77 Issue 6, August 2002, pp. 41–48.
8. "Overview of the Grid Security Infrastructure" at http://www-fp.globus.org/security/overview.html.
9. J.Y. Zhou and K.Y. Lam. "Securing digital signatures for non-repudiation", *Journal of Computer Communications*, Vol. 22, No. 8, 1999, pp. 710–716.
10. Internet Engineering Task Force. "Transport Layer Security (TLS)", http://www.ietf.org/html.charters/tls-charter.html.
11. The Open Mobile Alliance Ltd, "Wireless Application Protocol", http://www.wapforum.org.
12. ISO/IEC DIS 9798-3. "Information technology, security techniques, entity authentication, Part 3: mechanisms using digital signature techniques (Second Edition)", ISO/IEC, 1998.
13. K.Y. Lam, "Building an Authentication Service for Distributed Systems", *Journal of Computer Security*, Vol. 2, No. 1, 1993, IOS (Amsterdam).
14. K.Y. Lam and D. Gollmann, "Freshness Assurance of Authentication Protocols", *Proceedings of the 2nd European Symposium on Research in Computer Security*, Toulouse, France, November, 1992, LNCS 648, Springer-Verlag.

Reliable Cascaded Delegation Scheme for Mobile Agent Environments

Hyun-suk Lee[1], Hyeog Man Kwon[2], and Young Ik Eom[1]

[1] School of Information and Communication Engineering, Sungkyunkwan Univ.
Jangangu Chunchundong 300, Suwon Kyunggido, Korea
{ciga2000,yieom}@ece.skku.ac.kr
[2] HFR, Inc. 5F, Onse Bldg., Gumi-dong, Bundang-gu, Sungnam-si Kyunggi-do, 463-810,
Korea
hmkwon@hfrnet.com

Abstract. In mobile agent environments, migration of an agent occurs continuously due to the mobility of the agent. So, cascaded delegation can occur among places for delegating the privilege to execute the agent. Because the existing delegation scheme considers only the delegation between two places that participate in migration of an agent, it does not support secure cascaded delegation. In this paper, we propose a cascaded delegation scheme that provides agents with secure cascaded delegation in mobile agent environments. Depending on the trust-relationship among places, the proposed scheme achieves the goal by nesting each delegation token or by nesting only initial token signed by sender of the agent within the signed part of the next immediate delegation token. We prove that the proposed scheme is secure against the attack of replaying a message and the attack of substituting a delegation token.

1 Introduction

Mobile agents are defined as processes which can be autonomously delegated or transferred from node to node in network to perform some computations on behalf of the user. Compared with the client-server model, mobile agent technology has many advantages including reduction on network traffic, asynchronous interactions between clients and servers, and dynamic update server interfaces, so in recent years to guarantee the mobility of agents more securely several studies which have focused on authentication or protection of the hosts and agents have been performed [1-6].

In this paper, we propose a cascaded delegation scheme for mobile agents to perform cascaded delegation securely when a mobile agent migrates among several places continuously. *Delegation* is the process whereby a principal authorizes another principal to act on his behalf. *Cascaded delegation* is the process whereby the delegated principal delegates the rights of the delegating principal further [7,8].

*The rest of the paper is organized as follows. Section 2 outlines delegation between two places in mobile agent environments and cascaded delegation in distributed

---

*This work was supported by Korea Research Foundation Grant (KRF-2002-041-D00420).

K. Chae and M. Yung (Eds.): WISA 2003, LNCS 2908, pp. 55–68, 2004.

systems. Section 3 proposes a delegation scheme for cascaded delegation in mobile agent environments and describes how the proposed scheme works. Section 4 proves the security of our new scheme. Section 5 concludes this paper and proposes future works.

2 Backgrounds

The representative study for delegation in mobile agent environments is Berkovits et al.'s study [2]. But their study considers only the delegation between two places that participate in migration of an agent, and it does not support secure cascaded delegation. In this section, we describe existing delegation scheme between two places in mobile agent environments and cascaded delegation in distributed systems.

2.1 Mobile Agent Environments

In Berkovits et. al.'s study, according to the four distinct trust relationships between two principals that participate in migration of an agent, the principal of the executing agent becomes a compound principal in order for the agent to continue execution. Let us assume the situation where an agent A running on place I_1 as the principal P_1 migrates to the next place I_2 to execute itself as a new principal P_2. The four trust relationships are as follows:

(1) *Place Handoff* : I_1 can hand the agent off to I_2. I_2 will then execute the agent on behalf of P_1.
(2) *Place Delegation* : I_1 can delegate the agent to I_2. I_2 will combine its authority with that of P_1, and then execute the agent.
(3) *Agent Handoff* : The agent can directly hand itself off to I_2. I_2 will then execute the agent on behalf of A regardless of P_1.
(4) *Agent Delegation* : The agent can delegate itself to I_2. I_2 will combine its authority with that of A, and then execute the agent regardless of P_1.

According to the four distinct trust relationships between two principals that participate in migration of an agent, transformation of the executing principal of an agent is shown in Table 1. In this authentication scheme that Berkovits et. al. proposed, safeness is proved using Lampson et. al.'s authentication theory in distributed systems. Here A **for** S means authority of an agent signed by sender of the agent.

Table 1. Executing principal of an agent after migration of an agent

Agent Migration Request	Trust-relationship	Executing principal in place I_1	Executing principal in place I_2
Place	Place Handoff	P_1	$P_2 == P_1$
Place	Place Delegation	P_1	$P_2 == I_2$ **for** P_1
Agent	Agent Handoff	P_1	$P_2 == A$ **for** S
Agent	Agent Delegation	P_1	$P_2 == I_2$ **for** A **for** S

Because the existing delegation scheme considers only the delegation between two places that participate in migration of an agent, it does not support secure cascaded delegation.

2.2 Cascaded Delegation in Distributed Systems

Cascaded delegation in distributed systems can be defined as the process whereby the delegated principal delegates the rights of the delegating principal further [6,7]. Fig. 1 illustrates the situation where starting with grantor A the mobile agent migrates to another place B and C in sequence and requests a service to the end-server S.

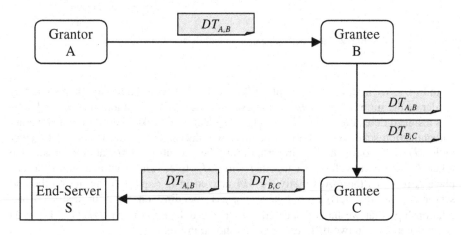

Fig. 1. Cascaded Delegation in mobile environments

Cascaded delegation occurs with the delegation token containing the privileges of the migrating place. However, in Fig. 2, the relationship among the delegation tokens is not formed, so this cascaded delegation can not be secure against the attack of substituting a delegation token.

3 Cascaded Delegation Scheme

This paper proposes a scheme for secure cascaded delegation in mobile agent environments. In this section, first we describe our system architecture and data structures necessary for secure cascaded delegation. Then we describe our proposed cascaded delegation scheme with an algorithm and example scenarios of cascaded delegation using our proposed scheme.

3.1 System Architecture

Fig. 2 shows the process that a mobile agent *MA* migrates from place I_1 eventually to I_n, then requests a service to the end server S with the delegation token DT_{In-1}.

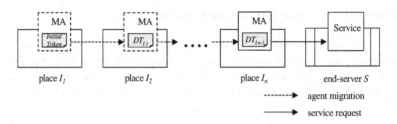

place I_1 place I_2 place I_n end-server S

- - - - - - ▶   agent migration

────────▶   service request

Fig. 2. Cascaded delegation in mobile agent environments

In Fig. 2, we assumes that the place I_1 executes *MA* with the initial token signed by sender of the mobile agent *MA*. In the event of the *MA*'s migration, the *MA* in I_1 creates a signed delegation token DT_{I1} to grant I_2. Here public-key based digital signature authentication scheme is used between the two places. Then I_1 transfers *MA* together with DT_{I1} to I_2 confidentially. In turn, during the execution of *MA* at I_2, I_2 creates the token DT_{I2}, then transfers *MA* together with DT_{I2} to I_3. This continues until the last place I_n receives the *MA*. Finally the *MA* arrived in I_n requests a service to the end server S with the delegation token DT_{In-1}. Depending on the four distinct trust-relationships that we have discussed earlier, the delegation token $DT_{Ik}(1 \le k \le n-1)$ can be generated in two different forms as shown in Fig. 3.

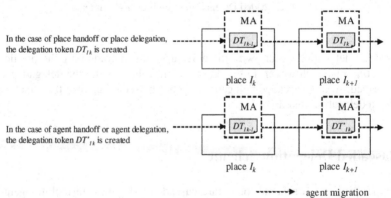

In the case of place handoff or place delegation, the delegation token DT_{Ik} is created

place I_k place I_{k+1}

In the case of agent handoff or agent delegation, the delegation token DT'_{Ik} is created

place I_k place I_{k+1}

- - - - - - ▶   agent migration

Fig. 3. Two way of the creation of token depending on the trust-relationships

The places which participate in this cascaded delegation process should figure out trust-relationships among the places that participate in migration of an agent. So, the structure shown as Fig. 4 is necessary.

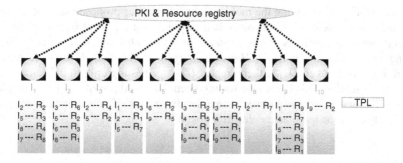

Fig. 4. Additional structure to figure out trust-relationship

Because, in our proposed scheme, public-key based digital signature authentication scheme is used between the delegating place and the delegated place, the places should be able to access PKI(Public Key Infrastructure). Also, the places should have TPL(Trustable Place List) and maintain it. TPL contains the information which places offer the resources that are required by the *MA*. So, the places should also access resource registry periodically to renew the information.

3.2 Data Structures

In this section, we describe the structures of the messages exchanged between places, the structure of the messages used to get the result which is offered by the end server, and the structure of the delegation token that is used in our proposed scheme. Fig. 5 shows the structure of the messages and the delegation token of our proposed scheme.

DR :	Delegator_ID	Migration_Type		Timestamp	Nonce	
DA :	Delegatee_ID	$Sig_{Delegatee}$(DR's Nonce)		Timestamp	Nonce	
SRR :	Requestor_ID	Timestamp	Nonce			
SRC :	Requested_ID	$Sig_{Requested}$(SRC's Nonce)		Timestamp	Nonce	
SR :	Requester_ID	$Sig_{Requester}$(Server's Nonce)	Delegation_token		Timestamp	Service_ID
SA :	Server_ID	Service_ID	Result			
DT_{li} :	Delegator_ID	Delegatee_ID	Privilege	$Sig_{Delegator}$(DA's Nonce)	Timestamp	DT_{li-1}
DT'_{li} :	Delegator_ID	Delegatee_ID	Privilege	$Sig_{Delegator}$(DA's Nonce)	Timestamp	Initial Token

Fig. 5. Data structures of the messages and the delegation token for the proposed scheme

The *DR* message and the DA message are used for authentication between places. On the contrary, the *SRC* message and *SRR* message are used for authentication between the last place on the delegation path and the end server. *SR* message and *SA* message are used to request a service and acknowledge a result of the service, respectively. The delegation token *DT* is created to authenticate the delegated place and delegate priority of executing the mobile agent *MA*. In our proposed scheme, there are two kinds of the delegation tokens. When migration of an agent occurs, if the relationship between places is *Place Handoff* or *Place Delegation*, I_i creates DT_{Ii} by nesting DT_{Ii-1}. But if it is *Agent Handoff* or *Agent Delegation*, I_i casts the previous nested delegation token DT_{Ii-1}, then creates DT'_{Ii} by nesting only initial token signed by the *MA*'s sender. This is because having been delegated priority by previous places is not necessary any more and secure against the attack of substituting a delegation token without the accumulated delegation token.

3.3 Algorithms

In our proposed scheme, we assume the delegation path is $I_1I_2I_3...I_{n-1}I_nS$. The mobile agent *MA* running on place I_1 as the principal P_1 migrates to I_2, $I_3,...,I_{n-1}$, I_n in sequence. At this moment, modified priority to execute *MA* is delegated to respective places $I_i(2 \le i \le n)$. Arriving at the last place I_n on the delegation path, *MA* requests a service to the end server S. Our proposed scheme can be divided into four different phases. (1) The delegation place I_1 initiates cascaded delegation with I_2. (2) The intermediary place I_i ($2 \le i \le n-1$) mediates cascaded delegation. (3) The final place I_n requests a service to the end server S. (4) The end server S performs the requested service and offers the result.

In the case of the situation where the delegating place I_1 executing *MA* on itself migrates *MA* to I_2 or *MA* running on place I_1 as the principal P_1 wants to migrate to I_2, I_1 initiates cascaded delegation using Algorithm 1. At the same time, the place I_2 uses the segment A of Algorithm 2 (see *Segment A: Contacting with I_{i-1}* of Algorithm 2) to authenticate I_1 and be authenticated by I_1. In the following Algorithms, TS means valid period of respective messages. MT of the *DR* message means Migration Type and the value of MT is one of PH(Place Handoff), PD(Place Delegation), AH(Agent Handoff) and AD(Agent Delegation). N_X means the nonce generated by the place X and $Sig_Y(N_X)$ means the place Y's public-key based digital signature on the nonce that is generated by the place X. Also, $Priv_X(Y)$ means the privilege that the place X granted to the place Y to act on his behalf and t_X means the period that the delegation token created by the place X is assumed to be valid.

As we comment earlier, the situation where migration of an agent occurs is divided into two cases. One is the delegating place executing *MA* on itself migrates *MA* and the other is *MA* requests migration to some place. In Algorithm 1, in the case that I_1 migrates *MA* to I_2, if the identity of I_2 is in TPL of I_1, then I_1 migrates *MA* with Place Handoff trust-relationship ①, else I_1 migrates *MA* with Place Delegation trust-relationship ②. However, in the case that *MA* running on I_1 requests migration to I_2, if the identity of I_2 is in TPL of I_1, then I_1 migrates *MA* with Agent Handoff trust-relationship ③, else I_1 migrates *MA* with Agent Delegation trust-relationship ④. If Algorithm 1 returns TRUE (this means that the cascaded delegation is initiated successfully), *MA* together with DT_{I1} arrives at I_2. Then the place I_2 resumes the execution of *MA* according to Migration Type within the *DR* message.

```
Algorithm 1 (Initiation Algorithm)
dispatch and execute MA with DT_I0 on I_1; // DT_P0 is the token of MA's sender
when (I_1 migrates MA to I_2) {
    if (I_2 is in TPL)
        send DR(I_1, PH, TS, N_I1) message to I_2;
    else
        send DR(I_1, PD, TS, N_I2) message to I_2;
}
when (migrate(I_2) is executed in MA) {
    if (I_2 is in TPL)
        send DR(I_1, AH, TS, N_I1) message to I_2;
    else
        send DR(I_1, AD, TS, N_I1) message to I_2;
}
wait for DA(I_2, Sig_I2(N_I1), TS, N_I2) message from I_2 during TS in DR;
if (DA message arrives from I_2 during TS) {
    auth_result ← verify (Sig_I2(N_I1));  // Sig_I2(N_I1) is in DA
    if (auth_result is FALSE) {
        discard MA;
        return FALSE;  // terminate cascaded delegation
    }
    if (MT == PH or PD) {  // MT is in DR
        DT_I1 ← createDT(I_1, I_2, Priv_I1(I_2), Sig_I1(N_I2), t_I1, DT_I0);
        send MA with DT_I1 to I_2;
    }
    else {
        DT'_I1 ← createDT(I_1, I_2, Priv_I1(I_2), Sig_I1(N_I2), t_I1, DT_I0);
        send MA with DT'_I1 to I_2;
    }
    return TRUE;
}
return FALSE;
```

Alg. 1. The initiation algorithm of cascaded delegation

That is, based on Lampson et. al.'s authentication theory, in the case of ① and ③, I_2 resumes MA with only the privilege in DT_{I1} as the principal I_1, A **for** S respectively. However, in the case of ② and ④, I_2 resumes MA with combination of its authority with the privilege in DT_{I1} as the principal I_2 **for** P_1, I_2 A **for** S respectively. In sequence, if migration of MA occurs, I_3 uses the segment B of Algorithm 2 (see *Segment B: Contacting with I_{i+1}* of Algorithm 2). At the same time I_3 uses the segment A of Algorithm 2 (see *Segment A: Contacting with I_{i-1}* of Algorithm 2) to authenticate I_2 and be authenticated itself by I_2. If Algorithm 2 returns TRUE, MA together with DT_{I2} arrives at the place I_3. This procedure is repeated for the place I_4, I_5, ..., I_{n-1} on the delegation path by using Algorithm 2. If this cascaded delegation is successful consecutively, MA eventually arrives at I_n together with DT_{In-1}.

If MA running on I_n requests a service to the end server S, I_n sends SRC message to the end server S for identification of S by using Algorithm 3. If SRR message arrives from S as a response of the SRC message, I_n sends SR message to the end server S by using Algorithm 3. Then the end server S verifies the digital signature $Sig_{Pn}(Ns)$ and the delegation token DT_{In-1} within the SR message by using Algorithm 4. If this procedure is successful, the end server S performs the requested service and responds to the request with the SA message including the result.

```
Algorithm 2 (Mediation Algorithm)
/* Iᵢ receives DR(Iᵢ₋₁, MT, TS, N_{Ii-1}) message from Iᵢ₋₁ */
/* Segment A: Contacting with Iᵢ₋₁ */
send DA(Iᵢ, Sig_{Ii} (N_{Ii}), TS, N_{Ii}) message to Iᵢ₋₁;
when (MA with DT_{Ii-1} arrives from Iᵢ₋₁ during TS in DA) {
    auth_result ⟵ verify Sig_{Ii}(N_{Ii});   // Sig_{Ii-1}(N_{Ii}) is in DT_{Ii-1}
    if (auth_result is FALSE) {
        discard MA;
        return FALSE;   // terminate cascaded delegation
    }
} /*End of segment A*/
if (MT == PH or AH) {   // MT is in DR
    resume execution of MA with the privilege in DT_{Ii-1};
else {   // MT == PD or AD
    new privilege ⟵ Iᵢ's own privilege for the privilege in DT_{Ii-1};
        // the for operator is defined in Lampson et al.'s Theory
    resume execution of MA with the new privilege;
}
/* Segment B: Contacting with Iᵢ₊₁ */
when (Iᵢ migrates MA to place Iᵢ₊₁) {
    if (Iᵢ₊₁ is in TPL)
        send DR(Iᵢ, PH, TS, N'_{Ii}) message to Iᵢ₊₁;
    else
        send DR(Iᵢ, PD, TS, N'_{Ii}) message to Iᵢ₊₁;
}
when (migrate(Iᵢ₊₁) is executed in MA) {
    if (Iᵢ₊₁ is in TPL)
        send DR(Iᵢ, AH, TS, N'_{Ii}) message to Iᵢ₊₁;
    else
        send DR(Iᵢ, AD, TS, N'_{Ii}) message to Iᵢ₊₁;
}
wait for DA(Iᵢ₊₁, Sig_{Ii+1}(N'_{Ii}), TS, N_{Ii+1}) message from Iᵢ₊₁ during TS in DR;
if (DA message arrives from Iᵢ₊₁ during TS) {
    auth_result ⟵ verify (Sig_{Ii+1}(N'_{Ii}));   // Sig_{Ii+1}(N'_{Ii}) is in DA
    if (auth_result is FALSE) {
        discard MA;
        return FALSE;   // terminate cascaded delegation
    }
    if (MT == PH or PD) {   // MT is in DR
        DT_{Ii} ⟵ createDT(Iᵢ, Iᵢ₊₁, Priv_{Ii}(Iᵢ₊₁), Sig_{Ii}(N_{Ii+1}), t_{Ii}, DT_{Ii-1});
        send MA with DT_{Ii} to Iᵢ₊₁;
    }
    else {   // MT == AH or AD
        DT'_{Ii} ⟵ createDT(Iᵢ, Iᵢ₊₁, Priv_{Ii}(Iᵢ₊₁), Sig_{Ii}(N_{Ii+1}), t_{Ii}, DT_{I0});
        send MA with DT'_{Ii} to Iᵢ₊₁;
    } /*End of segment B*/
    return TRUE;
}
return FALSE;
```

Alg. 2. The mediation algorithm of cascaded delegation

```
Algorithm 3 (Service Request Algorithm)
/* contacting with S */
when request (S, service) is executed in MA {
    send SRC(Iₙ, TS, N'_{In}) message to S;
    wait for SRR (S, Sigₛ(N'_{In}), TS, Nₛ) message from S during TS in SRC;
    if (SRR message arrives from Iᵢ₊₁ during TS in SRC) {
        auth_result ⟵ verify (Sigₛ(N'_{In}));   // Sigₛ(N'_{In}) is in SRR
        if (auth_result is FALSE) {
            discard MA;
            return FALSE;
        }
    }
    send SR (Iₙ, Sig_{In}(Nₛ), DT_{In-1}, TS, service) message to S;
    wait for SA (S, service, result) message from S during TS in SR;
}
return TRUE;
```

Alg. 3. Service Request Algorithm

```
Algorithm 4 (Service Response Algorithm)
/* S receives SRC(In, TS, N'ln) message from In */
send SRR (S, Sigs(N'ln), TS, Ns) message to In;
when (SR message arrives from In during TS in SRR) {
    auth_result  ←  verify (Sigln(N's));  // Sigln(N's) is in SR
    if (auth_result is FALSE) {
        discard MA;
        return FALSE;
    }
    else {
        if (DT0 exists) {    // DT0 exists in DTln within SR message
            execute the service requested from In;
            send SA (S, service, result) message to In;
        }
        else
            return FALSE;
    }
}
return TRUE;
```

Alg. 4. Service Response Algorithm

3.4 Example: Two Scenarios

In this section, we present two example scenarios of our scheme. In the following scenarios, X *migrates MA to Y* means that the place X tries to migrate the mobile agent MA running on itself to the place Y. And *migrate(Y)* means that MA requests the place that is executing itself to migrate itself to the place Y. Two scenarios are processes that the MA that is running on place A migrates to another place B, C and D in sequence and requests the service to the end-server S. However, in scenario 1, migration of an agent occurs Place Handoff, Place Delegation and Place Handoff between places in sequence, and in scenario 2, occurs Agent Delegation, Place Handoff and Agent Handoff in sequence. In scenario 1 (Fig. 6), A executes MA. Consider the situation that A tries to migrate MA to B. A confirms whether the identity of B is in its TPL. And because the identity of B is in the TPL, A creates the DR message that contains the identity of its own, PH, timestamp and the nonce N_A and sends the DR message to B. When the DR message arrives at B during the timestamp, B creates the DA message that contains the identity of its own, the signature on A's nonce, timestamp and the nonce N_B and sends the DA message to A as a response message. When the DA message arrives at A during the timestamp, A verifies the B's signature on its nonce $Sig_B(N_A)$. If the verification is successful, A creates the delegation token DT_A and sends MA along with the DT_A to B. DT_A contains the identity of A, the identity of B, the privilege that A delegates to B, its own signature on the nonce N_B, timestamp and initial token signed by sender of MA. Then B receiving MA along with DT_A verifies A's signature on its nonce $Sig_A(N_B)$ in DT_A. If the verification is successful, B calculates the privilege to execute MA. Because MT in the DR message sent from A is PH, B resumes the execution of MA on itself with the privilege in DT_A. Again, B tries to migrate MA to C. B confirms whether the identity of C is in its TPL. And because the identity of C is not in the TPL, B creates the DR message that contains the identity of its own, PD, timestamp and the nonce N'_B and sends the DR message to C. When the DR message arrives at C during the timestamp, C creates the DA message and

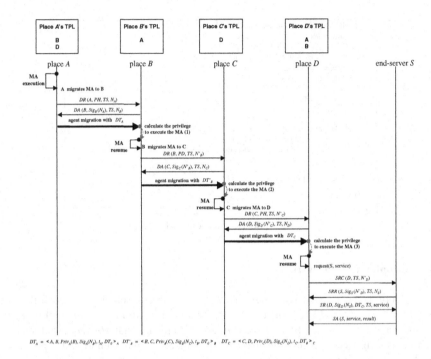

Fig. 6. Scenario

sends it to B in the similar way as B did. B receiving the DA message creates the delegation token DT'_B and sends MA along with the DT'_B to C. DT'_B contains the identity of B, the identity of C, the privilege that B delegates to C, its own signature on the nonce N_C, timestamp and initial token signed by sender of MA. In this case, DT_A is not nested within the signed part of DT'_B but initial token signed by sender of MA is nested, because the trust-relationship is Place Delegation. C receiving MA along with DT'_B verifies B's signature on its nonce $Sig_B(N_C)$ in DT'_B then combines its authority with that of the privilege in DT'_B then resumes the execution of MA on itself. Again, C tries to migrate MA to D. C sends MA to D in the similar way as A did. The delegation token DT_C created in this process contains DT_C contains the identity of C, the identity of D, the privilege that C delegates to D, its own signature on the nonce N_D, timestamp and the delegation token DT'_B. Because the trust-relationship is Place Handoff, DT'_B is nested within the signed part of DT_C. D receiving MA along with DT_C resumes the execution of MA on itself with the privilege in DT_C. Finally, when MA running on D requests a service to S, D creates the SRC message that contains the identity of its own, timestamp and the nonce N_D and sends it to S. S receiving the SRC message creates the SRR message that contains the identity of its own, its own signature on the nonce N_D, timestamp and the nonce N_S and sends the SRR message to D. D receiving the SRR message verifies the S's signature on its nonce $Sig_S(N_D)$. If the verification is successful, S creates the SR message that contains the identity of its own, D's signature of its own nonce, timestamp and the identity of requesting a service and sends the SR message to S. S receiving the SR message verifies the D's signature on its nonce $Sig_D(N_S)$. If the verification is successful, then confirms whether initial token signed by sender of *MA* is nested within DT_C in the SR message. If there is initial token, *S* performs the service requested from *D* and creates the *SA* message nesting the result of the service.

The process of scenario 2 (Fig. 7) is very similar to that of scenario 1. But there are some differences. Depending on the trust-relationship, the way of creation of the delegation token and the privilege that migrated place gets to resume *MA* are different with scenario 1. More details are as follows. When migration of *MA* from *A* to *B* occurs, in scenario 2, *MA* requests *A* that is executing itself to migrate itself to *B*. In this case, the identity of *B* is not in *A*'s TPL, so the trust-relationship is Agent Delegation. Therefore as shown in Table 2, the privilege of *MA* itself signed by sender of *MA* is appended to the part of the privilege of DT'_A. *B* receiving *MA* along with DT'_A resumes the execution of *MA* on itself with the privilege of combining its own authority with the privilege of *MA* itself signed by sender of *MA*. Again, B executing *MA* tries to migrate *MA* to *C*. And because the identity of *C* is in *B*'s TPL, the trust-relationship is Place Handoff. In this case, the cascaded delegation occurs in the same way how the cascaded delegation occurs from *A* to *B* or from *C* to *D* in scenario 1. Here, *C* resumes the execution of *MA* with the privilege in DT_B. In the case that *MA* running on *C* requests *C* to migrate itself to *D*, the process of delegation is same as that of delegation from *A* to *B*, and during *MA* resumed on D, the process of requesting a service to *S* is same as that in scenario 1.

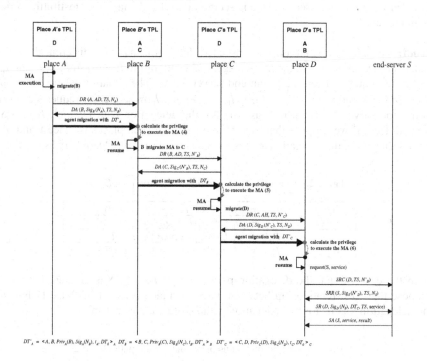

Fig. 7. Scenario 2

4 Safeness Proof

Because our proposed scheme uses public-key based digital signature authentication scheme, the fact that only authenticated places can participate in cascaded delegation is a premise. In this section, we prove that our proposed scheme is secure against the attack of replaying a message and the attack of substituting a delegation token.

Theorem 1: Our proposed scheme is secure against the attack of replaying a message.

Proof: Suppose that the delegation path is $I_1 I_2 I_3 ... I_{n-1} I_n S$ and a malicious place I'_i ($1 \leq i \leq n$) can attempt to make an attack of replaying a message. If I'_i can make a copy of the DT_{Ii} message or the SR message which is used on the normal delegation path $I_1 I_2 I_3 ... I_{n-1} I_n S$, I'_i can try to reuse those messages. But the nonce N_{I+1} of $Sig_{Ii}(N_{I+1})$ within the DT_{Ii} message or the nonce N_s of $Sig_{In}(N_s)$ within the SR message is randomly generated then used only once and discarded. Therefore the attack of replaying a message can not succeed. Thus, our proposed scheme is secure against the replay attack of a message.

$\square$

Theorem 2: Our proposed scheme is secure against the attack of substituting a delegation token.

Proof: Consider the situation that cascaded delegation has two different delegation paths. The situation where the mobile agent *MA*, migrating from I_1 to I_i, I_j, I_k and I_n in sequence, requests a service to the end server S (A). The situation where the mobile agent *MA*, migrating from I_1 to I'_i, I_j, I_h ($h \neq k$) and I_n in sequence, requests a service to the end server S (B). In the case of (A), the delegation path *Dpath1*: $I_1 I_i I_j I_k I_n S$ is created. Here if we suppose that trust-relationship between places is Place Handoff or Place Delegation, the delegation tokens for the delegation path *Dpath1* are as in Table 2.

Table 2. Delegation tokens of the delegation path *Dpath-1*

$I_1 \rightarrow I_i$	$DT_{I1} = <I_1, I_i, Priv_{I1}(I_i), Sig_{I1}(N_{Ii}), t_{I1}, DT_{I0}>_{I1}$
$I_i \rightarrow I_j$	$DT_{Ii} = <I_i, I_j, Priv_{Ii}(I_j), Sig_{Ii}(N_{Ij}), t_{Ii}, DT_{I1}>_{Ii}$
$I_j \rightarrow I_k$	$DT_{Ij} = <I_j, I_k, Priv_{Ij}(I_k), Sig_{Ij}(N_{Ik}), t_{Ij}, DT_{Ii}>_{Ij}$
$I_k \rightarrow I_n$	$DT_{Ik} = <I_k, I_n, Priv_{Ik}(I_n), Sig_{Ik}(N_{In}), t_{Ik}, DT_{Ij}>_{Ik}$

In the case of (B), the delegation path *Dpath2:* $I_1 I'_i I_j I_h I_n S$ is created. Here if we suppose that trust-relationship between places is Place Handoff of Place Delegation, the delegation tokens for the delegation path *Dpath2* are as in Table 3.

Table 3. Delegation tokens of the delegation path *Dpath-2*

$I_1 \rightarrow I'_i$	$DT_{I1} = <I_1, I'_i, Priv_{I1}(I'_i), Sig_{I1}(N_{I'i}), t_{I1}, DT_{I0}>_{I1}$
$I'_i \rightarrow I_j$	$DT_{I'i} = <I'_i, I_j, Priv_{I'i}(I_j), Sig_{I'i}(N_{Ij}), t_{I'i}, DT_{I1}>_{I'i}$
$I_j \rightarrow I_h$	$DT_{Ij} = <I_j, I_h, Priv_{Ij}(I_h), Sig_{Ij}(N_{Ih}), t_{Ij}, DT_{I'i}>_{Ij}$
$I_h \rightarrow I_n$	$DT_{Ih} = <I_h, I_n, Priv_{Ih}(I_n), Sig_{Ih}(N_{In}), t_{Ih}, DT_{Ij}>_{Ih}$

In the process of constructing the delegation path *Dpath1* and *Dpath2*, malicious place I'_1 can make each copy of the delegation tokens. In order to construct an invalid delegation path such as $Dpath3:I_1I_iI_jI_hI_nS$, I'_1 can attempt to substitute the delegation token $DT_{I'i}$ of the delegation path *Dpath2* with the delegation token DT_{Ii} of the delegation path *Dpath1*. However, when I_j creates DT_{Ij}, $DT_{I'i}$ is nested into DT_{Ij}, then I_j signature with own private key. However, I'_1 can not know I_j's private key. Therefore, the attempt to substitute the delegation token fails. Thus, our proposed scheme is secure against the attack of substituting a delegation token. This is caused by the characteristic that the attack of substituting a delegation token can be detected because our proposed scheme is based on nested token protocol. Also the detection is possible, regardless of trust-relationship between places.

$\square$

5   Conclusion

Because the existing delegation scheme considers only the delegation between two places that participate in migration of an agent, it does not support secure cascaded delegation. In this paper, we propose a cascaded delegation scheme that provides agents with secure cascaded delegation in mobile agent environments. Depending on the trust-relationship among places, when each place delegates the priority to the migrated place, to adapt the authentication scheme that Berkovits et. al. proposed the proposed scheme uses the delegation token created differently and priority changed and achieves the goal by nesting each delegation token or by nesting only initial token signed by sender of the agent within the signed part of the next immediate delegation token. We presented the mechanism of our scheme in detail. Also, we proved that the proposed scheme is secure against the attack of replaying a message and the attack of substituting a delegation token. Therefore our proposed scheme performs secure cascaded delegation. Further work will be aimed at managing a standard to update TPL.

References

1. C. Harrison, D. Chess, and A. Kershenbaum: Mobile Agents: Are they a good idea?. Research Report (1987), IBM Research Division (1994)
2. S. Berkovits, J. Guttman, and V. Swarup: Authentication for mobile agents. Lecture Notes in Computer Science #1419: Mobile Agents and Security, Springer-Verlag (1998) 114–136
3. W. Farmer, J. Guttman, and V. Swarup: Security for mobile agents: issues and requirements. Computer Communications: Special Issue on Advances in Research and Application of Network Security (1996)
4. W. Jansen: Countermeasures for mobile agent security. Computer Communications: Special Issue on Advances in Research and Application of Network Security (2000)
5. A. Corradi, R. Montanari, and C. Stefanelli: Mobile agents protection in the internet environment. Proc. 23th Annual International Computer Software and Applications Conference (1999) 80–85
6. U. Wilhelm, S. Stamann, and L. Buttyan: A pessimistic approach to trust in mobile agent platforms. IEEE Internet Computing, Vol. 4, No. 5 (2000) 40–48

7. Y. Ding and H. Petersen: A new approach for delegation using hierarchical delegation tokens. Proc. 2nd Conference on Computer and Communications Security (1996) 128–143
8. G. Vogt: Delegation of tasks and rights. Proc. 12th Annual IFIP/IEEE International Workshop on Distributed systems: Operations & Management (2001) 327–337
9. M. Abadi, M. Burrows, B. Lampson, and G. Plotkin: A calculus for access control in distributed systems. ACM Transactions on Programming Language and Systems, Vol. 15, No. 4 (1993) 706–734
10. B. Lampson, M. Abadi, M. Burrows, and E. Wobber: Authentication in distributed systems: theory and practice. Proc. 13th ACM Symposium on Operating Systems Principles (1991) 165–182

Practical Solution for Location Privacy
in Mobile IPv6

SuGil Choi, Kwangjo Kim, and ByeongGon Kim

International Research center for Information Security (IRIS)
Information and Communications University (ICU)
58-4 Hwaam-dong, Yusong-gu, Daejeon, 305-732, South Korea
{sooguri,kkj,virus}@icu.ac.kr

Abstract. Mobile IP (MIP) enables the Mobile Node (MN) to move
around without loosing their transport-layer connectivity by using resources in the foreign domain network. MIP is expected to be the core
infrastructure of future mobile communication, but certain level of security services must be provided before the wide deployment of MIP.
Security services, such as authentication and access control, have been
considered since the birth of MIP, but little attention has been given to
location privacy services despite of their increased significance in wireless
network. MIPv6 uses IPSec to provide data confidentiality and authentication between Home Agent (HA) and the Mobile Node (MN). However,
no practical solution was suggested for location information protection
in MIP. During the past years a variety of theoretical concepts for location privacy have been proposed, but most of them are not applicable
to MIP communication. So, in this paper, we identify required level of
location privacy, and propose new protocol for providing the identified
level of location privacy.

1 Introduction

Mobile IP is a protocol for passing IP datagrams between the MN and its Correspondent Node (CN) as the MN changes its attachment point on the Internet.
MIP is currently a hot research area and expected to be the core part of future
mobile communication. However, there are several issues that must be addressed
before the wide deployment of MIP. One of the important tasks is to provide
secure MIP communication.

Throughout the development of MIP, the following security services have
been considered useful for protecting a mobile Internet:

- Data integrity, origin authentication and anti-replay protection of MIP reg-
  istration and location update message
- Access control of the MN when they use resources on the foreign networks
- Location privacy and anonymity of the MN

Among these services, the first two are essential to secure MIP communications
and have been main research area in MIP security. On the other hand, location

K. Chae and M. Yung (Eds.): WISA 2003, LNCS 2908, pp. 69–83, 2004.
© Springer-Verlag Berlin Heidelberg 2004

privacy and anonymity have been largely ignored. But, these two services have a great significance especially in wireless network which is more vulnerable to eavesdropping attack than wired network. The disclosure of the MN's location or identity can be a serious violation of the MN's privacy.

In MIP communication, location privacy and anonymity are not independent security services because location privacy service can be provided on top of anonymity service. As long as the identity of the MN is kept secret, the disclosure of the MN's location is not a violation of the MN's privacy as nobody knows who is in the place. Therefore, we don't need to worry about location privacy while anaonymity is provided. To help understanding, before proceeding any further, we need to clarify the scope of anonymity and location privacy that we strive to achieve in a MIP communication.

- anonymity: no entity other than the MN should know any information regarding the user's identity, unless the MN decides to disclose such information.
- location privacy: any entity which is authorized to know the MN's real identity will not be able to know the exact physical location of the MN, unless the MN decides to reveal such information or another person physically sees the MN at that location.

As we can see in the definition, anonymity is prerequisite to location privacy.

During the past years a variety of theoretical concepts for location privacy and anonymity, such as Mix-network [9], Onion Routing [12], and Anonymizer [8], have been proposed. These can be classified into *Cascading Overlay Network based system* and *Single Trusted Entity based system*. *Cascading Overlay Network based system* can hide the location of communicating entities from strong attackers, but it is not suitable for real time communication. *Single Trusted Entity based system* is strong against only weak attacker, but it is more efficient and practical. We will explain those systems in Section 2.2 and the definition of strong attacker and weak attacker will be given in Section 4.1.

Our approach employs the concept of Single Trusted Entity and we would call the entity *Information Translating Proxy* (ITP). ITP makes the location information and identification information invisible to other communication participants and attackers by translating those information, unless the MN decides to disclose such information. This is similar to the function of Anonymizer, but our approach has several distinct characteristics such as:

- It operates on the network layer, so it uses only network layer information to process received information and forward it to final destination. It is compatible with IPv6 specifications.
- The operation of ITP doesn't require storing any session state information, so it doesn't need to worry about state information safeguarding as in Anonymizer.
- It authenticates every incoming request.

Our proposed scheme is focused on providing location privacy on network control messages, not content data. Also, it will provide revocable privacy rather than perfect privacy because, in case of serious crime, the location history and identity must be revealed.

Organization. The organization of this paper is as follows: In Section 2, we explain Mobile IP and location privacy providing systems. Section 3 classifies different requirements of location privacy in MIP communication. Considered factors for designing protocol are described in section 4, and our proposed protocol is presented in section 5. In Section 6, we conclude by mentioning a few directions about the following research.

2   Background

2.1   Mobile IP

Internet Protocol routes packets to their destination according to IP addresses which are associated with a fixed network. So, when the packet's destination is a mobile node, this means that each new point of access made by the node is associated with a new network number, hence, new IP address must be set to maintain connections as the MN moves from place to place. This makes transparent mobility impossible.

In MIPv4, MNs use two IP addresses: home address and care-of address (CoA). The home address is static and used to identify TCP connections. The CoA changes at each new point of attachment. MIP requires the existence of a network node known as the home agent (HA) and foreign agent (FA). Whenever the MN moves, it registers its new CoA with its HA and the HA redirects all the packets destined for the MN to the MN's CoA. In MIPv4, FA broadcasts agent advertisement at regular intervals and the MN gets network configuration information from the FA advertisement.

MIPv6 shares many features with MIPv4 but there are several major differences. First of all, MIPv6 uses IPv6 address structure [4]. Another difference is the support for "Route Optimization" as a built-in fundamental part of the MIPv6 protocol. The Route optimization allows direct routing from any CN to any MN without needing to pass through the MN's home network and be forwarded by its HA, and thus eliminates the problem of "triangle routing" present in MIPv4. And, there is no need to deploy special routers as FA.

2.2   Location Privacy Providing Systems

Mix-network. In [9], Chaum introduced the idea of mix-network. It is a set of servers that serially decrypt or encrypt lists of incoming messages and outputs them in a random order in such a way that attacker cannot correlate which output message belongs to which input message, without the aid of the mix nodes, when several messages are passed simultaneously. However, the goal of real time communication can't be achieved because it requires several public key encryption and decryption, and intentional time delay to defeat correlation attack.

Onion Routing. When using Onion Routing [12], a user sends encrypted data to a network of so-called Onion Routers. A trusted proxy chooses a series of these network nodes and opens a connection by sending a multiply encrypted data structure called an "onion" to the first of them. Each node removes one layer of encryption, which reveals parameters such as session keys, and forwards the encrypted remainder of the onion to the next network node. Once the connection is set up, an application specific proxy forwards HTTP data through the Onion Routing network to a responder proxy which establishes a connection with the web server the user wishes to use. The user's proxy multiply encrypts outgoing packets with the session keys it sent out in the setup phase; each node decrypts and forwards the packets, and encrypts and forwards packets that contain the server's response. In spite of the similar design to mix-network, Onion Routing cannot achieve the traffic analysis protection of an ideal mix-network due to the low-latency requirements.

Crowds. Crowds [11] consists of a number of network nodes that are run by the users of the system. Web requests are randomly chained through a number of them before being forwarded to the web server hosting the requested data. The server will see a connection coming from one of the Crowds users, but cannot tell which of them is the original sender. In addition, Crowds uses encryption, so that some protection is provided against attackers who intercept a user's network connection. However, this encryption does not protect against an attacker who cooperates with one of the nodes that the user has selected, since the encryption key is shared between all nodes participating in a connection. Crowds is also vulnerable to passive traffic analysis: since the encrypted messages are forwarded without modification, traffic analysis is trivial if the attacker can observe all network connections. An eavesdropper intercepting only the encrypted messages between the user and the first node in the chain as well as the cleartext messages between the final node and the web server can associate the encrypted data with the plaintext using the data length and the transmission time.

Anonymizer. Anonymizer [8] is essentially a server with a web proxy that filters out identifying headers and source addresses from web browsers' requests (instead of seeing the users true identity, a web server sees only the identity of the Anonymizer server). This solution offers rather weak security (no log safeguarding and a single point of vulnerability).

We classify the first three into *Cascading Overlay Network based system* and Anonymizer into *Single Trusted Entity based system*.

3   Classification of Location Privacy Requirements

Location privacy can be defined according to two different dimensional parameters: information related to the identification of the user and entities which are able to have access to these pieces of information. The required level of location privacy depends on various factors like the effect on performance incurred by providing this service, assumed attackers' capabilities and so on. To help choose the adequate level of location privacy necessary for a given environment, it is necessary to develop a classification scheme to represent the various possible levels of location privacy requirements.

A specific location privacy requirement is represented in terms of two dimensional matrix. If a particular class of entities knows a particular piece of information, the corresponding table entry is marked 1. Otherwise, it is marked 0.

In the case of Mobile IP communication, the different classes of entities which might know private information are: the home network provider (H), the foreign network provider (F), the correspondent node (C) and attacker (A).

The reason why we use the term private information, instead of location information, is that hiding location information alone can not guarantee location privacy and perfect protection of location information from all entities mentioned above is impossible because foreign network provider can always know the location of the MN. To provide location privacy against foreign network provider, the MN's identification information should not be disclosed. Without knowledge of the MN's real identity, it is not a violation of the MN's privacy to know the MN's physical location. In other words, as long as anonymity is provided, we don't need to try to protect location information. Therefore, we can define location privacy requirements on top of anonymity requirements and we will see possible levels of anonymity requirements first.

3.1 Possible Levels of Anonymity Requirements

The real identity of the MN may be discovered by the disclosure of identity itself or analyzing the traffic between the foreign and the home network. In other words, when the MN accesses the foreign network, if the identity of his home network is not protected, the information about the MN's real identity may be inferred. The home network address in address field of packet header or Network Access Identifier (NAI) [3] can reveal the identity of home network. NAI is formed like (username "@" realm). Example of valid NAI is fred@wisa.com. NAI is a standardized method for identifying users and enhances the interoperability of roaming and tunnelling services. So, we expect NAI will be used widely and assume identity is represented using NAI. Here is one example that the MN's real identity is inferred from the HN identity. If the MN visiting the foreign network in Japan wants to authenticate to his HN cwd.go.kr and an attacker happens to know that the only user from cwd.go.kr currently in Japan is president, the attacker can know that the the user of the MN is president. We call the MN identity Mi and the HN identity Hi.

We saw that Mi can be inferred from Hi. But, it is also true that, in most cases, Hi gives just rough idea about Mi. So, revealing Hi while keeping Mi secret is not so serious as disclosing Mi itself. But, hiding Hi while disclosing Mi is meaningless because NAI contains the HN identity. Hence, there are only two kinds of the MN identity protection. One is weak identity protection, hiding

Mi while revealing Hi, so others can know to which home network this MN belongs, but not exact the MN identity. The other is strong identity protection or *complete anonymity*, hiding both Mi and Hi.

The possible levels of anonymity requirements can be a combination of four different classes of entities and two kinds of the MN's identity protection mechanism. (Anonymity Level: AL)

Table 1. AL4

	H	F	C	A
Mi	1	0	0	0
Hi	1	1	1	1

AL1: hiding Mi from only attacker
AL2: hiding Mi from the FN and attacker
AL3: hiding Mi from the CN and attacker
AL4: hiding Mi from the CN, the FN, and attacker

Table 2. AL8

	H	F	C	A
Mi	1	0	0	0
Hi	1	0	0	0

AL5: AL4 + hiding Hi from attacker
AL6: AL4 + hiding Hi from the FN and attacker
AL7: AL4 + hiding Hi from the CN and attacker
AL8: AL4 + hiding Hi from the CN, the FN, and attacker

AL8 is the minimum set of requirement for *complete anonymity* against all entities except the HN. We assume that the HN should know the MN's real identity for authentication.

3.2 Possible Levels of Location Privacy Requirements

Various levels of anonymity requirements was identified in 3.1. We can provide location privacy just by hiding location information against entities which know the MN's identity because, without knowledge of the MN's real identity, it is not a violation of the MN's privacy to know the MN's physical location. So, there can be eight different location privacy requirements. We show two location privacy requirements built on top of AL6 and AL8. We call location information Li. (Location Privacy Level: LPL)

Table 3. LPL6

	H	F	C	A
Mi	1	0	0	0
Hi	1	0	1	0
Li	0	1	0	1

Table 4. LPL8

	H	F	C	A
Mi	1	0	0	0
Hi	1	0	0	0
Li	0	1	1	1

When any one of 8 LPLs is provided, no entities other than the MN can know the location information of the MN. However, LPL8 is the most desired level of location privacy requirement because it provides *complete anonymity* at the same time.

4   Practical Considerations

4.1   Threat Model

Potential entities that might try to collect location history of the MN can be classified into two groups: legitimate entities and illegitimate entities.

The HN, the FN, and the CN are legitimate entities. It is assumed that the maintainer of the FN and the CN are not necessarily trustworthy. Likewise, Home Network operator and thus home agent need not be trusted. These legitimate entities can collect location information from incoming messages without much effort and can use it against user's privacy. We assume these entities are passive in gathering location information, which means they don't take any other actions to get the information but extracting it from incoming messages.

Attackers are illegitimate entities. They can be roughly classified into strong attacker and weak attacker. Strong attacker is the one who is able to perform eavesdropping at arbitrary locations in the network and may trace messages while they traverse the network and thus link the sender of a message to its recipient. Eavesdropping at arbitrary locations in the network requires the capability of compromising arbitrary routers, which is very difficult if proper security measure is in place. We define weak attacker as the one who doesn't have the ability of compromising existing system, but just use exposed information. One example of the exposed information is the message transmitted over wireless network. Everyone with simple device can eavesdrop the communication. When we build security measure against strong attacker, location privacy can be guaranteed almost perfect, but strong security usually comes with high cost and low performance. So, in this paper, we develop protocol assuming weak attacker for practicality and wide deployment. We expect there will be other systems that provide location privacy against strong attacker.

- legitimate entities (HN, FN, CN): passive collection of location information from incoming messages
- illegitimate entities (attackers): no ability of compromising existing systems, just can eavesdrop messages transmitted over wireless network

4.2   Selection of Protocol Components

Return Routability (RR) Protocol. The RR procedure enables the CN to obtain some reasonable assurance that the MN is in fact addressable at its claimed care-of address (CoA) as well as its home address. Only with this assurance is the CN able to accept Binding Update from the MN which instructs the CN to direct that MN's data traffic to its claimed CoA. This is done by testing whether packets addressed to the two claimed addresses are routed to the MN. The MN can pass the test only if it is able to supply proof that it received certain data which the CN sends to those addresses. The below figure shows the message flow for the RR procedure. Due to space constraints, we do not go into the details of RR protocol. The reader is referred to the document [2] for more information.

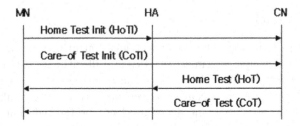

Fig. 1. RR Protocol

This protocol does not protect against attackers who are on the path between the HN and the CN. However, in our threat model, attackers don't have the ability of compromising existing systems, so attackers can't eavesdrop communication between the HN and the CN. RR protocol is not vulnerable in our threat model and it doesn't assume security associations or existence of authentication infrastructure between the MN and the CN. Therefore, RR protocol is just right fit in our model.

Information Translating Proxy. We classified location privacy providing systems into *Cascading Overlay Network based system* and *Single Trusted Entity based system*. *Cascading Overlay Network based system* assumes strong attackers, but can hardly provide real time service. *Single Trusted Entity based* *system* assumes relatively weak attackers, but provides practical solution. As we assumed weak attackers and passive collection of location information from incoming messages by legitimate entities, in our threat model, *Single Trusted Entity based system* can give enough level of security. We would call the system *Information Translating Proxy* (ITP).

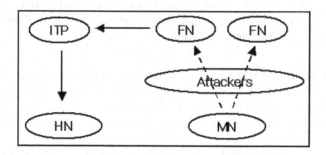

Fig. 2. Scenario based on ITP and weak attacker

5   Our Proposed Protocol

This section presents the way our proposed protocol provides location privacy in Home Binding Procedure and shows how location privacy can be revoked in case of serious crime. This protocol aims at providing LPL8 defined in section 3. We will use the following notations to describe the protocol.

Table 5. Notation

Symbol	Description
K_{AB}	Shared key between A and B
h()	One-way hash function
A | B	Concatenation of A and B
$prf(k, M)$	keyed pseudo random function. It accepts a secret key k and a message M, and generates a pseudo random output
$\{M\}_K$	Encryption of message M using key K

5.1   System Setup

Every message that needs special treatment for location privacy goes through ITP. ITP processes incoming messages and forwards it to the final destination. Hence, ITP needs association mechanism which enables bidirectional communication through ITP. In Anonymizer, system keeps track of source IP addresses and source port numbers of each request from users, and destination IP addresses and source port numbers of forwarded requests to the final destination. With those mapping information, Anonymizer can deliver received data to users in correct way.

As an association mechanism in ITP, we developed new mechanism. It operates on the network layer, so it uses only network layer information to associate incoming and outgoing traffic, not other layer element like port number. The operation of ITP doesn't require storing any session state information, so we don't need to worry about state information safeguarding as in Anonymizer and it becomes easy to manage the system.

New Association Mechanism. This requires secret key sharing between ITP and the MN. Each MN creates an ephemeral pseudonym (64 bit) randomly and ITP generates a secret key between ITP and the MN

$\qquad K_{IM} = \text{h}(K_I \mid \text{MN's pseudonym}) \qquad (K_I \text{ is the secret key of ITP})$

Initial Key Creation: When MN joins home network for the first time, it gets K_{IM}. MN shows that he belongs to the home network with the help of home network and delivers pseudonym and certificate to ITP. ITP authenticates the MN and his home network, and creates K_{IM} as shown above. K_{IM} is encrypted with the MN's public key, so nobody can know the key during delivery. This procedure is done just after the MN joins home network, so we can assume that the MN's communication doesn't need to go through ITP because the MN is in home network and, thus, the time delay for initial key setup doesn't cause a problem.

Key Update: When MN moves to different foreign network, it updates key K_{IM}.

- The MN creates new ephemeral pseudonym (64 bit)
- The MN creates care-of address (CoA) = FN subnet prefix (64 bit) | new pseudonym (64 bit)
- Duplication check of the CoA
- The MN sends Key Update Message to ITP
  Key Update Message = (previous CoA, $\{homeaddress, newCoA\}_{K_{IM}}$, MAC)
  MAC = $prf(K_{IM}, previousCoA|\{homeaddress, newCoA\}_{K_{IM}})$
- ITP verifies the Key Update Message, generates new K_{IM}, and sends Acknowledgement containing new K_{IM} encrypted with previous K_{IM}. (New pseudonym is contained in new CoA, so ITP can extract new pseudonym from new CoA)

Key update procedure includes normal MIP procedure. When MNs arrive at new foreign network, they create new CoA and check duplication of CoA. The process of Duplicate Address Detection is explained in the following paragraph. But, proposed key update procedure employs different way of CoA creation. The FN subnet prefix is obtained by listening to local router advertisement.

It is common practice to derive the remaining 64 bit *Interface Id* from the interface's MAC (EUI-64 global identifier) address [4], which guarantees the uniqueness of CoA. However, in this protocol, the *Interface Id* is a randomly generated ephemeral pseudonym. This pseudonym is 64 bit long and random collisions occur after 2^{32} pseudonyms have been generated. But, this is not a problem because it is not likely that 2^{32} addresses are used at the same time in a subnetwork and, if collisions occur, the collisions can be avoided through Duplicate Address Detection. The "u" and "g" bits of an IPv6 *Interface Id* have the semantics defined for EUI-64 global identifiers in which the "u" bit is set to one to indicate global scope, and it is set to zero to indicate local scope. "g" bit is the individual/group bit and is set to zero to indicate unicast address. (The "u" and "g" bits are the seventh bit and eighth bit of the first byte of *Interface Id* respectively) Therefore, in our way of CoA creation, "u" and "g" bits are always set to zero because its uniqueness is checked locally through Duplicate Address Detection [5]. In other words, the seventh and eighth bits of pseudonym must be zero. But, it should not be mistaken for locally routable address. For a set of addresses formed from the same subnet prefix, it is sufficient to check that the link local address generated from the subnet prefix is unique on the link to be a globally routable address. In this sense, the CoA generated in new way is globally routable address with locally unique *Interface Id*.

There is one thing that we have to be very careful in checking address duplication. For address duplication check, the MN sends a Neighbor Solicitation Message containing the tentative address as the target. If another node is already using that address, it will return a Neighbor Advertisement saying so. When globally routable address with locally unique *Interface Id* is used, this Duplicate Address Detection works fine in IPv6 communication. But, it can cause a problem in MIPv6 communication. When the MN sends a Neighbor Solicitation Message containing new CoA, if a node using the home address same as the CoA is visiting foreign network, the node can't respond to the Neighbor Solicitation Message though the CoA is same as his home address. If the MN uses the CoA, he can't receive any data from outside because HA will intercept every packet destined for the CoA and redirect it to outside. This problem happens because a network can be home network to a node and foreign network to visiting node at the same time. To solve this problem, HA must have the functionality to respond to the Neighbor Solicitation Message if there is a node using the requested CoA as the home address while the node is away from home network.

In Key Update Message, home address and new CoA are encrypted with K_{IM} to prevent correlation of CoAs of the MN. As only previous CoA appears in plaintext, others can not correlate the previous CoA to new CoA. But, care must be taken not to use new CoA as the source address of the packet containing Key Update Message. Otherwise, attacker can correlate previous CoA to new CoA. Temporary CoA must be used just for sending and receiving Key Update Message and Acknowledgement. ITP can generate key K_{IM} to decrypt the encrypted part of Key Update Message from previous pseudonym and its secret key as shown above.

In the verification of Key Update Message, it is not sufficient to check that the MN knows the K_{IM} corresponding to the claimed previous pseudonym. Let's suppose that the MN is not allowed to get service from home network any more due to some reason. If the current status of the MN in home network is not checked, the MN can send valid Key Update Message forever. Therefore, the current status of the MN in home network should be checked and ITP should keep the list of valid home address. But, we recommend the checking should be done after sending Acknowledgement to avoid time delay for that check. If the home address of the MN is known to be invalid in home network, the home address should be deleted from the list of valid home address and any Key Update Message containing a home address which is not in the list must be silently dropped.

However, there is still a problem. It is that we can't detect false Key Update Message, if valid home address of other nodes is used. In order to detect this, ITP has to keep home address-CoA binding information such as {*valid home address*, h(*the most recent CoA bound to the home address*)}. When the MN uses other nods's home address, ITP can detect this attempt because {*other node's home address*, h(*his CoA*)} would not appear in the *home address-CoA binding list*. Therefore, ITP should keep *home address-CoA binding list* rather than the list of valid home address.

When ITP verifies Key Update Message using *home address-CoA binding list*, Key Update process can go wrong if the Acknowledgement gets lost.

- ITP keeps {*home address*, h(*CoA #1*)}
- The MN sends Key Update Message = {CoA #1, {$homeaddress, CoA\#2$}$_{K_{IM}}$, MAC}
- ITP updates the list, {*home address*, h(*CoA #2*)}
- Acknowledgement gets lost
- The MN sends Key Update Message again as above
- Verification of Key Update Message fails because {*home address*, h(*CoA #1*)} is not valid any more

Therefore, ITP must keep both {*home address*, h(*CoA #1*)} and {*home address*, h(*CoA #2*)} until it receives Binding Update Message from the *CoA #2*. After that, ITP deletes {*home address*, h(*CoA #1*)} from the list. With this list, we can also defeat Key Update Message replay attack.

5.2   Location Privacy in Home Binding Procedure

Binding Update message must go through ITP to remove or translate information related to the MN identity or current location. We show how the Binding Update Message and Acknowledgement will look like.

<Binding Update Message>

IPv6 outer header (source = CoA, destination = ITP)
IPv6 inner header (source = ITP, destination = {$HAaddress$}$_{K_{IM}}$)

Destination options header
    Home address option ($\{homeaddress\}_{K_{IM}}$)
ESP header
Mobility header
    Binding Update
        Alternate care-of address option ($\{CoA\}_{K_{IM}}$)

<Binding Acknowledgement>

IPv6 outer header (source = HA address, destination = ITP)
IPv6 inner header (source = ITP, destination = $\{CoA\}_{K_{IM}}$)
Routing header (type2)
    home address
ESP header
Mobility header
    Binding Acknowledgement

Foreign network and attackers can't know the home agent address and home address because they are encrypted with K_{IM}. These are decrypted at ITP, outer header is removed, and remaining part is forwarded to HA. Home network can't know the location of the MN because CoA is encrypted. $\{CoA\}_{K_{IM}}$ in Alternate care-of address option is copied to destination address field of inner header of Binding Acknowledgement. ITP removes outer header of Binding Acknowledgement, decrypts $\{CoA\}_{K_{IM}}$ at inner header, encrypts home address at Routing header with K_{IM}, and forwards it to the MN's CoA.

Now, we are going to see how ITP can generate K_{IM} without any prior information. The source address of Binding Update Message is CoA of which pseudonym is *Interface Id*. ITP can know the MN's pseudonym, so it can generate $K_{IM} = h(K_I \mid$ MN's pseudonym$)$. The way to know the MN's pseudonym from Binding Acknowledgement is different. CoA should not appear at the header of Binding Acknowledgement, otherwise, home network can know the current location of the MN. So, ITP should find it out from other parts of header. We manipulate ITP address to carry pseudonym

ITP address = ITP subnet prefix (64 bit) | MN's pseudonym (64 bit)
We have mainly two benefits from forming ITP address as above:

- ITP subnet prefix is normally much more persistent than a ITP address, so the MN doesn't need to recognize reconfiguration of ITP address and doesn't need to try to find out new ITP address.
- ITP can extract the MN's pseudonym from ITP address and generate K_{IM}

When we use that form of ITP address, messages can be delivered to the network where ITPs reside by referring to just subnet prefix. But, the routers on the network should have the functionality to forward the messages to arbitrary ITPs because exact ITP address is not given.

5.3   Revocation of Location History

This protocol provides revocable location privacy rather than perfect location privacy. In case of serious crime, the location history must be revealed. The location privacy can be revoked this way:

- ITP stores (MN's pseudonym, $\{CoA\}_{K_{IM}}$, time in millisecond)
- The HN stores (home address, $\{CoA\}_{K_{IM}}$, time in millisecond)
- When there is quite enough reason to revoke location privacy, the HN asks ITP to decrypt the encrypted CoA.
- ITP looks up pseudonym by comparing $\{CoA\}_{K_{IM}}$ and time. If the time gap between the times recorded at ITP and the HN is within predefined value, the pseudonym is selected.
- ITP generates key using the pseudonym and decrypts the encrypted CoA

To minimize the time gap between the times recorded at ITP and the HN, it is required that ITP record the time when it receives Binding Update Message rather than Key Update Message. As the location history of the MN can be revealed only when the information at ITP and the HN was combined, keeping the information separately doesn't cause a problem. The clocks at ITP and HNs should be synchronized.

5.4   Discussion

In our protocol, the MN and ITP are not required to perform any public key cryptographic operations while the MN moves around foreign network, and traffic goes through just a single ITP. Only some parts of a packet are encrypted and decrypted, not multiple encryption and decryption of whole packet. Therefore this protocol can be very efficient.

We showed how location privacy can be provided in the Binding Update Procedure. We omitted how it can be provided in Route Optimization because of space constraints, though it would be better if it is seif-contained.

6   Conclusions

We realized an issue that has had little attention in MIP. That is location privacy which has increased significance in wireless network. We employed Single Trusted Entity based approach as the way of providing location privacy and it is quite efficient compared to Cascading Overlay Networks based approach. We identified adequate level of location privacy requirements and selected protocol components based on defined threat model.

Our protocol takes the initiative in providing practical solution for location privacy in MIP communication. Previous approach [13] is impractical because it performs multiple public key cryptographic operations and is based on Cascading Overlay Networks. However, this is the first proposal, so it might need to be improved. There are some open issues that need to be considered in the future work's agenda :

- including payment function for the use of foreign network resource
- providing location privacy in the Internet Key Exchange of IPSec
- ITP's secret key update
- ITP's survivability improvement

Acknowledgements. The authors are deeply grateful to the anonymous reviewers for their valuable suggestions and comments on the first version of this paper.

References

1. C. Perkins, "IP Mobility Support", IETF RFC 2002, October 1996
2. D. Johnson, C. Perkins, and J. Arkko, "Mobility Support in IPv6", IETF Internet-Draft, draft-ietf-mobileip-ipv6-21.txt, February 26, 2003
3. B. Aboba and M. Beadles, "The Network Access Identifier", IETF RFC 2486, January 1999
4. R. Hinden and S. Deering, "Internet Protocol Version 6 (IPv6) Addressing Architecture", IETF RFC 3513, April 2003
5. T. Narten, E. Nordmark, and W. Simpson, "Neighbor Discovery for IP Version 6 (IPv6)", IETF RFC 2461, December 1998
6. G. OShea and M. Roe, "Child-proof Authentication for MIPv6 (CAM)", Computer Communication Review, ACM SIGCOMM, volume 31, number 2, April 2001
7. D. Samfat, R. Molva, and N. Asokan, "Untraceability in Mobile Networks", Proceedings of the First Annual International Conference on Mobile Computing and Networking, ACM MOBICOM, November 13-15, 1995, pp. 26–36
8. Anonymizer.com, http://www.anonymizer.com
9. D. Chaum, "Untraceable electronic mail, return address, and digital pseudonyms", Communications of the ACM, Vol.24, No. 2, 1981, pp. 84–88
10. D. Chaum, A. Fiat, and M. Naor, "Untraceable Electronic Cash", Crypto, LNCS 0403, 1988, pp. 319–327
11. M. Reiter and A. Rubin, "Crowds: anonymity for web trasactions", ACM Transactions on Information System Security, Vol. 1, No. 1, November 1998, pp. 66–92
12. M. Reed, P. Syverson, and D. Goldschag, "Anonymous connections and Onion Routing", IEEE J. Selected Areas in Commun, Vol. 16, No. 4, May 1998, pp.482–494
13. T. Lopatik, C. Eckert, and U. Baumgarten, "MMIP-Mixed Mobile Internet Protocol", Communications and Multimedia Security (CMS), 1997

CTAR: Classification Based on Temporal Class-Association Rules for Intrusion Detection

Jin Suk Kim, Hohn Gyu Lee, Sungbo Seo, and Keun Ho Ryu

Database Laboratory, Chungbuk National University,
Cheongju , Korea
khryu@dblab.chungbuk.ac.kr
http://dblab.chungbuk.ac.kr

Abstract. Recently, increased number and diversity of network attack caused difficulties in intrusion detection. One of the intrusion detection, anomaly detection is a method of treating abnormal behaviors that deviate from modeled normal behaviors as suspicious attack. Research on data mining for intrusion detection focused on association rules, frequent episodes and classification. However despite the usefulness of rules that include temporal dimension and the fact that the audit data has temporal attribute, the above methods were limited in static rule extraction and did not consider temporal attributes. Therefore, we propose a new classification for intrusion detection. The proposed method is the CTAR(short for, Classification based on Temporal Class-Association Rules) and it extends combination of association rules and classification, CARs(short for, Class-Association Rules) by including temporal attribute. CTAR discovers rules in multiple time granularities and users can easily understand the discovered rules and temporal patterns. Finally, we proof that a prediction model (classifier) built from CTAR method yields better accuracy than a prediction model built from a traditional methods by experimental results.

1 Introduction

Intrusion detection is a process of identifying and coping injurious attack on computer and network resources and classified into misuse detection and anomaly detection techniques. Because of more complicated and sophisticated attacks, the system that can react quick and precise is demanded. Existing intrusion detection system is limited in speed for processing high capacity packet data and detection of new types of intrusion. The above problem can be solved by applying data mining technique that effectively analyze and extract meaningful data. Intrusion detection system equipped with above data mining technique uses association rule, frequent episodes and classification on syslog, TCP-dump and BSM(short for, Basic Security Module) audit data. Audit data is temporal data which has timestamp. Previous researches usually don't consider such time factor in temporal data or applied as static factor. Hence time to apply the generated rules was vague and useful rules for particular time points or time intervals could not be extracted [4]. Therefore, if we consider time intervals under multiple time granularities in order to apply data mining to audit data analysis with temporal

K. Chae and M. Yung (Eds.): WISA 2003, LNCS 2908, pp. 84–96, 2004.

attribute, we can discover useful rules during the given time interval. For example, we can clearly express time as it is abnormal behavior for some behavior on every first Monday of a week. Therefore we propose classification method and algorithms of data mining technique for analyzing timestamped audit data, CTAR which extended combination of association rules and classification, CARs by including temporal attribute. The proposed method is organized as follows.

First, we apply calendar pattern which proposed in [7] to timestamp of audit data for the time expression of temporal class-association rules. This calendar pattern is based on user-specified calendar pattern and represents cyclic pattern. TCARs(short for, Temporal Class-Association Rules) consists of rules that satisfy user-defined threshold and their calendar pattern. Therefore, it can discover rules in multiple time granularities. User can also easily understand the discovered rules. Second, we discover CARs in given time interval. CARs is a special subset of association rules with a consequent limited to class label values only. Finally, the generated TCARs is applied to build classifier for intrusion detection in audit data. Basically, the rule selection for building classifier is preferentially selected high confidence rules. But many rules are generated by TCARs algorithm result. Therefore, we propose a pruning technique for selection only useful rules in the generated rules. After this pruning process, the built classifier is applied for classifying new case. The proposed CTAR is applied to TCP-dump of DARPA data, and as a result TCP-dump data can be classified more accurately and efficiently than the previous method(C4.5). Considering temporal attribute of TCP-dump training dataset when generating rules for classifier guarantees the usefulness of the rules generated. Moreover, unlike the approach of decision tree which examines only the single variables, it generates the classifier based on the rules having the highest confidence among the various variables.

The rest of the paper is organized as follows. Section 2 presents related work. In section 3, we define calendar pattern and propose concept of the temporal class-association rules and algorithms. In section 4, we present rule selection algorithm for CTAR. In section 5, 6, we present the experimental result of our algorithms using the DARPA 1998 Intrusion Detection Evaluation data and then describe conclusion and future work the paper.

2 Related Works

2.1 Data Mining Techniques for Intrusion Detection System

In IDS(short for, Intrusion Detection System), detection techniques can be categorized into misuse detection and anomaly detection. Misuse detection aims to detect well-known attacks as well as slight variations of them, by characterizing the rules that govern these attacks. Anomaly detection is designed to capture any deviations from the established profiles of the system normal behavior. Recently, IDS has applied data mining techniques to efficient and automatic intrusion detection [2, 3, 8, 12].

IDSs use association rules and classification and frequent episodes in the audit data, applying data mining techniques. Association rules extracts to discover pattern between attributes from audit data and classification can be used to classify normal and anomaly behavior. Frequent episode is to discover set of patterns that occur frequently.

2.2 Temporal Association Rules

Time is an important aspect of all real world phenomena. Any systems, approaches or techniques that are concerned with information need to take into account the temporal aspect of data. Temporal data are now being viewed as invaluable assets from which hidden knowledge can be derived, so as to help understand the past and plan for the future [4, 11]. The previous researches for discovering temporal association rules which include temporal attribute can be categorized into cyclic and calendar based association rules. A cyclic association rule discovers regular cyclic variation [5]. Several algorithms and optimization techniques were presented in this paper. However, this work is limited in that it cannot treat multiple granularities and cannot describe real-life concepts such as the working hours of every day. Calendar association rules has been defined by combining the association rules with temporal features which represented by calendar time expression [6]. In this paper, for solving out the mining problem of temporal association rules, a framework for temporal data mining has been proposed. Also, this paper suggested a SQL-like mining language and shows architecture. However, the proposed method is just one kind of temporal pattern. In calendar based on temporal association rules [7], proposed the discovery of association rules along with their temporal patterns in terms of calendar schemas and identified two classes of rules, precise match and fuzzy match, to represent regular association rules along with their temporal patterns. An important feature of this paper representation mechanism is that the corresponding data mining problem requires less prior knowledge than the prior methods.

2.3 Classification Based on Association Rules

Associative classification is a combination of two data mining problems, association and classification, that uses association rules to predict a class label. CBA [9] (short for, Classification based on Association rules) method focuses on a special subset of association rules called CARs. CARs is association rules with a consequent limited to class label values only. CMAR [10] (short for, Classification Based on Multiple Association Rules) extends CBA by using more than one rule to classify a new case. The efficiency is also improved by applying FP-growth-like algorithm to rule generation. CMAR eliminates redundant rules by defining a new data structure, CR-tree and applies yet another type of pruning based on correlation analysis to prune noise rules. The experimental results showed that CMAR outperforms both C4.5 and CBA.

3 Temporal Class-Association Rules

In this section, we describe classification method and algorithms of TCARs. Fig. 1 shows a framework of classification process. We examine calendar-based pattern [7] and CARs [9] in section 3.1 and 3.2.

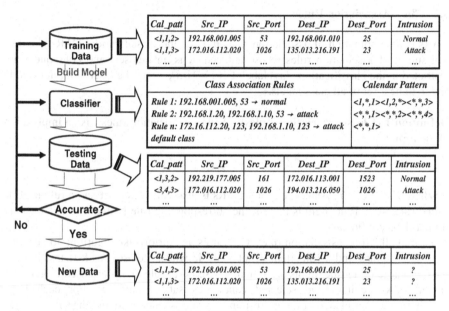

Fig. 1. CTAR process

3.1 Calendar Pattern

We present a class of calendar related temporal patterns called calendar patterns. Calendar pattern represents the sets of time intervals in terms of calendar schema specified by user. Calendar schema is a relational schema $R = (f_n:D_n, f_{n-1}:D_{n-1}, ..., f_1:D_1)$, where each attribute f_i is a time granularity name like year, month, day etc. Each domain D_i is a domain value corresponds to f_i. Given a calendar schema $R = (f_n:D_n, f_{n-1}:D_{n-1}, ..., f_1:D_1)$, a calendar pattern on the calendar schema R is a tuple on R of the form $<d_n, d_{n-1},...,d_1>$. Each d_i is a positive integer in D_i or the symbol "*". "*" denotes all values correspond to domain and means "every." Exactly, it represents periodic cycles on the calendar pattern as every week, every month, etc. For example, given the calendar schema (week, day, hour), the calendar pattern $<1,*,10>$ represents time intervals means the 10th hour of every day of week 1.

For presentation of calendar pattern, we call a calendar pattern with exactly k symbols a k-star calendar pattern (denoted e_k) and a calendar pattern with at least one symbol a star calendar pattern. In addition, we call a calendar pattern with no symbol a basic time interval. We say a calendar pattern e covers another calendar pattern e' in the same calendar schema if the set of time intervals of e' is a non-empty subset of the set of time intervals of e. For example, given the calendar schema (week, day, hour), $(1,*,10)$ covers $(1,1,10)$. It is easy to see that for a given calendar schema $(f_n, f_{n-1}, ... ,f_1)$, a calendar pattern $<d_n, d_{n-1}, ... , d_1>$ covers another calendar pattern $<d'_n, d'_{n-1}, ... , d'_1>$ if and only if for each i, $1 \leq i \leq n$ either $d_i = "*"$ or $d_i = d'_i$.

3.2 Class-Association Rules

CARs is a combination of association rules mining and classification. CARs is a special subset of association rules whose antecedent is an itemsets and consequent are restricted to the classification class label. Let $I = \{i_1,i_2, ... ,i_m\}$ be a set of all items in D and Y to be a set of all class labels.

Definition 1 (Class-Association Rules). A class association rules r is an implication of the form :

$$X => C$$

Where $X \subset I$, $C \subset Y$. Antecedent of a CARs is also called itemset and a rule itself is called rule_item. Rule_item is large if the corresponding rule is frequent and accurate if the rule is confident.

To find all strong association rules, CBA uses an Apriori-like algorithm to generate large rule_items. And k-rule_item denotes a rule whose itemset has k items. In each pass, all large (k-1)-rule_items are found. These (k-1)-rule_items are used to generate candidate k-rule_item and selected candidates satisfy min_sup. For each large rule_item, the confidence of the corresponding rule is calculated and the rule is added to the set of all rules if the confidence satisfies min_conf.

Definition 2 (CAR Support, Confidence). Support and confidence of rule_item in a transaction set D is the following :

$$Support = \frac{ruleCount}{|D|}, \quad Confidence = \frac{ruleCount}{itemsetCount}$$

where ruleCount is the number of items in D that contain the itemset and are labeled with class label and itemsetCount is the number of items in D that contain the itemset.

3.3 Concept of the TCARs

We assume that each transaction in associated with a timestamp that gives the time of the transaction. Given a basic time interval t (e_0) under a given calendar schema, we denote the set of transactions whose timestamps are covered by t (e_0) as $D[t](D[e_0])$. TCARs over a calendar schema R is a pair (r, e). Where r is a class-association rule and e is a calendar pattern on R. Thus, temporal class-association rule (r, e) holds in D if and only if the r satisfies min_sup and min_fre in $D[e_0]$ for each basic time interval e_0 covered by e. And TCARs is an implication of the form :

<X => C, e>, X: itemset, C: class label, e: star calendar pattern

However, in reality, all of the rules do not precisely hold during the time intervals. Thus, we define new threshold, minimum frequency.

Definition 3 (Minimum Frequency). Given a calendar schema R and a transaction set D, TCARs (r, e) satisfies min_sup and min_conf with respect to the minimum frequency min_fre in D if (r, e) holds during not less than 100 ·min_fre(%) of basic time intervals are covered by e.

For example, given the calendar schema (week:{1,...,4}, day:{1,...,5}) and minimum frequency mim_fre = 0.7, we may have a temporal class-association rule (S_IP: 172.016.112.020, D_IP: 192.168.001.020 => Intrusion: attack <*, 3>). This means that rule holds on at least 70% of the Wednesday of every week.

The purpose of using a temporal class-association rule is to predict future events. We are not interested in the class-association rules that only hold during basic time intervals because basic time interval may be too specific to be used in prediction of future events. So we are interested in the rule whose calendar pattern has at least 1 star symbol.

3.4 Generating the TCARs

We extend apriori [1] to discover large rule_items. The input of our algorithm consists of a calendar schema R, a set D of timestamped transactions, a minimum support, confidence and frequency. On the data mining tasks, our algorithm produces the rules $TCAR_k(e)$ that satisfies minimum support and confidence for all possible star calendar pattern on R. Let k-rule_item denote a rule_item whose itemset has k items. Let $L_k(e)$ denote the set of large k-rule_item for calendar pattern e. Each element of this set is of the following form :

$$< (itemset, itemsetCount), (class\_label, ruleCount) >$$

Let C_k be the set of candidate k-rule_item. The TCARs algorithm is given in algorithm 1. The algorithm generates all the large rule_items by making multiple passes over the data. In each passes, the basic time intervals in the calendar schema are processed one by one. During the processing of basic time interval e_0 in pass k, the set of large k-rule_items, $L_k(e_0)$ is first computed, and then $TCAR_k(e_0)$ is used to update the $TCAR_k(e)$ for all the calendar patterns that cover e_0. Assume that we have calendar schema (year, month, day). In the algorithm, we may need to consider, e.g., calendar pattern <2000,*,1> as well as <*,1,*>. These two patterns have an overlapping basic time interval, <2000,1,1>. In our algorithm, we use the large rule_items for <2000,1,1> to derive the large rule_items for <2000,*,1> and <*,1,*> to avoid duplicate tasks.

In the first pass, we compute the large 1-rule_items for each basic time interval by counting the supports (line 2). These 1-rule_items are used to generate candidate 2-rule_items by candidateGen($L_{k-1}(e_0)$) (line 7). The next scan of the data is performed to count which of the candidate 2-rule_items satisfy min_sup for each basic time interval (line 8-15). And then, the algorithm produces the rules $TCAR_k(e_0)$ using genRules function (line 16). The algorithm iterates in this fashion, starting each subsequent pass with the seed set of rules found to be large in the previous pass. Finally, large k-rule_items in $TCAR_k(e_0)$ is used to update the $TCAR_k(e)$ for each star calendar pattern that covers the basic time interval. After the basic time interval e_0 is processed in pass k, the large $TCAR_k$ for all the calendar patterns e that cover e_0 are updated as follows (line 18). We associate a counter count with each candidate $TCAR_k$ for each star calendar pattern. The counters are initially set to 1.

Input transaction (Training data set) D
Output <$TCAR_k(e)$, e> for all star calendar pattern e

1)   forall basic time intervals e_0 do
2) $L_1(e_0)$ = {large 1-rule_items in $D[e_0]$};
3) $TCAR_1(e_0)$ = genRules($L_1(e_0)$)
4)   end

5)   forall (k=2 ; $\exists$ a star calendar pattern e such that $L_{k-1}(e) \neq \emptyset$; k++) do
6)   forall basic time intervals e_0 do
7) $C_k(e_0)$ = candidateGen($L_{k-1}(e_0)$, min_sup);
8)   for each data case $d \in D(e_0)$ do
9) C_d = subset ($C_k(e_0)$, d);
10)   for each candidate $c \in C_d$ do
11)   c.itemsetCount ++;
12)   if d.class=c.class then c.ruleCount++;
13)   end
14)   end
15) $L_k(e_0)$ = {$c \in C_k$ | c.ruleCount $\geq$ min_sup};
16) $TCAR_k(e_0)$ = genRules($L_k(e_0)$, min_conf);
17)   forall calendar pattern e that cover e_0 do
18)   update $TCAR_k(e)$ using $TCAR_k(e_0)$;
19)   end
20) end

Algorithm 1. Generating TCARs algorithm

When $TCAR_k(e_0)$ is used to update $TCAR_k(e)$, the counters of the k-rule_items in $TCAR_k(e)$ that are also in $TCAR_k(e_0)$ are incremented by 1, and the k-rule_items that are in $TCAR_k(e_0)$ but not in $TCAR_k(e)$ are added to $TCAR_k(e)$ with the counter set to 1. Given threshold min_fre, suppose that there are totally N basic time intervals covered by e and that it is the n-th update to $TCAR_k(e)$. It is easy to see that a rule_item cannot be large for e if its counter does not satisfy $count+ (N-n) \geq min\_fre \cdot N$.

4 Building Classifier Using TCARs

In this section, we describe to build the efficient classifier using TCARs. Generated classifier for each calendar pattern is following format :

$$(r_1, r_2, \ldots , r_n, default\_class, e)$$

where, r_i is the generated TCARs and e is the calendar pattern. However, the number of rules generated by TCARs algorithm can be huge. To make the efficient classifier, we need to prune rules generated. To reduce the number of rules generated, we perform three types of rule prune. First rule prune is the pruning from calendar patterns of TCARs. After we discover all large rule_items, we remove all the TCARs (r, e) if we have other TCARs (r, e') and e is covered by e'. Second, we use general and high-confidence rule to prune more specific and lower confidence ones. Before the pruning, all rules are ranked according to the following criteria.

Definition 4 (Confidence-Support Ranking Criteria). Given two rules r_i and r_j, $r_i >$ r_j (or r_i is ranked higher than r_j) if

  1. conf(r_i) > conf(r_j) or
  2. conf(r_i) = conf(r_j), sup(r_i) > sup(r_j) or
  3. conf(r_i) = conf(r_j) and sup(r_i) = sup(r_j), but r_i is generated before r_j.

A rule r_1: X=>C is said a general rule w.r.t. rule r_2: X'=>C', if only if A is a subset of A'. First, we need to sort the set of generated rules for each calendar pattern. This sorting guarantees that only the highest rank rules will be selected into the classifier. And then, given two rules r_1 and r_2, where r_1 is a general rule w.r.t r_2. We prune r_2 if r_1 also has higher rank than r_2. The rationale behind the prune is the following: if rule r covers a case D then sub-rule also covers it, and sub-rule will always be selected since it has higher rank. Third, pruning rules based on database coverage [10]. We use a coverage threshold to select database coverage as shown in algorithm 2. The pruning method using database coverage is follows.

First for each case in D, set its cover-count(d.update) to 0. To the rules of each calendar pattern, if calendar pattern of r covers basic time interval of case and r can correctly classify at least one case then select r and increase the d.update of those cases matching r by 1. A case is removed if its d.update passes coverage threshold. The rule selection stops when either all of them are considered or no cases are left in D. A default rule is also selected. It has an empty ruleset and predicts a class label, which is a majority class among the case left in D or if none is left is the majority class in the original database.

After a set of rules is selected for classifier, we classify new cases. First, we select the rules whose calendar patterns can cover basic time intervals of cases. Then, we discover the rules matching case in the selected one and classify class labels of the discovered rules. If all the rules matching the new case have same class label, the new case is assigned to that label. Otherwise, we classify the new case as class label of the rule with higher confidence and support.

```
Input  a set of rules, coverage threshold δ
Output a subset of rules for classifier model

1)   forall case d ∈ D do
2)           d.update = 0;
3)   end
4)   for (the training data set and rule set ≠∅) do
5)          for each rule r ∈ rule set do
6)                for each case d ∈ D do
7)                      if (d.e₀∈r.e) and (d satisfies the conditions of r)
8)                            d.update ++;
9)                      select r;
10)              if d.update ≥ δ
11)                    delete case d in D;
12)          end
13)      end
14) end
```

Algorithm 2. Selecting rules based on coverage

5 Experiments and Results

In this section, we describe our experiments in building intrusion detection model on the dataset from the DARPA 1998 Intrusion Detection Evaluation [13].

The DARPA 1998 Intrusion Detection Evaluation Data consists of training data and test data. The training data consists of seven weeks of network-based attacks. Attacks are labeled in the training data. The test data consists of two weeks of data containing network-based attacks. To preprocessing the 7 weeks' training data, we define calendar schema and domain by a hierarchy of calendar concepts.

$$R=(week:\{1,...,7\}, day:\{1,...,5\}, group\_hour:\{1,...,5\})$$

where domain values of group_hour represent early morning(0-7hour), morning(7-9hour), daytime(9-18hour), evening(18-20hour), and late night(20-24hour).

We use connections as the basic granule, obtaining the connection from the raw packet data of the audit trail. We preprocess the packet data in the training data files in the following schema :

$$(Cal\_patt, S\_IP, S\_Port, D\_IP, D\_Port, Class\_label)$$

where Cal_patt is the basic time intervals of a network connection. S_IP and S_Port denote source address and Port number respectively, while D_IP and D_Port, represent the destination address and Port number. The attribute Class_label is class labels that are two categories: 'attack' and 'normal.' Fig. 2 shows the preprocessing results (TCP-dump data) from raw packet data of audit trail.

#	Start Date	Start Time	Duration	Service	Src Port	Dest Port	Src IP address	Dest IP address	Attack Score/Name
1	07/03/1998	08:00:01	00:00:01	http	1106	80	192.168.001.005	192.168.001.001	0 –
2	07/03/1998	08:00:01	00:00:02	domain/u	53	53	172.016.112.020	192.168.001.001	0 –
3	08/03/1998	08:00:01	00:00:01	smtp	1026	25	172.016.113.084	194.007.248.153	0 –
8383	07/03/1998	11:46:39	00:00:26	telnet	20504	23	197.218.177.069	172.016.113.050	laodmodule
9966	07/03/1998	11:49:39	00:00:01	tcpmux	1234	1	205.160.208.190	172.016.113.050	portsweep
...	...	...	...	...	...	...	...	...	...

Class Label

#	Cal_patt	Src_ip	Src_port	Dest_ip	Dest_port	Intrusion
1	<1,3,2>	192.168.001.005	1106	192.168.001.001	80	normal
2	<1,3,2>	172.016.112.020	53	192.168.001.001	53	normal
3	<1,3,2>	172.016.113.084	1026	194.007.248.153	25	normal
8383	<1,3,3>	197.218.177.069	20504	172.016.113.050	23	attack
9966	<1,3,3>	205.160.208.190	1234	172.016.113.050	1	attack
...	...	...	...	...	...	...

Fig. 2. Preprocessing of the training data

Our experiment has a two-step process. First, we build a classifier based on TCARs from the preprocessed 7 week's training data. Second, we classify 2 week' test data using class label after building classifier. We use two measure of the number of detected attacks and missed attacks to evaluate the performance. Fig. 3 shows the results of DARPA 1998 test data. Our experiments focused on detecting DOS and PROBE attacks form TCP-dump data and the result is more accurate than C4.5.

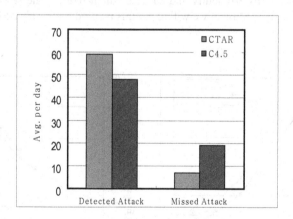

Fig. 3. Intrusion detection result

Also, we have three important thresholds for the classifier performance (minimum frequency, minimum confidence and database coverage thresholds.). These thresholds control the number of rules selected for building classifier so we used these thresholds. We had experiments about three thresholds using sample TCP-dump data list file of DARPA data. There is fixed minimum support value on 20. Fig. 4 and fig. 5 shows classifier accuracy according to minimum confidence and database coverage respectively. Fig. 4 is the result of testing accuracy according to minimum confidence where min_fre = 0.4 and database coverage = 1. Fig. 5 shows accuracy according to database coverage where min_conf = 0.4 and min_fre = 0.3.

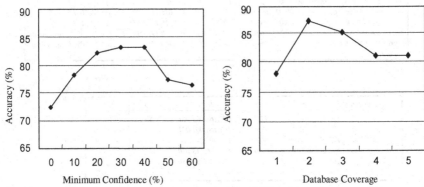

Fig. 4. The effect of confidence on accuracy   **Fig. 5.** The effect of coverage on accuracy

Fig. 6 illustrates that the generated large k-rule_items in each pass decreases by decreasing minimum confidence. Fig. 7 shows the comparing of execution times of large k-rule_item using previous apriori algorithm. In fig. 7, our algorithm spends more execution times than apriori algorithm because of discovering repeatedly each basic time interval when rule_items generate. So, we need an optimized algorithm pruning unnecessary candidate in candidates generating step. CMAR proposed FP-tree which generates large patterns efficiently and CF-tree which reduces the storing and search cost of generated rules. Maybe, we will apply this method on our algorithm to improve efficiency.

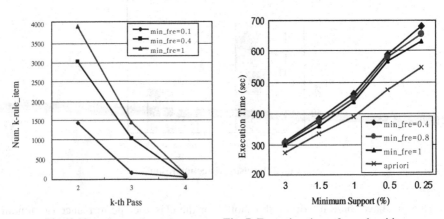

Fig. 6. Num. generating rules   **Fig. 7.** Execution time of our algorithm

6   Conclusion and Future Work

In this paper, we proposed new intrusion detection classification using data mining. The proposed classification is based on CTAR which considers temporal attribute of audit data. This method has been extended for time factors to be included in the CARs with integrated association and classification rules when building a prediction model. Also, regular exploration under various time units was possible with the way of expressing time factors and calendar pattern was applied for the users to easily understand the discovered rules. Therefore our proposed classification classified more accurate in terms of multiple time granularities. The proposed classification used 1988 DARPA Intrusion Detection Evaluation data and the results were more accurate than existing classification(C4.5). Moreover, we have found optimal threshold of audit data by experimenting about three thresholds which effect performance of classifier.

Currently, research on reducing cost of execution time for the proposed algorithm is doing. And we should design algorithms that generate TCARs and a way to store generated rules effectively.

Acknowledgment. This work was supported by University IT Research Center Project, KOSEF RRC Project(Cheongju Univ. ICRC) and ETRI in Korea.

References

1. R. Agrawal and R. Srikant.: Fast algorithms mining association rules in large databases, In Proc. of the 1994 International Conference on Very Large Data Bases, 1994.
2. W. Lee and S. Stolfo.: Data Mining Approaches for Intrusion Detection, In Proc. of the 7th USENIX Secunity Symposium, 1998.
3. W. Lee and S. Stolfo.: A Data Mining Framework for Building Intrusion Detection Models, IEEE Symposium on Security and Privacy, 1999.
4. J.F. Roddick and M. Spiliopoulou.: Temporal data mining : survey and issues, Research Report ACRC-99-007, University of South Australia, 1999.
5. B. Ozden and S. Ramaswamy.: Cyclic Association Rules, In Proc. of the 14th International Conference, 1998.
6. X. Chen and I. Petrounias.: A Framework for Temporal Data Mining, In Proc. of the 9th International Conference on Database and Expert Systems Applications, 1998.
7. Y. Li and P. Ning.: Discovering Calendar-based Temporal Association Rules, In Proc. of the 8th International Symposium on Temporal Representation and Reasoning, 2001.
8. D. Barbara, J. Couto and N. Wu.: ADAM: Detecting Intrusion by Data Mining, In Proc. of the 2th IEEE Information Assurance Workshop, 2001.
9. B. Liu, W. Hsu, and Y. Ma.: Integrating classification and association rule mining, In Proc. of the 4th International Conference Knowledge Discovery and Data Mining (KDD'98), 1998.
10. W. Li, J. Han, and J. Pei.: CMAR: Accurate and Efficient Classification Based on Multiple Class-Association Rules, In Proc. 2001 International Conference on Data Mining (ICDM'01), 2001
11. Y. J. Lee, S. B. Seo and K. H. Ryu.: Discovering Temporal Relation Rules form Temporal Interval Data, Korea Information Science Society (KISS), 2001.

12. M. S. Shin, E. H. Kim, K. H. Ryu and K. Y. Kim.: Data Mining Methods for Alert Correlation Analysis, International Journal of Computer and Information Science(IJCIS), to be appeared in 2003.
13. MIT Lincoln Laboratories DARPA Intrusion Evaluation Detection. In http://www.ll.mit.edu/IST/ideval/

Viterbi Algorithm for Intrusion Type Identification in Anomaly Detection System

Ja-Min Koo and Sung-Bae Cho

Dept. of Computer Science, Yonsei University
Shinchon-dong, Seodaemoon-ku
Seoul 120-749, Korea
icicle@candy.yonsei.ac.kr,
sbcho@cs.yonsei.ac.kr

Abstract. Due to the proliferation of the infrastructure of communication networks and the development of the relevant technology, intrusions on computer systems and damage are increased, resulting in extensive work on intrusion detection systems (IDS) to find attacks exploiting illegal usages or misuses. However, many IDSs have some weaknesses, and most hackers try to intrude systems through the vulnerabilities. In this paper, we develop an intrusion detection system based on anomaly detection with hidden Markov model and propose a method using the Viterbi algorithm for identifying the type of intrusions. Experimental results indicate that the buffer overflow is well-identified, while we have some difficulties to identify the denial of service attacks with the proposed method.

1 Introduction

As the worldwide proliferation in network environments, a variety of faster services have become a reality. However, the higher the reliance on computers, the more crucial security problems such as the overflow or manipulation by external aggression occur. Korea Computer Emergency Response Team and Coordination Center (CERTCC-KR) reports that hacking damages are significantly increased from 1998: 1,943 attempts in 2000, 5,333 attempts in 2001 and 15,192 attempts in 2002 [1]. In addition, anyone who has little basic knowledge on hacking can easily intrude computer system with tools for hacking, which will lead to the increase of the damage by hacking in the near future. As demand and interest in intrusion detection are raised, the most active effort in this area has mainly developed the system security mechanisms like firewalls. Especially intrusion detection system (IDS) is one of them [2]. Intrusion detection techniques are divided into two groups according to the type of data they use: misuse detection and anomaly detection. The former uses the knowledge about attacks, and the latter uses normal behaviors [3].

The intrusion detection markets have been grown rapidly from 183 million dollars in 2000 to 422 million dollars in 2002 [4], so that new products related with IDS are released continuously. In 2001, there are 15 classes of IDS for commercial, 8 classes

K. Chae and M. Yung (Eds.): WISA 2003, LNCS 2908, pp. 97–110, 2004.

of IDS for information, 58 classes of IDS for research and 12 classes of IDS are released to Korean market. Most of IDSs have been developed to improve the detection rates, and they have some technical inertia such as inability of detecting the cause and the path of intrusion. As a result, when intrusion is happened, even if an intrusion is detected by IDSs, it takes long time to do appropriate actions. Moreover, it is hard to get the data that include the type of attempted intrusion mainly in specific system. Therefore, we cannot consider appropriate countermoves of how to cope with the attacks.

In this paper, normal behaviors are modeled by using system call events included in BSM (Basic Security Module) auditing data from Solaris. It checks the auditing data for detecting the intrusion, and the Viterbi algorithm traces the state sequence of current intrusion to compare with the sequences of known intrusions to determine the type of intrusions.

2 Background

2.1 Anomaly Detection System

There are four representative approaches based on anomaly detection system such as expert system approach, statistical approach, neural network approach and hidden Markov model (HMM), and Table 1 summarizes them.

Table 1. Research of the representative anomaly detection system

Organization	Name	Period	Approach			
			A	B	C	D
AT&T	Computer Watch [5]	1987-1990	X			
UC Davis	NSM [6]	1989-1995			X	
	GrIDS [7]	1995-	X			
SRI International	IDES [8]	1983-1992			X	
	NIDES [9]	1992-1995			X	
	EMERALD [10]	1996-			X	
CS Telecom	Hyperview [11]	1990-1995		X	X	
New Mexico Univ.	C.Warender et. Al [12]	1999			X	X
Yonsei Univ.	Park and Cho [13]	2002				X

(A: Expert system; B: Neural network; C: Statistical approach; D: HMM)

First of all, statistical approach is the most widely used in IDS. It uses some information such as login and logout time of the session, continuation of the resources and so on. It detects the intrusion by analyzing the time of resources and pattern of the command of normal users.

Second, NIDES (Next-generation Intrusion Detection Expert Systems), sets a standard of the intrusion detection with the similarities between profiles of short time and long time [9]. It can be widely applied and it has very high detection rate because of processing based on the past data. However, it has some disadvantages such as insensitive for the event sequence of specific behavior and limited to modeling the intrusion behavior.

Third, neural network approach is similar to statistical one but it is easier to represent non-linear relationship. There is an example of Hyperview developed in CS Telecom, which consists of 2 neural network modules and an expert system module [11]. Neural network modeling is good at representing the non-linear relationship and training automatically but the relationship modeled is usually in blackbox.

Finally, HMM proposed by C. Warender in New Mexico University is good at modeling and estimating with event sequence of which is the underlying unknown. It performs better to model the system than any others [12]. However, it takes long time to train and detect intrusions. To overcome such disadvantages, we can extract the events of changing the privilege before and after them, and we are able to model the normal behavior with them. By using this method, we can reduce the time to model and maintain good performance [13].

2.2 Intrusion Type

The main purpose of intrusion is to acquire the authority of roots, and buffer overflow is one of the main vehicles to do that. An intruder uses the buffer overflow with a general ID that is hardly used or has no password, and acquires the root privileges with advanced techniques. Hence, we must analyze the type of intrusions to make the host-based IDS to detect the intrusions. Intrusion types mainly used are classified by Markus J. Ranum who developed the open software of firewall at first and CERTCC-KR extended the intrusions into 10 classes [1]. Among these intrusions, prevalent are 4 types of intrusions such as buffer overflow, denial of service, setup vulnerability and S/W security vulnerability.

- Buffer overflow: This intrusion type is one of the most difficult things to be dealt with, because we have to understand the execution sequence of specific programs and structures of memory, and memory or stack structures are dependent on operating system. However, anyone can download and use it easily, because source codes of the buffer overflow and bugs of operating systems are opened at internet. Consequently, this attack is widely used for hacking. Especially, in the case of root program which sets the SETUID, someone can easily acquire the shell having the authority of roots easily using buffer overflow [14]. There are three kinds of vulnerabilities of the buffer overflow.

  - xlock vulnerability: It is program that locks local x display until a password is entered. Due to in sufficient bound checking on arguments which are supplied by users, it is possible to overwrite the internal stack space of thx lock program while it is executing. By supplying a carefully designed argument to the xlock program, intruders may be able to force xlock to execute arbitrary command. As xlock is setuid root, this may allow intruders to run arbitrary commands with root privileges.

- lpset vulnerability: Solaris's lpset allows setting of printing configuration in /etc/printers.conf or FNS. This product has been found to contain a security vulnerability that allows a local user to obtain root privileges.

- kcms_sparc vulnerability: Solaris contains support for the Kodak Color Management System (KCMS), a set of openwindows compliant API's and libraries to create and manage profiles that can describe and control the color performance of monitors, scanners, printers and film recorders. It also allows obtaining root privileges.

• S/W security vulnerability: This intrusion plays a major role in the bugs to cause the failures of programs: security errors on programming and on execution.

• Setup vulnerability: It happens when we setup a specific system without considering security. Some intrusions are included in this class related with various kinds of disadvantages of services provided by system. These can be used easily because there is no need of execution codes for hacking.

• Denial of service: It is used to make a specific system not to provide services normally. This is different from the usual intrusions which acquire the authority of system administrators. This attack inflicts a loss on specific host by exhausting all the resources of system not to provide service completely [15].

2.3 Solaris Basic Security Modules

Unix system provides the log information of wtmp, utmp and sulog in some directories such as /var/log/message or /var/adm/. It has some advantages to obtain easily whenever we want but some weak points. For example, when intruders succeed to intrude they can delete their log files. Due to this reason, we use the audit data of system call level to detect intrusions: Basic Security Module (BSM) which is provided by Sun Microsystems.

The algorithms presented in this paper which operate on audit data use logs produced by the BSM of the Solaris operating system. Each event generates a record, where the record is composed of different types of tokens depending on the event and the type of data needs to be included in the record.

The user audit ID is a useful piece of information included in the audit records of all events which can be attributed to a specific user. It is a unique identification number assigned to every user when they login and inherited by all processes descended from the login shell. This number allows an intrusion detection system to easily identify which user caused a specific event, even if that user has changed identities (through the su command, for example).

The log files are initially written in a binary format by the auditing process. Sun provides a tool, named praudit, which reads the binary log files and produces a human readable ASCII equivalent. This ASCII representation is what the algorithms working with the BSM data use. While having to convert to ASCII text slows down the algorithms somewhat, it makes coding and debugging much easier. Furthermore, once an algorithm has been prototyped and found promising, extending it to directly read the binary files would eliminate the praudit text conversion overhead [16]. Figure 1 shows the audit data record of BSM.

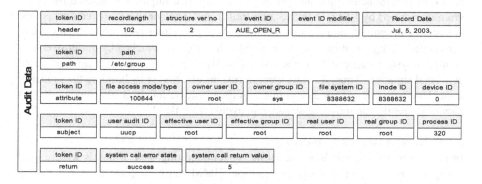

Fig. 1. BSM audit data record

3 Proposed Method

An IDS based on HMM collects and abridges normal auditing data, and it makes normal behavior models for a specific system. And then it detects intrusions with auditing data to detect the intrusions from it. Finally, to identify the type of intrusions, we analyze the state sequences of the system call events using the Viterbi algorithm.

Figure 2 shows the entire system structure. The proposed method consists of 4 parts: normal behavior modeling, intrusion detection, state sequence analysis and identification of the intrusion types.

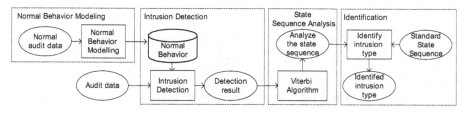

Fig. 2. System structure

3.1 Intrusion Detection

The basic log files can be easily obtained without any significant effort, but mostly it is hard to locate any evidence of privilege acquisition when buffer overflow attacks are attempted, and after a successful intrusion the attacker can easily erase his or her traces from those essential log files [17]. Because of the drawback, system call level audit data are used [12].

Especially, Sun Microsystems' BSM provides adequate representation of the behavior of programs, because any privileged activity that might be generated by a program is captured by BSM. Usually, audit trail from BSM consists of several measures. A system call, one of the measures from BSM, can be either perfectly normal or dangerous depending on situations. For example, the program attacked by buffer overflow generates system call events that are significantly different from the events generated at normal situation. Thus, we can detect intrusions effectively by building the model of normal system call events and noting significant deviation from the model. In this paper, we use the audit data of system call events from BSM.

3.1.1 Normal Behavior Modeling

In this paper, we use HMM to model the system auditing data, which is widely used for speech recognition or image recognition. HMM can be applied to model the sequence of system call events because it is very useful for modeling the sequence information [18].

An HMM λ is described as $\lambda = (A, B, \Pi)$. An HMM is characterized by a set of states Q, a set of possible observation symbols V, a number of observation symbols M, state transition probability distribution A, observation symbol probability B and initial state distribution Π [19]. The set of all system call events in audit data corresponds to that of possible symbol observations V, and a number of events correspond to M. The length of observation sequence T corresponds to the length of windows. The type of HMM that we use is a left-to-right model, which is known for modeling temporal signals better than any other models [20].

This phase is to model the normal behavior, which determines HMM parameters to maximize $P(O|\lambda)$ with which input sequence O, because no analytic solution is known for it, by an iterative method called Baum-Welch reestimation [18]. Figure 3 shows an example of the left-to-right model of HMM.

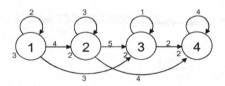

Fig. 3. Left-to-right model of HMM with 4 states

3.1.2 Intrusion Detection

Given λ, forward procedure can be used to calculate the probability $P(O|\lambda)$ with which input sequence O is generated out of model λ using forward variables [19]. The probability is used to decide whether normal or not with a threshold. Forward variable $a_t(i)$ denotes the probability at which a partial sequence $O_1, O_2, \cdots, O_t$ is observed and stays at state q_i.

$$\alpha_t(i) = P(O_1, O_2, \cdots, O_t, s_t = i \mid \lambda) \tag{1}$$

According to the above definition, $a_t(i)$ is the probability with which all the symbols in input sequence are observed in order and the final state reached at i. Summing up $a_t(i)$ can be calculated by the following procedure [18][19].

• Step 1. Initialization:

$$\alpha_1(i) = \pi_i b_i(O_1) \tag{2}$$

• Step 2. Induction:

$$\alpha_{t+1}(j) = \left[\sum_{j=1}^{N} \alpha_t(i) a_{ij} \right] b_j(O_{t+1}), \quad 1 \le t \le T \cdot \tag{3}$$

• Step 3. Termination:

$$P(O \mid \lambda) = \sum_{i=1}^{N} \alpha_T(i) \cdot \tag{4}$$

Finally, if calculated value $P(O|\lambda)$ calculated log scale is smaller than the threshold, we decide that intrusion is occurred.

3.2 Intrusion Type Identification

3.2.1 Sequence Analysis with Viterbi Algorithm

The detected intrusion at the previous phase triggers to analyze the current state sequence of events. To identify the type of intrusions, we must know the state sequence, but HMM does not provide the state sequence explicitly. However, we can estimate the state sequence of the most probable ones using the Viterbi algorithm which finds the most-likely state transition path in a state diagram, given a sequence of symbols [20, 21]. It has been applied to speech and character recognition tasks where the observation symbols are modeled by HMM [22, 23]. The Viterbi algorithm can be easily combined with other information in real-time. In this paper, we apply the Viterbi algorithm to find optimal state sequence. Figure 4 shows the result of the Viterbi algorithm based on the HMM in Figure 3.

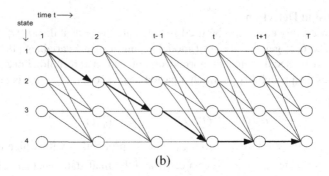

(b)

Fig. 4. Process of the viterbi algorithm

In left-to-right model of HMM, transition can only take place in a left to right manner and just one state can be skipped, thus only state transition a_{ij}, a_{ij+1} and a_{ij+2}.
For example in Figure 3, because we must start the state having the highest initial state distribution, we can do in state 1 at time 1 and transit with the highest transition probabilities among state 1, 2, 3 and 4 at time 2.

The procedures of Viterbi algorithm are as follows.

• Step 1: Initialization

$$\delta_1(i) = \pi_i b_i(O_1), \quad 1 \le i \le N$$
$$\Psi_q(i) = 0 \tag{5}$$

$\delta_1(i)$ is the probability that symbol O_1 occurs at time $t=1$ at state i. The variable $\psi_t(j)$ stores the optimal states. In Figure 2(a) can be seen above $\delta_1(i)$ assigns a number which is beside each state. In Figure 2(a), $\delta_1(1)=3$, $\delta_1(2)=2$, $\delta_1(3)=2$ and $\delta_1(4)=2$.

• Step 2: Recursion

$$\delta_t(j) = \max_i [\delta_{t-1}(i)a_{ij}]\, b_j(O_t), \qquad 2 \le t \le T, 1 \le j \le N$$
$$\Psi_t(j) = \arg\max_i [\delta_{t-1}(i)a_{ij}]\, b_j(O_t), \quad 2 \le t \le T, 1 \le j \le N \tag{6}$$

$\delta_t(i)$ denotes the weight accumulated when we are in state i at time t as the algorithm proceeds, and $\psi_t(j)$ represents the state at time t-1 which has the lowest cost corresponding to the state transition to state j at time t. In Figure 2(a), $\delta_2(1)=5$, $\delta_2(2)=7$, $\delta_2(3)=6$ and $\delta_2(4)$ is not defined. Therefore, $\psi_2(2)=2$.

• Step 3: Termination

$$P* = \max_{s \in S_F} [\delta_T(s)]$$
$$S_T* = \arg\max_{s \in S_F} [\delta_T(s)] \tag{7}$$

At the final time T, there are N probabilities δ_t, $t=1, 2, \cdots, N$. The highest probability among these probabilities becomes the candidate for the optimal state sequence. S_T^*

stores the corresponding state. Now, the final task is to backtrack to the initial state following the variable named ψ_t .

• Step 4: Backtracking

$$s_t^* = \Psi_{t+1}(s_{t+1}^*), \quad t = T - 1, T - 2, \cdots, 1 \tag{8}$$

When step 4 is finished, we can get the optimal state sequence '1-2-3-4-4-4' as shown in Figure 4.

3.2.2 Intrusion Type Identification

After backtracking, the similarity is compared between the average state sequence for every intrusion type and the state sequence of current intrusion using Euclidean distance. The formula is as follows.

$$d = \sqrt{\sum_{i=1}^{N} (x_i - y_i)^2} \tag{9}$$

By assigning the analyzed state sequence of current intrusion to x_i, and doing the state sequence of every intrusion type to y_i, we calculate the Euclidean distance d. The smaller the value is, the higher similarity is. Hence, the intrusion type that we have found has the least value d.

Table 2. The state sequence of intrusions of buffer overflow
(A: xlock, B: lpset, C: kcms_sparc)

	1	2	3	4	5	6	7	8	9	10
A	0	2	4	6	8	10	12	14	16	17
B	0	2	2	2	4	6	8	10	12	14
C	0	2	4	6	8	10	11	13	15	17

Table 3. The similarity with actual intrusion

	Distance
A – actual	1.732
B – actual	9.381
C – actual	0

Table 2 shows the state sequence of each type of intrusions. For instance, if the state sequence of current intrusion is "0-2-4-6-8-10-11-13-15-17" the similarity between kcms_sparc and actual intrusion becomes 0, between xlock and actual intrusion is 1.732, and between lpset and actual intrusion is 9.381 as shown in Table 3. Actual intrusion is identified as kcms_sparc intrusion, because the Euclidean distance is smaller than anything else.

4 Experimental Results

4.1 Experimental Environments

We have collected normal behaviors from six users for 2 weeks using Solaris 7 operating system. They have mainly used text editor, compiler and program of their own writing. In total 13 megabytes (160,448 events are recorded) of BSM audit data are used. Main types of intrusions are used: Buffer overflow gets root privileges by abusing systems' vulnerability. Denial of service is a kind of intrusions which disturbs to provide the service well. These are the main intrusions which are subject to happen in host based systems. The attack types and the number of attempts are shown in Table 4.

Table 4. Intrusion types and the number of trials

Attack Category	Intrusion Type	Count
	OpenView xlock Heap Overflow	9
Buffer Overflow	Lpset –r Buffer Overflow Vulnerability	7
	Kcms_sparc Configuration Overflow	4
	Process creation	9
Denial Of Service	Exhausting the memory	7
	Fill the Disk	9

4.2 Results

We conduct experiments of the HMM with different number of states and observation lengths. Table 5 shows the result of the HMM-based IDS, and we experiment with the

Table 5. The performance of HMM-based IDS (no. of states is 20)

Length	Threshold	Detection Rate	F-P Error
10	-9.43	100%	2.626
15	-9.43	100%	3.614
10	-14.42	100%	1.366
15	-14.42	100%	2.718
10	-16.94	100%	0.789
15	-16.94	100%	2.618
10	-18.35	100%	0.553
15	-18.35	100%	2.535
10	-19.63	100%	0.476
15	-19.63	100%	2.508
10	-20.83	100%	0.372
15	-20.83	100%	2.473

threshold value of -20.83 which minimizes the false-positive error rate. The state symbol sequence of each intrusion type is as shown in Figure 5, where their values are from 30 runs.

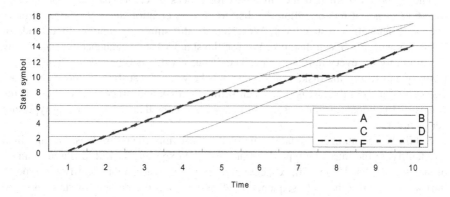

Fig. 5. State transition with 20 states and observation length of 10 (A:xlock, B: lpset, C: kcms_sparc, D: processe creation, E: fill the disk, F: exhausting the memory)

We make experiments to identify the intrusion type with auditing data for detecting the intrusion. Table 6 and Table 7 show the results.

Table 6. Result when state is 20 and observation length is 10

	A	B	C	D	E	F	Rate
A	8	1	-	-	-	-	88%
B	-	6	1	-	-	-	86%
C	-	-	4	-	-	-	100%
D	-	-	-	3	-	6	33%
E	-	-	-	4	-	3	0%
F	-	-	-	2	1	6	86%

Table 7. Average of results

Attack	Trial	Correct	Incorrect	Rate
Buffer Overflow	20	18	2	90%
Denial of Service	25	9	16	36%
Total	45	27	18	60%

A, B, C, D, E and F are the type of intrusions such as xlock Heap overflow, lpset overflow, kcms_configure buffer overflow, processes creation, fill the disk intrusion and exhausting the memory, respectively. Columns indicate the type of intrusions that we use actually and rows indicate the identified type of intrusions from experiments.

As a result, buffer overflow such as xlock, lpset and kcms_sparc intrusion are identified effectively. On the other hand, it is hard to identify the specific intrusion type of denial of service. The state sequence is analyzed to find the reason. In case of having the low identification rate for the intrusions of denial of service is relatively low, because their state sequences are very identical.

The proposed method makes mistakes for processes creation to exhaust memory over 60%. Also, it misses filling the disk to process creation and exhausting memory over 40% and 50%, respectively. We calculate the similarity among three kinds of intrusions with Euclidean distance. We use the standard state sequence for calculating the similarity for every intrusion type. The distance value is 0 between exhausting the memory and filling the disk, and the one is 0 between exhausting memory and processes creation, and the last is 0 between filling the disk and processes creation. Three values of Euclidean distance are 0, so that we discover that three intrusion types are very similar.

Similarly, the number of states, one of the most important variables, has an effect on identifying the intrusion type. We carry out the experiments with different number of states to 5, 10, 15 and 20, respectively. However, we cannot identify the type of intrusions, because the state sequence is identical when the number of states is 5, 10 and 15. On the other hand, the state sequences are different for every intrusion type in case of the number of states is 20.

5 Concluding Remarks

In this paper, we have proposed a method to identify the type of intrusions in the anomaly detection system based on HMM. The proposed process calculates the Euclidean distance to compare the similarity between the standard state sequence and current state sequence which are obtained by using Viterbi algorithm when intrusion occurs. Experiments are executed in the intrusion detection system based on HMM with 100% intrusion detection rates. We change the number of states from 5 to 30 and the length of observation symbols from 10 to 20 in the experiments. As a result, the system detects all the intrusions when the number of states is more than 20.

However the deviation of identification rates is very extreme for the type of intrusions. Especially, identification rates of intrusions belonging to denial of service are very low, because the state sequence among three intrusion types – processes creation, exhausting the memory and filling the disk – are identical. In addition, the number of states which is one of the most important variables has an effect to identify the type of intrusions. The proposed system needs more than 20 states. Moreover, it has difficulty to identify various types of intrusions of denial of service. Therefore, we must investigate to identify types of intrusions with HMM in smaller number of states.

Acknowledgement. This research was supported by University IT Research Center Project.

References

1. CERTCC-KR, Korea Computer Emergency Response Team and Coordination Center, http://www.certcc.or.kr, 2003.
2. H. S. Vaccaro and G. E. Liepins, "Detection of anomalous computer session activity," *In Proc. of IEEE Symposium on Research in Security and Privacy*, pp. 280–289, 1989.
3. T. F. Lunt, "A survey of intrusion detection techniques," *Computers & Security*, vol. 12, no. 4, pp. 405–418, June 1993.
4. IDC, *Plugging the Holes In eCommerce: The Market for Intrusion Detection and Vulnerability Assessment Software,* 1999-2003.
5. C. Dowel and P. Ramstdet, "The computer watch data reduction tool," *In Proc. of the 13th National Computer Security Conference,* pp. 99-108, Washington DC, USA, October 1990.
6. T. Heberlein, G. Dias, K. Levitt, B. Mukherjee, J. Wood and D. Wolber, "A network security monitor," In *Proc. of the 1990 IEEE Symposium on Research in Security and Privacy,* pp. 296–304, Los Alamitos, CA, USA, 1990.
7. S. Stanford-Che, S. Cheung, R. Crawford, M. Dilger, J. Frank, J. Hoagland, K. Levitt, C. Wee, R. Yip and D. Zerkle, "GrIDS-A graph based intrusion detection system for large networks," *In Proc. of the 19th National Information Systems Security Conference,* vol. 1, pp. 361–370, October 1998.
8. T. F. Lunt, A. Tamaru, F. Gilham, R. Jagannathan, C. Jalali and P. G. Neuman, "A real-time intrusion-detection expert system (IDES)," *Technical Report Project 6784,* CSL, SRI International, Computer Science Laboratory, SRI International, February 1992.
9. D. Anderson, T. F. Lunt, H. Javits, A. Tamaru and A. Valdes, "Detecting unusual program behavior using the statistical components of NIDES," *NIDES Technical Report,* SRI International, May 1995.
10. P. A. Porras and P. G. Neumann, "EMERALD: Event monitoring enabling responses to anomalous live disturbances," *In Proc. of the 20th National Information Systems Security Conference,* pp. 353–365, Baltimore, Maryland, USA, October 1997.
11. H. Debar, M. Becker and D. Siboni, "A neural network component for an intrusion detection system," *In Proc. of 1992 IEEE Computer Society Symposium on Research in Security and Privacy,* pp. 240–250, Oakland, CA, May 1992.
12. C. Warrender, S. Forrest and B. Pearlmutter, "Detecting intrusion using calls: Alternative data models," *In Proc. of IEEE Symposium on Security and Privacy,* pp. 133–145, May 1999.
13. S.-B. Cho and H.-J. Park, "Efficient anomaly detection by modeling privilege flows using hidden Markov model," *Computers & Security*, vol. 22, no. 1, pp. 45–55, 2003.
14. D. Larochelle and D. Evans, "Statically detecting likely buffer overflow vulnerabilities," *In Proc. of USENIX Security Symposium,* pp. 177–190, August 2001.
15. F. Lau, S. H. Rubin, M. H. Smith and L. Trajkovic, "Distributed denial of service attacks," *2000 IEEE International Conference on Systems, Man and Cybernetics,* pp. 2275–2280, 2000.
16. S. E. Webster, "The development and analysis of intrusion detection algorithms," *S. M. Thesis, Massachusetts Institute of Technology,* June 1998.
17. S. Axelsson, "Research in intrusion detection system: A survey," *Chalmers University of Technology,* 1999.
18. L.R. Rabiner, "A tutorial on hidden markov models and selected applications in speech recognition," *Proc. of IEEE*, vol. 77, no. 2, pp. 257–286, February 1989.
19. L. R. Rabiner and B .H. Juang, "An introduction to hidden markov models," *IEEE ASSP Magazine,* vol. 3, no. 1, pp. 4–16, 1986.

20. G. D. Forney Jr., "Maximum-likelihood sequence detection in the presence of intersymbol interference," *IEEE Transactions on Information Theory,* vol. 18, no. 30, pp. 363–378, May 1972.
21. G. D. Forney Jr., "The viterbi algorithm," *Proc. of IEEE,* vol. 61, no. 3, pp. 268–278, March 1973.
22. L. R. Rabiner and B. H. Juang, *Fundamentals of Speech Recognition,* Chapter 6, Prentice Hall, Englewood Cliffs, New Jersey, 1993.
23. J. Picone, "Continuous speech recognition using hidden markov models," *IEEE ASSP Magazine,* vol. 7, no. 3, pp. 26–41, July 1990.

Towards a Global Security Architecture for Intrusion Detection and Reaction Management

Renaud Bidou[1], Julien Bourgeois[2], and Francois Spies[2]

[1] Iv2 Technologies, 20, rue du Colombier, 94360 Bry sur Marne, France
Renaud.Bidou@iv2-technologies.com
http://www.iv2-technologies.com
[2] LIFC, Universite de Franche-Comte, 4, place Tharradin, 25211 Montbeliard, France
{Julien.Bourgeois,Francois.Spies}@univ-fcomte.fr
http://lifc.univ-fcomte.fr

Abstract. Detecting efficiently intrusions requires a global view of the monitored network. This can only be achieved with an architecture which is able to gather data from all sources. A Security Operation Center (SOC) is precisely dedicated to this task. In this article, we propose our implementation of the SOC concept that we call SOCBox.

1 Introduction

Ensuring network security requires two modules: protection and supervision. Protection is composed of hardware, software and a security policy that must be followed. Even the best protection is always vulnerable to attacks due to unknown security bugs. Besides, the network configuration is subject to constant changes and possibly adds security holes. That is why the network supervision is an essential part of the security process and is realized by security experts.
In order to help the supervisors, Intrusion Detection Systems (IDS) have been developed [1], but these systems have several flaws. First of all, IDSs have an insufficient rate of detection: either too many intrusions are detected or missed [2]. Besides, simple IDSs have no sufficient information to detect coordinated attacks. Other types of IDS has been created and tested like distributed ones [6] [9] [5]. Cooperation of IDSs is still an on going work [3].

We propose here the implementation of a completely integrated Security Operation Center (SOC), called SOCBox in order to overcome the limitations of IDS. The SOCBox gathers data from a wide range of sources (IDS, Firewall, router, workstation, etc.) and therefore has a global view of the network. Its analysis engine can then correlate all messages generated by all the network components and find patterns of intrusion. Section 2 designs the global architecture of the SOCBox. We then focus on the collection and the analysis of the data generated by sensors in sections 3 and 4. A short conclusion will describe further research and analysis to be performed in the field of SOCBox design.

K. Chae and M. Yung (Eds.): WISA 2003, LNCS 2908, pp. 111–123, 2004.
© Springer-Verlag Berlin Heidelberg 2004

2   Global Architecture

The SOCBox implements the different box types defined in [7]. However, beside
the pure technical aspects involved in such an implementation, it is necessary to
consider the supervision of an IT infrastructure as a full operational project. We
will thus follow the functional steps of such a project in order to describe both
the purpose and the concepts of selected parts of the architecture described in
figure 1.

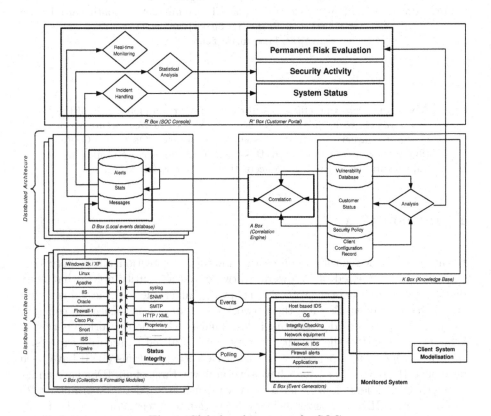

Fig. 1. Global architecture of a SOC

2.1   Data Acquisition

Before setting up sensors and designing any correlation or analysis rule, it is
necessary to evaluate the overall security level of the IT infrastructure to be
supervised. This will make it possible to determine if an intrusion path may
effectively lead to an intrusion on the target system and the criticality associated
to such an intrusion attempt.

Another point to be defined is the security policy, mostly in terms of access rights, permitted operations, etc.

Vulnerability database. The vulnerability database holds information about security breaches and insecure behavior that would either impact the overall security level or that could be exploited by an attacker in order to perform an intrusion. The database format must make it possible to include the following types of vulnerabilities :

- Structural vulnerabilities, i.e. vulnerabilities internal to specific software such as a buffer overflow, format string, race conditions, etc.
- Functional vulnerabilities, depending on configuration, operational behavior, users, etc. These vulnerabilities differ from the previous ones as they deeply depend on the environment in which they lie.
- Topology-based vulnerabilities, including networking impact on intrusions and their consequences.

Security policy. The next step of the supervised system inventory is an organizational one and, more specifically, a review of security policy aspects that would impact either event generation and/or the reaction-reporting processes.

It is clear that the two major aspects of security policy that need to be reviewed are authorization and testing/audit procedures. These two aspects will provide information concerning behavior that sensors would detect. Events generated (administrator login, portscans, etc.) will then be marked as matching with security policy criteria. Others will be analyzed as possible part of an intrusion attempt.

This information is stored in the Knowledge Base.

Status evaluation. The last part of the Knowledge Base is a detailed security level evaluation of the systems to be monitored. The objective is to process such an evaluation through an analyzing engine capable of integrating the three kinds of vulnerabilities as seen above, as well as security policy constraints. The engine should provide a list of vulnerabilities each system is exposed to, the relative impact of each vulnerability and intrusion paths leading to the activation of "inactive" vulnerabilities.

In order to be reliable, such an evaluation must be re-generated each time a new vulnerability is found or one of the monitored systems is changed.

2.2   Data Analysis and Reporting

Structural and behavior-lead alerts. The main operations performed that generate alerts are the following: correlation, structural analysis, intrusion path analysis and behavior analysis. Correlation is a stand-alone operation leading to the creation of contexts against which further analysis will be made, in order to check if they match the characteristics of an intrusion attempt. Structural analysis may be compared to an advanced pattern matching process, used to determine if events stored within a certain context lead to a known intrusion path or to an attack tree [8]. Intrusion path analysis is the next step whose output provides information about the exposure of the target system to the intrusion attempt detected. Then, the behavior analysis integrates elements from the security policy in order to determine if the intrusion attempt is allowed or not.

The purpose of such operations is to generate alerts that not only match the structural path of intrusion (i.e. scan, fingerprinting, exploiting, backdooring and cleaning), but also take care of the security policy defined, as well as criticality of targets systems.

3 Collection and Storage

3.1 Data Collection

Collecting data from heterogeneous sources implies the setup of two kinds of agents: protocol and application. The former collects information from E Boxes, the latter parses information for storage in a "pseudo-standard" format. These two modules are connected by a dispatcher. Such an architecture allows high-availability and load-balancing systems to be set at any level into the architecture.

Figure 2 shows some architecture examples, based on the details provided below.

Protocol agents. Protocol agents are designed to receive information from specific transport protocols, such as syslog, snmp, smtp, html, etc. They act like server side applications and their only purpose is to listen to incoming connexions from E Boxes and make collected data available to the dispatcher.

The simplicity of such agents make them easy to implement and maintain.

The raw format storage is usually a simple file, though direct transfer to the dispatcher through named pipes, sockets or shared memory ensures better performance.

From a security point of view, the most important point is to ensure the integrity of data collected by agents. Therefore, data is encapsulated into a secure tunnel.

Dispatcher and application agents. The dispatcher's purpose is to determine the source-type of an incoming event and then forward the original message to the appropriate application agent. Once again, implementation is relatively trivial, once a specific pattern has been found for each source-type from which the data may be received.

Autonomous operations performed by the dispatcher are the following:

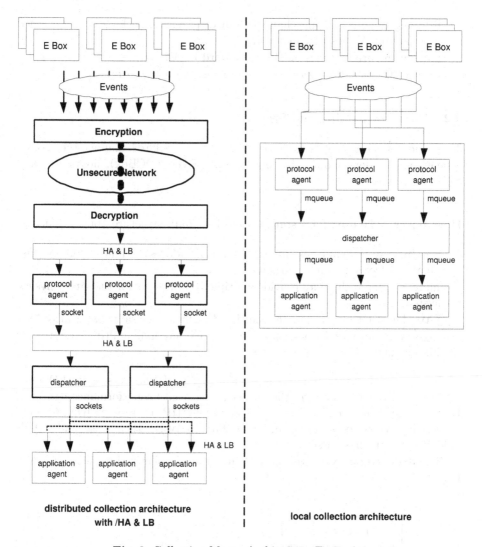

Fig. 2. Collection Macro Architecture Examples

- listening to an incoming channel from protocol agents, such as socket, named pipe, system V message queue, etc.
- checking pattern matching against a patterns database that should be pre-loaded in memory for performances considerations.
- sending the original message to an E Box specific application agent through any suitable outgoing channel.

Application agents perform formatting of messages so that they match with the generic model of the message database.

Autonomous operations performed by application agents are:

- listening to an incoming channel from dispatchers, such as socket, named pipe, system V message queue etc.
- parsing the original message into standard fields.
- transmitting the formatted message to corresponding D Boxes.

3.2 Data Formatting and Storage

Two kinds of data have to be formatted in a "standard" manner (i.e. homogeneous and understandable by any module of the SOCBox): host entry and collected messages.

Host entry. The need for a standardized host data structure appears since:

- sensors may transmit host information in IP address format or FQDN (Full Qualified Domain Name) format.
- multi-homing techniques provide multiple IP addresses for the same physical system.
- virtual host techniques provide multiple FQDN for the same physical system.
- high availability and load balancing systems may hide multiple systems behind a single IP address or FQDN.

It appears that identifying a host either by its IP address or its FQDN is not reliable. What is more, in the never-ending need for performance, (reverse) DNS lookup cannot be performed for each new (IP address) FQDN detected in logs. It is then necessary to rely on a third-party ID, IP address and FQDN independent: the host token.

The data structure for storing host information follows the scheme given in Figure 3.

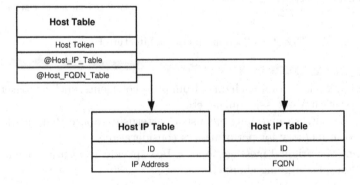

Fig. 3. Host Entry Data Structure

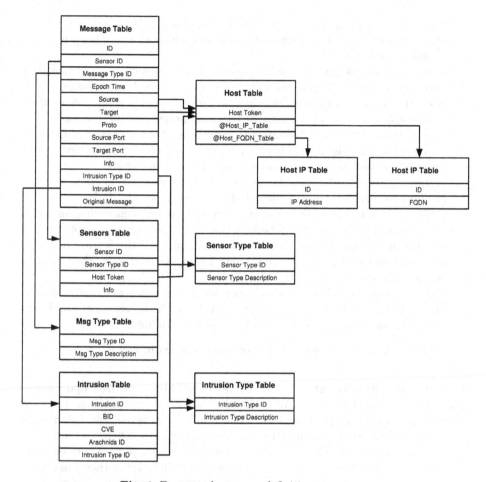

Fig. 4. Formatted message definition structures

Messages. Working on the data generated by the different types of equipment, transmitted via different protocols requires "standard" formatting. Although an effort has been made to define a worldwide standard with IDMEF [4], it appears that the XML bus used is too heavy and resources consuming, for our purposes of event correlation. However, a separate translation process must be implemented for IDMEF compliance. Relations between each structure are given in Figure 4.

4   Correlation

4.1   Overview

Operating the Correlation. The correlation's purpose is to analyze complex information sequences and produce simple, synthesized and accurate events. In order to generate such qualified events, five operations are to be performed:

- the first, obvious, operation is to identify duplicates and set a specific flag in order to keep the information and continue without the need keep multiple identical messages.
- sequence patterns matching is the most common operation performed by a correlation engine. Its purpose is to identify a sequence of messages which would be characteristic of an intrusion attempt. It makes it possible to identify on-going intrusion processes, as well as complex intrusion scenarios.
- time pattern matching is designed to include another important dimension in intrusion analysis: time. This is mainly used for context (see below) management, as well as slow and distributed intrusion processes.
- system exposure and criticality analysis, provide information about the target system's vulnerability to detected intrusion attempts. Indeed, it seems inappropriate to have the SOCBox generating alarms concerning an intrusion scenario based on a vulnerability that the target system is not exposed to. Another piece of information is the criticality of the intrusion i.e. its overall impact on the supervised system. This helps to manage the priorities in terms of reaction to multiple incidents.
- security policy matching, is a behavior-based filter that eliminates specific events if they match security policy criteria such as administrator login, identification processes and authorizations / restrictions.

A global overview of correlation operations is given in figure 5 below.

Introduction to contexts. The analysis defined above is based upon a specific structure called contexts. All correlation operations are performed against these structures. In simple terms, the definition of a context is the following: a container of formatted data matching a common criteria. Therefore, any message stored in the formatted message database is to be part of one or more contexts. Correlation operations will be done in parallel so that they can be run simultaneously on each context. Two kinds of context management approaches can be implemented. The first one is to define independent and distinct contexts. Each context will contain messages matching every criteria. We define such an architecture as an array of contexts. The second approach is a hierarchical one. Top level contexts matching a limited number of criteria are defined. Then sub-contexts, based on different criteria, are created and so on. This will be defined hereafter as context tree. As is to be expected, none of the preceding approaches meet all needs, be they in terms of performance or functionality. A mixed architecture will thus have to be defined.

4.2   Contexts

Context definition criteria. Defining context criteria is done according to security related events that the SOCBox must react to, even if they are distributed scanning operations, fingerprinting, massive exploit testing, account brute forcing, spamming and so on. A full functional architecture of contexts is given in figure 6.

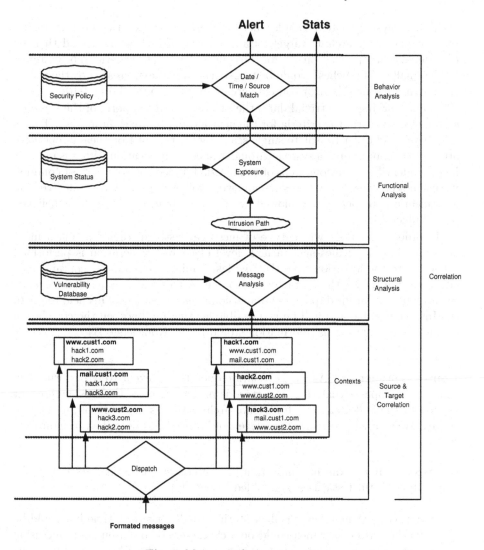

Fig. 5. Main correlation operations

The first obvious criteria is the attacking and attacked host's ID, which has to be standardized:

- source, defining source as a context creation criteria allows sweeps detection, identification of the systems used as attack relays or compromised by worms and targeted hack-proofing.
- target, contexts created by target criteria will provide information on scans (be they distributed, slow or "normal") and, should it even be noticed, intrusion attempts and system compromises.

Two arrays of context should then be defined, one with context matching sources, another matching targets. Each context of each array should then be considered as a top-level context for the context trees. The criteria to be matched by the smallest "branches" would be target ID (for contexts created by the source ID match) or source ID (for contexts created by the source ID match).

While working with trivial data, the protocols and the ports of the targeted systems should form the criteria for the next level of context "branches". This is mainly done in order to isolate single scanning operations from heavy repetitive attempts to compromise a system through a specific application. What is more, it helps to identify the various steps of an intrusion. Indeed one of the most common intrusion scenarios, is a wide portscan sweep followed by fingerprinting/version identification on open ports followed by an exploit launched on systems believed to be vulnerable.

In order to identify which type of message is stored, thus starting a more accurate analysis of messages, a next level of context generation is performed according to the intrusion type ID. The last "branch" of contexts contains specific intrusion ID, i.e. the characterization of each message. At this level we reach the atomic (except for duplicates) dimension of each message. This field refers to the Intrusion Table and will be responsible for the link between the correlation engine and system status information stored in the Knowledge Base.

Contexts structure. As any correlation operation is exclusively performed on contexts, it appears that their structure is probably one of the most important aspects of the SOCBox. The functional architecture is made up of an array of context trees. Each tree contains 4 levels of branches, as described in figure 6.

Contexts status. Another important characteristic of context is its status. We define three distinct statuses as detailed below:

− active, context matches specific criteria (usually based on time but could be any other criteria), which could be a characteristic of an on-going intrusion process. Typically, such a context appears to be under a heavy load from the arrival of new messages and its analysis by the correlation engine should be set to the highest possible priority.
− inactive, such a context either does not match "active" criteria or did not receive a specific closure code. This means that it is no longer analyzed by the correlation engine, but that it can be reactivated by the next message matching the same context criteria.
− closed, in this state a context is completed. Any new message matching this context criteria will create a new context.

Context status management is summarized in figure 7.

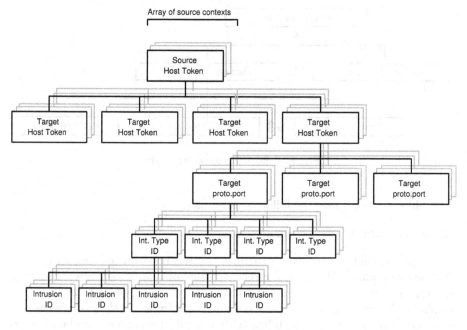

Fig. 6. Contexts functional architecture

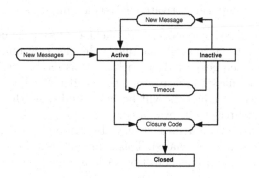

Fig. 7. Context status management

4.3   Analysis

Structural analysis. The purpose of structural analysis is to identify on going intrusion attempts, manage context inactivity status and context closure conditions. In simple terms, structural analysis is a set of operations performed by independent modules on each context. Each module is activated by a specific message and performs analysis using a "standard" semantic.

The output of the analysis modules is the result of several logical operations between autonomous conditions against fields of contexts. Figure 8 describes members of such operations.

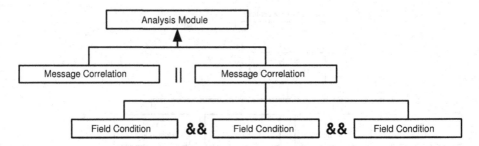

Fig. 8. Analysis module structure

Field conditions have the following structure:

```
field operator <field | value> [!]
```

It appears that the power of structural analysis relies on the number of operators made available. However, the very structure of contexts provides embedded operations such as source, target, port correlation. This not only increases the number of "native" operators but also significantly improves the performances of structural analysis. The ! sign indicates that the field condition is to be matched in order to activate the module.

Two kinds of events can activate analysis modules: messages and time.

- messages, as described above, some field conditions must be matched in order to activate an analysis module. A header containing field conditions to be met, is then generated for each analysis module. Given the structure of analysis module, it appears that the header will be a set of logical OR operations, whose members will be field conditions that require the least amount of resources to be evaluated.
- time, the analysis module header may also contain timer information forcing the correlation to be evaluated. This is mainly used for context closure and time dependent intrusions detection such as (slow) portscans, brute forcing, etc.

Advanced correlation. Advanced correlation operations are performed in order to define the criticality of an intrusion attempt and evaluate if such an intrusion attempt is permitted according to the security policy.

The functional analysis step is performed in order to evaluate system exposure to the intrusion and the overall impact of such an intrusion on the supervised system. Once the structural analysis has provided information about an occurring intrusion attempt, a request is made to Customer Status part of the K Box. This request contains the Intrusion ID and the Host token of the target. The response provides the following pieces of information:

- criticality, is a value from an arbitrary scale, typically info-warning-minor-major-critical based.

- closure code, if the context is to be closed, usually because the target is not impacted by the intrusion attempt.
- message, a new formatted message to be appended to the actual context, that may activate additional analysis modules.

The purpose of this last analysis is to define if the attempts match the security policy. This is mainly used to manage access to accounts but can also be implemented in the case of pre-programmed audits, portscans, etc. In such a situation a closure code is sent to the context. Technically, this analysis is performed in exactly the same way as structural analysis i.e. via specific modules whose structure is loaded from the security policy part of the K Box.

5   Conclusion

Intrusions are clearly taking place and there is thus a need for operational supervision systems today. Experience shows that a pragmatic approach needs to be taken in order to implement a professional SOC that can provide reliable results. The SOCBox is our response to these new threats.

However, some research are still to be conducted to improve our architecture. Firstly, functionalities of the SOCBox have to be distributed on different network components. This will ensure the system scalability and messages will be better processed. Secondly, the correlation process could include a more sophisticated process in order to be more accurate.

References

1. J.P. Anderson. Computer security threat monitoring and surveillance. Technical report, James P. Anderson Company, Fort Washington, Pennsylvania, April 1980.
2. F. Cuppens. Managing alerts in a multi-intrusion detection environment. In *17th Annual Computer Security Applications Conference*, New-Orleans, December 2001.
3. F. Cuppens and A. Miege. Alert correlation in a cooperative intrusion detection framework. In *IEEE Symposium on Research in Security and Privacy*, Mai 2002.
4. D. Curry and H. Debar. Intrusion detection message exchange format data model and extensible markup language (xml) document type definition. Technical report, IETF Intrusion Detection Working Group, January 2003.
5. Peter G. Neumann and Phillip A. Porras. Experience with EMERALD to date. In *First USENIX Workshop on Intrusion Detection and Network Monitoring*, pages 73–80, Santa Clara, California, apr 1999.
6. P. Ning, S. Jajodia, and X.S. Wang. Design and implementation of a decentralized prototype system for detecting distributed attacks. *Computer Communications*, 25:1374, August 1970.
7. Stephen Northcutt and Judy Novak. *Network Intrusion Detection*. ISBN: 0-73571-265-4. New Riders, third edition edition, 2002. September.
8. B. Schneier. Attack trees. *Dr. Dobb's Journal*, December 1999.
9. S. Staniford-Chen, S. Cheung, R. Crawford, M. Dilger, J. Frank, J. Hoagland, K. Levitt, C. Wee, R. Yip, and D. Zerkle. Grids - a graph based intrusion detection system for large networks. In *Proceedings of the 19th National Information Systems Security Conference*, volume 1, pages 361–370, October 1996.

Intrusion-Tolerant System Design
for Web Server Survivability

Dae-Sik Choi, Eul Gyu Im, and Cheol-Won Lee

National Security Research Institute
62-1 Hwa-am-dong, Yu-seong-gu
Daejeon, 305-718, Republic of Korea
{dschoi,imeg,cheolee}@etri.re.kr

Abstract. Internet becomes more and more popular, and most companies and institutes use web services for e-business to promote their business. As results, Internet and web services become core infrastructure for a business and become more and more important, but attacks against web services increase as the popularity of web services grows. Therefore, there are increasing needs of undisrupted web services despite of attacks. In this paper, contrast to previous approaches that detect and filter known attacks using known vulnerabilities and patterns, we proposed an intrusion tolerant system that can tolerate known vulnerabilities as well as unknown vulnerabilities by providing adaptation, redundancy and diversity. After detecting attacks, the system provides continuous web services using server adaptation and request filtering.

Keywords: intrusion tolerance, survivability, web services.

1   Introduction

Advances of Internet make more people to use Internet services, and among these Internet services, web services are most popular and become important business tools. Web services disruptions can cause many problems, such as reduced number of accesses, restoration costs, degradation of company credibility, and the like. According to the reports of CSI/FBI in 2001, 38 percent of web sites were affected by hacking, and among these sites 21 percent of them were not aware of hacking in their sites [1]. The Symantec/Riptech report published in January 2002 says that 100 percent of web users experienced hacking incidents and 43 percent of users experienced serious hacking incidents in 2001 [2].

Defense directions against hacking incidents can be divided into two categories: the first one is intrusion blocking mechanisms, such as firewalls, user authentication, and virus scanning, and the second one includes intrusion detection mechanisms.

Since systems and networks become more and more complicated with the advance of technologies, the above mechanisms will have more limitations for

K. Chae and M. Yung (Eds.): WISA 2003, LNCS 2908, pp. 124–134, 2004.
© Springer-Verlag Berlin Heidelberg 2004

protecting resources as time goes by. Despite of lots of research efforts on computer security, there are many limitations to eliminate all the vulnerabilities of computer systems and networks [3]. Because of widespread uses of integration of COTS components and various distributed resources, defense mechanisms against attacks become incomplete and more vulnerable [4].

According to CSI/FBI reports, even though 95 percent of organizations have firewalls, 61 percent of them have IDS, 90 percent of them use access control, and 42 percent of them use digital signatures, attacks still occurred. These data indicate that both intrusion detection mechanisms and intrusion blocking mechanisms apparently have limitations, so there should be new directions toward research areas, such as intrusion tolerant systems.

Intrusion tolerant systems(ITS's) are defined as systems that provide continuous services using filtering, recovery, and adaptation techniques even though attacks are occurred on the server [5,6,7,8]. ITS's can be composed with the following components: a resistance module, a recognition module, a recovery module, and an adaptation module. A resistance module is used to tolerate attacks, a recognition module is used to detect intrusions, a recovery module is used to recover damages caused by attacks, and an adaptation module is used to reconfigure components for continuous services after attacks.

In this paper, we propose an intrusion tolerant system that can handle known vulnerabilities as well as unknown vulnerabilities using redundancy and diversity. Client categorization and adaptation techniques are also used to defend and adapt against attacks.

The rest of this paper is organized as follows: After reviewing previous approaches in Section 2, Section 3 shows an overall structure of our intrusion tolerant system, and each module is explained in detail in Section 4, followed by conclusions and future directions in Section 5.

2   Related Work

Feiyi Wang et. al [9,10,11] proposed an intrusion tolerant system called SITAR. In their approach, requests are forwarded to several web servers through acceptance monitors, and responses are monitored in acceptance monitors and ballot monitors. An adaptive reconfiguration module takes care of reconfiguration and adaptation when attacks are detected. There are several problems with their approach. 1) Their modules lack detailed design and implementation descriptions, and many issues are not addressed in their paper. It is not clear how the reconfiguration module works. 2) Since a request is forwarded to several web servers simultaneously, there is performance problem for handling requests.

Partha P. Pal et. al at BBN Technologies explained intrusion tolerant systems [4]. But their paper shows system strategies and requirements without any detailed system design, so it is just a preliminary report about intrusion tolerant systems.

Even though there are some previous researches on intrusion tolerant systems, more research and experiments are in need. Therefore, after reviewing previous approaches, we designed an intrusion tolerant system and plan to implement a prototype.

3   Overall System Structure

Figure 1 shows a logical view of the proposed system which is called WITS, i.e. web server intrusion tolerant system. An intrusion tolerant server lies in front of more than one web server, and these web servers share a database. Each server can have more than one identical web service for redundancy and diversity, and more than one web server runs simultaneously. An intrusion tolerant server acts as a proxy server, and it relays requests and responses between clients and servers.

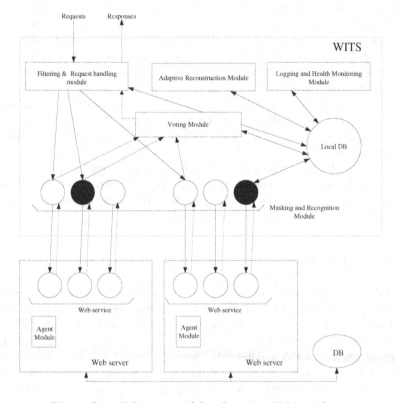

Fig. 1. Overall Structure of Our Intrusion Tolerant System

Data flow in this system is as follows: For requests from each client in the Internet, a new FRM (filtering and request handling module) process and a new VOM (voting module) process are created. An FRM process forwards requests to MRM (masking and recognition module) according to policies of ARM (adaptive reconstruction module) or administrator's manual settings. FRM runs request validation procedures which will be explained later, and if the request passed validation tests, the request is forwarded to a web server through MRM. After that, the MRM gets results from the web server and runs result validation procedures. If the results are ok, then they are forwarded to VOM. Otherwise, the validation test results are sent to ARM and the ARM performs filtering and reconstruction. In VOM, a selected result through voting is transmitted to the client that sent the request. AM's(agent modules) reside in web servers, and collect information about web servers.

Based on results of request and response validations, 'black' lists are maintained. These 'black' lists are created using statistical information of relations between clients and URLs or between clients and web servers, and these lists allow system administrators to establish policies of filtering requests, restricting services, or selecting a web server for a request. The policies established here are used by FRM when requests are forwarded to MRM. Unknown attacks are detected through the response validation process.

LHM(logging and health monitor) is responsible for collecting logs from modules in the system as well as checking web server status or contents of web servers. To check integrity of contents, LHM keep MD5 hash values of contents that must be protected, and AM's periodically recalculate hash values and send them to LHM.

4   Web Server Intrusion Tolerant System (WITS)

Our proposed intrusion tolerant system is mainly designed for web servers. In this section, we will address each module in WITS in detail.

Main modules of WITS are FRM that filters known attacks and requests from clients in the black lists, MRM that detects intrusions or server faults, and ARM that performs adaptation and recovery functions. Other modules in WITS include VOM, LHM, and AM's.

4.1   Filtering and Request Handling Module (FRM)

When FRM get web service requests from a client, a new FRM process is created to handle these requests. Main functions of FRM are to detect and filter known attacks against WITS and web servers, to transmit requests to MRM in accordance with policies of the system, and to send responses back to clients. In addition, FRM also synchronizes web sessions and cookies of clients.

4.2   Masking and Recognition Module (MRM)

The MRM exists between FRM and web servers, and it relays requests and responses after validating them. Figure 2 shows detailed data flows in FRM and MRM especially regarding validations. Objectives of validation checks are to

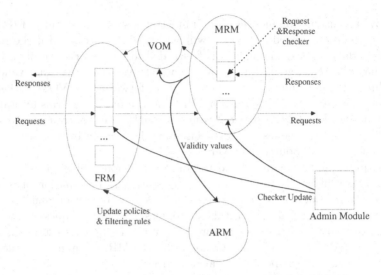

Fig. 2. Request and Response Checkers in FRM and MRM

provide resistance against attacks and to provide validation values for ARM so that ARM can update policies.

Validation checks can be divided into two kinds: request validation and response validation. Request validation procedures are performed in FRM. Request validation examines attack patterns and filters malicious requests to WITS and web servers. Results calculated in request validation are used to perform response validation. Both Request validation and response validation are executed in MRM. Results of validation procedures are sent to VOM and ARM.

Request validation can prevent only know attacks. In contrast, since response validation examines responses of web servers, it can detect some unknown attacks and filter out these attacks in future. For example, if packets are generated in web servers without corresponding requests as CodeRed worm does, the packets can be regarded as attack packets and these packets can be dropped in VOM.

4.3   Voting Module (VOM)

A VOM process is created with a FRM process when requests from a new client arrive. Main functions of VOM are to collect validity values from MRM processes, to send a selected response to FRM, and to send voting results to ARM. Voting enables WITS to provide continuous web services even though there are attacks against some of web servers. As an example, when one web service is affected by attacks, if a request is forwarded to more than one web services, VOM can be able to select responses from unaffected web services using validity tests.

Since a same attack will have different effects on different web servers, more robust web services can be provided by running diverse replicated web servers with same contents. In addition, replication of web contents gives redundancy to the system, and correct contents can be selected by validation testing despite one of contents is modified by an attacker. The contents checking procedure compares modified time and MD5 hash values of response contents with pre-saved values. This procedure applies only to static web contents, and dynamically changing web pages cannot be examined.

Statistical data generated in VOM are sent to ARM so that ARM updates policies of request filtering. To collect statistical data, the following validity scores are collected:

- Web server : Validity scores of each server are collected, and the average scores are calculated. The higher validity score of a web server, the more requests are assigned to the server.

- URL : Validity scores per URL are collected.

- Client : Validity scores per client are collected and they are used for ARM to build the 'black' lists.

- URL vs web server : If one URL is replicated into several servers and requests to the URL are forwarded to more than one server, URL validity scores per web server are collected.

- Client vs web server : Client validity scores per web server are also collected.

Based on collected validity scores, scores per web server, URL, and client are calculated. These calculated scores are used to update policies for filtering requests, assigning MRM processes for requests, and the like. If more than one web server is running and the average validity score of a web server within a certain time frame is less than a threshold, the number of requests that the web server receives is decreased, and vice versa.

4.4   Adaptive Reconstruction Module (ARM)

ARM gets inputs from LHM, VOM, MRM, and Admin Module, and it updates filtering policies and executes reconstructions of web servers and data flows when necessary. Details about adaptations are addressed in the subsequent paragraphs.

Changes of Web Server Assigning Methods. There are two kinds of web server assigning methods: *all active* and *primary/backup*. Initially, web servers are set as *all active*. As attacks increase, the assigning method is changed to the *primary/backup* method.

Degree of Replication. Depending on intensity of attacks, the degree of replication changes for a web server that is less vulnerable to that attack. Policies to determine the degree of replication are decided by administrators or statistical information from VOM.

For intrusion tolerance, our system provide different kinds of web servers, and if the validity score of a web server is higher than a certain threshold, the number of replicated servers is increased by one, and vice versa.

Blacklist. Statistical information gathered from VOM is used to update policies and the blacklist.

– IPs in the blacklist are filtered for accesses of a certain URL.
– An item in the blacklist is a certain IP, a URL for a certain IP, or a certain URL.
– A certain URL is registered to the blacklist when the URL is under development or bugs are found in the URL, so that the URL is not accessible from outside.
– For example, if the ratio of invalid ones is greater than 50 percent, put the requesting IP in the blacklist for request masking.

Period of Health Monitoring. The period of health monitoring for web servers is reduced when the intensity of attacks is increased.

4.5   Agent Module(AM)

AM is communicated with other modules such as Admin module, MRM, and ARM. AM exists in a web server as a process, and its main functions are the following:

– MD5 checksums are calculated for web pages, and the checksums are sent to LHM.
– AM recovers web pages when the pages are affected by attacks.
– AM executes reconstructions of the web server when reconstruction requests are received from ARM.

4.6   Logging and Health Monitoring Module(LHM)

Main functions of LHM which is executed as a process in WITS are to monitor health of web servers and other modules as well as to save logs of WITS. The period of health monitoring is dynamically changed based on conditions of WITS. Other functions of LHM are as follows:

– LHM checks hash values of web pages periodically. If LHM finds errors in any web pages, it notifies AM so that AM can restore the pages.
– If LHM finds errors or performance degradation from any modules, LHM notifies ARM for reconstructions or adaptation.

4.7   Other Components and Functions of WITS

Administration Console. The administration console provides the following functions:

- Interfaces to each module in WITS
- To set and update policies in ARM
- To monitor LHM
- To select web pages to be protected
- To checks logs gathered in LHM

Unfiltered Transfer of Requests. To provide continuous web services, when WITS has problems and cannot provide proper services or WITS fails, requests and responses are relayed without any filtering.

Recovery. When system faults occur, the recovery process is executed based on current recovery policies. The following activities are executed for recovery.

- Administrators can select operating modes of web servers: *all active* or *primary/backup*.
- When a server was down due to a certain request, the following sequence of actions is taken for recovery.
  - In case of the *primary/backup* mode
    1. Stop the affected server.
    2. Make a backup server as a primary server. Send messages to filter requests from the source IP of the request, and notify administrators.
    3. Recover the affected server. If successful, make the server as a backup server.
  - In case of the *all active* mode
    1. Stop the affected server.
    2. Send messages to filter requests from the source IP of the request, and notify administrators.
    3. Recover the affected server. If successful, put the server to the active server list.
- Contents are recovered using backup data when LHM finds content damages.

Adaptation. ARM changes configurations such as web server operating modes and degree of replication, to respond to attacks, based on information about current server states and administrator's commands.

Figure 3 shows decision factors of adaptation. Reconstruction is done based on statistical data, system performance, and commands from administrators. If validity scores of a server are lower than a certain threshold, the number of requests that are assigned on the server will be reduced by one, and vice versa.

Impact masking is used to filter a certain client for a certain URL. To decide impact masking, validity scores of client vs. URL are used. If the score is lower than a certain threshold, the client will be filtered.

Table 1. Comparisons of Information Assurance Systems

	WITS	Intrusion Detection Systems (IDS's)	IDS and Firewall	Secure OS
Summary	Without changes of servers, WITS protects them against known attacks as well as unknown attacks.	IDS detects only known attacks, and sends alert messages to administrators.	Firewalls can block unused ports so that they cannot be used by attackers. Application-level firewalls are not feasible for high-speed networks.	Secure OS is directly installed in a target server, and parts of the server can be protected by Secure OS even though attacks are successful.
Attack Detection	WITS examines requests to a server as well as responses from the server so that WITS can filter out both known attacks and unknown attacks.	Based on known patterns of attacks, IDS detects and sends alerts to administrators. Alerts include a large portion of false positives.	Same as IDS. It may get fewer attacks because firewalls may filter out some of attacks.	Attacks are detected using known patterns of attacks.
Stability	Automatic recovery and adaptation allow WITS to provide more stable and continuous services to clients.	Even though IDS fails, a server can continue its services.	If firewalls fail, no network traffics can pass through firewalls.	It may cause new vulnerabilities as well as performance problems in the server.
Attack Blocking	Request and response validation is used in WITS. ARM also filters clients according to policies.	None	Firewalls can filter specific IPs.	It provides access control mechanisms.
Against New Vulnerabilities	WITS has a way of handling new vulnerabilities.	Only known attacks are detected.	Only known attacks are detected.	Only known attacks are detected, but parts of the server can be protected by Secure OS even though attacks are successful.

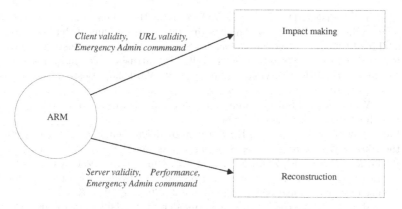

Fig. 3. Decision Factors of Adaptation

4.8 Summary and Advantages of WITS

WITS executes passive protections against attacks, and it is designed to provide continuous web services and higher availability of data. Table 1 shows comparisons WITS with other information assurance systems. As it is shown in Table 1, WITS has better than other systems in many aspects. The main advantages of WITS are 1) it can provide more continous service than other IA systems, 2) it can block some unknown attacks, and 3) it can adapt against attacks.

5   Conclusions and Future Directions

Advances of Internet make more people use Internet services, and among these Internet services, web services are most popular and become important business tools or infrastructure. Web services disruptions can cause many problems, such as reduced number of accesses, restoration costs, degradation of company credibility, and the like.

In this paper, we proposed an intrusion tolerant system, called WITS (Web Server Intrusion Tolerant System) that can handle known vulnerabilities as well as unknown vulnerabilities using redundancy and diversity. Client categorization and adaptation techniques are also used to defend and adapt against attacks.

As future directions, with more various experiments, adaptation and recovery procedures must be strengthened.

References

1. Computer Security Institute/Federal Bureau of Investigation: Computer crime and security survey (2001)
2. Symantec Corp.: Symantec internet security threat report, volume i (2002)

3. Ellison, B., Fisher, D.A., Linger, R.C., Lipson, H.F., Longstaff, T., Mead, N.R.:
   Survivable network systems: An emerging discipline. Technical Report CMU/SEI-
   97-TR-013, Carnegie-Mellon University Software Engineering Institute (1997)
4. Pal, P., Webber, F., Schantz, R.E., Loyall, J.P.: Intrusion tolerant systems. In: Proceedings of the IEEE Information Survivability Workshop, Boston, Massachusetts,
   U.S.A. (2000)
5. Lee, W., Fan, W.: Mining system audit data: opportunities and challenges. ACM
   SIGMOD Record **30** (2001) 35–44
6. Pal, P., Webber, F., Schantz, R.: Survival by defense-enabling. In: Proceedings of
   the 2001 workshop on New security paradigms, ACM Press (2001) 71–78
7. Rathi, M., Anjum, F., Zbib, R., Ghosh, A., Umar, A.: Investigation of intrusion
   tolerance for COTS middleware. In: Proceedings of the IEEE International Conference on Communications 2002. Volume 2. (2002) 1169–1173
8. Stavridou, V., Dutertre, B., Riemenschneider, R.A., Saidi, H.: Intrusion tolerant
   software architectures. In: Proceedings of the DARPA Information Survivability
   Conference & Exposition (DISCEX) 2001. Volume 2. (2001) 230–241
9. Wang, F., Upppalli, R.: SITAR: a scalable instrusion-tolerant architecture for
   distributed services - a technology summary. In: Proceedings of the DARPA Information Survivability Conference & Exposition (DISCEX) 2003. Volume 2. (2003)
   153–155
10. Wang, R., Wang, F., Byrd, G.T.: Design and implementation of acceptance mon-
    itor for building scalable intrusion tolerant system. In: Proceedings of the Tenth
    International Conference on Computer Communications and Networks, Scottsdale,
    AZ, USA (2001) 200–205
11. Wang, F., Gong, F., Sargor, C., Goseva-Popstojanova, K., Trivedi, K., Jou, F.:
    SITAR: A scalable intrusion-tolerant architecture for distributed services. In:
    Proceedings of the 2001 IEEE Workshop on Information Assurance and Security,
    United States Military Academy, West Point, NY (2001) 38–45

PANA/IKEv2:
An Internet Authentication Protocol for Heterogeneous Access

Paulo S. Pagliusi and Chris J. Mitchell

Information Security Group
Royal Holloway, University of London
Egham, Surrey TW20 0EX, UK
{P.S.Pagliusi, C.Mitchell}@rhul.ac.uk
http://www.isg.rhul.ac.uk

Abstract. Currently there are no Internet access authentication protocols available that support both symmetric and asymmetric cryptographic techniques, can be carried over arbitrary access networks, and are flexible enough to be re-used in all the likely future ubiquitous mobility access contexts. This article proposes the PANA/IKEv2 authentication protocol for heterogeneous network access as a step towards filling this gap. A security analysis of the PANA/IKEv2 protocol is also provided. This article aims primarily at contributing to the design of authentication protocols suitable for use in future heterogeneous Internet access environments supporting ubiquitous mobility.

1 Introduction

According to the PAMPAS Project [1, p135], "the increasing heterogeneity of the networking environment is one of the long-term trends which requires new security approaches. The main challenges include the investigation and development of unified, secure and convenient authentication mechanisms that can be used in different access networks". Authentication and key agreement are the central components of secure access procedures for heterogeneous network access supporting ubiquitous mobility.

Currently there are no authentication protocols available that can be carried over arbitrary access networks, and are flexible enough for use with all the various access technologies likely to be deployed to support future ubiquitous mobility. Furthermore, existing access procedures need to be made resistant to Denial-of-Service (DoS) attacks; they also do not provide non-repudiation. In addition to being limited to specific access media (e.g. 802.1aa [2] for IEEE 802 links), some of these protocols are limited to specific network topologies (e.g. PPP [3] for point-to-point links) and are not scalable.

Additionally, the cryptography used to support the access procedures can be based either on secret key (symmetric) or public key (asymmetric) techniques. Whereas the former requires the involvement of the home network during the

K. Chae and M. Yung (Eds.): WISA 2003, LNCS 2908, pp. 135–149, 2004.
© Springer-Verlag Berlin Heidelberg 2004

initial authentication process between a user and visited network, the latter allows for architectures that avoid on-line involvement of the home network, since authentication may then be based on certificates. Nevertheless, asymmetric techniques typically require a Public Key Infrastructure to support key distribution, and use of this PKI may require on-line certificate status checking. While symmetric techniques are used almost exclusively today, it seems likely that asymmetric techniques will gain greater importance in future ubiquitous mobility access networks because of their greater flexibility.

The recent IETF PANA (Protocol for carrying Authentication for Network Access[1]) work aims to provide a protocol [4] that will be a flexible and scalable network-layer authentication carrier for access networks that support IP. PANA will be capable of transporting any EAP (Extensible Authentication Protocol) method [5] to enable access authentication. In addition, the EAP-IKEv2 protocol [6] specifies a way of encapsulating the first phase of the Internet Key Exchange (IKEv2) Protocol [7], which supports both symmetric and asymmetric authentication, within EAP. Once inside EAP, the IKEv2 parameters can thus be carried by PANA. In this paper we present a proposal for combining IKEv2 authentication with EAP-IKEv2 and PANA, which we call PANA/IKEv2.

The goal of the PANA/IKEv2 protocol is to provide an IP compatible, flexible and scalable authentication method that allows a client to be authenticated by either symmetric or asymmetric techniques in a heterogeneous network access environment. The proposal adapts the security techniques used in IKEv2 to the PANA structure. The protocol runs between a client device and an agent device in the access network, where the agent may be a client of an AAA (Authentication, Authorization and Accounting) infrastructure.

Section 2 summarises the authentication and key exchange phase of the IKEv2 protocol, Section 3 describes the EAP-IKEv2 method, and Section 4 explains the PANA protocol. Section 5 then describes the proposed new PANA/ IKEv2 authentication scheme. Section 6 analyses the threats to the PANA/IKEv2 protocol, Section 7 considers its advantages and disadvantages and, finally, Sections 8, 9, and 9 present possible further work, conclusions and acknowledgements.

2   Authentication and Key Exchange via IKEv2 Protocol

IKEv2 [7] is a component of IPsec (IP Security Protocol[2]) used for performing mutual authentication and establishing and maintaining security associations (SAs). IKEv2 is a protocol which consists of two phases:

1. An authentication and key exchange protocol, which establishes an IKE-SA,
2. Messages and payloads which allow negotiation of parameters (e.g. algorithms, traffic selectors) in order to establish IPsec SAs (i.e. Child-SAs).

---

[1] http://www.ietf.org/html.charters/pana-charter.html
[2] http://www.ietf.org/html.charters/ipsec-charter.html

In addition, IKEv2 also includes certain payloads and messages which allow configuration parameters to be exchanged for remote access scenarios. The PANA/IKEv2 protocol defined here uses the IKEv2 payloads and messages from phase 1.

IKEv2 is designed to address certain issues with IKEv1 [8], as described in Appendix A of [7]. Important here are the reduced number of initial exchanges, support of legacy authentication, decreased latency of the initial exchange, optional DoS protection capability, and the resolution of certain known security defects. IKEv2 is a protocol that has received a considerable amount of expert review, and that benefits from the experience gained from IKEv1. The goal of PANA/IKEv2 is to inherit these properties through the EAP-IKEv2 method.

IKEv2 also provides authentication and key exchange capabilities which allow an entity to use symmetric as well as asymmetric cryptographic techniques, in addition to legacy authentication[3] support, within a single protocol. Such flexibility seems likely to be important for heterogeneous network access supporting ubiquitous mobility, and is provided by PANA/IKEv2.

For further information on IKEv2 and its design rationale, see Perlman [10].

3   An EAP Mechanism for Carrying IKEv2

The EAP-IKEv2 protocol [6] is an EAP mechanism for authentication and session key distribution that uses IKEv2 [7]. It offers the security benefits of IKEv2 without aiming to establish IPsec SAs. The authentication method used within EAP-IKEv2 differs from IKEv2 only in the computation of the $AUTH$[4] payload.

Figure 1 shows an EAP-IKEv2 message flow, which occurs between the Initiator (I) and the Responder (R). I is also referred to here as the *Client* (acting on behalf of a user), whereas R is referred to as the *Authenticating Party*. R may be co-located with the *EAP server*, which is the network element that terminates the EAP protocol [5]. However, the EAP server is typically implemented on a separate AAA server in the user's home Internet AAA network, with whom R communicates using an AAA protocol. The core EAP-IKEv2 exchange (1) consists of three round trips, which may be reduced to two if the optional IKEv2 DoS protection (2) is not used.

In the EAP/IKEv2 authentication procedure, an identity request/response message pair (a, b) is first exchanged. Next, R sends (c) an EAP-Request/EAP-IKEv2 (Start) message. I sends back (d) a message that contains an IKEv2 header (HDR[5]), a payload with the cryptographic suites supported by I for

---

[3] *Legacy authentication* involves methods that are not strong enough to be used in networks where attackers can easily eavesdrop and spoof on the link (e.g. EAP-MD5 [9] over wireless links). They also may not be able to produce enough keying material. Use of legacy methods can be enabled by carrying them over a secure channel (see also [4,7]).

[4] $AUTH$ contains data used for authentication purposes; see subsection 3.8 of [7].

[5] HDR contains Security Parameter Indexes (SPIs), version numbers, and flags of various sorts. SPIs are values chosen by I and R to identify a unique IKE_SA.

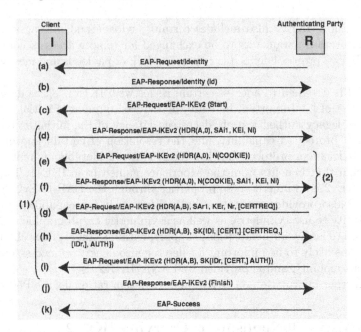

Fig. 1. EAP-IKEv2 message flow. The name of each message is shown, followed by the contents of the message in round brackets. Square brackets are used to denote optional fields.

the IKE_SA ($SAi1$), a Diffie-Hellman [11] value (KEi), and a nonce (Ni). Next, we may optionally have an IKEv2 DoS protection round trip (e, f) based on 'cookies' [7]. After that, R sends a message (g) that contains its choice of a cryptographic suite from among I's offers ($SAr1$), its value to complete the Diffie-Hellman exchange (KEr), and its nonce[6] (Nr). At this point, each party can generate the $SKEYSEED$ value (computed as a pseudo random function (prf) of Ni, Nr and the Diffie-Hellman shared secret), from which the keying material for the IKE_SA is derived. All but the IKEv2 headers of the messages that follow are encrypted and integrity protected[7], and this is indicated using the notation $SK\{\dots\}$.

I sends back (h) a message to assert its identity (IDi), to prove knowledge of the secret corresponding to IDi, and to integrity protect the contents of the first two messages with $AUTH$ (see subsection 2.15 of [7]). It may also send its certificate ($CERT$) and a list of its 'trust anchors', i.e. the names of the CAs whose public keys it trusts [12] ($CERTREQ$); the optional IDr payload

---

$HDR(A,0)$ means that I assigned the SPI 'A' and R did not assign its SPI yet, while $HDR(A,B)$ means that I assigned the SPI 'A' and R assigned the SPI 'B'.

[6] *Nonces* are inputs to cryptographic functions; they contain pseudo random data used to guarantee liveliness during an exchange, and protect against replay attacks.

[7] The recipients must verify that all signatures and *MACs* are computed correctly, and that the *ID* names correspond to the keys used to generate the *AUTH* payload.

enables I to specify which of R's identities it wants to talk to (e.g. when R is hosting multiple IDs at the same IP address). R then asserts its identity (IDr), optionally sends one or more certificates ($CERT$), and authenticates its identity with $AUTH$ (i). Start (c) and Finish (j) messages are required due to the asymmetric nature of IKEv2, and due to the Request/Response message handling of EAP. The message flow finishes with an EAP-Success message (k).

Man-in-the-middle attacks discovered in the context of tunnelled authentication protocols (see [13] and [14]) are applicable to IKEv2 if legacy authentication is used with the inner EAP [9]. To counter this threat, IKEv2 provides a compound authentication by including the inner EAP session key inside the $AUTH$ payload (see Subsection 6.1).

4   Protocol for Carrying Authentication for Network Access (PANA)

This section briefly introduces the draft PANA protocol [4], a link-layer agnostic transport for EAP to enable client-to-network access authentication. PANA runs between a PaC (PANA Client) and a PAA (PANA Authentication Agent) situated in the access network, where the PAA may optionally be a client of an AAA infrastructure. PANA carries any authentication mechanism that can be specified as an EAP method (e.g. EAP/IKEv2), and can be used on any link that supports IP. The header of every PANA packet contains two sequence numbers to provide ordered delivery of EAP messages: one transmitted sequence number (tseq), and one received sequence number (rseq). The payload of any PANA message consists of zero or more Attribute Value Pairs (AVPs), e.g. an optional cookie AVP, used for making an initial handshake robust against 'blind DoS attacks' [4], a MAC AVP, protecting the integrity of a PANA message, or an EAP AVP, which transports an EAP payload.

Two important features of PANA, namely the security association (SA) and re-authentication, are now described. Once the EAP method has completed, a session key (e.g. the EAP/IKEv2 MSK) is shared by the PaC and the PAA. The session key is provided to the PaC as part of the EAP key exchange process, and the PAA can obtain the session key from the EAP server via the AAA infrastructure (if used). PANA SA establishment based on the EAP session key is required where no physical or link layer security is available. Two types of re-authentication (or fast reconnection) are supported by PANA. The first type enters the chosen EAP method (e.g. EAP/IKEv2) at the authentication phase, where the initial handshake phase can be omitted. If there is an existing PANA SA, PANA_auth messages carrying the EAP fast reconnection process can be protected with a MAC AVP. The second type is based on a single protected PANA message exchange without entering the authentication phase. If there is an existing PANA SA, both PaC and PAA can send a PANA_reauth_request to the communicating peer and expect the peer to return a PANA_reauth_answer, where both messages are protected with a MAC AVP.

5   PANA/IKEv2 Authentication Procedure

The PANA/IKEv2 mechanism proposed here involves three functional entities, namely the *PaC* (also referred to here as the *client, user* or *subscriber*), the *PAA* (or *authenticating party*) and the *EAP server*. The *PaC* is associated with a network device and a set of credentials that are used to prove the PaC identity for network access. The *PAA* authenticates the credentials provided by the PaC and grants network access. In the context of this article, the *EAP server* is assumed to be implemented on the AAA server. The PAA is thus an AAA client that communicates with the user's EAP server through an AAA protocol supporting EAP (e.g. Diameter EAP [15]) and key wrap (e.g. Diameter CMS [16], where this involves encrypting a content-encryption key using a key encrypting key).

PANA/IKEv2 also involves a further entity, namely the EP (Enforcement Point), which may be co-located with the PAA, which applies per-packet enforcement policies (i.e. filters) to the traffic of the PaC's devices.

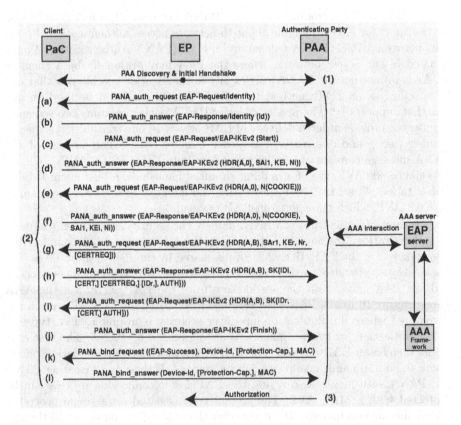

Fig. 2. PANA/IKEv2 full authentication procedure. The name of each message is shown, followed by the contents of the message in round brackets. Square brackets are used to denote optional fields.

Figure 2 shows the PANA/IKEv2 full authentication procedure, which has three main phases: (1) Discovery and initial handshake, (2) Authentication, and (3) Authorization. In the *Discovery* phase, an IP address for the PAA is identified, and a PANA/IKEv2 session is established between the PaC and the PAA, following the PANA model (see subsection 4.2 of [4]). In the *Authentication* phase, the main focus of this article and further explained below, EAP/IKEv2 messages encapsulated in PANA/IKEv2 are exchanged between the PaC and the PAA. At the end of this phase, a PANA SA is established, including the provision of a shared secret EAP/IKEv2 session key, called the 'Pre-Master-Secret' [6] or $KEYMAT^8$, exported as part of the EAP keying framework [17] for further key derivation; we call this the PANA/IKEv2 SA. During the *Authorization* phase, a separate protocol is used between the PAA and the EP to manage the PaC network access control. After this phase, the established PANA/IKEv2 session as well as the PANA/IKEv2 SA is deleted, following the PANA standard (see subsection 4.5 of [4]).

During the *Authentication* phase, the first PANA_auth_request message (a) issued by the PAA encapsulates an EAP-Request/Identity payload. The PaC responds (b) with a PANA_auth_answer, which carries an EAP-Response/Identity payload including the user identifier Id. After that, an EAP-Request/EAP-IKEv2 (Start) packet is transported in a PANA_auth_request (c). The PaC sends back (d) a PANA_auth_answer carrying the EAP-Request/EAP-IKEv2 payload, which contains HDR, $SAi1$, KEi, and also Ni, the random number chosen by the PaC. Next, we may optionally have an IKEv2 DoS protection round trip (e, f). The next PANA_auth_request message (g) issued by the PAA includes the EAP-Request/EAP-IKEv2 packet that contains $SAr1$, KEr, the random number Nr chosen by the PAA, and $CERTREQ$, an optional list of the PAA trust anchors. At this point, each party can derive the keying material for that IKE_SA. All but the $HDRs$ of the messages that follow are encrypted and integrity protected.

On receipt of this message, the PaC sends back (h) a PANA_auth_answer message with its identity IDi, an $AUTH$ value, and the following optional payloads: $CERT^9$, $CERTREQ$, and IDr, which enables the PaC to specify which of PAA's identities it wants to talk to. The notation $SK\{\dots\}$ here indicates that the content between brackets is encrypted and integrity protected. The PAA then sends a PANA_auth_request to assert its identity (IDr); this message also includes $AUTH$ and optionally $CERT$(i). An EAP-Response/EAP-IKEv2 (Finish) packet is transported in a PANA_auth_answer (j).

Finally the PAA encapsulates the EAP-Success packet in a PANA_bind_request message sent to the PaC (k), and receives back an acknowledge through a PANA_bind_answer (l). Both PANA_bind messages are

---

[8] $KEYMAT$ is derived from Ni, Nr, and a temporary key called SK_d using a pseudo random function. The key SK_d is taken from the bits output by another pseudo random function, using $SKEYSEED$, Ni, Nr, $SPIi$, and $SPIr$ as inputs [7].

[9] If any CERT payloads are included, the first certificate provided will contain the public key required to verify the AUTH field. For symmetric techniques, $CERT$ and $CERTREQ$ payloads are not required in IKEv2 (see [7]).

protected by a MAC AVP; they may optionally contain a Protection-Capability AVP to indicate if link-layer or network-layer encryption should be initiated after PANA/IKEv2. They are also used for binding device identifiers of the PaC and the PAA, via Device-Id AVP, to the PANA/IKEv2 SA established at the end of the authentication phase.

6 Security Analysis

In this section, security threats to the proposed PANA/IKEv2 protocol are considered. The security of the proposed PANA method is based on IKEv2 [7].

6.1 Man-in-the-Middle Attacks

Care has to be taken to avoid man-in-the-middle attacks arising when tunnelling is used, e.g. when using the Protected Extensible Authentication Protocol (PEAP) [18], or when EAP/IKEv2 is part of a sequence of EAP methods. Such vulnerabilities can arise (see, for example, Asokan et al. [13]) even when the authentication protocols used at the various 'levels' are in themselves secure (the man-in-the-middle attack described is taken into account in IKEv2). When such attacks are successfully carried out, the attacker acts as an intermediary between a PaC victim and a legitimate PAA. This allows the attacker to authenticate successfully to the PAA, as well as to obtain access to the network.

As a solution to the problem, Asokan et al. [13] and Puthenkulam et al. [14] suggest to cryptographically bind the session keys of the two phases. This can be achieved by binding together the tunnel session key T (a typical example of T is the TLS master key derived in the TLS handshake of PEAP) and the $KEYMAT$ derived from the EAP/IKEv2 method, to generate an ultimate session key K. There are two ways to achieve the necessary binding between $KEYMAT$ and K. In the first method the binding is established directly by taking $KEYMAT$ in addition to T as input to the computation of the session key K. This provides *implicit authentication* of the PaC. The second method is to make use of a cryptographic check value to verify that the PaC who is in possession of T is also in possession of $KEYMAT$. This second type of binding provides *explicit authentication* of the PaC.

In addition to authentication based on secret key or public key techniques, IKEv2 supports authentication using EAP [9] legacy mechanisms. Using PANA/IKEv2 in these scenarios leads to an outer EAP/IKEv2 exchange transporting an inner EAP legacy method, such as the example provided by Tschofenig and Kroeselberg [6], where EAP/IKEv2 encapsulates an EAP/SIM [19] message flow. For inner EAP legacy methods that create a shared key as a side effect of authentication (e.g. the MSK derived from EAP/SIM), that shared key must be used by both the PaC and PAA to generate an $AUTH$ payload.

Even when tunnelling, an EAP sequence of methods, or EAP legacy mechanisms are not used with PANA/IKEv2, user data need to be integrity protected on physically insecure networks to avoid man-in-the-middle attacks and session hijacking.

6.2 Identity Confidentiality and Integrity Protection

In PANA/IKEv2, a large number of identities are required due to nesting of authentication methods, and due to multiple uses of identifiers for routing (i.e. authentication end point indication). The identifier types and their requirements for confidentiality and integrity protection are as follows.

The identifier Id, used in the first round trip of the PANA/IKEv2 authentication phase (b), indicates where the EAP messages terminate; it is not used to identify the PaC, and thus it does not allow the adversary to learn the identity of the PaC. The identifiers IDi and IDr are used respectively to identify the PaC and PAA; IDi can be associated with a user identifier (e.g. an email address), and IDr can be a fully-qualified domain name (FQDN). Both identifiers are of importance for the PANA/IKEv2 Authorization phase (3), and are thus encrypted and integrity protected by PANA/IKEv2.

The transport of inner EAP legacy methods by PANA/IKEv2 adds further identifiers: the inner EAP identifier (i.e. an NAI [20]), and a separate identifier for the selected EAP legacy method (e.g. an $IMSI$ [19]). These identifiers are also encrypted and integrity protected by the PANA/IKEv2 SA up to the PANA/IKEv2 endpoint.

In summary, PANA/IKEv2 includes identity confidentiality and integrity protection support, which protects the privacy of the PaC and PAA identities against *passive* (e.g. eavesdropping) and *active* attackers (e.g. impersonation of the access network).

6.3 Mutual Authentication

PANA/IKEv2 provides mutual authentication via the IKEv2 mechanisms. The PaC believes that the PAA is authentic because the network sent a correct IDr name, which corresponds to the input used to generate the $AUTH$ value. The PAA believes that the PaC is genuine because the received IDi matches the input used to compute the $AUTH$ value. Moreover, PANA/IKEv2 validates the EAP AVP exchanges through its PANA message validity check scheme (Section 4.1.6 of [4]).

6.4 Key Derivation

PANA/IKEv2 supports session key derivation through the EAP/IKEv2 method. It is good security practice to use different keys for different applications. To export an IKEv2 session key as part of an EAP keying framework [17], Tschofenig and Kroeselberg [6] suggest deriving another session key for use with EAP, referred to as the 'Pre-Master-Secret'. They reuse the IKEv2 key derivation function, specified in Section 2.17 of [7], to export a freshly generated $KEYMAT$ as a 'Pre-Master-Secret' for further EAP/IKEV2 key derivation.

6.5   Service Theft and Dictionary Attacks

PANA/IKEv2 does not specify any mechanism for preventing service theft. Therefore an attacker can gain unauthorized access to the network by stealing service from another user, spoofing both the IP and MAC addresses of a legitimate PaC to gain unauthorized access. In a non-shared medium, service theft can be prevented by simple IP address and MAC address filters. In shared links, filters are not sufficient to prevent service theft as they can easily be spoofed (as described by Parthasarathy [21]). A recent draft [22] describes how an IPsec[10] SA can be established to secure the link between the PaC and the EP, which can be used to prevent service theft in the access network.

Because PANA/IKEv2 is not a password protocol, it is not vulnerable to dictionary or social engineering attacks, assuming that the pre-shared secret or the key used for digital signature are not derived from a weak password, name, or other low entropy source.

6.6   Perfect Forward Secrecy, Brute-Force Attacks, and Generation of Random Numbers

PANA/IKEv2 generates IKEv2 keying material using an ephemeral Diffie-Hellman exchange, in order to gain the property of "perfect forward secrecy" [7]. Support of this property requires that, when a connection is closed, each endpoint forgets not only the keys used by the connection but any data that could be used to recompute those keys.

The Diffie-Hellman exchange must be based on one of the groups defined in [7], where all but the first of the groups (which is only present for historical reasons) offers security against any computationally feasible brute force attack. It is assumed that all Diffie-Hellman exponents are erased from memory after use.

In the context of the PANA/IKEv2 SA, four cryptographic algorithms are negotiated: an encryption algorithm, an integrity protection algorithm, a Diffie-Hellman group, and a pseudo-random function (prf). The prf is used for the construction of keying material for all of the cryptographic algorithms used. The strength of all IKEv2 keys is limited by the size of the output of the negotiated prf function. For this reason, a prf whose output is shorter than 128 bits (e.g. a CBC-MAC derived using a 64-bit block cipher) shall never be used with the PANA/IKEv2 protocol. Finally, a PANA/IKEv2 implementation also needs to use a good source of randomness to generate the random numbers (nonces) required in the protocol[11].

6.7   Integrity, Replay Protection, and Confidentiality

The protection of signaling packet exchanges through the PANA/IKEv2 SA prevents an opponent from acting as a man-in-the-middle adversary, from session

---

[10] http://www.ietf.org/html.charters/ipsec-charter.html
[11] See [23] for details on generating random numbers for security applications.

hijacking, from injecting packets, from replaying messages, and from modifying the content of the exchanged messages. Also, as with all PANA methods, in PANA/IKEv2 an integrity object is defined, supporting data-origin authentication, replay protection based on sequence numbers, and integrity protection based on a keyed message digest.

Moreover, in PANA/IKEv2 all but the headers of the IKEv2 messages that follow the Diffie-Hellman exchange are encrypted and integrity protected. The recipients must verify that all signatures and MACs are computed correctly, and that the *ID* names correspond to the keys used to generate the *AUTH* payload. The use of nonces guarantees liveliness during an exchange, and also protects against replay attacks.

6.8   Negotiation Attacks and Fast Reconnection

EAP method downgrading attacks might be possible because PANA/IKEv2 does not protect the EAP method negotiation, especially if the user employs the EAP/IKEv2 identifier with other EAP methods. Nevertheless, the EAP document [5] describes a method of avoiding attacks that negotiate the least secure EAP method from among a set. If a particular peer needs to make use of different EAP authentication methods, then distinct identifiers should be employed, each of which identifies exactly one authentication method. In any case, some protection against such an attack can be offered by repeating the list of supported EAP methods protected with the PANA/IKEv2 SA.

PANA/IKEv2 does not support EAP/IKEv2 protocol version negotiation, but supports cipher suite negotiation through IKEv2.

In line with Section 4, PANA/IKEv2 supports two types of fast reconnection. Since fast reconnection does not involve the entire AAA communication, it gives performance benefits.

6.9   Denial-of-Service Attacks and Use of Cookies

PANA sequence numbers and cookies provide resistance against blind resource consumption DoS attacks, as described in [4]. But PANA does not protect the EAP/IKEv2 method exchange itself. Since in particular the PAA is not allowed to discard packets, and packets have to be stored or forwarded to an AAA infrastructure, the level of risk of DoS attacks largely depends on the chosen EAP/IKEv2 message flow.

The EAP/IKEv2 method offers an optional DoS protection capability inherited from IKEv2, which also uses cookies and keeps the responder stateless when it receives the first IKEv2 message. If DoS protection is required then an additional round trip is necessary.

It follows that in PANA/IKEv2 there can be at most two levels of cookies: PANA cookie and IKEv2 cookie. Since both cookies are optional, there are theoretically four possibilities:

a) Both PANA and IKEv2 cookies are used,

b) Only PANA cookies are used,

c) Only IKEv2 cookies are used,

d) Cookies are not used by either PANA or IKEv2.

Option *a*) is redundant, and option *d*) should only be employed when the access network is physically secure and there is no risk of DoS attacks.

The PANA/IKEv2 protocol also enables both the PaC and the PAA to transmit a tear-down message [4]. This message causes state removal, a stop to the accounting procedure, and removes the installed packet filters. Thus such a message needs to be protected to prevent an adversary from deleting state information and thereby causing DoS attacks. PANA/IKEV2 supports protected tear-down messages by using a MAC AVP, which neutralizes this threat.

7   Advantages and Disadvantages

In this section, the PANA/IKEv2 proposal is assessed with respect to how well it addresses security issues arising in future heterogeneous network access scenarios supporting ubiquitous mobility. The main advantages of PANA/IKEv2 in this context are as follows.

- PANA/IKEv2 is implemented using PANA, a flexible and scalable network-layer access authentication protocol. Such a protocol is necessary when link-layer authentication mechanisms are either not available or unable to meet the overall requirements, or when multi-layer authentication is needed.
- PANA/IKEv2 also derives from IKEv2, which supports both symmetric and asymmetric mutual authentication, in addition to legacy authentication support, within a single protocol. Because of its greater flexibility, it seems likely that public key authentication will gain greater importance in future ubiquitous mobility access networks.
- PANA/IKEv2 is based on the EAP/IKEv2 method. This method enables the use of the existing IKEv2 infrastructure (e.g. the use of X.509 certificates [12]) in a number of new scenarios; it also enables use of IKEv2 in a transparent way. PANA/IKEv2 also includes identity confidentiality and integrity protection support, has the perfect forward secrecy property, and is not vulnerable to brute-force or dictionary attacks.
- The PANA/IKEv2 SA prevents man-in-the-middle attacks, session hijacking, packet injection, message replay, and content modification of the exchanged packets. The PANA/IKEv2 integrity object supports data-origin authentication, replay protection based on sequence numbers, and integrity protection. The use of nonces guarantees liveliness during an exchange, and also protects against replay attacks.
- PANA/IKEv2 provides ordered delivery of messages with sequence numbers, which along with cookies provides protection against blind DoS attacks. PANA/IKEv2 also offers an optional IKEv2 DoS protection capability.
- PANA/IKEv2 provides confidentiality and integrity protection of the IKEv2 payload, and includes IKEv2 cipher suite negotiation. PANA/IKEv2 also supports two types of fast reconnection, resulting in performance benefits.

The disadvantages of the proposed PANA/IKEv2 protocol are as follows:

- PANA/IKEv2 does not specify any mechanism for supporting EAP/IKEv2 version negotiation.
- PANA/IKEv2 does not specify any mechanism for preventing service theft. On the other hand, because PANA/IKEv2 is just a signalling protocol and does not carry user data traffic, in fact it does not have to formally specify any mechanism for preventing service theft. However, since EAP/IKEv2 has key derivation functionality, it is possible to establish a local IPsec tunnel to provide service theft prevention.

8   Further Work

The session key derivation procedure in the current version of PANA/IKEv2 depends heavily on the EAP/IKEv2 protocol. Therefore one interesting alternative may be to adopt one of the unified EAP session key derivation approaches for multiple applications currently being investigated (see, for example, Salowey and Eronen [24]), instead of adopting the existing scheme from EAP/IKEv2. An analogous scheme to PANA/IKEv2 would be to specify the GPRS GMM authentication protocol [25] as an EAP method (e.g. Buckley et al. [26]), enabling its use with PANA. Another interesting new application would be the transport of EAP Archie (see Walker and Housley [27]) by PANA.

9   Conclusions

"Heterogeneous network access control security" received the highest rating value in the list of open research issues for future mobile communication systems produced by the PAMPAS Project [1, p65]. In this paper, we have proposed the new PANA/IKEv2 protocol, in order to provide an IP compatible, flexible and scalable authentication method that allows a client to be authenticated using either symmetric or asymmetric techniques to an arbitrary access network.

The protocol is based on PANA, a network-layer access authentication protocol carrier, which communicates, via EAP, with an AAA infrastructure. PANA/IKEv2 is also based on EAP-IKEv2, which permits use of the IKEv2 infrastructure in future heterogeneous Internet access scenarios. PANA/IKEv2 prevents man-in-the-middle attacks, session hijacking, packet injection, message replay, content modification, and blind DoS attacks. It provides data-origin authentication, replay protection using sequence numbers and nonces, and integrity protection. As well as supporting identity and IKEv2 payload confidentiality, it allows IKEv2 cipher suite negotiation, and is not vulnerable to brute-force or dictionary attacks.

The performance gains arising from the two types of fast reconnection, the increase in flexibility provided by the public key based authentication option, and the benefits of security given by the PANA/IKEv2 SA make the PANA/IKEv2 scheme potentially attractive to all operators wishing to offer to their users heterogeneous Internet access in ubiquitous mobility networks.

Acknowledgements. The authors would like to acknowledge the many helpful insights and corrections provided by Hannes Tschofenig and Yoshihiro Ohba. The first author would like to thank the Brazilian Navy, particularly the military organizations EMA, DGMM, DTM, and CASNAV, for sponsoring his PhD in Information Security course at Royal Holloway, University of London.

References

1. C. Guenther. Pioneering advanced mobile privacy and security (PAMPAS) refined roadmap. Deliverable D03 IST-2001-37763, PAMPAS Project, http://www.pampas.eu.org/, February 2003.
2. Institute of Electrical and Electronics Engineers. *IEEE P802.1aa/D5-2003 DRAFT Standard for Local and Metropolitan Area Networks - Port Based Network Access Control - Amendment 1: Technical and Editorial Corrections*, February 2003.
3. W. Simpson. The point-to-point protocol (PPP). Request For Comments 1661 (STD 51), Internet Engineering Task Force, July 1994.
4. D. Forsberg, Y. Ohba, B. Patil, H. Tschofenig, and A. Yegin. Protocol for carrying authentication for network access (PANA). Internet draft (work in progress), Internet Engineering Task Force, July 2003.
5. L. Blunk, J. Vollbrecht, B. Aboba, J. Carlson, and H. Levkowetz. Extensible authentication protocol (EAP). Internet draft (work in progress), Internet Engineering Task Force, June 2003.
6. H. Tschofenig and D. Kroeselberg. EAP IKEv2 method. Internet draft (work in progress), Internet Engineering Task Force, June 2003.
7. C. Kaufman (editor). Internet key exchange (IKEv2) protocol. Internet draft (work in progress), Internet Engineering Task Force, May 2003.
8. D. Harkins and D. Carrel. The Internet key exchange (IKE). Request For Comments 2409, Internet Engineering Task Force, November 1998.
9. L. Blunk and J. Vollbrecht. PPP extensible authentication protocol (EAP). Request For Comments 2284, Internet Engineering Task Force, March 1998.
10. R. Perlman. Understanding IKEv2: Tutorial, and rationale for decisions. Internet draft (work in progress), Internet Engineering Task Force, February 2003.
11. W. Diffie and M. Hellman. New directions in cryptography. *IEEE Transactions on Information Theory*, IT-22(6):644–654, June 1976.
12. R. Housley, W. Polk, W. Ford, and D. Solo. Internet X.509 public key infrastructure certificate and certificate revocation list (CRL) profile. Request For Comments 3280, Internet Engineering Task Force, April 2002.
13. N. Asokan, V. Niemi, and K. Nyberg. Man-in-the-middle in tunnelled authentication. In *the Proceedings of the 11th International Workshop on Security Protocols*, Cambridge, UK, April 2003. To be published in the Springer-Verlag LNCS series.
14. J. Puthenkulam, V. Lortz, A. Palekar, D. Simon, and B. Aboba. The compound authentication binding problem. Internet draft (work in progress), Internet Engineering Task Force, October 2002.
15. T. Hiller and G. Zorn. Diameter extensible authentication protocol (EAP) application. Internet draft (work in progress), Internet Engineering Task Force, March 2003.
16. P. Calhoun, S. Farrell, and W. Bulley. Diameter CMS security application. Internet draft (work in progress), Internet Engineering Task Force, March 2002.

17. B. Aboba and D. Simon. EAP keying framework. Internet draft (work in progress), Internet Engineering Task Force, March 2003.
18. A. Palekar, D. Simon, G. Zorn, and S. Josefsson. Protected EAP protocol (PEAP). Internet draft (work in progress), Internet Engineering Task Force, March 2003.
19. H. Haverinen and J. Salowey. EAP SIM authentication. Internet draft (work in progress), Internet Engineering Task Force, February 2003.
20. B. Aboba and M. Beadles. The network access identifier. Request For Comments 2486, Internet Engineering Task Force, January 1999.
21. M. Parthasarathy. PANA threat analysis and security requirements. Internet draft (work in progress), Internet Engineering Task Force, April 2003.
22. M. Parthasarathy. Securing the first hop in PANA using IPsec. Internet draft (work in progress), Internet Engineering Task Force, May 2003.
23. D. Eastlake 3rd, S. Crocker, and J. Schiller. Randomness recommendations for security. Request For Comments 1750, Internet Engineering Task Force, December 1994.
24. J. Salowey and P. Eronen. EAP key derivation for multiple applications. Internet draft (work in progress), Internet Engineering Task Force, June 2003.
25. ETSI. *GSM Technical Specification GSM 04.08 (ETS 300 940): "Digital cellular telecommunication system (Phase 2+); Mobile radio interface layer 3 specification" (version 7.8.0).* European Telecommunications Standards Institute, June 2000.
26. A. Buckley, P. Satarasinghe, V. Alperovich, J. Puthenkulam, J. Walker, and V. Lortz. EAP SIM GMM authentication. Internet draft (work in progress), Internet Engineering Task Force, August 2002.
27. J. Walker and R. Housley. The EAP Archie protocol. Internet draft (work in progress), Internet Engineering Task Force, February 2003.

An Automatic Security Evaluation System for IPv6 Network

Jaehoon Nah[1], Hyeokchan Kwon[1], Sungwon Sohn[1],
Cheehang Park[1], and Chimoon Han[2]

[1] Information Security Research Division,
Electronics and Telecommunications Research Institute
161 Gajeong-dong, Yuseong-gu, Daejeon, Korea
{jhnah,hckwon,swsohn,chpark}@etri.re.kr
[2] HanKook University of F.S
270 Imun-dong, Dongdaemun-gu, Seoul, Korea
cmhan@hufs.ac.kr

Abstract. IP version 6 is a new version of the Internet Protocol, designed as the successor to IP version 4(IPv4). IPv6 is now a deployment phase. For Security of IPv6 network, IPsec(IP Security) is designed by IPsec Working Group of IETF. IPsec(IP Security) offers not only Internet security service such as Internet secure communication and authentication but also the safe key exchange and anti-replay attack mechanism. Recently, Several Project implement IPv6 IPsec on the various Operating Systems. But there is no existing tool that checks the servers, which provide IPsec services, work properly and provide their network security services well. In this paper, we design and implement an automatic security evaluation system for IPv6 network. This system is operated on Windows and UNIX platform and operated on IPv6 network. We developed the system using Java and C language.

1 Introduction

IP version 6(IPv6) is a new version of the Internet Protocol, designed as the successor to IP version 4(IPv4). IPv6 is finally gaining market momentum after many years of getting attention mainly in the standard forums, due to two recent market trends: the growing shortage of available IP addresses, mainly in the Far East, and the upcoming deployment of 3G mobile networks with IP address assignment per individual wireless phone or handheld device[1]. The changes from IPv4 to IPv6 fall primary into the following categories: Expanded Addressing Capabilities, Header Format Simplification, Improved Support for Extensions and Options and Flow Labeling Capability. Currently 43 RFCs and 22 Internet drafts related to IPv6 have been made by IETF Internet Area IPv6 Working Group.[2] IPv6 is now a deployment phase. Several pieces of network equipment that support IPv6 have been shipped, and some network providers have started IPv6 commercial services. However, more implementations

K. Chae and M. Yung (Eds.): WISA 2003, LNCS 2908, pp. 150–161, 2004.
© Springer-Verlag Berlin Heidelberg 2004

and experiments are necessary in some areas. One such ongoing field is Security for IPv6

For Security of IPv6 network, IPsec(IP Security) is designed by IPsec Working Group of IETF. Currently nearly 18 RFCs and 30 Internet drafts related to IPsec protocols have been made[2-7]. IPsec is a method of protecting IP datagrams. This protection takes the form of data origin authentication, connectionless data integrity, data content confidentiality, anti-replay protection, and limited traffic flow confidentiality. IPsec can protect any protocol that runs on top of IPv4 and IPv6 such as TCP(Transmission Control Protocol), UDP(User Datagram Protocol) and ICMP(Internet Control Message Protocol). Recently, Several Projects such as KAME, USAGI [8-9] implement IPv6 IPsec on the various Operating Systems.

In order to maintain the security of the network, we need the security evaluation tool that can check current security status of the network. But there is no existing such a tool which checks the IPv6 servers that provide IPsec services work properly and provide their network security services as well.

In this paper, we design and implement an automatic security evaluation system for IPv6 network. This system is originally intended for testing Universal IPv6 security Engine that is developed by ETRI. But this evaluation system can be applied to any IPv6 security engine because it exists independently and it is up to standard document such as IETF RFC 2401, 2402, 2406, 2407 and so on.

The Security Evaluation System is based on rule, so it is able to automate the security test of the network and it can cope with new vulnerability easily without modifying the system. If its users get information about new vulnerability, then they can add Security Test Rules that can handle the new vulnerability.

The Paper is organized as follows. Section 2 presents the architecture of the security evaluation system. Section 3 presents the implementation of the system. Finally the conclusion is given in section 4.

2 Architecture of the Security Evaluation System

Figure 1 shows the architecture of the security evaluation system. The system is divided into following parts.
- Evaluation Engine, controlling the whole system
- DBMS (Data Base Management System)
- Agent
- Security Evaluation Modules

2.1 Evaluation Engine

Evaluation Engine consists of System Configuration, Database Control and Rule Interpreter.

System Configuration. System configuration can be divided into four units: Access Control, Agent Registration, Module Registration and Directory Setup. Access Control Unit provides user authentication service. Agent Registration Unit performs registration of agent name, agent type, DB name and host information in which agent has been installed. Module Registration Unit registers information about a module such as module name, installation path and description of a module. Directory Setup Unit defines the directory path for storing data such as temporal data and packet data generated during the evaluation process.

Database Control. Database Control Unit in Fig.1 generates and manages database. A System Administrator can define, modify and delete Security Evaluation Rules with Rule DB Control Unit. Result Search Unit has the functions of search and display the test results. Collection Data Control Unit receives the packet by using Socket Handler from agents that is installed in a remote host during the test process, and stores received data and its information into Collection Data DB.

Rule Interpreter. Rule Interpreter will be described in section 2.2

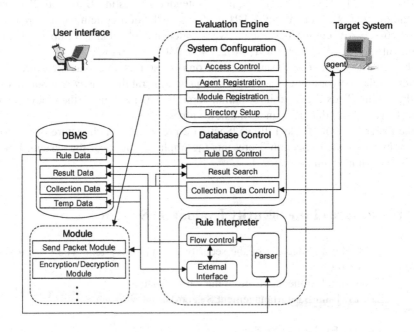

Fig. 1. Architecture of the Automatic Security Evaluation System

2.2   Rule Interpreter

Rule Interpreter reads test rule from Rule Data DB and then interprets and performs the rules. Parser in Rule Interpreter has the function of analyzing the syntax of the Test Rules from the Rule Data DB that are selected for the security evaluation. Flow

Control Block performs the Control Command and calls the External Interface Block when Test Rule requests the execution of specific Security Analysis Module. Control Commands are shown in Table 1. External Interface Block controls the agent and operates DB such as Temp Data and Collection Data. And it manages and executes the modules. The processing flow of Rule Interpreter is shown in Fig. 2.

Table 1. Control Command

Command	Syntax

IF	IF *condition* THEN
	    statements ...
	[ELSE]
	    statements ...
	ENDIF

FOR	FOR *initial value, final value* [STEP *step-value*] statements ... NEXT
DO	DO [WHILE *condition*] statements ... LOOP [UNTIL *condition*]
BREAK	BREAK
PRINT	PRINT display statement
COMMENT	// ... or /* ... */

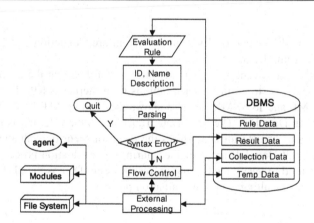

Fig. 2. Processing Flow of Rule Interpreter

External Interface Block contains predefined functions. Table 2 shows the list of predefined functions that can be executed by External Interface Block.

We implemented sniffer and sndpkt function that could be contained to the command field in Table 2. Sniffer function is used for a sniffing packet, in accordance with the specified rule, from the network, a remote host or Database. Currently, sniffer function can sniff the packets generated by the protocols that are used by IPsec such as ISAKMP(Internet Security Association and Key Management Protocol), AH(Authentication Header), ESP(Encapsulating Security Payload), SNMP(Simple Network Management Protocol), IP(Internet Protocol), ICMP(Internet Control Message Protocol) and so on.

Sndpkt function is used for sending a packet that is stored in its system to the target host by Raw Socket interface. Current the sendpkt function can send the packet such as AH, ESP, ISAKMP, IP, ICMP. You can see the examples of test rule in section 3.

Table 2. Predefined Functions of External Interface Block

SQL(output DB, Query, input DB)
Process the query from input DB and stores the results in the output DB so that the next Test Rule can use them.
AGENT(command, START[or STOP])
Start or stop execution of agent, and it is possible to specify an execution option by its command field.
MODULE(command)
Execute Module, and it is also possible to specify Module name and execution option by its command field.
SAVE(filename, query, input DB)
Process the query from input DB and stores the results in the file specified by its filename field. This file is used for sending a packet for the security test.

2.3 DBMS

The Databases used by Security Evaluation System are Collection Data, Rule Data, Result Data and Temp Data.

Collection Data stores the various kinds of protocol data that the agent transmits. The protocol which is stored in the each table is the Ethernet, ARP, IPv6, AH, ESP, TCP, UDP, ICMP and ISAKMP. Table 3 shows the field of AH, ESP, ISAKMP tables of Collection Data DB. The Rule Data Table stores the rule that is used for the security evaluation. The Result Data stores the result of security evaluation. The values stored in Result Data DB are displayed during the evaluation process and sometimes later it is used to verify the evaluation result. Temp Data is the place that stores the temporary data resulting from the evaluation process.

Table 3. Collection Data DB

• AH Table

Field Name	Type	Description
ID	INTEGER	ID of Packet
NEXTHDR	CHAR	Type of Next Header
PAY_LEN	INTEGER	Length of AH Header
SPI	INTEGER	Security Parameter Index
SEQUENCE	INTEGER	Sequence Number
AUTHENTICATION	MEDIUMTEXT	Authentication Data (ICV)
TIME	VARCHAR	Sniffing Time

- ESP Table

Field Name	Type	Description
ID	INTEGER	ID of Packet
SPI	INTEGER	Security Parameter Index
SEQUENCE	INTEGER	Sequence Number
ENCRYPTION	MEDIUMTEXT	Encryption Data
TIME	VARCHAR	Sniffing Time

- ISAKMP Table

Field Name	Type	Description
ID	INTEGER	ID of Packet
INIT_COOKIE	CHAR	Initial Cookie
RESPOND_COOKIE	CHAR	Respond Cookie
NEXT_PAY	CHAR	Type of Next Payload
MAJ_VER	INTEGER	Major version of ISAKMP
MIN_VER	INTEGER	Minor version of ISAKMP
EXCHANGE_TYPE	CHAR	The Exchange Type that currently used
FLAGS	CHAR	Flags about Exchange
MESSAGE_ID	INTEGER	Message ID
TOTAL_LEN	INTEGER	Total Payload length
ENCRYPTION	MEDIUMTEXT	Encrypted data
TIME	VARCHAR	Sniffing time

2.4 Agent

Agent sniffs the packets generated by the protocols that are used by IPsec such as AH, ESP, ISAKMP, IP, ICMP, TCP, and send them to the Security Evaluation System in order to check whether security hosts provide proper IPsec services to the network or not. When the connection is established with evaluation system, agent waits a command from the evaluation system. The Security Evaluation System can send four types of command - START, STOP, HALT, RESUME - to the agent. Fig. 3 shows the flow of agent execution.

3   Implementation

The Automatic Security Evaluation System has been implemented in Java and C language and the Database has been implemented in My-SQL. And we implemented packet-sniffing component in agent with libpcap for the IPv6 network, a system independent interface for user-level network packet capturing developed by the Network Research Group at the Lawrence Berkely Laboratory. This system operated on Windows and UNIX platform. You can see the main window in Fig. 4.

Using the three windows that are located on the left side in the main window in Fig. 4, we may select or view a list of Agent, module and rule. Upper and right side window displays execution log or collected protocol data. If we want to see only the specified protocol data or log, we uses the buttons such as 'log', 'Packet data', 'AH', 'ESP', 'ARP' and so on. And they are located in the bottom of the window. In lower and right side window displays the process of sniffing protocol packet data.

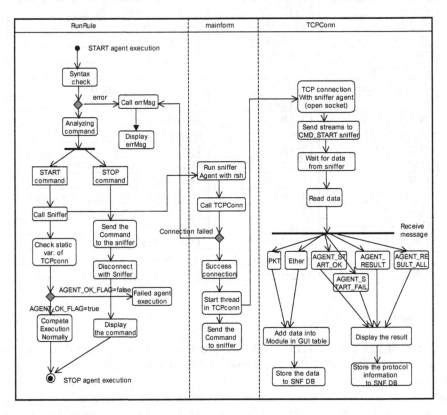

Fig. 3. The Process of Agent Execution

3.1 Management of Agent, Module, Host, and Packet

Users can manage agent, module, host and packet by clicking the menus in figure 4. The menus are listed below.

'Agent', 'Module' 'Rule': addition, selection, deletion or modification of Agent, Module or Rule.
'Host': register target host or edit agent information that is installed in target host
'Tool': Set up the Preference of the user or the DB, and manage packets.

Fig. 5 is the window for managing packet. In Fig. 5, the packet management window has the function that displays the collected packet and stores the packet with changing the value of some fields. Using the left window in Fig. 4, we may select or view a list of packet file, and using the upper and right window we may edit packet and lower and right window shows the list of stored packet in selected file.

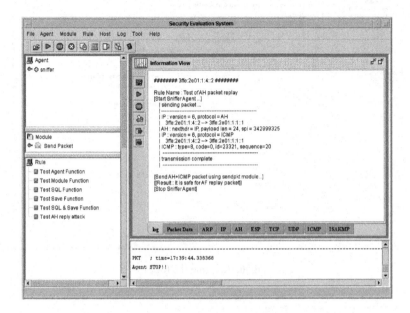

Fig. 4. Main Window & Test Result

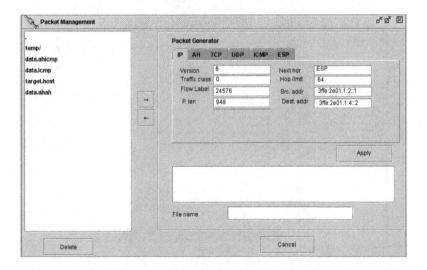

Fig. 5. Packet Management Window

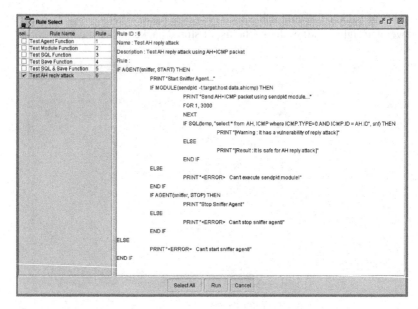

Fig. 6. Selecting the Rule

Fig. 7. Sniffed AH Packet

3.2 Editing and Executing the Rule

Users may register, modify, select or delete the rule by clicking the 'rule' menu in Fig. 4. Fig. 6 is an example of selecting a rule. The meaning of the rule displayed in Fig. 6 is as follows.

- Sniff and store the AH+ICMP packet whose destination is target host, and send it to the target host again.
- And see what happens to the target host.
- If target host responds to this trial, the Security Evaluation System displays the warning message "It has a vulnerability of replay-attack".
- Otherwise, the Security Evaluation System displays the message "It is safe for replay-attack"

Fig. 4 shows the result of this test. Fig. 7 shows sniffed AH packet during the execution of the rule in Fig. 6. As a result of this test item, Universal IPv6 IPsec Server is safe for replay attack.

3.3 Security Evaluation

The method of evaluating the four representative security services that are provided by IPsec protocol can be summarized below.

Confidentiality: Sniff the any ESP packet, whose source or destination is target host, from network, and check the packet whether it is readable or not, and try to decrypt it by using arbitrary key.

Data Origin Authentication: Sniff AH or ESP packet whose destination is target host, from network by real time, and modify source IP address in sniffed packet, and try to send it to the target host, and see what happens to the target host.

Access Control: Generate ICMP packet with AH or ESP by using arbitrary key, and send it to the target host, and see what happens to the target host.

Connectionless Integrity: Modify arbitrary field of sniffed packet, and re-calculate ICV value, and change the ICV value with the newly calculated ICV value, and send it to the target host, and see what happens to the target host.

Anti-replay: Monitor SN(Sequence Number) value in sniffed AH/ESP packet header, and guess and change the SN value of the packet, and send it to the target host, and see what happens to the target host.

At first, we evaluate Universal IPv6 Security Server that is developed by ETRI. The test environment is shown in Fig. 8. For this work, we defined test suite that is consists of 80 test items. Table 4 shows a part of security test suite. For each test item, we check the security services of IPv6 Security Server by using automatic security

Evaluation System. In our experience, Universal IPv6 Security Server passed 75 items and failed 3 items.

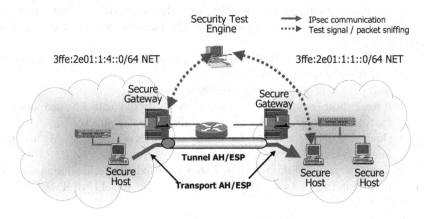

Fig. 8. Test Environment

Table 3. Security Test Suites (H: Host, GW: Gateway)

1. Detect modified AH packet (Modification of IP dst.) 　　H1 =======> H2   ICMP Echo request (with AH, modification of IP dst.) 　　H1 <===X=== H2   No ICMP Echo reply (Drop packet)
2. Inbound ESP packet with Fragmentation (Auth.: NONE, Encrypt.: 3DES-CBC) 　　H1 ==============> H2   Send Fragmented TCP message (with ESP) 　　(1st /2nd / 3rd ... fragment)
3. Inbound Tunnel AH packet (Auth.: HMAC-SHA1) 　　H1 ===> GW1 ===> GW2 ===> H2   ICMP Echo request (with Tunnel AH) 　　|---------------Tunnel AH----------| 　　H1<=== GW1 <=== GW2 <=== H2   ICMP Echo reply (with Tunnel AH)
4. Outbound AH+ESP packet with SA bundles 　　H1 ==> GW1 ==> GW2 ==> H2   ICMP Echo request (with SA bundles) 　　　　|---ESP SA--| 　　|------------AH SA---------------| 　　H2 <== GW1 <== GW2 <== H1   ICMP Echo reply (with SA bundles) 　　　　|---ESP SA--| 　　|------------AH SA--------------|
5. Inbound AH+ESP (policy=drop) 　　H1 ======> H2   ICMP Echo request (with AH+ESP) 　　H1 <==X == H2   No ICMP Echo reply (drop packet) 　　. . .

4 Conclusions

In this paper, we design and implement the Automatic Security Evaluation System for IPv6 network. This system is originally intended for testing IPv6sec Engine that is developed by ETRI. But the this system can be applied to any IPv6 security engine because it exists independently and it is up to standard document such as IETF RFC 2401, 2402, 2406, 2407 and so on.

The characteristics of the Automatic Security Evaluation System that is presented in this paper are as follows.

- It can be operated on IPv6 network
- It is able to collect and analyze various protocol packets from network
- It provides security evaluation of the specific hosts that provide security services to the network domain based on IPsec service.
- It is rule based system, so it is able to automate the security evaluation of the network and it can cope with new vulnerability easily without modifying the system. If its users get information about new vulnerability, then they can add Security Evaluation Rules that can handle the new vulnerability.
- The grammar of the security evaluation rule is very simple, so we can define evaluation scenario easily.
- It is very scalable because it manages the functions that are needed for security test system with the modules. Additional Security Evaluation Modules that have new functions can be added to the Security Evaluation System easily without modifying the whole system.

In the future work, we will upgrade the system by adding rules and modules, and we will study on AI(Artificial Intelligence) technology for intelligent security evaluation.

References

1. White Paper, IPv6 to IPv4 is Not Merely 50% More, Ezchip Technologies.
2. IETF, http://www.ietf.org
3. S.Deering, R.Hinden, Internet Protocol, Version 6(IPv6) Specification, RFC2460, Dec. 1998
4. S.Kent and R.Atkinson, Security Architecture for the Internet Protocol, RFC2401, Nov. 1998
5. S.Kent and R.Atkinson, IP Authentication Header, RFC2402, Nov. 1998
6. S.Kent and R.Atkinson, IP Encapsulating Security Payload, RFC2406, Nov. 1998
7. D.Harkins, D.Correl, Internet Key Exchange, RFC2409, Nov. 1998
8. KAME, http://www.kame.net
9. USAGI, http://www.linux-ipv6.org/
10. A.Conta, S.Deering, "Internet Control Message Protocol (ICMPv6) for the Internet Protocol Version 6 (IPv6) Specification, RFC2463, Dec. 1998
11. R.Hinden, S.Deering, IP Version 6 Addressing Architecture, RFC2373, Jul. 1998

A Location Privacy Protection Mechanism for Smart Space

Yeongsub Cho, Sangrae Cho, Daeseon Choi, Seunghun Jin,
Kyoil Chung, and Cheehang Park

Electronics and Telecommunications Research Institute,
161 Gajeong-dong, Yuseong-gu, Daejeon, 305-350 KOREA
{yscho,sangrae,sunchoi,jinsh,kyoil,chpark}@etri.re.kr

Abstract. Ubicomp (Ubiquitous Computing) makes computers ubiquitous in anywhere and anytime, and so provides users with seamless
services. In this paper, we present a user location privacy protection
mechanism for Smart Space which is a feasible Ubicomp environment.
At first, we present a feasible Ubicomp use scenario and define Smart
Space to support this derived scenario. Then, we analyze security requirements for Smart Space and derive conceptual security model for
that Space. Among the conceptual security model, we focus on user location privacy protection. In order to protect user location privacy, we
propose a location privacy protection mechanism based on policy. We
classify the policy as user policy and space policy and present policy resolution mechanism to resolve policy conflicts. Further we present system
configuration to execute the proposed mechanism.

1 Introduction

Ubicomp began with the easy computing as next generation computing vision. It
was proposed by Mark Weiser[1] at XEROX Palo Alto Research Institute in 1991.
Currently, Ubicomp concept has been developed as anytime, anywhere service
by making computer ubiquitous and implanted in all things and all spaces[2][3].

10 years ago, many people thought the vision of Mark Weiser as impossible.
However, now the price of microprocessor is lower and its size is smaller. This
makes it possible to embed the chips in more electronic devices than before.
Furthermore, the functionality of the sensor is enhanced, which makes it easy
to identify the shapes and location of things. In addition, as the communication
technology enhances, it is much easier to communicate with the other things.
As these technologies enhances, the realization of the Ubicomp concept is more
feasible than before [4]. Many people consider Ubicomp as the fourth revolution following the first urban revolution, the second industrial revolution and
the third information revolution in human. That is, many people expect that
the Ubicomp will have influence on all social areas. Therefore, many countries
have been carrying out researches on Ubicomp [2]. Nowadays, the researches on
Ubicomp include wearable computing, nomadic computing, pervasive computing
and other various computing areas [2][3].

K. Chae and M. Yung (Eds.): WISA 2003, LNCS 2908, pp. 162–173, 2004.

The realization of Ubicomp means that computing services are ubiquitously provided for users. To minimize or remove user interaction, these services are commonly invisible to users. To provide these services, Ubicomp generally collect more and more users data. User location data collection may be used to expose user information such as user hobby, health and life pattern and so user location data may be critical information from the users point of view. In addition, when the collected data may be misused or abused, Ubicomp may take a role of surveillance system on users. Due to these characteristics, privacy protection is an essential requirement to realize and deploy Ubicomp.

Various researches have been done in order to solve privacy problems in Ubicomp. Researches have been made to present privacy model and develop privacy system for Ubicomp [5][6]. Also, Researches have been made to protect users location information [7][8]. However, these researches are targeted for general Ubicomp environment and so it may be unsuitable for real application area.

In this paper, we present a user location privacy protection mechanism for Smart Space which is a feasible Ubicomp environment. At first, we present a feasible Ubicomp use scenario and define Smart Space to support this derived scenario. Then, we analyze security requirements for Smart Space and derive conceptual security model for that Space. Among the conceptual security model, we focus on user location privacy protection. In order to protect user location privacy, we propose a location privacy protection mechanism based on policy. We classify the policy as user policy and space policy and present policy resolution mechanism to resolve policy conflicts. Further we present system configuration to execute the proposed mechanism

We organize this paper as follows. In section 2, we describe privacy concept and Ubicomps implications on privacy. We also specify current researches on Ubicomp privacy. In section 3, we present a feasible Ubicomp use case scenario and define Smart Space to support the scenario. We analyze security requirements for Smart Space and present conceptual security model for the Space in section 4. We also propose a location privacy protection mechanism and present a system configuration to support such a mechanism. In section 5, we conclude this paper.

2   Privacy in Ubicomp

2.1   Privacy Concept and Laws

The concept of privacy was well described by Lousi Brandeis and Alan Westin [9]. Lousi Brandeis described privacy as "The right to be left alone." Alan Westin described privacy as "The desire of people to choose freely under what circumstances and to what extent they will expose themselves, their attitude and their behavior to others."

To protect these traditional privacy concepts, many countries have made laws. Among these, two important laws has been affected other countries privacy law enactment and privacy protection policies.

The first important law is "US Privacy Act, 1974" enacted in 1976. OECD presented "Fair Information Practices" based on this law [10]. Fair Information Practices presented the following principles on privacy protection [9].

- **Openness and transparency.** There should be no secret record keeping. This includes both the publication of the existence of such collections, as well as their contents.,
- **Individual participation.** The subject of a record should be able to see and correct the record.,
- **Collection limitation.** Data collection should be proportional and not excessive compared to the purpose of the collection.,
- **Data quality.** Data should be relevant to the purposes for which they are collected and should be kept up to date.
- **Use limitation.** Data should only be used for their specific purpose by authorized personnel.,
- **Reasonable security.** Adequate security safeguards should be put in place, according to the sensitivity of the data collected.,
- **Accountability.** Record keepers must be accountable for compliance with the other principles.

The second important law is "The Directive" by EU [11]. The Directive's main impact is two-fold. Firstly, its article 24/1 limits data transfers to non-EU countries only to those with an adequate level of privacy protection. Secondly, the Directive not only subsumes and refines the fair information practices described above, but its article 7 adds the notion of explicit consent: personal data may only be processed if the user has unambiguously given his or her consent. This practically disallows all types of data collection (except for when required by law) and requires a case-by-case explicit consent by the data subject.

2.2   Ubicomp Privacy and Researches

Ubicomp provides users with various services by making computer ubiquitous in real world. Ubicomp has the following characteristics.

- **Ubiquity.** Computers are ubiquitous in real world. This means that sensors sensing users as well as computers are ubiquitous in real world.,
- **Invisibility.** Ubicomp has a goal to provide users with least-intrusive or non-intrusive service. So, users are commonly unaware of the fact that Ubicomp collects their own data.

Web computing collects users' data which are mainly related to their digital life and whose boundary has limited. However, Ubicomp collects users' everyday life. The traditional computing collects users data such as social security number, credit card number and so on. However, Ubicomp may collect detailed and refined user information such as location and image through enhancements of sensor facility and ubiquitous existence. These characteristics of Ubicomp enlarge the possibility of the privacy violation on users.

Nowadays, there have been various researches to protect privacy in Ubicomp. In these researches, Privacy Awareness System describes the architecture and functionalities of privacy protection system for Ubicomp [5]. In addition, six principles are presented for Ubicomp privacy in this paper. The principles are Notice, Choice and consent, Anonymity and Pseudonymity, Proximity and Locality, Security Access and Recourse. These six principles give guideline for other privacy protection researches Another project called Mist provides a location protection mechanism [6]. This project describes the mechanism to prevent service system from obtaining users exact location. In the research called Loc-Server [8], the notice/consent mechanism similar to P3P [12] are described. P3P is a notice/consent mechanism for web service.

3 Smart Space: A Feasible Ubicomp Environment

3.1 Feasible Scenarios

Ubicomp may be realized in all social areas such as transportation, health care, shopping center, corporate, government and so on. Ubicomp can be constructed in the various shapes according to target environments. The shopping mall is considered as a real world place where the characteristics of Ubicomp environment can be demonstrated appropriately. For that reason, we suggests that USM (Ubiquitous Shopping Mall) is the right choice as a feasible ubiquitous application environment. In the USM, various transactions and interactions take place such as the purchase of goods and services, and activities related to personal affairs. The feasible scenario that is selected from the various possible scenarios is as follows.

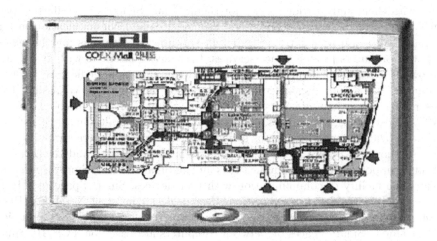

Fig. 1. An Example Map on Alice'PDA (Origin: http://www.coexmall.com)

User Alice enters the USM. The USM provides basic map information for her PDA. The map will include locations of shops and passageways. The Figure 1 shows an example USM map on her PDA.

After providing map information, the USM queries Alice shopping list and tell her optimal shopping route. Alice confirms the USM-presenting route and then decides it is better to visit video shop first. As soon as Alice enters the shop, the shop senses her entrance and obtains her preferences. In doing so, as the shop figure out that Alice likes animation movie, it displays a location for animation booth on her PDA and directs her to that place. While Alice chooses videos, Bob who is a friend of Alice enters the USM. Bob made an appointment to meet her in the USM. So, he asks his PDA her location and in turn his PDA sends a request for her location to the USM. The USM informs Alice of Bobs entrance and then she sends a message to meet in restaurant A. Both of them confirm the location of the restaurant displayed on their PDA, respectively. They meet together in the restaurant a few minutes later. As soon as they sit on a table, the menu of the restaurant displays on their PDAs. If they select a menu item, the detailed description of the food is displayed on their PDAs. They choose and order crab meat. After eating the food, they visit aquarium. When they approach each section of the aquarium, detailed information on the fishes of the section is automatically displayed on their PDAs. In aquarium, Bob has a sudden stomachache. So, Alice asks the USM of the location of the nearest drugstore and confirms the location through her PDA. She takes him to the drugstore. Due to his pain, they decide to exit the USM. When they exit the USM, it calculates the total expense they have spent in the shopping mall. If the expense meets the shopping discount policy, then the USM can discharge the parking fee.

3.2   Smart Space

Smart Space is defined to be minimal physical unit space to contain users, interact with them and provide service for them. Smart Space is a intelligent space which consists of sensors, computers, user devices and communication media. Sensor can sense user entrance/exit and capture the locations and images of users. Computers provide space services. User device interacts with spaces and provides users with adequate information. Communication media take a role to communicate among user device, sensors and computer system. We assume that user devices have some computation power, being PDA or Notebook. In the USM, video shops, restaurants, aquarium and so on fall under Smart Space. The USM provides users with various services through mutual interactions.

As shown in Figure 2, the USM consists of Smart Spaces and Bridges. The bridge support mutual communications among Smart Spaces. Smart Space provides the facility of communication with user devices. Smart Space uses Bluetooth or Infrared for communication. User devices consist of Notebook, PDA, cellular phone, and so on which have some computation power. The communications among Smart Spaces or between computers are based on TCP/IP. Smart Space provides its own and specific service according to its goal such as food sales, clothing sales and so on.

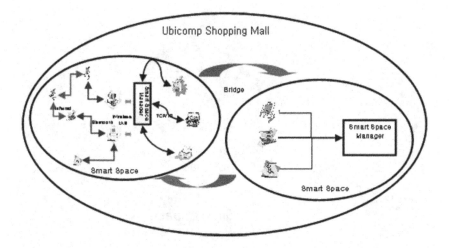

Fig. 2. Conceptual Model of Ubicomp Shopping Mall

There are two methods to connect two or more Smart Spaces. The one is simple connection. In this method, Smart Spaces share simple information which is user location or trace information. The other is intelligent connection. In this method, Smart Space obtains a users context information and provides proactive service for him. The USM combines the existing cyber space and the physical space using Smart Spaces and Bridges. Consequently, the USM provide intelligent services for users.

4   A Location Privacy Protection Mechanism

4.1   Location Privacy Requirements in Smart Space

In the USM, a user stores on its PDA such information as her or his identifier, attributes and preference and so on. Such information falls under personal privacy data, so Smart Space configures a PPS (Privacy Protection Space). PPS protects users private information not to be exposed. When a user enters a Smart Space, it knows his entrance and gives non-intrusive authentication facility to remove or minimize users interaction with the Space. Once authenticated, the user receives various services, interacting with the Space with direct negotiation or with indirect negotiation. Indirect negotiation means that users device negotiates with the Space on behalf of the user. In this time, other users or service providers are also authenticated and authorized. Smart Space forms TS (Trust Space) which makes mutual authentication and authorization possible. In summary, various security functionalities must be provided in order to manage Smart Space well.

The one is non-intrusive authentication. The others are access control based on the contexts of users and spaces, trust management and privacy protection mechanism. The Figure 3 shows conceptual security model of Smart Space. As

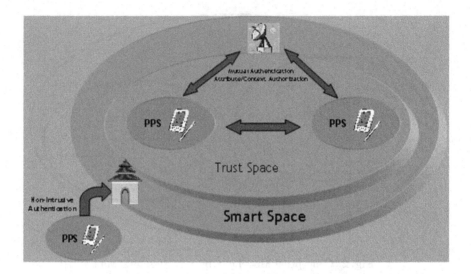

Fig. 3. Conceptual Security Model of Smart Space

specified in previous section, privacy becomes more and more important issue according to enhancement of Ubicomp environments. Smart Space must collect some user information in order to minimize user's intrusion and to provide invisible and proactive services. However, these data collections may bring about users privacy violation due to the misuse or abuse of the collected data. To solve these problems, Smart Space must notify users the fact that it collects data on users and get users'explicit consents on data collection. Smart Space senses user location and give service according to the location, so being always aware of user location. The collected user location data may be used not only for service providing but also for privacy exposure. For example, if a user visits a specific hospital, the Space can infer his health condition. If a user visits in stores in shopping mall, the Space can infer his purchase patterns and in turn life style. If a user goes to a golf shop, the Space can infer his hobby. That is, the collected information of Smart Space will violate human's privacy. Therefore, a location privacy protection mechanism must be the prime security requirement.

4.2 Policy-Based Location Privacy Protection Mechanism

In Smart Space, a user must be able to control her or his location information. For example, Alice must be able to decide according to her preferences that Bob is allowed to know her location but Carol is not allowed to know her location. In addition, Smart Space must be able to control the location information of users within its boundary. When Alice and Bob is within Space A, the Space must be able to decide according to its preferences that it informs Carol of the existence of Alice and Bob in response to Carol's inquiry, but that it informs Dave of only the two persons existence in response to Dave's inquiry. We propose a mechanism which defines the location privacy based on policy of Smart Space including users and Smart Space itself. The policy is classifies as ULP (User Location Policy) and SLP (Space Location Policy). ULP means the location policy of a user. SLP means the location policy of the Smart Space. When a user set up her or his location policy as to who know her or his location, the user can set up the policy based on user or user group. In addition, the user selects the location granularity such as space or shopping mall. This means one person is informed of the name of the space in which the user is, and the other person is informed the fact that the user is within the shopping mall. In addition, time zone can be set up in establishing a location policy. A user can put a priority into the policy to be established.

ULP is defined as follows.
ULP = Set of ULPE
ULPE = {UserId, Granularity, TimeZone, Priority}
UserId = User | UserGroup | Any
Granularity = SpaceName | ZoneName
TimeZone = { startTime, endTime }
Priority = High | Mid | Low

ULP is made up of ULPE set. ULPE is a location policy corresponding to each user. ULPE includes UserId, Granularity, TimeZone and Priority. UserId has a value among User, UserGroup and Any. User represents one user identifier such as real name and social security number. UserGroup represents a group including some related users such as friends or colleague. Any means all people. Granularity is classified as SpaceName and ZoneName. The former represent the name of Space which is some information on space location. The latter means that its policy allows inquirer only to know that the policy owner is within the shopping mall. All inquirers are allowed to get the user location information only within TimeZone. TimeZone consists of startTime and endTime. The former means beginning time and the latter ending time. In addition, Priority means a value of importance about the policy. Priority has a value among High, Mid and Low. High takes precedence over Mid and Low. Mid has priority to Low.

SLP is defined as follows.
SLP = Set of SLPE
SLPE = {SLPUserId, Granularity, TimeZone, Priority}
SLPUserId = SpaceId | SpaceGroup | User | UserGroup | ShopManager | Any
Granularity = UserName | UserCount
Priority = Emergency | High | Mid | Low

The configuration of SLP is similar to ULP with some difference. SLPuserId has a value among SpaceId, User, ShopManager and Any. SpaceId represents one Space identifier such as real name of the Space. SpaceGroup represents a group whose members are in the same category of business such as food shops, video shops and etc. ShopManager means the manager or manager space of the shopping mall. Granularity is classified as UserName and UserCount. The former means that the space informs inquirers of the real names of the users within it. The latter means that the space informs inquirers of the count of the users within it. In SLP, Priority may have an additional value, Emergency. Emergency may be used for emergent cases such as fire in the shopping mall. So, Emergency takes highest priority to other priority values.

ULP and SLP define the location policy of users and Smart Space, respectively. So, their policies possibly come into conflict with each other. For example, a user allows exposure of her or his location by ULP. But the Space which the user is within, set up SLP not to inform the locations of its users. Such a case creates a conflict between ULP and SLP. Many resolution methods are acceptable. We think that user private decision takes precedence over the decision of a Space. But emergency case such as fire must be firstly treated than other case. So, we give ULP a high priority over SLP except for the emergency case of the shopping mall. We solve the conflicting policies as following resolutions rules

1. The Emergency of SLP takes highest priority.
2. In case the priorities of ULP and SLP are different, the one with higher priority takes precedence over the other.
3. In case the priorities of ULP and SLP are the same, ULP takes precedence over SLP.

Assume that the ULP of Alice and SLP of Space A are set up as follows. Alice'ULP = { {Bob, SpaceName, (0000, 2400), High}, {Carol, ZoneName, (0000, 2400) Mid}}

Space A's SLP = { {Any, UserCount, (0000, 2400), Mid}, {Carol, UserName, (0000, 2400), Mid}, {ShopManager, UserName, (0000, 2400), Emergency}}

If Alice enters Space A, RLP (Resolved Location Policy) are determined according to the above policy resolution rules.

RLP of Alice at Space A: { {Bob, SpaceName, (0000, 2400)}, {Carol, ZoneName, (0000, 2400) }, {ShopManager, SpaceName, (0000, 2400) }}

We can answer various queries by the derived RLP. When Bob asks the location of Alice, Space A informs him of the name of the Space. When Carol asks the location of Alice, Space A informs her of the fact that Alice is within the shopping mall. In case ShopManager asks the location of Alice, Space A responds with exact location of the Space.

4.3   Privacy Protection System Architecture

Figure 4 shows the architecture of location service system where the proposed location privacy protection mechanism is adapted.

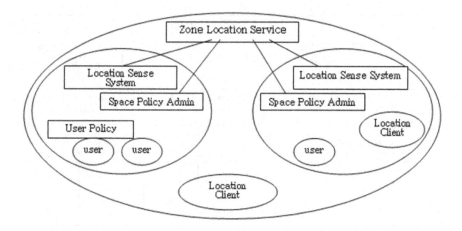

Fig. 4. The Architecture of Location Service System

- **Zone Location Service** provides the location information as to users.,
- **Location Sense System.** The subject of a record should be able to see and correct the record.,
- **Location Client** is a client to ask Zone Location Service about the locations of users and Smart Space.,
- **Space Policy Admin** is a tool to set up and manage location privacy policies of user.

Location service is provided in the next steps

1. When a user enters a Smart Space, Zone Location Service interacts with User Policy Agent and retrieves her or his ULP. Then, the Space resolves the ULP and its SLP, and calculates a RLP to be applied while the user is in the Space. The Space maintains a record until the user exits the Space. The record consists of user id, space name and RLP.
2. When a Location Client asks for the location information of specific user, the Space provides location information according to the stored record with user id, space name and RLP.

Figure 5 shows detailed architecture of location service system. If a user enters a new Space, Location Monitor which monitors Location Sense System, senses users entrance and asks policy resolution of Policy Manager. Policy Manager retrieves the SLP to be set up and stored by Space Policy Admin. Policy Manager interacts with User Policy Agent and then acquires the ULP of the user. Then, Policy Manager calculates user's RLP at the Space and returns the RLP to Location Monitor. Location Monitor stores the returned RLP together with user id and space name in User Location DB.

If Location Client asks for the location information of specific user, Privacy Controller searches User Location DB for a record with appropriate RLP and

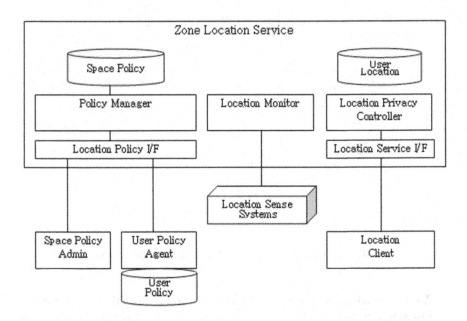

Fig. 5. The Detailed Architecture of Location Service System

provides proper location information according to retrieved RLP. If Client asks the count of users within specific Space, Location Privacy Controller asks SLP of Privacy Manager and then provides proper location information by retrieved RLP.

5   Conclusion

In this paper, we proposed a location privacy protection mechanism based on policy for Ubicomp. At first, we derived a feasible scenario for Ubiquitous Shopping Mall where users took shopping or did some business works. Then, we defined Smart Space to realize the derived scenario into Ubicomp. After that, we presented conceptual security model for Smart Space. Smart Space consists of Privacy Protection Space and Trust Space as well as Non-Intrusive Authentication and Access Control mechanism. Among the various security requirements, we focused on location privacy. The reason is that the location information in Ubicomp is collected more extensively than before and this increases the possibility to violate personal privacy. The proposed mechanism was based on policies of user and Smart Space. We define ULP as user location policy and SLP as Space location policy. When a user enters a Smart Space, we calculate Resolved Location Policy by using the users ULP and the Space'SLP. If the polices conflicts with each other, we solve the problem with Policy Resolution Rules. The rules give the highest priority to emergent affairs such as fire. If the polices are equal with each other, we give higher priority to users policy because we think that the privacy of a user is more important than the normal policy of shopping mall. In addition, we presented system architecture for the proposed mechanism.

In the future, we need to design the system for the proposed mechanism and implement the system to demonstrate a feasibility of the mechanism. We need further researches for the prevention mechanism of location privacy tracing. Moreover, privacy assurance framework is required so that the privacy is properly enforced based on location privacy policy.

References

[1] Weiser, M.: The Computer for the Twenty-First Century. Scientific American, Vol. 256, No. 3, pp. 94–104, September (1991)
[2] Ha, W., et at.: Confusion of Physical Space and Electronic Space: Ubiquitous IT Revolution and the Third Space. Korean Electronic Times, (2002)
[3] Sakamura, K.: Ubiquitous Computing. Dongbang Media Books, (2002)
[4] Techno-Economics Research Department.: Ubicomp Research Trends. ETRI (2002)
[5] Langheinrich, M.: A Privacy Awareness System for Ubiquitous Computing Environments. UbiComp 2002:Ubiquitous Computing, LNCS 2498, pp. 237 245, (2002)
[6] Al-Muhtadi, J., et al.: A Flexible, Privacy-Preserving Authentication Framework for Ubiquitous Computing Environments. IEEE ICDCSW Proc of the 22nd, (2002)
[7] Hengartner, U., Steenkiste, P.: Protection People Location Information. Proc. of Workshop on Security in Ubiquitous Computing, September, (2002)
[8] Myles, G., et al.: Preserving Privacy in Environments with Location-Based Applications. Pervasive Computing, IEEE, Vol. 2, No. 1, pp. 56–64, (2003)
[9] Langheinrich, M.: Privacy by Design - Principles of Privacy-Aware Ubiquitous System. UbiComp 2001:Ubiquitous Computing, LNCS 2201, pp. 273–291, (2001)
[10] OECD.: Recommendation of the council concerning guidelines governing the protection of privacy and transborder flows of personal data. September (1980)
[11] European Commission.: Directive 95/46/ec of the European parliament and of the council of 24 October 1995 on the protection of individuals with regard to the processing of personal data and on the free movement of such data. November (1995)
[12] Cranor, L., et al.: The Platform for privacy preferences 1.0(P3P1.0) specification. W3C Recommendation, HTML Version at www.w3.org/TR/P3P/, April (2002)

Secure System Architecture
Based on Dynamic Resource Reallocation

Byoung Joon Min[1], Sung Ki Kim[1], and Joong Sup Choi[2]

[1]Dept. of Computer Science and Engineering, University of Incheon,
177, Dohwa-dong, Nam-gu, Incheon 402-749, Republic of Korea
{bjmin, proteras}@incheon.ac.kr
[2]Korea Information Security Agency,
78, Karak-dong, Songpa-gu, Seoul 138-160, Republic of Korea
jschoi@kisa.or.kr

Abstract. A secure system architecture using a two-level approach is presented in this paper. At the node level, by means of dynamic resource reallocation within a computing node, the critical services previously selected are to survive even after the occurrence of an attack. If it becomes impossible to find enough resources for the services within the node in spite of the adaptive actions taken at the node level, it moves to the system level. The system level mechanism is to deliver the intended services transparently to the clients even when a node fails by means of inter-node resource reallocation. An architecture adopting diverse redundant computing nodes is proposed for that purpose. Through the experiments on a test-bed, especially, for web services, the approach turned out very effective to cope with not only denial of service attacks but also confidentiality and integrity attacks.

1 Introduction

Most of networked information systems adopt intrusion prevention mechanisms such as cryptography and authentication for the purpose of the confidentiality and the integrity of the information. Nevertheless, many successful attacks exploiting various vulnerabilities are found in the systems. Intrusion detection systems can effectively detect pre-defined attacks but have limitations in responding to continuously created novel attacks.

In the mean time, the concept of intrusion tolerance has been presented in recent researches [7]. The purpose of the intrusion tolerance is to maintain critical services at the acceptable level of service quality even in the presence of compromised components in a system due to intrusions. It urges to change the objective of security. The objective of security has been primarily elimination of the intentional threats on the operation of a system by creating barriers between the system and the threats. For complex open systems the barriers may be undesirable and impractical. Now, we need to consider applying some of fault tolerant techniques to the system security for the construction of the system that can tolerate intrusions. In mission critical systems, the need for intrusion tolerance is very high. In order to enforce the survivability of the

K. Chae and M. Yung (Eds.): WISA 2003, LNCS 2908, pp. 174–187, 2004.

critical services that have to be maintained under any circumstances, the concept of adaptability and diversity from fault tolerance can be used.

The goal of the research presented in this paper is to enforce the survivability of pre-defined mission critical services. In order to achieve this goal, two fundamental techniques from the fault-tolerance and dependable computing researches are adopted. One is reallocating resources within a computing node, which is to enable the critical services to survive in the node even after the occurrence of a successful system attack. The resource reallocation may accompany the degradation of overall performance and the sacrifice of non-critical services. The other technique is applying diverse redundant servers at the system level. This is to continue mission critical services transparently to the clients even when a node fails.

When a computing node is attacked, the impacts within the node can be classified into the following three groups in general. An attack called DOS(Denial of Services) exhausts resources such as CPU power, memory space, and I/O bandwidth. Or, some attacks may create unauthorized files or modify existing files. Lastly, by some attacks, system calls and commands are executed in the node [2].

In general, we need to take the following three major steps to respond to system attacks for the purpose of intrusion tolerance: intrusion detection, isolation of compromised components, and recovery [5]. The basic idea of the approach proposed in this paper is to adopt the mechanisms developed at the node-level and at the system-level as summarized in Figure 1.

	Detection	Isolation	Recovery
Node Level • Resource reallocation	Monitoring resource usage	Reallocating resources for critical services	
System Level • Diverse redundant servers • Surveillance through out of band network	Both acceptance testing on results and comparing results of servers	Cutting-off the compromised node by reconfiguration	Rejoining the recovered node under the control of the surveillant

Fig. 1. Basic idea of the proposed approach. A two-level approach for the intrusion tolerance is presented in the paper. It aims at enforcing the survivability of critical services even in the presence of compromised component in computing nodes.

At the node level, each node tries to adaptively reallocate its resources for the critical services selected by the system manager. A reallocation algorithm within a node is proposed. The algorithm is helpful when enough resources are found in the computing node after the reallocation procedure. If it becomes impossible, delivery of the services should rely on another computing node. For the system level, redundant computing nodes are applied. The redundant architecture proposed in the paper is composed of N concurrent active nodes and one hot standby backup node. There is also a surveillance node to control and mediate the computing nodes. The servers running on the computing node are based on diversity. They use different software modules on different platforms with the same design goals. Both acceptance test and vote are used to detect the abnormal situation. Upon the detection, the suspect node is isolated and the backup newly joins as one of active nodes. When the suspected node is repaired, it becomes a new backup under the supervision of the surveillance node.

The rest of the paper is organized as follows. Section 2 summarizes related research results and explains the contribution of the research presented in the paper. In Section 3, a resource reallocation algorithm is presented. It describes the actions to be taken at the node level in order response to the attacks exhausting resources in the node. Section 4 is to explain an architecture adopting diverse replication. It includes the operational steps in detail for the system level response. For the validation of the approach, a test-bed has been implemented and experiments have been conducted. In Section 5, the results of the experiments are presented. Finally, Section 6 concludes the paper.

2   Related Works

Intrusion tolerance is to be prepared for the still remaining vulnerabilities of a system. Unless identifying all the vulnerabilities of the system, intrusion prevention and intrusion detection cannot be perfectly worked out [1].

One of important research efforts related the intrusion tolerance has been conducted in IST(Information Security Technologies) programs at European Commission [9]. It has contributed toward the dependability support to enforce the trust of systems. Another important research activities have been carried out with the support of DARPA.

In [3], the concept of resource reallocation is presented as a security responsive technology. A managing controller of a system decides which action should be taken with a limited amount of communication and computing resources. With the proper resource reallocation, predefined critical processes can be protected from a certain type of security attacks. The concrete algorithm and demonstration of resource reallocation, however, have not been fully presented yet.

One of the previous researches on diverse replication is found in HACQIT(Hierarchical Adaptive Control of Quality of service for Intrusion Tolerance) project [6]. In the architecture, a firewall controls the access to the servers. The primary and backup servers provide the desired services. A monitor controls the servers, and has an out-of-bands communication channels so that services can be reconfigured dynamically as needed. The intrusion detection relies on the conventional error detection mechanism. If the results of the two servers are not same, it decides that one of the two is compromised based on a fairly simple comparison of the status codes generated from HTTP servers. The architecture can be easily constructed with COTS (Commercial Off The Shelf) servers. However, the detection mechanism is too weak to handle more complicated situations. Besides, it is hard to extend the architecture once an attack is treated since the goal itself of the architecture is to provide four hours of intrusion tolerance.

Another example of diverse replication is SITAR(Scalable Intrusion-Tolerance Architecture) [8]. This architecture is composed of proxy servers, acceptance monitors, ballot monitors, an audit controller, and an adaptive reconfiguration module with COTS servers. Proxy servers provide public access points for COTS servers. The acceptance monitors apply certain validity check to the responses, and forward them to the ballot monitors along with an indication of the check results. The ballot monitors serve as representatives for the respective COTS servers and decide on a final response. The adaptive reconfiguration module receives intrusion trigger information from other module, and generates a new configuration according to the evaluation. This architecture is scalable. The configuration is very flexible. However, it seems very hard to implement and impractical because of its cost and complexity.

The contribution of this paper is demonstrating a practical approach to intrusion tolerance. A concrete algorithm for resource reallocation is developed as an adaptive response to the attacks exhausting resources. By combining the adaptability of each server and the diversity of replicated servers, we can reduce the cost incurred by frequent system reconfiguration while considering the aggregated user performance. The approach proposed in the paper aims at handling not only denial of service attacks but also confidentiality and integrity attacks with reasonable amount of timing overheads.

3   Resource Reallocation Algorithm

In this section, an algorithm for resource reallocation within a node is presented. It is to maintain critical services even after the occurrence of intrusion, especially DOS compromise, in a computing node.

The services are divided into two classes: critical and non-critical. The algorithm is concerned with the critical services. Executing non-critical services in a node is just to obtain better aggregate user performance.

The resource reallocation in a node is to provide enough resources for the critical services. This can be achieved by sacrificing non-critical services. One important issue here is how to evaluate the survivability of critical services, that is, whether enough resources for the critical services exist or not. Another important issue is which non-critical service should be terminated first in the reallocation procedure.

For the execution of a service in a computing node, it has to provide a certain level of resources including CPU, memory, and I/O. However, it is not easy to assert the exact level of the required resources for each critical service. Of course, it is impractical to reserve resources in advance for all critical services. In order to resolve the first issue mentioned above, baseline and ATEEB (accumulated time elapsed in excess of the baseline) are used in the algorithm. The baseline of a service implies the minimum amount of resource shares required in order to provide the service at the minimal acceptable level of the service quality. It can be established for each resource, for example, CPU, memory, and I/O. The ATEEB is used to compromise the abruptness that may happen in an instant. It is assumed that the ATEEB of a service should be greater than a threshold when the service is delivered properly.

In order to resolve the second issue mentioned above, the accumulated times not only for critical services but also for non-critical services with default baselines are measured periodically. When a critical service needs more resources, a non-critical service holing the most of the resources is sacrificed first. The algorithm works as follows;

(1) Baseline for the resource usage in total is also established. When the ATEEB for the total usage is below the threshold, which means that there exist plenty of unoccupied resources, the algorithm keeps on monitoring the resource usage.

(2) When the ATEEB for the total usage becomes above the threshold, the amount of resources occupied by each critical service should be checked. If the ATEEB of a critical service is above the threshold, the algorithm keeps on monitoring the resource usage. Otherwise, the algorithm needs to figure out the reason why it cannot obtain enough resources.

(3) In order to recognize the circumstance, the algorithm withdraws some amount of resources intentionally by controlling the priority of the process for the non-critical service occupying the most of the resources. If the ATEEB of the critical service does not increase even when more resources become available, the algorithm concludes that the critical service does not require more resources, and it returns the withdrawn resources to the non-critical service before gets back to the monitoring stage.

(4) However, if the ATEEB of the critical service increases after taking resources from the non-critical service, which means that they have been competing for the resources, the algorithm tries to terminate the non-critical service by force.

Figure 2 depicts the detail of the algorithm presented in a pseudo code.

```
{resource reallocation algorithm}
{assume that there are m critical service processes and n non-critical service processes}

var
  EP[m] : array of essential process id's;
  DP[n] : array of dispensable process id's;
  TotalResourceUsage, BaselineTotal, ResourceUsage[], Baseline[] : integer;

procedure Resource_Reallocation(m, n : integer);
var
  i : integer;
begin
  if CheckTotalResourceUsage(mon_slot, threshold) then
  begin
    if (CheckEssentialServiceResourceUsage(m, mon_slot, threshold) < > m) then
    begin
      sort dispensable processes stored in DP[n] in descending order of resource
        usage;
      for  i := 1 to n do
      begin
        withdraw resource of DP[i];
        if EssentialServiceResourceUsage has increased then
          terminate DP[i];
        else
          restore the withdrawn resource to DP[i]
      end;
    end;
  end;
end;
```

Fig.2. Resource reallocation algorithm in a node. In the pseudo code, we assume that there exist m critical service processes and n non-critical service processes.

```
function CheckTotalResourceUsage(mon_slot, threshold : integer) : boolean;
var
  i, excessCount : integer;
begin
  excessCount := 0;
  for i := 1 to mon_slot do
    if TotalResourceUsage > BaselineTotal then
      excessCount := excessCount + 1;
  if excessCount > threshold then
    CheckTotalResourceUsage := true;
  else
    CheckTotalResourceUsage := false
end;

function CheckEssentialServiceResourceUsage(m, mon_slot, threshold[m] : integer) :
integer;
var
  i, j, k, excessCount : integer;
begin
  k := 0;
  for i := 1 to m do
   begin
    excessCount := 0;
    for j := 1 to mon_slot do
      if ResourceUsage[EP[i]] > Baseline[EP[i]] then
        excessCount := excessCount + 1;
    if excessCount > threshold[i] then
      k := k + 1
   end;
  CheckEssentialServiceResourceUsage := k
end;
```

Fig.2. Resource reallocation algorithm in a node. In the pseudo code, we assume that there exist m critical service processes and n non-critical service processes.

With this algorithm, resources for critical services can be provided. When a critical service selected by the system manager depends on other services, they also should be protected as critical services. This algorithm assumes that there is no threat within the critical services. If an attack sneaks into a critical service component to exhaust resources, the algorithm would not be able to allocate enough resources for other un-compromised critical services. This is the limitation of the algorithm. Nevertheless, it will be a cost-effective protection mechanism within a node for critical services against DOS attacks.

4 Replicated Server Architecture

When it becomes impossible to find enough resources for the execution of critical services within a node, the critical services should rely on another computing node prepared in the system. This section presents the architecture for the system level response.

In general, we can divide the replication into two classes according to the status of the replicated node. One is active replication and the other is passive replication. In the active replication, a set of active nodes executes the request concurrently, and majority is voted as the result. The number of replicated nodes depends on the fault model and the execution conditions. A failed node may roll back to a safe state called checkpoint and retry the execution for the recovery. In the passive replication, one primary node is in active while other backup nodes are in passive. The primary node that has passed its acceptance test delivers the result. If the primary fails its acceptance test, one of backup nodes takes the role of the primary. Again, the status of the backup nodes can be either hot standby or cold standby. A hot standby backup node is always ready to be in the active state, while a cold standby backup node needs some amount of time to make its proper status.

An architecture based on N+1 replication using both acceptance test and vote is proposed in this paper. It has the following characteristics:

• The architecture consists of N active nodes and one hot standby backup node. A front-end node provides clients with the access point on behalf of the server nodes. A surveillance node is connected with the other nodes through a separate out of band network.

• Since the backup node is always ready to be in active, not only the fast reconfiguration is possible but also consecutive attacks can be treated with the architecture.

• By utilizing both acceptance test and vote for the intrusion detection triggering, it is possible to reduce the latency incurred by the replication and to increase the detection coverage with the reduced dependency of acceptance test on the application.

• In order to raise the aggregate performance of the replicate nodes, synchronization among active nodes is very restricted. Most of the time, each computing node asynchronously responds to the requests as they arrive in the node. Only the responses of critical services are collected and forwarded by the surveillance node.

Using both acceptance test and vote is also to overcome their limitations. In general, two aspects have been tested by the acceptance test, one is testing logical reasonableness of the result and the other is testing on the bound of the execution time. Since the test requires a certain level of understanding of the application, it is hard to generate a high coverage acceptance test in a systematic way. In the vote, since it waits all the results from the replicas, the system performance is tied up with the slowest node. As we adopt both acceptance test and vote for the intrusion detection, the acceptance test doesn't have to be complicated to produce the high coverage and at the same time the voter has little chance to wait in vain for the result from a failed node.

The number N depends on the number of intrusions to be tolerated during the execution time of a request. According to the Byzantine algorithm in [4], the following formula satisfies: $3t \leq N$, where t is the number of nodes which could go wrong in an arbitrary manner except disturbing the execution of other normal nodes. With this assumption, if two thirds of N nodes have passed their acceptance with the same result on a request, the surveillance node can deliver the result to the client without waiting other responses from the rest.

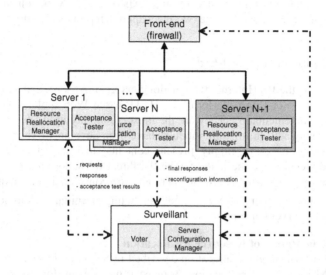

Fig. 3. Replication architecture proposed in the paper. In the figure, initially, Sever 1 to Server N are concurrent active nodes and Server N+1 is a hot standby backup node. Since the surveillant is connected to other nodes through a separate network as denoted with dotted lines, the clients including malicious attackers cannot access the surveillant.

The operational scenario is as follows:

(1) The clients' requests to critical services are delivered to N active nodes through the front-end node. Active servers execute the same requests to critical services autonomously. Results of requests to the critical services are forwarded to the surveillant along with the acceptance test results. One the other hand, a request to a non-critical service is responded by one of active nodes and the response is delivered to the client through the front-end node.

(2) Intrusion detection can be triggered either by an acceptance tester in each node or by the voter in the surveillant. Once an intrusion is detected, the compromised node is isolated from the system by the surveillant, and the backup node replaces it immediately. In order to do that, the backup node has kept on updating its status with the help of the surveillant.

(3) When the compromised node is repaired, it rejoins the system as a new backup node. Again this backup node updates its status with the coordination of the surveillant.

5   Implementation and Experiments

This section presents the results of the experimental work on a tested-bed implemented in order to validate the two-level approach proposed in the paper.

5.1   Implementation of a Test-Bed

For the diversity, the IIS (Internet Information Services), Apache, and Tomcat servers on either Windows or Linux platforms for HTTP-based Web applications have been chosen in the implementation. They are the most commonly used Web servers in the Internet and many add-on software modules have been developed. The server has two types of codes: one is to simply present contents, and the other is to provide functional services. Since the latter can be the threat to the system, service requests containing script codes with data write operations are considered in the experiment.

The test-bed consists of four server nodes including an initial backup node, a front-end node, and a surveillance node.

5.1.1   Implementation of Resource Reallocation

The algorithm for resource reallocation described in Section 3 has been implemented as the RRM(Resource Reallocation Manager) module in Figure 2. The RRM implemented as an application object provides a user interface to establish critical services with the baseline and the ATEEB. The RRM uses services internally provided by two threads called HMT(Health Monitor Thread) and SET(Survivability Evaluation Thread). The internal relationship among these components is described in Figure 4.

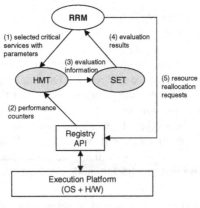

HMT : Health Monitor Thread
SET : Survivability Evaluation Thread

Fig. 4. The HMT collects performance related counters from the operating system through API(Application Program Interface). The information is forwarded to the SET that is actually executing the testing part of the algorithm. The result of the evaluation is reported to RRM. Then the RRM uses the API to control the priorities of services or to terminate services. The RRM reports its status periodically to the SCM(Server Configuration Manager) in the surveillant.

5.1.2 Implementation of Replicated Server Architecture

The architecture presented in Section 4 has been implemented as the Front-end, the Agent, and the Surveillant.

(1) Implementation of Front-end

The Front-end receives requests from clients. First, it recognizes the service class. For the request to a critical service, it puts a unique identification number and the arrival time to the request before forwards the request to all active nodes. In order to process multiple requests simultaneously, it uses a pool of connection objects. A message format is used to forward the information to the Agent in each active node. The message contains not only the request and response data but also the information on each node's role and status. On the other hand, a request to non-critical service is distributed to one of active nodes in a Round Robin style.

(2) Implementation of Agent

The Agent receives the message containing the client's request. After the request is executed, it conducts acceptance test on the result. Test is based on the specification of the Web application. Another function of the Agent is to forward the execution and acceptance test results to the surveillant. Before forwarding the message to the surveillant, the agent unifies various URL extensions caused by diversity of Web servers and platforms.

(3) Implementation of Surveillant

As the surveillant receives messages from Agents of actives nodes, it conducts vote. The vote is completed with the first two identical responses arrived. The voted response is stored in its own database and also forwarded to the backup node and the Front-end node.

SCM controls the reconfiguration of the system. When intrusion detection is triggered, it isolates the suspected active node from the system. The isolated node is replaced with the backup node.

5.2 Experimental Results

Experiments have been conducted in order to verify the ability of the system to respond to simulated attacks and to measure the timing overheads or the loss in throughput introduced by the mechanisms explained so for.

For the experimentation, various Web servers including IIS and tomcat were used on diverse platforms as shown in Figure 5.

	Server 1	Server 2	Server 3	Server 4
CPU	P3-600MHz	P4-1.7GHz	P3-833MHz	Duron-800MHz
Memory	128MByte	256MByte	256MByte	256MByte
Operating System	Linux 7.0	Windows2000	Linux 7.0	WindowsXP

Fig. 5. Platform used for the experimentation.

On the platforms, the following three types of service requests were considered.

• Type A : Simple read of HTML file or DB data only

• Type B : Script execution, mainly simple computation

• Type C : DB write operation included

In order to check the responsiveness of the system, the following two types of attacks have been simulated in the experiments.

(1) DOS attack

The attack is simulated by introducing a heavily resource consuming process into a computing node, such as video streaming. By triggering the process as a critical and/or non-critical service in the middle of normal operation, a DOS attack can be simulated.

(2) Integrity attack

By inserting a program that modifies files or data in the database, integrity attack can be simulated.

Figure 6 shows an example of results of experiments on resource reallocation. For the experiment, a video application as a non-critical service is triggered to operation in order to simulate a DOS attack. In the figure, horizontal axis represents time and the vertical axis represents CPU usage. The sampling of monitored information is done in every 0.5 second. The RRM makes decision to control the priorities of services in every 25 seconds in the example. The baseline of the critical service is set to 25 percent. The amount of CPU resources used by the critical service is denoted by darker line. The thinner dotted line represents the resource used by a non-critical service. At the point of 25 second, since ATEEB is down below the threshold, the RRM puts lower priority on the non-critical service. During next 25 seconds, the resource usage of the critical service has increased. Therefore, RRM decided to terminate the non-critical service at the point of 50 seconds.

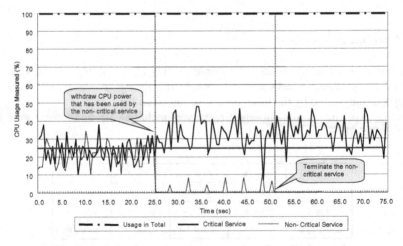

Fig. 6. A result of experiment on resource reallocation in a node.

The sampling rate affects the timing overheads. The RRM decision period should be selected carefully. If it is too short, RRM may make a misjudgment inducing unnecessary termination of non-critical services. On the other hand, it reacts very slowly if it is too long.

In order to measure the timing overhead incurred by the resource reallocation and diverse replication, the average execution time (turn around time) of above three types of requests on a typical clustered server architecture first. Data consistency is maintained, and the requests are distributed in the Round Robin fashion. The average turn around times for request type A, B, and C when the proposed approach is not applied are 21.9msec, 12.3msec, and 28.1msec, respectively. The numbers were obtained through more than 10 times measurements during 120 seconds interval each.

Request Pattern	Time Elapsed in Each System Component			Total Time	Overhead (Overhead / Total Time)
	Front-end	Server including RRM	Surveillant		
A	1.7	41.6	1.4	44.7	22.8 (51%)
B	1.9	18.8	1.0	21.7	9.4 (43%)
C	1.8	49.2	1.3	52.3	24.2 (46%)

(unit : msec)

Fig. 7. Timing overhead measured.

With the same condition of the request generation, average turn around times on each request type were measured on the test-bed implemented. The results are summarized in Figure 7. As shown in the figure, most of the timing overhead is introduced in the execution of the server nodes, which consist of RRM, Agent, and Service objects.

Since the Java language was used for the implementation, the execution speed was dragged down especially for the monitoring in RRM. Another obstacle is from the difference of the platforms. The Agent wastes times to maintain connections with diverse servers. It seems the limitation in utilizing COTS components in the implementation.

In order to make the approach more practical some other aspects should be considered in further study. Front-end can be implemented in hardware to reduce both timing overhead and security vulnerabilities. Coordination with IDS will be desirable. A smart vote is needed rather than a brute force comparison of the result data.

6 Conclusion

An approach to intrusion tolerance has been presented in this paper. The approach functions in two levels. At the node level, the dynamic resource reallocation algorithm helps the critical services previously selected by the system manager survive even after the occurrence of DOS attacks. If an attack sneaks into a critical service component to exhaust resources, the algorithm would not be able to allocate enough resources for other un-compromised critical services. In such a case, a system level mechanism is needed to keep on delivering the intended critical services transparently to the clients. The N+1 replication architecture has been proposed in this paper to provide a system-level support. As long as we can assume that only one computing node out of three nodes with diversity is compromised during one execution cycle, concurrent diverse replicas can continue the mission. By utilizing both acceptance test and vote for the intrusion detection triggering, it is possible to reduce the latency incurred by the replication and to increase the detection coverage and accuracy with the reduced dependency of acceptance test on the application.

Experimental results obtained on a test-bed reveal the validity of the proposed approach. Especially, for web applications, it can handle not only DOS attacks but also confidentiality and integrity attacks with reasonable amount of timing overheads. By combining the adaptability of each server and the diversity of replicated servers, we can reduce the cost incurred by frequent system reconfiguration. In order to make the approach more practical, we will need to consider a tradeoff between the throughput of the system and the prompt responsiveness to attacks in the further study.

Acknowledgements. This work is supported by University IT Research Center Project, by RRC at the University of Incheon, and by Korea Information Security Agency Research Project.

References

1. Matti A. Hiltunen, et. al, "Survivability through Customization and Adaptability: The Cactus Approach", DARPA Information Survivability Conference & EXposition, pp.294–306, 0-7695-0490-6/99 1999.
2. Andrew P. Moore, "Attack Modeling for Information Security and Survivability", Technical Node, CMU/SEI-2001-TN-001, CMU 2001.
3. National Security Agency, Defence Advanced Research Projects Agency, Office of the Assistant Secretary of Defence, "Securing the U.S Defence Information Infrastructures: A Proposed Approach", Technical Report, 1998.
4. Marshall Pease, Robert Shostak, Leslie Lamport, "Reaching Agreement in the Presence of Faults", Journal of the ACM 27/2 pp. 228–234 1980.
5. Brian Randell, "Dependability - Unifying Concept", Computer Security, Dependability & Assurance: From Needs to Solutions, ISBN 0-7695-0337-3/99, 1998.
6. J. Reynolds, et. al, "The Design and Implementation of an Intrusion Tolerant System", Proc. of Int'l Conference on Dependable Systems and Networks, pp. 258–290, Washington D.C., June 2002.

7. V. Stavridou, et. al, "Intrusion Tolerant Software Architectures", DARPA Information Survivability Conference & EXposition, ISBN 0-7695-1212-7/01, Anaheim, June 2001.
8. Feiyi Wang, et. al, "SITAR: A Scalable Intrusion-Tolerant Architecture for Distributed Services", Proc. of 2001 IEEE Workshop on Information Assurance and Security US Military Academy, pp.38–45, West Point, NY, June 2001.
9. Marc Wilikens, et. al., "Defining the European Dependability Initiative", Dependability & Assurance: From Needs to Solutions, Report of the Workshop on Dependability of Critical Systems and Services in the Information Society, Italy, Dec. 1997.

Fair Exchange with Guardian Angels

Gildas Avoine and Serge Vaudenay

Swiss Federal Institute of Technology (EPFL)
lasecwww.epfl.ch

Abstract. In this paper we propose a new probabilistic Fair Exchange Protocol which requires no central Trusted Third Party. Instead, it relies on a virtually distributed and decentralized Trusted Third Party which is formalized as a Guardian Angel: a kind of Observer e.g. a tamper proof security device. We thus introduce a network model with Pirates and Guardian Angels which is well suited for Ad Hoc networks.
In this setting we reduce the Fair Exchange Problem to a Synchronization Problem in which honest parties need to eventually decide whether or not a protocol succeeded in a synchronous way through a hostile network which does not guaranty that sent messages will be eventually received. This problem can be of independent interest in order to add reliability of protocol termination in secure channels.

Keywords: Fair Exchange, Security Module, Synchronization, Distributed Systems.

1 Introduction

In the Fair Exchange problem, two participants A and B wish to exchange items k_A and k_B in a fair way, i.e. such that either both participants receive the expected item, or nobody can obtain anything valuable. In addition to the fairness property, we generally require that a fair exchange protocol should obey the following properties:

- **Completeness:** the exchange always succeeds when the involved participants behave honestly.
- **Timeliness:** the participants always have the ability to reach, in a finite amount of time, a step in the protocol where they can fairly stop the exchange.

The completeness property avoids the trivial fair protocol where no information at all is exchanged. On the other hand, protocols with infinite communication complexity are avoided by the timeliness property. With regard to the fairness property, literature brings a lot of general or specific definitions [16,22,23,26,29, 36,37].

The basic exchange scheme, where the participants send their items one after the other, is obviously unfair: neither A and B would like to be first to send its item since the first receiver can disrupt the protocol without sending its own item.

K. Chae and M. Yung (Eds.): WISA 2003, LNCS 2908, pp. 188–202, 2004.

Non-perfect fair exchange protocols were proposed in the early eighties in order to decrease the unfairness, involving a complexity cost in term of exchanged messages. These *gradual protocols* are based on the following scheme: each entity alternatively transmits successive bits of the item to exchange until the last bit of each item was sent (the lengths of the items are supposedly equal). (See for example [8,10,11,25,30].) In order to improve this kind of protocol, fractions of bits can be transmitted instead of real bits [31,32]. When the protocol aborts and one party receives the exchanged item, the *a posteriori* computation of the missing bits is made possible to the other party by the protocol. This induces a computation cost. Hence, real fairness of gradual protocols relies on A and B having approximately the same computational power.

The introduction of perfect fairness in these protocols faces to the impossibility result of Even-Yacobi [13], without the help of third parties.

One can achieve perfect fairness with the help of a *Trusted Third Party* (TTP) in the scheme. The first proposed protocols used an *on-line* Trusted Third Party which assures the fairness during the exchanges. The main drawback with this kind of protocol is that it creates a communication bottleneck: TTP must interfere at least once during the protocol. A great improvement of TTP protocols is to use *off-line* Trusted Third Party. Asokan introduced the notion of *optimistic* fairness where the TTP is required only in case of dispute. (See e.g. [1,2,3,4,5,24,28,29,33].) The efficiency of this approach relies on the fact that the environment is mostly honest.

Even if there exists a great body of literature on fair exchange, only one fair exchange protocol, up to our knowledge, tries to take advantage of the presence of security modules [34,35] to enforce fairness, by devising an optimistic fair exchange protocol for electronic commerce. We briefly describe it here. In this protocol, four entities interfere in the exchange: the client, his security module (e.g. a smart card), the vendor (which does not have security module), and the vendor's bank (which is called only in case of conflict). The sketch of the protocol is the following. (1) The vendor sends the item and its description to the client's security module. (2) The client sends the payment and the expected item's description to his security module. (3) After checking item and payment, the security module sends the payment to the vendor. (4) Finally, if the payment is correct, then the vendor must send a payment acknowledgment to the security module, and then later gives the expected item to the client. If the vendor does not send the acknowledgment (he already has the payment), the bank is called in order to restore the fairness. Thus this falls into the optimistic fair exchange protocols category which requires an (off-line) TTP and the assumption that vendors are mostly honest.

All those protocols rely on the assumption that both parties can have access to the TTP though a channel which achieves timeliness: any request to the TTP gets addressed, eventually. This is quite a strong assumption, for instance in mobile systems where an adversary may control all communications in one network cell. In some environments, like mobile ad hoc networks [19,20], introducing a timely-available unique Trusted Third Party is not desirable nor possible; therefore optimistic protocols are not suitable. We rather concentrate on a Chaum *et Al.*'s observer-based third party. We assume that all participants have one timely-available observer (e.g. a smart card). The originality of this model for fair exchange is that one party may not be able to contact the observer of another party though a timely channel. We can still propose a protocol which ensures probabilistic fairness, without centralized Trusted Third Party, and without assumption on the participants' computational power.

This paper is organized as follow: in Section 2 we first describe the Synchronization Problem, design a probabilistic protocol — the Keep-in-Touch (KiT) Protocol — and analyze it. Section 3 addresses the fair exchange problem in the Pirates and Guardian Angels model. Section 4 illustrates this protocol bringing applications to the Mobile Ad Hoc Networks. We finally conclude.

2   Synchronization Protocol

2.1   Security Model

In this part, we consider two participants A and B who want to achieve a secure transaction in a fair way through a malicious network N. In our model we assume that A and B are able to communicate through two secure channels (one from A to B, the other from B to A) providing confidentiality, integrity, authentication, and sequentiality.

- **Confidentiality** ensures that the message is kept secret from any third party.
- **Integrity** ensures that the message cannot be modified by any third party.
- **Authentication** ensures that no third party can insert a forged message in the channel.
- **Sequentiality** ensures that at any time, the sequence of messages which were received by one party was equal at some time to the sequence of messages which were sent by the other party in the same ordering. In particular, no messages can be replayed, erased, or swapped by any third party.

Note that one important security property is missing in the channel: **timeliness**. Actually, some sent messages can never reach their final destination. Therefore, the only way for a malicious man-in-the-middle N to make the protocol fail is to stop transmitting messages in one direction or another by cutting the channel. Hence our adversarial model for N is a malicious algorithm which decides to cut one channel at some time, or the two channels at the same or at different times. Due to the confidentiality property, the choice on when to cut channels cannot depend on the content of the messages, but only on the number of exchanged messages.

Here is an example of a secure communication channel from A to B. Let m be the message to send and *seq* a sequence number which is incremented each time after a message is sent.

A: increase *seq* by 1
      encrypt m for B
      authenticate $(B, seq, \mathrm{ENC}_B(m))$

$A \to B$:   transmission of $\mathrm{AUT}_A(B, seq, \mathrm{ENC}_B(m))$

B: check the identity B
      check the authentication from A
      check $seq = \ previous\_seq + 1$
      set $previous\_seq \leftarrow seq$
      decrypt $\mathrm{ENC}_B(m)$

Here $\mathrm{ENC}_B(m)$ means m encrypted for B and $\mathrm{AUT}_A(m)$ means m authenticated by A. This kind of secure channel can be implemented, for instance by using the SSL/TLS protocol [12].

2.2   Synchronization Problem

We focus here on the synchronization problem[1] which is defined as follows.

Definition 1. *A synchronization protocol between A and B is a protocol which eventually ends with A and B on two possible terminal states: either* success *or* failure. *We say that the protocol is*

1. **complete** *if A and B always end on the* success *state when there is no malicious misbehavior;*
2. **non-trivial** *if either A or B cannot end on the* success *state without receiving at least one message;*
3. **fair** *if A and B always end on the same state even in case of misbehavior;*
4. **timely** *if A and B eventually end.*

We say that the protocol is *perfectly fair* when it follows all these properties. When it is not perfectly fair, we define two measures of unfairness.

– P_a *(probability of asynchronous termination) is the maximum of the probability that the protocol ends on an unfair state over all possible misbehavior of N.*
– P_c *(probability that crime pays) is the maximum of the conditional probability that the protocol ends on an unfair state conditioned on N deviating from the protocol over all possible misbehavior of N.*

We recall that we are interested here in honest participants A and B who communicate through an untrusted network but can establish a channel which achieves confidentiality, integrity, authentication, sequentiality, but not timeliness. Perfect fair protocols are impossible in this setting. This motivates our measures for unperfect protocols.

---

[1] This is equivalent to the well known *Non-Blocking Atomic Commitment* problem in the fault-tolerance literature [17,18].

Note that there is a tricky distinction between P_a and P_c as will be shown in the sequel. The P_a gives confidence to A and B in the fairness of the protocol while P_c gives measures the incentive for a misbehavior.

In order to illustrate the synchronization problem, let's consider the TLS protocol. In TLS 1.0 [12], the client and the server have to close some connections during the execution of a session. To achieve this task, "the client and the server must share knowledge that the connection is ending in order to avoid a truncation attack" [12]. A quite simple procedure is proposed in [12] which consists in sending a `close_notify` message from the initiator to the other party. This prevents from opening new connections in the session until the `close_notify` is properly acknowledged. If the session goes on with new connections it means that the closed connections was fair. This scheme is however not standard and obviously lacks of fair termination, at least for the very last connection. Here fairness of non-terminal connections is guaranteed by the fact that the client and the server keep-in-touch. To keep-in-touch is actually the key idea to solve the synchronization problem.

2.3 Keep-in-Touch Protocol

Our Keep-in-Touch protocol, depicted on Fig. 1, is a quite simple synchronization protocol: the initiator of the protocol picks a random number C which says how many messages will be exchanged. In case of time-out while expecting a message, a participant ends into a failure state. One can notice that, except the first message, the exchanged messages are really empty ones! The participants just keep-in-touch by exchanging sequential authenticated empty messages.

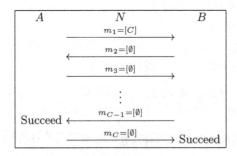

Fig. 1. Keep-in-Touch (KiT) Protocol

Termination side channel protection. In the case that N has access to a side channel saying whether A or B ended in some terminal state, we propose that after the required number of exchanges, the two participants wait for a timeout τ then decide that they succeeded. This extra time prevents a malicious N from trying to get a side channel from the behavior of the two participants within the time-out interval.

Bit-messages variant. Instead of picking C once and sending it at the beginning of the protocol, we can just ask each participant to toss a biased coin before sending the ith message and sending the output bit in the message. A 0 bit means "let's keep-in-touch" and a 1 bit means "so long". Obviously, if the bit is 1 with probability $\Pr[C = i/C \geq i]$, this variant is fully equivalent to the above protocol.

Since the channel provides confidentiality, the hackers have no clue what C is. The integrity, authentication and sequentiality of messages is also protected, so participants are ensured that (empty) messages were exchanged. The sequence number also prevents from replay attacks. Therefore, the only misbehaving strategy to end up the protocol in an unfair state is to end transmitting messages at some point. If the first dropped message is not the last one, the two participants will end up on a failure state. If it is the last one, the protocol becomes unfair. In other cases, the protocol succeeds before the hackers decide to drop messages. In the analysis of the protocol we will only discuss index number of the first message that hacker drops and the chosen distribution for C.

2.4   Analysis of the KiT Protocol

Here we analyze the Keep-in-Touch Protocol depending on the distribution choice for C.

Complexity. When A, B, and N are honest, the complexity in terms of exchanged messages is exactly equal to C. When someone misbehaves by cutting channels, the complexity is smaller, so we can just focus on C. We let p_i be the probability $\Pr[C = i]$. By definition, the average complexity is

$$E(C) = \sum_{i=1}^{+\infty} i p_i.$$

Note that the communication and time complexities are linear in terms of C due to the simplicity of the message contents and the computations to perform.

Completeness. Obviously, the protocol eventually succeeds with a complexity of C when everyone is honest. Hence the protocol is complete.

Non-triviality. Obviously, the protocol fails if B does not receive C.

Fairness (P_a computation). We assume that N is willing to misbehave the ith message, i.e. to cut the channel which is assumed to transmit this message. If $C < i$ then the misbehavior of N has no influence and the protocol succeeds. If $C > i$, the participant who is expecting the ith message cannot send the next one, so both participants are blocked and the protocol fails in a fair state. Clearly, the protocol is unfair if $C = i$, thus with probability p_i. Therefore we have

$$P_a = \max_i p_i.$$

Fairness (P_c computation). With the same discussion we can show that the above misbehavior has a conditional probability of success of $\Pr[C = i/C \geq i]$. Hence we have

$$P_c = \max_i \frac{p_i}{\sum_{j \geq i} p_j}.$$

Timeliness. Obviously, the protocol eventually ends due to the timeout management.

Theorem 1. *The KiT Protocol is a complete, non-trivial and timely synchronization protocol. Let $p_1, p_2, \ldots$ denote the probability distribution of C in the protocol. The expected complexity is $E(C) = \sum_{i=1}^{+\infty} i p_i$ and the probability of unfairness is $P_a = \max_i p_i$. The probability that the crime pays is $P_c = \max_i \frac{p_i}{\sum_{j \geq i} p_j}$.*

Example 1. For any n, when $p_1 = \ldots = p_n = \frac{1}{n}$ and $p_i = 0$ for $i > n$ we have an expected complexity of $E(C) = \frac{n+1}{2}$ and a probability of unfairness of $P_a = \frac{1}{n}$. However we have $P_c = 1$ for $i = n$: if the strategy of N is not to forward the nth message, then his risk is void since this is the last message for sure. Hence the protocol is unfair with probability $\frac{1}{n}$ but with no risk at all for Pirates.

Example 2. For any p, when $p_i = (1-p)^{i-1} p$ for $i > 0$ we have an expected complexity of $E(C) = \frac{1}{p}$ and a probability of unfairness of $P_a = p$. In this case we also have $P_c = p$. The equivalent bit-messages variant is where each participant flips a coin of distribution $(1-p, p)$ in every step.

2.5   Optimal Distributions for the KiT Protocol

The distribution choice plays on the complexity and fairness parameters. Obviously there is a trade-off. The optimal case is studied in the following theorem.

Theorem 2. *Let $p_1, p_2, \ldots$ denote the probability distribution of C in the KiT Synchronization Protocol. We have $E(C) \geq \frac{1}{2}\left(\frac{1}{P_a} + 1\right)$ and $E(C) \geq \frac{1}{P_c}$ where P_a and P_c are the highest probability of unfairness and that the crime pays respectively.*

This shows that Example 1 is the optimal case for P_a and that Example 2 is the optimal case for P_c.

Proof. We want to minimize $E(C)$ with $P_a \leq \varepsilon$. It is equivalent to finding $p_1, p_2, \ldots$ such that $0 \leq p_i \leq P_a$ for all i, $\sum p_i = 1$, and $\sum i p_i$ minimal.

Let ε be a probability smaller than P_a. Let $n = \lfloor \frac{1}{\varepsilon} \rfloor$ and $\alpha = \frac{1}{\varepsilon} - n$. We have $\alpha \in [0, 1[$.

Obviously $\sum i p_i$ is minimal when the first p_is are maximal, i.e. when $p_1 = p_2 = \ldots = p_n = \varepsilon$. The sum of all remaining p_i is equal to $1 - n\varepsilon$. Thus we have

$$E(C) \geq \varepsilon + 2\varepsilon + \ldots + n\varepsilon + (n+1)(1 - n\varepsilon).$$

Hence $E(C) \geq \frac{n(n+1)}{2}\varepsilon + (n+1)(1 - n\varepsilon)$. If we substitute $\frac{1}{\varepsilon} - \alpha$ to n we obtain

$$E(C) \geq \frac{1}{2}\left(\frac{1}{\varepsilon}+1\right) + \alpha + \frac{\alpha\varepsilon}{2}(1 - \alpha).$$

Since $0 \leq \alpha < 1$ we have $E(C) \geq \frac{1}{2}\left(\frac{1}{\varepsilon}+1\right)$. Since this holds for any $\varepsilon \leq P_a$, it holds for $\varepsilon = P_a$. This proves the first bound.

For the second bound we notice that

$$E(C) = \sum_{i=1}^{+\infty}\sum_{j\geq i} p_j.$$

Since we have $\sum_{j\geq i} p_j \geq \frac{p_i}{P_c}$ by definition of P_c, we obtain that $E(C) \geq \frac{1}{P_c}$. $\square$

3   Fair Exchange with Observers

3.1   Fair Exchange Problem

Several (different) definitions for the fair exchange are available in the literature. Most of them are context-dependent. For completeness we provide an informal one for our purpose.

Definition 2. *An exchange protocol between A and B is a protocol in which A and B own some items k_A and k_B respectively and aim at exchanging them. We say that the protocol is*

1. **complete** *if A gets k_B and B gets k_A at the end of the protocol when there is no malicious misbehavior;*
2. **fair** *if its terminates so that either A gets k_B and B gets k_A (success termination), or A gets no information about k_B and B gets no information about k_A (failure termination) even in case of misbehavior;*
3. **timely** *if A and B eventually end.*

We say that the protocol is *perfectly fair* when it follows all these properties. When the protocol is not perfectly fair, we define two measures of unfairness.

- P_a *(probability of unfair termination) is the maximum of the probability that the protocol ends on an unfair state over all possible misbehaviors.*
- P_c *(probability that crime pays) is the maximum of the conditional probability that the protocol ends on an unfair state conditioned on someone deviating from the protocol over all possible misbehaviors.*

The fair exchange problem looks trivial when A and B are honest: they can just exchange their items one after the other and commit to discard them if the protocol fails. However, if timeliness is not guaranteed for the communication channel, N can just discard the last message and the protocol becomes insecure despite A and B being honest. We solve this here by using the synchronization protocol.

3.2   Security Model: Pirates and Guardian Angels

Our model, based on the notion of "observer" introduced by Chaum and Pedersen [9], considers that both participants own a security module. Contrarily to
[9] we assume that the security modules are honest. For this reason, participants
and security modules are respectively named "Pirates" and "Guardian Angels".
We describe now the properties of these entities.

We assume that the Pirates are powerful in the sense that they are able to
communicate with all other devices and their own Guardian Angel. We require no
assumption on the computational capabilities of the Pirates, in particular Pirates
can have very different capabilities. We have no assumption at all for the inter-
Pirates communication channels. In particular they can be totally insecure. On
the other hand, the Pirate-Guardian Angel communication channel is assumed to
be fully secure: it provides confidentiality, integrity, authentication, sequentiality,
and timeliness.

Guardian Angels fulfill the following requirements: they are *tamper-proof*,
that is any potential attacker could not have access to the stored data or change
the Guardian Angel's behavior. Full access stays possible, but limited to some
authorized parties, e.g. for set up. Since the cost for making a tamper-proof
device increases steadily with its capabilities, we assume that Guardian Angels
are simple and limited devices: their computational and storage ability are low.
Moreover they have a single i/o port which is connected to their own Pirate only:
they have no other information source about the outside world. In particular we
will assume that they have no notion of time but a clock signal which is provided
by the pirate. From a practical point of view, Guardian Angels should be some
smart cards.

Obviously, Guardian Angels can play the role of a distributed trusted third
party. They can establish secure channels between them, providing confidentiality, integrity, authentication, and sequentiality. The originality of our model is
that those channels require the cooperation of Pirates, so we cannot assume timeliness. Hence the inter-Guardian angels communication channels can be assumed
to correspond to the model of Section 2.

3.3   Fair Exchange with Two Guardian Angels

Let us denote P the Pirates and G the Guardian Angels. In this section we focus
on the fair exchange problem between P_A and P_B using G_A and G_B. Note that
this can be adapted in a straightforward way for the exchange problem between
P_A and G_B or between G_A and G_B.

If P_A and P_B wish to exchange k_A and k_B, they ask their Guardian Angels
for assistance. Then, G_A simply sends k_A to G_B through their secure channel,
and G_B transmits k_B to G_A. After the exchange itself, they perform a synchronization by using the KiT Protocol. Then, if the protocol succeeded G_A and G_B
disclose the received items to the Pirates. This protocol is illustrated on Fig. 2.

To keep our protocol easily readable, some important issues are not depicted
on Fig. 2. Firstly, we assume that the Guardian Angels have means to check

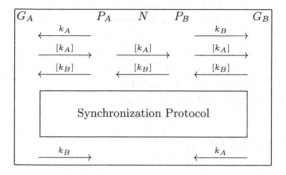

Fig. 2. Fair Exchange Protocol

that the received item is the expected one: Pirates can sent the descriptions of the items to their Guardian Angel. Secondly, since items have an arbitrary size and that Guardian Angels are assumed to have a limited storage facility, we assume that the Guardian Angels forward the received item by encrypting it on-the-fly with a freshly picked key. The key then takes place of the item in the above protocol. Thirdly, the lack of timeliness in the synchronization should be managed by timeouts. But since Guardian Angels are not assumed to have internal clocks, timeouts should be yield by Pirates. Similarly, the end of the synchronization protocol (at least for the Guardian Angel who sends the very last message) should occur only after the Pirate yields a timeout by using the termination side channel protection of the KiT Protocol since the Pirate can detect his state from the behavior.

We give here the initiator's Fair Exchange and Synchronization programs. We assume that P_A is the initiator of the exchange.

G_A's Synchronization Program

- send a random value C to G_B
- while $C > 0$ do
    - standby {wait for a message or a timeout}
    - if a timeout from P_A is received then the synchronization failed
    - {a message from G_B is received} decrement C
    - if $C = 0$ then the synchronization succeeded
    - send an message to G_B and decrement C
- end while
- standby {wait for a timeout}
- the synchronization succeeded

G_A's Fair Exchange Program

- receive k_A from P_A
- establish a secure channel with G_B through P_A

- send k_A to G_B through the channel
- receive k_B from G_B through the channel
- check k_B, if incorrect, abort
- encrypt k_B with a random secret key K
- send k_B encrypted with K to P_A
- execute the Synchronization Protocol
- if the synchronization failed then abort
- send K to P_A

P_A's Fair Exchange Program

- send k_A to G_A
- forward messages between G_A and P_B for the channels between G_A and G_B
- if timeout then
  - send timeout signal to G_A
  - if receive K then decrypt k_B else the protocol failed

3.4 Analysis of Our Protocol

Obviously, our fair exchange protocol inherits Theorems 1 and 2 from the KiT Protocol.

Let us assume that we have a fair exchange protocol. We describe the following synchronization protocol between A and B: they decide to exchange some value. If the exchange succeeds, they enter into a `success` state. Otherwise, they enter into a `failure` state. This is obviously a synchronization protocol which inherits his parameters from the fair exchange protocol.

4 Applying to the Mobile Ad Hoc Networks

4.1 Applications

Current Mobile Networks rely on a heavy fixed infrastructure which connects the users through relays. Installing such an infrastructure is often either too expensive or technically impossible and hence some areas are not reachable. Ad Hoc Wireless Networks mitigate this problem by allowing users to route data through intermediate nodes: the network is furthermore self-organized and rely on any established infrastructure anymore.

In such a network, cryptographic protocols cannot use on-line Trusted Third Party for some obvious reasons. One can think that optimistic protocol may run properly. Besides that using off-line Trusted Third Party does not come up to the Mobile Ad Hoc Networks requirements, we cannot assume that most of the nodes will be honest. Indeed, the nodes have to forward the packets of the other ones to keep alive the community, but they will try to cheat as soon as possible in order to save their battery life since forwarding packets have a substantial cost: nodes will become selfish. Participants will have then to require the Trusted Third Party in each transaction. On the other hand we cannot reasonably use

Gradual Fair Exchange Protocols since no assumption have been done on the computational power of the nodes: the latter could be mobile phones, but also PDAs, laptops, etc.

Additionally, extreme case of fully self-organized networks aim at getting rid of any central service. Our model is then fully relevant to this environment since it achieves probabilistic fairness without Trusted Third Party, assuming only that a secure channel between the Guardian Angels is available. Even if economic and practical aspects are not fully designed yet, it makes sense to imagine the following scenario. Some company builds and sells guardian angels who becomes the virtually distributed TTP. This company (who was the network provider in earlier wireless networks) simply makes community rules and install an accounting service. Guardian Angels are responsible for community rules enforcement and keep local accounting in their lifetime. When they expire, their successor keep track of accountings. Users can thus just buy and plug Guardian Angels into their device in order to control fairness, security, accounting, services,... We can later imagine several Guardian Angels manufacturer with specific trade exchange protocols.

As an application we can exchange an inexpensive service against a micropayment with the protocol of Example 2 with $p = \frac{1}{2}$. The risk for both participants is to loose small valuables, but with a probability bounded by $\frac{1}{2}$ instead of a probability which may be equal to 1.

4.2   Improvements

We would like to notice that, besides the exchanged messages during the synchronization step are empty, the complexity of our protocol can be improved by performing several parallelized Fair Exchanges and by factorizing the synchronization steps: if A and B need to perform a new synchronization despite the previous one is not finished, they can just merge the two KiT protocols into a single one. If they need C_1 remaining messages for the previous protocol to end up and C_2 messages for the new one to end up, they perform a protocol with $\max(C_1, C_2)$ messages. The ith protocol will end up when $C_i = \min(C_1, C_2)$ messages will be exchanged. We have already implemented our protocol in a PDAs network and so we have shown that our protocol is practicable [7]. This way the synchronization protocol induces a constant overhead to serial Fair Exchange Protocol.

Note that we can easily design a protocol which involves one Guardian Angel instead of two. This will be detailed in the full paper version.

5   Conclusion

In this paper, we first recalled the definitions and properties related to Fair Exchange Problem and described the main existent ways to achieve fairness. We introduced then the Synchronization Problem devising such a Gradual Synchronization Protocol and shown that the Fair Exchange Problem can be reduced to the Synchronization Problem in our model based on Chaum *et Al.*'s observer. We designed in this model a Fair Exchange Protocol which provides arbitrarily low unfairness. Our protocol does not require Trusted Third Party and does not come up to computational power assumptions. Even if there exists a great body of literature on Fair Exchange, our protocol is the first non-optimistic one taking advantage of the presence of security modules. Finally, we analyzed the protocol complexity, the probability of unfairness, but also the probability that an attack could achieve.

We also introduced a communication network model with Pirates and Guardian Angels. This model is well suited to Ad Hoc networks and may deserve future research.

Acknowledgment. We are thankful to the students Jérôme Berclaz and Steve Vaquin for their implementation of the protocol.

The work presented in this paper was supported (in part) by the National Competence Center in Research on Mobile Information and Communication Systems (NCCR-MICS), a center supported by the Swiss National Science Foundation under grant number 5005-67322.

References

1. N. Asokan, Matthias Schunter, and Michael Waidner. Optimistic protocols for fair exchange. Research Report RZ 2858, IBM Research Division, Zurich, Switzerland, September 1996.
2. N. Asokan, Matthias Schunter, and Michael Waidner. Optimistic protocols for multi-party fair exchange. Research Report RZ 2892, IBM Research Division, Zurich, Switzerland, December 1996.
3. N. Asokan, Matthias Schunter, and Michael Waidner. Optimistic protocols for fair exchange. In *Proceedings of 4th ACM Conference on Computer and Communications Security*, pages 7–17, Zurich, Switzerland, April 1997. ACM Press.
4. N. Asokan, Victor Shoup, and Michael Waidner. Asynchronous protocols for optimistic fair exchange. In *Proceedings of the IEEE Symposium on Research in Security and Privacy*, pages 86–99, Oakland, California, USA, May 1998. IEEE Computer Society Press.
5. N. Asokan, Victor Shoup, and Michael Waidner. Optimistic fair exchange of digital signatures. In Kaisa Nyberg, editor, *Advances in Cryptology – EUROCRYPT'98*, volume 1403 of *Lecture Notes in Computer Science*, pages 591–606, Helsinki, Finland, May 1998. Springer-Verlag.
6. Michael Ben-Or, Oded Goldreich, Silvio Micali, and Ronald L. Rivest. A fair protocol for signing contracts. *IEEE Transactions on Information Theory*, 36(1):40–46, January 1990.
7. Jérôme Berclaz and Steve Vaquin. Fair exchange between iPAQs. Semester project, Swiss Federal Institute of Technology (EPFL), Lausanne, Switzerland, http://lasecwww.epfl.ch, February 2002.
8. Ernest F. Brickell, David Chaum, Ivan B. Damgård, and Jeroen van de Graaf. Gradual and verifiable release of a secret. In Carl Pomerance, editor, *Advances in Cryptology – CRYPTO'87*, volume 293 of *Lecture Notes in Computer Science*, pages 156–166, Santa Barbara, California, USA, August 1988. IACR, Springer-Verlag.

9. David Chaum and Torben P. Pedersen. Wallet databases with observers. In Ernest F. Brickell, editor, *Advances in Cryptology – CRYPTO'92*, volume 740 of *Lecture Notes in Computer Science*, pages 89–105, Santa Barbara, California, USA, August 1992. IACR, Springer-Verlag.

10. Richard Cleve. Controlled gradual disclosure schemes for random bits and their applications. In Gilles Brassard, editor, *Advances in Cryptology – CRYPTO'89*, volume 435 of *Lecture Notes in Computer Science*, pages 573–588, Santa Barbara, California, USA, August 1990. IACR, Springer-Verlag.

11. Ivan B. Damgård. Practical and probably secure release of a secret and exchange of signatures. In Tor Helleseth, editor, *Advances in Cryptology – EUROCRYPT'93*, volume 765 of *Lecture Notes in Computer Science*, pages 200–217, Lofthus, Norway, May 1993. IACR, Springer-Verlag.

12. Tim Dierks and Christopher Allen. The TLS protocol – version 1.0, January 1999.

13. Shimon Even and Yacov Yacobi. Relations amoung public key signature systems. Technical Report 175, Computer Science Department, Technicon, Israel, 1980.

14. Matt Franklin and Michael K. Reiter. Fair exchange with a semi-trusted third party. In *Proceedings of the 4th ACM Conference on Computer and Communications Security*, pages 1–5, Zurich, Switzerland, April 1997. ACM Press.

15. Matt Franklin and Gene Tsudik. Secure group barter: Multi-party fair exchange with semi-trusted neutral parties. In Rafael Hirschfeld, editor, *Financial Cryptography – FC'98*, volume 1465 of *Lecture Notes in Computer Science*, pages 90–102, Anguilla, British West Indies, February 1998. IFCA, Springer-Verlag.

16. Felix C. Gärtner, Henning Pagnia, and Holger Vogt. Approaching a formal definition of fairness in electronic commerce. In *Proceedings of the International Workshop on Electronic Commerce – WELCOM'99*, pages 354–359, Lausanne, Switzerland, October 1999. IEEE Computer Society Press.

17. Rachid Guerraoui. Revisiting the relationship between non-blocking atomic commitment and consensus. In Jean-Michel Hélary and Michel Raynal, editors, *Proceedings of the 9th International Workshop on Distributed Algorithms – WDAG'95*, volume 972 of *Lecture Notes in Computer Science*, pages 87–100, Le Mont Saint Michel, France, September 1995. Springer-Verlag.

18. Rachid Guerraoui. Non-blocking atomic commit in asynchronous distributed systems with failure detectors. *Distributed Computing*, 15(1):17–25, February 2002.

19. Jean-Pierre Hubaux, Jean-Yves Le Boudec, Silvia Giordano, and Maher Hamdi. The terminode project: Toward mobile ad-hoc wans. In *Proceedings of the Sixth IEEE International Workshop on Mobile, Multimedia Communications – MoMuC'99*, San-Diego, California, USA, 1999.

20. Jean-Pierre Hubaux, Thomas Gross, Jean-Yves Le Boudec, and Martin Vetterli. Towards self-organizing mobile ad-hoc networks: the terminodes project. *IEEE Comm Mag*, 39(1):118–124, January 2001.

21. Markus Jakobsson. Ripping coins for a fair exchange. In Louis C. Guillou and Jean-Jacques Quisquater, editors, *Advances in Cryptology – EUROCRYPT'95*, volume 921 of *Lecture Notes in Computer Science*, pages 220–230, Saint Malo, France, May 1995. IACR, Springer-Verlag.

22. Steve Kremer, Olivier Markowitch, and Jianying Zhou. An intensive survey of non-repudiation protocols. Technical Report ULB–474, Université Libre de Bruxelles, Bruxelles, Belgium, 2001.

23. Olivier Markowitch. *Les protocoles de non-répudiation*. PhD thesis, University of Bruxelles, Bruxelles, Belgium, January 2001.

24. Olivier Markowitch and Shahrokh Saeednia. Optimistic fair exchange with transparent signature recovery. In *Financial Cryptography – FC'01*, Lecture Notes in Computer Science, Cayman Islands, February 2001. IFCA, Springer-Verlag.
25. Tatsuaki Okamoto and Kazuo Ohta. How to simultaneously exchange secrets by general assumptions. In *Proceedings of the 2nd ACM Conference on Computer and Communications Security*, pages 184–192, Fairfax, Virginia, USA, November 1994. ACM Press.
26. Henning Pagnia, Holger Vogt, and Felix C. Gärtner. Fair exchange. *The computer Journal*, 46(1):55–75, January 2003.
27. Michael O. Rabin. Transaction protection by beacons. *Journal of Computer and System Science*, 27(2):256–267, October 1883.
28. Indrakshi Ray and Indrajit Ray. An optimistic fair exchange e-commerce protocol with automated dispute resolution. In Kurt Bauknecht, Sanjay Kumar Madria, and Günther Pernul, editors, *Electronic Commerce and Web Technologies – EC-Web 2000*, volume 1875 of *Lecture Notes in Computer Science*, pages 84–93, London, United Kingdom, September 2000. DEXA Association, Springer-Verlag.
29. Matthias Schunter. *Optimistic Fair Exchange*. PhD thesis, University of Saarlandes, Saarbruken, Germany, October 2000.
30. Paul Syverson. Weakly secret bit commitment: Applications to lotteries and fair exchange. In *Proceedings of the 11th Computer Security Foundations Workshop – PCSFW*, pages 2–13, Rockport, Massachusetts, USA, June 1998. IEEE, IEEE Computer Society Press.
31. Tom Tedrick. How to exchange half a bit. In David Chaum, editor, *Advances in Cryptology – CRYPTO'83*, pages 147–151. Plenum Press, August 1983.
32. Tom Tedrick. Fair exchange of secrets. In George Robert Blakley and David Chaum, editors, *Advances in Cryptology – CRYPTO'84*, volume 196 of *Lecture Notes in Computer Science*, pages 434–438, Santa Barbara, California, USA, August 1985. IACR, Springer-Verlag.
33. Holger Vogt. Asynchronous optimistic fair exchange based on revocable items. In Rebecca N. Wright, editor, *Financial Cryptography – FC'03*, volume 2742 of *Lecture Notes in Computer Science*, Le Gosier, Guadeloupe, French West Indies, January 2003. IFCA, Springer-Verlag.
34. Holger Vogt, Felix C. Gärtner, and Henning Pagnia. Supporting fair exchange in mobile environments. *Journal on Mobile Networks and Applications*, 8(2):127–136, April 2003.
35. Holger Vogt, Henning Pagnia, and Felix C. Gärtner. Using smart cards for fair exchange. In L. Fiege, G. Mühl, and U. Wilhelm, editors, *Proceedings of 2nd International Workshop on Electronic Commerce – WELCOM 2001*, volume 2232 of *Lecture Notes in Computer Science*, pages 101–113, Heidelberg, Germany, November 2001. Springer-Verlag.
36. Jianying Zhou, Robert Deng, and Feng Bao. Evolution of fair non repudiation with TTP. In Josef Pieprzyk, Reihaneh Safavi-Naini, and Jennifer Seberry, editors, *Proceedings of Fourth Australasian Conference on Information Security and Privacy – ACISP 1999*, volume 1587 of *Lecture Notes in Computer Science*, pages 258–269, Wollongong, Australia, April 1999. Springer-Verlag.
37. Jianying Zhou, Robert Deng, and Feng Bao. Some remarks on a fair exchange protocol. In Hideki Imai and Yuliang Zheng, editors, *Proceedings of Third International Workshop on Practice and Theory in Public Key Cryptography – PKC 2000*, volume 1751 of *Lecture Notes in Computer Science*, pages 46–57, Melbourne, Australia, January 2000. Springer-Verlag.

Sign-Based Differential Power Analysis

Roman Novak

Jozef Stefan Institute, Jamova 39, 1000 Ljubljana, Slovenia,
Roman.Novak@ijs.si

Abstract. Differential Power Analysis (DPA) by Paul Kocher et al. is expanded with the information that is hidden in the sign of power biases. The latter reveal values that collide with the DPA target value within the circuitry. With the help of cross-iteration comparisons, the interpretation of those values can provide significant amounts of the information required to reverse engineer secret algorithm. We have successfully launched a demonstration attack on a secret authentication and session-key generation algorithm implemented on SIM cards in GSM networks. The findings provide guidance for designing tamper resistant devices that are secure against this kind of attack.

1 Introduction

Any real cryptographic device provides more information to a determined adversary than just the input plaintext and output ciphertext. This side-channel information is available as the timing of operations [1], power consumption of the devices [2], electromagnetic emanations [3], etc. Very little side-channel information is required to break many common ciphers. Non-invasive attacks and their accompanying countermeasures have been studied extensively over the past few years. Systems that rely on smartcards are of particular concern.

Most of the side-channel based methods deal with the extraction of cryptographic material, such as keys, from the implementations of well-known algorithms. A fundamental rule of cryptography is that one must assume that the cryptanalyst knows the general method of encryption used. Experts have learned over the years that the only way to ensure security is to follow an open design process, encouraging public review to identify flaws while they can still be fixed. However, many cryptographic algorithms are still kept secret. For instance, GSM network operators use an updated version of COMP128-1, designated as COMP128-2, as an authentication algorithm, but the algorithm remains unpublished. Some network operators even develop a proprietary algorithm in secrecy. In either case, the algorithm used has not been publicly reviewed.

The purpose of this paper is to show that secret algorithms offer very little protection. We expand the well-known Differential Power Analysis (DPA) attack [2] with the information that is hidden in the sign of power biases. An adversary can use a method similar to the proposed Sign-based Differential Power Analysis (SDPA) to reverse engineer secret algorithms. A sign of power biases has been already used in other contexts, e.g. in a power based attack on the Twofish

K. Chae and M. Yung (Eds.): WISA 2003, LNCS 2908, pp. 203–216, 2004.
© Springer-Verlag Berlin Heidelberg 2004

reference code [4], but its use for reverse engineering is new. Experiments on reverse engineering using side-channel information have been conducted by other authors, i.e. in [5] neural networks are used to automate reverse engineering of software code. Strength comparison of known methods has not been performed yet.

An example is given on the secret authentication and session-key generation algorithm implemented on SIM (Subscriber Identity Module) cards that are used in GSM networks. Specification of the algorithm was not available. Correctness of the restored algorithm was checked by means of plaintext/ciphertext pairs. As the algorithm is not well-known COMP128-1, only small parts of the code are given in order to keep the algorithm secret and be clear enough.

The rest of the paper is structured as follows. Section 2 gives a short introduction to power analysis techniques. In Sect. 3 we introduce the theoretical basis of Messerges et al. for the DPA attack [6], invented by Kocher et al. [2]. We expand the method to create a more powerful SDPA attack in Sect. 4. In Sect. 5 the leaked information that can be captured by the SDPA is detailed. In order to improve the interpretation of SDPA vectors, cross-iteration comparisons are suggested in Sect. 6. An example is given on an unknown GSM authentication algorithm. Usually, supplementary methods have to be employed to completely restore the algorithm under attack. Some of them are mentioned in Sect. 7. Section 8 expands the SDPA with iteration independent SDPA matrices and shows how they can be used to extract permutations from side-channel information. Countermeasures against the proposed side-channel attack are discussed in Sect. 9. The findings are summarised in Sect. 10.

2   Power Analysis

Smart cards consist of logic gates, which are basically interconnected transistors. During operation, charges are applied to or removed from transistor gates. The sum of all charges can be measured through power consumption, on which power analysis techniques are based.

Several variations of power analysis have been developed [2,7]. The power consumption measurements of smart card operations are interpreted directly in Simple Power Analysis (SPA). SPA can reveal hidden data in algorithms in which the execution path depends on the data being processed. More advanced techniques, like Differential Power Analysis (DPA) and Inferential Power Analysis (IPA), allow observation of the effects correlated to the data values being manipulated.

Power analysis attacks have been known for a while and effective countermeasures exist that pose difficulties, even to a well-funded and knowledgeable adversary [8,9,6]. However, many providers for cryptographic tokens are still convinced that implementation of secret algorithms provide a sufficient level of protection against low-cost side-channel attacks. The results presented here speak against attempts to establish secrecy by keeping cryptographic algorithms undisclosed.

3   DPA Attack

A DPA attack begins by running the encryption algorithm for N random values of plaintext input. For each of the N plaintext inputs, PTI_i, a discrete time power signal, $P_i[j]$, is collected. The corresponding ciphertext output may also be collected. The power signal $P_i[j]$ is a sampled version of the power being consumed during the portion of the algorithm that is under attack. The index i corresponds to the PTI_i that produced the signal and the index j corresponds to the time of the sample. The $P_i[j]$ are split into two sets using a partitioning function, $D(\cdot)$:

$$P_0 = \{P_i[j]|D(\cdot) = 0\}$$
$$P_1 = \{P_i[j]|D(\cdot) = 1\} \ . \tag{1}$$

The partitioning function can take plaintext input or ciphertext output as a parameter. The next step is to compute the average power signal for each set:

$$A_0[j] = \tfrac{1}{|P_0|}\sum_{P_i[j]\in P_0} P_i[j]$$
$$A_1[j] = \tfrac{1}{|P_1|}\sum_{P_i[j]\in P_1} P_i[j] \ , \tag{2}$$

where $|P_0| + |P_1| = N$. Note that it is not necessary for the sets P_0 and P_1 to be exactly equal. By subtracting the two averages, a discrete time DPA bias signal, $T[j]$, is obtained:

$$T[j] = A_0[j] - A_1[j] \ . \tag{3}$$

Selecting an appropriate function $D(\cdot)$ results in a DPA bias signal that can be used to verify guessed portions of the secret key. For instance, the partitioning function can differentiate power traces into two groups based on the predicted value of a bit of some intermediate variable, which in turn depends on a portion of the secret key. At some point during execution, the software needs to compute the value of this bit. When this occurs, or when any data containing this bit is manipulated, there will be a slight difference in the amount of power dissipated, depending on whether this bit is a 0 or a 1. As the number N of PTI inputs is increased, $T[j]$ converges to the expectation equation:

$$\lim_{N\to\infty} T[j] = E\{P_i[j]|D(\cdot) = 0\} - E\{P_i[j]|D(\cdot) = 1\} \ . \tag{4}$$

If enough PTI samples are used and a correct guess as to the value of the intermediate variable has been made, $T[j]$ will show power biases of ε at times j' and will converge to 0 all other times. Time indices j' are those indices at which the instructions manipulating the observed bit occur. Due to weakly correlated events, $T[j]$ will not always converge to 0 for $j \neq j'$; however, the largest biases will occur at times j'. Figure 1 shows power biases for a correct guess on the value of the secret and a signal without biases for an incorrect guess.

4   Sign of Power Biases

The DPA method as described does not put any significance on the sign of biases in $T[j]$. However, the sign carries additional information about the algorithm

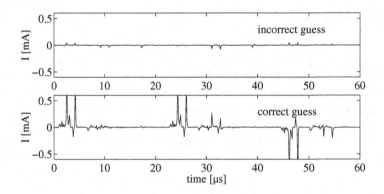

Fig. 1. Example of experimental DPA power biases

under attack. Biases are of different signs, positive or negative, as can be clearly seen from Fig. 1.

The different sign of biases can be explained by a closer look at semiconductor technology, the source of power dissipation. In [6] a simple model of CMOS circuit is proposed as a basis for understanding power dissipation measurements. CMOS logic has almost no static power dissipation, but there is dynamic power dissipation. The gate of a transistor forms a small capacitor. When switching an input, not only the transistor gate capacities but also the whole wire needs to be charged or discharged. Note that the wires connecting the gates have even bigger capacities than the gates themselves. There are also short-circuit currents during switching due to the way CMOS logic is designed.

Suppose the partitioning function $D(\cdot)$ returns the value of a bit that occurs on the input of CMOS gate at time j'. The impact on power dissipation will occur only if the state of the input changes. Let the initial state of the input be 0. There is then an increase in power dissipation in power traces selected to set P_1, hence negative power bias at time j'. On the other hand, when the initial state of the CMOS input is 1, the reverse is true and positive power bias is observed at time j'. The above explanation holds when the difference of the two sets is computed as in (3). If the difference is computed in a different way, the signs have to be interpreted accordingly.

It is evident from the above that the sign of DPA bias carries information about the initial state of the circuitry. Furthermore, a similar effect on power dissipation may be observed when the circuitry that already holds the bit under observation is assigned the next value. Again, the sign of DPA bias reveals this next value.

Suppose the correct guess as to the value of the intermediate has been made, or that the intermediate is not secret at all. Note that the term 'intermediate' refers to the value of the intermediate variable within the algorithm. By performing sign analysis of power biases for all bits of the intermediate, values can be revealed that collide with the observed value in the same circuitry.

Definition 1 (of the SDPA vector). *Let $D_{I_b}(\cdot)$ be a partitioning function that splits power traces as regard to the value of the b-th bit of an intermediate I and the j' time index at which DPA power bias is observed for at least one bit of the intermediate. Let $T_{I_b}[j']$ be a DPA bias signal for $D_{I_b}(\cdot)$. An SDPA vector $\mathbf{s}_{j'} \in \{0, 1, \sim\}^{n+1}$ is defined as*

$$\mathbf{s}_{j'} = [sgn(T_{I_n}[j']), \ldots, sgn(T_{I_1}[j']), sgn(T_{I_0}[j'])] , \tag{5}$$

where the bit length of the intermediate I is $n + 1$ and sgn is defined as

$$sgn(x) = \begin{cases} 1 & x > threshold \\ 0 & x < -threshold \\ \sim & otherwise . \end{cases} \tag{6}$$

Definition 2 (of the SDPA value). *When $\mathbf{s}_{j'}$ is completely defined, i.e. $\mathbf{s}_{j'} \in \{0, 1\}^{n+1}$, an SDPA value can be extracted by computing the dot product*

$$s_{j'} = \mathbf{s}_{j'} \cdot [2^n, ..., 2, 1] . \tag{7}$$

Note that the intermediate can be handled internally as a bit complemented value, in which case the SDPA value is also bit complemented.

5   Leaked Information

Basically DPA is used as a tool for testing various hypotheses about secret values in cryptographic algorithms. This is done through selection of the partitioning function. On the other hand, SDPA is performed on known variables within an algorithm in order to deduce further knowledge about the algorithm. In this way secret values can be detected as well, however, they are revealed through collision with known values.

Empirical evidence is provided on the kind of information that can be revealed through SDPA in the following sections. The method has been validated on an unknown authentication and session-key generation algorithm (A3A8) implemented on SIM card. The algorithm's specification was not made available in advance. All that was known was that the algorithm was not COMP128-1. The experiment was part of a larger ongoing project in which the significance of the side-channel information is evaluated in various reverse engineering techniques.

Experiments in [6] showed that, in a typical smart card, a large portion of the power dissipation occurs in the gates attached to internal busses. However, when a precharged bus design is used, SDPA values caused by bus activity are of limited usability because the bus is driven to a constant value before and after each transfer. This is not the case for internal busses and other circuitry, including microcontroller registers. We could not establish the exact source of SDPA information as we were experimenting with smart card of unknown architecture. Future research into this area is required.

When the algorithm is secret, the plaintext input can be selected as a known intermediate variable. The input can usually be split into n-bit blocks, where n depends on the microcontroller architecture; today 8-bit microcontroller architecture is the most common. Applying SDPA to input blocks results in a set of SDPA vectors $s_{j'}$ with different time indices j'. Not all of them are completely defined.

It is difficult to deduce the meaning of SDPA values, as there can be many explanations. For instance, a constant may be a real constant used by the algorithm, but it can also be the memory address of a variable, value of a variable, opcode, or just the effect of a precharged bus. Other more complex explanations are possible. Note that events that correlate with the observed value, i.e. selected bit of the intermediate, also result in non-zero power biases.

Moreover, the collision of the observed value with its transformed counterpart produce very distinct SDPA vectors, which can be considered as a signature of the transformation. First results based on simulation suggest that various arithmetic and logic operations may be identified by analysing SDPA vectors. For example, suppose that input value i collides with its shifted counterpart, $i \gg 3$. Then the following SDPA vector $s_{j'}$

$$s_{j'} = [0, 0, 0, \sim, \sim, \sim, \sim, \sim] \tag{8}$$

is expected, where the number of consecutive zeros equals the number of places shifted to the right.

Proof. The upper three bits of input collide with zero due to a right shift, therefore, zero components are expected. On the other hand, the lower bits of input collide with shifted bits. There is a transition on a gate if one of the collided bits is 1 and another is 0. When input values are evenly distributed, approximately half the power traces in each partition show power bias due to transition. Therefore, the DPA power signal for the lower five bits at time j' converges to zero, hence neither positive nor negative bias.   □

Note that the same signature would be obtained if zero collided with masked input. Signatures for other typical logical and arithmetic operations may be derived. They are very dependent on the value with which the transformed value collides. Similar signatures may result from different transformations, while some transformations cannot be identified in this way. For instance, when the rotated value collides with its original, the DPA power bias limits to zero. Furthermore, many signatures, like those for addition and multiplication, have an effect on the size of a bias and not only on its sign. When the transition of some bits leak more information than others, i.e. power bias is dependent on bit position [10], the interpretation of magnitudes in addition to signs may appear difficult. Further research is required in order to include the information about magnitudes into signatures.

6   Cross-Iteration Analysis

Many ciphers implement complex compositions of simple operations through different levels of iterated code. In order to correctly interpret fully defined SDPA vectors, the investigation of similar vectors from multiple iterations can be very helpful. We define the SDPA matrix that captures sign information for cross-iteration comparisons.

Definition 3 (of the SDPA matrix). *Let m be the number of iterations in which similar patterns of SDPA responses have been observed. Suppose the iterations are of fixed length l. An SDPA matrix $\mathbf{S}_{j'}$ is a collection of transposed SDPA vectors*

$$\mathbf{S}_{j'} = [\mathbf{s}_{j'}^T, \mathbf{s}_{j'+l}^T, \mathbf{s}_{j'+2l}^T, \dots, \mathbf{s}_{j'+(m-1)l}^T] \,, \tag{9}$$

where time index j' refers to the first iteration. The SDPA vectors are computed for intermediates that are expected to be processed within each iteration.

We have applied SDPA to an unknown GSM authentication algorithm that has been deployed by different service providers. The algorithm is a keyed hash function. It takes a 16-byte key (128 bits) and 16-byte of data (128 bits) to output a 12-byte (96 bits) hash. The key $k_0 - k_{15}$, as used in the GSM protocol, is unique to each subscriber and is stored in the SIM card. The input data $i_0 - i_{15}$ is a random challenge supplied by the base station. The first 32 bits of the hash are used as a response to the challenge and sent back to the base station. The remaining 64 bits are used as a session key for voice encryption using the A5 algorithm.

The following SDPA matrices are identified at the beginning of the algorithm:

$$\mathbf{C}_0 = [0, 0, 0, 0, \dots, 0, 0, 0, 0]$$
$$\mathbf{CNT}_{0-15} = [0, 1, 2, 3, \dots, 12, 13, 14, 15]$$
$$\mathbf{KEY} = [76, 157, 145, 129, \dots, 217, 109, 31, 224] \tag{10}$$
$$\mathbf{CNT}_{0-15} \oplus \mathbf{KEY} = [76, 156, 147, 130, \dots, 213, 96, 17, 239]$$
$$\mathbf{CNT}_{69-84} \oplus \mathbf{KEY} = [9, 219, 214, 201, \dots, 136, 63, 76, 180] \,,$$

where the matrix columns are written as the SDPA values. 8-bit blocks of plaintext input $i_0 - i_{15}$ were selected as known intermediate variables, one per iteration. The time index j' of the above matrices is omitted as the matrices repeat several times. In Fig. 2 a temporal ordering of the matrices within the algorithm's first iterations is shown.

When only one iteration is observed, the SDPA values are just different constants that collided with the input. The matrix representation gives more information. For instance, $\mathbf{CNT}_{0-15}$ can be interpreted as a loop counter in collision with the plaintext input. This explanation is very likely as both input and counter are handled within a typical loop. In the middle of the iteration a SDPA matrix that appears to contain random SDPA values is identified three times. Our prediction that a key $k_0 - k_{15}$ collided with the input has proven correct, hence the label **KEY**. At the end of the iteration two different matrices were

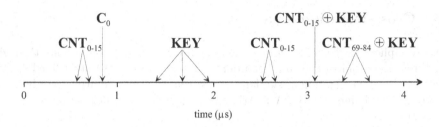

Fig. 2. Temporal ordering of the SDPA matrices within the first iterations

identified. The first can be calculated as a bitwise exclusive or between $\mathbf{CNT}_{0-15}$ and $\mathbf{KEY}$, $\mathbf{CNT}_{0-15} \oplus \mathbf{KEY}$, and the second as $\mathbf{CNT}_{69-84} \oplus \mathbf{KEY}$. It is highly unlikely that these values actually collided with the input; however, the same matrices are obtained if $\mathbf{KEY} \oplus i_0 - i_{15}$ collides with $\mathbf{CNT}_{0-15}$ and $\mathbf{CNT}_{69-84}$, respectively. This is due to the property of exclusive or. When SDPA is performed on an intermediate xored by a constant C without modification of the partitioning function, the partitions P_0 and P_1, and thus the signs, are swapped for all ones in C; the same effect would have the exclusive or between the initial state and C. There is also a third option according to which $\mathbf{CNT}_{0-15} \oplus i_0 - i_{15}$ collided with $\mathbf{KEY}$, but it is less probable. The $\mathbf{CNT}_{69-84}$ may show the memory range where the results of the computation are stored. Other explanations are also possible. From the above conclusions, one can write the Alg. 1 that would cause a similar response to SDPA.

Algorithm 1. Initial computation in unknown algorithm
FOR j from 0 to 15
    $x[j] = i[j] \oplus k[j]$
END FOR

Note that the flow of the operations is in agreement with the temporal ordering of the SDPA matrices. First, the input is read. After that, the key is accessed. Computation of the exclusive or follows. Finally, the results are stored in the memory.

In the above example, SDPA reveals information about keys, counters, memory ranges, operations and their temporal ordering.

7   Supplementary Methods

As shown by a simple example, SDPA can be used in the reverse engineering attempts of an adversary to reveal secret code. After new intermediate values have been discovered, SDPA is performed on those values instead of on blocks of plaintext input. The intermediates can be deduced from the information in SDPA matrices and by testing the most probable hypotheses about transformations. SDPA signatures of various logical and arithmetic operations can provide significant help in selecting the right hypothesis.

Supplementary methods have to be employed to completely restore the algorithm under attack. For instance, simple power analysis (SPA) and the use of correlation techniques may help in identifying the algorithm's loops.

The next major difficulty in restoration attempts are substitution blocks, which are usually implemented as lookup tables. Modern cryptography uses substitution as a building block in complex compositions of strong ciphers. Substitution tables are considered to provide a high security level because they contribute effectively to data diffusion. A substitution block is a very effective countermeasure against SDPA as it prevents intermediates from being tracked through the algorithm. However, many implementations of lookup operation are insecure. An attack on substitution blocks is proposed in [12]. The attack is based on identifying equal intermediate results from power measurements while the actual values of these intermediates remain unknown.

We managed to completely restore the unknown GSM authentication algorithm using the above methods. In Fig. 3 a detail of the algorithm is shown that includes four lookup operations. Only a small fraction of the sixteen similar iterations is shown. The code is executed at the beginning of the algorithm and can be restored only by combining SDPA, SPA and substitution block attack.

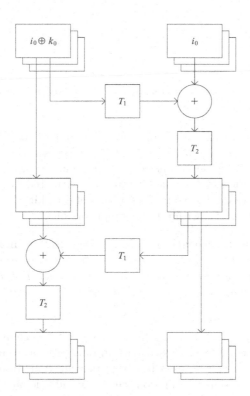

Fig. 3. Computation in the GSM authentication algorithm

8   Iteration Independent SDPA

The code from Fig. 3 is repeated five times within eight iterative loops. Each inner iteration is followed by a permutation while each outer iteration completes with a compression. The compression is a permutation on a subset of bits.

We define iteration independent SDPA matrices and show how they can be used to extract permutation or compression from side-channel information. We demonstrate the method on a detail of the compression from Fig. 4.

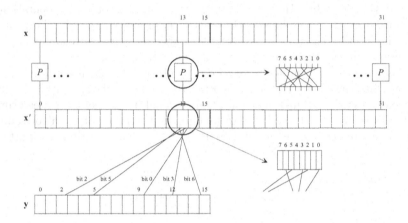

Fig. 4. Detail of the outer compression in the GSM authentication algorithm

The algorithm was extracted from the outer loop of our GSM authentication algorithm. A 32-byte (256 bits) vector $\mathbf{x}$ is compressed in a 16-byte (128 bits) vector $\mathbf{y}$. First, bit permutations within the components of $\mathbf{x}$ are performed using the permutation P. Half the bits are then extracted from the vector $\mathbf{x}'$ and recomposed in $\mathbf{y}$. In the last step, the position of each bit within the components of $\mathbf{y}$ remains the same as within the components of $\mathbf{x}'$.

Definition 4 (of the iteration independent SDPA matrix). *When specific intermediates to be processed within each iteration cannot be determined, SDPA vectors for a fixed intermediate could be computed regardless of the iteration. Let $\mathbf{S}_j^I$, designate an iteration independent SDPA matrix computed on fixed intermediate I.*

Iteration independent matrices have usually only one column defined because the intermediate is often processed only in one, previously unknown iteration. This type of matrix can be used to reveal permutations from the side-channel information. Again, sign information can be an additional help in making hypotheses about the algorithm.

The following matrices were obtained when iteration independent SDPA was applied to x_{13}:

$$\mathbf{A}_1^{x[13]} = [\sim, \ldots, \sim, 13, \sim, \sim, \sim, \sim, \sim, \sim]$$
$$\mathbf{B}_1^{x[13]} = [\sim, \ldots, \sim, 0, \sim, \sim, \sim, \sim, \sim, \sim]$$
$$\mathbf{C}_1^{x[13]} = [\sim, \ldots, \sim, \mathbf{c}_1^T, \sim, \sim, \sim, \sim, \sim, \sim] \qquad \mathbf{c}_1 = [0, 0, 0, 0, \sim, 0, 0, 0]$$
$$\mathbf{D}_1^{x[13]} = [\sim, \ldots, \sim, \mathbf{d}_1^T, \sim, \sim, \sim, \sim, \sim, \sim] \qquad \mathbf{d}_1 = [\sim, \sim, \sim, \sim, 0, \sim, \sim, \sim]$$
$$\mathbf{A}_2^{x[13]} = [\sim, \sim, 13, \sim, \ldots, \sim] \tag{11}$$
$$\mathbf{B}_2^{x[13]} = [\sim, \sim, 0, \sim, \ldots, \sim]$$
$$\mathbf{C}_2^{x[13]} = [\sim, \sim, \mathbf{c}_2^T, \sim, \ldots, \sim] \qquad \mathbf{c}_2 = [0, 0, 0, 0, 0, 0, \sim, 0]$$
$$\mathbf{D}_2^{x[13]} = [\sim, \sim, \mathbf{d}_2^T, \sim, \ldots, \sim] \qquad \mathbf{d}_2 = [\sim, \sim, \sim, \sim, \sim, \sim, 0, \sim] .$$

Note that the vector $\mathbf{x}$ is already known to an adversary. Temporal ordering of the matrices is given in Fig. 5. Only a subset of matrices is shown in order to demonstrate the reconstruction of the compression algorithm. Below the time axis the positions of other matrices are marked for the intermediates $x_0 - x_{31}$. Eight groups were detected, but only three are shown.

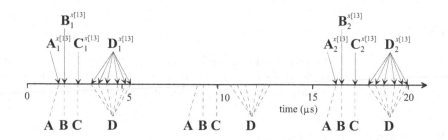

Fig. 5. Temporal ordering of the iteration independent matrices

From the above, several conclusions about the algorithm can be made. Here, we give the most probable explanation, which led to the reconstruction of the compression algorithm in Fig. 4.

The compression is performed in a part of the algorithm where 16 iterations were detected; hence 16 columns in the matrices. The intermediate, in our case x_{13}, appears in different iterations, i.e. different columns are defined. We concluded that a sort of permutation is performed, with each iteration computing one component of the output vector $\mathbf{y}$. Eight groups of matrices were identified within the iterations; only some groups were present for a given intermediate. We made an assumption that the 8-bit components of $\mathbf{y}$ are computed one bit per group.

Each group starts with matrix $\mathbf{A}$ for which the only defined vector contains the address of the intermediate. Confirmation that the value is really an address, and not just a constant, could be found in the matrices for other intermediates. The collision of the intermediate with its address suggests that, within each group, an independent computation is performed on the intermediate value.

Matrices $\mathbf{C}$ and $\mathbf{D}$ can be signatures of various masking operations. For instance, when a constant collides with an intermediate that has been previously masked, only corresponding components of the SDPA vector are defined. Therefore, bit 3 of x_{13} could be extracted in the 10th iteration, as one can deduce from the matrices $\mathbf{C}_1^{x[13]}$ and $\mathbf{D}_1^{x[13]}$. A similar conclusion, based on the matrices $\mathbf{C}_2^{x[13]}$ and $\mathbf{D}_2^{x[13]}$, can be made for bit 1 in the 3rd iteration.

The temporal ordering of the extracted bits within the iteration can be the ordering of bits in the result, i.e. iteration j computes value y_j by bit composition from bit 0 to bit 7. Consequently, bit 3 of x_{13} maps to bit 0 of y_9 while bit 1 of x_{13} maps to bit 2 of y_2.

The described response to iteration independent SDPA could be achieved by implementation of Alg. 2.

Algorithm 2. Restored compression algorithm
FOR j from 0 to 15
$\quad y[j] = (x[b_0[j]] \ \& \ 0x08) \gg 3) \ |$
$\quad\quad\quad (x[b_1[j]] \ \& \ 0x40) \gg 5) \ |$
$\quad\quad\quad (x[b_2[j]] \ \& \ 0x02) \ll 1) \ |$
$\quad\quad\quad \ldots$
END FOR

The first level permutation is performed by masking and shifting operations. $b_0 - b_7$ are the second level permutation tables and can be defined from the information in the iteration independent SDPA matrices.

9   Countermeasures

Designers must not rely on secrecy of the algorithm because the algorithm may be reverse-engineered in the presence of side-channel information leakage. Only low-cost equipment is needed to perform this kind of attack. Even when well-tested public algorithms are used, there is a chance that SDPA may reveal sensitive information or break a layer of protection. Techniques for preventing SDPA attacks, as described in this paper, fall roughly into two categories.

The first approach is to prevent information leakage, using the general techniques that protect the algorithm as a whole. Well-known techniques are signal size reduction, introducing noise into power consumption, randomised execution timing and order, balancing state transitions, key use counters, physically shielding the device, blinding, multithreaded applications, etc [13,2,8,9].

On the other hand, many techniques can be used to bypass or compensate for these countermeasures. We suggest the use of as many redundant countermeasures as available resources permit, because many of the countermeasures can be compensated for if they are implemented alone [11]. The best way to eliminate an attack would be adherence to the cardinal principle [9], which is hard to achieve. According to the cardinal principle, if differential attacks are to be completely eliminated, relevant bits of all intermediate cycles and their values should be statistically independent of the inputs, outputs and sensitive information.

A second category of countermeasures against SDPA attacks involves measures that prevent leakage of sensitive information through the sign of power biases. Due to the presence of unexpected sign-based leakages, a comprehensive vulnerability assessment has to be an integral part of any effort to protect specific implementation. In order to prevent collisions of sensitive information with well-known intermediates, the use of precharged busses is suggested. A similar action should be carried out in all parts of the circuitry where sign-based leakage is observed. An even better solution is to feed registers and busses with random values. The countermeasures should be implemented in hardware, however software based solutions can also provide a significant level of protection.

10   Conclusion

The realities of a physical implementation can be extremely difficult to control. The level of tamper resistance offered by any particular product can be measured by the time and cost penalty that the protective mechanisms impose on the attacker. When the method is known, a side-channel attack on a moderately protected smartcard typically requires a few minutes to several hours to complete, while the cost of the sampling equipment falls in the range from several hundred to several thousand dollars.

We have introduced a sign extension to the differential power analysis. The sign of DPA biases reveal values that collide with the DPA target value within the circuitry. Basically, DPA is used as a tool for testing various hypotheses about secret values in cryptographic algorithms. On the other hand, SDPA is performed on known variables within an algorithm in order to deduce further knowledge about the algorithm. The method is formalised through definitions of SDPA vectors, values and matrices.

SDPA vectors could reveal memory addresses, variable values, counters, operations, permutations etc. Cross-iteration comparisons performed through SDPA matrices improve the interpretation of the SDPA values and provide a significant amount of the information required to reverse engineer a secret algorithm.

Clearly, the actual attack would be highly dependent on the algorithm being implemented, the types of countermeasures and the hardware architecture being used, and would require some guesswork on the part of the attacker. In addition to SDPA, supplementary methods like simple power analysis and substitution block attack, would be needed to completely restore the algorithm under attack.

Countermeasures against side-channel attacks may be based on secret code. Such implementations may be the subject of the SDPA as well; however, the efficiency of the method on those algorithms should be studied further. Further research should also be done on operation signatures, in order to capture the information about power bias magnitudes.

The best way to eliminate attack is strict adherence to the cardinal principle. However, the fundamental rule is that the designers must not rely on secrecy of the algorithm, as the algorithm may be reverse-engineered in the presence of side-channel information leakage.

References

1. Kocher, P.: Timing Attacks on Implementation of Diffie-Hellman, RSA, DSS and Other Systems. In: Koblitz, N. (ed.): Advances in Cryptology - Crypto'96. Lecture Notes in Computer Science, Vol. 1109. Springer-Verlag, Berlin Heidelberg New York (1996) 104–113
2. Kocher, P., Jaffe, J., Jun, B.: Differential Power Analysis. In: Wiener, M. (ed.): Advances in Cryptology - Crypto'99. Lecture Notes in Computer Science, Vol. 1666. Springer-Verlag, Berlin Heidelberg New York (1999) 388–397
3. Agrawal D., Archambeault B., Rao J.R., Rohatgi P.: The EM Side-Channel(s): Attacks and Assessment Methodologies. In: Cryptographic Hardware and Embedded Systems - CHES'2002
4. Chari S., Jutla C., Rao J.R., Rohatgi P.: A Cautionary Note Regarding Evaluation of AES Candidates. In: AES Second Candidate Conference, Rome, Italy, March 22–23 (1999) 133–147
5. Quisquater J.J., Samyde D.: Automatic Code Recognition for Smartcards Using a Kohonen Neural Network. Proceedings of the 5th Smart Card Research and Advanced Application Conference - CARDIS'02, San Jose, CA, USA, November 21–22, USENIX Association (2002)
6. Messerges T.S., Dabbish E.A., Sloan R.H.: Examining Smart-Card Security under the Threat of Power Analysis Attacks. IEEE Transactions on Computers, **51(5)** (2002) 541–552
7. Fahn, P.N., Pearson, P.K.: IPA: A New Class of Power Attacks. In: Koc, C.K., Paar, C. (eds.): Cryptographic Hardware and Embedded Systems - CHES'99. Lecture Notes in Computer Science, Vol. 1717. Springer-Verlag, Berlin Heidelberg New York (1999) 173–186
8. Kömmerling, O., Kuhn, M.G.: Design Principles for Tamper-Resistant Smartcard Processors. Proceedings of the USENIX Workshop on Smartcard Technology - Smartcard'99, Chicago, Illinois, May 10–11, USENIX Association (1999) 9–20
9. Chari S., Jutla C.S., Rao J.R., Rohatgi P.: Towards Sound Countermeasures to Counteract Power-Analysis Attacks. In: Wiener, M. (ed.): Advances in Cryptology - Crypto'99. Lecture Notes in Computer Science, Vol. 1666. Springer-Verlag, Berlin Heidelberg New York (1999) 398–412
10. Akkar M.L., Bevan R., Dischamp P., Moyart D.: Power Analysis, What Is Now Possible. In: Okamoto T. (ed.): ASIACRYPT 2000. Lecture Notes in Computer Science, Vol. 1976. Springer-Verlag, Berlin Heidelberg New York (2000) 489–502
11. Clavier C., Coron J.S., Dabbous N.: Differential Power Analysis in the Presence of Hardware Countermeasures. In: Koc C.K., Paar C. (ed.): Cryptographic Hardware and Embedded Systems - CHES'2000. Lecture Notes in Computer Science, Vol. 1965. Springer-Verlag, Berlin Heidelberg New York (2000) 252–263
12. Novak, R.: Side-Channel Attack on Substitution Blocks. In: 1st MiAn International Conference on Applied Cryptography and Network Security - ACNS'2003, Kunming, China. Lecture Notes in Computer Science. Springer-Verlag, Berlin, Heidelberg, New York (2003) in print
13. Anderson, R., Kuhn, M.: Low Cost Attacks on Tamper Resistant Devices. In: Lomas, M. et al. (ed.): Security Protocols. Lecture Notes in Computer Science, Vol. 1361. Springer-Verlag, Berlin Heidelberg New York (1997) 125–136

Asymmetric Watermarking Scheme
Using Permutation Braids

Geun-Sil Song, Mi-Ae Kim, and Won-Hyung Lee

Graduate School of Advanced Imaging Science, Multimedia & Film, Chung-Ang
University, 221 Hukseok-Dong, Dongjak-Gu, Seoul, Korea
ylem74@netsgo.com,
kimma@deramwiz.com,
whlee@cau.ac.kr

Abstract. In this paper, we propose asymmetric watermarking system using
permutation braids. Asymmetric watermarking system uses different keys for
watermark embedding and detection. In such a scheme, the detector only needs
to know a public key, which does not give enough information to make
watermark removal possible. The proposed watermarking scheme can match
requirements of asymmetric watermarking system. Our experimental result
shows that this scheme provides security from any attempts to identify or
remove the secret key.

1 Introduction

Recently various kinds of digital multimedia data have been widely distributed
through internet. As the commercial price of multimedia data is increased and the
resulting multimedia data can be easily duplicated via network, the importance of
copyright protection for multimedia data becomes more crucial. For this reason,
researcher have started looking for techniques that allow copy control of digital
multimedia data and enable copyright enforcement. It was realized that common
cryptographic means are not displayed in the case of image or video data. To solve
this problem, the digital watermarking techniques have been investigated [8].

Digital watermarking technique embeds an imperceptible secret signal, which
asserts the ownership or intellectual property rights of the media creator or owner. In
order to be effective, a digital watermarking must satisfy the following requirements
[9]:

Imperceptibility: The embedded watermark must be perceptually invisible or
inaudible to maintain the quality of the host media under typical perceptual
conditions. That is, human observers cannot distinguish the original host media from
the watermarked data.

Robustness: The digital watermark is still present in the image after attacks and
can be detected by the watermark detector, especially on the attacks from
compression. Possible attacks include linear or nonlinear filtering, image
enhancements, requantization, resizing, and image compression.

K. Chae and M. Yung (Eds.): WISA 2003, LNCS 2908, pp. 217–226, 2004.
© Springer-Verlag Berlin Heidelberg 2004

Unambiguity: Retrieval of the watermark should unambiguously identify the owner. Furthermore, the accuracy of owner identification should degrade gracefully in the face of attack.

Most existing watermarking schemes are symmetric. Symmetric means that the detection process make use of the parameters used by the embedding process. The knowledge of these parameters allow pirates to forge illegal data by modifying or removing watermark. Using watermark technology for copy protection, the watermark detector needs to be implemented in many cheap consumer devices all over the world. A symmetric watermarking scheme presents a security risk, since the detector has to know the required secret key. However, cheap tamper-proof devices are hardly produceable, and thus, pirates can obtain the secret key from such devices and use them to outwit the copy protection mechanism [4][5]. A solution to this problem is the asymmetric scheme that uses two different keys for embedding and detection process. Detector needing a set of parameters is called the public key. Knowing the public key, it should be neither possible to deduce the secret key nor possible to remove the watermark. Fig.1 shows symmetric and asymmetric watermarking schemes.

In this paper, we propose a new asymmetric watermarking system which renders asymmetry through a permutation braids.

This paper is organized as follows. In section 2, we are described characteristics of proposed asymmetric watermarking schemes. In section 3, we are introduced the asymmetric watermarking scheme using permutation braids. In section 4, the experimental results are shown. The conclusions of our study are given in section 5.

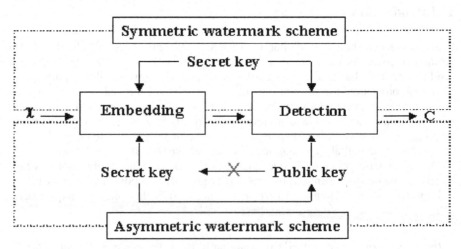

Fig. 1. Symmetric vs asymmetric watermark scheme

2 Review on Asymmetric Watermarking Scheme [3][4][6]

The asymmetric watermarking schemes proposed until now can be classified as two categories. The one is watermark-characteristics-based-method to use as watermarks the signals which have special characteristics such as periodicity. The other is transform-based-method to make a detection key from a given embedding key by a proper transform. In this classification, Legendre-sequence-key by Van Schyndel et al. and eigenvector key by J. Eggers et al. belong to the first category. Hartung and Girod's method, Furon and Duhamel's power spectrum method, and Picard and Robert's neural network method belong to the second category.

In the following, we will briefly present these systems and recall some of their known limitations.

2.1 Hartung and Girod's Method

This is first suggestion of asymmetric watermarking system. Given the secret embedded watermark w and a random vector r uncorrelated with w, the idea is to build the public key p from subsets of r and from w: $p = t\,w + (1 - t)\,r$, where t is a secret binary $(0,1)$ vector. This way, the user does not know which parts of p correspond to the secret key, even though there is sufficient correlation between the watermarked signal and p to ensure detection. However, an attacker can easily remove this correlation by small modifications to the watermarked signal.

2.2 Van Schydel's Method

Van Schydel et al. suggested an asymmetric watermarking system using a length N Legendre sequence a. Legendre sequences have the following features: $Fa = a_{DFT} = ca^*$, where F is DFT matrix, the scalar c can be complex, and a a^* denotes the complex conjugate Legendre sequence. Van Schydel et al. proposed to use the Legendre sequence as a watermark $w = a$, so that the watermarked signal is $y = x + a$.

In detection of the watermark from the transmitted signals r, the correlation between the transmitted signals and its Fourier transformed signals was used as follows: $C = (r^t Fr) / N \approx (ca^h a) / N$. Here, r^h denotes the complex conjugate transpose of r. A large correlation value indicates the existence of the embedded Legendre watermark. The detecting device does not use information on the inserted Legendre sequence. Only the length of the inserted sequence is given.

2.3 Eiggers's Method

The Eigenvector approach extends the initial idea of Legendre watermarking, where the watermark vector w is chosen as an eigenvector of a transform matrix G, i.e. $Gw = \lambda w$. Therefore some correlation can be expected between a watermarked signal $x + w$ and its transform $G(x + w) = Gx + \lambda w$. This allows detection of the watermark knowing only G, which is in the public domain. This technique was thoroughly explored by its authors, and several weaknesses were found: high sensibility to host signal noise, attacks by confusing the detector with a fake watermark w_f with the property that $G\,w_f = -\lambda\,w_f$.

2.4 Furon and Duhamel's Method

Furon and Duhamel suggested a watermarking method using power density spectrum (PDS). We briefly describe the basic principle of the proposed scheme. First, the host signal is permuted to get rid of the statistical dependencies between adjacent signal samples, supposing that the PDS of the permuted signal is flat. Next, a colored noise signal with a specific PDS form is inserted into the permuted host signal. The watermark w is obtained by filtering a white noise signal z of power P_z. Let $H(\Omega)$ denote the frequency response of the selected filter. The PDS of the watermark signal is given by $\Phi_{ww}(\Omega) = P_z |H(\Omega)|^2$. Since the watermark signal w is independent from the host signal x, the PDS of the public signal y is straightforwardly derived as $\Phi_{yy}(\Omega) = P_x + P_z |H(\Omega)|^2$.

In the detection process, the transmitted signal is substituted as in the insertion process, and then the PDS of the permuted received signal r is arrived at. Its similarity to the watermark PDS is measured. If the shape of the PDS of the permuted signal is quite similar to that of the watermark, it is judged that a watermark is inserted. If the permuted signal shows flatness, it is judged that there is no watermark. In this method, the PDS shape of the watermark becomes the public key. The authors said that it is not possible to reveal the embedded watermark as the shape of the spectrum alone does not allow perfect reconstruction due to the loss of the signal phase.

2.5 Simith's Method

J. Simith and C. Dodge suggested a very simple form of an asymmetric scheme. The same watermark is inserted twice. The detection is made by using the correlation of the twice-inserted watermark. That is, the embedding process hides a watermark w of length $\frac{N}{2}$ (N is even) two times in a signal r of length N.

$$r(n) = x(n) + w(\mathrm{mod}(n, \frac{N}{2})) \qquad \forall \in 0, \cdots, N-1$$

where, $\mathrm{mod}(.\,,.)$ is the modulo function.

The detector arrives at the correlation between the two partial sequences r_1 and r_2 by dividing the transmitted signal r into two. The detection process is then :

$$C = \frac{r_1^t r_2}{N/2}$$

A large correlation value indicates the existence of the embedded watermark, which need not be known for the detection process.

2.6 Picard and Robert's Method

Picard and Robert suggested an asymmetric watermarking method using neural network function. The neural network is used as a projection function of an input space into an output space. In a single layer linear neural network, the linear projection function G projects an input space of size N into an output space of size M. The $N \cdot M$ parameters of G, u, are initially generated randomly, and a watermark w of size N is projected using G into the public key p of size M. For a given host x, a watermark w is added to the host to produce the watermarked content $r = x + w$. The detector receives r, and computes its projection r'. The projected content is then correlated with the public key. Then a large correlation value identify an embedded watermark. The public key p and the neural network parameters u are public and the watermark w is secret. Not to determine the secret key, knowing the public key: $p = G(w, u)$, M is lower than N.

3 Asymmetric Watermarking Scheme Using Permutation Braids

In this section, asymmetric watermarking scheme using permutation braids is presented.

3.1 Definition of the n-Braid Group [7]

A braid can be understood as the intertwining or crossing over of parallel strands or strings. The number of strands is called the braid index, and the set of all braids on n strands is denoted $_n$. In an effort to align the algorithm presentation with source code implementation we will use a zero-based indexing convention.

The n-braid group $_n$ is defined by the following group presentation.

$$B_n = \left\langle \sigma_1,...,\sigma_{n-1} \;\middle|\; \begin{array}{l} \sigma_i\sigma_j\sigma_i = \sigma_j\sigma_i\sigma_j, if |i-j| = 1 \\ \sigma_i\sigma_j = \sigma_j\sigma_i, if |i-j| \geq 2 \end{array} \right\rangle$$

Braids have the following geometric interpretation: an n-braid is a set of disjoint n strands all of which are attached to two horizontal bars at the top and at the bottom such that each strand always heads downward as one walks along the strand from the top to the bottom. The braid index is the number of string.

3.2 Describing Braids Using Permutations [7]

The n-braid group $_n$ is an infinite non-commutative group of n-braids defined for each positive integer n. We introduce the notations of the permutation braids. To each permutation $\pi = b_1, b_2, ..., b_n$, we associate an n-braid A that is obtained by connecting the upper i-th point to the lower b_i-th point by a straight line and then making each crossing positive, i.e. the line between i and b_i is under the line between j and b_j if $i < j$. For example if $\pi = 4213$, then $A = \sigma_1\sigma_2\sigma_1\sigma_3$ as in Fig. 2.

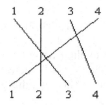

Fig. 2. The braid $A \in \sum n$ corresponding to $\pi = 4213$

The braids made as above is called a permutation braid and $\sum n$ denotes the set of all permutation braids. The correspondence from permutation π to a canonical factor A is a right inverse of $\rho: B_n \rightarrow \sum n$ as a set function. So the cardinality of $\sum n$ is $n!$. The permutation braid can be characterized by the property that every crossing is positive and any pair of strands crosses at most once.

So we can describe a braid $s = \Delta^u A_1 A_2 \ldots A_n$ by a tuple $(u, \pi_1, \pi_2, \ldots, \pi_n)$, where the canonical factor A_n corresponds to the permutation π_n. Here n is called the canonical length, denote by $len(s)$, of s.

3.3 Asymmetric Watermarking Scheme Using Permutation Braids

Asymmetric watermarking systems require that the embedding and detection keys should be different, but that they should be related for proper correlation detection. The watermark embedding process is as follow:

-   Define a braid group binary operations and parameters. We standardize zero based indexing. That means all arrays and consequently strands of a braid start at the label 0.
-   Generate a watermark using a secret key and compute the public key as the projection of the secret key into the permutation braids algorithms. In order to be specific, let a secret key set $s = \{s_i, i=0, 1, \ldots, n-1\}$ be a sequence of length n. The latter is projected using G into the associated public key $p=G(s)$ of length m, where G is the projection function. Here, public key p is a permutation braids. For $j = 0,1, \ldots, m-1$ we have :

$$p_j = \sum_{i=0}^{n-1} s_i \tag{1}$$

-   Embed the watermark by adding it into the host content. The described embedding scheme is analogous to that for common spread spectrum watermarking. Let χ denote the host signal in which the watermark is to be embedded. Then the embedder output is:

$$y_j = x_i + \alpha_i \cdot s_i \tag{2}$$

where, α is a constant number. α is a scaling factor which is the watermark strength and can be adjusted to achieve a reasonable compromise between the robustness of the watermark and its visibility.

The detection operation is a usual correlation process between the decoder input y and the public key, and we call it the public detection. However, must hold to enable the watermark detection without explicit access to the embedded sequence s. With help of G, the embedded watermark s can be detected by measuring the correlation between the received content y and public key : this gives a detection statistic c :

$$c = corr(y \cdot p) = \sum_{j=1}^{M} y_j \cdot p_j \tag{3}$$

As n grows in the braid groups B_n, the computation of group operations become harder in $O(n \log n)$. On the other hand, a naïve computation of the inverse of one-way functions are seem to be at least $O(n!)$. Therefore, it is not possible to determine the secret key, knowing only public key.

3.4 Brute Force Attack

The most important feature of a watermarking system is its ability to withstand attempts to break it. In contrast, the goal of any attack will be removing the embedded watermark. The removal of the watermark without destroying the host signal quality requires the knowledge of the secret key s_i. Since the watermarked signal y and the public keys, p_j ($j = 0, ..., n-1$), are open to attackers, it is required that s_i should not be computed from y and p_j. Any attacker will try to compute the secret watermark from the public watermark.

But in a practical system, the adversary can generate all braids $s = \Delta^u A_1 A_2 \ldots A_n$ in the canonical form with some reasonable bound for n. The number of n-braids A of canonical length n is at least $\left(\dfrac{\ell-1}{2}! \right)^n$. For example, if $\ell = 45$ and $n = 2$, then $\left(\dfrac{\ell-1}{2}! \right)^n > 2^{139}$, which shows that the brute force attack is of no use. The security of the braid groups asymmetric watermarking system, therefore, is inherent in the sense that s_i can not be computed from p_i.

4 Implementation and Results

We present the results of the braid groups asymmetric watermarking system experiments on still images. Experiments is performed on 512×512 Lena image. The experiments method uses discrete wavelet transform (DWT) to decompose the original image into 3-levels. The length of watermark is about 1000.

The watermarked image quality is measured using PSNR(Peak Signal to Noise Ratio) by the equation (6) where MSE is the mean-square error between a watermarked image and original image.

$$PSNR = 10 \cdot \log_{10} \frac{255^2}{MSE^2} = 10 \cdot \log_{10} \frac{255 \cdot 255}{\sum (f(x) - f(x)')^2} \tag{6}$$

The PSNR of Lena image is 42.82(dB). Fig. 3 (a) is the original Lena image and (b) is the watermarked image.

Fig. 3. Experimental results: (a) Original Lena image, (b) Watermarked Lena image

We assume that there are no geometrical alterations on the images. We made both the public detection and the secret detection, under the influence of JPEG coding. The detection was reliable in every case as shown in Fig.4.

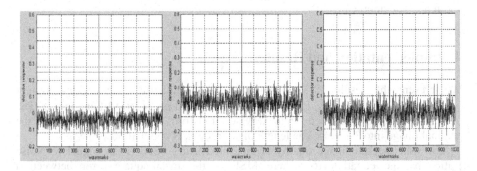

Fig. 4. Watermark detection results. (Left) Symmetric watermark detection, (Middle) Asymmetric watermark detection: public detection, (Right) Asymmetric watermark detection: secret detection

The public detection statistic is computed after JPEG compression with different quality factors, see Fig.5. The watermark can still be detected in the image compressed at the 0 quality factor.

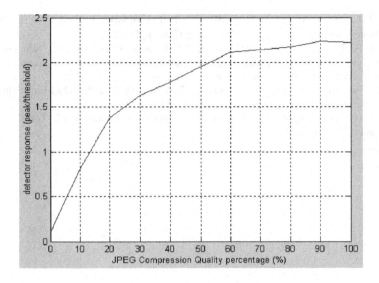

Fig. 5. Robustness comparison against JPEG (Asymmetric watermark detection)

5   Conclusions

In this paper, we propose an asymmetric watermarking system using permutation braids. We use the public key and the watermarked image to detect the secret key. Since the public key is open to the public, the detection is called the public detection. Although the attacker has a public key or original image, it is very difficult to find a secret key. Because permutation braids used to public key have characteristic of one-way function that is based on group operation.

Acknowledgement. The Ministry of Education, Seoul, Korea, supported this research under the BK21 project, and the Industry Research Consortium, the affiliated organization of the Small and Medium Business Administration, supported this research too.

Reference

1. Cox, I. J., Kilian, J., Leighton, T. and Shamoon, T.: Secure Spectrum Watermarking for Multimedia. IEEE Trans. on Image Processing (1997) 1673–1687
2. Cox, I. J., Miller, M. L. and Bloom, J. A.: Digital Watermarking. Morgan Kaufmann Publishers (2001)
3. Eggers, J. J., Su, J. K., and Girod, B.: Public key watermarking by eigenvectors of linear transforms. In Proc. of European Signal Processing Conf., Tampere, Finland (2000)
4. Eggers, J. J., Su, J. K., and Girod, B.: Asymmetric watermarking schemes. Tagungsband des GI Workshops Sicherheit in Mediendaten, Berlin, Germany (2000) 107–123
5. Furon, T., Duhamel, P.: Robustness of asymmetric watermarking technique. In Proc. of the Int. Conf. on Image Processing, Vancouver, Canada (2000)

6. Picard, J., Robert, A.: On the Public Key Watermarking Issue. In Proc. of SPIE , Security and Watermarking of Multimedia Contents III (2001) 290–299
7. Ko, K. H., Lee, S. J., Cheon, J. H., Han, J. W., Kang, J. S., and Park, C.: New public-key Cryptosystem Using Braid Groups. Advances in Cryptology- Crypto 2000, Lecture Notes in Computer Science 1880 (2000) 166–183
8. M.D. Swanson, M. Kobayasi, and A. Tewfik: Multimedia Data-Embedding and Watermarking Technologies. Proc. of IEEE (1998)
9. C.T. Hus and J. L. Wu: Hidden Digital Watermarks in Images. IEEE Trans. on Image Processing (1999) 58–56

Low-Power Design of a Functional Unit for Arithmetic in Finite Fields GF(p) and GF(2^m)

Johann Großschädl and Guy-Armand Kamendje

Graz University of Technology
Institute for Applied Information Processing and Communications
Inffeldgasse 16a, A–8010 Graz, Austria
{Johann.Groszschaedl,Guy-Armand.Kamendje}@iaik.at

Abstract. Recent multi-application smart cards are equipped with powerful 32-bit RISC cores clocked at 33 MHz or even more. They are able to support a variety of public-key cryptosystems, including elliptic curve systems over prime fields GF(p) and binary fields GF(2^m) of arbitrary order. This flexibility is achieved by implementing the cryptographic primitives in software and taking advantage of dedicated instruction set extensions along with special functional units for low-level arithmetic operations. In this paper, we present the design of a low-power multiply/accumulate (MAC) unit for efficient arithmetic in finite fields. The MAC unit combines integer arithmetic and polynomial arithmetic into a single functional unit which can be configured at run-time to serve both types of fields, GF(p) and GF(2^m). Our experimental results show that a properly designed unified (dual-field) multiplier consumes significantly less power in polynomial mode than in integer mode.

Keywords: Multi-application smart cards, elliptic curve cryptography, finite fields, unified multiplier datapath, instruction set extensions.

1 Introduction

In general, embedded systems incorporate a mixture of general-purpose hardware (e.g. processor core, memory, etc.), application-specific hardware[1] (e.g. special functional unit or co-processor), and software. An example for such embedded systems are smart cards, whereby the application-specific hardware may include a cryptographic co-processor or a random number generator. The majority of the smart cards on the market today are equipped with 8-bit micro-controller cores such as Intel's 8051, Motorola's 6805, or Hitachi's H8. More sophisticated smart cards contain a cryptographic co-processor for enhanced arithmetic computation capabilities [12].

The smart card market is currently shifting from the traditional 8-bit smart cards to 16 and 32-bit cards equipped with powerful RISC processors. "Second

---

[1] Application-specific hardware shall be understood as hardware tailored to a certain application or application domain like multimedia processing or cryptography.

K. Chae and M. Yung (Eds.): WISA 2003, LNCS 2908, pp. 227–243, 2004.
© Springer-Verlag Berlin Heidelberg 2004

generation" operating systems like *MULTOS* or *Windows for Smart Cards* sit on top of the card's proprietary system and can host several applications separated by secure firewalls. The RISC cores of these multi-application smart cards support advanced cryptography processing by means of dedicated instruction set extensions, following the idea of multimedia extensions found in today's high-end processors (e.g. Intel's MMX). Well-known microprocessor vendors such as ARM Limited or MIPS Technologies developed optimized 32-bit RISC cores for smart cards with advanced security features and custom instructions for accelerating both symmetric and asymmetric cryptosystems [1,18].

Integrating security technology into the processor core is necessary because cryptographic co-processors are inadequate for next-generation multi-application cards due to limitations in scalability and algorithm agility. For instance, elliptic curve cryptosystems [3] offer a variety of implementations options, which calls for more flexible solutions than fixed-function hardware blocks allow. Augmenting a general-purpose processor with special instructions for performance-critical operations facilitates fast yet flexible implementations of elliptic curve cryptography. Typical candidates for custom instructions are the inner loop operations of low-level arithmetic primitives (e.g. multiplication in finite fields).

The circuitry that actually executes a given kind of instruction is called a *functional unit* (FU). There are two fundamental differences between an FU and a co-processor. Firstly, an FU is tightly coupled to the processor core and directly controlled by the instruction stream, which eliminates the hardware cost of a co-processor interface and dedicated control logic. Secondly, FUs have access to the register file and perform their operations on operands stored in general-purpose registers, whereas a co-processor typically incorporates extra registers for holding the operands involved in the computations.

In this paper, we present a special functional unit (FU) for multiplications and multiply-and-add operations on signed/unsigned integers and binary polynomials. The FU is realized in terms of a multiply/accumulate (MAC) unit and uses the same datapath for both types of operands, i.e. it consists of a so-called unified multiplier datapath. A custom instruction for the word-level multiplication of binary polynomials is very useful for an efficient software implementation of elliptic curve cryptosystems over binary extension fields $GF(2^m)$ [19]. The basic building block of the MAC unit is a (32×32)-bit array multiplier made up of radix-4 partial product generators and unified (4:2) compressors. Our design is optimized for low power consumption and exploits the fact that a properly designed dual-field multiplier consumes significantly less power in polynomial mode than in integer mode. A general-purpose RISC processor equipped with this MAC unit allows fast yet flexible implementations of elliptic curve cryptography over $GF(2^m)$, thereby eliminating the need for a co-processor.

1.1   Related Work

The first approach for combining the hardware of a conventional multiplier with a multiplier for finite fields $GF(2^m)$ was introduced by Drescher *et al.* [6]. They investigated the implementation of arithmetic in $GF(2^m)$, $m \leq 8$, on a DSP datapath for signal coding, in particular BCH codes. Later, polynomial arithmetic was also integrated into the datapath of modular multipliers for cryptographic applications [4]. Savaş et al. presented a scalable and unified architecture for Montgomery multiplication in finite fields $GF(p)$ and $GF(2^m)$ [26]. Their design is based on the observation that polynomial addition can be realized by using an integer addition circuit and simply disabling the carry path. The basic building block of their processing unit (PU) is a so-called dual-field adder (DFA), which is nothing else than a full adder with a small overhead of logic for setting the carry output to zero.

Goodman and Chandrakasan described the implementation of a domain-specific reconfigurable cryptography processor (DSRCP) capable of performing a number of different public-key cryptosystems [8]. The major component of the DSRCP is a reconfigurable 1024-bit datapath made up of simple computation units (CUs), each consisting of two full adders and two NAND gates. These CUs can be reconfigured on the fly to carry out radix-2 Montgomery multiplication of integers modulo a prime p, MSB-first bit-serial multiplication in $GF(2^m)$, as well as inversion in $GF(2^m)$ according to the binary extended Euclidean algorithm. During multiplication in $GF(2^m)$, the CUs use one full adder to compute a 3-input $GF(2)$ addition, whereas the second full adder is disabled to avoid unnecessary switching activities.

A completely different approach for combining integer and polynomial addition was introduced by Au and Burgess [2]. They implemented the addition of integers by using a *redundant binary representation* based on the digit set $\{0, 1, 2\}$, whereby the digits have the following encoding: $0 \sim (0, 0)$, $1 \sim (0, 1)$, and $2 \sim (1, 0)$. A fourth digit, denoted 1* and encoded as $(1, 1)$, represents the 1 in $GF(2)$, which means that the addition of binary polynomials is performed with the digit set $\{0, 1^*\}$. Taking advantage of this special encoding, Au and Burgess proposed a unified (4:2) adder for integers and binary polynomials. The (4:2) adder has a critical path of only three XOR gates and does not need extra control logic to suppress the carries for polynomial addition.

Satoh and Takano presented a scalable elliptic curve cryptographic processor for finite fields $GF(p)$ and $GF(2^m)$, which is able to handle arbitrary field orders without changing the hardware configuration [25]. The core of the processor is a fully parallel $(r \times r)$-bit multiplier based on a Wallace tree architecture, whereby the word-size r is either 8, 16, 32, or 64 bits, depending on the desired trade-off between area and performance. Satoh and Takano's tree network is made up of standard full and half adders, respectively. The adders of the first stage (i.e. the leaf cells) take in three partial products and produce a sum and carry vector. In the subsequent stages, the sum and carry vectors are processed in separate datapaths, i.e. separate sub-trees of the multiplier. That way, the delay for summing up r binary polynomials is only $\lceil \log_3 r \rceil$ full adder delays since any full adder performs a 3-input $GF(2)$ addition. On the other hand, an integer multiplication has a delay of about $\lceil \log_{3/2} r \rceil$ adder stages, coming from the fact that not only sum but also carry vectors need to be processed. Satoh and

Takano's design is highly scalable and can be used for a variety of applications, ranging from embedded micro-controllers to high-speed security servers.

1.2 Our Contributions

Arithmetic in $GF(2^m)$ has several advantages over conventional integer arithmetic used for prime fields. For instance, Satoh and Takano demonstrated that polynomial multiplication is much faster (i.e. allows higher clock frequencies) than the multiplication of integers, simply because of the "carry-free" addition of binary polynomials. Integer multipliers typically use a redundant representation (e.g. carry save form) to avoid time-consuming carry propagation, which causes extra delay in a tree multiplier since both sum and carry vectors must be processed.

In the present paper, we show that polynomial arithmetic has another major advantage over integer arithmetic, namely *less power consumption* and therefore better energy efficiency. The proliferation of portable battery-driven devices makes a good case to design low-power functional units, especially multipliers since they can make a notable contribution to the total power consumption of a RISC processor. We demonstrate that a properly designed dual-field multiplier consumes about 30% less power in polynomial mode than in integer mode.

Furthermore, we present a unified radix-4 partial product generator (PPG) for signed and unsigned integer multiplication as well as for multiplication of binary polynomials. The PPG is based on our previous work [9], but extended to support also the processing of signed operands. In integer-mode, the generation of partial products is performed according to the modified Booth recoding technique [15]. In polynomial mode, on the other hand, the PPG works like a digit-serial polynomial multiplier with a digit-size of $d = 2$ (see [16]). Note that all designs mentioned in the previous subsection are based on radix 2.

2   Architecture of the MAC Unit

Various RISC processors tailored to the embedded systems field contain a fast multiply/accumulate (MAC) unit to facilitate common DSP routines like computation of matrix multiplies, vector dot products, or fast Fourier transforms (FFT). For instance, the MIPS32 4Km features a MAC unit consisting of a 32×16 Booth recoded multiplier, result/accumulation registers (referenced by the names HI and LO), and the necessary control logic [17]. The multiply-and-add (MADD) instruction multiplies two 32-bit words and adds the product to the 64-bit concatenated values in the HI/LO register pair. Then, the resulting value is written back to the HI and LO registers. In other words, the MADD instruction can carry out computations of the form $A \times B + Z$, whereby the operand Z is a double-precision (i.e. 64-bit) quantity. Various signal processing kernels can make heavy use of that instruction, which optimizing compilers automatically generate when appropriate.

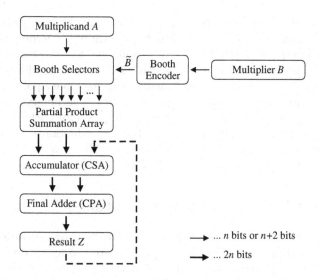

Fig. 1. Main components of the multiply/accumulate unit

In the following sections, we present the design and implementation of a single-cycle $(32 \times 32 + 64)$-bit MAC unit that can execute multiply (MULT) as well as multiply-and-add (MADD) instructions on three different kinds of operands: Unsigned integers, signed integers in two's complement representation, and binary polynomials. The core of the proposed MAC unit is a unified (32×32)-bit multiplier made up of so-called dual-field adders (DFAs). Figure 1 illustrates the architecture of the MAC unit with its main components. Modified Booth recoding [15] is widely employed in parallel multipliers because it reduces the number of partial products by half. We present a unified Booth selector (partial product generator) for signed/unsigned integers and binary polynomials in Section 3. The partial products are summed up by using a redundant representation (e.g. carry-save form) to avoid the time-consuming carry propagation.

A multitude of efficient techniques for partial product summation have been proposed in literature, see e.g. [22] and the references therein. In the simplest case, the addition of partial products can be accomplished with (3:2) counters (carry-save adders) arranged in an array or tree structure. Higher-order counters or compressors generally help to reduce the cycle time. Array multipliers are simple to implement and result in a very regular layout, whereas tree multipliers allow to reach much higher clock frequencies, but at the expense of irregular wiring. We decided to implement the multiplier by means of an array architecture since smart cards, in general, are clocked at moderate frequencies (typically less than 33 MHz).

An Accumulator, which is nothing else than a carry-save adder (CSA), allows the addition of the product to a 64-bit cumulative sum when a MADD instruction is executed[2]. The outputs of the Accumulator represent the result in carry-save

---

[2] MIPS32 processors store the 64-bit cumulative sum in the HI/LO register pair.

form. Now we have convert the sum and carry vector to a standard binary number to obtain the final result. This final addition is accomplished with a carry-propagation adder (CPA). The key point is that the carry-propagation delay occurs only once, at the very end, rather than in each addition step.

The availability of MULT and MADD instructions for binary polynomials allows very efficient implementation of arithmetic operations in binary extension fields $GF(2^m)$. Many standard algorithms for multiple-precision arithmetic of integers — such as Montgomery multiplication or Barrett reduction — can be applied to binary polynomials as well [14,5]. We refer to [10] for a detailed description of word-level algorithms for arithmetic in $GF(2^m)$.

3   Radix-4 Partial Product Generation

The multiplication of two numbers A and B is realized by generation and summation of partial products. Consequently, there are two major options to speed up multiplication: Reduce the number of partial products or accelerate their summation. For the former we need a higher-radix multiplication scheme where two or more bits of the multiplier B are examined at a time. Well-known examples include Booth's algorithm and modified Booth's algorithm (also called Booth-MacSorley algorithm [15]). Figure 1 indicates that modified Booth recoding is performed within two steps: Encoding and Selection (partial product generation).

A unified partial-product generator (PPG) that works for both unsigned integers and binary polynomials was presented in [9]. In this section, we extend the unified PPG to support also signed integers. This is necessary because most modern RISC processors, including the MIPS32 4Km, can deal with both signed and unsigned multiplication. We introduce a radix-4 encoding and partial product generation technique for handling three different types of operands: unsigned integers, signed integers in two's complement form, and binary polynomials. In any case, the number of partial products is reduced by one half compared to the conventional radix-2 (binary) multiplication scheme.

Encoding of Unsigned Integers. The Booth Encoder depicted in Figure 1 converts the n-bit multiplier B into an equivalent radix-4 number $\widetilde{B}$ with digits in $\{-2, -1, 0, 1, 2\}$. From a mathematical point of view, the digit set conversion is performed according to the following equation.

$$B = \sum_{i=0}^{n-1} b_i \cdot 2^i = \sum_{k=0}^{\lfloor n/2 \rfloor + 1} \widetilde{b}_k \cdot 4^k \quad \text{with} \quad \widetilde{b}_k = -2 \cdot b_{2k+1} + b_{2k} + b_{2k-1} \quad (1)$$

We set $b_{n+1} = b_n = 0$ when B is an n-bit unsigned integer. Furthermore, b_{-1} is always 0, and therefore the least significant digit of the encoded multiplier can be computed as $\widetilde{b}_0 = -2 \cdot b_1 + b_0$. Given an n-bit unsigned multiplier B, radix-4 Booth recoding reduces the number of partial products to $\lfloor n/2 \rfloor + 1$. Applying radix-4 Booth recoding to (32×32)-bit multiplication means that we have to

Table 1. Partial product generation for integers and binary polynomials

Multiplier bits			Integer mode (*fsel* = 1)				Polynomial mode (*fsel* = 0)			
b_{2k+1}	b_{2k}	b_{2k-1}	P_k	*inv*	*trp*	*shl*	$P_k(t)$	*inv*	*trp*	*shl*
0	0	0	0	0	0	0	0	0	0	0
0	0	1	$+A$	0	1	0	0	0	0	0
0	1	0	$+A$	0	1	0	$A(t)$	0	1	0
0	1	1	$+2A$	0	0	1	$A(t)$	0	1	0
1	0	0	$-2A$	1	0	1	$t{\cdot}A(t)$	0	0	1
1	0	1	$-A$	1	1	0	$t{\cdot}A(t)$	0	0	1
1	1	0	$-A$	1	1	0	$t{\cdot}A(t){\oplus}A(t)$	0	1	1
1	1	1	0	0	0	0	$t{\cdot}A(t){\oplus}A(t)$	0	1	1

generate and sum up 17 partial products $P_k = \tilde{b}_k \cdot A$ for $0 \le k \le 16$. Note that the partial product P_{16} is either 0 or the multiplicand A since $b_{33} = b_{32} = 0$ and consequently $\tilde{b}_{16} = b_{31} \in \{0,1\}$. The fourth column of Table 1 shows the value of the partial product P_k depending on the multiplier bits b_{2k+1}, b_{2k}, and b_{2k-1}. Using the digit set $\{-2,-1,0,1,2\}$ for the encoded multiplier $\tilde{B}$ has the advantage that only the multiples $\pm 2A$, $\pm A$ of the multiplicand A are required when a radix-4 multiplication is performed with $\tilde{B}$. The generation of partial products is therefore simply a matter of shifting and/or inverting[3] the multiplicand A.

Encoding of Signed Integers. A Booth multiplier requires to handle singed numbers properly since the partial products can have positive or negative values (see Table 1). The two's complement (TC) form is the most widespread method for representing signed numbers because it allows to treat addition and subtraction equally [22]. On the other hand, radix-4 multiplication of TC numbers requires a different Encoding since the MSB of a number in TC form has a negative weight, whereas the weight of an unsigned number's MSB is positive.

$$B = b_{n-1} \cdot (-2^{n-1}) + \sum_{i=0}^{n-2} b_i \cdot 2^i = \sum_{k=0}^{\lceil n/2 \rceil} \tilde{b}_k \cdot 4^k \; ; \quad \tilde{b}_k = -2 \cdot b_{2k+1} + b_{2k} + b_{2k-1} \quad (2)$$

For an n-bit signed multiplier B given in TC form, the encoded version $\tilde{B}$ can be computed according to Equation (2). However, it is important to consider that modified Booth's algorithm yields the correct result only if the sign bit b_{n-1} is extended properly, i.e. we have to set $b_{n+1} = b_n = b_{n-1}$ when B is represented in TC form (b_{-1} is always 0). A second difference between unsigned and signed (TC) Booth multiplication is the number of digits in the radix-4 representation of the multiplier. Applying Equation (2) to encode an n-bit TC number B leads

---

[3] Negative multiples (in two's complement form) can be obtained by inverting the corresponding positive multiple (i.e. producing the one's complement) and adding a "1" at the least significant position of the partial product [22]. This addition is typically performed in the partial product summation array or tree.

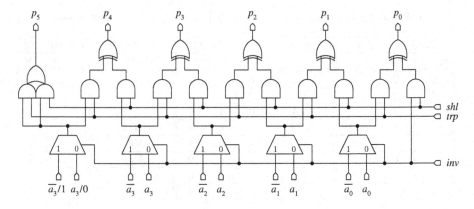

Fig. 2. Unified radix-4 PPG for signed/unsigned integers and binary polynomials

to a radix-4 representation $\widetilde{B}$ consisting of exactly $\lceil n/2 \rceil$ digits $\widetilde{b}_k$. Given a 32-bit multiplier B, we have to sum up 17 partial products when B is unsigned, but only 16 partial products when B is a signed number in TC form. Therefore, Booth multipliers for both signed and unsigned multiplication are generally designed to sum up $\lfloor n/2 \rfloor + 1$ partial products, whereby the last partial product is set to 0 when a signed multiplication has to be performed [7]. This requires no extra control logic since the last partial product is automatically 0 due to the sign extension of B, e.g. for $n = 32$ we get $\widetilde{b}_{16} = -2 \cdot b_{33} + b_{32} + b_{31} = 0$ because $b_{33} = b_{32} = b_{31}$.

Encoding of Binary Polynomials. The multiplication of two binary polynomials $A(t), B(t)$ is performed in a similar way as integer multiplication, namely by generation and addition of partial products. However, signed-digit recoding techniques like Booth recoding do not work for binary polynomials [9]. On the other hand, the generation of partial products for high-radix (digit-serial) multiplication of binary polynomials is simply a matter of AND and XOR operations [16]. Digit-serial polynomial multiplication with a digit-size of $d = 2$ requires a two-coefficient operand scan in which either 0, 1, t, or $t+1$ times the multiplicand $A(t)$ is added, depending on the corresponding coefficients of $B(t)$.

$$B(t) = \sum_{i=0}^{n-1} b_i \cdot t^i = \sum_{k=0}^{\lceil n/2 \rceil} \widetilde{b}_k(t) \cdot t^{2k} \quad \text{with} \quad \widetilde{b}_k(t) = b_{2k+1} \cdot t + b_{2k} \quad (3)$$

Consequently, any partial product $P_k(t) = \widetilde{b}_k(t) \cdot A(t)$ is a polynomial from the set $\{0, A(t), t \cdot A(t), t \cdot A(t) \oplus A(t)\}$. The multiplication of $A(t)$ by t is nothing else than a 1-bit left shift of the coefficients of $A(t)$.

Design of a Unified PPG. Figure 2 shows a partial product generator for signed/unsigned integers and binary polynomials. The PPG is controlled by an

Encoder circuit via the three signals *inv* (invert), *trp* (transport), and *shl* (shift left). These signals depend on the multiplier bits b_{2k+1}, b_{2k}, and b_{2k-1} according to Equations (4)-(6), as can be easily derived from Table 1. An additional control signal, *fsel* (field select), allows to switch between integer-mode ($fsel = 1$) and polynomial-mode ($fsel = 0$). The circuit shown in Figure 2 needs A (the multiplicand) and $\overline{A}$ as an input, and the multiplexors select between A and $\overline{A}$. The AND/XOR combination allows to perform a 1-bit left-shift operation.

$$inv = fsel \cdot \left(b_{2k+1} \cdot \overline{b}_{2k} + b_{2k+1} \cdot b_{2k} \cdot \overline{b}_{2k-1} \right) \tag{4}$$

$$trp = fsel \cdot \left(\overline{b}_{2k} \cdot b_{2k-1} + b_{2k} \cdot \overline{b}_{2k-1} \right) + \overline{fsel} \cdot b_{2k} \tag{5}$$

$$shl = fsel \cdot \left(\overline{b}_{2k+1} \cdot b_{2k} \cdot b_{2k-1} + b_{2k+1} \cdot \overline{b}_{2k} \cdot \overline{b}_{2k-1} \right) + \overline{fsel} \cdot b_{2k+1} \tag{6}$$

In integer mode ($fsel = 1$), the PPG works as follows: When $inv = 1$, the corresponding partial product is negative, i.e. $P_k = -2A$ or $-A$. Control signal $trp = 1$ means $P_k = \pm A$ (no left-shift). On the other hand, when $shl = 1$, a 1-bit left-shift has to be performed, i.e. $P_k = \pm 2A$. Last but not least, $P_k = 0$ is generated by $trp = shl = 0$. In integer mode, it is possible that *inv* and *trp* or *shl* are equal to 1 at the same time, but $trp = shl = 1$ will never occur. In polynomial mode ($fsel = 0$), the signal *inv* is always 0 and the PPG is directly controlled by the multiplier bits, i.e. $trp = b_{2k}$ and $shl = b_{2k+1}$. Therefore, the unified PPG works like a digit-serial polynomial multiplier with a digit-size of $d = 2$.

A parallel $(n \times n)$-bit multiplier for signed/unsigned multiplication contains $\lfloor n/2 \rfloor + 1$ PPGs and the same number of Encoder circuits. The partial products are $n + 2$ bits long as they are represented in two's complement form. However, the generation of partial products for signed multiplication differs slightly from unsigned multiplication. To process a signed multiplicand A, the sign bit a_{n-1} must be extended by one position. The leftmost multiplexor of the PPG is either connected to a_{n-1} (signed multiplication), or to 0 (unsigned multiplication).

4   Addition of Partial Products

A standard $(n \times n)$-bit radix-4 array multiplier consists of $n/2$ stages of carry-save adders (CSAs) [22]. Higher-order counters or compressors can be used to reduce the cycle time. Each CSA stage takes three inputs of the same weight and generates two outputs, i.e. the intermediate result is kept in redundant representation (the so-called carry-save form) to avoid carry propagation.

The rules of two's complement arithmetic demand an extension of the sign bit. Therefore, the $(n + 2)$-bit partial products have to be sign extended up to the $2n$-th bit position as illustrated in Figure 3. However, the actual width of the sign bit extension depends on the chosen addition method [24]. In general, sign extension should be minimized since the addition of extended sign bits increases the hardware cost and contributes to power consumption. On the other hand, the sign bits are necessary to process partial products which have a negative value. As mentioned in Section 3, a typical Booth PPG performs merely an inversion when the generation of a negative partial product is intended. This requires that

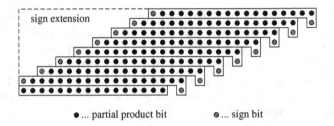

● ... partial product bit   ◎ ... sign bit

Fig. 3. Radix-4 multiplication of 16-bit unsigned integers

a "1" is added at the least significant position of the partial product in order to get the correct two's complement representation. Most Booth multipliers do this "correction" at the CSA stage where the partial product is added, e.g. by setting the LSB of the output carry vector to 1.

Each partial product, except for the last one, is $n + 2$ bits long. The partial products are added according to their "weight" (i.e. in the appropriate relative position) to obtain the correct result. For instance, partial product P_1 has four times the weight of P_0, which means that it is offset by two bit positions. Note that the last partial product (i.e. P_{16} in our case) is either 0 or the multiplicand A, and hence it can never have a negative value[4]. The cumulative sum Z is a 64-bit quantity and added in the Accumulator. In our implementation, we merged the CSA stages for partial product summation with the Accumulator in order to reduce overall hardware cost and delay.

The first three partial products, P_0, P_1, and P_2, can be summed up in one CSA stage [11]. All remaining partial products require an additional CSA stage, which means that we need 16 CSA stages altogether to sum up the 17 partial products and the cumulative sum Z. The datapath of an $(n \times n + 2n)$-bit MAC unit consists of $(\lfloor n/2 \rfloor - 1) \cdot (n + 2)$ adder cells to sum up the $\lfloor n/2 \rfloor + 1$ partial products. Furthermore, $2n$ adder cells are required to add the $2n$-bit quantity Z. The overall delay of the array including Accumulator is $\lfloor n/2 \rfloor$ adder cells.

We will not discuss further details in this paper since the implementation of an array multiplier is fairly simple. However, we refer the interested reader to Huang's thesis [13], which serves as an extensive and state-of-the-art reference for low-power multiplier design.

4.1   Counters and Compressors for Dual-Field Arithmetic

Savaş *et al.* define a dual-field adder (DFA) as *a full adder which is capable of performing addition both with carry and without carry* [26]. A DFA has an extra input, called *fsel* (field select), that allows to switch between integer mode and polynomial mode. When *fsel* = 1 (integer mode), the DFA operates like a standard full adder, i.e. it performs a bitwise addition with carry. On the other

---

[4] Recall that a radix-4 Booth multiplier has to sum up $\lfloor n/2 \rfloor + 1$ partial products when the operands are unsigned, but only $\lceil n/2 \rceil$ partial products for signed integers.

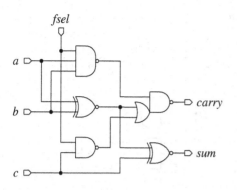

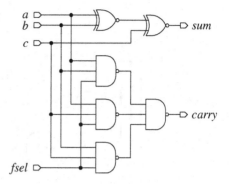

Fig. 4. Dual-field adder presented in [10]   **Fig. 5.** DFA for (4:2) compressor design

hand, when $fsel = 0$, the DFA's *carry* output is always 0, regardless of the input values. The *sum* output computes a 3-input XOR operation, which corresponds to the addition of binary polynomials. Therefore, we can use exactly the same hardware for the addition of both integers and binary polynomials.

Figure 4 shows a DFA for standard cell implementation, which was first presented in our previous work [10]. An important aspect when designing a DFA is not to increase the critical path of the circuit compared to a conventional full adder. The critical path of the DFA depicted in Figure 4 is determined by the two XNOR gates. Thus, the delay of the DFA is not larger than that of a standard full adder. We point out that in polynomial mode ($fsel = 0$), the outputs of the two NAND gates are forced to 1 and the output *cout* is always 0. Hence, only the two XNOR gates are active and contribute to power consumption. Simulations with random input patterns show that this DFA consumes approximately 42% less power in polynomial mode than in integer mode.

The DFA illustrated in Figure 5 also avoids unnecessary switching activities when polynomial addition is performed. This design has the advantage that it allows very efficient implementation of (4:2) compressors. In the past, (4:2) compressors have been widely used in tree multipliers, whereas there is relatively little previous work on applying them in array multipliers. A (4:2) compressor has the same gate complexity as two carry-save adders, but is typically faster than two cascaded CSAs because an efficient design has only three XOR delays, while each single CSA has a delay of two XORs. Consequently, when (4:2) compressors are used in an array multiplier, the delay for partial product summation is reduced by about 25%. This also reduces the power consumption as less switching activities arise when signals propagate fewer stages [13].

The DFA illustrated in Figure 5 was motivated by the balanced (4:2) compressor presented in [21]. The efficiency of the design is based on the observation that NAND gates are typically much faster than XOR/XNOR gates (in typical standard cell libraries up to twice as fast). Under this assumption, the DFA shown in Figure 5 has "fast" and "slow" inputs and outputs, respectively. For instance, input c is a fast input since the delay from c to either output is only

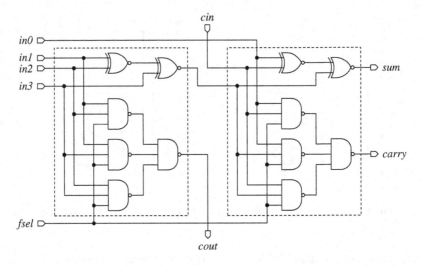

Fig. 6. Balanced (4:2) compressor composed of dual-field adders

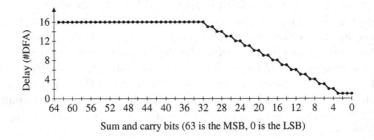

Sum and carry bits (63 is the MSB, 0 is the LSB)

Fig. 7. Signal arrival profile of a $(32 \times 32 + 64)$-bit array multiplier

one equivalent XNOR delay. Inputs a and b are slow inputs because their path to the *sum* output contains two XNOR gates. Similarly, the output *carry* is a fast output, whereas *sum* is a slow output. Oklobdžija *et al.* introduced an algorithmic approach for designing high-speed multipliers, taking the different input-to-output delays of counters or compressors into account [21]. By connecting slow outputs with fast inputs and vice versa, as shown in Figure 6, a fast (4:2) compressor can be built with two DFAs. The delay of this "balanced" (4:2) compressor is only three XNOR gates (provided, of course, that two NANDs do not cause more delay than an XNOR gate).

5 Final Adder

When designing a final adder, it is important to consider the signal arrival profile of the sum and carry vector [20]. Figure 7 shows the signal arrival profile of a $(32 \times 32 + 64)$-bit array multiplier as described in Section 4. The low-order bits

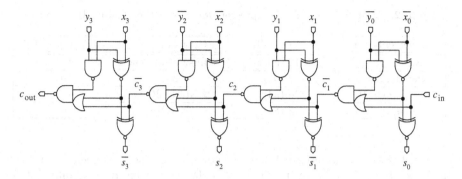

Fig. 8. Example of a 4-bit ripple-carry adder for standard-cell implementation

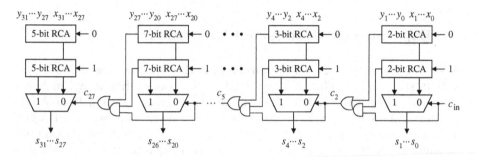

Fig. 9. Typical implementation of a 32-bit carry-select adder (see [23] for details)

arrive sequentially, whilst the upmost 32 bits of the sum and carry vector arrive simultaneously. It is easily observed from Figure 3 that the first four bits have to pass only the DFA stage of the Accumulator, i.e. they arrive after a delay of one DFA cell. The next two bits of the sum and carry vector have an additional delay of one DFA cell, and the following two bits have an overall delay of three DFA cells, etc. Finally, the upmost 32 bits arrive after passing 16 DFA cells.

Our final adder is realized in the same way as described in [11], namely by means of a "hybrid" adder made up of elements of carry-select addition and ripple-carry addition. For the redundant to non-redundant conversion of the topmost 32 bits, we employ a carry-select adder composed of "small" ripple-carry adders (RCAs). A carry-select adder divides the words to be added into blocks (not necessarily of the same size) and forms two sums for each block in parallel, one with a carry-in of "0" and the other with a carry-in of "1". When the actual carry of the previous block arrives, the appropriate result is selected with the help of multiplexors [22]. A major attraction of carry-select adders is the regularity of the layout.

Considering the non-equal arrival times of the low order bits, it becomes evident to use concatenated 2-bit ripple-carry adders (RCAs) for the final addition of these bits. Ripple-carry adders are generally designed so that the carry-in to

Table 2. Comparison of (4:2) compressors for unified (i.e. dual-field) arithmetic

Implementation	#Gates (#Tr.)	Critical path	Act. gates GF(2)
Savaş et al. [26]	10 (60)	XOR+2AOI+2NOR	6
Au & Burgess [2]	10 (56)	3XOR	10
Prev. work [10]	10 (64)	2XNOR+2OAI	4
This work	12 (80)	3XNOR	4

carry-out delay is minimized. Figure 8 shows a possible implementation of an RCA, whereby the carry-in to carry-out delay of a k-bit RCA is only k OAI gates (excluding inverters). Figure 9 depicts the carry-select adder that we use to convert the 32 MSBs of the redundant result into binary representation.

6   Experimental Results and Discussion

We developed a $(32 \times 32 + 64)$-bit prototype of the MAC unit based on a 0.6 μm CMOS standard cell library. The partial product summation array (including Accumulator) consists of 572 DFA cells and has a critical path of 16 DFA cells for the addition of 17 partial products along with the extra operand Z. Measured in terms of gate delays, the critical path of the partial product summation array is only 24 XNORs since we used the balanced (4:2) compressors described in Subsection 4.1. The overall gate count of the MAC unit is roughly 10k.

Simulations based on a netlist with extracted parasitics show that the delay of our prototype is slightly less than 30 ns, which corresponds to a maximum clock frequency of 33 MHz. This clock speed is sufficient for smart card applications, even though a significant performance gain could be achieved by using a state-of-the-art CMOS technology. We also simulated the power dissipation of the MAC unit for both integer and polynomial mode. Our results indicate that the overall power consumption of the MAC unit is about 30% lower when polynomial multiplications are executed. This is primarily because the dual-field adders were designed to suppress all unnecessary switching activities when polynomial arithmetic is performed (see Figure 5)

Table 2 provides a comparison of our design with previous works that disclosed gate-level schematics of the implemented dual-field adders. We analyzed four different (4:2) compressors based on the DFAs published in [26], [2], and our previous work [10] (i.e. the DFA depicted in Figure 4). The second column indicates the gate and transistor count of the compressors. The critical path shown in the third column was determined by interconnecting two DFAs so that the overall delay is minimized. The fourth column lists the number of active gates in polynomial mode, which is an indicator for the power consumption.

The (4:2) adder introduced by Au and Burgess is small and very fast, but has high power consumption in polynomial mode, which is due to the encoding they used. Savaş et al's design has a longer critical path and does also show unnecessary power consumption in polynomial mode. The critical path of our previous design [10] is slightly longer than the minimum of three XOR/XNOR gates. Note that unnecessary switching activities do not take place in our previous design, which is also the case for the design described in this paper. The present design features the minimum delay of three XNOR gates, i.e. it combines a short critical path with low power consumption. However, the gate count of the proposed (4:2) compressor is slightly higher than that of the others.

7 Conclusions

We presented the design of a $(32 \times 32 + 64)$-bit multiply/accumulate (MAC) unit for signed/unsigend integers and binary polynomials. It performs multiply and multiply-and-add operations within one clock cycle and can be easily integrated into general-purpose RISC processors. The datapath of the MAC unit is modular, consists of only very few basic cells, and results in a very regular and compact layout. Our design is based on a unified radix-4 partial-product generator in combination with an optimized (4:2) compressor for signed/unsigned integers and binary polynomials. The extra functionality for polynomial arithmetic is very simple to integrate into a standard multiplier and causes virtually no speed penalty. A slight increase in silicon area is tolerable for most applications, especially when considering that a cryptographic co-processor would require much more silicon area than the modification of a standard multiplier datapath for dual-field arithmetic.

The main result of our work is that a properly designed dual-field multiplier consumes significantly less power in polynomial mode than in integer mode (approximately 30% in our implementation). Instruction set extensions along with low-power functional units open up new options for fast and energy-efficient software implementation of elliptic curve cryptography. For many applications, including smart cards and other kinds of embedded systems, the functional unit can eliminate the need for a cryptographic co-processor.

References

1. ARM Limited. ARM SecurCore Solutions. Product brief, available for download at http://www.arm.com/aboutarm/4XAFLB/$File/SecurCores.pdf, 2002.
2. L.-S. Au and N. Burgess. A (4:2) adder for unified GF(p) and GF(2^n) Galois field multipliers. In *Conference Record of the 36th Asilomar Conference on Signals, Systems, and Computers*, vol. 2, pp. 1619–1623. IEEE, 2002.
3. I. F. Blake, G. Seroussi, and N. P. Smart. *Elliptic Curves in Cryptography*. Cambridge University Press, 1999.
4. M. Bucci. Dual mode (integer, polynomial) fast modular multipliers. Presentation at the Rump Session of EUROCRYPT '97, Konstanz, Germany, May 13, 1997.
5. J.-F. Dhem. Efficient modular reduction algorithm in $\mathbb{F}_q[x]$ and its application to "left to right" modular multiplication in $\mathbb{F}_2[x]$. In *Cryptographic Hardware and Embedded Systems — CHES 2003*, LNCS 2779, pp. 203–213. Springer Verlag, 2003.

6. W. Drescher, K. Bachmann, and G. Fettweis. VLSI architecture for datapath integration of arithmetic over GF(2^m) on digital signal processors. In *Proceedings of the 22nd IEEE Int. Conference on Acoustics, Speech, and Signal Processing (ICASSP '97)*, vol. 1, pp. 631–634. IEEE, 1997.

7. A. A. Farooqui and V. G. Oklobdžija. General data-path organization of a MAC unit for VLSI implementation of DSP processors. In *Proceedings of the 31st IEEE Int. Symposium on Circuits and Systems (ISCAS '98)*, vol. 2, pp. 260–263. IEEE, 1998.

8. J. R. Goodman and A. P. Chandrakasan. An energy efficient reconfigurable public-key cryptography processor architecture. In *Cryptographic Hardware and Embedded Systems — CHES 2000*, LNCS 1965, pp. 175–190. Springer Verlag, 2000.

9. J. Großschädl. A unified radix-4 partial product generator for integers and binary polynomials. In *Proceedings of the 35th IEEE Int. Symposium on Circuits and Systems (ISCAS 2002)*, vol. 3, pp. 567–570. IEEE, 2002.

10. J. Großschädl and G.-A. Kamendje. Instruction set extension fast elliptic curve cryptography over binary finite fields GF(2^m). In *Proceedings of the 14th IEEE Int. Conference on Application-specific Systems, Architectures and Processors (ASAP 2003)*, pp. 455–468. IEEE Computer Society Press, 2003.

11. J. Großschädl and G.-A. Kamendje. A single-cycle ($32 \times 32 + 32 + 64$)-bit multiply/accumulate unit for digital signal processing and public-key cryptography. Accepted for presentation at the 10th IEEE Int. Conference on Electronics, Circuits and Systems (ICECS 2003), scheduled for Dec. 14-17, 2003 in Sharjah, U.A.E.

12. H. Handschuh and P. Paillier. Smart card crypto-coprocessors for public-key cryptography. In *Smart Card Research and Applications — CARDIS '98*, LNCS 1820, pp. 372–379. Springer Verlag, 2000.

13. Z. Huang. *High-Level Optimization Techniques for Low-Power Multiplier Design.* Ph.D. Thesis, University of California, Los Angeles, CA, USA, 2003.

14. Ç. K. Koç and T. Acar. Montgomery multiplication in GF(2^k). *Designs, Codes and Cryptography*, 14(1):57–69, Apr. 1998.

15. O. L. MacSorley. High-speed arithmetic in binary computers. *Proceedings of the IRE*, 49(1):67–91, Jan. 1961.

16. M. C. Mekhallalati, A. S. Ashur, and M. K. Ibrahim. Novel radix finite field multiplier for GF(2^m). *Journal of VLSI Signal Processing*, 15(3):233–245, Mar. 1997.

17. MIPS Technologies, Inc. MIPS32 4Km^{TM} processor core family data sheet. Available for download at http://www.mips.com/publications/index.html, 2001.

18. MIPS Technologies, Inc. SmartMIPS Architecture Smart Card Extensions. Product brief, available for download at http://www.mips.com/ProductCatalog/P_SmartMIPSASE/SmartMIPS.pdf, 2001.

19. E. M. Nahum, S. W. O'Malley, H. K. Orman, and R. C. Schroeppel. Towards high performance cryptographic software. In *Proceedings of the 3rd IEEE Workshop on the Architecture and Implementation of High Performance Communication Subsystems (HPCS '95)*, pp. 69–72. IEEE, 1995.

20. V. G. Oklobdžija. Design and analysis of fast carry-propagate adder under non-equal input signal arrival profile. In *Conference Record of the 28th Asilomar Conference on Signals, Systems, and Computers*, vol. 2, pp. 1398–1401. IEEE, 1994.

21. V. G. Oklobdžija, D. Villeger, and S. S. Liu. A method for speed optimized partial product reduction and generation of fast parallel multipliers using an algorithmic approach. *IEEE Transactions on Computers*, 45(3):294–306, Mar. 1996.

22. B. Parhami. *Computer Arithmetic: Algorithms and Hardware Designs.* Oxford University Press, 2000.

23. J. M. Rabaey. *Digital Integrated Circuits – A Design Perspective*. Prentice Hall, 1996.

24. O. Salomon, J.-M. Green, and H. Klar. General algorithms for a simplified addition of 2's complement numbers. *IEEE Journal of Solid-State Circuits*, 30(7):839–844, July 1995.

25. A. Satoh and K. Takano. A scalable dual-field elliptic curve cryptographic processor. *IEEE Transactions on Computers*, 52(4):449–460, Apr. 2003.

26. E. Savaş, A. F. Tenca, and Ç. K. Koç. A scalable and unified multiplier architecture for finite fields $GF(p)$ and $GF(2^m)$. In *Cryptographic Hardware and Embedded Systems — CHES 2000*, LNCS 1965, pp. 277–292. Springer Verlag, 2000.

Efficient Implementation of Relative Bid Privacy in Sealed-Bid Auction

Kun Peng, Colin Boyd, Ed Dawson, and Kapalee Viswanathan

ISRC, IT Faculty, Queensland University of Technology
2 Goerge Street, Brisbane, QLD4000, Australia
{k.peng,c.boyd,e.dawson,k.viswanathan}@qut.edu.au
http://www.isrc.qut.edu.au

Abstract. The concept of relative bid privacy in auction is proposed, which does not conceal the bids, but conceals the link between them and the corresponding bidders. Relative bid privacy leads to three advantages: high efficiency, the bidding values can be very precise and any auction rule can be applied. A new mix network is designed and applied to implement relative bid privacy efficiently. Two rounds of shuffling are employed in the mix network, so that fairness can be achieved in the auction without any trust and relative bid privacy is achieved even in abnormal situations.

1 Introduction

In a sealed-bid auction, every bidder offers a sealed bid for some merchandise on sale and after the bids are open the wining price and the winner can be determined according to a pre-defined auction rule. A sealed-bid auction is usually composed of four phases. In the preparation phase, the auction system is set up (e.g. parameter generation) and prepared for bidding. Next every bidder submits a sealed bid in the bid submission phase. Then in the bid opening phase, the bids are opened. Finally in the winning price and winner determination phase, the result of the auction is determined.

The following properties are often required in sealed-bid auction schemes. Some properties are compulsory in any auction applications. They must be satisfied without trust on any party.

1. Correctness: Correct winning price and winner(s) are determined according to the auction rule.
2. Confidentiality: Each bid remains confidential to other bidders and the auctioneer(s) before the bid opening phase starts.
3. Fairness: No bidder can choose his bid according to other bidders' bids.
   - No bidder has any knowledge of any other bids before the bid submission phase ends.
   - After the bid submission phase ends, no bidder can change his bid.
4. Non-repudiation: The winner cannot deny his bid.

K. Chae and M. Yung (Eds.): WISA 2003, LNCS 2908, pp. 244–256, 2004.

5. Robustness: Any malicious behaviour of any party cannot compromise the system or lead to an incorrect result.

Other properties can be selected to be satisfied in different applications. Their achievement can be based on trust in some parties (e.g. a threshold trust on the auctioneers).

1. Public Verifiability: The validity of the auction result can be publicly verifiable.
2. Price Flexibility: The biddable prices are not limited to a fixed set of prices. The bids can be as precise as the bidders like.
3. Rule Flexibility: The auction protocol is independent of the auction rules. The simplest auction is first bid auction, in which a single item is on sale and the bidder with the highest bid wins and pays his bidding price for the item. In a Vickrey (second-bid) auction, a single item is on sale and the bidder with the highest bid wins but pays the second highest bidding price for the item. In k^{th} bid auction, $k - 1$ identical items are on sale, the kth bidding price is the clearing price and bidders with higher bids are winners.
4. Privacy: There are several ways to define the privacy of losing bids. In our paper only relative bid privacy, namely the unlinkability between the true identity of bidders and the values of their bids, is achieved.

It is required that all these properties are achieved in a computationally and communicationally efficient manner. In this paper, an auction scheme achieving relative bid privacy is proposed. To hide the link between the bids and the bidders, a new mix network is designed to realize an anonymous channel for the bidders to submit and open the bids anonymously. All the bids are published in plaintext after the bid opening phase, so that any auction rules can be applied. Moreover, there is no limitation on the values of the bids and they can be as precise as the bidders require. Due to the high efficiency of the mix network, the proposed auction scheme is very efficient.

2   Background

2.1   Absolute Bid Privacy and Relative Bid Privacy

Bid privacy is a very important and frequently required property in sealed-bid auction schemes. It has a great influence on other properties, especially computational efficiency. Bid privacy may be strong (little or no trust is needed) or weak (strong trust is needed).

According to the motivation behind it, bid privacy can be classified into absolute bid privacy and relative bid privacy. There are many motivations to support this property. The following are the most common two.

1. Bidders want their bidding behaviours to be untraceable. Especially they do not want their evaluations of items to be collected, which is a violation of their personal privacy and may violate their benefit in a later auction.

2. Sellers should be prevented from knowing the bidding values or their distribution. Otherwise they may gain some advantage when selling an identical or similar item in the future.

Absolute bid privacy requires that after the auction is finished:

- a bidder knows only his own bidding value, the results (the clearing price and identity of the winner(s)) and information that can be deduced from them;
- seller, auctioneers or other parties only know the results and information that can be deduced from them.

However, in some applications, only the first motivation is required and the second is not necessary. In this case, only relative bid privacy need be employed. Relative bid privacy means at the end of the auction, although the bids are opened and published in plaintext, the only information revealed from the auction about the link between bidders and their bids is:

- each winner has a bid no less than the winning price;
- each loser has a bid less than the winning price.

Schemes only achieving relative bid privacy inherently achieve price flexibility and rule flexibility because any bid values can be used, and since they are published, any formula can be used to find the winner. However, there must be an anonymous channel between the bidders and the published plaintext bids.

2.2   Mix Networks

A mix network shuffles a number of ciphertext inputs, each from a user, to the same number of plaintext outputs, so that

1. the output is a permutation of the plaintexts of the input;
2. the permutation between the inputs and the outputs is unknown, so that the users cannot be linked to their outputs.

These two properties are called *correctness* and *privacy*. A mix network obtains *robustness* if it can still work properly in abnormal situations (e.g. invalid shuffling occurs). A mix network is *publicly verifiable* if its correctness can be publicly verified. A mix network is secure if it is correct, private, robust and publicly verifiable. A mix network is usually composed of a few servers, working in sequence. Each server gets its inputs from the previous server and permutes them to a set of outputs, which are inputs to the next server.

Since the first mix network proposed by Chaum [6], many mix networks have been proposed [1,2,4,6,9,10,11,12,13,20,21,22,27]. However, most of them failed to achieve publicly and efficiently verifiable strong correctness while maintaining strong privacy.

Park *et al* [24] proposed a mix network that employs two rounds of shuffling. In the first round, short-term public keys of the users are shuffled and the servers do not prove correctness of their shuffling. Each user checks that his public key is among the published results of the first round shuffling and protests if the check fails. In the second round, the users' inputs signed by their short-term private keys are shuffled and the outputs are published in plaintext. Again the servers do not prove correctness of their shuffling, which can be verified by anyone using signature verification. A cut-and-choose mechanism is used in the second round to prevent outputs of the mix network from being revealed when a malicious server performs an invalid shuffling. This scheme is correct and private. However, the cut-and-choose mechanism is inefficient. Moreover, when used in auction, this scheme is vulnerable to an attack against fairness. A user (bidder) can collude with some servers (auctioneers) to decrypt the inputs (bids) of other users (bidders) before he submits his own bid. This attack compromises fairness in the auction.

2.3 Related Work

The following parameters are used in auction schemes.

- n is the number of bidders;
- m is the number of auctioneers if more than one auctioneer is employed to share the trust (in our scheme the number of servers in the mix network);
- w is the number of biddable prices in an auction scheme not achieving price flexibility; k is the trust threshold of the auctioneers;
- t means t^{th} bid auction rule is applied.

Bid privacy is achieved in all the known auction schemes with very few exceptions [8]. Most published sealed-bid auction schemes [3,5,7,14,15,16,23,26,28,29,31] achieve absolute bid privacy. However, absolute bid privacy is inherently inconsistent to rule flexibility and price flexibility as all auction schemes with absolute bid privacy limit biddable prices to a small finite set and follow different search routes when the auction rules differ[1]. More seriously, no published scheme can achieve absolute bid privacy efficiently.

Some schems employ downward searching strategy. For example, [28] achieved all the desired properties without any trust except efficiency, rule flexibility and price flexibility. The auction scheme in [28] is an interactive protocol (the bidders must stay on-line during the bid-opening phase) and costs $O(nw)$ exponentiations. A few following auction schemes with absolute bid privacy tried to improve efficiency of [28], but were only partially successful. For example, [26] and [31] improved communicational efficiency on [28], but failed to improve computational efficiency. The scheme in [29] improved computational efficiency on [28], but failed to improve communicational efficiency.

Some schemes employ homomorphic bid opening [3,5,7,14,15,16,23], so that the computational cost for bid opening is more efficient, which is $O(mn + m\log_2 w)$ exponentiations, a great improvement on $O(nw)$ exponentiations. But

---

[1] Many auction schemes [31,26,28,29] cannot deal with any other auction rule except first bid rule.

in these schemes, validity of bids must be proved by the bidders and verified by the auctioneers, which cost $O(nw)$ exponentiations. So, those schemes cannot achieve an improvement on efficiency if they intend to be correct and robust. After all, this strategy moves nearer to rule flexibilty. Two of them [3,15] can deal with t^{th} bid auction. However, in these two schemes, the searching routes under different rules are still different. In this paper, these two schemes are described as achieving semi-rule-flexibility.

Some schemes employ an evaluation circuit to determine the winning price and identity of the winner without revealing losing bids. The bids are encrypted and input into the circuit, the corresponding decryption key is shared among a few auctioneers and a multiparty decryption protocol is used to conduct a distributed circuit evaluation. As a representative in this category, Naor et al [19] uses an oblivious third party to construct the circuit, which is then used by the auctioneers. However, it is costly in communication and computation although efficiency was not concretely and comprehensively analysed in [19]. Lipmaa et al [17] improved [19] by saving communicational cost and avoiding threshold trust. These improvements are achieved at a cost that the auctioneer learns the bid statistics, a phenomenon called relative bid privacy in this paper. However, [17] is still not efficient enough to be superior to some of the schemes employing downward search or homomorphic bid opening, although again a concrete and comprehensive efficiency analysis was not provided in [17]. Moreover, neither of there two schemes can provide price flexibility or rule flexibility.

To achieve high efficiency, rule flexibility and price flexibility, a different idea was presented: in the bid opening phase to publish the bids in plaintext. This idea was originally proposed by Viswanathan et al [30]. The same method was used in the scheme proposed by Mu and Varadharajan [18]. Although the concept of relative bid privacy was not explicitly defined in their schemes, there is no doubt they had this concept in mind.

In [18], it was suggested that pseudonyms distributed by a third party in the form of its blind signature are used by the bidders to submit their bids through an anonymous channel. However, neither a detailed implementation (an anonymous channel must be included) of relative bid privacy nor a comprehensive analysis of efficiency (cost of the anonymous channel must be included) is provided. So high efficiency, a supposed advantage of relative bid privacy over absolute bid privacy, was not illustrated convincingly in their scheme.

In [30], blind signature by a third party was used to distribute the pseudonyms as well. However, [30] is more advanced in that the anonymous channel for bid submission was described briefly. It was suggested [30] that the pseudonym for a bidder was actually a short-term public key signed by the pseudonym distributor blindly. Every bidder uses his short-term private key to sign his bid before sending it through a mix network. As the signature is not forgeable, integrity of the bids (equivalent to correctness of the mix network) can be verified when they are published in plaintext. As the short-term keys are anonymous, relative bid privacy is achieved. Implementation of the mix network was not described and the computational cost of the anonymous channel was not taken into account in efficiency analysis. Although high efficiency can be achieved in their proposal as the actioneers need not prove correctness of shuffling, this scheme cannot prevent a bidder from colluding with a server in the mix network to change his bid when it is sent through the anonymous channel. As the bids can be unsealed by malicious auctioneers when they are sent through the anonymous channel (although still in the bid submission phase), fairness is achieved only when the auctioneers are trusted.

The implicit mix network in [30] is actually very similar to that of Park [24]. They both employ two rounds (pseudonym distribution is also one round). The first round is anonymous distribution of short-term keys (by blind signature or mix shuffling). The second round is shuffling of inputs signed by the short-term keys. Correctness proof is not needed for the servers as it can be guaranteed by the correctness of signatures. However, neither of them can provide fairness in an auction without trust.

3   Auction with Relative Privacy

A sealed-bid auction scheme is presented in this paper, which achieves relative bid privacy, robustness, public verifiability, and especially rule flexibility, price flexibility, high efficiency and fairness without trust.

3.1   A New Mix Network

A new mix network is designed to implement auction with relative bid privacy. The mix network is not complex and its security is straightforward.

1. Each user P_i chooses an input b_i and commits to it as $c_i = H(b_i, v_i)$ where $H()$ is a one-way and collision-resistant hash function and v_i is a random number.
2. All the c_i for $i = 1, 2, ...n$ are shuffled and then published on a bulletin board by a set of m servers. The servers do not need to prove correctness of the shuffling. Each user verifies that his commitment is among the published shuffled commitments.
3. Then (b_i, v_i) for $i = 1, 2, ...n$ are shuffled by the same set of servers in a second round and then published on the bulletin board. Again, the servers do not have to prove the correctness of shuffling. Anyone can verify that every published output is correctly committed to some commitment.

The shuffling can be realized by either decryption chain [6] or re-encryption [24]. If decryption chain is applied, the private key of each server must be shared in a threshold method among all the other servers to achieve robustness. The properties of this mix network are as follows.

1. If the hash function is one-way and collision-resistant and every user is honest, incorrect shuffling by any malicious server will be detected.
2. It is efficient as no proof of shuffling correctness is needed.

3. Privacy can be achieved if at least one server conceals his shuffling.
4. Every user's commitment is published (anonymously) before any other user's input is submitted to the mix network. So, even though a malicious user can collude with a server to change its input (violating correctness) without being detected, this change is restricted as follows.
   - During the first round of shuffling, the malicious user can collude with a server to change its commitment, thus actually changing its committed input. However, during the first round of shuffling, even if he can get collusion from all the servers the malicious user has no information about the other users' inputs if the hash function is one-way.
   - During the second round of shuffling, the malicious user may get some information about the other users' inputs if he gets collusion of some parties processing the decryption key(s) of the mix network. However, if the hash function is collision-resistant he cannot change his input during the second round as his commitment has been published in the first round.

   Therefore, a malicious user cannot change his input according to some other users' inputs if those users do not collude with him and the hash function is one-way and collision-resistant. This is the advantage over the schemes by Chaum [6], Park et al [24] and Viswanathan et al [30]. This advantage makes the proposed mix network especially suitable for auction applications, as fairness can be guaranteed without any trust.

3.2   The Proposed Auction Scheme

In this section, an auction scheme achieving relative bid privacy is proposed by utilizing the new mix network. Any auction rule can be applied. Either decryption chain or re-encryption can be adopted in the shuffling. In the following, a detailed auction scheme employing ElGamal encryption algorithm and re-encryption mechanism is described. Let q be a large prime. If not specified, all the computations take place in $G = Z_q^*$. Let g be a generator of G. The auction protocol is realized as follows where there are n bidders B_i for $i = 1, 2, \ldots, n$ and m auctioneers A_j for $j = 1, 2, \ldots, m$, who act as the servers in the mix network.

1. Preparation Phase
   A public key $y \in Z_q^*$ is published, while the corresponding private key $x = \log_g y$ is shared among the auctioneers by $k\_out\_of\_m$ verifiable secret sharing [25]. Each A_j gets a share x_j while $y_j = g^{x_j}$ is published for $j = 1, 2, \ldots, m$.
2. Bid submission phase
   - Submitting the bid commitments
     Each bidder B_i chooses a bid $b_i \in Z_q^*$. An appropriate mapping[2] is used to transform the biddable prices to the elements in Z_q^*. B_i also chooses a random value $v_i \in Z_q^*$. Each B_i calculates his commitment $c_i = H(b_i, v_i)$

---

[2] For example, suppose the biddable prices are $p_1, p_2, \ldots, p_w$. B_i's evaluation p_j with $1 \le j \le w$ is mapped to $b_i \in Z_q^*$, so that $b_i \bmod w = j$.

and encrypts it as $e_i = (\alpha_i, \beta_i) = (g^{r_i}, c_i y^{r_i})$ where r_i is chosen randomly from Z_q^*. B_i signs e_i and submits it to the first server in the mix network. The signed e_i for $i = 1, 2, \ldots, n$ are published on the bulletin board and anyone can verify that they are validly signed by the bidders.

- Shuffling the commitments

  Inputs to auctioneer A_j are $e_{j-1,i}$ for $i = 1, 2, \ldots, n$ and his outputs are $e_{j,i}$ for $i = 1, 2, \ldots, n$ while inputs to the first auctioneer A_1 are $e_{0,i} = e_i$ for $i = 1, 2, \ldots, n$. Auctioneer A_j performs the following operations:

  - obtains input $e_{j-1,i}$ for $i = 1, 2, \ldots, n$ published by A_{j-1} on the bulletin board;
  - performs re-encryption $e_{j,i} = (\alpha_{j,i}, \beta_{j,i}) = (g^{r_{j,i}} \alpha_{j-1,\pi_j(i)},$ $y^{r_{j,i}} \beta_{j-1,\pi(i)})$ for $i = 1, 2, \ldots, n$ where π_j is a random permutation from $\{1, 2, \ldots, n\}$ to $\{1, 2, \ldots, n\}$ and $r_{j,i}$ for $i = 1, 2, \ldots, n$ are randomly chosen.

- Decrypting the commitments

  A_m's outputs $e_{m,i}$ for $i = 1, 2, \ldots, n$ are decrypted by the auctioneers. Each auctioneer A_j publishes $d_{i,j} = \alpha_{m,i}^{x_j}$ and proves $\log_g y_j = \log_{\alpha_{m,i}} d_{i,j}$ for $i = 1, 2, \ldots, n$. This proof of correct decryption can be verified by anybody. If there exist a set $S = \{s \mid 1 \leq s \leq n, \ d_{i,s} \text{ is correct}\}$ with order more than k, c_i can be recovered as $c_i = \beta_{m,i} / \prod_{s \in S} d_{i,s}^{u_s}$ where $u_s = \prod_{l \in S, l \neq s} (s - l)/l$.

- Checking the shuffled commitments

  Every bidder checks that his commitment is among the published commitments. If a bidder B_i fails in the check, he can protest by revealing his encrypted commitment (input to the mix network) $\hat{e}_i$, his commitment (respected output of the mix network) $\hat{c}_i$ and the random value (he used in the encryption) $\hat{r}_i$. If $\hat{e}_i = (g^{\hat{r}_i}, \hat{c}_i y^{\hat{r}_i})$, $\hat{e}_i$ is among the encrypted commitments and $\hat{c}_i$ is not among the shuffled and decrypted commitments, the shuffling is proved to be incorrect. In that case, every auctioneer has to prove that he re-encrypted $\hat{e}_i$ correctly by zero knowledge proof of equality of logarithms. Any auctioneer failing to prove validity of his shuffling is removed. After removal of the malicious auctioneer, e_i for $i = 1, 2, \ldots, n$ are re-shuffled (if necessary, a new auctioneer can replace the malicious auctioneer).

3. Bid opening phase

   - Providing the committed bidding values

     Each bidder B_i calculates $e1_i = (\alpha 1_i, \beta 1_i) = (g^{r1_i}, b_i y^{r1_i})$ and $e2_i = (\alpha 2_i, \beta 2_i) = (g^{r2_i}, v_i y^{r2_i})$ where $r1_i$ and $r2_i$ are chosen randomly from Z_q^*. B_i signs $(e1_i, e2_i)$ and submits it to the first server in the mix network. The signed $(e1_i, e2_i)$ for $i = 1, 2, \ldots, n$ are published on the bulletin board and anyone can verify that they are validly signed by the bidders.

   - Shuffling the bids

     Auctioneer A_j with $j > 1$ gets $(e1_{j-1,i}, e2_{j-1,i})$ for $i = 1, 2, \ldots, n$ from A_{j-1} and shuffles them to $(e1_{j,i}, e2_{j,i})$ for $i = 1, 2, \ldots, n$. A_1 gets $(e1_{0,i}, e2_{0,i}) = (e1_i, e2_i)$ for $i = 1, 2, \ldots, n$ from the bidders and shuffles them to $(e1_{1,i}, e2_{1,i})$ for $i = 1, 2, \ldots, n$. Re-encryption and permutation in the shuffling are the same as in the first round.

- Decrypting the bids
  A_m's outputs $(e1_{m,i}, e2_{m,i})$ for $i = 1, 2, \ldots, n$ are decrypted by the auctioneers. Like in the first round, if more than k auctioneers are honest, b_i and r_i for $i = 1, 2, \ldots, n$ can be recovered correctly.
- Verifying validity of the bids
  Suppose $(\hat{b}_i, \hat{v}_i)$ for $i = 1, 2, \ldots, n$ are the results of bid decryption. If $H(\hat{b}_i, \hat{v}_i)$ is not among the published commitments in the first round, $(\hat{b}_i, \hat{v}_i)$ is traced in a reverse direction through the mix network and every auctioneer is required to reveal his shuffling in regard to $(\hat{b}_i, \hat{v}_i)$. Any auctioneer failing to prove correctness of his shuffling is removed from the mix network. If all the auctioneers prove correctness of their shuffling successfully, B_i is accused of submitting invalid bid and removed from the auction. After the malicious party (auctioneer or bidder) is removed, $(e1_i, e2_i)$ for $i = 1, 2, \ldots, n$ are re-shuffled (if necessary, a new auctioneer can replace the malicious auctioneer). After valid bids are obtained, they are mapped back to a price in $\{p_1, p_2, \ldots, p_w\}$.

4. Winning price and winner determination phase
   The auction rule is applied to the opened bids and the winning price and the winner's price. The winner B_I has to prove his identity by revealing $r1_I$ and illustrating the winner's price is encrypted in $e1_I$. Anyone can verifiy that the winner's price is encrypted in $e1_I$ and the $(e1_I, e2_I)$ on the bulletin board is signed by B_I. If the winner refuses to cooperate, the auctioneers can trace the winner's bid through the mix network (revealing their shuffling in regard to the winner's bid) to identify the winner.

4   Analysis of the Scheme

4.1   Security Analysis

The desired properties introduced in Section 1 are satisfied in the proposed scheme.

1. Satisfaction of correctness is straightforward.
2. In the bid submission phase the bids are sealed by hash function $H()$. As $H()$ is one-way, any bidder's bid is kept confidential in the bid submission phase no matter how many auctioneers and other bidders conspire against him.
3. As confidentiality is achieved, no bidder has any knowledge of other bidders' bids during the bid submission phase. As all the commitments are published in plaintext in the end of the bid submission phase, no bidder can change his bid after the bid submission phase ends, if $H()$ is collision-resistant. So fairness is achieved.
4. As illustrated in Section 3.2, the auctioneers can cooperate to identify the winner when he refuses to claim the winner's bid. So, non-repudiation is achieved.

5. Signature, shuffling and bid decryption can be verified publicly.
6. As illustrated in Section 3.2, incorrect shuffling and invalid bid can be discovered. After the identified malicious auctioneer or bidder is removed, the auction can run on correctly. So the proposed scheme is robust.
7. Every bid is decrypted into plaintext in the bid opening phase, so any auction rule can be applied and any bidding value can be submitted. That means rule flexibility and price flexibility are obtained.
8. If at least one auctioneer is honest, the bids cannot be linked to the bidders and relative bid privacy is achieved. A very slight trust is needed, so the achieved relative bid privacy is strong.

4.2 Efficiency Analysis

The proposed auction scheme is actually composed of two rounds of shuffling and distributed decryptions of the bids. As the correctness verification mechanism does not require the auctioneers (servers in the mix network) to prove the correctness of their shuffling, the scheme is very efficient.

- Two rounds of communication are needed between the bidders and auctioneers.
- Every bidder has to perform three encryptions and two signature generations (the computation of hash function is negligible compared to public key encryptions), which cost eight exponentiations if ElGamal encryption and RSA encryption are employed.
- Each auctioneer has to perform $3n$ re-encryptions, which costs $6n$ exponentiations if ElGamal encryption is employed.
- Each auctioneer has to perform $3n$ distributed decryptions and prove their correctness, which costs $9n$ exponentiations if ElGamal encryption is employed.
- A verifier of correctness of the auction only needs to verify the correctness of distributed decryption by $k+1$ auctioneers, which costs $12n(k+1)$ exponentiations.

4.3 Comparison

In Table 1, our scheme is compared against the currently known schemes in relation to achieved properties.

The comparisons clearly illustrate that relative privacy is the only available solution to achieve high efficiency, price flexibility and rule flexibility simultaneously. Actually, among the currently known auction schemes only [30] and our scheme can achieve these three properties. As fairness in [30] is not strong, our scheme is the only one to achieve high efficiency and fairness without trust. Moreover, price flexibility and rule flexibility are also obtained in our scheme.

In Table 2, our scheme is compared against the currently known schemes in regard to efficiency. Recall that n is the number of bidders; m is the number of auctioneers if more than one auctioneer is employed to share the trust (in our

Table 1. Comparison of properties

Schemes	Bid privacy	Rule flexibility	Price flexibility	Fairness
[31,5,14,16,7,3] [15,23,26,19,17]	absolute	no	no	conditional
[28,31,29]	absolute	no	no	unconditional
[3,15]	absolute	semi	no	conditional
[18,30]	relative	yes	yes	conditional
Proposed scheme	relative	yes	yes	unconditional

scheme the number of servers in the mix network); w is the number of biddable prices in an auction scheme not achieving price flexibility. t means t^{th} bid auction rule is applied, so $t = 1$ in first bid auction and $t = 2$ in second bid auction. Suppose ElGamal encryption and RSA signature are employed to encrypt and sign the bids and bid validity check is used in schemes employing homomorphic bid sealing. Usually $w > n \gg m > t$.

Table 2. Comparison of Efficiency

Schemes	Computation of a bidder	Computation of the auctioneers	Communication
[28]	average $2w + 2$	average $(4w + 1)n$	interactive average $w/2$ rounds
[29]	1	n	interactive average $w/2$ rounds
[26]	3	average $(2.5w + 1)n$	non-interactive
[31]	$8w + 1$	average $5.5nw + w + 4n$	non-interactive
[15,16,23] [14,3,7,5]	$\geq 6w + 1$	$\geq 4wn + 3m \log_2 w$ $+3mn + n$	non-interactive
[30,18]	3	unspecified	non-interactive
Proposed	8	$15mn$	non-interactive

As in most applications $w \gg m > t$, schemes achieving relative bid privacy like the proposed scheme are more efficient in computation than schemes achieving absolute bid privacy except [29], which is very inefficient in communication.

5   Conclusion

A new concept proposed in this paper—relative bid privacy—is described and a method implementing this auction scheme is proposed by employing a new mix network. Rule flexibility, price flexibility and high efficiency are achieved easily as absolute bid privacy is not necessary. The achieved relative bid privacy is based on minimal trust: at least one auctioneer is honest. Correctness, confidentiality, fairness, non-repudiation and public verifiability are also achieved.

References

1. M Abe. Mix-networks on permutation net-works. In *Asiacrypt 98*, pages 258–273, Berlin, 1999. Springer-Verlag. Lecture Notes in Computer Science 1716.
2. Masayuki Abe and Fumitaka Hoshino. Remarks on mix-network based on permutation networks. In *Public Key Cryptography 2001*, pages 317–324, Berlin, 2001. Springer-Verlag. Lecture Notes in Computer Science 1992.
3. Masayuki Abe and Koutarou Suzuki. M+1-st price auction using homomorphic encryption. In *Public Key Cryptology 2002*, pages 115–124, Berlin, 2002. Springer-Verlag. Lecture Notes in Computer Science Volume 2288.
4. Dan Boneh and Philippe Golle. Almost entirely correct mixing with applications to voting. In *Proceedings of the 9th ACM conference on Computer and communications security*, pages 68–77, 2002.
5. Felix Brandt. Cryptographic protocols for secure second-price auctions. 2001. Available at http://wwwbrauer.in.tum.de/~brandtf/papers/cia2001.pdf.
6. D Chaum. Untraceable electronic mail, return address and digital pseudonym. In *Communications of the ACM, 24(2)*, pages 84–88, 1981.
7. Koji Chida, Kunio Kobayashi, and Hikaru Morita. Efficient sealed-bid auctions for massive numbers of bidders with lump comparison. In *Information Security, 4th International Conference, ISC 2001*, pages 408–419, Berlin, 2001. Springer-Verlag. Lecture Notes in Computer Science Volume 2200.
8. Matthew K Franklin and Michael K Reiter. The design and implementation of a secure auction service. In *IEEE Transactions on Software Enginerring*, volume 5, pages 302–312, May 1996.
9. Jun Furukawa and Kazue Sako. An efficient scheme for proving a shuffle. In *CRYPTO2001*, volume 2139 of *Lecture Notes in Computer Science*, pages 368–387. Springer, 2001.
10. Philippe Golle, Sheng Zhong, Dan Boneh, Markus Jakobsson, and Ari Juels. Optimistic mixing for exit-polls. In *ASIACRYPT 2002*, pages 451–465, Berlin, 2002. Springer-Verlag. Lecture Notes in Computer Science Volume 1592.
11. Jens Groth. A verifiable secret shuffle of homomorphic encryptions. In *Public Key Cryptography 2003*, pages 145–160, Berlin, 2003. Springer-Verlag. Lecture Notes in Computer Science Volume 2567.
12. Markus Jakobsson, Ari Juels, and Ronald L. Rivest. Making mix nets robust for electronic voting by randomizsed partial checking. In *Proceedings of the 11th USENIX Security Symposium, San Francisco, CA, USA, August 5-9, 2002*, pages 339–353. USENIX, 2002.
13. Ari Juels and Markus Jakobsson. An optimally robust hybrid mix network. In *Proc. of the 20th annual ACM Symposium on Principles of Distributed Computation*, pages 284–292. ACM, 2001.
14. H Kikuchi, Michael Harkavy, and J D Tygar. Multi-round anonymous auction. In *Proceedings of the First IEEE Workshop on Dependable and Real-Time E-Commerce Systems*, pages 62–69, June 1998.
15. Hiroaki Kikuchi. (m+1)st-price auction. In *The Fifth International Conference on Financial Cryptography 2001*, pages 291–298, Berlin, February 2001. Springer-Verlag. Lecture Notes in Computer Science Volume 2339.
16. Hiroaki Kikuchi, Shinji Hotta, Kensuke Abe, and Shohachiro Nakanishi. Distributed auction servers resolving winner and winning bid without revealing privacy of bids. In *proc. of International Workshop on Next Generation Internet (NGITA2000), IEEE*, pages 307–312, July 2000.

17. H Lipmaa, N Asokan, and V Niemi. Secure vickrey auctions without thresh-old trust. In *Proceedings of the 6th Annual Conference on Financial Cryptography, 2002*, Berlin, 2002. Springer-Verlag.
18. Yi Mu and Vijay Varadharajan. An internet anonymous auction scheme. In *International Conference on Information Security and Cryptology 2000*, pages 171–182, Berlin, 2000. Springer-Verlag. Lecture Notes in Computer Science Volume 2015.
19. Moni Naor, Benny Pinkas, and Reuben Sumner. Privacy perserving auctions and mechanism design. 1999. Available from http://www.tml.hut.fi/~helger/crypto/link/protocols/auctions.html.
20. C. Andrew Neff. A verifiable secret shuffle and its application to e-voting. In *ACM Conference on Computer and Communications Security 2001*, pages 116–125, 2001.
21. W Ogata, K Kurosawa, K Sako, and K Takatani. Fault tolerant anonymous channel. In *Proc. of International Conference on Information and Communication Security 1997*, pages 440–444, Berlin, 2000. Springer-Verlag. Lecture Notes in Computer Science Volume 1334.
22. Miyako Ohkubo and Masayuki Abe. A length-invariant hybrid mix. In *ASIACRYPT 2000*, pages 178–191, Berlin, 2000. Springer-Verlag. Lecture Notes in Computer Science Volume 1976.
23. Kazumasa Omote and Atsuko Miyaji. A second-price sealed-bid auction with the discriminant of the p-th root. In *Financial Cryptography 2002*, Berlin, 2002. Springer-Verlag.
24. C. Park, K. Itoh, and K. Kurosawa. Efficient anonymous channel and all/nothing election scheme. In Tor Helleseth, editor, *Advances in Cryptology - EuroCrypt '93*, pages 248–259, Berlin, 1993. Springer-Verlag. Lecture Notes in Computer Science Volume 765.
25. Torben P. Pedersen. Distributed provers with applications to undeniable signatures. In *EUROCRYPT 91*, pages 221–242, Berlin, 1991. Springer-Verlag. Lecture Notes in Computer Science Volume 547.
26. K Sako. An auction scheme which hides the bids of losers. In *Public Key Cryptology 2000*, pages 422–432, Berlin, 2000. Springer-Verlag. Lecture Notes in Computer Science Volume 1880.
27. K. Sako and J. Kilian. Receipt-free mix-type voting scheme–a practical solution to the implementation of a voting booth. In *EUROCRYPT '95*, pages 393–403, Berlin, 1995. Springer-Verlag. Lecture Notes in Computer Science Volume 921.
28. Kouichi Sakurai and S Miyazaki. A bulletin-board based digital auction scheme with bidding down strategy -towards anonymous electronic bidding without anonymous channels nor trusted centers. In *Proc. International Workshop on Cryptographic Techniques and E-Commerce*, pages 180–187, Hong Kong, 1999. City University of Hong Kong Press.
29. Koutarou Suzuki, Kunio Kobayashi, and Hikaru Morita. Efficient sealed-bid auction using hash chain. In *International Conference on Information Security and Cryptology 2000*, pages 183–191, Berlin, 2000. Springer-Verlag. Lecture Notes in Computer Science 2015.
30. Kapali Viswanathan, Colin Boyd, and Ed Dawson. A three phased schema for sealed bid auction system design. In *Information Security and Privacy, 5th Australasian Conference, ACISP'2000*, pages 412–426, Berlin, 2000. Springer-Verlag. Lecture Notes in Computer Science 1841.
31. Yuji Watanabe and Hideki Imai. Reducing the round complexity of a sealed-bid auction protocol with an off-line ttp. In *STOC 2000*, pages 80–86. ACM, 2000.

Multi-dimensional Hash Chain for Sealed-Bid Auction

Navapot Prakobpol and Yongyuth Permpoontanalarp

Logic and Security Laboratory
Department of Computer Engineering, Faculty of Engineering
King Mongkut's University of Technology Thonburi
91 Pracha-Uthit Road, Bangkok 10140, Thailand
navapot_p@hotmail.com
yongyuth@cpe.eng.kmutt.ac.th

Abstract. Sealed-bid electronic auction is an electronic auction where each submitted bid can be opened only after the closing time of the bid. A number of hash-based approaches were proposed which have advantages over non hash-based approaches due to the simplicity and efficiency of hash. We argue that the existing hash-based approaches do not offer both the security and efficiency at the acceptable level. Then, we propose a new hash-based approach which provides the two properties at more acceptable level than the existing approaches. In particular, we show that with the high level of security offered, our approach is more efficient than the existing approaches.

1 Introduction

Electronic auctions (e-auction) are auctions where bidders can bid over the Internet. E-auctions are a fundamental technology for electronic commerce [2]. Sealed-bid auction eg. [1, 2, 3, 4, 5] is an auction where each bid submitted can be opened only after the closing time of the bid. After the bid opening phase, the auctioneer announces the winner along with her winning price. Most sealed-bid auctions are classified according to the amount of money paid by the bid winner. For example, in first-price sealed-bid auction the winner pays at the first highest price and in second-price sealed-bid (Vickrey) auction the winner pays at the second highest price.

The following are desirable security properties proposed for sealed-bid auctions.

Anonymity of bidders [2, 4, 5]: Each bid must be submitted anonymously. Furthermore, after the closing of bidding, both auctioneer and bid winner can prove to each other the identity of the bid winner, but none of them knows the identity of the other bidders.

Secrecy of bids [1, 3, 4, 5]: Any submitted bids cannot be changed by someone and must not be opened until the close of auction.

Privacy of bidding price [2, 3, 4, 5]: Even after the close of auction, all of bidding prices must be kept in secret except for the winning price

Bidder Authentication [4, 5]: Any bidder (and auctioneers) can verify the authenticity of submitted bids.

Verifiability of the correctness of the auction [3,4,5]: All of bidders can observe each step of determining the winner and can verify the correctness of the auction

K. Chae and M. Yung (Eds.): WISA 2003, LNCS 2908, pp. 257–271, 2004.
© Springer-Verlag Berlin Heidelberg 2004

Undeniability of bids [1, 4, 5]: Any bidders (winner or losers) cannot repudiate their own submitted bid. In addition, the auctioneer cannot refuse receiving some bids

There is a plenty of research on sealed-bid auction [1, 2, 3, 4, 5]. They can be classified broadly into two main kinds, namely, advanced cryptography-based [1, 2, 3] and standard cryptography-based [4, 5] approaches. Advanced cryptography-based approach employs sophisticated cryptography, such as threshold secret sharing [1] and distributed computation [2], to realize the desirable properties of sealed-bid auctions. However, standard cryptography-based approach uses only ordinary yet standard cryptography, for example hashing functions and public key cryptography.

Advanced cryptography-based approach has a number of disadvantages in that it is complicated and requires a large amount of computation. Furthermore, it is difficult to implement due to the complexity of cryptography employed.

Since standard cryptography approach [4, 5] employs mainly hashing functions to realize sealed-bid auction, it is more efficient than the advanced cryptography approach and it is also easier to implement.

[4] is the first who proposed the use of hash for sealed-bid auction. In particular, bidding prices are represented using some iterations of a hashing function, which is a *linear hash chain*. However, the approach requires a large number of iterations to represent a large price. Thus, it is not very efficient. However, it offers a *strong* privacy property in that only information on winning bid such as price is revealed.

Later, [5] proposed an improved scheme of [4] by using *a binary tree* to represent a bidding price. As a result, the improved scheme uses much less amount of iterations than [4] to represent a large bidding price. Thus, [5] is more efficient than [4]. However, it provides a *very weak* privacy property in that some information on all losing bids can be revealed. In particular, bidding prices for losing bids which are closed to winning bids can be guessed by auctioneers with high probability.

In this paper, we propose a new hash-based approach for sealed-bid auction. In particular, we propose multi-dimensional hash chain to represent a bidding price, and our multi-dimensional hash chain corresponds to m-ary tree structure. Our approach is slightly less efficient than [4] but is much more secure than [4]. In particular, our approach is as secure as [5] but is much more efficient than [5]. Thus, with the high level of security offered, our approach is more efficient than the existing approaches. After our approach is discussed, we show the analysis on both the security and the computation of our approach in comparison to the existing approaches [4, 5].

2 Background

2.1 Previous Work

We will explain two standard cryptography-based approaches that employ mainly hashing function in order to compare with our approach.

Suzuki et.al. [4]. This approach achieves all above properties, however it suffers weak anonymity of bidders and low efficiency. Conceptually, bidding prices are represented using some iterations of a hashing function, which is a linear hash chain from a bidding price to the maximum price for a bid. Thus, a number of iterations in each bid are the length between bidding price and the maximum price. Conversely, in the opening phase it opens any bids from the maximum to minimum price to find out the winning price.

Bidding Phase. After each bidder i generates a hash chain from her bidding price P_i to the maximum price M for a bid, the bidder submits the last iteration of hash L_M as the commitment of bid as well as bidder's signature on L_M. Each bidder generates a chain as follows:

$$
\begin{aligned}
L_{P_{i-1}} &= R \\
L_j &= h(Yes \parallel L_{P_{i-1}}) && j = P_i \\
&= h(No \parallel L_{j-1}) && j = P_i + 1,\, P_i + 2,\, \ldots,\, M
\end{aligned}
$$

where *Yes means this is my bidding price*
    No means this is not my bidding price
    h = cryptographic hash function
    M = maximum price
    R = random number

Opening Phase. Each bidder sends each $L_{j,i}$ for $j = M, M-1,\ldots, 1$ until the auctioneer finds the winning bid by obtaining *Yes* from a bidder. Given L_j that the auctioneer already has, and L_{j-1} that the auctioneer has just received, the auctioneer checks for Answer in $L_j = h(Answer \parallel L_{j-1})$. If Answer is *Yes*, then the winner is found and the auctioneer stops opening.

Advantage
1. It offers strong bid privacy that is *"any information of losing bids is not leaked at anytime"*.

Disadvantage
1. It requires a lot of computation for constructing a hash chain for a bidding price, especially the bidding price that differs greatly from the maximum price.
2. It requires a lot of communication, and also requires online interaction between all bidders and the auctioneer during the opening phase.
3. It requires a special trusted third party which keeps identity of bidders and their public keys to prove bids' owners to auctioneer, and the third party must not collude with auctioneers in order to offer anonymity.

Omote et.al. [5]. This second method offers also all properties, however it provides a *very weak* privacy property in that some information on all losing bids can be revealed. Conceptually, bidder' bidding price is represented in binary number that can be understood by a binary tree and the binary number is hashed bit by bit. Thus, a number of hash iterations are equal to the number of bits. In opening phase, a biding price is opened consecutively bit by bit from the most significant bit to the least significant provided that bit that is just opened is 1.

Bidding Phase. First, a bidder i converts her bidding price into binary number $b = [b_k, b_{k-1}, \ldots, b_1]$, then the bidder computes her bid $M_i = M_{(i,1)}, \ldots, M_{(i,k+1)}$ corresponding to her bidding price as follows.

$$
\begin{aligned}
M_{(i,s)} \quad &= \; h^{k-s+1}(r_i) + h^{k-s}(r_i) \quad &\text{if } b_s = 1 \text{ and for } 1 \le s \le k \\
&= \; h^{k-s+1}(r_i) + R_{i,k-s} \quad &\text{if } b_s = 0 \text{ and for } 1 \le s \le k \\
M_{(i,k+1)} \quad &= \; r_i + x_i \\
\text{where} \quad & h^j(r) \text{ means } r \text{ is hashed } j \text{ times,} \\
& r_i, R_{i,k-s} \text{ are random numbers, and} \\
& x_i \text{ is } Bi\text{'s private key, and } k \text{ is the number of bits}
\end{aligned}
$$

After M_i is generated, it is sent together with bidder's public key to auctioneer.

Opening Phase. As soon as the auctioneer receives $h^k(r_i)$ from each bidder, the auctioneer uses this information to open bits in M_i by using subtraction operations. Note that all consecutive 1 bits in each M_i of each bidder are opened (revealed) at once. Such consecutive 1 bits represent partial information on bidding prices. Thus, they are used by the auctioneer to determine the winner. If the winner cannot be determined, then winner candidates need to send more information to the auctioneer to open the next consecutive 1 bits in M_i.

After the winner is found, the auctioneer can extract winner's private key from M_i and the private key is verified with the corresponding public key sent earlier.

Advantage
1. It requires a little amount of computation to generate the hash chain for a large bidding price and a small amount of communication for bid opening.

Disadvantage
1. Bidding prices for some losing bids can be guessed and an order of prices for (many) losing bids can be determined.

For example, suppose that *M1, M2, M3, M4* and *M5* are bids represented in binary number as shown in table 1. In table 1, the size of search space means the number of all possible prices for losing bid, *and* * stands for an unknown bit. Notice that *M2* is closed to *M1* and has only one unknown bit. Even though one bit is unknown, the auctioneer can guess the price of *M2* with probability ½. Therefore, prices of losing bids which are very closed to winning price can be guessed by auctioneers with high probability. After the end of opening bid, the auctioneer can determine an order of losing bids that is *M1* > *M2* > *M3* > *M4* > *M5*.
2. The approach is vulnerable to denial of service in that attackers can use any private key to submit arbitrary bids (called faked bids). Since each bid is initially anonymous, all those faked bids will be processed and discovered later. As a result, faked bids waste computation of the system.

Table 1. This table shows the representation of bidding price in Omote's approach

Bids	Binary Numbers	Size of Search Space	Probability
M1	1 1 0 1 1 1 1 1 1		
M2	1 1 0 1 1 1 1 0 *	$2^1 = 2$	1/2
M3	1 1 0 1 1 1 0 * *	$2^2 = 4$	$1/(2^2)$
M4	1 1 0 1 0 * * * *	$2^4 = 16$	$1/(2^4)$
M5	0 * * * * * * * *	$2^8 = 256$	$1/(2^8)$

2.2 Homomorphic Property of Public Key Cryptography

The homomorphic encryption (eg. [6]) in public key cryptography is an encryption algorithm $En\{M\}_K$ that can satisfy the *multiplicative property* that is $En\{M_1\}_K \times En\{M_2\}_K = En\{M_1 \times M_2\}_K$ where $En\{M\}_K$ stands for encryption using public key K. Our approach employs public key cryptography which has the homomorphic property. Also, our approach requires that the public key cryptography used is *semantic secure*, such as Elgamal [7].

3 Multi-dimensional Hash Chain and M-ary Tree Structure

In our approach, a bidding price is represented by using multi-dimensional hash chain which corresponds to m-ary tree structure. We discuss the corresponding between them here.

Conceptually, in a tree structure each leaf node represents a specific price and such prices are ordered incrementally from left nodes to right nodes. Given a maximum price M, such an m-ary tree is generated such that the maximum can be represented in the tree. A non-leaf node represents a range of prices denoted by all its children. A path from the root node to a leaf node identifies the bidding price represented by the leaf uniquely. Such path simply consists of a collection of branches that are visited at each level of the tree.

Such m-ary tree structure can be understood as multi-dimensional hash chain also. Multi-dimensional hash chain is a hash chain with two directions. A level of a tree corresponds to a *dimension* in multi-dimensional hash chain. Nodes at the same level in a tree are used to generate a linear hash chain and such node is called a *column* in multi-dimensional hash chain. In multi-dimensional hash chain, there are two directions of hash chains : *horizontal* and *vertical* chains. Horizontal chain is a linear hash chain in a dimension whereas vertical chain is a linear hash chain from one dimension to another. Horizontal chain in the last dimension stands for an increment of specific prices since an element in the chain denotes a specific price. In other than last dimensions, horizontal chain represents an increment of ranges of prices. However, vertical chain stands for a decrement of ranges of prices, that is from a larger range of prices to a smaller range of prices. A price can be identified uniquely by both horizontal and vertical chains from the first dimension to the last dimension. Such chains simply can be constructed by a collection of columns in each dimension.

Figure 1 shows an example of m-ary tree structure for bidding price. There are 3 levels of height in the tree. Leaf nodes in the figure represent specific prices from 37 to 40. Non-leaf node 2 in 2nd dimension represents the range of prices 37 – 40 which are prices for its children. Suppose that winning price is 38. A path to the winning price 38 is (3, 2, 2). For the rest of the paper, we shall use the terminology in m-ary tree and multi-dimensional hash chain interchangeably.

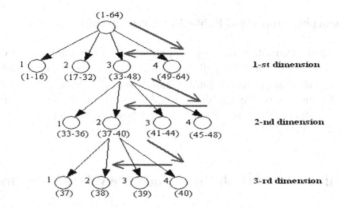

Fig. 1. An 4-ary tree structure of bidding price.

3.1 Bid Opening in Multi-dimensional Hash Chain

The purpose of bid opening process is for an auctioneer to find a bid winner. In our approach, the bid winner is the person who proposes the highest bidding price. Before the closing time of bidding, each bidder submits a bidding price to an auctioneer. At the closing time, the auctioneer starts bid opening process.

Bid opening is carried out dimension by dimension starting from the first dimension to the last dimension.

For any other than last dimension, auctioneer queries all bidders whether their bidding prices fall into a specific range of prices represented by each node in the dimension. The range of prices queried starts from the highest range of prices to the lowest range of prices in the dimension. A bidder replies "*Yes*" if bidder's bidding price falls into a range of prices being queried, and "*No*", otherwise. Note that such answer is called *individual answer*. If at least one bidder's reply is "*Yes*", then the bid opening process moves to next dimension by using the vertical chain.

For the last dimension, auctioneer queries bidders whether their bidding prices are just particular price represented by each leaf node. Similarly to other than last dimensions, the query in the last dimension starts from the highest price to the lowest price. The bidder(s) with "*Yes*" answer is the bid winner(s).

However, in other than last dimensions, if bidders give their *individual answers* to auctioneer, the auctioneer would know the number of bidders who bid for a specific range of prices. This information allows the auctioneer to infer information on losing bids such as the number of bid losers whose bidding prices are in a range of prices.

For example, consider figure 1. Suppose that there are three bids : $B1$ for 36, $B2$ for 32 and $B3$ for 40. At the first dimension, auctioneer obtains individual answers "*Yes*", "*No*" and "*Yes*" from $B1$, $B2$ and $B3$, respectively. Then, the auctioneer can infer that $33 \leq B1 \leq 48$ and $33 \leq B3 \leq 48$. At the second dimension, the auctioneer obtains individual answers "*No*", "*No*" and "*Yes*" from $B1$, $B2$ and $B3$, respectively. Hence, the auctioneer can infer further that $33 \leq B1 \leq 36$ and $37 \leq B3 \leq 40$. Therefore, the auctioneer knows that there are two bidders whose bidding prices are in 33-48.

Therefore, to prevent auctioneers to infer such information on losing bids, we employ the concept of *group answers*, instead of individual answers, for queries in other than last dimensions. Group answers are answers that hide the number of bidders who give a specific reply. Group answer "*Yes*" means that there exists a bidder who gives individual "*Yes*" answer whereas group answer "*No*" means that all bidders give individual "*No*" answer. Since the number of bidders with "*Yes*" individual answers cannot be inferred from the group answer, auctioneer cannot know the information on losing bids. Hence, in any other than last dimensions, all bidders calculate group answer and reply it to the auctioneer.

We employ the homomorphic property of public key encryption to implement group answer. In particular, each individual answer from a bidder is encrypted with auctioneer's public key. Then, group answer from all bidders is calculated by multiplying all encrypted individual answers.

3.2 Notations for Multi-dimensional Hash Chain

We discuss notations for multi-dimension hash chain. To represent all bidding prices $= (1, ..., M)$, the number of dimension needed is D

$$D = \lceil \log_m M \rceil$$

where D = *the total number of dimensions*
m = *the total number of columns in a dimension*
M = *maximum price*

To determine if bidding price P_i is located in column t at dimension d, we need to know a sequence of column numbers $(k_1, k_2, ..., k_{d-1})$ which are column numbers in all previous dimensions of d. We assume that such a sequence is given. We use $PATH(1,d-1)$ to denote the sequence. More generally, for any P_i, $PATH(1,D)$ is $(k_1, k_2, ..., k_D)$ where k_i, $1 \leq i \leq D$, is the column number in dimension i in which P_i locates in.

Firstly, the maximal price of q-th column at d-th dimension is denoted by $S_{d,q}$ which is defined as follows.

$$S_{d,q} = S_{PATH(1,d-1)} - (m-q).n_d$$

Where $1 \leq d \leq D$, $1 \leq q \leq m$,

$$S_{PATH(1,d-1)} = M - \sum_{j=1}^{d-1}(m-k_j).n_j \text{ , and}$$

$n_j = m^{D-j}$ = *the number of prices represented by a column in j-th dimension.*

Note that $S_{PATH(1,d-1)}$ is the maximal price in $(d-1)$th dimension according to $PATH(1,d-1)$.

For example, consider figure 1. Suppose that $d = 2$, $q = 3$ and $PATH(1,1) = (3)$. Clearly, $n_2 = 4$, $S_{PATH(1,1)} = 48$, $S_{2,3} = 48 - (4-3).(4) = 44$ which is the maximal price of 3rd column at 2nd dimension given that the column number in 1st dimension is 3.

Note that we need $PATH(1,d-1)$ to determine $S_{d,q}$. This is because $S_{2,3}$ where $PATH(1,1) = (3)$ is different from $S_{2,3}$ where $PATH(1,1) = (1)$. Clearly, if $PATH(1,1)$

$= (1)$, the maximal price for any further dimension is not more than 16 which is the maximal price of 1st column in 1st dimension.

Thus, the column number in which P_i locates is t such that $S_{d,t-1} < P_i \le S_{d,t}$ where $1 \le t \le m$. For example, suppose that $P_i = 38$. Thus, P_i locates in 2nd column at 2nd dimension where $PATH(1,1)=(3)$.

3.3 Protocol Details

Overview

There are mainly three entities in our sealed-bid auction, namely bidders, auctioneer and bidder agents. The bidder agents are agents working on behalf of bidders and are able to move from one location to another. Initially, a bidder agent operates at a bidder. After the bidder agent receives bid information from the bidder, it travels to auctioneer. Bid information includes bidder's public key certificate and bidder's signature on bidding price, and it is encrypted by a (symmetric) session key.

At the auctioneer, each bidder agent generates a horizontal hash chain for each dimension and takes part in bid opening phase. After bid winner is found, the auctioneer can obtain the session key used to retrieve winner's bid information. Note that auctioneer can obtain winner's session key only, not bid losers' session keys.

Table 2. Table of Notation

Symbol	Meaning	Symbol	Meaning
N	The number of bidders participated in the auction	$GA_{d,q}$	group answer of q-th column and d-th dimension
i	bidder index that ranges over $\{1, ..., N\}$	$Pri\text{-}X$ $Pub\text{-}X$	party X's private key party X's public key
B_i	bidder i	$En\{M\}_K$	asymmetric encryption of message M with key K
P_i	bidding price of bidder B_i		
Bid_i	hash-chain bid	$De\{M\}_K$	asymmetric decryption of message M with key K
d	dimension index that ranges over $\{1,...,D\}$		
t	the column number in which P_i is located for each dimension	$Sign\{M\}_K$	signature message M with key K
		$E(M, K)$	symmetric encryption of message M with key K
BA_i	bidder i's agent (or bidder agent i) auctioneer	$h(M)$	collision resistant hash function of message M
A	(symmetric) session key of bidder i	R_i	bidder i's random seed
K_i	(symmetric) key initially sharing among all bidder agents	$Cert_i$	bidder i's public key certificate
	individual answer of q-th column and d-th dimension	$BA_i Cert$	bidder agent i's public key certificate
K_b		$A \to B{:}M$	A send B message M
		Set_Yes	set of all possible individual "Yes" answers
$IA_{d,q}$			

Our Protocol

1) Initialization
    1.1)   Bidder agent receives bid information from bidder.

$$B_i \rightarrow BA_i : P_i, BidCert_i$$
$$\text{where } BidCert_i = Sign\{ h(P_i), K_i\}_{Pri\text{-}Bi}, Cert_{Bi}$$

1.2) Each BA_i moves to the auctioneer site

2) Bidding Process
Repeat the following (2.1 and 2.2) for each dimension $d = 1...D$

2.1) Generating Bid information

a) Broadcast individual answers for all columns in a dimension

$$(\text{for } d = 1...D\text{-}1)$$
$$BA_i \rightarrow BA_{j,} : E(IA_{d,q}, K_b) \qquad \text{for } q = 1, ..., m$$
$$where$$
$$IA_{d,q} = En\{Yes\}_{Pub\text{-}A} \qquad \text{if } q = t$$
$$= En\{No\}_{Pub\text{-}A} \qquad \text{otherwise, and}$$
$$No = 1 \text{ and } Yes \in Set\_Yes \text{ and}$$
$$Set\_Yes = \{ x \mid x \in Z_p^* \text{ and } x \neq No\} \text{ and}$$
$$\neg \exists x_1,...,x_a \in Set\_Yes \left(De\{En\{x_1\}_{Pub\text{-}A} \times...\times En\{x_a\}_{Pub\text{-}A} \}_{Pri\text{-}A} = No \right)$$
$$j \neq i, \text{ and } d \in \{1, ..., D-1\}$$

Note that here we assume that the public key cryptography used is Elgamal in which p stands for prime modulus. Note also that since we do not require group answer for the last dimension, the following generation of group answers is not applied for the last dimension.

b) Generate group answer for each column at a dimension.
    Each bidder computes the following

$$GA_{d,q} = \prod_{i=1}^{N} (IA_{d,q})_i \qquad \text{for } q = 1, ..., m$$

    where $(IA_{d,q})_i$ means B_i's answer, $d \in \{1, ..., D-1\}$,
        $GA_{d,q} = 1$ (for answer= "No") and $GA_{d,q} \neq 1$ (for answer="Yes").

c) Generating a horizontal hash chain for each dimension. (for $d = 1...D$)
    Each bidder computes $L_d = L_{d,m}$ by the following

For $d = 1,..., D-1$ (other than last dimension)

$$L_{d, q-1} = R_d$$
$$L_{d, q} = h(GA_{d,q} \| L_{d,q-1} \| S_{d,q})$$

where $R_d = h^{D-d}(R_i)$, R_i *is* B_i'*s random,*

$$t \leq q \leq m \qquad if\ S_{d,t-1} < Pi \leq S_{d,t}\ (P_i\ is\ in\ column\ t\ at\ d)$$
$$1 \leq q \leq m \qquad otherwise$$

For $d = D$ *(last dimension)*

$$\left. \begin{array}{l} L_{d,t-1} = R_i \parallel K_i \\ L_{d,t} \quad = h(Yes \parallel L_{d,t-1}) \end{array} \right\} \qquad if\ S_{d,\ t-1} < Pi \leq S_{d,\ t}\ (P_i\ is\ in\ column\ t\ at\ d)$$

$$L_{d,\ q-1} \quad = R_i \qquad\qquad\qquad\qquad Otherwise$$

$$L_{d,\ q} \quad = h(No \parallel L_{d,\ q-1})$$
where $t+1 \leq q \leq m$,   *if* $S_{d,t-1} < Pi \leq S_{d,t}$
$\qquad 1 \leq q \leq m$,   *otherwise*

2.2) Opening bids

        a)   Agents submit initial bid information for a dimension

$$BA_i \rightarrow A\ :(bid\text{-}information)_d$$
Where $bid\text{-}information_1 = (Bid_i,\ Sign\{h(Bid_i)\}_{Pri\text{-}BAi},\ BA_i\ Cert\ )\ and$
$$Bid_i = (L_1,\ E(BidCert_i\ ,K_i)),$$
$$bid\text{-}information_j = \ L_j\ for\ 2 \leq j \leq D,\ and\ 1 \leq d \leq D.$$

Repeat the following until $(Answer)_{d,q} = $ "*Yes*" for $q=m...1$ and for a dimension d.

        b)   Agents submit bid information for each column in the dimension

$$BA_i \rightarrow A\ :(bidding)_{d,q}$$
where $bidding_{d,q} = (GA_{d,q} \parallel L_{d,q-1} \parallel S_{d,q})$ *for* $1 \leq d \leq D\text{-}1$, *and*
$$bidding_{d,q} = L_{d,q-1}\ \ for\ d = D$$

        c)   Auctioneer calculates the answer and informs all bidding agents.

for $1 \leq d \leq D\text{-}1$
$$(Answer)_{d,q} = De\{GA_{d,q}\}_{Pri\text{-}A} \qquad if\ bidding_{d,q} = h(bidding_{d,q\text{-}1})$$

for $d=D$

$$\left. \begin{array}{l} (Answer)_{d,q} \ = \ Yes \\ R_i \parallel BidKey \ = \ bidding_{d,q\text{-}1} \end{array} \right\} if\ bidding_{d,q} = h(Yes \parallel bidding_{d,q\text{-}1})$$

$$(Answer)_{d,q} = No \qquad\qquad if\ bidding_{d,q} = h(No \parallel bidding_{d,q\text{-}1})$$

3)   Announcement of Bid winner

    a)   Obtain $BidCert_w$ from Bid_w by using $BidKey$ where w is a bid winner.

$$\left.\begin{array}{l} BidWinner \; = \; B_w \\ WinningPrice \; = \; (S_{D-1,k_D-1}) \; - \; (m-k_D) \end{array}\right\} \quad \text{if } BidCert_w \text{ contains } w\text{'s signature}$$

       where $PATH(1,D) = (k_1, ...,k_{D-1}, k_D)$.

    b)   Check the validity of $WinningPrice$

$$h(WinningPrice) = h(P_i) \qquad\qquad \text{if } WinningPrice \text{ is valid}$$

4   Discussion

Our protocol satisfies all desirable properties with the following reasons.

Collusion between bidder and auctioneer: In our approach discussed above, bidder (or bidder agent) may collude with auctioneer in order to reveal all bidders' individual answers. Such collusion would destroy bid privacy since auctioneer can then guess some bidders' bidding prices. Thus, to prevent the collusion between bidder and auctioneer, we employ blinding [8] on bidders' individual answers as follows.

At initial stage, a trusted authority generates blind factor b_i for each bidder B_i by computing $b_1 \times b_2 \times ... \times b_N \equiv GB \pmod p$ where p stands for prime modulus in Elgamal and GB stands for group blind factor. Also, the authority calculates GB^{-1} such that $GB.GB^{-1} \equiv 1 \pmod p$ and give it to all bidders. During the bidding process, each bidder agent broadcasts *blinded* individual answers as follows:

$$BA_i \text{ -> } BA_j : BlindedIA_{d,q} \qquad\qquad \text{for } q = 1, ..., m$$
$$\text{where } BlindedIA_{d,q} = En\{b_i \times IA_{d,q}\}_{Pub\text{-}A}$$

Furthermore, each bidder calculates *unblinded* group answer for each column at a dimension.

$$GA_{d,q} = GB^{-1}.\prod_{l=1}^{N}(BlindedIA_{d,q})_l \qquad \text{for } q = 1, ..., m$$

Even though our approach requires all bidders to collaborate to generate unblinded group answers, such collaboration does not use a large amount of resources. This is because all bidder (mobile) agents operate at auctioneer.

Anonymity of bidders: $BidCert_i$ for each bidder i is encrypted with a session key. Only when the winner is found, auctioneer can obtain the session key. Thus, before the winner is found, all bidders are anonymous.

Secrecy of bids: Winning price obtained during the bid opening can be checked with bidding price the winner has submitted initially in $BidCert_i$. Thus, a bidder in particular bid winner cannot change bidding price after the bid is submitted.

Privacy of bidding price: By using multi-dimensional hash chain, group answer and collision resistant hash, auctioneer can obtain the winner's session key only, not losers' session keys. Thus, only information about bid winner is revealed. Note that during the bid opening since bidder's individual answers are encrypted by agents' session key (K_b) which is known to all agents initially, auctioneer cannot infer information about losing bids during the opening.

Bidder Authentication: Any submitted bid is authenticated by using bidder agent' private key, not its bidder' private key. Thus, our approach prevents the denial of service problem (fake bids) occurred in Omote's approach.

Verifiability of the correctness of the auction: Since bidder agents observe the number of iterations of published hashes, they can compare current bidding price with their submitted bidding prices. So bidder agents can verify the outcome of the bid.

Undeniability of bids: Since $BidCert_i$ contains bidder's signature, bid winner cannot refuse her submitted bid.

5 Analysis

In this section we will analyze the security, computation and communication of our approach in comparison with the existing hash-based approach.

5.1 Security

We measure the security of the three approaches by using the size of search space of prices for losing bids. If the size of search space of losing prices is small, then the bid privacy property is weak. As shown in Table 3, our size of search space for losing prices is as large as Suzuki's and it depends on only the winning price. In Omote's approach, the size of search space depends upon the number of revealed bits. The nearer losing prices to the winning price, the more bits are revealed and the smaller the size of search space.

Table 3. The security analysis of our approach, Suzuki's and Omote's.

Approach	Range Search Space of Possible Losing Price	Size of Search Space
Suzuki	$1, ..., P_w-1$	P_w-1
Omote	$\sum_{j=0}^{v} b_{c-j} 2^{c-j} + 0, \quad \cdots, \sum_{j=0}^{v} b_{c-j} 2^{c-j} + 2^{c-v} - 1$	$2^{c-v} < P_w-1$
Ours	$1, ..., P_w-1$	P_w-1

where P_w = the winning price, b = the value of bits (0 or 1)
         c = the maximal number of bits representing bidding price
         v = the number of revealed bits

5.2 Computation

We use the number of iterations of hash to measure the computation required in each approach. Such number of hash iterations is used to represent bidding prices and it designates the required steps for the bid opening. Table 4 shows the computation required in the three approaches. In particular, it shows the number of hash iterations required to represent any bidding price P_i.

Table 4. The computation of the three approaches

Approach	Number of Hash Computation
Suzuki	$= M - P_i + 1$
Omote	$= \lceil \log_2(M) \rceil$
Ours	$\leq m. \lceil \log_m(M) \rceil$

In our approach, the computation depends on the parameter m which is the number of columns in a dimension. The smaller the number of column, the less the number of hash required. In our experiment where M is 1,000,000, the optimal value for m is 4. Details of our experiment can be found in [9].

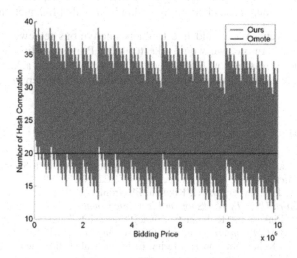

Fig. 2. The number of hash iterations.

In table 4, the computation for our approach is the worst case analysis in that it shows the number of hash iterations required to generate a horizontal hash chain for all columns in every dimension. However, some winning prices do not require the generation of a horizontal hash chain for all columns, but just some columns, in every dimension. Note that bid losers need to generate such kinds of horizontal hash chain.

Figure 2 shows the actual number of hash iterations required to represent each winning price in our approach in comparison with Omote's. It shows that for some cases, we use less amount of computation than Omote's. Note that in figure 2, we use $m = 4$ and $M=1,000,000$. And the average of computation in our approach is 25.173.

5.3 Communication

Although our opening phase may require communication between bidder agents and auctioneer, such communication is internal within auctioneer. This is because all bidder agents operate at the auctioneer site.

6 Conclusion

In this paper, we propose a new hash-based approach for sealed-bid auction. Our approach is based on multi-dimensional hash chain which corresponds to m-ary tree structure to represent a bidding price. We show that our approach satisfies all desirable properties of sealed-bid auctions, and offers both the security and efficiency at the acceptable level. Then, we show that our approach is as secure as Suzuki's but much more efficient than Suzuki's. Furthermore, we show that even though our approach is slightly less efficient than Omote's, it is much more secure than Omote's. At the moment, we are implementing a prototype of our approach and aims to apply the multi-dimensional hash chain for other kinds of sealed-bid auctions.

Acknowledgement. We would like to thank anonymous reviewers for their helpful comments. Furthermore, we would like to thank Professor Hiroaki Kikuchi for his kindly productive discussion. The second author would like to acknowledge financial support from National Research Council of Thailand and his department.

References

1. M. Franklin and M. Reiter, The Design and Implementation of a Secure Auction Service, *IEEE Transactions on Software Enginerring*, Vol. 22, No. 5, 1996.
2. M. Harkavy, J. D. Tygar, and H. Kikuchi, Electronic Auctions with Private Bids, *Proceeding of the Third USENIX Workshop on Electronic Commerce*, pp. 61–74, 1998
3. M. Naor, B. Pinkas, and R. Sumner, Privacy Preserving Auctions and Mechanism Design, *Proceeding of ACM Conference on Electronic Commerce*, pp. 129–139, 1999
4. K. Suzuki, K. Kobayashi, and H. Morita, Efficient Sealed-Bid Auction Using Hash Chain, *Proceeding of Third International Conference on Information Security and Cryptology*, pp. 183–191, 2000
5. K. Omote and A. Miyaji, An anonymous auction protocol with a single non-trusted binary trees, *Proceeding of Third International Workshop on Information Security* pp. 108–120, 2000

6. Alfred J. Menezes, Paul C. van Oorschot, Scott A. Vanstone, *Handbook of Applied Cryptography*, CRC Press, 1996
7. Y. Tsiounis and M. Yung, On the Security of Elgamal based Encryption, *Proceeding of First International Workshop on Practice and Theory in Public Key Cryptography*, 1998.
8. D. Chaum, R.L. Rivest, and A.T. Sherman, Blind Signatures for Untraceable Payments, In *Proceeding of Crypto*, pp 199–203, 1982
9. N. Prakobpol, Multi-dimensional Hash Chain for Sealed-Bid Auction, *Master Thesis, Department of Computer Engineering, King Mongkut's University of Technology Thonburi, Thailand, 2003, (In preparation)*.

An Improved Forward Integrity Protocol for Mobile Agents

Ming Yao, Ernest Foo, Kun Peng, and Ed Dawson

Information Security Research Centre
Queensland University of Technology
Brisbane, QLD, 4000, Australia
{m.yao,e.foo,k.peng,e.dawson}@qut.edu.au
http://www.isrc.qut.edu.au

Abstract. Forward integrity is an important mobile agent security property. Forward integrity in mobile agents guarantees that results contained in a mobile agent from previously visited servers cannot be changed by a malicious server. Many mobile agent forward integrity protocols are based on a protocol family proposed by Karjoth et al.. This paper identifies a "colluding servers" attack on these protocols where two (or more) visited servers can conspire to modify the existing collected data from other servers. We propose an improved Karjoth protocol by applying split-knowledge when constructing digital signatures, which can defend against the colluding servers attack.

1 Introduction

Mobile agents are executable code which can migrate from one server to another. They have great potential for electronic commerce applications. A shopping agent can travel the Internet in order to buy a specific product on behalf of the user at the most convenient price. The agent migrates to multiple servers, collects price quotes and is free to choose its next move dynamically based on a predefined itinerary choosing algorithm.

Forward integrity is an important security property for mobile agents. The notion of forward integrity was first introduced by Bellare and Yee in [1]. It was described as "a generalisation of the notion 'forward secrecy' ". In forward integrity, keys used for maintaining integrity and privacy are generated in a way that even if the key generating server is later compromised, it is not possible to forge previously obtained data. This contrasts with simple digital signature schemes, where if an attacker compromises the server storing the signing key, the authenticity of all the messages signed with that key becomes questionable.

Yee [10] later employed the concept of forward integrity in the context of mobile agents to provide data integrity protection, particularly to non-static data. Non-static data is not known by the originator in advance and will be generated and involved in an agent's future execution. In the shopping agent scenario non-static data are the offers from each server. In general, Yee defines forward integrity in the following manner "if a mobile agent visits a sequence

K. Chae and M. Yung (Eds.): WISA 2003, LNCS 2908, pp. 272–285, 2004.
© Springer-Verlag Berlin Heidelberg 2004

of servers S_1, S_2, ..., S_n, and the first malicious server is S_m, then none of partial results (non-static data) generated at server S_i, where i < m, can be forged". In other words, the *first* encountered malicious server can not modify or forge any existing partial results generated by any of the *upstream* servers. However, partial results for servers visited after the first malicious server cannot be trusted. Because of the assumption of an "honest prefix", Yee's proposal is defined as *weak forward integrity*.

Karjoth *et al.* [4] proposed a notion of *strong forward integrity* where an attacker S_m can not forge any of partial results generated at server S_i, where i < m, even by colluding with one (or more) other visited server(s) S_j, where j < i. Therefore, despite the presence of more than one malicious server in an agent's itinerary, the partial results can still be preserved intact. This ensures that all the partial results can only be generated once and can not be changed after the data is collected by the agent. In other words, S_i can not make another offer by modifying the previous offer or replacing it with a new offer to the same agent after it has made a commitment, unless the originator requires it.

Protocols that achieve forward integrity of partial results carried by multi-hop agents were first published by Yee [10]. Yee's protocols were based on *partial result authentication codes* (PRACs), which were constructed in similar forms to MACs and digital signatures verified with PKI public keys. The notable difference is the secret keys used by PRACs were destroyed prior to the agent's migration, contrasting with the private keys in a normal digital signature system where private keys are stored on the servers for a long term. Thus in some sense PRAC keys are one-time keys.

Karjoth, Asokan and Gülcü [4] extended Yee's results and proposed a family of protocols, which are directed at preserving the integrity of intermediate computed data acquired by multi-hop agents. Some of their protocols also possess additional features such as data confidentiality, forward privacy and public verifiability. We have particular interest in publicly verifiable forward integrity, since it allows other servers on the agent's itinerary to help detect tampering. In this paper, we concentrate on Karjoth, Asokan and Gülcü's fourth protocol because it contains publicly verifiable chained signatures. For convenience, we refer to this protocol as KAG.

It will be demonstrated that the KAG protocol is vulnerable to a "colluding servers" attack which occurs when a server plots with another server positioned later in the agent's itinerary to alter the data accumulated between visits to the two servers. To the best of our knowledge, there have been no effective solutions proposed to counter these attacks on a single agent [2].

Based on the "colluding servers" attack and other known attacks, this paper proposes four requirements (R1 - R4) for the design of protocols that provide forward integrity of data in mobile agents. Another contribution of this paper is the proposal of a strengthened KAG protocol which defends against the "colluding servers" attack.

The paper is organised as follows: Section 2 describes the KAG protocol and some known attacks. It also includes the "colluding servers" attack. Proposed protocol design rules are presented in Sect. 3. In Sect. 4, we present a new protocol, which can defend against some of the discussed attacks. We have some concluding remarks and plans for future work in Sect. 5.

Notation. For ease of reading, we refer to the entities appeared in our demonstrated application by their names. Alice is the owner of the agent. Adam, Bob and Dave are shops's owners who will be visited by Alice's agent. Carol is the adversary who may be a server in the agent's itinerary or an external attacker.

The notation used in the paper are listed in Table 1.

Table 1. Notation used in this paper ($0 \leq i \leq n$ unless i is indicated)

Notation	Meaning
$\prod$	An agent's code.
S_0	ID of the originator.
$S_i, 1 \leq i \leq n$	ID of server i.
o_0	A secret possessed by S_0. It can be regarded as a dummy offer and is only known to the originator.
$o_i, 1 \leq i \leq n$	An offer (a partial result) from S_i .
O_i	An encapsulated offer (cryptographically protected) from S_i.
$O_0, O_1, O_2,...,O_n$	The chain of encapsulated offers from the originator and shops $S_1, S_2,..., S_n$.
h_i	Message integrity check value associated with O_i.
r_i	A nonce generated by S_i.
H(m)	A one-way collision-free hash function.
(K_Pub_i, K_Priv_i)	A public/private key pair of server S_i.
$(t\_Pub_{i+1}, t\_Priv_{i+1})$	A one-time key pair to be used by S_{i+1}. The key pair is generated by S_i.
$\{t\_Priv_{i+1}\}_{K_{i,i+1}}$	One-time private key is sent by using some key establishment protocol between S_i and S_{i+1}.
(j_Pub_i, j_Priv_i), $1 \leq i \leq n$	A one-time key pair for constructing the proposed signature/verification is generated by S_i.
$\{m_i\}_{K\_Pub_i}$	Message m_i encrypted with the encryption key associated with S_i.
$\mathrm{Sig}_{K\_Priv_i}(m_i)$	A signature of S_i on the message m_i with K_Priv_i.
$\mathrm{Ver}_{K\_Pub_i}(s_i, m_i) =$ true or false	Verification of the signature s_i on the message m_i. It is true when $\mathrm{Sig}_{K\_Priv_i}(m_i) = s_i$; false otherwise.
Alice $\rightarrow$ Bob: m	Alice sending a message m to Bob.

2   The KAG Protocol

The KAG protocol is an extension of *publicly verifiable partial result authentication codes* published by Yee [10]. The protocol aims to allow any intermediate server (either trusted or untrusted) to detect the tampering of the previously computed partial results contained in the agent.

One-time digital signatures are deployed in the KAG protocol. Public key algorithms are used but the public key used to verify the signature is passed by the agent and not certified through a public key infrastructure. Each shop generates a private/public key pair for constructing the one-time signature and its verification, and also certifies the public key to be used by its successor. The successor server uses the received private key to sign the partial result it computed. The private key is subsequently erased.

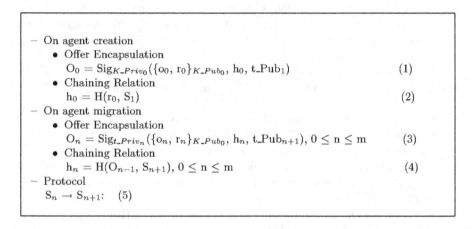

Fig. 1. The KAG Protocol

The KAG protocol is summarised in Fig. 1. Let us assume the agent will visit m servers. The originator S_0 initialises the protocol by randomly generating r_0 and a one-time private/public key pair (t_Priv$_1$, t_Pub$_1$) for the first server S_1. S_0 also computes a checksum h_0 from r_0 and the identity of S_1. S_0 then encrypts a secret token o_0 and r_0 with its own public key. S_0 signs this encrypted value together with h_0 and t_Pub$_1$ to construct a dummy encapsulated offer O_0. Finally S_0 sends O_0 to the first server S_1. With a key establishment protocol, the one-time private key t_Priv$_1$ can be sent securely over the insecure channel to S_1.

As such a list of encapsulated offers are generated. Note lines (2) and (4) in Fig. 1 indicate that a chaining relationship is built up. The chaining relationship is constructed in the following way: A hash chain h_n at server S_n is composed of the encapsulated offer O_{n-1} of its predecessor and some unique data linking to its successor and/or S_n itself. In the KAG protocol, the unique data is the identity of the next server. The hash chain h_n together with the current server's partial result o_n are then signed by S_n (if we do not consider r_n and t_Pub$_{n+1}$ in figure 1), and become an encapsulated offer O_n. O_n will be added into the hash chain by the successor server S_{n+1}. We can generally express the hash chain h_{n+1} at S_{n+1} as :

$$h_{n+1} = H(O_n, \text{unique linking data})$$
$$= H(\text{Sig}_{t\_Priv_n}(o_n, h_n), S_{n+2})$$

It is observed that the link has been built upon three consecutive servers S_n, S_{n+1} and S_{n+2} $(n \geq 0)$.

If an attacker wishes to replace o_n with o'_n without being detected, the change must not affect the rest of the chain. As the attacker does not know the private key of S_n, providing K_Priv$_n$ is not compromised, he can only replace the entire signed partial result O_n with O'_n. The attacker has to find a $h'_{n+1} = H(O'_n$, unique linking data) where $h_{n+1} = h'_{n+1}$. This contradicts the assumption that hash function H is collision free.

During the agent's execution, the list of one-time public keys (for verifying the signature) should be either published and/or carried with the agent. When these one-time public keys are available to all the servers on the agent's itinerary, at server S_n, partial results obtained at server S_j can be verified, where $j < n$.

When the agent arrives at server S_{n+1}, carrying a set of previously collected encapsulated offers $\{O_0, O_1, \dots O_n\}$, S_{n+1} can conduct verification as follows:

- S_{n+1} obtains O_n from the chain and searches for the corresponding one-time public key t_Pub$_n$ from the key list. If Ver$_{t\_Pub_n}$ (O_n) = true, S_{n+1} can ensure that the signature is authentic. S_{n+1} recovers $\{o_n, r_n\}_{K\_Pub_0}$, h_n and t_Pub$_{n+1}$. S_{n+1} can not view o_n since it was encrypted using K_Pub$_0$. Only the originator is able to decrypt the offer o_n, hence it provides data confidentiality.
- S_{n+1} obtains O_{n-1} from the chain and computes $h'_n = H(O_{n-1}, S_{n+1})$. If $h'_n = h_n$, the hash chain is valid at S_n. The valid hash chain proves that no illegal modification, insertion or deletion has occurred at S_n as we have discussed above. As such S_{n+1} keeps tracing untill O_0. If S_{n+1} can successfully verify the signature on O_0 and check the validity of h_0, S_{n+1} then ensures that the agent is genuinely sent by the originator.

If no integrity violation is detected, the agent continues its execution; otherwise, the agent's computation can abort early, instead of having to finish the computation and detecting integrity violations when the agent returns to the originator.

S_{n+1} has also received the one-time private key t_Priv$_{n+1}$ from S_n. When the agent is ready to leave S_{n+1}, it chooses a new one-time private/public key (t_Priv$_{n+2}$, t_Pub$_{n+2}$) pair (either on the fly or by means of precomputation [7]) for S_{n+2}. S_{n+1} constructs its encapsulated offer O_{n+1} with t_Priv$_{n+1}$ and sends t_Priv$_{n+2}$ to the next server. Lastly, before the agent migrates to the server S_{n+2}, t_Priv$_{n+1}$ is destroyed.

3 Security Requirements for Forward Integrity

The primary aim of this section is to define a set of requirements for a robust security protocol of forward integrity. This section first examines some known attacks on the KAG protocol and their countermeasures. A new "colluding servers" attack is then identified and demonstrated. We introduce our design rules as well.

3.1   Some Known Attacks and Countermeasures

Some attacks on the integrity of intermediate computed data addressed by Karjoth [4] *et al.* include:

- *Modification of partial results.* This attack occurs when an entity maliciously alters previously generated partial results. The KAG protocol protects agents against this attack by establishing a chaining relationship. Each entry of the chain depends on some of the previous and/or succeeding members. In Sect. 2 when we discussed the KAG protocol, we have demonstrated that the chaining relationship can effectively prevent attackers from tampering with the signed data without being noticed.
- *Insertion.* This attack takes place when an entity inserts offers which would not have been included without the intervention of the malicious entity. This attack can be countered by applying the chaining relationship. No one can insert an offer anywhere between O_0 and O_m if given a chain of signed partial results $O_0, O_1,... O_m$; otherwise the chain will be invalid at the element with the inserted data. Consequently the illegal insertion will be noticed by the verifier. Insertion is allowed only at the last node of the chain.
- *Deletion.* This attack is similar to the insertion attack where an attacker deletes previously generated partial results instead of inserting a new offer. Following the same line of reasoning, if the chaining relationship is constructed, it is impossible to delete some offers from the chain without being detected. However in the KAG protocol, security relies on the assumption that an attacker does not change the last signed partial result O_m. There is no obligation that an attack will not do so. A *"truncation attack"* [4] is a type of deletion attack where the adversary cuts off the offers from S_i to S_m and append fake offers. The KAG protocol can not defend against the "truncation attack" because it only provides a "weak chain relationship". We will define the "weak chain relationship" in Sect. 3.3.

3.2   Colluding Servers Attack

The security assurance of the KAG protocol relies on the assumption that the predecessor does not leak the secret used by its successor. However, there is no reason why a malicious shop would be so obliging. In contrast, if the malicious shop, say S_j is willing to change its successor's offer O_{j+1}, he can conspire with S_{j+2} and divulge S_{j+1}'s private key because S_j generates the one-time public/private key pair for S_{j+1}. We identify this attack as a "colluding servers" attack.

We assume that Carol attempts to alter Bob's offer. Let Carol be S_j, Bob be S_{j+1}, and Dave S_{j+2}, $j > 1$. Carol always knows the secret of her next hop - Bob's one-time public/private key pair $(t\_Pub_{j+1}, t\_Priv_{j+1})$ because the key pair is generated at her server. However she does not know any other one-time key pairs used by other servers; thus she is not able to alter other offers.

When Carol first receives Alice's agent, she is unable to change Bob's offer because the one-time key pair used by Bob has not been generated yet. Nevertheless if she bribes Dave and sends Bob's private key to him, Dave can easily replace Bob's offer by faking an offer and signing with Bob's one-time private key without being noticed by Bob, Alice or other verifiers (see Fig. 2).

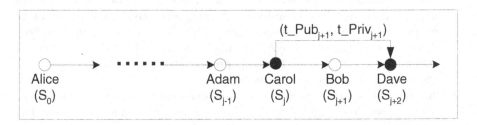

Fig. 2. "Colluding servers" attack on the KAG protocol (Black dots mean colluding servers)

Carol Sends Her Encapsulated Offer to Bob

Following the same steps in Sect. 2, upon the received agent, Carol (S_j) computes O_j, generates one-time key pair for Bob and sends message (1).

$$\text{Carol } (S_j) \rightarrow \text{Bob}(S_{j+1}): \prod, \{O_0, O_1, O_2, ..., O_j\}, \{t\_Priv_{j+1}\}_{K_{j,j+1}} \quad (1)$$

Bob Verifies the Integrity

Bob receives the agent from Carol. He verifies Carol's signature using her public key and follows the same procedures that we have described in Sect. 2 to validate the chain relationship.

Prior to agent's migration, Bob (S_{j+1}) generates the key pair (t_Pub_{j+2}, t_Priv_{j+2}) and includes t_Pub_{j+2} in the encapsulated offer.

Attack on Bob

We have assumed that Carol is colluding with Dave. Once Dave receives the agent, he can notify his colluding partner Carol to send him Bob's private key.

$$\text{Bob } (S_{j+1}) \rightarrow \text{Dave}(S_{j+2}): \prod, \{O_0, O_1, ..., O_j, O_{j+1}\}, \{t\_Priv_{j+2}\}_{K_{j+1,j+2}} \quad (2)$$
$$\text{Carol } (S_j) \rightarrow \text{Dave}(S_{j+2}): (t\_Pub_{j+1}, t\_Priv_{j+1}) \quad (2')$$

Dave can randomly choose a r'_{j+1}, make a fake offer o'_{j+1} for Bob (S_{j+1}) and sign them with Alice's public key. As Dave always knows Carol's encapsulated offer O_j and his own ID S_{j+2}, with information in (2') he is able to reconstruct a fake offer for Bob $O'_{j+1} = Sig_{t\_Priv_{j+1}}(\{o'_{j+1}, r'_{j+1}\}_{K\_Pub_0}, h_{j+1}, t\_Pub_{j+2})$ where $h_{j+1} = H(O_j, S_{j+2})$ without being noticed by any verifier.

3.3   Security Requirements

After observing these possible attacks and their countermeasures, we sum up a few requirements which may be good practice for future protocol design.

- R1: require unique commitment of the current server;
- R2: require commitment of previous server in chain to travel to the next intended server;
- R3: require commitment of next server in chain;
- R4: require commitment of the originator.

R1 ensures that no replay or impersonation attack can take place. As discussed above, a chaining relationship specifies the dependency. If defined properly, any modification of the chain, including deletion or insertion of elements, will invalidate the link for all members dependent on the altered element. R1, R2 and R3 make sure that a "strong chain relationship" is established. Suppose a chain contains elements $e_1 \dots e_n$. A strong chain relationship indicates any e_i ($1 \leq i \leq n$) in the chain relies on both e_{i-1} and e_{i+1}. One can not alter e_i without affecting e_{i-1} and e_{i+1}. In contrast with a strong chain relationship, in a "weak chain relationship" e_i depends on either e_{i-1} or e_{i+1}, or none of them. A weak chain relationship could lead to a truncation attack, to which the KAG protocol is vulnerable. A "weak chain relationship" does not satisfy all of R1, R2 and R3.

R4 guarantees that the chain is verifiable and traceable.

It is observed in Fig. 1 that the KAG protocol satisfies the security requirements R2 in lines (3) and (4), and satisfies R4 in lines (1) and (2). However it lacks commitment from the current server and the next server, which result in a vulnerability to the "colluding servers" attack and the "truncation" attack. It only provides a "weak chain relationship".

Note that these requirements aim at providing forward integrity to the partial results, however integrity of execution and integrity of an agent's code are beyond the scope of this paper. Thus we assume execution integrity and code integrity when we discuss the forward integrity protocols.

4   Our Solution

We have devised a new protocol extended from the KAG protocol to defend against the "colluding servers" attack and some of the other attacks described in Sect. 3.1. The main goal is to provide robust forward integrity. The idea is to involve the predecessor server and the successor server to participate in the partial results signing. The predecessor's knowledge about the secret is restricted to his part. Therefore the malicious server can not tamper with the data by colluding with other servers.

4.1   Publicly Verifiable Signature Scheme Using Split Knowledge

The new protocol is based on the concept of a split-knowledge scheme [6] where knowledge of the secret S is split among two people. Any action requiring S needs two people to trigger it. Despite the resemblance, the proposed scheme differs from split-knowledge schemes in fundamental aspects: The secret is not known beforehand; instead two shares of the secret are provided by the involved parties independently in advance. The secret is thereafter constructed by one involved party using two shares. There is no trusted third party needed.

In the proposed scheme, we keep the main part of the KAG protocol, however the keys used for constructing signatures and the corresponding verification are generated in a different way. We use a "joint" private key (the secret) j_Priv_n to generate signatures for S_n. j_Priv_n is composed of two parts: a one-time private key t_Priv_n generated by the predecessor and its own long-term private key K_Priv_n. The corresponding public key j_Pub_n can be deduced from the public keys t_Pub_n and K_Pub_n. The proposed signature scheme can be achieved using the ElGamal signature scheme [6]. In the ElGamal signature scheme, K_Pub_n can be expressed as (p, g, y_n) and t_Pub_n can be (p, g, u_n), where p is a large random prime and $g \in Z_p^*$ is a generator of Z_p^*.

We have detailed each stage of the KAG protocol during the agent's journey in Sect. 2. Following the same lines, we elaborate our new scheme as follows (see Fig. 3):

- Agent's creation stage. Same as in the KAG protocol, the originator constructs a dummy encapsulated offer O_0 and initialises the hash chain h_0.
- Agent's migration stage. S_n constructs a joint private key j_Priv_n used for signing its offer as: $\mathbf{j\_Priv}_n = \mathbf{t\_Priv}_n + \mathbf{K\_Priv}_n$. S_n then signs its offer with j_Priv_n, as well as adding its hash chaining element h_n to the chaining relationship. Prior to the agent's migration, S_n chooses a one-time key pair $(t\_Priv_{n+1}, t\_Pub_{n+1})$ for S_{n+1}. S_n at last sends the agent with all the encapsulated offers and the one-time private key to S_{n+1}.
- Verification stage. Any entity S_i is able to verify any offer contained in the agent. To verify O_n, S_i needs to construct a joint verification function. S_i obtains S_n's long-term public key K_Pub_n and the one-time public key t_Pub_n from the key lists. S_i assembles the joint verification as: $\mathbf{j\_Pub}_n = (p, g, j_n)$ **where** $j_n = \mathbf{y}_n \times \mathbf{u}_n$. If S_i computes $Ver_{j\_Pub_n}(O_n) = true$, it can prove that the signature is authentic. S_i checks the validity of hash chain at S_n as well. Following the same procedures as the KAG protocol, S_i is able to check all the partial results and the entire hash chain.

We detail the key generation and signature generation/verification in the following section.

Key Generation with ElGamal Signature Scheme

Assume p and g are system parameters for all the servers in the agent's itinerary. A server S_{n+1} has a long term private key K_Priv_{n+1} and a long-term public key $K\_Pub_{n+1} = (p, g, y_{n+1})$ where $y_{n+1} = g^{K\_Priv_{n+1}} \bmod p$.

- On agent creation
  - Offer Encapsulation
    $$O_0 = Sig_{K\_Priv_0}(\{o_0, r_0\}_{K\_Pub_0}, h_0, t\_Pub_1) \tag{1}$$
  - Chaining Relation
    $$h_0 = H(r_0, S_1) \tag{2}$$
- On agent migration
  - **Joint Private Key Generation**
    $$j\_Priv_n = t\_Priv_n + K\_Priv_n \tag{3}$$
  - Offer Encapsulation
    $$O_n = Sig_{j\_Priv_n}(\{o_n, r_n\}_{K\_Pub_0}, h_n, t\_Pub_{n+1}), 0 < n \le m \tag{4}$$
  - Chaining Relation
    $$h_n = H(O_{n-1}, S_{n+1}) \tag{5}$$
- On verification
  - **Joint Verification Generation**
    $$j\_Pub_n = (p, g, j_n) \text{ where } j_n = y_n \times u_n \tag{6}$$

    $$Ver_{j\_Pub_n}(O_n, m_n) = \begin{cases} true, & if \quad Sig_{j\_Priv_n}(m_n) = O_n \\ false, & otherwise \end{cases}$$

    where $m_n = (\{o_n, r_n\}_{K\_Pub_0}, h_n, t\_Pub_{n+1})$
- Protocol
  $$S_n \rightarrow S_{n+1}: \textstyle\prod, \{O_0, O_1, \ldots O_n\}, \{t\_Priv_{n+1}\}_{K_{n,n+1}}, 0 \le n \le m \tag{7}$$

Fig. 3. The New Signature Scheme using Split-knowledge

The one-time private/public key for S_{n+1} is generated by S_n. S_n chooses the same random prime p and a generator g as above. S_n generates one-time private/public key pair for S_{n+1} as follows: one-time private key is t_Priv_{n+1} where t_Priv_{n+1} is a random integer $(1 \le t\_Priv_{n+1} \le p - 2)$; and one-time public key is $t\_Pub_{n+1} = (p, g, u_{n+1})$ where $u_{n+1} = g^{t\_Priv_{n+1}} \bmod p$. S_n sends the key pair to S_{n+1}.

Upon received message from S_n, S_{n+1} computes $j\_Priv_{n+1} = t\_Priv_{n+1} + K\_Priv_{n+1}$. The *joint verification* is generated by computing:

$$
\begin{aligned}
j_{n+1} &= g^{(t\_Priv_{n+1} + K\_Priv_{n+1})} \\
&= g^{t\_Priv_{n+1}} g^{K\_Priv_{n+1}} \\
&= u_{n+1} y_{n+1} \bmod p. \\
j\_Pub_{n+1} &= (p, g, j_{n+1})
\end{aligned}
$$

Signature Generation and Verification

Prior to the agent's migration, server S_n signs the message m_n including j_Pub_n using j_Priv_n. To produce the proposed signature, server S_n conducts the following process: S_n selects a random secret integer k, $1 \le k \le p - 2$, with $\gcd(k, p - 1) = 1$. Then S_n does these computations:

- $c = g^k \bmod p$.

- k^{-1} mod $(p - 1)$.
- $s = k^{-1}\{h(m_n) - j\_Priv_n\ c\}$ mod $(p - 1)$.

S_n's signature for m_n is the pair (c, s).

Similar to the KAG protocol, the list of joint public keys should be publicly accessible. To verify S_n's signature (c, s) on m_n, server S_i should do the following: S_i obtains S_n's joint public key $j\_Pub_n = (p, g, j_n)$ from the joint public key list. S_i checks if $1 \leq c \leq p - 1$; if not, then S_i rejects the signature and notifies the agent's owner that signature (c, s) has lost its authenticity. S_i computes $v_1 = (j_n)^c c^s$ mod p. Then S_i computes $h(m_n)$ and $v_2 = g^{h(m_n)}$ mod p. S_i compares v_1 and v_2. The signature is accepted if and only if $v_1 = v_2$.

4.2   Security Analysis

Since the publicly verifiable signature using split-knowledge is based on ElGamal signature scheme, it is as secure as ElGamal encryption.

Theorem 1. *Without collusion with S_{j-1} and compromise of S_j's private key α_j, it is impossible for S_{j+1} to tamper O_i if DL problem is intractable and ElGamal signature scheme is secure.*

Proof: We assume that ElGamal signature scheme is secure (it is computationally intractable to generate a valid signature without knowledge of the private key)[1]. Therefore, in the new scheme, integrity of the signed data relies on the confidentiality of the private key $(t\_Priv_n + K\_Priv_n)$.

Suppose given y_j and u_j, S_{j+1} successfully extracts $(t\_Priv_n + K\_Priv_n)$ using an algorithm A without knowledge of either α_j or r_{j-1}, or both. As a result, S_{j+1} can employ A to break DL problem as follows: Given β, S_{j+1} chooses γ and calculates $\delta = g^\gamma$. Then S_{j+1} employs A to extract $\log_g \beta + \log_g \delta = \log_g \beta + \gamma$. Therefore, S_{j+1} can extract $\log_g \beta$ as S_{j+1} knows γ. Namely, S_{j+1} can solve discrete log problem. This is contradictory to the assumption that discrete log problem is intractable. □

From Theorem 1, it is observed that the new scheme has advantage over the KAG protocol in that to compromise the integrity of O_i, S_{j+1} needs to not only conspire with S_{j-1}, but also compromise S_j's long-term private key.

Complexity of the new scheme. Suppose the KAG protocol and the new scheme are both implemented using ElGamal signature scheme. Compared to the KAG protocol, the new scheme has two more operations: one addition (referring to line (3) in Fig. 3) to generate the private key, and one multiplication (referring to line (6) in Fig. 3) to produce the verification (the public key) of the signature for every server. These two operations are negligible in the entire computational cost of the protocol.

---

[1] The problem of breaking ElGamal encryption is equivalent to solving the Diffie-Hellman problem [6]

The publicly verifiable signature using split-knowledge can effectively prevent the "colluding servers" attack and some other attacks.

- *colluding servers* attack

  In Sect. 4.1 we reconstructed the private key used for a digital signature to be: one-time private key + server's own private key. The cause of colluding servers attack on the KAG protocol lies in the fact that the knowledge of the one-time public/private key pair used by the successor server is also known to the predecessor server. In the new scheme, the knowledge of key used for digital signature is composed of two secrets:
  - one-time private key known by the predecessor and the successor
  - private key **only** known by the successor

  Therefore, a server only knows part of key knowledge can not reconstruct the key by colluding with the other server.

- *modification, insertion and deletion* attacks

  As we discussed in Sect. 3.1, a chaining relationship can effectively prevent these three attacks. The new protocol inherits this feature from the KAG protocol and can also defend these attacks. However, the new protocol also receives the vulnerability to the "truncation" attack from the KAG protocol because any server in the chain can truncate all offers following its own, the protocol allows the attacker to insert other fake offers before the agent is sent back to the originator.

  Our approach satisfies some of our design rules:
  - R1 requires the current server to make a unique commitment to prevent replay or masquerade attack. In the proposed protocol, lines (3) and (4) indicate that the digital signature includes the server's own long-term private key, which is only known to the server. Therefore a malicious server can not impersonate the legitimate server to sign the message.
  - R2 requires a commitment from the previous server to honestly transfer the agent to the intended server. The commitment is the encapsulated offer signed by the previous server which includes an indication of next intended server within the hash element. Line (5) presents this commitment. The encapsulated offer is ensured of its order integrity by the hash chain.
  - R4 is to ensure that the agent is truly from the originator. Like the KAG protocol, R4 is satisfied in the new protocol as the hash chain presented in line (2) contains a secret only known to the originator. When the originator checks the returned hash chain, it can determine if the hash chain remains intact by verifying the integrity of the secret.

R3 is not satisfied in the new protocol as the next server does not make any commitment. The unique identity of the next server included in the hash chain does not provide proof that the agent will execute on the next server chosen by the agent. The next server's identity is only signed by the current server. R3 is also not satisfied in the KAG protocol. Like the KAG protocol, the new protocol only provides a "weak chain relationship". This results in a vulnerability to the "truncation" attack. Table 2 summarises how the KAG protocol and the new scheme satisfy the security requirements.

Table 2. Comparison of the KAG protocol and the new protocol on security requirements

	R1	R2	R3	R4
the KAG protocol		✓		✓
the New Scheme	✓	✓		✓

5   Conclusion and Future Work

Karjoth *et al.* [4] proposed a scheme to achieve publicly verifiable forward integrity. We have exposed some vulnerabilities of their scheme resulting from some subtle problems overlooked during design. In spite of these problems, we believe that the security of their core scheme remains intact. We proposed a strengthened scheme to prevent some potential attacks. The new scheme uses a joint public/private key to generate and verify a signature. The joint key contains a component generated by the previous server and a secret generated by the current server. The proposed publicly verifiable signature scheme using split-knowledge is more robust against the colluding servers attack.

However the new scheme only provides a "weak chain relationship". As a consequence, it can not effectively defend against "truncation" attacks [4] where a malicious server discards all the entries after its own, and grows a fake stem. Maggi *et. al* [5] proposes a solution to the truncation attack. We will conduct further investigation on this issue. The new scheme is not able to protect code integrity and execution, which is difficult to protect as it involves run-time compilation data. These problems are still open issues.

References

1. Bellare, M., Yee, B. S.: Forward Integrity for Secure Audit Logs. Technical report. Computer Science and Engineering Department, University of California. San Diego, USA (1995)
2. Cheng, J. S. L., Wei, V. K.: Defenses against the Truncation of Computation Results of Free-Roaming Agents. In: Deng, R. H., Qing, S., Bao, F., Zhou, J.(ed.): Information and Communications Security, 4th International Conference, ICICS 2002, Singapore. Lecture Notes in Computer Science, Vol. 2513. Springer-Verlag, Berlin Heidelberg (2002) 1–12
3. ElGamal, T.: A Public-Key Cryptosystem and a Signature Scheme based on Discrete Logarithms. IEEE Transactions on Information Theory, Vol. 31, Number 4. IEEE Computer Society Press, Phoenix(1985) 469–472
4. Karjoth, G., Asokan, N., Gülcü, C.: Protecting the Computation Results of Free-Roaming Agents. In: Rothermel, K., Hohl, F.. (eds.): Proceedings of the 2nd International Workshop on Mobile Agents (MA '98). Lecture Notes in Computer Science, Vol. 1477. Springer-Verlag, Berlin Heidelberg New York (1998) 195–207

5. Maggi, P., Sisto, R.: A Configurable Mobile Agent Data Protection Protocol Proceedings of the 2nd International Conference on Autonomous Agents and Multiagent Systems (AAMAS'03), Melbourne, Australia. ACM Press, New York, USA (2003) 851–858
6. Menezes, A., Oorschot, P. van, Vanstone, S.: Handbook of Applied Cryptography. CRC Press Inc. (1996)
7. Roth, V.: On the Robustness of some Cryptographic Protocols for Mobile Agent Protection. Proceedings Mobile Agents 2001. Lecture Notes in Computer Science, Vol. 2240. Springer-Verlag, Berlin Heidelberg (2001) 1–14
8. Roth, V.: Programming Satan's agents. In: Fischer, K., Hutter, D.. (eds.): Proceedings of 1st International Workshop on Secure Mobile Multi-Agent Systems (SEMAS 2001). Electronic Notes in Theoretical Computer Science, Vol. 63. Elsevier Science Publishers (2002).
9. Roth, V.: Empowering Mobile Software Agents. Proceedings 6th IEEE Mobile Agents Conference. Lecture Notes in Computer Science, Vol. 2535. Springer-Verlag, Berlin Heidelberg (2002) 47–63
10. Yee, B. S.: A Sanctuary for Mobile Agents. Secure Internet Programming. Lecture Notes in Computer Science, Vol. 1603. Springer-Verlag, Berlin Heidelberg (1999) 261–273

Taming "Trusted Platforms" by Operating System Design

Ahmad-Reza Sadeghi[1] and Christian Stüble[2]

[1] Ruhr-University Bochum,
Institute for Information and Communication Security,
44780 Bochum, Germany
sadeghi@crypto.rub.de
[2] Saarland University,
Security and Cryptography Group,
66041 Saarbrücken, Germany
stueble@acm.org

Abstract. Experiences of the past have shown that common computing platforms lack security due to architectural problems and complexity. In this context, Microsoft Palladium (Pd) and TCPA are announced to be the next-generation computing platforms, and claimed to improve users' security. However, people are concerned about those capabilities of TCPA/Pd that may allow content providers to gain too much power and control over the use of digital content and users' private information. In this paper, we argue that TCPA/Pd can increase the security of computing platforms by faithfully designing the operating system. Moreover, we discuss how interferences between digital rights management capabilities and end-user security can be prevented. Our results are based on the fact that even with TCPA/Pd platforms the operating system has enough control over the platform to prevent misuse by both content providers and end-users.

We argue that such a trustworthy operating system, that is secure in the sense of multilateral security, can be developed without much effort by efficiently combining the ideas of security kernels and state of the art of operating system technology. We propose a new architecture for a trustworthy security platform that uses TCPA/Pd hardware features in conjunction with an open-source security kernel we have developed. Our security kernel provides backward-compatibility to the Linux operating system. The layered design and its lightweightness allows an easy migration to other hardware platforms like PDAs, mobile phones, and embedded systems.

1 Introduction

The advent of e-commerce and the rapid expansion of world-wide connectivity demands end-user systems that can guarantee authenticity, integrity, privacy, anonymity, and availability. While cryptographic and security research communities have provided solutions to a variety of security related problems, all these solutions depend upon the security of the underlying computing platform.

K. Chae and M. Yung (Eds.): WISA 2003, LNCS 2908, pp. 286–302, 2004.
© Springer-Verlag Berlin Heidelberg 2004

Existing computing platforms, in particular common operating systems, neither offer appropriate mechanisms to enforce adequate security policies, nor can they be maintained by non-experts. Additionally, they suffer from several vulnerabilities in hardware and software: beside architectural security problems and the inherent vulnerabilities resulting from complexity [31], common operating systems require careful and competent system administration and will still not effectively protect individuals from executing malicious code. This situation brings about the need for developing a new generation of secure computing platforms.

A lot has been reported about Microsoft's Next-Generation Secure Computing Base for Windows (NGSCB, former Palladium or Pd) [10,14] and the specification proposed by the Trusted Computing Platform Alliance[1] (TCPA) [36,35]. The stated goal of these systems is to improve security and trustworthiness of computing platforms [13,27,31,30]. However, since their announcement, there is an ongoing public debate about the negative economical, social and technical consequences of these platforms [3,7,32]. There are many concerns regarding their capabilities, in particular, in conjunction with Digital Rights Management (DRM). People are worried about the potential negative consequences of TCPA/Pd and believe that these platforms may give vendors and content providers too much control over personal systems and users' private information: they may allow commercial censorship[2], political censorship, or destroy innovation.[3] Especially, the open-source community seems to resist against TCPA/Pd, mainly because they are more sensitive regarding user security and privacy issues.

To clarify this situation, we briefly recapitulate requirements of secure end-user computing platforms and evaluate on a technical level to what extend common hardware architectures like PCs satisfy them. After a short review on TCPA/Pd based on available technical documentations, we analyze whether and how they can be used to improve end-user security of existing computing platforms. In this context, we argue that the functionalities provided by TCPA and Pd are completely under control of the operating system. As a consequence, users can benefit from the security features of TCPA/Pd, as long as their operating system is trustworthy. Although this statement seems to be obvious at first glance, the trustworthiness of existing and future operating systems is questionable.

Therefore, we propose a new architecture of a trustworthy security platform that uses TCPA/Pd hardware features in conjunction with an open-source security kernel [28] we have developed. Our proposed architecture demonstrates the following important issues. On the one hand, one can build highly secure

---

[1] www.trustedcomputing.org

[2] Microsoft, as the vendor of Palladium, is able to remotely delete documents that are locally stored on a Pd-machine.

[3] For instance, word could encrypt all documents using keys only known to Microsoft, making it impossible for rival products (e.g., OpenOffice or StarOffice) to be compatible or undermine the General Public License (GPL).

systems based on TCPA/Pd hardware without much effort. On the other hand, the security concerns mentioned above can effectively be prevented by a careful operating system design.

Furthermore, we propose design criteria to provide DRM features on our security platform that avoid conflicts between DRM policies and end-user security (privacy). In this way, the proposed trustworthy DRM platform fulfills security requirements of end-users and content providers in the sense of multilateral security.

2   The Need for Secure Hardware

In the conventional sense, secure platforms are systems that enforce user-defined security policies to protect them against attacks from inside and outside of the platform, e.g., against other users, remote adversaries and malicious applications such as a virus or worm.

Traditional security targets of secure platforms are authenticity, integrity, privacy, anonymity, and availability. In general, the measures applied to achieve them are information flow control and access control mechanisms [12]. For a secure realization of these mechanisms, the underlying platform has to fulfill appropriate security requirements.

It is sometimes stated that these security requirements can be fulfilled based on common hardware architectures. However, this is not true, since in the era of smartphones, notebooks and PDAs the untrusted environment does not physically protect the device anymore. However, untrusted adversarial environments require tamper evidence or tamper resistance, which is not provided by common hardware architectures. Even the certain degree of tamper-resistance provided by smartcards (e.g., to protect unauthorized access to cryptographic keys) do not help here, since they cannot offer other important security features such as *trusted path*[4] (see below).

2.1   Types of Threads

We informally distinguish between two types of threats, called Adv_1 and Adv_2.

– In Adv_1, adversaries cannot gain physical access to the device. Thus, attacks can only be performed remotely, e.g., via remote shell, Trojan horse or virus. Further, it is assumed that users do not break their own security policy[5]. An example of Adv_1 is a desktop computer that is connected to the Internet but physically protected by the environment, e.g., a locked room.
– In Adv_2, adversaries have physical access to the device, which requires tamper evidence or tamper resistance to protect its integrity. As in Adv_1, it is assumed that users do not break their own security policy.

---

[4] This is the reason why smartcard applications based on insecure operating systems can easily be broken.
[5] Nevertheless, inexperienced users may break their security policy by mistake.

2.2 Problems of Common Hardware

Since the functional security requirements to be fulfilled by a secure platform are well known (see, e.g., [17,12,28]), the following discussion focuses on their technical feasibility based on common hardware architectures:

Trustworthiness (R1): The most important requirement is the trustworthiness of all components that can break the security policy. These components are generally called the trusted computing base (TCB). The size and complexity of security-critical implementations directly influences their reliability and thus the trustworthiness of TCBs. As stated in [31] a typical Unix or Windows system (including major applications) consists of about 100 Million lines of code (MLOC). An analysis of a common Linux distribution using *sloc* [39] counts about 55 MLOC and that the TCB counts more than 5 MLOC[6]. According to [31], several studies have shown that typical software consists of about one security critical bug per 1000 lines of code. Thus, we have to assume that more than 5000 security critical bugs are part of the TCB of a typical Linux distribution.

Further methods to increase the trustworthiness of critical components is the evaluation according to the common criteria [12] and to make source code and design decisions publicly available [3,29].

Confidentiality and integrity of application code and data (R2): This requirement should hold during the execution and during the storage.

The former is required to prevent concurrent processes from accessing confidential information. Unfortunately, with common hardware architectures it is very difficult to prevent untrusted components from accessing data. For example, an untrusted process must never be allowed to control DMA-enabled devices[7]. As long as common hardware architectures contain these difficulties, the only solution is to put critical code (e.g., every device driver) into the TCB.

The latter requirement (protection during storage) can be realized in Adv_1 based on existing hardware architectures using cryptographic primitives. However, for this to be realized under the adversary model Adv_2 more effort is required. In theory, it would suffice to have a *complete* tamper-resistant platform including the whole TCB, but the reality shows that this is a strong assumption [5,2]. Thus, common solutions are to encrypt critical data and to protect the master encryption key either by entering it at system startup, or by protecting it by tamper-resistant components.

---

[6] The Linux kernel 2.4 contains about 2.4 MLOC, but any application that is executed with root rights and libraries used by this applications can directly manipulate the kernel and are therefore part of the TCB. For example, alone the XServer extends the size of the TCB by about 1.3 MLOC.

[7] DMA (Direct Memory Access) allows peripheral hardware, e.g., the video adapter or the sound card, to directly access physical memory circumventing memory protection mechanisms. Thus, malicious modules which control DMA-enabled hardware (e.g., a device driver), can bypass policy enforcing mechanisms.

Integrity of the TCB (R3): The enforcement of security policies can only be guaranteed as long as the TCB is not manipulated. Since existing hardware architectures does not provide mechanisms to protect the integrity of critical components, adversaries can easily manipulate software components of the TCB, e.g., by exploiting design and implementation failures like /dev/kmem or buffer overflows. An important aspect in this context is a secure bootstrap architecture to prevent adversaries from manipulating the TCB when it is inactive. If the adversary has no physical access (Adv_1), a secure bootstrap architecture can for instance be provided by using a read-only boot medium, e.g., a CD-ROM. Obviously, this is impossible under Adv_2. Another important issue in this context is to provide users with a mechanism to securely verify the results of the integrity check [1].

Enforcing least privilege (R4): Many security flaws concerning viruses and Trojan horses result from the fact that common operating systems do not enforce the concept of least privileges. The underlying access control mechanisms, originally designed to separate different users from each other, are based on access control lists (ACL). As a result, every application has all privileges of the invoking user, which makes it very easy for malicious software to bypass confidentiality or integrity policies.

Trusted path to user (R5): A trusted path prevents unauthorized applications from accessing passwords entered by the ordinary user. Further, it is a prerequisite for application authentication to prevent faked dialogs [37,9]. Application authentication also requires a secure application manager that provides the necessary information about the applications, e.g., a unique, user-defined application name.

Secure channel to devices and between applications (R6): Integrity, confidentiality and authenticity of inter-application communication is required to prevent malicious applications from deceiving honest applications, e.g., by faked process numbers. Further, it has to be ensured that unauthorized components can neither read nor write to buffers of peripheral devices.

Secure Random Numbers (R7): To be able to use cryptographic primitives, a secure generation of random numbers is required to generate secure cryptographic keys. With existing deterministic computer architectures the generation of secure random numbers is very difficult, if not impossible [15,19].

As a bottom line of this section, we can stress that the development of a secure system based on existing hardware architectures under Adv_1 is difficult, but possible. Research results in operating system security have shown that this is also possible in practice [28,34,21]. Under threat type Adv_2 a secure system can by no means be developed without hardware extensions, since tamper-resistance or at least tamper-evidence is required. As we have already stated above, Adv_2 is important whenever the system cannot be protected by the environment, e.g.,

PDAs, mobile phones, notebooks, embedded systems or pervasive computing. Thus, we require hardware architectures that under Adv_2 offer features which can be deployed to fulfill the above mentioned requirements.

Next, we consider the TCPA and Palladium and briefly discuss what features they provide to overcome some of the shortcomings of the conventional hardware architectures.

3   TCPA and Palladium

Since NGSCB and TCPA are announced to improve user's security, this sections discusses on a more technical level to what extend TCPA/Pd can keep their promises. We review only the architecture of TCPA and briefly outline known differences to Pd. The reasons are that TCPA and Pd provide similar functionality (on technical level) and that only the full TCPA specification is publicly available.

Figure 1 outlines the components of a TCPA-compatible PC platform [35]. Beside the conventional hardware, TCPA consists of two tamper-resistant modules called TPM (Trusted Platform Module)[8] and CRTM (Core Root Trust Module). The operating system supporting these modules is not part of the TCPA specification.

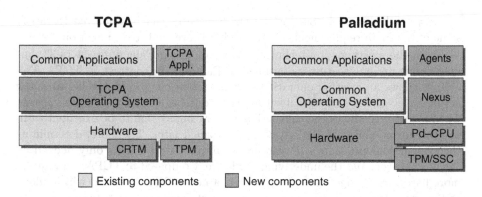

Fig. 1. Comparison between the TCPA and the Palladium architectures. Palladium allows a common operating system to be executed in parallel but requires more changes to hardware components to prevent the common operating system to bypass security policies.

The TCPA specification [36,35] extends the PC architecture by the following functionalities:

- **System configuration authentication (attestation):** The TPM contains a certified and unique signature key that can sign the current system

---

[8] Some documents on Palladium call it the Security Support Component (SSC).

configuration H stored in protected TPM registers $h_1 \ldots h_n$. H is determined by the bootstrap process using a SHA-1 hash function. When the CRTM is invoked on system startup, it determines the BIOS configuration, writes the result into h_1 and invokes the system BIOS which itself determines the configuration of the boot sector, writes it to h_2, invokes the boot loader and so on [40]. This procedure is continued until the operating system is loaded.[9]

- **Sealing:** The integrity preserving mechanism of TCPA does not protect the TCB directly, but ensures that data that was encrypted under a configuration H cannot be revealed under another configuration H'. This is realized by cryptographically binding relevant information (e.g., the system configuration and the identifier of the invoking application) to the data to be encrypted. Note that the TPM cannot distinguish between different applications. Thus, the application identifier (e.g., a hash value of the application code) has to be provided by the operating system.

- **Protection of cryptographic keys:** The identifying signature key and the keys used to seal data are protected by the TPM which they never leave. Instead, the TPM itself provides cryptographic functions to operate on the cryptographic keys.

- **Secure random numbers:** Beside cryptographic functions used to determine and sign the system configuration and to seal data, the TPM contains a secure random generator to generate secure cryptographic keys.

As we will discuss in Section 4.3 these features can be deployed to satisfy some of the main requirements on secure hardware we listed in Section 2.2.

From the existing (non-technical) descriptions on Palladium [11,14,33] one may derive an architecture as outlined in Figure 1. In contrast to TCPA, Palladium allows an existing operating system to be executed in parallel to a new kernel called *nexus*[10], which itself executes critical applications called *agents*. The architecture allows the conventional operating system to be executed without the nexus, and that the nexus can be loaded later. Therefore, determining the system configuration in Palladium is simpler, since agents only depend on the nexus kernel and the underlying hardware. Compared to TCPA, Pd requires more hardware changes than TCPA: first, a new CPU is required which allows the nexus to be executed. Second, to prevent interferences between the conventional operating system and the nexus, nearly every hardware device has to support Palladium by providing a "nexus-mode".

A major benefit of Palladium is an extension of the mainboard chipset that allows the nexus to control DMA cycles [11,33] (see Section 2). Since TCPA does

---

[9] The functionality of the bootstrap process is similar to those described in [8].

[10] This is done by adding a new mode of operation that allows the nexus to protect itself (and applications for which the nexus acts as the operating system) against the conventional operating system. A possible implementation of the extension is to add another CPU protection ring, e.g. r_{-1} *below* protection ring r_0 [6] and give it capabilities to hide memory pages and process structures to protect itself and critical applications from code executed on r_0 or above (the conventional operating system).

not contain such a functionality, appropriate drivers and hardware devices have to be part of the TCB which enormously increases its size and complexity.

As a result, we can outline that the functionality provided by TCPA and Pd is completely under the control of the operating system. This moves the question, whether end-users can trust TCPA/Pd platforms or not, to the question, whether they can trust their operating systems. Therefore, the next section proposes an architecture of a security platform that uses the features of TCPA/Pd to increase the overall operating system security without allowing to realize those capabilities of TCPA/Pd people are concerned about.

4   Towards Personal-Secure Systems

As we have discussed in Section 2, many requirements to build secure computing platforms are difficult to fulfill using existing hardware architectures, especially, if the adversary has physical access to the system's hardware (Adv_2). Moreover, we discussed that TCPA/Pd offer prospective properties to build secure systems as long as the underlying operating system can be trusted by the user. In this section we propose an architecture for a secure computing platform in the sense of Adv_2 using TCPA/Pd in conjunction with a security kernel called PERSEUS we have developed. First, we shortly explain the architecture of this security kernel.

4.1   The PERSEUS Security Architecture

PERSEUS[11] [28] is a minimal open-source security kernel providing all operating system services required to protect security critical applications executed on top of it. The main idea is to let common operating systems run as applications on the top of the security kernel, since the past has shown that secure operating system architectures live in the shadow if they are incompatible to a common operating system. Therefore, a tamed[12] operating system (Client OS) provides users with a common user interface and a *backward-compatible interface* to reuse all uncritical standard applications and services.

One main design goal of the PERSEUS security architecture was the realization of a minimal and therefore manageable, stable and evaluable security kernel for conventional hardware platforms such as IBM-PC and mobile devices like PDA's and smartphones. This requirement was fulfilled by extracting only security-critical operations and data to the security kernel. The Client OS still provides all uncritical operating system services like a filesystem, network support, etc.[13] Our decision to use this hybrid architecture is motivated, among others, by the following two facts: Firstly, the development of a completely new

---

[11] www.perseus-os.org

[12] Currently, a slightly modified user-space Linux adapted to the L4 microkernel, L4-Linux [20], is used.

[13] The hardware access used to provide this high-level services is controlled by low-level services of PERSEUS.

secure operating system that provides backward-compatibility is too costly. Secondly, improving the existing operating systems, e.g., like SE-Linux [26], are too inflexible[14]. The high-level PERSEUS architecture is illustrated in Figure 2.

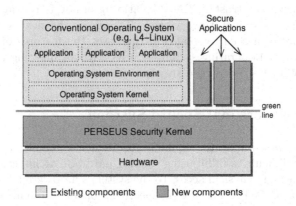

Fig. 2. An overview over the PERSEUS architecture. The green line indicates the border between trusted and untrusted components.

The PERSEUS security kernel is based on the efficient L4 microkernel [25,18] that provides (i) a hardware abstraction, (ii) elementary mechanisms, and (iii) flexible policies that are required to control and protect critical system services, device drivers and resource managers as separated user-space processes (a so-called multi-server system). This prevents that errors of one component can affect others, ensures that only authorized processes can access the hardware and guarantees that only the microkernel itself is executed in the supervisor mode of the CPU.

Also security-critical applications and the conventional operating system are implemented as separated user-space processes which can only communicate to each other or to the underlying hardware using services provided by the secure kernel. This allows PERSEUS to enforce its own user-defined security policy independent of the conventional operating system.

The PERSEUS security kernel currently consists of the following components (see Figure 3):

- **Microkernel.** The only component that is executed in supervisor mode. It contains about 7100 lines of code (LOC) and provides basic process, inter-process communication (IPC), thread, memory and exception support. Furthermore, capabilities to processes, interrupts and I/O ports and a process-level access control mechanism [24,22] is provided.

---

[14] On the one hand, it is questionable whether, e.g., a trusted path can be provided without many changes to core components. On the other hand, these improvements do not decrease the complexity.

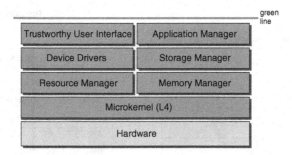

Fig. 3. A more detailed illustration of the PERSEUS security kernel. Again, the green line indicates the border between application layer and trusted computing base.

- **Resource Manager.** The resource manager enforces security policies on low-level hardware resources like interrupts, processes and I/O ports. It consists of about 5600 LOC.
- **Memory Manager.** This module ensures that different services and applications do not share memory pages. The size of the implementation is currently about 654 LOC.
- **Device Drivers.** Because of the security problems with DMA-enabled devices discussed in Section 2, every device driver that accesses DMA-enabled devices (or at least the critical parts) has to be isolated in the secure environment to be protected against malicious modifications. The size depends on the size of the original drivers.[15]
- **Trustworthy User Interface.** The trustworthy user interface provides a *trusted path* by controlling the hardware of input devices (keyboard and mouse) and the video adapter. The implementation ensures that only the active application receives user input and exclusively controls a small region of the output device used for application authentication. For larger screen resolutions (e.g., PC's), a minimal implementation of a secure window manager is provided. The current implementation has a size of about 5400 LOC.
- **Application Manager.** The application manager controls installation and removal of security critical applications based on code signing. It enforces user-defined installation policies and assigns predefined sets of permissions to new applications. The implementation is currently in beta-state; we expect an overall size of about 5000 LOC.
- **Storage Manager.** This module encrypts/decrypts memory pages of other applications/services and persistently stores them using the filesystem of the Client OS. Its size is currently about 500 LOC.
- **Secure Booting.** Because of lack of hardware support, secure booting is currently only provided marginally. The storage manager uses cryptographic

---

[15] This is especially a problem of common PCs, because they can have a huge amount of DMA-enabled devices which enormously increases the size and complexity of the TCB. For mobile devices like PDAs, this is not so important, since they have a relatively fixed hardware architecture.

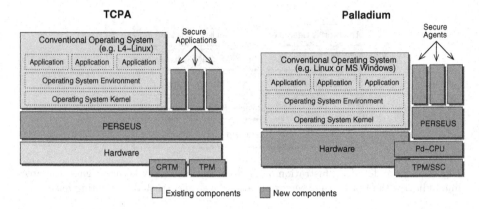

Fig. 4. When the PERSEUS architecture is combined with TCPA or Pd hardware, the resulting architectures are somewhat similar. The Pd approach allows the reuse of every conventional operating system, but requires more changes to the hardware.

key derived from a passphrase entered by the user at system startup. Additionally, all critical components can be stored onto a read-only medium, e.g., a CD-ROM.

- **DGP.** DGP is a PERSEUS application that provides users compatibility to PGP [41]. Security-critical data, e.g., cryptographic keys, never leave the PERSEUS application, since also security-critical operations are performed by the PERSEUS service. Additionally, DGP provides a trusted viewer/editor to verify, e.g., information to be signed, and to enter confidential data.

For more information on PERSEUS and to download the current source code, see the PERSEUS homepage[16].

4.2   Improving Security with TCPA/Pd

To obtain a secure platform in the sense of Adv_1 and Adv_2, we can extend the PERSEUS security kernel to support TCPA and Pd. The latter, however, requires that Microsoft publishes technical specification about Pd, as promised [14]. Since PERSEUS separates critical from uncritical components, the resulting architectures look very similar (see Figure 4).

The only difference is that Pd allows the trusted kernel to control the conventional operating system by extending the CPU hardware, while the TCPA approach reuses exiting protection mechanisms but requires the conventional operating system to be modified.

Table 1. Fulfilling security requirements by the functions of the proposed architecture

	R1	R2	R3	R4	R5	R6	R7
Random Generator		x	x				x
Sealing		x	x				
Attestation			x				
CPU		x	x				
Microkernel	x			x	x		
PERSEUS	x				x		

4.3 How Existing Security Problems Are Solved

The combination of the security functions provided by a minimal, highly secure operating system kernel and those provided by TCPA/Pd hardware allows us to offer a security platform that fulfills all security requirements that have been demanded in Section 2.2. Table 1 outlines which properties resp. functions of the proposed architecture are deployed to fulfill the corresponding requirement.

The trustworthiness of the proposed architecture is improved, since the reuse of an existing operating system allows us to keep the size and the complexity of the TCB very small (currently, about 25.000 LOC). Moreover, the attestation functionality of the underlying TCPA/Pd hardware allows also external systems to trust our architecture. Application code and data is protected during runtime by existing CPU memory protection mechanisms (e.g., virtual address spaces). Persistently stored data is protected by the extended Storage Manager that uses sealing to ensure that users cannot bypass security mechanisms by booting another operating system. The same mechanism is used by the bootstrap architecture to protect the integrity of the TCB. To allow reusing of existing device driver implementations, DMA has to be tamed as, e.g., proposed in [23,16]. Obviously, the proposed architecture cannot directly solve security problems of viruses, since viruses exploit security flaws on the application layer (e.g., a Word macro-viruses). Nevertheless, the proposed architecture reduces the potential damage caused by such attacks by enforcing its own security policy and separating code and data of different applications from each other. For example, the Client OS cannot access data of another PERSEUS application. A trusted path is provided by the TCB that controls a subset of the user interface and prevents Trojan horses attacks. Since secure IPC is the only communication mechanisms of the underlying microkernel a secure channel to devices and between applications can be provided. Finally, the random generator of the TCPA/Pd hardware is used to securely create cryptographic keys.

To be able to use the security features provided by our proposed architecture, security-critical applications have to be adapted to the interface of PERSEUS. To achieve this efficiently, we only need to move the security-critical data and the operations performed on this data to a compartment protected by PERSEUS. For example, consider a signature application: the critical data to be moved to the protected compartment is the signing key. The security critical operations are the generation of the signature and, to prevent attacks performed by an insecure Client OS, the verification of the document to be signed (trusted viewer).

5   Multilateral Secure DRM Platforms

Digital technology and media offer content providers and producers many business opportunities and users many advantages towards the realization of new electronic marketplaces. In this context, trading digital goods over open networks, such as the Internet, plays an important role. However, all these technological possibilities for comfortable handling and trading digital goods face us also with challenging problems regarding copyright protection of digital properties. *Digital Rights Management (DRM) platforms* are often considered as systems that should realize the appropriate environment for trading digital works while protecting the rights of authors and copyright holders. This is what we call a *DRM policy*.

To enforce DRM policies, one actually requires an ideal *trusted media player*, also called *trusted viewer* enabling only the authorized users to "view" (watch, listen to, edit, execute, etc.) digital works[17] while controlling the use of works according to the specified DRM policy.

5.1   Consequences of DRM

DRM policies and (user) security policies often conflict, e.g., if the external copyright control or system-wide censorship contradicts with a locally defined availability requirement of a user, or if a software product can prevent the installation of competitive products. While users are interested in unrestricted use, copying and even redistributing digital works, the providers want to protect their digital goods against misuse to limit financial damage. However, providers are not always the victims: they may also become the delinquents, and misuse DRM policies against users (see also [4] and [32]).

In DRM systems, providers are capable of enforcing any kind of policy within their specific media player. This is independent of any technical design and has many implications: For instance, a media player can censor the documents that it controls and a DRM-wordprocessor can encrypt its documents in such a way that other products like open-office cannot read them. If users desire to use DRM-enabled platforms and if they accept the underlying DRM conditions, then the only possibility to prevent issues such as censorship is the regulation by law.

5.2   Towards Trustworthy DRM Systems

Although the potentially negative consequences of DRM platforms mentioned above cannot be prevented on a technical level, a careful design of the TCB

---

[17] Note that the media player can control access to information only within the platform. Users may still be able to make unauthorized copies by using cameras or audio recorders.

(which now has to be trusted by users and providers) can prevent most of the dangerous consequences regarding user security. Most functions for controlling the system from outside, for instance a system-wide censorship, require a reference monitor located at the operating system layer or below. To enforce DRM policies such a system-wide reference monitor under control of content providers is not required, since the context to enforce DRM policies is only available at the application layer (the media players).

Therefore, we propose a multilateral secure operating system based on the PERSEUS security kernel that allows content providers to enforce DRM policies by guaranteeing that users cannot bypass enforcement mechanisms provided by the application layer, e.g., by patching media players. This can be provided by the sealing mechanism offered by TCPA and Pd, but requires a TCB that cannot be modified afterwards.[18] The enforcement of system-wide security policies, e.g., access control between applications and their data or the decision on which application are to be installed, can be kept under control of local users. This is by no means a restriction on providers, because the media player applications have to be trusted by providers at this layer anyway. The PERSEUS kernel is extended by services that provide sealing and attestation functions to be used by the application layer. This prevents users from bypassing DRM policies, e.g., by rebooting another operating system after the system was authenticated, since applications can still *bind* their contents to a specific system configuration. To allow applications to enforce their own access control policy, the Application Manager offers an application identification mechanism based on hash values.

This is what we call a *trustworthy DRM platform*. The important aspect about trustworthy DRM platforms is that they allow users to freely decide whether to accept or to reject applications that use DRM policies. Especially, it allows users to remove such an application without consequences for the other applications or system components.

The resulting architecture of a multilateral secure DRM platform is similar to the one outlined on Figure 2 and Figure 3. The only difference is that the TCB (all components below the green line) has to ensure that users cannot (i) manipulate application code and (ii) access application data. For instance, the user interface service must not allow other applications to create screenshots, and the storage manager resp. the memory manager have to strictly separate data of different applications. All these requirements are still fulfilled by the existing implementation of the PERSEUS security kernel.

As a bottom line of this section, we stress that security and DRM requirements are not mutually exclusive. Therefore, by strictly separating the enforcement of DRM policies and (user-defined) security policies, it is possible to provide a platform that allows external providers to enforce their policies without allowing them to misuse these mechanisms against users (privacy issues).

---

[18] Device drivers or Linux' kernel modules are negative examples. Microkernel systems that provide system services by user-space processes are more promising in this regard.

Many potential dangers of DRM systems debated in the press (see, e.g., [3, 32]) can be efficiently avoided using the proposed architecture of a trustworthy operating system. The proposed architecture provides only a minimal set of operating system functions, allowing different conventional operating systems to be developed (or ported) on top of it.

In this context, an important political and social issue to be considered is the use of an open-source security kernel that is not under control of one (or a few) vendors, avoiding monopolies. This may solve certain conflicts, since DRM platforms have to be trusted by both users and content providers.

6   Conclusion

In this paper, we discuss the capabilities of Microsoft Next-generation Secure Computing Base for Windows and TCPA based on the available documentation. Based on common security requirements we discuss why common hardware architectures in untrusted environments are unable to provide users with adequate security properties if the adversary has physical access to the device. Examples of untrusted environments are the use of mobile devices like smartphones, PDAs, notebooks and applications in pervasive computing.

Our analysis of TCPA/Palladium shows that their hardware architectures can be used to improve end-user security, but we also conclude that the DRM capabilities of TCPA/Palladium can be misused against users, if the underlying operating system does not prevent it. Therefore, we propose an open security architecture that relies on TCPA/Palladium hardware and an open-source security platform called PERSEUS we have developed. TCPA/Pd support can be implemented without much effort, providing the open-source community an alternative to commercial TCPA/Pd products. With the proposed architecture we also demonstrate that highly secure systems can profit from the features of TCPA or Palladium. However, the border between security and censorship is small and the community should observe further developments in this area carefully.

Since there is a need for DRM platforms, we emphasize that a careful design of a DRM kernel, what we call a trustworthy DRM platform, can prevent most of the negative consequences on the operating system level. The philosophy behind it is the strict separation between the enforcement of DRM policies and personal security policies. This allows user security policies and DRM policies to coexist and gives users the freedom to accept or reject a DRM application without further consequences. Furthermore, we have evaluated which negative consequences cannot be prevented on a DRM system on a technical level.

References

1. A. Alkassar and C. Stüble. Towards secure IFF — preventing mafia fraud attacks. In *Proceedings of IEEE Military Conference (MILCOM)*, 2002.
2. R. J. Anderson. *Security Engineering — A Guide to Building Dependable Distributed Systems*. John Wiley & Sons, 2001.

3. R. J. Anderson. Security in open versus closed systems — the dance of Boltzmann, Coase and Moore. Technical report, Cambridge University, England, 2002.
4. R. J. Anderson. The TCPA/Palladium FAQ. http://www.cl.cam.ac.uk/~rja14/tcpa-faq.html, 2002.
5. R. J. Anderson and M. Kuhn. Tamper resistance – a cautionary note. In *Proceedings of the 2nd USENIX Workshop on Electronic Commerce* [38], pages 1–11.
6. J. L. Antonakos. *The Pentium Microprocessor*. Prentice Hall Inc., 1997.
7. W. A. Arbaugh. Improving the TCPA specification. *IEEE Computer*, pages 77–79, Aug. 2002.
8. W. A. Arbaugh, D. J. Farber, and J. M. Smith. A reliable bootstrap architecture. In *Proceedings of the IEEE Symposium on Research in Security and Privacy*, pages 65–71, Oakland, CA, May 1997. IEEE Computer Society, Technical Committee on Security and Privacy, IEEE Computer Society Press.
9. N. Asokan, H. Debar, M. Steiner, and M. Waidner. Authenticating public terminals. *Computer Networks*, 31(8):861–870, May 1999.
10. A. Carroll, M. Juarez, J. Polk, and T. Leininger. Microsoft "Palladium": A business overview. Technical report, Microsoft Content Security Business Unit, August 2002.
11. A. Carroll, M. Juarez, J. Polk, and T. Leininger. Microsoft "Palladium": A business overview — combining microsoft windows features, personal computing hardware, and software applications for greater security, personal privacy and system integrity. White paper, Microsoft Windows Trusted Platform Technologies, July 2002.
12. Common Criteria Project Sponsoring Organisations. *Common Criteria for Information Technology Security Evaluation*, Aug. 1999. Version 2.1, adopted by ISO/IEC as ISO/IEC International Standard (IS) 15408 1–3. Available from http://csrc.ncsl.nist.gov/cc/ccv20/ccv2list.htm.
13. M. Corporation. Building a secure platform for trustworthy computing. White paper, Microsoft Corporation, Dec. 2002.
14. M. Corporation. Microsoft "Palladium" technical FAQ. http://www.microsoft.com, Aug. 2002.
15. D. E. Eastlake, S. D. Crocker, and J. I. Schiller. Randomness requirements for security. Internet Request for Comment RFC 1750, Internet Engineering Task Force, Dec. 1994.
16. L. Fraim. SCOMP: A solution to the multilevel security problem. In *IEEE Computer*, pages 26–34, July 1983.
17. M. Gasser. *Building a Secure Computer System*. Van Nostrand Reinhold Co., New York, USA, 1988.
18. A. Gefflaut, T. Jaeger, Y. Park, J. Liedke, K. J. Elphistone, V. Uhlig, J. E. Tidswell, L. Deller, and L. Reuter. The SawMill multiserver approach. ACM SIGOPS European Workshop, Sept. 2000.
19. P. Gutmann. Software generation of practically strong random numbers. In *Proceedings of the 7th USENIX Security Symposium*, San Antonio, Texas, USA, Jan. 1998. USENIX.
20. H. Härtig, M. Hohmuth, and J. Wolter. Taming linux. In *Proceedings of PART'98*. TU Dresden, 1998.
21. H. Härtig, O. Kowalski, and W. Kühnhauser. The BirliX security architecture. *Journal of Computer Security*, 2(1):5–21, 1993.
22. T. Jaeger, K. Elphinstone, J. Liedtke, V. Panteleenko, and Y. Park. Flexible access control using IPC redirection. In *Hot Topics in Operating Systems (HotOS VII)*, pages 191–196, Rio Rico, AZ, Mar. 1999.

23. B. Leslie and G. Heiser. Towards untrusted device drivers. Technical Report UNSW-CSE-TR-0303, School of Computer Science and Engineering, Mar. 2003.
24. J. Liedke. Clans and Chiefs. a new kernel level concept for operating systems. Working paper, GMD, 1991.
25. J. Liedke. Towards real micro-kernels. *Communications of the ACM*, 39(9), 1996.
26. P. Loscocco and S. Smalley. Integrating flexible support for security policies into the Linux operating system. Technical report, U.S. National Security Agency (NSA), Feb. 2001.
27. C. Mundie, P. de Vries, P. Haynes, and M. Corwine. Microsoft whitepaper on trustworthy computing. Technical report, Microsoft Corporation, Oct. 2002.
28. B. Pfitzmann, J. Riordan, C. Stüble, M. Waidner, and A. Weber. The PERSEUS system architecture. Technical Report RZ 3335 (#93381), IBM Research Division, Zurich Laboratory, Apr. 2001.
29. E. S. Raymond. The cathedral and the bazaar.
    http://www.openresources.com/documents/cathedral-bazaar/, August 1998.
30. D. Safford. Clarifying misinformation on TCPA. White paper, IBM Research, Oct. 2002.
31. D. Safford. The need for TCPA. White paper, IBM Research, Oct. 2002.
32. B. Schneier. Palladium and the TCPA.
    http://www.counterpane.com/crypto-gram-0208.html\#1.
33. S. Schoen. Palladium details.
    http://www.activewin.com/articles/2002/pd.shtml, 2002.
34. J. S. Shapiro, J. M. Smith, and D. J. Farber. EROS: a fast capability system. In *Proceedings of the 17th ACM Symposium on Operating Systems Principles (SOSP'99)*, pages 170–185. Kiawah Island Resort, near Charleston, Sout Carolina, Dec. 1999. Appeared as ACM Operating Systems Review 33.5.
35. Trusted Computing Platform Alliance (TCPA). TCPA PC specific implementation specification, Sept. 2001. Version 1.00.
36. Trusted Computing Platform Alliance (TCPA). Main specification, Feb. 2002. Version 1.1b.
37. J. D. Tygar and A. Whitten. WWW electronic commerce and Java Trojan horses. In *Proceedings of the 2nd USENIX Workshop on Electronic Commerce* [38], pages 243–250.
38. USENIX. *Proceedings of the 2nd USENIX Workshop on Electronic Commerce*, Oakland, California, Nov. 1996.
39. D. A. Wheeler. More than a gigabuck: Estimating GNU/Linux's size.
    http://www.dwheeler.com/sloc/, June 2001.
40. Wintermute. TCPA and Palladium technical analysis.
    http://wintermute.homelinux.org/miscelanea/TCPASecurity.txt, Dec. 2002.
41. P. Zimmerman. *The Official PGP User's Guide*. prz@acm.org, 1994. The MIT Press In press. More in
    http://www.pegasus.esprit.ec.org/people/arne/pgp.html.

A Software Fingerprinting Scheme for Java Using Classfiles Obfuscation

Kazuhide Fukushima[1] and Kouichi Sakurai[2]

[1] Graduate School of Information Science and Electrical Engineering, Kyushu University, Japan,
fukusima@tcslab.csce.kyushu-u.ac.jp,
http://itslab.csce.kyushu-u.ac.jp/\%7Efukusima/index.html
[2] Faculty of Information Science and Electrical Engineering, Kyushu University, Japan,
sakurai@csce.kyushu-u.ac.jp,
http://itslab.csce.kyushu-u.ac.jp/\%7Esakurai/index.html

Abstract. Embedding a personal identifier as a watermark to Java classfile is effective in order to protect copyrights of them. Monden et al.[1] proposed watermarking scheme that embeds arbitrary character sequence to the target method in a Java classfiles. But the scheme can be only used to embed the same watermark to each user's classfiles. Therefore, if we apply this scheme for embedding each user's personal identifier, the watermarks can be specified by comparing two or more users' Java classfiles. In this paper solve the problem by using "Classfiles Obfuscation" which is our obfuscation scheme for Java sourcecodes. By the scheme, we distribute all the methods among the all the Java classfiles at random. Evrey user's Java classfiles will have different structures respectively by appling "Clasfiles Obfuscation". As the result, to specify watermark by compareing classfiles will be difficult.

1 Introduction

1.1 Background and Motivation

Recently, Java has spread widely. Java sourcecodes are compiled to Java classfiles which are independent of machines or operating systems. And they are executed on the Java Virtual Machine (JVM). The same Java classfiles can run on different platforms without recompiling because the JVM for each platform is prepared. Java programs can run on portable phones and small information terminals such as Personal Digital Assistants (PDA) as well as PCs and Workstations.

On the other hand, Java classfiles contain information such as the name of the class, the name of the super class and names of the methods and the fields defined in the class. Moreover, the description of a classfile can be divided into description of the field and the methods. Therefore, Java classfiles have high readability. As the result, an attacker can obtain Java source codes easily by decompiling Java classfiles. He can crib secret data and key algorithms by his reverse engineering of the obtained source code.

K. Chae and M. Yung (Eds.): WISA 2003, LNCS 2908, pp. 303–316, 2004.
© Springer-Verlag Berlin Heidelberg 2004

Software developers are frightened by the prospect of a competitor being able to extract secret data and key algorithm in order to incorporate them into their own programs. The competitor may intercept their commercial edge by cutting development time and cost. To make matters worse, it is difficult to detect and pursue the injustice.

Software obfuscation[2,3,4,5,6] is a scheme to solve the problem. Software obfuscation makes sourcecode difficult to analysis, while its functionalitys are preserved. We can apply these techniques for protecting the copyright of software. However, it is impossible to specify the person who copied software illegally.

Moreover, an other attecker may steal Java classfiles in a program and create a new Java program using the Java classfiles. Software wartermarking scheme can be applied for stand up to this problem[7,1]. Even if an attacker steals Java classfiles and distributes a new program using them, the fact of the crib can be proved by extracting the watermark from the program. However in this case, since the information embedded is a developer's identifier, it is impossible to specify the person who copied the program illegally.

In this paper, we propose a digital fingerprinting scheme for Java. We improve the watermarking scheme by Monden et al. to embed user's identifier. But, this scheme has the big problem that the embedded position of personal identifiers can be easily specified. In order to solve the problem, we apply the 'Classfiles Obfuscation. This obfuscation make to specify the embedding position of software fingerprinting difficult, even when two or more users conspire.

1.2 Related Work

Digital watermarking scheme. Most of digital watermarking schemes for pictures and sounds have been studied. However, digital watermarking schemes for software have been proposed. Digital watermarking scheme for Java is [7,1].

Kitagawa et al[7] proposed the watermarking scheme which embeds arbitrary sequences as a watermark. In this scheme, variables are prepared and sequences are stored as watermark the variables. When extracting the watermark, specific, a certain class file is change into special class file for extraction.

Monden et al[1] proposed the watermarking scheme which embeds watermarks to numerical operands or opcodes in the class files. In this scheme, a dummy method is injected to the target source code as a space for a watermark. In this scheme, even if only one class file is stolen, the watermark can be extracted from the dummy method. Furthermore, the watermarking scheme is implemented as the tools "jmark" and "jdecode" [8].

However we need to embed not the developer's identifier but the personal identifier to the program to prevent illegal copies and unjust distributions.

Obfuscation schemes. On the other hand, there many researches about obfuscation schemes. Many obfuscation tool have been developed such as Don Quixote[9] and Zelix KlassMaster[10].

Collberg and Low proposed an obfuscation scheme for Java programs by injecting dummy codes and complicating data structures and control flows[2,3]. Monden et al. proposed an obfuscation scheme for C programs contain loops .

Few obfuscation schemes have basis of security. On the other hand, Myers[11] had came up with the negative result that many interprocedual Static Analysis problem are NP-complete in 1981. Later, Wang et al. proposed an obfuscation scheme based on the fact that the problem of determining precise indirect branch target addresses is NP-hard[4]. They used global arrays and pointers of C programs in their scheme. Ogiso et al[6]. extended this technique by using function pointer. If we use this technique, since neither control flow graph nor call graph of the obfuscated program settled statically, static analysis of the program becomes remarkably difficult. These technique have the basis of security. But we cannot introduce pointers to Java programs by the problem of the grammer. Then Sakabe et al[5] proposed the technique that makes static analysis of the obfuscated program much more difficult, by using method overloading and interfaced.

Barak et al. show that there are no obfuscator that satisfy "virtual black box" property. (i.e. there is no obfuscator $\mathcal{O}$, such that for any program P, Anything that can be efficiently computed from $\mathcal{O}(P)$ can be efficiently computed given oracle access to P.

Recently, many analysis tools for Java classfiles, including decompiler (such as Mocha[12] and Jad[13]), have been developed and they are improved rapidly. In the near future those scheme may be broken. On the other hand, few tools that can analyze the role of classfiles, which is abstract notion, automatically.

1.3   Challenging Issues

When we apply watermarking scheme by Monden et al.[1] for embedding personal identifier, we have two problems.

One is the vulnerability of watermark itself. An attacker can specify the dummy method by investigating all the methods in every Java classfiles. If he can specify dummy methods (in which a personal identifier is embedded), he can eliminate or tamper the fingerprint. The time he needs for this attack is proportional to the number of the methods in a class file. This attack is effective because the number of the methods in every class file is generally at most dozens of pieces. Actually we can specify the dummy method in which embedded watermarking from a class file by investigating the method which is not called. and we can eliminate or tamper easily. This is a fatal problem, because a personal identifier embedded in Java classfiles is used to specify the user who distribute program illegally.

Another is the vulnerability over two or more user's conspiracy. The Java classfiles distributed to users are the same when the developer's identifier is embedded as a watermark. The dummy method of a class file will differ for every user when the personal identifier is embedded as fingerprinting. In this case, the dummy method can be specified by comparing each of class file of two or more users. Actually we can specify the dummy method by taking difference of two Java classfiles.

1.4   Our Contribution

We pointouted two problems of watermarking scheme. The first one is vulnerability over brute force attack. We can specify the dummy method embeded watermark effectively, because there are not so many methods contained in a class file. The second one is vulnerability over conspiracy attack. We can specify the dummy method by comparing two or more Javas classfiles.

We improve the watermarking Monden et al to embed personal identifier to Java Program. In this paper, we solve the problem by using "Classfile Obfuscation" that is an obfuscation scheme. By the scheme, we distribute all the methods among the all the Java classfiles at random. Every user Java classfiles of different structure respectively by carrying out this scheme. As the result, to specify watermark by compareing Java classfiles comes to difficult even when two or more persons conspire. And we restrict the retern value of dummy methods to void, dummy method comes to called at any site.

2   Watermarking Scheme by Monden et al.

We use the watermarking scheme by Monden et al to embed personal identifier to Java Program. In Java, verifier check bytecodes before programs are executed. Therefore, it is necessary to be careful for embed personal identifier to Java classfiles.

2.1   Encoding Procedure

Their watermark encoding procedure consists of following three phases.

1. Inject of dummy methods
   In the first phase of watermarking, the dummy method, which will never be executed actually, is to a target Java program. Dummy method is a space for watermark codeword. Dummy method must be large enough to embed watermark.
2. Compilation
   In the second phase, the Java source program in which dummy method was injected, is compile with Java compiler.
3. Watermark injection
   In this phase they need to take account of the bytecode verifier. When execute a Java application or applet, the bytecode verifier checks the syntactical rightness and type consistency of the program. In order to keep them, they use following two approaches.

(1) Overwriting numerical operands
A numerical operand of an opcode that pushes a value to stack, and of an opcode that pushes a value to the stack, can be overwritten any other value without syntactical incorrectness and type inconsistency. For example, an operand xx of the opcode iinc xx can be overwritten into any single byte.

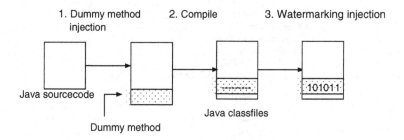

1. Dummy method   2. Compile   3. Watermarking injection
    injection

Java sourcecode

Dummy method

Java classfiles

101011

Fig. 1. Overview of watermarking scheme by Monden et al.

On the other hand, most of other operands that indicate a position or and index of class table or location variable can not be overwritten because of syntactical incorrectness.

(2) Replacing operands
In odder to increase the place for watermark injection, they replace some of the opecodes into other kind of opcode. For example, an opcode iadd can be replaced to anything among isub, imul, idiv, irem,iand, ior and ixor. This indicates that above eight opcode can be replaced mutually. They can encode 3 bits information into these opecodes by assigning 000 to iadd, 001 to isub, 010 to imul, $\cdots$, and 111 to ixor. Such information assignment and opcode replacement can be also done in other opecodes groups.

2.2   Decoding Procedure

In the watermark decoding phase, there is an assumption that they know the relation between bytecode and their assigned bits and their assigned bits, and also the relation between bit sequence and alphabet. The decoding algorithm is very simple. They simply do the exactly opposite procedure of watermark injection procedure, from top of every method. Both opcode and operand in each class method should be replaced into bit sequence, and then they should be replaced into alphabet sequence. After that, watermark will appear from the dummy method.

2.3   Our Attack to Their Scheme

We can attack to their scheme by taking advantage of vulnerability of their scheme mentioned in section 1.3. We can remove or tamper, if we can specify the dummy method by brute force attack or conspiracy attack of two or more users. We attack to their sample program TEST0 that can convert midi to text. The program has one class file and twelve methods (include the one dummy method).

```
#classfile: TEST0.class
#key: default
#algorithm: 0 (default)
#begin{watermark}
1          " B2VL"
2          "))VXVXV771XV771XFIF3H3X6XF"
3          " BO"
4          "F(J1GJ"
5          ""
6          ""
7          " B,2K 4C"
8          "6BK2V 7N"
9          "0VO7"
10         "ALICE ALICE ALICE ALICE AL"
11         " B,2K I3"
12         " JHJ1J JX1V1"
#end{watermark}
```

Fig. 2. The output of 'jdecode' for TEST0.class

Brute force attack. We assume that watermark string ALICE is embedded to the target class file, TEST0.class. The output of jdecode, that is the decode tool realizing their scheme, is shown by Fig.2.

The watermark is embedded in the tenth method. We can specify the dummy method by Brute force attack. The attack consists of four phases.

1. Decompilation
   In the first phase of our attack, the class file(s) is decompiled to Java source code(s). We used Jad[13] that is a one of famous Java decompiler, in this Phase.
2. Extraction of methods
   In the second phase, we extract method from Java source code(s), obtained in first phase. And we make the list of the methods those are defined in this class.
   Twelve methods are defined in the class, TEST0.class. The list of method is as follows.
   main, TEST0, handleEvent, action, f021, m2t, check_STD_header, check_format, write_STD_header,check_std, check_TRK_header, length
3. Searching the dummy method
   In this phase, we investigate whether each method is used actually. We use grep command of unix.
   The method f021 is not the dummy method because it called the form of f021(smf0.getText(), smf1.getText()). One the other hand, we see grep check_std is the dummy method, because the method is never called.
4. Attacking to the watermark
   Finally we can attack to the watermark by eliminating the dummy method or tampering operands and opcode in the dummy code. The output of jdecode is change into

Conspiracy attack. We assume that watermark string ALICE is embedded to the class file, TEST0_A.class and string BOB is embedded to the class file TEST0_B.class. The outputs of jdecode for TEST0_A.class and TEST0_B.class are demonstrated by Fig.5.

We can attack to the scheme by conspiracy attack The attack is consisted of three phases.

1. Decompilation
   In the first phase of our attack, the class files is decompiled to Java source code(s). We obtain TEST0_A.Java from TEST0_A.class and TEST0_B.Java from TEST0_B.class.
2. Taking the difference of class file
   We take advantage of the fact that watermarks are different for every user. We take the difference of class file using diff command of UNIX. The output of diff is shown by Fig.6.
   According to the output, we see that position of the dummy code (from 240th line to 259th line).
3. Attacking to the watermark
   Finally we can attack to the watermark by eliminating the dummy method or tampering operands and opcode in the dummy code.

3   Classfiles Obfuscation for Java

3.1   Our Proposed Obfuscation Scheme

Data structures (fields) and procedures (methods) are defined all together in Java. This is called encapsulation. The exterior of the class doesn't need to take into consideration the processing which is executed inside. This is called abstraction in Java. In our proposed scheme, relation during a class file can be made unclear by distributing methods between class files and destroying abstraction. By operation 1 and 2 shown bellow, we make preparations for distributing methods (operation 3) between class files. Furthermore, after distributing methods, We have to correct a call side by opration 4.

1. Destruction of encapsulation

```
% less TEST0.JAVA | grep handleEvent
    f021(smf0.getText(), smf1.getText());
    System.out.println("ERROR! in calling f021");
    private void f021(String filename1, String filename2)  throws IOException{
% less TEST0.JAVA | grep check_std
    private void check_std(int k){
```

Fig. 3. The output of grep

```
¥begin{verbatim}
#classfile: TEST0.class
#key: default
#algorithm: 0 (default)
#begin{watermark}
1           " B2VL"
2           "))VXVXV771XV771XFIF3H3X6XF"
3           " BO"
4           "F(J1GJ"
5           ""
6           ""
7           " B,2K 4C"
8           "6BK2V 7N"
9           "0VO7"
10          "BBOX XBJVS SEFE JREYU SS"
11          " B,2K I3"
12          " JHJ1J JX1V1"
#end{watermark}
```

Fig. 4. The output of `grep`

TEST0_A.class

```
#classfile: TEST0_A.class
#key: default
#algorithm: 0 (default)
#begin{watermark}
1           " B2VL"
2           "))VXVXV771XV771XFIF3H3X6XF"
3           " BO"
4           "F(J1GJ"
5           ""
6           ""
7           " B,2K 4C"
8           "6BK2V 7N"
9           "0VO7"
10          "ALICE ALICE ALICE ALICE AL"
11          " B,2K I3"
12          " JHJ1J JX1V1"
#end{watermark}
```

TEST0_B.class

```
#classfile: TEST0_B.class
#key: default
#algorithm: 0 (default)
#begin{watermark}
1           " B2VL"
2           "))VXVXV771XV771XFIF3H3X6XF"
3           " BO"
4           "F(J1GJ"
5           ""
6           ""
7           " B,2K 4C"
8           "6BK2V 7N"
9           "0VO7"
10          "BOB BOB BOB BOB BOB BOB BO"
11          " B,2K I3"
12          " JHJ1J JX1V1"
#end{watermark}
```

Fig. 5. The output of 'jdecode' for `TEST0_A.class` and `TEST0_B.class`

a) Publication of the fields

Modifiers of all the fields of all classes are changed into `public`. By this change, all fields can be accessed from all the sites of the program.

b) Publication of methods

Modifiers of all the methods of all classes are changed into `public static`.

By this change, all methods can be accessed from all the sites of a program. These are called in the form of `(class name).(method name)`.

```
240c240
< for(int j = -1; j < 25; j -= 128)
---
> for(int j = 2; j >= 101; j -= 115)
242,243c242,243
<    for(int i1 = 2; i1 >= 76; i1 += 6)
<      i += (j - 38) % i1;
---
>    for(int i1 = 0; i1 > 1; i1 -= 98)
>      i &= (j | 0x1a) * i1;
248c248
< for(int k = 2; k <= 100; k += 0)
---
> for(int k = 1; k < -32; k += 89)
250,251c250,251
<    for(int j1 = -1; j1 > 49; j1 += 25)
<      i += (k | 3) + j1;
---
>    for(int j1 = 0; j1 >= -42; j1 += 104)
>      i += (k | 4) + j1;
```

```
256c256
< for(int l = -1; l > 49; l += 25)
---
> for(int l = 0; l >= -42; l += 104)
258,259c258,259
<    for(int k1 = 0; k1 < 96; k1 += 76)
<      i |= 1 + 4 + (k1 + 3);
---
>    for(int k1 = 1; k1 < -32; k1 += 89)
>      i -= (1 + 4) / (k1 & 4);
```

Fig. 6. The result of `diff TEST0_A.Java TEST_B.Java`

2. Change of the methods

An instance method may be changed into a class method when encapsulation breaks in operation 1. Therefore, an instance needs to be added as a new argument of methods. An example is shown in Fig.7.

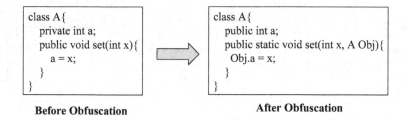

Before Obfuscation   **After Obfuscation**

Fig. 7. The transformation of the code.

After change, Methods `set` must newly take as a parameter `Obj` which is the instance of class `A`. Furthermore, it must be shown that the substitution to the field `a` is the field `a` of the Instance `Obj`.

3. Distribution the Methods

All methods are changed into the class method which can call from anywhere by operation 1 and 2. Thereby, all methods can be placed in arbitrary classes.

4. Change of the arguments

The methods are changed and distributed by operation 1, 2 and 3. We have to correct a call side for this reason. For example, the instance method of class A must have been called in the form of "obj_A.setA(3);" through the instance of class A (say *Obj_a*). However, after applying obfuscation, the instance of the class is added as a parameter and it is changed into the class method of other class (for example, class B). The method comes to be called in the form of "B.set(3,Obj_A);".

3.2 Experiments

In this section we present application of our obfuscation scheme to five programs, that is, BinTree, BinSearch, HuffmanEncoding, TopologicalSort and HeapSort[14]. Table 1 shows the differences between the original programs and the obfuscated programs. We compare the number of lines, the number of classes, the number of methods, execution time [ms] and size of source code[KB]. The experiments were conducted on Intel Pentium III 1GHz with RedHat Linux 8.

We can readily see from the table that the number of lines and the size of source code does not increase so much. And the number of methods never increase because we only change the position of method. Moreover, the obfuscation does not affect the execution time. Rather, it becomes better. The improvement due to change from instance methods to class methods.

Table 1. The property the programs

Program	Before Obfuscation					After Obfuscation				
---------	#lines	#classes	#methods	time	size	#lines	#classes	#methods	time	size
BinTree	201	3	24	6100	3.46	227	14	24	5640	4.34
BinSearch	99	2	11	4250	1.76	108	11	6	3960	2.18
HuffEnc	226	3	31	6290	3.83	280	17	31	6090	4.76
TopSort	156	3	18	2940	2.51	187	10	18	2870	2.71
Heapsort	203	3	18	3010	3.48	228	12	18	2890	4.34

4   Our Proposed Scheme

4.1   The Procedure

Our fingerprinting encoding procedure consists of following four phase.

1. Inject of dummy method

In the first phase of watermarking, the dummy method, which will never be executed actually, is inserted to a target Java program.

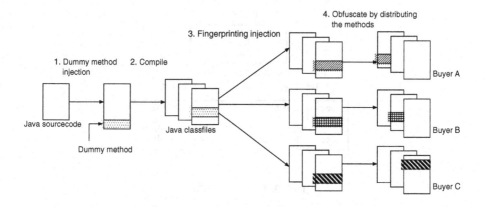

Fig. 8. Overview of our fingerprinting scheme

2. Compilation
   In the seconds phase, the Java source program (in which dummy method was injected) is compiled. We can obtain the Java class files.
3. Fingerprinting injection
   In the third phase, we embedded personal identifier to Java program by the same method as Monden et al.
4. Obfuscation Finally we apply our obfuscation scheme as mentioned above. The all methods in the program is distributed between the all class files.

1. Search the dummy method, to which we embedded personal identifier.
2. Decode I work in the decode to found met

4.2   Consideration of Our Proposed Method

Now we consider a program which is embed personal identifier by the our proposed scheme.

The dummy method, which is embedded as personal identifier, does not have an influence on the execution time, because it isn't executed actually. And we consider that the execution time increases hardly, because the obfuscation scheme, we apply in pile, change only position where methods are placed. The following five advantages lie in changing a class file by the dispersion of the way. By changing the class files distribution of the methods, we can get the following four advantages.

1. Preventing the theft of class files.
   The class files before applied obfuscation conversion contains data structures and algorithms. For this reason, other users can steal some class files and use them as parts of another program. However, after applied the obfuscation, since the data structures and the algorithms will be separated, it becomes

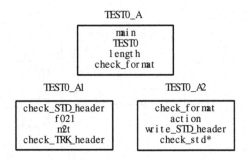

Fig. 9. Classes of TESTO_A

impossible to use each class file as a parts of program. Therefore, the our proposed scheme is considered to be an effective measure to theft of class files.

2. The fall of the readability of class files

   Since the data structures and the algorithms are separated by conversion, the readability of a program falls remarkably. Therefore, we can prevent a malicious third persons' reverse engineering.

3. Deletion of the number of dummy methods

   In the scheme of Monden et al. there is a dummy method in each class file. But after conversion, some dummy method is enough for program since the surreptitious use of every class file can be prevented. Therefore, it is necessary to find one dummy method from all the methods in all the class files.

4. Preventing two or more users' conspiracy

   Before applying obfuscation conversion, we were able to pinpoint the position of the dummy method (in which personal identifier are embedded) by comparing two or more users' class files. However, after methods are distributed between class files, it becomes difficult to pinpointing of the position of the watermark by comparison.

We solved two problems, the vulnerability of watermark itself and the vulnerability over two or more users' conspiracy, in Section 1.3. We can solved these problems with advantage 3 and 4 as mention above. We summarize the above result in a table.

4.3   The Example of Application

We obfuscate classes TESTO_A.class and TESTO_B.class in section 2.3. For example, we can divide TESTO_A.class into three class TESTO_A, TESTO_A1 and TEST_A2 and TESTO_B.class can be divide TESTO_B and TEST_B1 as following.

The dummy method is chech_std. Since the structures of a class file differ, the attack by comparison is not effective.

TEST0_B

TEST0_B1

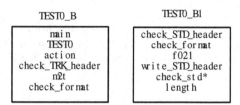

Fig. 10. Classes of TEST0_B

5 Conclusion

We proposed the scheme by which we can embed personal identifier to a Java program. It was impossible to apply existing watermarking scheme as it is, because of attack by two or more users' conspiracy. However, we were able to not only solve this problem by applying the obfuscation scheme using class file conversion in piles, but also raise the security of the class files.

Acknowledgement. This research was partly supported by the 21st Century COE Program "Reconstruction of Social Infrastructure Related to Information Science and Electrical Engineering".

References

1. Monden, A., Iida, H., Matsumoto, K., Inoue, K., Torii, K.: A practical method for watermarking java programs. In: compsac2000, 24th Computer Software and Applications Conference. (2000)
2. C.Collberg, C.Thomborson, D.Low: A taxonomy of obfuscating transformations. Technical Report of Deptartment of Computer Science 148, University of Auckland, New Zealand (1997)
3. Low, D.: Java control flow obfuscation (1998)
4. Wang, C., Hill, J., Knight, J., Davidson, J.: Software tamper resistance: Obstructing static analysis of programs. Technical Report CS-2000-12 (2000)
5. Sakabe, Y., Soshi, M., Miyaji, A.: Software obfuscation for object oriented languages. Technical report of ieice (2002)
6. Ogiso, T., Sakabe, Y., Soshi, M., Miyaji, A.: A new approach of software obfuscation based on the difficulty of interprocedural analysis. IEICE Transactions on Fundamentals **E86-A** (2003) 176–186
7. Kitagawa, T., Kaji, Y., Kasami, T.: Digital watermarking method for java programs. Symposium on cryptography and information security (scis1998) (1998)
8. : (jmark: A lightweight tool for watermarking java class filess) http://se.aist-nara.ac.jp/jmark/.
9. : (Don quixote) http://oikaze.com/tamada/Products/DonQuixote/.
10. : (Zelix klassmaster) http://www.zelix.com/klassmaster/.
11. Myers, E.M.: A precise inter-procedural data flow algorithm. In: Proceedings of the 8th ACM SIGPLAN-SIGACT symposium on Principles of programming languages, ACM Press (1981) 219–230

12. : (Mocha, the java decompiler)
http://www.brouhaha.com/eric/computers/mocha.html.
13. : (Jad - the fast java decompiler) http://kpdus.tripod.com/jad.html.
14. Lafore, R.: Data Structures and Algorithms in Java (2nd Edition). (Sams)

Reducing Storage at Receivers in SD and LSD Broadcast Encryption Schemes

Tomoyuki Asano

Sony Corporation
6-7-35 Kitashinagawa, Shinagawa-ku, Tokyo 141-0001, Japan
tomo@arch.sony.co.jp

Abstract. A broadcast encryption scheme allows a sender to send information securely to a group of receivers while excluding other designated receivers over a broadcast channel. The most efficient methods currently proposed are the Subset Difference (SD) method and the Layered Subset Difference (LSD) method. In these methods, each receiver must store $O\left(\log^2 N\right)$ and $O\left(\log^{1+\epsilon} N\right)$ labels, respectively, where N is the total number of receivers and ϵ is an arbitrary number satisfying $\epsilon > 0$. In this paper we apply the Master Key technique to the SD and LSD methods in order to reduce the number of labels a receiver stores by $\log N$ in exchange for an increase in the computational overhead. In order to reduce a receiver's memory requirements in another modification, we apply a version of the Complete Subtree method using trapdoor one-way permutations to the SD and LSD methods.

Keywords. Digital rights management, key management, broadcast encryption, revocation, stateless receiver, master key, subset difference

1 Introduction

Digital rights management and copyright protection have become topics of considerable interest. *Broadcast encryption* technology is useful for protection and management of copyrighted data. This technology allows a sender to send information securely to a group of receivers while excluding other receivers (called *revoked receivers*) over a broadcast channel.

Broadcast encryption schemes have many applications in the real world such as a scheme to protect copyrighted content stored on recordable media from unauthorized copying [6]. In this scheme, only authorized receivers (i. e. players or recorders) are given a set of keys so they can retrieve a session key which can be used to encrypt or decrypt the content file stored on a medium. If it is found that there is a receiver which treats the content in an unauthorized way (e. g. making unauthorized copies and transmitting them over the Internet), the receiver will be revoked, and as a result it will not be able to retrieve session keys from the media which are produced after the revocation.

We now have two simple methods to realize a broadcast encryption scheme. The first method gives a unique key to each receiver. A sender broadcasts secret

K. Chae and M. Yung (Eds.): WISA 2003, LNCS 2908, pp. 317–332, 2004.

information encrypted under each of the keys possessed by unrevoked receivers. This method requires a receiver to store only one key, but the sender must transmit $N - r$ ciphertexts, where N and r denote the total number of receivers in the system and the number of revoked receivers, respectively.

The other method is called the Power Set method. It defines a power set of N receivers, i.e. $\{S_{b_1...b_i...b_N}\}$ where $b_i \in \{0, 1\}$. Each b_i indicates whether or not a receiver i belongs to a subset $S_{b_1...b_i...b_N}$. It assigns a subset key for each subset and gives the subset key to receivers which belong to the subset. To send secret information, a sender chooses an appropriate subset key and encrypts the information with it, then broadcasts the ciphertext. Though the communication overhead of this method is minimal, each receiver must store 2^{N-1} keys.

The notion of broadcast encryption was introduced by Berkovits [3] and Fiat et al. [7] independently. An administrator or a broadcaster usually has much greater memory and computing resources than receivers. Therefore, the main criteria for this technology are the upper bound of the number of ciphertexts to be broadcast (the communication overhead), the number of keys or labels each receiver stores (the storage overhead), and the computational overhead at each receiver. Berkovits devised a broadcast encryption method using a secret sharing scheme. This method requires each receiver to store one key, however the communication overhead is $O(N)$. Fiat et al. proposed an r-resilient method which is resistant to a collusion of at most r revoked receivers by combining their 1-resilient methods hierarchically. Its communication and storage overhead are $O(r^2 \log^2 r \log N)$ and $O(r \log r \log N)$, respectively.

Efficient broadcast encryption methods using a logical key tree structure were independently proposed by Wallner et al. [17] and Wong et al. [18]. Their methods define a node key for each node in a tree. Each receiver is assigned to a leaf and given a set of node keys defined for the nodes on the path from the root to the leaf. Namely, each receiver stores $\log N + 1$ keys. This method revokes one receiver at a time, and updates all keys stored by unrevoked receivers, keys which are also possessed by the revoked receiver. A sender must broadcast $2 \log N$ ciphertexts and a receiver must perform at most $\log N$ decryptions for a single revocation.

Even though their methods are very efficient, several modifications using a similar structure have been proposed [2,4,8,9,11,12,14]. Some of these modifications reduce the number of messages for a single revocation to $\log N$ by combining the key tree structure with another cryptographic primitive such as a one-way function [11], a pseudo-random generator [4], or the Diffie-Hellman key exchange scheme [9]. The number of keys a receiver stores remains $\log N + 1$, however these modifications increase the computational overhead at a receiver. Similar to the methods of Wallner et al. [17] and Wong et al. [18], these modifications assume state relevant receivers, i.e. the receivers can change their keys.

The easiest way for receivers to store secret information such as receiver keys is storing it as part of the initial configuration at the time of manufacture. Giving receivers a mechanism to change their keys increases the production cost and might also weaken their security. Therefore it is reasonable to assume that most receivers cannot change their keys. Such receivers are called *stateless receivers*.

If receivers are state relevant, they can use keys (e. g. shared keys established among the sender and a group of receivers) they have previously stored in order to obtain the current session key. This may contribute to reducing the size of the broadcast. However, stateless receivers can store only the keys given at the initial stage. Hence every broadcast message must contain sufficient information to enable all unrevoked receivers to obtain the current session key using their initial receiver keys.

Naor et al. [12] proposed two efficient methods suitable for stateless receivers using a binary key tree structure. The Complete Subtree (CS) method requires a sender to broadcast $r \log (N/r)$ ciphertexts and each receiver to store $\log N + 1$ keys, whereas the Subset Difference (SD) method requires $2r - 1$ ciphertexts, $\frac{1}{2} \log^2 N + \frac{1}{2} \log N + 1$ labels and $O (\log N)$ computational overhead at a receiver. Halevy et al. [8] modified the SD method to include the concept of a *layer*. The Layered Subset Difference (LSD) method reduces the number of keys a receiver stores to $O (\log^{1+\epsilon} N)$, where ϵ is an arbitrary positive number, while maintaining the communication overhead and the computational overhead in $O (r)$ and $O (\log N)$, respectively.

Asano [2] improved the CS method and proposed two methods using an a-ary tree, the Master Key technique [5] and the Power Set method. One of them requires a storage for one key and $O \left(\frac{2^a \log^5 N}{\log a} \right)$ computational overhead at a receiver, where a is an arbitrary integer satisfying $a > 1$. The other requires $\frac{\log N}{\log a}$ keys and $O (2^a)$ computation. In both methods the number of broadcast ciphertexts is $r \left(\frac{\log(N/r)}{\log a} + 1 \right)$. Another concept to reduce the number of keys in the CS method was introduced by Nojima et al. [14]. As we describe in Section 5, they used two trapdoor one-way permutations with identical domains. Unfortunately, the security of this method has not been established.

Among the currently proposed methods, the SD and LSD methods are considered the most efficient due to their good balance in the the communication and storage overhead. In this paper we apply the Master Key technique [5] to these methods in order to reduce the storage at receivers. Table 1 summarizes the properties (the number of broadcast ciphertexts, the number of labels a receiver stores, and the computational overhead at a receiver) of the original SD and Basic LSD methods and their modifications proposed in this paper. Our modifications reduce the number of labels by $\log N$ while maintaining their communication complexity, in exchange for an increase in the computational overhead. When applied to the General LSD method, this construction reduces the number of labels by $\log N$ from $O (\log^{1+\epsilon} N)$. In addition, we apply to the SD and LSD methods the concept which reduces the number of keys a receiver stores in the CS method proposed by Nojima et al. [14].

Table 1. The properties of original methods and modifications proposed in this paper. N, r and M denote the total number of receivers, the number of revoked receivers and the modulus of RSA cryptosystem, respectively

SD	original [12]	modified (this paper)
Number of ciphertexts	$2r - 1$	$\leftarrow$
Number of labels	$\frac{1}{2}\log^2 N + \frac{1}{2}\log N + 1$	$\frac{1}{2}\log^2 N - \frac{1}{2}\log N + 1$
Computational overhead	$O(\log N)$	$O\left(\max\{\log^5 N, \log^2 N \log^2 M\}\right)$
Basic LSD	original [8]	modified (this paper)
Number of ciphertexts	$4r - 2$	$\leftarrow$
Number of labels	$\log^{3/2} N + 1$	$\log^{3/2} N - \log N + 1$
Computational overhead	$O(\log N)$	$O\left(\max\{\log^5 N, \log^2 N \log^2 M\}\right)$

2   Modification of the Subset Difference Method

In this section we present a modification which reduces the storage at receivers in the SD method [12]. All methods described below use a binary key tree structure. For clarity, we assume that the total number of receivers N is a power of 2. We call the entity which manages the broadcast encryption scheme *Trusted Center* *(TC)*. In the setup phase, TC defines a binary tree with N leaves and assigns a receiver to each leaf. Let $path_m$ be the path from the root to a leaf to which a receiver u_m is assigned. In order to represent the relationships of nodes, let $P(i)$, $S(i)$, $LC(i)$ and $RC(i)$ denote the parent node, sibling node, left child node and right child node of a node i, respectively.

2.1   The SD Method

In this section we give a brief explanation of the original SD method. In this method, a subset $S_{i,j}$, which is defined as $S_{i,j} = S_i \setminus S_j$, is represented by two nodes i and j, where S_i and S_j are sets of receivers assigned to the leaves of a subtree rooted at nodes i and j, respectively. The method defines all subsets $S_{i,j}$ such that i is an ancestor of j. In this arrangement, each receiver belongs to $O(N)$ subsets. If independent subset keys are assigned to these subsets, each receiver must store $O(N)$ subset keys securely so a large N is impractical.

The method uses a mechanism for generation of subset keys based on a pseudo-random sequence generator. Given C bits input, the pseudo-random generator G outputs $3C$ bit sequence. Let $G_L(S)$ denote the left third of the output of G on seed S, $G_M(S)$ the middle third, and $G_R(S)$ the right third.

TC picks up an internal node i as a starting point and sets a randomly chosen element $S \in \{0,1\}^C$ as a label of i, $LABEL_i$. Then TC evaluates $G(S)$ and sets $LABEL_{i,LC(i)} = G_L(S)$ and $LABEL_{i,RC(i)} = G_R(S)$, where labels $LABEL_{i,LC(i)}$ and $LABEL_{i,RC(i)}$ correspond to subsets $S_{i,LC(i)}$ and $S_{i,RC(i)}$, respectively. Similarly, labels corresponding to subsets $S_{i,LC(j)}$ and $S_{i,RC(j)}$ are generated as $LABEL_{i,LC(j)} = G_L(LABEL_{i,j})$ and $LABEL_{i,RC(j)} =$

$G_R(LABEL_{i,j})$, respectively, where i is an ancestor of j. TC continues inputting a label to the generator G in order to generate the labels $LABEL_{i,j}$ corresponding to all subsets $S_{i,j}$ such that j is a descendant of i. TC repeats this process for all internal nodes i including the root so that it generates all labels $LABEL_{i,j}$ for all subsets $S_{i,j}$. A subset key $SK_{i,j}$ corresponding to a subset $S_{i,j}$ is defined as $SK_{i,j} = G_M(LABEL_{i,j})$.

Since the generator G is public, a receiver given a label $LABEL_{i,j}$ can derive any label $LABEL_{i,k}$ and the corresponding subset key $SK_{i,k}$ such that $k = j$, or k is a descendant of j. Therefore, it is sufficient for a receiver u_m to store labels $LABEL_{i,j}$ defined by two nodes i and j in order to derive a subset key corresponding to any subset to which u_m belongs, where i is a node on $path_m$ and j is a descendant of i just hanging off $path_m$.

For a node i located on level l (where the leaf level is considered as level 0), there are l choices for j. Therefore, the number of labels a receiver stores (including a label for the case where no receivers are revoked) is

$$1 + \sum_{l=1}^{\log N} l = \frac{1}{2} \log^2 N + \frac{1}{2} \log N + 1$$

Since one can derive subset keys from these labels using the public generator G, receivers must store them in a secure manner.

2.2   Modification

We can observe the following as regards labels in the SD method. There are two cases in which a label is obtained by a receiver: a label $LABEL_{i,j}$ is (case I) directly given to a receiver by TC, or (case II) derived from another label using the generator G by a receiver. If i is a parent of j, there only exists case I. In other words, such labels are not derived from another label by a receiver. We consider such labels *special*.

It is obvious for each internal node i on $path_m$ for a receiver u_m there is only one choice for j such that u_m belongs to a subset $S_{i,j}$ and i is a parent of j. Therefore a receiver stores $\log N$ special labels. We apply the Master Key technique to these special labels and a label for the case of no revocation in order to reduce the storage at receivers. Our method combines $\log N + 1$ labels into one master label, so that it reduces $\log N$ labels from a receiver's storage. Our construction consists of three phases: setup, broadcast and decryption.

Setup

Step 1. TC, which is a sender of secret information, defines a rooted full binary tree with N leaves. Each node is numbered l ($l = 1, 2, \ldots, 2N - 1$) where the root is 1 and other nodes are numbered with breadth first order. A receiver u_m ($m = 1, 2, \ldots, N$) is assigned to each leaf of the tree. For each internal node i ($i = 1, 2, \ldots, N - 1$), TC defines subsets $S_{i,j}$ such that j is a descendant of *i.* Let $SS_{i,k}$ denote a special subset such that i is a parent of k among the subsets defined above. Since each node except the root has one parent node, each k ($k = 2, 3, \ldots, 2N - 1$) appears exactly once in representation of all special subsets $SS_{i,k}$. TC also defines a subset $S_{1,\phi}$ including all receivers for the case where there are no revocations.

Then TC selects large primes q_1 and q_2, a pseudo-random sequence generator G which outputs $3C$ bit sequence given C bits input, and a pairwise independent hash function H which maps $|M|$ bits randomly distributed elements into C bit strings, where $M = q_1 q_2$. Note that similar functions are also used in the original paper [12]. TC publishes M, G and H.

Step 2. TC chooses $2N - 1$ primes p_k ($k = 1, 2, \ldots, 2N - 1$), and assigns a prime p_1 to a subset $S_{1,\phi}$, and p_k to $SS_{i,k}$, where $k = 2, 3, \ldots, 2N - 1$, then publishes this assignment.

TC randomly chooses an element $K \in \mathbb{Z}_M^*$ and sets a label $LABEL_{1,\phi}$ corresponding to a subset $S_{1,\phi}$ and labels $LABEL_{i,k}$ corresponding to special subsets $SS_{i,k}$ such that i is a parent of k as $LABEL_{1,\phi} = H\left(K^{T/p_1} \bmod M\right)$ and $LABEL_{i,k} = H\left(K^{T/p_k} \bmod M\right)$, respectively, where $T = \prod_{k=1}^{2N-1} p_k$.

Step 3. Using the generator G and the labels $LABEL_{i,k}$ for special subsets $SS_{i,k}$, TC generates all labels $LABEL_{i,j}$ for the subsets $S_{i,j}$ defined in Step 1, where j is a descendant of k. This process is the same as in the SD method.

Step 4. For a receiver u_m, TC selects labels corresponding to subsets to which u_m belongs (in other words, labels given to the receiver in the original SD method). These are $LABEL_{1,\phi}$ and $LABEL_{i,j}$ for subsets $S_{i,j}$ which are determined by two nodes i and j, where i is an internal node on $path_m$ and j is a descendant node of i just hanging off $path_m$.

Then TC computes a master label ML_m of $LABEL_{1,\phi}$ and the labels corresponding to special subsets among the subsets selected for a receiver u_m as $ML_m = K^{T/w_m} \bmod M$, where w_m is a product of p_1 and p_k assigned to the special subsets to which u_m belongs.

TC gives u_m the master label ML_m, and labels selected above except $LABEL_{1,\phi}$ and labels corresponding to special subsets. In other words, TC gives u_m the master label and labels for non-special subsets $S_{i,j}$.

Example. Figure 1 depicts a binary tree with $N = 16$. In the original SD method, a receiver u_4 assigned to a leaf 19 stores 11 labels: $LABEL_{i,j}$ such that

$$(i, j) = \{(1, 3), (1, 5), (1, 8), (1, 18), (2, 5), (2, 8), (2, 18), (4, 8), (4, 18), (9, 18)\}$$

and $LABEL_{1,\phi}$. In our method, $LABEL_{1,3}$, $LABEL_{2,5}$, $LABEL_{4,8}$, $LABEL_{9,18}$ and $LABEL_{1,\phi}$ are combined into a master label ML_4. Therefore, a receiver u_4 stores a master label ML_4 and 6 labels: $LABEL_{1,5}$, $LABEL_{1,8}$, $LABEL_{1,18}$, $LABEL_{2,8}$, $LABEL_{2,18}$ and $LABEL_{4,18}$.

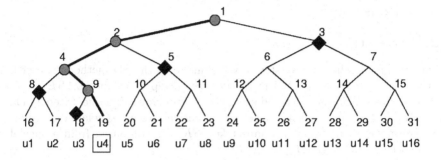

Fig. 1. A binary tree and receivers

Broadcast. TC broadcasts one or more ciphertexts. Each ciphertext is an encryption of the secret information under a subset key. The way to find the subset keys to be used for this encryption is the same as in the original SD method. Note that a subset key $SK_{i,j}$ corresponding to a subset $S_{i,j}$ is derived from a label $LABEL_{i,j}$ in the same way as in the SD method as $SK_{i,j} = G_M (LABEL_{i,j})$.

Decryption. An unrevoked receiver belongs to a subset corresponding to a subset key used for encryption in the broadcast phase. The way for a receiver to find a ciphertext to decrypt is the same as in the original SD method. After finding an appropriate ciphertext, a receiver derives the corresponding subset key from its master label or a label it stores then decrypts the ciphertext. The derivation of a subset key is performed as follows.

If no receivers are revoked and a subset key $SK_{1,\phi}$ is used, a receiver u_m computes a label $LABEL_{1,\phi}$ from its master label ML_m as $LABEL_{1,\phi} = H\left(ML_m^{w_m/p_1} \bmod M\right)$, then computes the subset key $SK_{1,\phi} = G_M (LABEL_{1,\phi})$. Otherwise, a receiver u_m checks that the node j for the subset $S_{i,j}$ corresponding to the subset key used for the ciphertext is either (a) a descendant of a node k (including the case $j = k$) such that u_m stores a label $LABEL_{i,k}$, or (b) a descendant of a node k (including the case $j = k$) such that the subset $S_{i,k}$ is a special subset and the corresponding special label $LABEL_{i,k}$ is combined into its master label ML_m (in other words, j is equal to k or its descendant where k is a child node of i and not located on $path_m$). In the case of (b), a receiver u_m derives the special label $LABEL_{i,k}$ as

$$LABEL_{i,k} = H\left(ML_m^{w_m/p_k} \bmod M\right) \tag{1}$$

The remaining process is common to both cases (a) and (b), and it is the same as in the original SD method: the receiver applies the generator G to the label $LABEL_{i,k}$ the necessary times to obtain $LABEL_{i,j}$, then derives the subset key $SK_{i,j} = G_M (LABEL_{i,j})$ and decrypts the ciphertext using the subset key.

3 Discussion

3.1 Security

Our method applies the Master Key technique to the SD method. Subset keys in our method are generated in three steps: (Step 1) a label $LABEL_{i,k}$ for a special subset $SS_{i,k}$ is generated using the Master Key technique, (Step 2) a label $LABEL_{i,j}$ for a non-special subset $S_{i,j}$ is derived from a special label using the generator G, then (Step 3) a subset key $SK_{i,j}$ is computed from a special or non-special label $LABEL_{i,j}$ using G.

In this section we analyze the security of each step. Broadcast encryption methods using the Master Key technique have been proposed by Asano [2]. The security analysis of these methods based on the discussion by Akl et al. [1] is applicable for Step 1. Namely, under the assumption that "If factors q_1, q_2 of a large composite $M = q_1 q_2$ are unknown, then computing p^{th} roots (mod M) for integral $p > 1$ is difficult." related to RSA cryptosystem [15], it is difficult for any coalition of receivers to obtain an intermediate label $IL_{i,k}$ corresponding to a special subset $SS_{i,k}$ to which no receivers in the coalition belong, where the intermediate label is defined as $IL_{i,k} = K^{T/p_k} \mod M$. We refer to Section 3 of [2] for a proof of this part. A special label $LABEL_{i,k}$ is derived from the intermediate label using the hash function H as $LABEL_{i,k} = H(IL_{i,k})$. Since the output of H is pairwise independent, we can say that it is difficult for any coalition with no receivers belonging to a special subset $SS_{i,k}$ to obtain the corresponding label $LABEL_{i,k}$.

Then the label $LABEL_{i,k}$ is fed to the generator G in Step 2 in order to derive a label $LABEL_{i,j}$ for a non-special subset $S_{i,j}$ determined by two nodes i and j, such that j is a descendant of k in the same way as in the SD method. The process in Step 3 is also the same as in the original. Since the output of H is pairwise independent, the discussion of the security of the SD method by Naor et al. [12] is applicable to Steps 2 and 3 in order to show the indistinguishability of subset keys.

3.2 Communication Overhead

In our method, the way to define subsets and to select subset keys used for encryption of secret information is the same as in the original SD method. Therefore, the upper bound of the number of ciphertexts is also the same, i.e. $2r - 1$, where r is the number of revoked receivers. Each broadcast ciphertext is an encryption of secret information I under a subset key. Any secure encryption algorithm can be used for this encryption. For example, we can use a block cipher algorithm with the block size $|I|$ and the key size C.

3.3 Storage and Computational Overhead

Let us first study the size of a secure memory at a receiver which is used to store labels. As described in Section 2.1, the number of labels a receiver stores in a secure manner is $\frac{1}{2}\log^2 N + \frac{1}{2}\log N + 1$ in the SD method. Our method uses a master label as a substitution for $\log N + 1$ (i. e. $LABEL_{1,\phi}$ and $\log N$ special labels). Therefore the number of labels a receiver stores in our method is $\frac{1}{2}\log^2 N - \frac{1}{2}\log N + 1$. Since the Master Key technique is based on RSA cryptosystem, the size of a master label is the size of a secure RSA modulus. As an example, if we set parameters as the total number of receivers $N = 2^{25}$, the size of a label $|LABEL_{i,j}| = C = 128$ bits and the size of a master label $|ML_m| = |M| = 1024$ bits, then the size of a secure memory of a receiver in our method is about 5.5 % smaller than in the original.

Next, when a receiver stores primes it needs, we consider an increase in the size of a memory which does not need secrecy. The total number of primes assigned to special subsets and a subset $S_{1,\phi}$ is $2N - 1$. Since the size of the nth prime is $O(n \log n)$ [10], we roughly estimate that the size of each prime is at most $O(N \log N)$. A receiver belongs to $\log N$ special subsets and a subset $S_{1,\phi}$, hence it needs $\log N + 1$ primes assigned to these subsets. In order to store them, it needs storage of $O(\log^2 N)$ bits. Since a combination of subsets to which a receiver belongs is unique, a combination of primes each receiver needs is also unique. Note that these primes and their assignments to subsets are public, therefore receivers do not need to store them in a confidential manner.

On the other hand, there is a situation where it is difficult for receivers to have such storage for uniquely assigned primes but it is possible to prepare a sufficient size of memory which is common to all receivers (e. g. a usual mask ROM storing program codes). In that case, receivers can store all $2N - 1$ primes assigned to the subsets. Kunth [10] introduced several techniques designed to reduce the size of memory for either of the above cases.

There may be another case where it is difficult for receivers to possess either type of memory noted above. In that case, we can define the assignment of the primes to the subsets as follows. A prime p_k is the smallest prime larger than $(k - 1)L$, where L is a positive integer such that an interval $((k - 1)L, kL]$ contains at least one prime. If a number p is chosen at random, the probability that it is prime is about $1 / \ln p$ [16]. Recall that the size of a prime used in the method is at most $O(N \log N)$. Therefore, if we use L satisfying $L > \ln(N \log N)$, it is expected that the interval $((k - 1)L, kL]$ contains at least one prime.

Each receiver can compute p_k from k in an on-the-fly manner by testing each number from $(k - 1)L + 1$ using a primality testing algorithm until it finds a prime. An example of a probabilistic primality testing algorithm is the Miller-Rabin algorithm. Since the complexity of the algorithm for testing a number p is $O(\log^3 p)$ [16], it is expected that the computational overhead for finding a prime is $O(\log^4 p)$. In order to compute w_m/p_k in the equation (1), a receiver must find $\log N$ primes, since w_m is a product of $\log N + 1$ primes. Therefore the total computational overhead for generation of primes is roughly $O(\log^5 N)$.

After finding these primes, the computational overhead for a receiver for derivation of a special label is a multiplication of $\log N$ primes whose size is at most $O(\log N)$ bits (the overhead of this computation is estimated as $O(\log^4 N)$), a modular exponentiation over a modulus M with an index of size

$O\left(\log^2 N\right)$ bits (the overhead is estimated as $O\left(\log^2 N \log^2 M\right)$), and an evaluation of the hash function H. It has been reported that the computational overhead for an evaluation of a pairwise independent hash function is much smaller than a modular exponentiation [13].

Note that a receiver needs to find primes and derive a special label only in case (b) in the decryption phase. In addition, in either case (a) or (b), a receiver must derive a subset key from the special label or a non-special label it stores using the generator G at most $\log N$ times. The computational overhead for the derivation of a subset key from a label is the same as in the original SD method.

4   Modification of the Layered Subset Difference Method

The LSD method is an extension of the SD method based on the concept of a layer. Halevy et al. [8] proposed two methods, the Basic and General LSD methods. These methods use a key tree structure similar to the SD method, however some levels in the tree are defined as special. The Basic LSD method uses only one kind of special level, whereas the General LSD method adopts several kinds of special level.

4.1   The Basic LSD Method

In the Basic LSD method, the root is defined as a special level, and in addition, every level of depth $l \log^{1/2} N$ for $l = 1, 2, \ldots, \log^{1/2} N$ is defined as special (assuming that $\log^{1/2} N$ is an integer). The set of levels between adjacent special levels (including two special levels) is defined as a layer. This method uses only a part of subsets defined in the SD method. A subset $S_{i,j}$ is defined in the Basic LSD method only if it satisfies at least one of the following conditions: both i and j belong to the same layer, or i is located on a special level.

In this setting, any subset defined in the SD method can be described as a disjoint union of at most two subsets defined in the Basic LSD method. Suppose that nodes i, k, j occur in this order on a path from the root to a leaf, i is not located on a special level, i and j do not belong to the same layer, and k is located on the first special layer from i to j. In this case a subset $S_{i,j}$ is not defined in the Basic LSD method but it is described using two defined subsets as $S_{i,j} = S_{i,k} \cup S_{k,j}$. Instead of a ciphertext encrypted under a subset key $SK_{i,j}$ in the SD method, two ciphertexts under $SK_{i,k}$ and $SK_{k,j}$, respectively, are broadcast in the Basic LSD method. Therefore the communication overhead increases at most twice compared with in the SD method, and the storage overhead at a receiver is reduced.

The number of labels a receiver stores is calculated as follows. First, consider the number of labels $LABEL_{i,j}$ such that both nodes i and j belong to the same layer. For a node i located on level h in a layer (where the bottom of the layer is considered as level 0), we have h choices for j. Therefore the number of labels is $\sum_{h=1}^{\log^{1/2} N} h = \frac{1}{2}\left(\log N + \log^{1/2} N\right)$. There are $\log^{1/2} N$ layers in the tree, hence the total number becomes $\frac{1}{2}\left(\log^{3/2} N + \log N\right)$. Second, consider the number of labels $LABEL_{i,j}$ such that i is located on a special level. For a node i located on level l (from the leaf level) in the entire tree, we have l choices for j. Hence there are $\sum_{l=1}^{\log^{1/2} N}\left(\log^{1/2} N\right) l = \frac{1}{2}\left(\log^{3/2} N + \log N\right)$ labels. We have counted labels which satisfy both conditions two times. The number of such labels is $\log N$, since there are $\log^{1/2} N$ such labels in each layer. Therefore, the total number of labels a receiver stores in the Basic LSD method including a label $LABEL_{1,\phi}$ is

$$\frac{1}{2}\left(\log^{3/2} N + \log N\right) + \frac{1}{2}\left(\log^{3/2} N + \log N\right) - \log N + 1 = \log^{3/2} N + 1$$

4.2   Modification of the Basic LSD Method

The modification of the SD method described in Section 2.2 uses the Master Key technique in order to combine a label $LABEL_{1,\phi}$ and special labels $LABEL_{i,j}$ for special subsets $SS_{i,j}$ into a master label. We can apply the same technique to the Basic LSD method.

The modification of the Basic LSD method is almost same as the modification of the SD method. The only difference is the condition for subsets. In the Basic LSD method, only the subsets satisfying the condition noted in Section 4.1 are defined, therefore the total number of subsets as well as the number of labels which are given to a receiver is smaller compared with that in the SD method. Our construction uses the same subsets as in the Basic LSD method.

In the example tree depicted in Fig. 1, three levels, where the root, nodes 4 to 7, and the leaves are located are considered as special. In the Basic LSD method, a receiver u_4 stores 9 labels: $LABEL_{i,j}$ such that

$$(i,j) = \{(1,3),(1,5),(1,8),(1,18),(2,5),(4,8),(4,18),(9,18)\}$$

and $LABEL_{1,\phi}$. Similar to in the modified SD method, $LABEL_{1,3}$, $LABEL_{2,5}$, $LABEL_{4,8}$, $LABEL_{9,18}$ and $LABEL_{1,\phi}$ are combined into a master label ML_4. Therefore, a receiver u_4 stores a master label ML_4 and 4 labels: $LABEL_{1,5}$, $LABEL_{1,8}$, $LABEL_{1,18}$ and $LABEL_{4,18}$ in our modification.

We are interested in how many labels we can eliminate from a receiver's storage. Consider how many special labels $LABEL_{i,j}$ a receiver stores in the original Basic LSD method. If a node i is a parent of a node j, we have three cases: i is located on a special level, j is located on a special level, or neither of them is located on a special level. In any case, both nodes belong to the same layer since they are adjacent to each other. Therefore, any subset $S_{i,j}$ such that i is a parent of j satisfies the condition and it is defined in the Basic LSD method. This means that the number of these special subsets to which a receiver belongs is $\log N$ and a receiver must store $\log N$ special labels in the Basic LSD method, just as in the SD method.

As noted in Section 4.1, the number of labels a receiver stores in the original Basic LSD method is $\log^{3/2} N+1$. Our modification combines $\log N$ special labels

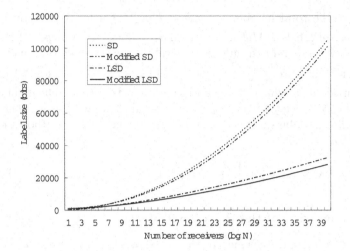

Fig. 2. The number of receivers and the label size

and a label $LABEL_{1,\phi}$ into a master label. Therefore it reduces the number to $\log^{3/2} N - \log N + 1$. If we consider the same parameters as in Section 3.3, i. e. the total number of receivers $N = 2^{25}$, the size of a label $|LABEL_{i,j}| = C = 128$ bits and the size of a master label $|ML_m| = |M| = 1024$ bits, the size of a secure memory for storing labels is reduced about 14 % compared with in the original method.

Figure 2 shows the relationship between the number of receivers (in log) and the size of labels a receiver stores (in bits) in the SD, Basic LSD, modified SD and modified Basic LSD methods under the same parameters as the previous example. The figure shows that the modification of the Basic LSD method provides a higher reduction rate of a receiver's storage than the modified SD method.

The other discussions on security, the size of non-secret storage and the computational overhead for the modified SD method in Section 3 are applicable to this modification of the Basic LSD method, as well as the modification of the General LSD method presented in Section 4.4.

4.3 The General LSD Method

The General LSD method uses several kinds of special level reflecting their different degrees of importance. We use the explanation given in [8] to describe the method.

Consider a path from the root to a leaf in the tree as a line graph. One end of the graph is the root and the other end is a leaf, and this graph has nodes corresponding to nodes located on the path in the tree. Each node in the graph is represented by its distance from the root, expressed as a d digit number in base $b = O\left(\log^{1/d} N\right)$. Hence the root is represented by $0\ldots00$, its child node is represented by $0\ldots01$, etc.

A subset defined in the SD method is represented as a disjoint union of at most d subsets defined in the General LSD method, i.e. if nodes $i, k_1, k_2, \ldots, k_{d-1}, j$ occur in this order on a path, a subset $S_{i,j}$ is represented as $S_{i,j} = S_{i,k_1} \cup S_{k_1,k_2} \cup \cdots \cup S_{k_{d-1},j}$. The broadcaster must send at most d ciphertexts as a substitute for one ciphertext in the SD method.

A subset $S_{i,j}$ defined in the General LSD method satisfies the following condition: if a node i in the graph is represented as a d digit number in base b by $\overrightarrow{x} a \overrightarrow{0}$ then a node j is represented either by $\overrightarrow{x + 10}\,\overrightarrow{0}$ or by any number $\overrightarrow{x} a' \overrightarrow{y}$, where a is the rightmost nonzero digit, $\overrightarrow{x}$ is a sequence of arbitrary digits, $\overrightarrow{0}$ is a sequence of zeroes, $a' \geq a$ and $\overrightarrow{y}$ is an arbitrary sequence of digits of the same length as $\overrightarrow{0}$. Note that the number of trailing zeroes in the representation of a node i determines how special it is. A node j of a defined subset $S_{i,j}$ can be any number from $i + 1$ to the first node which is even more special than i (including both nodes at the end).

As we enlarge a parameter d, the number of labels a receiver stores in the General LSD method decreases. Finally it becomes $O\left(\log^{1+\epsilon} N\right)$, where ϵ is an arbitrary positive number.

4.4 Modification of the General LSD Method

The Master Key technique can also be applied to the General LSD method as well as the SD and Basic LSD methods. We omit the detailed modification of the General LSD method since the difference between the Basic and General LSD methods is only the condition of defined subsets: the way to apply the Master Key technique is the same.

We want to know how many labels a receiver must store can be eliminated in this modification. For any internal node i, a subset $S_{i,j}$ such that $j = i+1$ (i.e. j is a child of i) satisfies the condition in the General LSD method. Similar to the Basic LSD method, a receiver must store $\log N$ labels corresponding to such special subsets. These special labels and a label $LABEL_{1,\phi}$ are combined using the Master Key technique, hence our method eliminates $\log N$ labels a receiver stores from $O\left(\log^{1+\epsilon} N\right)$ labels. Since ϵ can be an arbitrary positive number, this reduction can be very significant.

5 Approach Based on Trapdoor One-Way Permutations

Nojima et al. [14] introduced a concept to reduce the number of keys a receiver stores in the Complete Subtree method [12] to one using two trapdoor one-way permutations F_L and F_R with identical domains. Using a node key NK_i for a node i, node keys $NK_{LC(i)}$ and $NK_{RC(i)}$ for child nodes of i are generated as $NK_{LC(i)} = F_L^{-1}(NK_i)$ and $NK_{RC(i)} = F_R^{-1}(NK_i)$, respectively, where F_L^{-1} and F_R^{-1} are inverse permutations of the public permutations F_L and F_R, respectively, and which are known only to TC. After choosing an element randomly from the domain and setting it as a node key NK_1 for the root, TC generates all node keys from the root to the leaves using F_L^{-1} and F_R^{-1}. Then TC gives a receiver u_m a node key corresponding to a leaf to which u_m is assigned, so that u_m can derive any node key for a node on $path_m$ from its node key using the public permutations F_L and F_R.

The concept is based on the fact that if a node i is an ancestor of a node j, a leaf of a subtree rooted at j is also a leaf of a subtree rooted at i. In the SD method, we observe that if a node i is a parent of two nodes j and k, and j is also a parent of another node n, then a receiver which belongs to a subset $S_{j,n}$ also belongs to a subset $S_{i,k}$. Moreover, from the observation noted in Section 2.2 we can say that labels $LABEL_{j,n}$ and $LABEL_{i,k}$ for these subsets are directly given to receivers by TC, and not derived from another label by a receiver. These observations enable us to apply the concept by Nojima et al. to the SD method in order to reduce the number of labels a receiver stores as follows.

TC publishes two trapdoor one-way permutations F_L and F_R with identical domains, keeping their inverse permutations F_L^{-1} and F_R^{-1} secret. TC chooses an element S randomly from the domains, sets an intermediate label $IL_{1,\phi}$ for a subset $S_{1,\phi}$ as $IL_{1,\phi} = S$, then generates intermediate labels for special subsets $SS_{1,2}$ and $SS_{1,3}$ as $IL_{1,2} = F_L^{-1}(IL_{1,\phi})$ and $IL_{1,3} = F_R^{-1}(IL_{1,\phi})$, respectively. TC repeats invocations of the secret permutations in order to generate intermediate labels for special subsets $SS_{i,LC(i)}$ and $SS_{i,RC(i)}$ as $IL_{i,LC(i)} = F_L^{-1}(IL_{P(i),S(i)})$ and $IL_{i,RC(i)} = F_R^{-1}(IL_{P(i),S(i)})$, respectively, until it generates all intermediate labels $IL_{i,j}$ such that i is a parent of j. TC gives a receiver u_m assigned to a leaf j an intermediate label $IL_{P(j),S(j)}$. This enables u_m to derive any intermediate label for a special subset to which it belongs using the public permutations F_L and F_R. Note that a label $LABEL_{i,j}$ for a special subset $SS_{i,j}$ is derived from an intermediate label $IL_{i,j}$ as $LABEL_{i,j} = H(IL_{i,j})$ using the same hash function as in Section 2.2.

In Sections 4.2 and 4.4 we observed that a receiver in the Basic and General LSD methods stores $\log N$ special labels, just as in the SD method. This means that the construction described above can also be applied to the Basic and General LSD methods. Similar to the modifications using the Master Key technique presented in Sections 2 and 4, the modification based on trapdoor one-way permutations reduces $\log N$ labels from a receiver's storage in the SD and LSD methods.

Note that the permutations F_L and F_R need to satisfy various conditions. For example, the probability that $F_L^{-1}(F_R^{-1}(x)) = F_R^{-1}(F_L^{-1}(x))$ should be negligible for any intermediate label x. The strict conditions for the F_L and F_R, or the concrete permutations which are useful to construct a secure broadcast encryption scheme are currently not known.

6   Summary

In this paper we have proposed modifications of the SD, Basic LSD and General LSD methods. Using the Master Key technique, our methods reduce the number of labels a receiver must store in a secure manner by $\log N$ while maintaining their communication complexity, in exchange for an increase in the computational overhead. We have also applied another concept based on trapdoor one-way permutations to the SD and LSD methods in order to reduce the number of labels a receiver stores by $\log N$. Consequently, we have given another trade-off in the requirements of broadcast encryption methods.

References

1. S. G. Akl and P. D. Taylor, "Cryptographic Solution to a Problem of Access Control in a Hierarchy," ACM Transactions on Computer Systems, Vol. 1, No. 3, pp. 239–248, 1983.
2. T. Asano, "A Revocation Scheme with Minimal Storage at Receivers," Advances in Cryptology - Asiacrypt 2002, Lecture Notes in Computer Science 2501, Springer, pp. 433–450, 2002.
3. S. Berkovits, "How to Broadcast a Secret," Advances in Cryptology - Eurocrypt '91, Lecture Notes in Computer Science 547, Springer, pp. 535–541, 1991.
4. R. Canetti, T. Malkin and K. Nissim, "Efficient Communication-Storage Tradeoffs for Multicast Encryption," Advances in Cryptology - Eurocrypt '99, Lecture Notes in Computer Science 1592, Springer, pp. 459–474, 1999.
5. G. C. Chick and S. E. Tavares, "Flexible Access Control with Master Keys," Advances in Cryptology - Crypto '89, Lecture Notes in Computer Science 435, Springer, pp. 316–322, 1990.
6. "Content Protection for Recordable Media Specification," available from http://www.4centity.com/tech/cprm/.
7. A. Fiat and M. Naor, "Broadcast Encryption," Advances in Cryptology - Crypto '93, Lecture Notes in Computer Science 773, Springer, pp. 480–491, 1994.
8. D. Halevy and A. Shamir, "The LSD Broadcast Encryption Scheme," Advances in Cryptology - Crypto 2002, Lecture Notes in Computer Science 2442, Springer, pp. 47–60, 2002.
9. Y. Kim, A. Perrig and G. Tsudik, "Simple and Foult-Tolerant Key Agreement for Dynamic Collaborative Groups," Proceedings of ACM Conference on Computer and Communication Security, CCS 2000.
10. D. E. Knuth, "The Art of Computer Programming," vol. 2, Addison-Wesley, 1981.
11. D. A. McGrew and A. T. Sherman, "Key Establishment in Large Dynamic Groups Using One-Way Function Trees," Manuscript, available from http://www.csee.umbc.edu/~sherman/Papers/itse.ps, 1998.
12. D. Naor, M. Naor and J. Lotspiech, "Revocation and Tracing Schemes for Stateless Receivers," Advances in Cryptology - Crypto 2001, Lecture Notes in Computer Science 2139, Springer, pp. 41–62, 2001.
13. M. Naor and O. Reingold, "Number-Theoretic Constructions of Efficient Pseudo-Random Functions," Proceedings of 38th IEEE Symposium on Foundations of Computer Science, pp. 458–467, 1997.
14. R. Nojima and Y. Kaji, "Tree Based Key Management Using Trapdoor One-Way Functions," (in Japanese), Proceedings of the 2003 Symposium on Cryptography and Information Security, pp. 131–136, 2003.
15. R. L. Rivest, A. Shamir and L. Adleman, "A Method for Obtaining Digital Signatures and Public-Key Cryptosystems," Communications of the ACM, 21, pp. 120–126, 1978.

16. D. R. Stinson, "Cryptography: Theory and Practice," CRC Press, 1995.
17. D. Wallner, E. Harder and R. Agee, "Key Management for Multicast: Issues and Architectures," IETF Network Working Group, Request for Comments: 2627, available from `ftp://ftp.ietf.org/rfc/rfc2627.txt`, 1999.
18. C. K. Wong, M. Gouda and S. S. Lam, "Secure Group Communications Using Key Graphs," Proceedings of ACM SIGCOMM '98, 1998.

3D Face Recognition under Pose Varying Environments

Hwanjong Song, Ukil Yang, and Kwanghoon Sohn*

Biometrics Engineering Research Center
Department of Electrical & Electronics Engineering,
Yonsei University, Seoul, 120-749, Korea
khsohn@yonsei.ac.kr

Abstract. This paper describes a novel three-dimensional (3D) face recognition method when the head pose varies severely. Given an unknown 3D face, we extract several invariant facial features based on the facial geometry. We perform a Error Compensated Singular Value Decomposition (EC-SVD) for 3D face recognition. The novelty of the proposed EC-SVD procedure lies in compensating for the error for each rotation axis accurately. When the pose of a face is estimated, we propose a novel two-stage 3D face recognition algorithm. We first select face candidates based on the 3D-based nearest neighbor classifier and then the depth-based template matching is performed for final recognition. From the experimental results, less than a 0.2 degree error in average has been achieved for the 3D head pose estimation and all faces are correctly matched based on our proposed method.

1 Introduction

Face recognition technologies have made great progress using 2D images for the past few decades. They played an important role in many applications such as identification, crowd surveillance and access control [1,2]. Although they show reasonable performance under varying inner and outer environments such as the face expression and illumination change, it still remained as an unsolved problem when the position or pose of a face is severely varied. In other words, it is difficult to recognize a face when the face pose is not frontal. In 2D face recognition, we already know that approximately 20 percent of the recognition rate has been degraded when the head position is deviated from 10–15 percent off the frontal orientation, thus it cannot be utilized for the face recognition system. Therefore, the head pose estimation is an inevitable step for the pose invariant face recognition system which cannot be effectively achieved in a 2D domain.

Many approaches have been reported about the head pose estimation based on 2D images and video sequences [3,4,5,6]. Most of them exploited facial features to estimate the head pose, but they showed poor performances for pose invariant

---

* Corresponding author

K. Chae and M. Yung (Eds.): WISA 2003, LNCS 2908, pp. 333–347, 2004.

face recognition systems. In recent years, more attention has been focused on
3D head pose estimation for face recognition based on a 3D face model. Few
approaches have been done regarding 3D head pose estimation. Q. Chen et al.
[7,8] used the skin and hair regions of a face which are extracted with color
information. They detected facial features in those regions to estimate the 3D
head pose. However, this method is sensitive to the change of hairstyle and
illumination variations due to color information. K. Hattori et al. [9] proposed
a method to estimate the pose of a 3D face using the symmetry plane based
on range and intensity images. However, the error increases when the head pose
variation is over 20 degrees for each rotation axis.

In the field of face recognition,3D face recognition has attracted the attention
of many researchers. In the 3D domain, many researchers have treated 3D face
recognition problems using differential geometry tools of computing curvatures
[10,11,12]. S. Lao et al. [13] used stereo images and performed 3D face recognition by calculating the mean differences in depth between corresponding data
points in the test 3D model and all the models in the database. However, 3D
range images recently have gained much attention in the face recognition field
due to some advantages over the grey level and color images. For example, the
explicit representation of the 3D shape is invariant under the change of color
or reflectance properties [12]. Unfortunately, few researchers have focused on
the 3D facial range images. C.S. Chua et al. [14] used 3D range images for face
recognition using point signature and explored a technique dealing with different
facial expressions. H.T. Tanaka et al. [11] treated the face surface as a 3D rigid
free-form surface. However, these approaches regarding 3D face recognition have
not taken into considerations for compensating the 3D head pose estimation.
Therefore, it is essential to have an accurate 3D head pose estimation for face
recognition and also an efficient normalization process of input data which is
required for 3D pose variations.

In this paper, we concentrate on the accurate 3D head pose estimation algorithm using the extracted facial feature points and perform the pose invariant
face recognition. Figure 1 briefly presents the whole process to build facial feature
extraction, perform the 3D head pose estimation, and accomplish face recognition. It is important to explore the capability of 3D face recognition based on
3D techniques. Therefore, we explored based on a 3D input image and 3D face
database for 3D face recognition. First, the 3D facial feature extraction technique using the facial geometry is described in this paper. We automatically
extract maximum and minimum curvature points which are denoted by convex
and concave points, and a Nose Peak Point (NPP). To estimate the initial head
pose and more accurate head pose of an input image, we propose the Error Compensated SVD algorithm which first minimizes the least square error and then
compensates for the head pose error in the established 3D normalized space. We
compare the facial feature points of the 3D input face with the 3D average head
in the database to estimate the head pose. We perform an accurate pose refinement procedure for each axis with the acquired angles from the SVD method.
It recovers the error angle for the accurate head pose in the 3D normalized face

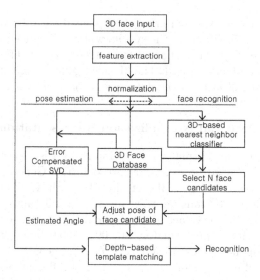

Fig. 1. The block diagram of the proposed method

space and enables robust face recognition. In addition, we present a 3D-based nearest neighbor classifier to select face candidates in the database based on extracted feature points. The distances between the selected features such as the eyebrow center point, the minimum point of nose ridge, and a NPP are pose invariant measurements. The proposed algorithm selects N similar face candidates from the database. This procedure decreases the computation time for 3D head pose estimation and efficiently performs depth-based template matching with regard to selected 3D face candidates.

The remainder of this paper is organized as follows: Section 2 describes the extraction of 3D facial feature points using geometrical characteristics of 3D face and explains 3D normalized face space for pose estimation and recognition. Section 3 introduces a 3D head pose estimation procedure based on the proposed EC-SVD (Error Compensated SVD) in detail. In Sec. 4, face recognition algorithm based on 3D-based nearest neighbor classifier and 3D template correlation matching are described. In Sec. 5, test performance is analyzed to explain the efficiency of the proposed algorithm. Finally, Sec. 6 concludes by suggesting future directions in which the method can be extended.

2 3D Facial Feature Extraction

2.1 3D Laser Scanned Face Data

Although many algorithms have been developed for 2D images, approaches using 3D face data have been increased to overcome the shortcomings of 2D images, and 3D input devices are getting more popular [15]. The face database consists of highly realistic 3D laser-scans of individual heads with both shape and texture data. We have available a model of a person's head with 3D vertex points and texture image data. The input to the system will be 3D range image and texture data. For each face, a sequence of poses from -90 degrees to +90 degrees for each X, Y, and Z axis can be generated. The 3D average face which is computed over all the vertex points of faces in the database is constructed.

2.2   3D Face Space and Normalization Representation

For 3D face recognition, normalization of input data is especially required for the estimation of 3D head poses and face recognition. Generally, 3D face input data is accompanied by complex 3D rotations for each X, Y, and Z axis. In our experiments, we use a 3D range data as an input for 3D head pose estimation, and it will be used for the face recognition task as well. Our 3D face data in the database include approximately 70,000 – 200,000 vertex points for each person and corresponding texture image. However, geometrical coordinates of the vertex points of each person are in a wide and different range (variation up to 100,000 for each axis). It takes a great computational effort to calculate them and different scales exist on each face.

Thus, we normalize the face data to make all the 3D face on the same object/face space. Different scale factors may occur when we acquire input data, so they should be fixed into a normalized face space through this 3D face normalization step. We define a 3D face space that normalizes the face representation for head pose estimation and face recognition. Given a 3D face F, which is defined by a point set of Cartesian coordinates, we consider the range of coordinates on the X, Y and Z axis being infinite. However, we normalize these input data to a defined range for each axis, which we denote as 3D normalized face space. Figure 2 shows the example of a 3D normalized face space that we have established. All the faces that we consider are in this normalized face space and are

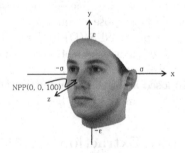

Fig. 2. 3D normalized face space

proportionally located based on the original face data in the limited range of $[-x_n, x_n]$, $[-y_n, y_n]$, $[0, z_n]$ for the X, Y, and Z axis, respectively. We especially locate the NPP as a fixed point on the Z axis, which makes a reliable and efficient task to estimate head poses. It will be discussed more in detail in Sec.3. We first normalize 3D faces with depth information (Z value) and then proportionally adjust the X and Y range. We acquire the limited range for each axis as follows:

$$F\left(x_i, y_i, z_i\right) = \left[\frac{F_x - F_{x_{\min}}}{F_{x_{\max}} - F_{x_{\min}}} \times x_n, \frac{F_y - F_{y_{\min}}}{F_{y_{\max}} - F_{y_{\min}}} \times y_n, \frac{F_z - F_{z_{\min}}}{F_{z_{\max}} - F_{z_{\min}}} \times z_n \right], \quad (1)$$

where $F\left(F_x, F_y, F_z\right)$ is an input data point.

2.3   Extracting 3D Facial Feature Points

The availability of 3D data can help to reduce the influence of the viewpoint through the use of viewpoint invariant geometrical features. We extract facial feature points using 3D geometric information, especially depth information to find the key features such as the nose peak point (NPP). The Euclidean distance (radius) of the NPP is maximal from the Y axis among the vertex points of the 3D face. We can vertically and almost symmetrically divide the face using the YZ plane which includes the NPP and Y axis, and obtains the face dividing line/curvature. On the face center curve, we use curvature characteristics to extract facial feature points, which are convex and concave points except for the nose peak point. We automatically extract six points which are a center point between the left and right eyebrows, a minimum point of the nose ridge, the nose peak point, the upper lip, the mouth center point, and the lower lip point as shown in Fig. 3. We assume that the face expression does not change and consider only a neutral face.

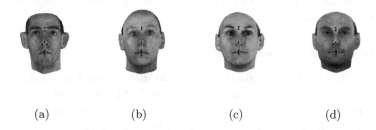

| (a) | (b) | (c) | (d) |

Fig. 3. 3D facial feature extraction(frontal). (a)Volker (b)Barbara (c)Isabelle (d)Thomas

3   3D Head Pose Estimation

In most problems of face recognition, the face is considered as a frontal and the effect of head rotations are ignored. Though 3D head pose estimation and normalization in 3D space are important, they have not been considered in the previous research on 3D face recognition [11,14,16,17]. It is obvious that accurate head pose estimation not only enables robust face recognition but also critically determines the performance of the face recognition system.

In this section, we apply a 3D head pose estimation algorithm which uses 3D facial features. We make up of 3D feature point vectors and use them for calculating the initial head pose of the input face based on the Singular Value Decomposition (SVD) method [18,19]. The SVD method uses a 3D-to-3D feature point correspondence matching scheme to estimate the rotation angle relative to the average frontal 3D face in the database with respect to minimize the error of all extracted facial feature points [20,21]. Although the error is minimized by the SVD method, it still has some errors which may cause serious problems in face recognition. To achieve reliable face recognition results, these errors must be reduced as much as possible.

We propose an Error Compensated SVD (EC-SVD) to compensate for the rest of the errors which were not yet recovered from the SVD method. The proposed EC-SVD procedure compensates for the error rotation angles for each axis after acquisition of the initial head pose from the SVD method. It geometrically fits the feature points in the 3D normalized face space using an error rotation matrix for each axis. In this method, we build a complete rotation matrix R which consists of six rotation matrices for each axis. They are three rotation matrices from three SVD methods and three error rotation matrices for each axis. We compensate for the error rotation matrix in the order of the X, Y, and Z axis, and this is the reverse order of the forward rotation of an input image. We independently calculate the error rotation matrix for the X and Y axis using the geometrical location of the NPP in the 3D normalized face space, and finally calculate the error angle between a face normal vector which is made up of extracted facial features and the Y axis to compensate for the error angle of the Z axis.

3.1   Error Compensated SVD

Although the SVD method finds the rotation matrix based on the least-squares approach, we empirically know that there still exist some errors which often cause serious problems in face recognition. The estimated angles for each X, Y, and Z axis from the SVD method become unacceptable when a large pose variation occurs for a certain axis or the extracted 3D facial features are not located on the face center line/curve, which means that the 3D input face is not symmetric. These errors may produce a face recognition rate which is severely low. Thus, we cannot classify the faces efficiently even if we adopt a powerful face recognition algorithm when a head pose of the face is not exact. We need to compensate for the error in each axis and compensate the error angle which has not been recovered from the SVD method.

In the proposed EC-SVD algorithm, we independently refine/compensate for this error rotation matrix for each axis in order to obtain the complete rotation matrix with the aid of the SVD method. Figure 4 illustrates the proposed 3D

EC-SVD procedure. The proposed algorithm first infers the initial head pose by using the SVD method. Then, we establish a complete rotation matrix with an assumption that there still exist some errors to compensate for as,

$$R = R_X R_Y R_Z = R_{\text{SVD}_X} R_{\theta_X} R_{\text{SVD}_Y} R_{\theta_Y} R_{\text{SVD}_Z} R_{\theta_Z}, \tag{2}$$

where R is a 3×3 complete rotation matrix, $R_X = R_{\text{SVD}_X} R_{\theta_X}$, $R_Y = R_{\text{SVD}_Y} R_{\theta_Y}$ and $R_Z = R_{\text{SVD}_Z} R_{\theta_Z}$. $R_{\text{SVD}_X}, R_{\text{SVD}_Y}, R_{\text{SVD}_Z}$ are rotation matrices obtained from SVD method for the X, Y, and Z axis,respectively. $R_{\theta_X}, R_{\theta_Y}, R_{\theta_Z}$ are error rotation matrices that must be compensated for each axis.

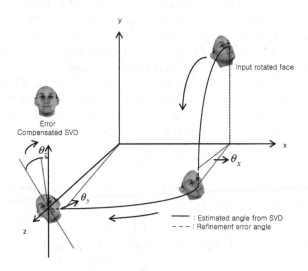

Fig. 4. Error Compensated SVD procedure

Utilizing a R complete rotation matrix , we can write a rigid transformation as follows:

$$f'_i = R f_i + t = R_X R_Y R_Z f_i + t = R_{\text{SVD}_X} R_{\theta_X} R_{\text{SVD}_Y} R_{\theta_Y} R_{\text{SVD}_Z} R_{\theta_Z} f_i + t, \tag{3}$$

where f'_i and f_i are feature vectors before and after rotation.

As the translation vector can be easily obtained after finding a complete rotation matrix and we found $R_{\text{SVD}_X}, R_{\text{SVD}_Y}$, and R_{SVD_Z} for X, Y, and Z axis respectively, the purpose of the proposed EC-SVD is to evaluate $R_{\theta_X}, R_{\theta_Y}$, and R_{θ_Z} using the geometry of the 3D normalized face space and a facial feature point. Since we know that the inverse of the complete rotation matrix must be an input rotated face of frontal view, we use the inverse transform of the complete rotation matrix as follows:

$$p_i = R^{-1} p'_i = R_Z^{-1} R_Y^{-1} R_X^{-1} p'_i = R_{\text{SVD}_Z}^{-1} R_{\theta_Z}^{-1} R_{\text{SVD}_Y}^{-1} R_{\theta_Y}^{-1} R_{\text{SVD}_X}^{-1} R_{\theta_X}^{-1} p'_i, \tag{4}$$

where $p_i = f_i - \bar{f}$ and $p'_i = f'_i - \bar{f}$.

From Eq. 4, we can utilize the rotation matrix R^{-1} to rotate input feature vectors to the frontal view. That is, we compensate for the error rotation matrix using the geometry of the 3D normalized face space in the order of each X, Y, and Z axis. We now describe the proposed EC-SVD procedure for each axis in detail.

Estimation of the Error θ_x. After rotating the estimated angle obtained from the SVD method about the X axis, we denote the angle as θ_{SVD_x}, the error θ_x is supposed to be computed for compensating for the existing error. In order to estimate θ_x in the X axis, we exploit the X axis rotation matrix for evaluation. The key feature point that we use for input is the NPP because all the NPPs of the 3D face model and the input are normalized to the fixed point $p(0, 0, z)$ when the face is frontal. In this paper, we use 100 as the z value. If the NPP of an input face, denoted by $n(x, y, z)$, is rotated fully backward around the X axis, it must be on the XZ plane and the coordinate of the NPP must b, is rotated fully backward around the X axis, it must be on the XZ plane and the coordinate of the NPP must be $p'(x, 0, z)$. We can move the point $n(x, y, z)$ to the point $p'(x, 0, z)$ by rotating angle θ_{SVD_x} and then compensate for the error angle, θ_x. We can estimate θ_x from the following equation:

$$\mathbf{p'} = R_X^{-1}\mathbf{n} = R_{\theta_x}^{-1}R_{SVD_x}^{-1}\mathbf{n} . \tag{5}$$

For the rotation matrix, an inverse matrix can be easily acquired by transposing the X axis rotation matrix as follows:

$$R_X^T = R_X^{-1} \text{,where } R_X = \begin{bmatrix} 1 & 0 & 0 \\ 0 & \cos\theta_x & \sin\theta_x \\ 0 & -\sin\theta_x & \cos\theta_x \end{bmatrix} , \tag{6}$$

$$\begin{bmatrix} x \\ 0 \\ z' \end{bmatrix} = \begin{bmatrix} 1 & 0 & 0 \\ 0 & \cos\theta_x & -\sin\theta_x \\ 0 & \sin\theta_x & \cos\theta_x \end{bmatrix} \begin{bmatrix} 1 & 0 & 0 \\ 0 & \cos\theta_{SVD_x} & -\sin\theta_{SVD_x} \\ 0 & \sin\theta_{SVD_x} & \cos\theta_{SVD_x} \end{bmatrix} \begin{bmatrix} x \\ y \\ z \end{bmatrix} . \tag{7}$$

Using the Eq. 6, we can solve the equation

$$\begin{bmatrix} 1 & 0 & 0 \\ 0 & \cos\theta_{SVD_x} & -\sin\theta_{SVD_x} \\ 0 & \sin\theta_{SVD_x} & \cos\theta_{SVD_x} \end{bmatrix} \begin{bmatrix} x \\ y \\ z \end{bmatrix} = \begin{bmatrix} 1 & 0 & 0 \\ 0 & \cos\theta_x & \sin\theta_x \\ 0 & -\sin\theta_x & \cos\theta_x \end{bmatrix} \begin{bmatrix} x \\ 0 \\ z' \end{bmatrix} , \tag{8}$$

where $z' \neq 0$. Therefore,

$$\theta_x = \arctan\left(\frac{y\cos\theta_{SVD_x} - z\sin\theta_{SVD_x}}{y\sin\theta_{SVD_x} + z\cos\theta_{SVD_x}}\right) . \tag{9}$$

Estimation of the Error θ_y. When the error θ_x has been refined, the same refinement procedure is applied to estimate the error θ_y. As we have rotated the input features θ_{SVD_y} inversely, we have to rotate the input data around the Y axis for θ_y inversely as well. Then the rotated point of $p'(x, 0, z')$ can be determined which is almost on the XZ plane. We exploit this point $p'(x, 0, z')$ for refining the error θ_y. We can now estimate θ_y as follows:

$$\mathbf{p} = R_Y^{-1}\mathbf{p}' = R_{\theta_y}^{-1} R_{\text{SVD}_y}^{-1} \mathbf{p}' \,, \tag{10}$$

$$\begin{bmatrix} 0 \\ 0 \\ z'' \end{bmatrix} = \begin{bmatrix} \cos\theta_{SVD_y} & 0 & -\sin\theta_{SVD_y} \\ 0 & 1 & 0 \\ \sin\theta_{SVD_y} & 0 & \cos\theta_{SVD_y} \end{bmatrix} \begin{bmatrix} \cos\theta_y & 0 & -\sin\theta_y \\ 0 & 1 & 0 \\ \sin\theta_y & 0 & \cos\theta_y \end{bmatrix} \begin{bmatrix} x \\ 0 \\ z' \end{bmatrix}, \tag{11}$$

$$\theta_y = \arctan\left(\frac{x\cos\theta_{SVD_y} - z'\sin\theta_{SVD_y}}{x\sin\theta_{SVD_y} + z'\cos\theta_{SVD_y}}\right). \tag{12}$$

Estimation of the Error θ_z. When the X and Y axis rotation are refined, we finally estimate the error θ_z However, we cannot use the point NPP, since it is not affected by the Z axis rotation. We utilize a face vector $\overrightarrow{F}(a, b, c)$ which is a vertical vector connected from the minimum point of the nose ridge to the center point of the left and right eyebrow. These two features are located on the XY plane. In other words, they have almost the same depth information. Thus, we can easily estimate the error θ_z by matching the face normal vector with the Y axis. We write a normalized face vector $\overrightarrow{F'}$ as

$$\overrightarrow{F'} = \left[\frac{a}{\sqrt{a^2+b^2+c^2}}, \frac{b}{\sqrt{a^2+b^2+c^2}}, \frac{c}{\sqrt{a^2+b^2+c^2}}\right] \cong \left[\frac{a}{\sqrt{a^2+b^2+c^2}}, \frac{b}{\sqrt{a^2+b^2+c^2}}, 0\right], \tag{13}$$

where $c \approx 0$. The error angle θ_z must be rotated as to match the $\overrightarrow{F'}$ with the Y axis and we use the Z axis rotation matrix to calculate θ_z. If we denote $\overrightarrow{F'}(f_x, f_y, 0)$ as a normalized face vector, then

$$\overrightarrow{F'} = \begin{bmatrix} f_x \\ f_y \\ 0 \end{bmatrix} = \begin{bmatrix} \cos\theta_z & -\sin\theta_z & 0 \\ \sin\theta_z & \cos\theta_z & 0 \\ 0 & 0 & 1 \end{bmatrix} \begin{bmatrix} 0 \\ 1 \\ 0 \end{bmatrix} = \begin{bmatrix} -\sin\theta_z \\ \cos\theta_z \\ 0 \end{bmatrix}, \tag{14}$$

$$f_x = \frac{a}{\sqrt{a^2 + b^2 + c^2}} = -\sin\theta_z, \tag{15}$$

$$\theta_z = \arcsin\left(\frac{-a}{\sqrt{a^2 + b^2 + c^2}}\right). \tag{16}$$

As a result, the final estimated 3D head pose is obtained when we inversely rotate the error angle θ_z.

4   3D Face Recognition

In this section, we present a two-stage method of 3D face recognition algorithm. For the first step, we utilize a 3D-based nearest neighbor classifier for selecting N similar face candidates. The objective of this method is to reduce computational time for template matching by selecting most similar faces in the database.

With selected face candidates, the final recognition stage based on a depth-based template matching is performed. As we have shown in Fig. 1, we simultaneously perform face recognition steps with the 3D head pose estimation.

4.1   3D-Based Nearest Neighbor Classifier

At present, we need a large computational time if we estimate the head pose and match the input data with all the faces in the database simultaneously. It is a critical problem to reduce the computational time when the size of the face database becomes larger. Therefore, efficiently selecting face candidates in the database must be an crucial part for 3D face recognition.

In this paper, to select face candidates, we adopt a 3D-based nearest neighbor classifier which utilizes some of the extracted facial feature points to calculate the feature distances. As we mentioned in Sec. 2, the value of feature distance of the input head are pose invariant because the extracted feature points are invariant. We exploit them to acquire N face candidates in the database which must be within the limited range that we have defined. We perform both a template matching stage and a 3D head pose estimation based on the proposed EC-SVD with only those N face candidates.

Three features that we select for calculating the distances are an NPP, the center point of the left and right eyebrow, and a minimum point of the nose ridge. The Euclidean distance of the selected feature points is computed as

$$D(f) = \sqrt{\left\| \hat{f}_1 - \hat{f}_2 \right\|^2 + \left\| \hat{f}_2 - \hat{f}_3 \right\|^2}, \qquad (17)$$

where $\hat{f}_1, \hat{f}_2$ and $\hat{f}_3$ indicate the center point of the left and right eyebrow, the minimum point of the nose ridge, and the nose peak point, respectively.

We determine those N face candidates as most similar or a similar configuration to the input face. Therefore, we choose them if the distance measure satisfies the following condition:

$$0 \leq D(f) \leq \delta, \qquad (18)$$

where δ is a threshold value for selecting face candidates. With selected face candidates, we then go to the next step for the final recognition stage.

4.2   Depth-Based Template Matching

After selecting N face candidates based on the 3D-based nearest neighbor classifier, we perform the depth-based template matching for final face recognition as shown Fig. 5. The depth-based template matching is applied to compare face candidates in the database which are passed from the previous step with the input face data. At this stage, we already know the pose of an input head

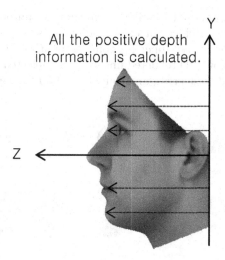

All the positive depth
information is calculated.

Fig. 5. Depth-based template matching

and rotate the face candidates based on the angle acquired from the proposed EC-SVD method.

We can measure the difference between them by calculating the sum of squared distance (SSD) in depth between data points of an input data and all the face candidates. We take into considerations of data points which are in the correspondence, which are a pair of nearest data points in the 3D normalized face space. Depth-based template matching is done by following procedure:

1. Both the input face data and the face candidates are expressed in the 3D normalized face space.
2. Divide the matching area into $m \times n$ of the XY plane.
3. For each 3D data point of the input data, find the nearest data points in the face candidates.
4. Calculate the sum of squared distance(SSD) in depth between all the face candidates and the input data.
5. Choose the face candidate with which of the smallest distance in depth as the final answer.

5   Experimental Results

We test the proposed EC-SVD and two-step 3D face recognition based on enrolled 3D faces for database against the pose varying environments. As mentioned in Sec.2, we adopt a 3D face range image as an input. We use the laser scanned 3D heads of 14 people for database which are 5 downloaded faces from the Max Planck Institute (MPI) and 9 face data of our own.

To evaluate the proposed EC-SVD algorithm, we automatically extract six facial feature points which are a center point of two eyebrows, a nose ridge point, a nose peak point, an upper lip point, a mouth center point and a lower lip point. Figure 6 shows 2D rendered images of the selected facial feature points of frontal, left 15 and 30 degrees, and right 15 and 30 degrees. For 3D head pose

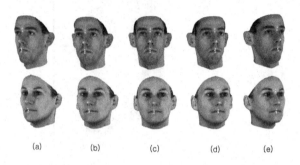

(a)   (b)   (c)   (d)   (e)

Fig. 6. 3D facial feature extraction on various head poses:(a)-30 degree,(b)-15 degree, (c) frontal,(d)15 degree,(e)30 degree

estimation, we synthesize various poses for each head model. We use them to compare the SVD method with the proposed EC-SVD algorithm. In order to estimate the head pose of an input data, we test 3D face input data on various rotation angles. We generate various head poses in 15-degree steps for the Y, Z axis and 10-degree step for the X axis, and obtain 23 different head poses. We examine 3D input faces and compare them with the average face in the database to acquire an initial head pose based on the SVD method. In addition, the proposed EC-SVD algorithm estimates the head pose in each X, Y, and Z rotation axis by compensating for the error angle.

Table 1 shows our test result by comparing the SVD and EC-SVD based on the Mean Absolute Error (MAE) in degree. It also includes the number of face

Table 1. Mean Absolute Error for test faces (in degree) and selecting face candidates based on the 3D-based nearest neighbor classifier.

Test Images	MAE using SVD	MAE using EC-SVD	Number of Face Candidates
Volker	0.442	0.033	7
Barbara	1.424	0.000	6
Isabelle	0.218	0.003	2
Thomas	0.206	0.009	3

candidates that we select. We can confirm that the EC-SVD algorithm provides an accurate head pose for a wide range of head poses.The error angle is almost perfectly compensated for any head poses when we normalize the NPP to the fixed point on the Z axis. Less than a 2 degree error is resulted from our test results for Z axis and we almost perfectly reconstruct for the X and Y axis, respectively. The proposed EC-SVD algorithm recovers the error angle caused from the SVD method very well, and it can be efficiently applied to pose invariant face recognition.

For 3D face recognition, we test the proposed 3D-based nearest neighbor classifier for selecting face candidates. The Euclidean distance of the input feature is first calculated and then compared with those of 3D faces in the database. We select some face candidates which are within the threshold($\delta = 5$). Among them, we have the Euclidean distance of the matching face in the database with the minimum value, at most 6×10^{-6}. The number of face candidates highly depends on the threshold of the feature distance. As presented in table 1, the proposed 3D-based nearest neighbor classifier adaptively selects the face candidates for the purpose of reducing computation time for depth-based template matching.

To identify an input face, we test our method with 14 persons' head for various head poses. We perform the depth-based template matching for N selected face candidates and final matching results are indicated in table 2. As we can see from the table 2, the SSD of matched face is the minimum value among the face candidates, which explains correct matching for recognition.

Table 2. Face recognition based on the depth-based tenplate matching. (Note: '•' denotes exclusion as a face candidate.)

Test	Face Candidates						
Images	Average	Volker	Thomas	Barbara	Isabelle	Charlie	Julian
Volker	1.47232	**0.00577**	3.98343	4.06863	•	•	4.88611
Thomas	•	3.98343	**0.00078**	3.58796	•	•	•
Barbara	•	4.06864	3.58796	**0.00065**	4.93118	4.15420	•
Isabelle	•	•	•	4.93118	**0.00170**	•	•

Since we have accurate pose estimation results, depth-based template matching becomes effective for recognition. Almost all the input faces are recognized correctly in a first or a second face when the face candidates are sorted by the similar configuration. However, we still have a small database that we have a limit to test our face recognition algorithm. We can evaluate the depth-based template matching in the order of similarity for final recognition with more 3D faces in near future.

6   Conclusions

In this paper, we proposed the robust 3D face recognition method under pose varying environments. We extracted several geometrical 3D facial feature points that lie on the face center line such as the nose peak point, the mouth center, and concave and convex points. In order to cope with the effect of pose varying conditions, we proposed the EC-SVD for the 3D head pose estimation using extracted facial feature points. These feature points also can be utilized in the face recognition step as a method of 3D-based nearest neighbor classifier for selecting face candidates. This procedure is a crucial step, since we can confirm that computational time for the 3D template correlation matching can be reduced by selecting only few face candidates from the database. For final face recognition, we exploited the depth-based template matching.

Based on the experimental results, we obtained accurate 3D head pose estimation results based on the proposed EC-SVD procedure. In addition, our 3D facial feature extraction is automatically performed and assures that geometrically extracted feature points are efficient to estimate the head pose. From the viewpoint of pose invariant face recognition, the final estimation errors of the 3D head pose determination in our proposed method were less than a 0.2 degree in average. In addition, we obtained correctly matching results based on the depth-based template matching for final recognition.

At present, we have 14 faces for database for pose invariant face recognition we need more 3D faces for the database. Therefore, for future research, we investigate for the robust face recognition algorithm with more 3D faces in order to achieve accurate face recognition and also consider illumination invariant face recognition in 3D space.

Acknowledgement. This work was supported by Korea Science and Engineering Foundation (KOSEF) through Biometrics Engineering Research Center (BERC) at Yonsei University. We would like to thank the Max-Planck Institute for Biological Cybernetics for providing some 3D head data.

References

1. R. Chellappa, C.L. Wilson, S. Sirohey: Human and machine recognition of faces: A survey. Proceedings of the IEEE, Vol. 83. (1995) 705–740
2. W. Zhao, R. Chellappa, A. Rosenfeld,P.J. Phllips: Face recognition: A survey. CVL Tech. Report, Center for Automation Research, University of Maryland at College Park (2000)
3. T. Maurer and C. Malsburg: Tracking and learning graphs and pose on image sequences on faces. Proceedings of the Second International Conference on Automatic Face and Gesture Recognition, Vermont, USA, (1996) 176–181
4. T. Horprasert, Y. Yacoob, L.S. Davis: Computing 3-D head orientation from a monocular image sequence. Proceedings of the Second International Conference on Automatic Face and Gesture Recognition, Vermont, USA, (1996) 242–247
5. D. Machin: Real-time facial motion analysis for virtual teleconferencing. Proceedings of the Second International Conference on Automatic Face and Gesture Recognition, Vermont, USA, (1996) 340–344

6. E. Elagin, J. Steffens, and H. Neven: Automatic pose estimation system for human faces based on bunch graph matching technology. Proceedings of the Third International Conference on Automatic Face and Gesture Recognition, Nara, Japan, (1998) 136–141.

7. Q. Chen, H. Wu, T. Fukumoto, and M. Yachida: 3D head pose estimation without feature tracking. Proceedings of the Third International Conference on Automatic Face and Gesture Recognition, Nara, Japan, (1998) 88–93

8. Q. Chen, H. Wu, T. Shioyama, and T. Shimada: Head pose estimation using both color and feature information. Proceedings of the Fifteenth International Conference on Pattern Recognition, Barcelona, Spain, (2000) 2842–2847

9. K. Hattori, S. Matsumori, and Y. Sato: Estimating pose of human face based on symmetry plane using range and intensity images. Proceedings of the Fifteenth International Conference on Pattern Recognition, Brisbane, Australia Vol. 2. (1998) 1183–1187

10. J.C. Lee and E. Milios: Matching range image of human faces. Proceedings of the Third International Conference on Computer Vision, (1990) 722–726

11. H. T. Tanaka, M. Ikeda and H. Chiaki: Curvature-based face surface recognition using spherical correlation. Proceedings of the Third International Conference on Automatic Face and Gesture Recognition, Nara, Japan, (1998) 372–377

12. B. Achermann, X. Jiang, and H. Bunke: Face recognition using range images. International Conference on Virtual Systems and MultiMedia '97 (VSMM '97), Geneva, Switzerland, (1997) 129–136

13. S. Lao, Y. Sumi, M. kawade, and F. Tomita: 3D template matching for pose invariant face recognition using 3D facial model built with isoluminance line based stereo vision. Proceedings of the Fifteenth International Conference on Pattern Recognition, Barcelona, Spain, (2000) 2911–2916

14. C.S. Chua, F. Han, and Y.K. Ho: 3D human face recognition using point signature. Proceedings of the Fourth International Conference on Automatic Face and Gesture Recognition, Grenoble, France, (2000) 233–238

15. T.K Kim, S.C. Kee and S.R. Kim: Real-Time normalization and feature extraction of 3D face data using curvature characteristics. Proceedings of the Tenth IEEE International Workshop on Robot and Human Interactive Communication, Paris, France, (2001) 74–79

16. T. Nagamine, T. Uemura and I. Masuda: 3D facial image analysis for human identification. Proceedings of the International Conference on Pattern Recognition, Amsterdam, Netherlands, (1992) 324–327

17. C. Beumier and M. Acheroy: Automatic 3D face authentication. Image and Vision Computing 18(4) (2000) 315–321

18. B.K.P. Horn, H.M. Hilden, and S. Negahdaripour: Closed-form solution of absolute orientation using orthonormal matrices. J. Optical Soc. Am. 5 (1988) 1127–1135

19. K.S. Arun, T.S. Huang, and S.D. Blostein: Least-squares fitting of two 3D point sets. IEEE Trans. Pattern Analysis and Machine Intelligence, 9 (1987) 698–700

20. R.M. Haralick, H.N. Joo, C.N. Lee, X. Zhuang, V.G. Vaidya, M.B. Kim: Pose estimation from corresponding point data. IEEE Trans. On Systems, Man and Cybernetics 19(6) (1989) 1426–1446

21. T.S. Huang, A.N. Netravali: Motion and structure from feature correspondences: A Review. Proceedings of the IEEE 82(2) (1994) 252–268

An Empirical Study of Multi-mode Biometric Systems Using Face and Fingerprint

H. Kang[1], Y. Han[1], H. Kim[1], W. Choi[2], and Y. Chung[3]

[1] Graduate School of Information Technology & Telecommunication, Inha University
Biometrics Engineering Research Center, Korea
kanghyosup@krpost.net, g1983673@inhavision.inha.ac.kr,
hikim@inha.ac.kr

[2] School of Info. And Control Eng., MyougJi University
hschoi@wh.myongji.ac.kr

[3] Korea University, Dept. of Computer Information Science
ychungy@korea.ac.kr

Abstract. Recent deployments of biometrics application systems have revealed various limitations of the person authentication technology based on a single biometric feature. This paper empirically studies a multi-mode system by integrating face and fingerprint recognition to overcome the limitations of individual single-mode biometric systems and to achieve an increase in performance. This also proposes a framework of the performance evaluation of multiple biometric systems. The multi-mode system has been tested and evaluated by fusion of confidence levels in scenario and operational tests. The results of this research on combining two biometric modalities demonstrate a considerable amount of improvement in EER (Equal Error Rate) and ROC (Receiver Operating Characteristic) curves than single-mode biometric systems.

1 Introduction

As the development in technological cultures of human society, biometrics has been considered as a promising technology for person identification and verification, and In general, the requirements for biometrics as a person identification technology are *universality, uniqueness, permanence,* and *collectability* [1-4][11-12]. However, it has been acknowledged that most of the single-mode biometric systems have their own limitations. Hence, it cannot be said that one person identification technology based on a certain biometric mode is better than another of a different biometric mode because each biometric technology has its own strength and weakness depending on user habits and environmental factors as shown in table 1.

The purpose of this research is to demonstrate the feasibility of improving the performance and availability of biometric technology by integrating face and fingerprint recognition.

In this research, a multi-mode system has been implemented using a fingerprint reader and a web camera, and tested and evaluated by fusing the confidence levels

K. Chae and M. Yung (Eds.): WISA 2003, LNCS 2908, pp. 348–354, 2004.
© Springer-Verlag Berlin Heidelberg 2004

produced from individual recognition systems. The performance of the multi-mode system is represented by EER (Equal Error Rate) and ROC (Receiver Operating Characteristic) curves compared with those of the single-mode biometric system.

The next section introduces multiple biometric technologies and its performance evaluation model. And, the following section describes the experimental procedures and summarizes the results. The last section concludes the work by proposing further studies.

Table 1. Limitations of single-mode biometric systems [2]

Mode	Limitation
Fingerprint	3% of fingerprint are unacceptable
Face	Lighting, Background, Make-up
Voice	Easily variable in body condition
Iris & Retina	Focusing
Signature	Language (Alphabet)

2 Multiple Biometric Systems

In general, multiple biometric systems provide either higher security or better convenience, but not both at the same time. Higher security can be reached by requiring that *all* of the individual single-mode biometric authentication processes must be passed, which may decrease the user convenience by raising FRR. To the contrary, better convenience can be achieved by requiring that *one* or *some* of the individual single-mode biometric authentication processes must be passed, which may decrease the security level by raising FAR.

Figure 1 introduces the five different schemes in multiple biometric systems proposed by Prabhkar and Jain [5-7]. This research focuses on the scheme of the multi-mode system based on the face and the fingerprint recognition. This is the scheme among the multiple biometric systems which is able to increase the system availability by adopting different biometric modes. The multi-mode system implemented in this research integrates a commercial face recognition system with a fingerprint recognition system developed by the authors.

As depicted in figure 2, there are three levels of fusion in combining a multiple biometric system: (a) fusion at the *feature extraction* level, where features extracted using multi sensors are concatenated, (b) fusion at the *confidence* level, where matching scores produced by multiple matchers are combined, and (c) fusion at the *abstract* level, where the accept/reject decisions of multiple systems are consolidated [6].

AND or OR rules are the typical methods of the fusion in the abstract level. Although they are simple and improve either user convenience or security level, they are expected to elevate the overall error rate - the sum of FAR and FRR. For the confidence level, however, either the Bayesian updating rule or the weighted sum can be employed to improve the overall error rate.

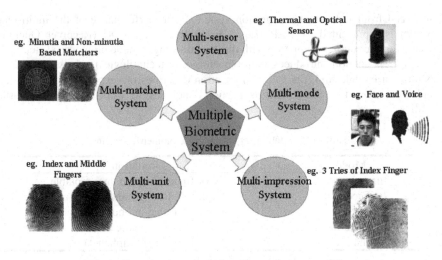

Fig 1. Classification of multiple biometric systems [5]

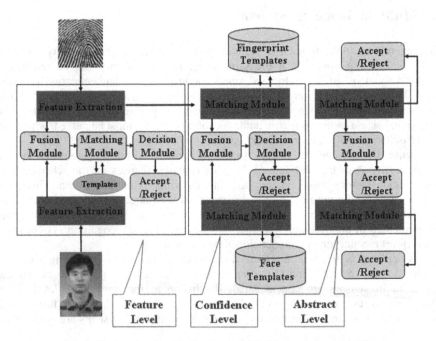

Fig 2. Various levels of fusion for multiple biometric systems [6]

In this study, the weighted sum as defined in equation (1) is applied to combine the individual confidence levels, S_{fi}, S_{fa}, produced by the fingerprint and the face recognition systems, respectively into a merged confidence, S_M. p denotes the weighting factor.

$$S_M = p \cdot S_{fi} + (1-p) \cdot S_{fa} \quad (0 \le p \le 1) \tag{1}$$

The components in performance evaluation of multiple biometric systems are *evaluation mode, evaluation target, evaluation method*, and *database*, and its process consists of five steps as shown in figure 3, determination of evaluation mode and target, selection of evaluation method and indices, construction of database, evaluation, and presentation of results [8-10]. In our framework of evaluating the performance of a multi-mode system, the evaluation target is a face-fingerprint combined multi-mode system, the evaluation method is the weighted sum of confidence levels, and the evaluation index is the EER in the combined score obtained by the weighted sum. Upon the determination of the evaluation target and the method, a database of fingerprint and face images is constructed using the multi-mode system under evaluation.

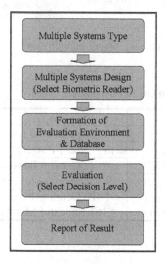

Fig. 3. Process of performance evaluation of multiple biometric systems

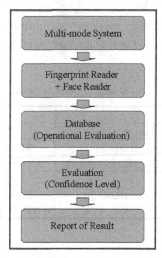

Fig. 4. Process of performance evaluation of a face-fingerprint combined multi-mode systems

3 Experimental Results

The multi-mode system under evaluation consists of a commercial face recognition system and a fingerprint recognition system developed by the authors as show in figure 5. For the face recognition system, a cheap web-camera is used, while a sweeping-type thermal sensor is used for the fingerprint recognition system. The fingerprint recognition system uses a minutiae-based fingerprint matching algorithm based on type and angle information. It consists of three stages, alignment stage, matching stage, and scoring stage[11]. The first experiment is a scenario test, where the multi-mode biometric system is placed in a controlled office environment and the test population consists of only experienced people. The second experiment, however, is an operational test, where the system is placed in an uncontrolled indoor environment and the test population consists of unexperienced people. They are summarized and compared in table 2.

Each test has been operated for several months while recording the matching scores from both the face and the fingerprint recognition systems. Figure 6 shows the score distribution of the first experiment.

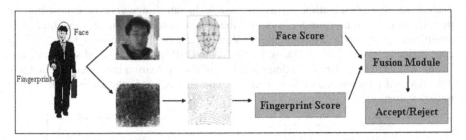

Fig 5. Multi-mode biometric system by combining fingerprint with face

Table 2. Experiment environments of the multi-mode biometric system

	Test 1	Test 2
Test method	Scenario test	Operational test
Test Mode	Multi-mode biometric system (Face + Fingerprint)	
Operating Environment	Controlled illumination	Ambient light
Database	25 Experienced Subjects 3228 Genuine Matching 488 Impostor Matching	59 Unexperienced Subjects 1810 Genuine Matching 361 Impostor Matching

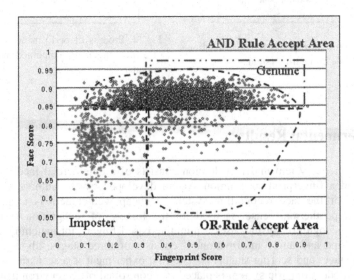

Fig 6. Distribution of scores in a scenario test and AND & OR voting areas

As the results of the experiments shown in figure 7, the EER of the weighted sum of the confidence levels in test 1 has decreased to 1.66% (when p is 0.7) compared to the EER of the fingerprint system, 5.49% (p=0) and the face system's EER 4.88% (p=1). Similarly in test 2, the EER of the combined score has reduced to 5.93% (when p is 0.6) from the fingerprint system's EER 11.04% and the face system's EER 12.85%.

Furthermore, as demonstrated by the ROC curves in figure 8, the multi-mode biometric system always produces lower FMR and FNMR.

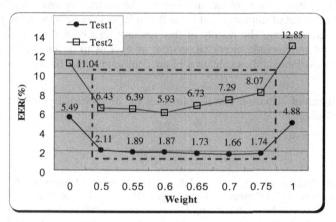

Fig 7. Change in EER according to the change of p

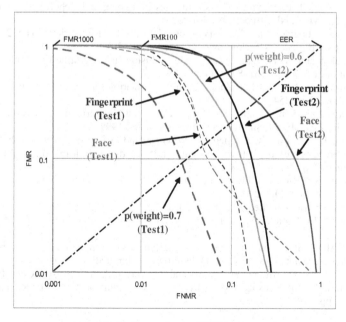

Fig 8. Comparison of ROC curves

4 Conclusions

In this paper, we have proposed a performance evaluation model for multiple biometric systems and carried out the performance testing of a multi-mode system by combining a fingerprint recognition system and a face recognition system. We tested the scenario and operational evaluation. This study tested on real environments which are carefully considering the outbreak situations such as lighting shortage, temperature changes, user habituation, and so on. The results of the experiments to evaluate the performance of a multi-mode biometric system demonstrates a considerable amount of improvement in EER and ROC curve compared to any single-mode biometric system. The results of this research can be utilized to improve the performance of multi-mode biometric system as well as to develop fusion methods. The future works include the evaluation of the combining three biometric systems.

Acknowledgement. This work was supported by Biometrics Engineering Research Center, KOSEF.

References

1. R. Clarke, "Human Identification in Information Systems: Management Challenges and Public Policy Issues," Information Technology & People, vol. 7, no. 4, pp. 6–37, 1994
2. Lin Hong and Anil Jain, "Integrating Faces and Fingerprint for Personal Identification", IEEE Transaction on Pattern Analysis and Machine Intelligence, vol. 19, no 12, December 1998
3. A.J. Mansfiled, J. L. Wayman, "Best Practices in Testing and Reporting Performance of Biometric Device", NPL Report, August 2002
4. Jung Soh, Younglae Bae, "A Survey of Multi-Modal Biometrics", The 2nd Korean Workshop on Biometrics Technology, pp.1–5, January 2002.
5. S. Prabhakar and A. K. Jain, "Decision-level fusion in fingerprint verification", Pattern Recognition, vol. 35, pp.861–874, 2002
6. Arun Ross, Anil Jain and Jian-Zhong Qian, "Information Fusion in Biometrics", AVBPA 2001 Halmstad, pp.354–359, June 2001
7. Lin Hong, Anil Jain, Sharath Pankanti, "Can Multibiometric Improve Performance?", Proceed-ings AutoID'99, Summit, NJ, pp. 59–64, , Oct 1999.
8. D. Mario, D. Maltoni, R. Cappelli, J. Wayman and A.K. Jain, "FVC2002: fingerprint verification competition", Pattern Recognition, Proceedings. 16th International Conference on, Volume: 3, pp. 811–814, 2002
9. BioIS Project, "BIOIS Study Comparative Study of biometric Identification system", Public Final Report, May 2000
10. Hyosup Kang, Bongku Lee, Hakil Kim, Daecheol Shin, and Jaesung Kim, "A Study on Performance Evaluation of Fingerprint Sensors", AVBPA 2003 Surrey, pp.574–584, June 2003
11. Dosung Ahn, "Study on fingerprint recognition algorithm based on cliques asnd its performance evaluation system", Ph D dissertation submitted to Inha University, 2001
12. S. Pan, Y. Gil, D. Moon, Y. Chung and C. Park, "A Memory-Efficient Fingerprint Verification Algorithm using a Multi-Resolution Accumulator Array", ETRI Journal, Vol. 25, No. 3, pp. 179–186, 2003. 6.

Fingerprint-Based Authentication
for USB Token Systems

Daesung Moon[1], Youn Hee Gil[1], Dosung Ahn[1], Sung Bum Pan[1],
Yongwha Chung[2], and Chee Hang Park[1]

[1] Biometrics Technology Research Team, ETRI, Daejeon, Korea
{daesung,yhgil,dosung,sbpan,chpark}@etri.re.kr
[2] Dept of Computer Information Science, Korea University, Korea
ychungy@korea.ac.kr

Abstract. In the modern electronic world, the authentication of a person is an important task in many areas of day-to-day. Using biometrics to authenticate a person's identity has several advantages over the present practices of Personal Identification Numbers (PINs) and passwords. To gain maximum security in the authentication system using biometrics, the computation of the authentication as well as the store of the biometric pattern has to take place in the security token(e.g., smart card, USB token). However, there is an open issue of integrating biometrics into the security token because of its limited resources(processing power and memory space). In this paper, we describe our implementation of the USB token system having 206MHz StrongARM CPU, 16MBytes Flash memory, and 1MBytes RAM. Then, we describe a fingerprint enrollment algorithm that can check false minutiae detected and true minutiae missed by using multiple impressions. Also, to meet the memory space specification and processing power of the security token in fingerprint verification algorithm, we describe a memory-efficient alignment algorithm. Based on experimental results, we confirmed that the RAM requirement of the proposed algorithm is about 16 KBytes, and the Equal Error Rate(EER) is 1.7%. Therefore, our fingerprint authentication algorithm can be executed in real-time on the developed USB token.

1 Introduction

In the modern electronic world, the authentication of a person is an important task in many areas of day-to-day life such as E-commerce and E-business. Using biometrics to authenticate a person's identity has several advantages over the present practices of Personal Identification Numbers (PINs) and passwords [1-7].

In typical biometric authentication systems, the biometric patterns are often stored in a central database. With the central storage of the biometric pattern, there are open issues of misuse of the biometric pattern such as the "Big Brother" problem. To solve these open issues, the database can be decentralized into millions of security token such as smart card, USB token[8-10]. USB token is technologically identical to smart

K. Chae and M. Yung (Eds.): WISA 2003, LNCS 2908, pp. 355–364, 2004.
© Springer-Verlag Berlin Heidelberg 2004

cards, with the exception of the interface to the computer. The smart card requires an additional card reader, whereas the USB token having about the size of a house key is designed to interface with the universal standard bus (USB) ports found on millions of computers and peripheral devices.

Most of the current implementations of USB token using biometrics have a common characteristic that the biometric authentication process is solely accomplished out of the USB token. This system is called Store-on-Token because USB token is used only as a storage device to store the biometric pattern. For example, in a fingerprint-based Store-on-Token, the fingerprint pattern stored in USB token needs to be insecurely released into a host PC to be compared with an input fingerprint pattern.

To heighten the security level, the verification operation needs to be performed by in- USB token processor, not the host PC. This system is called Match-on-Token because the verification operation is executed on USB token. Note that standard PCs on which typical biometric verification systems have been executed have 1GHz CPU and 128MBytes memory. On the contrary, the system specification of the USB token that we have developed is 206MHz CPU, 16MBytes Flash memory, and 1MBytes RAM. Therefore, the typical biometric verification algorithms may not be executed on the USB token successfully.

In this paper, we present a minutiae-based fingerprint authentication algorithm for the Match-on-Token system that can be executed in real-time on the resource-constrained environments. We first develop a fingerprint enrollment algorithm which can check false minutiae detected and true minutiae missed by using multiple impresssions. Then, to meet the processing power and memory space specification of the USB token, we develop a memory-efficient alignment algorithm by using a data structure, called a multi-resolution accumulator array. Based on the experimental results, we confirmed that the memory requirement of the proposed algorithm is about 16KBytes, and the Equal Error Rate(EER) is 1.7%.

The rest of the paper is structured as follows. Section 2 explains structural elements and system specification of our USB token, and Section 3 describes the enrollment algorithm. In Section 4, verification for USB token is explained, and the experimental results are given in Section 5. Finally, conclusions are given in Section 6.

2   USB Token Authenticated by Fingerprint Recognition

The fingerprint authentication system can divide into two phases of enrollment and verification, and the verification algorithm consists of three parts: Image Pre-Processing, Minutiae Extraction and Minutiae Matching. To assign the verification steps to the USB token or the host PC, we evaluate first the resource requirements of each step. Gil et al.[10] reported that the Pre-processing and Extraction steps cannot be executed on the resource-constrained environments such as USB token. Thus, we determined the Minutiae Matching step is executed on the USB token. Especially, the Minutiae Matching step is most important for the security.

Note that the Minutiae Matching step(alignment and matching stages) to compute the similarity between the enrolled minutiae and the input minutiae is executed on the

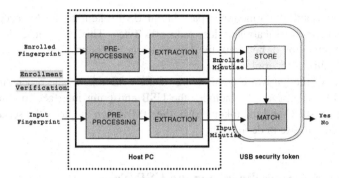

Fig. 1. Fingerprint-based Match-on-Token

Match-on-Token, whereas the Image Pre-Processing and Minutiae Extraction steps are executed on the host PC.

Fig. 1. shows a fingerprint-based Match-on-Token system. In the off-line enrollment phase, an enrolled fingerprint image is preprocessed, and the minutiae are extracted and stored. In the on-line verification phase, the minutiae extracted from an input fingerprint are transferred to the USB token. Then, the similarity between the enrolled minutiae and the input minutiae is examined in the USB token.

Table 1. System Specification of the USB token

CPU	32-bit RISC Processor (StrongARM, 206MHz)
Flash Memory	16 Mbyte
RAM	1 Mbyte
Physical Size	7cm×2cm×1cm

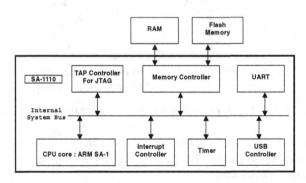

Fig. 2. Architecture of the USB Token

Table 1 shows the system specification of the USB token we developed. The USB token employs 206MHz CPU, 16MBytes Flash memory, and 1MBytes RAM. The size of the USB token is 7cm×2cm×1cm. The reason that we adopt the powerful StrongARM processor[11] is to execute many other applications in real-time such as speaker verification, face verification, and PKI, in addition to fingerprint verification.

Though there is sufficient memory space in our USB token, the RAM space available to the fingerprint verification is less than 50KBytes. This is because the 1MBytes RAM memory should be used by Linux Kernel version Embedded Linux 2.4. (717Kbytes) and other applications.

Fig. 2. shows the hardware architecture of the USB token. The processing core of The Intel SA-1110 processor includes the USB end-point interface to communicate between the host PC and the token. Also, the USB token employs the serial port and JATG interface to use in debugging.

3   Fingerprint Enrollment for the USB Token

As the minutiae-based fingerprint authentication systems rely on the comparison between two minutiae sets, a reliable minutiae extraction algorithm is critical to the performance of the system.

In general, minutiae are detected from the raw image through the preprocessing and extraction stage. However, the extraction stage has some false minutiae detected, and true minutiae missed as well. Thus, performance of a fingerprint authentication system is influenced by three kinds of errors. In particular, if they occur during an enrollment phase and are stored as enrolled template, they will degrade the overall performance significantly, i.e., the falsely detected minutiae will affect the matching phase continuously. Therefore, the falsely detected minutiae need to be discarded and the missed ones need to be compensated prior to be stored as enrolled minutiae.

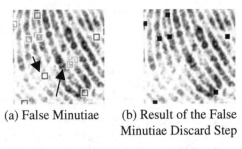

(a) False Minutiae   (b) Result of the False
                           Minutiae Discard Step

Fig. 3. Discard of Falsely Extracted Minutiae.

Fig. 3 illustrates the discard of false minutiae. In Fig. 3(a), false minutiae are pointed out with black arrows. They are neither an ending nor a bifurcation which should not have been detected.

There are couples of reasons of these errors in the extraction stage like miss thinning or noise of fingerprint image itself. However, these can be eliminated based on the fact that they are temporal. A false minutia in one fingerprint image may not be detected from the same position in another image. Therefore, plural fingerprint images are used on the enrollment phase in order to discard the false minutiae. Also, missed one can be compensated using the plural fingerprint images.

Fig. 4 shows the fingerprint-based authentication system using plural fingerprint images during enrollment. Enrolled minutiae are generated from several genuine fingerprint images, which can prevent false minutiae from being stored as enrolled minutiae and true minutiae missed.

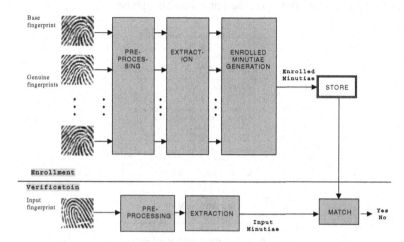

Fig. 4. Fingerprint-based Authentication System using Multiple Impressions.

In our method, the first fingerprint impression acquired is set as a base fingerprint image, and minutiae are extracted from it. After the segmentation of the image, a center of foreground which will be a reference point of the polar coordinate system is found. The last step applied to the base fingerprint image is a transformation into the polar coordinate system. Once Completing the processing with the base image, N genuine fingerprint images are acquired. Minutiae set from each fingerprint image are extracted, and they are aligned with the base fingerprint image. Then, they are converted to the polar coordinate system with respect to the center of the base fingerprint image.

Now, it is examined whether each minutia of the base fingerprint image is a false minutia and any true minutia is missed. For the examination, a similarity between the base minutiae set and each genuine minutiae set is computed. A minutia is regarded as a false minutia if it has not been mated with any minutia during N examinations. And, the points which have not been detected as minutiae on the base image are regarded as true minutiae if they are extracted as minutiae from at least two of the genuine images. The flowchart of the false minutiae discard and missed minutiae compensation algorithm is shown in Fig. 5.

4   Fingerprint Verification for the USB Token

The fingerprint matching stage is composed of two phases: minutiae alignment and point matching. In general, the stored template and the input minutiae cannot be compared directly because of random noise or deformations. The minutiae alignment phase computes the shift and rotation parameters in order to align the two fingerprints. Then, the point matching phase counts the overlapping minutia pairs in the aligned fingerprints. Typically, the minutiae alignment phase requires a lot of memory space and execution time than the point matching phase.

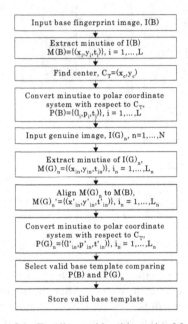

Fig. 5. Flow Chart of the Enrollment Algorithm using Multiple Impressions.

Our alignment algorithm employs an accumulator array in order to compute the shift and rotation parameters[12]. When the two fingerprints are from the same fingerprint. The input to the alignment phase consists of two sets of minutiae points P and Q extracted from fingerprint images[5].

We assume that the second fingerprint image can be obtained by applying a similarity transformation (rotation and translation) to the first image. The second point set Q is then a rotated and translated version of the set P, where points may be shifted by a random noise, some points may be added and some points deleted. The task of fingerprint alignment is to recover this unknown transformation. Since we do not know whether the two fingerprints are the same or not, we try to find the best transformation in the sense.

We discretize the set of all possible transformations, and the matching score is computed for each transformation. The transformation having the maximal matching score is believed to be the correct one. Let's consider a transformation,

$$F_{\theta,\Delta x,\Delta y}\begin{pmatrix} x \\ y \end{pmatrix} = \begin{pmatrix} \cos\theta & \sin\theta \\ -\sin\theta & \cos\theta \end{pmatrix}\begin{pmatrix} x \\ y \end{pmatrix} + \begin{pmatrix} \Delta x \\ \Delta y \end{pmatrix} \tag{1}$$

where θ and $(\Delta x, \Delta y)$ are the rotation and translation parameters, respectively. The space of transformation consists of $(\theta, \Delta x, \Delta y)$, where each parameter is discretized into a finite set of values :

$$\theta \in \{\theta_1, ... \theta_L\}, \; \Delta x \in \{\Delta x_1, ... \Delta x_M\}, \text{ and } \Delta y \in \{\Delta y_1, ... \Delta y_N\},$$

where L, M and N are the allowable range of the parameters.

Matching scores for the transformations are collected in the accumulator array A, where the entry $A(l,m,n)$ counts the evidence for the transformation $F_{\theta, \Delta x, \Delta y}$. For each pair (p,q), where p is a point in the set P and q is a point in the set Q, we find all possible transformations that map p to q. Then, is incremented the evidence for these transformations in the array A.

In this straightforward implementation of the accumulator array A, the requirement memory size is $O(LMN)$. If the numbers of L, M and N are 64, 128 and 128, respectively, the memory size of accumulator array A is 1,048,576 bytes. It can not be executed on the Match-on-Card or Security Token. Therefore, we develop a fingerprint matching algorithm using a multi-resolution accumulator array as shown in Fig. 6.

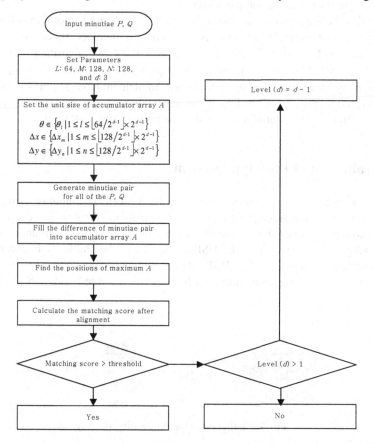

Fig. 6. Flow Chart of the Verification Algorithm using Multi-Resolution Accumulator Array

In the first level with the coarse resolution, considering search range and unit size, find the maximum bin of the accumulator array is found, that is approximate alignment parameter. To obtain more exact alignment parameter using the same memory space, our algorithm iterates the same process with the finer resolution than the first level with the half search range and the half unit size around the positions found in the first level. Finally, in the third level with the finest resolution, quarter search range and quarter unit size, the exact alignment parameter is found.

We can align two fingerprints by selecting the reference minutia pair and getting the difference of position and direction of the selected minutia pair. However, it is difficult to select the reference minutiae pair because fingerprints tend to be deformed irregularly. Therefore, all of the possible minutia pairs of two fingerprints have to be considered. The corresponding minutia pairs usually have the similar difference, and this difference can be used as the shift and rotation parameters in order to align the two fingerprints. The accumulator array is used to find the difference. After computing the difference for the minutia pair, each of the entry of array is increased. At the end of the accumulating processing, the array index with the maximum value is selected as the shift and rotation parameters.

Note that the requirement of memory space of the proposed algorithm is the same at each level. For example, In level 3, the required memory space is 16,384B, (($64/2^{3-1}$)*($128/2^{3-1}$)*($128/2^{3-1}$)). Also, in level 2 and 1, our algorithm uses 16,384B, (($32/2^{2-1}$)*($64/2^{2-1}$)*($64/2^{2-1}$)) and (($16/2^{1-1}$)*($32/2^{1-1}$)*($32/2^{1-1}$)). On the contrary, the memory space of the straightforward implementation requires 1,048,576B. Moreover, the accuracy of our fingerprint verification algorithm is similar to the typical algorithm, because our algorithm takes the unit size 1 in last level.

5   Evaluation of Prototype System

Fig. 7. shows the system environments of our USB token. The input fingerprint image is captured from the fingerprint sensor, and then input minutiae are extracted from input fingerprint image in the host PC. The minutiae extracted from an input fingerprint image are transferred to the USB token. Then, the similarity between the enrolled minutiae that stored in the USB token and the input minutiae is examined in the USB token. Finally, the verification result is transfer again red back to host PC.

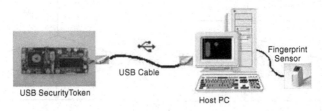

Fig. 7. Configuration of the security token system

We have tested our fingerprint verification algorithm on the fingerprint images captured with an optical scanner manufactured by SecuGen[13], which has resolution of 500dpi. The size of captured fingerprint images was 248×292. The image set is composed of four fingerprint images per one finger from 100 individuals for a total of 400 fingerprint images. When these images were captured, no restrictions on the spatial position and direction of fingers were imposed. Also, the captured fingerprint images vary in quality.

According to the evaluation, the required working memory space of the proposed algorithm is about 16KBytes, and the total number of instruction is about 80MBytes. Thus, it is executable in real-time on the USB token. The straightforward implementation requires about 300KBytes RAM and 20Mbytes instruction, respectively. Also, the EER(Equal Error Rate) of the proposed algorithm was 1.7%.

6 Conclusions

USB token is a model of very secure device, and the biometrics is the promising technology for verification. These two can be combined for many applications to enhance both the security and the convenience. However, typical biometric verification algorithms that have been executed on standard PCs may not be executed in real-time on the resource-constrained environments such as USB token.

In this paper, we have presented a fingerprint enrollment algorithm which can improve the accuracy and a memory-efficient fingerprint verification algorithm which can be executed in real-time on the USB token. To improve the accuracy, we employ multiple impressions to check false minutiae detected and true minutiae missed. Then, to reduce the memory requirement, we employ a small-sized accumulator array. To compute the alignment parameters more accurately, we perform more computations at from a coarse-grain to a fine-grain resolution on the accumulator array. Currently, we are porting memory-efficient speaker and face verification algorithms to the USB token for multi-modal biometric authentication. We believe that such multi-modal algorithms can improve the accuracy of the biometric authentication significantly.

References

[1] A. Jain, R. Bole, and S. Panakanti,: Biometrics: Personal Identification in Networked Society, Kluwer Academic Publishers, (1999)
[2] L. Jain, et al.,: Intelligent Biometric Techniques in Fingerprint and Face Recognition, CRC Press, (1999)
[3] F. Gamble, L. Frye, and D. Grieser,: Real-time Fingerprint Verification System, Applied Optics, Vol. 31, No. 5, pp. 652–655, (1992)
[4] A. Jain, L. Hong, and R. Bolle,: On-line Fingerprint Verification, IEEE Trans. on Pattern Analysis and Machine Intelligence, Vol.19, No.4, pp.302–313, (1997)

[5] N. Ratha, K. Karu, and A. Jain,: A Real-Time Matching System for Large Fingerprint Databases, IEEE Transactions on Pattern Analysis and Machine Intelligence, Vol. 18, No. 8, August (1996)

[6] S. Lim, and K. Lee, : Efficient Iris Recognition through Improvement of Feature Vector and Classifier. ETRI Journal, Vol. 23, No. 2, (2001)

[7] S. Im, et. al.,: A Direction Based Vascular Pattern Extraction Algorithm for Hand Vascular Pattern Verification , ETRI Journal, Vol. 25, No. 2, (2003)

[8] Kingpin,: Attacks on and Countermeasures for USB Hardware Token Devices, Proceedings of the Fifth Nordic Workshop on Secure IT Systems Encouraging Co-operation, Reykjavik, Iceland, pp 35-57, October 12–13. (2000)

[9] M. Janke, FingerCard Project Presentation, http://www.finger-card.org, (2001)

[10] Y. Gil, et. al.,: Performance Analysis of Smart Card-based Fingerprint Recognition for Secure User Authentication, in Proc. of IFIP on E-commerce, E-business, E-government, pp. 87–96, (2001)

[11] Intel, http://www.intel.com.

[12] S. Pan, et. al.,: A Memory-Efficient Fingerprint Verification Algorithm using A Multi-Resolution Accumulator Array, ETRI Journal, Vol. 25, No. 3, June (2003)

[13] SecuGen, http://www.secugen.com.

Iris Recognition System Using Wavelet Packet and Support Vector Machines

Byungjun Son[1], Gyundo Kee[1], Yungcheol Byun[2], and Yillbyung Lee[1]

[1] Division of Computer and Information Engineering, and of BERC,
Yonsei University, 134 Shinchon-dong, Sudaemoon-ku, Seoul, 120-749, Korea,
{sonjun,kigd,yblee}@csai.yonsei.ac.kr,
http://csai.yonsei.ac.kr
[2] Division of Communication & Computer Engineering,
Cheju National University, 66 Jejudaehakno, Jeju-si, Jeju-do, Korea,
ycb@cheju.ac.kr

Abstract. In this paper, iris recognition system using wavelet packet and support vector machines is presented. It specifically uses the multiresolution decomposition of 2-D discrete wavelet packet transform for extracting the unique features from the acquired iris image. This method of feature extraction is well suited to describe the shape of the iris while allowing the algorithm to be translation and rotation invariant. The SVM approach for comparing the similarity between the similar and different irises can be assessed to have the feature's discriminative power. We have showed that the proposed method for human iris recognition gave a way of representing iris patterns in an efficient manner and thus had advantages of saving both time and space. Thanks to the efficiency of the proposed method, it can be easily applied to the real problems.

1 Introduction

Controlling the access to secure areas or transacting electronically through the internet, a reliable personal identification infrastructure is required. Conventional methods of recognizing the identity of a person by using a password or cards are not altogether reliable.

Biometrics measurements such as fingerprints, face, or retinal patterns are common and reliable ways to achieve verification of an individual's identity with a high level of accuracy. It provides a better way for the increased security requirements of our information society than traditional identification methods such as passwords or ID cards.

Since each individual has a unique and robust iris pattern, it has been considered as a good information for the identification of individuals among the various biometrics features. The highly randomized appearance of the iris makes its use as a biometric well recognized. Its suitability as an exceptionally accurate biometric derives from its extremely data-rich physical structure, stability over time, and genetic independence - no two eyes are same [1].

K. Chae and M. Yung (Eds.): WISA 2003, LNCS 2908, pp. 365–379, 2004.

Most of works on personal identification and verification by iris patterns have been done in 1990s, and recent noticeable studies among them include those of [1], [2] and [3].

In this paper we present iris recognition system using wavelet packet and support vector machines. We give the following techniques; an evaluation method for the quality of images in the image acquisition stage to determine whether the given images are appropriate for the subsequent processing or not and then to select the proper ones, a bisection-based Hough transform method in the iris localization stage for detecting the center of the pupil and localizing the iris area from an eye image, and a compact and effective feature extraction method which is based on 2D multiresolution wavelet packet transform. The SVM approach for comparing the similarity between the similar and different irises is presented.

The contents of this paper are as follows. In the following section, some related works are briefly mentioned. Section 3 gives a method of evaluating the quality of an image and iris localization in detail. In section 4, we overview wavelet and explain the application strategy including the method to choose an optimal features set on the selected wavelet transformed subimages. Section 5 describes the SVM-based classification and classifier evaluation techniques. Experimental results and analysis will be stated in section 6, and finally the conclusions are given in section 7.

2   Related Works

Some works on human iris recognition have been found in the literatures [1]-[4]. We will take a brief look at the overall process from some of the representative systems.

Daugman used the circular edge detector to find out the boundaries and developed the feature extraction process based on information from a set of 2-D Gabor filter. He generated a 256-byte code by quantizing the local phase angle according to the outputs of the real and imaginary part of the filtered image, and compared by computing the percentage of mismatched bits between a pair of iris representation via XOR operator and by selecting a separation point in the space of Hamming distance.

On the contrary, the Wildes system exploited the gradient-based Hough transform for localizing the iris area, and made use of Laplacian pyramid constructed with four different resolution levels to generate iris code. It also exploited a normalized correlation based goodness-of-match values and Fisher's linear discriminant for pattern matching. Both of the iris recognition systems made use of bandpass image decompositions to avail multiscale information.

Boles used the knowledge-based edge detector for iris localization, and implemented the system operating the set of 1-D signals composed of normalized iris signatures at a few intermediate resolution levels and obtaining the iris representation of these signals via the zerocrossing of the dyadic wavelet transform. It made use of two dissimilarity functions to compare a new pattern and the reference patterns.

Boles' approaches have the advantage of processing 1-D iris signals rather than 2-D image used in both [1] and [2]. However, [1] and [2] proposed and implemented a whole system for personal identification or verifications including the configuration of image acquisition device, but [3] only focused on the iris representation and matching algorithm without an image acquisition module.

3   Image Acquisition and Preprocessing

3.1   Evaluation of Image Quality

For fully automated systems for recognizing iris patterns to identify a person, it is required to minimize person's intervention in the image acquisition process. One simple way is to acquire a series of images within the specific interval and select the best one among them, but its approach is strongly required to have reasonable computational time for real applications.

In this paper, we propose a method for checking the quality of images to determine whether the given images are appropriate for the subsequent processing or not and then to select the proper ones among them in real time. Some images asserted to inappropriate ones are excluded from the next processing.

The images excluded from the subsequent processing include as follows; the images with the blink(Fig. 1(a)), the images whose the pupil part is not located in the middle thus some parts of the iris area disappear(Fig. 1(b)), the images obscured by eyelids or the shadow of the eyelids(Fig. 1(c)), and the images with severe noises like Fig. 1(d). Fig. 1 shows the examples of images with bad quality, and they can be caused to decrease the recognition rate and the overall system performance if they are excluded by the proposed method.

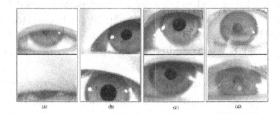

Fig. 1. Examples of images with bad quality: (a)the images with the blink (b)the images whose the pupil part is not located in the middle (c)the images obscured by eyelids or the shadow of the eyelids (d)the images with severe noises

We define some basic cases of the inappropriate images for the recognition and then develop straightforward and efficient sub-modules to deal with each case by considering the pixel distribution and the directional properties of edge only on regions of interest. Each sub-module is combined in parallel and sequential depending on the characteristics of information used in the sub-modules. Our approach has the great potential of extending the functional modules simply by adding the corresponding mechanisms.

The eye image, at first, is divided into $M \times N$ blocks to get the pixel distribution of the specific areas. The process of the quality evaluation consists of three stages by combining three sub-modules sequentially. The first stage is to detect the blink using the information that the intensity of the eyelids is lighter than those of the pupil and the iris. The second stage is related to detect the location of the pupil approximately. The brightness of the pupil area is darker than those of the other areas in the normal cases, accordingly the darkest block around the center of the given image would be the best candidate of the pupil area. After finding out the darkest block, we give the score to other blocks depending on the distance from the center of the image. The third stage is to get the vertical and horizontal edge components using Sobel edge detector to compute the ratio of directional components as the form of score. Just applying the threshold to the sum of the scores obtained from each stage, we can decide the appropriateness of the given image eventually.

3.2   Iris Localization

The iris localization is to detect the iris area between pupil and sclera from an eye image. To find out that area exactly, it is important to precisely detect the inner boundary (between pupil and iris) and the outer boundary(between iris and sclera). At first, we need to get the exact reference point, the center of the pupil, and then compute the distance from that point to the boundaries as the radius.

We propose a three-step technique for detecting the reference point and localizing the iris area from an eye image. In the first step, the Canny edge detector is applied to the image to extract edge components and then the connected components are labeled. The next step is to use a 2D bisection-based Hough transform, not a 2D gradient-based Hough transform [5], to get the center of the pupil. The basic idea of the bisection method is that any line connecting to two points on the circle is bisected the perpendicular line to that line which passes through the center of the circle.

The frequency of each intersecting point among the perpendicular lines formed by two points at a specific distance on the edge components is computed. The most frequently intersected point above a threshold indicates the existence of a circle from the edge components, and the corresponding point can be considered as the center of the circle, the reference point. After detecting the candidate of the center, the radius histogram technique is applied to validate the existence of a circle and calculate its radius.

In order to compute the radius of the tentative circle, the inner boundary, one simple method is to average all of the distance from the center to the points on the connected edge components, but its method is sensitive to noise. Therefore, we propose a new method what we called the maximal frequency determination. The method is to divide the possible range of radius into lots of sub-ranges, and to select a sub-range with the maximal frequency and then determine the median of the corresponding sub-range as the radius. By using this method, we can get the radius less sensitive to noise. After determining the radius, we can easily find the inner boundary using the center of the pupil and the radius. For the outer boundary, the similar process of getting the inner boundary is applied. Finally, the iris area can be localized by separating the part of an image between the inner boundary and the outer boundary.

Fig. 2 shows each stage of the bisection-based Hough transform method.

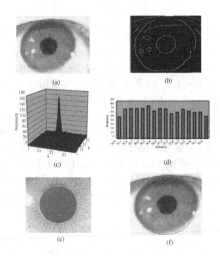

Fig. 2. Each stage of the bisection-based Hough transform: (a)Original image (b)Edge detected image (c)Plot of the frequency of the intersecting points (d)Radius histogram (e)Detected inner boundary (f)Detected outer boundary

4 Feature Extraction

4.1 Wavelet Packet

The hierarchical wavelet functions and its associated scaling functions to decompose the original signal or image into different subbands. The decomposition process is recursively applied to the subbands to generate the next level of the hierarchy. The traditional pyramid-structured wavelet transform decomposes a signal into a set of frequency channels that have narrower bandwidths in the lower frequency region.

However, it may not be suitable for signals that dominant frequency channels are located in the middle frequency region. To analysis signals, the concept of wavelet bases has been generalized to include a library of modulated waveform orthonormal bases, called wavelet packet [6] or simply wavelet packet. Wavelet packet have been shown to be useful for texture classification in the literature [8] possibly due to their finite duration, which provides both frequency and spatial locality. The library of wavelet packet basis functions $\{W_n\}_{n=0}^{\infty}$ can be generated from a given function W_0 as follows:

$$W_{2n}(x) = \sqrt{2} \sum_k h(k) W_n(2x - k)$$

$$W_{2n+1}(x) = \sqrt{2} \sum_k g(x) W_n(2x - k) \tag{1}$$

where the function $W_0(x)$ can be identified with the scaling function ϕ and W_1 with the mother wavelet ψ. Then, the library of wavelet packet bases can be defined to be the collection of orthonormal bases composed of functions of the form $W_n(2^l x - k)$, where $l, k \in Z, n \in N$. The three parameter $\{k, n, j\}$ have physical interpretations of scale, frequency, and position, respectively. Thus each library of wavelet packet bases can be organized as a subset of a full binary tree.

In the case of discrete 2-D signals or images, the wavelet coefficients can be computed in a manner similar to the 1-D case. The 2-D wavelet packet basis functions can be expressed by the product of two 1-D wavelet packet basis functions along the horizontal and vertical directions. The corresponding 2-D filters can be also obtained by the tensor product of the low-pass filter $h(x)$ and the high-pass filter $g(x)$:

$$h_L L(k, l) = h(k)h(l)$$
$$h_L H(k, l) = h(k)g(l)$$
$$h_H L(k, l) = g(k)h(l)$$
$$h_H H(k, l) = g(k)g(l) \tag{2}$$

Fig. 3 (a) shows the full balanced tree of pyramid-structured wavelet decomposition and Fig. 3 (b) shows the 2-level full tree of wavelet packet decomposition applied to an iris image.

The wavelet packet transform is a generalized version of the wavelet transform: it retains not only the low but also the high frequency subband, performing a decomposition upon both at each stage. As a result, the tiling of the time-frequency plane is configurable: the partitioning of the frequency axis may take many forms to suit the needs of the application.

4.2   Wavelet Feature Generation

Aside from the main idea of the algorithm, one can argue about the appropriate choice of the feature set for each node. In order to generate the wavelet features, one can use the statistical properties of the wavelet coefficients for each resolution and orientation. Iris images are two-dimensional signals. Since the pixels of these detail images are the decomposition coefficients of the original image in an

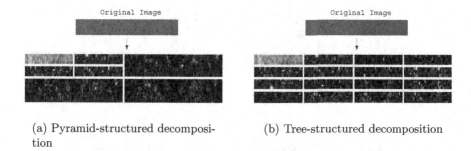

(a) Pyramid-structured decomposi-   (b) Tree-structured decomposition
tion

Fig. 3. Example of a 2-level wavelet transform of the iris image.

orthonormal family, they are not correlated. In practice, for all resolutions and orientations, these histograms are symmetrical peaks centered in zero.

Mallat's experiment [7] suggests that by using wavelet representation, statistics based on first order distribution of grey-levels might be sufficient for preattentive perception of textual difference. Hence we use moments as feature sets, that is, mean, standard deviation coefficients of the subband images.

In this paper, each iris image was decomposed into three levels using Daubechies tap-4 filter which resulted in 12 subimages from pyramid-structured wavelet in 84 subimages from tree-structured wavelet so as to generate feature set. By applying the method of wavelet basis selection, subimages which have high discriminant power are selected. We used the statistical features to represent feature vectors, thus statistical features were computed from each subband image.

Furthermore, we divide the subimages into local windows in order to get robust feature sets against shift, translation and noisy environment (Fig. 4). We extracted first-order statistics features, that is, mean and standard deviation from local windows on the corresponding subimages to represent feature vectors. If the local window is $W(M,N)$, with $1 \leq m \leq M$ and $1 \leq n \leq N$, the moments are

$$\sigma = \sqrt{\frac{1}{MN}\sum_{i=1}^{M}\sum_{j=1}^{N}(W(m,n)-\mu)^2}. \tag{3}$$

The mean extract low spatial-frequency features and the standard deviation can be used to measure local activity in the amplitudes from the local windows.

4.3   Wavelet Feature Selection

Well known in the pattern recognition is the curse of dimensionality, which dictates that classification performance not necessarily increases with an increasing

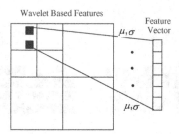

Fig. 4. Arrangement of feature vectors by local windows.

number of features(given a fixed amount of data samples) [9]. Therefore, given a feature extraction scheme and a finite number of training samples , there exists an optimal number of features for a particular task.

First, we proposed the wavelet basis selection method based on recognition rate for each subimages. By applying the proposed method of wavelet basis selection, subimages which have high discriminant power are selected. Fig. 5 presents the recognition rate map of 2-level wavelet packet decomposition using a Daubechies's 4-taps wavelet. We used the statistical features to represent feature vectors. Furthermore, we divide the subimages into local windows in order to get global and local feature from each subimages.

Second, energy map based classification method is compared with the proposed method of wavelet basis selection based on recognition rate. We perform a full wavelet packet decomposition for each class iris and used energy measure as signatures for the coefficients. However, the full wavelet packet decomposition will produce many coefficients and so a large feature set will be obtained. As proposed [10], the most dominant frequency channels obtained from tree-structured wavelet transform are should be applicable. Hence, we can reduce the feature set by means of choosing the signatures with highest energy values as wavelet basis features (as shown in Fig. 6). And the classification process was performed by SVM.

It is important to adopt a feature selection scheme to find a sub-optimal set of features. In this work we shall adopt the Sequential Floating Forward Selection scheme(SFFS) [11], which has recently been found to outperform other selection schemes [12]. This algorithms is initialized by taking the best feature. The term "best" is defined as giving the best recognition performance. The selection then continues by iteratively adding (or deleting) a feature in each step to obtain a subset of all available features which gives the highest classification performance.

After the full tree of wavelet basis functions is selected, to simplify the feature vector, those nodes that do not actively contribute the overall classification performance can be discarded.

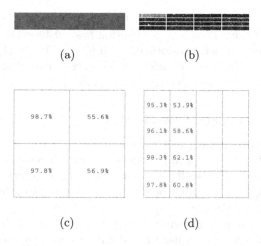

(a)   (b)

98.7%	55.6%
97.8%	56.9%

95.3%	53.9%		
96.1%	58.6%		
98.3%	62.1%		
97.8%	60.8%		

(c)   (d)

Fig. 5. Recognition rate map of 2-level wavelet packet decomposition using a Daubechies's 4-taps wavelet. (a) An iris image. (b) wavelet packet decomposition of (a) 2-level. (c) A recognition table of 1-level subimages. (d) A recognition rate table of 2-level subimages.

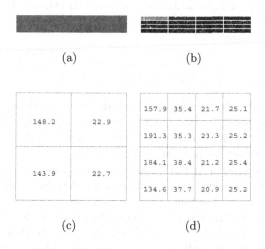

(a)   (b)

148.2	22.9
143.9	22.7

157.9	35.4	21.7	25.1
191.3	35.3	23.3	25.2
184.1	38.4	21.2	25.4
134.6	37.7	20.9	25.2

(c)   (d)

Fig. 6. Energy map of 2-level wavelet packet decomposition using a Daubechies's 4-taps wavelet. (a) An iris image. (b) wavelet packet decomposition of (a) level-2. (c) A energy map of 1-level subimages. (d) A energy map of 2-level subimages.

5   Pattern Matching

Once an appropriate set of iris features is computed, the next step is to adopt a suitable classification algorithm to asses the feature's discriminative power. The process of pattern matching consists of two phases: training and classification.

In the training phase, we construct the registered patterns corresponding to the enrollment process of an iris recognition system based on a set of features obtained from the wavelet transformation on images. In the classification phase, the feature representation of an unknown iris is constructed in order to compare with the registered ones for identifying a person.

5.1 SVM Training and Classification

The main pattern matching method investigated in this paper is SVM. SVM is widely used for variety of applications in pattern recognition nowadays. In the face recognition, especially, these methods have shown good results and performance [13], and also high possibility of applying to other area of pattern recognition such as biometrics [14].

SVM perform pattern recognition for two-class problems by determining the optimal linear decision hyperplane based on the concept of structural risk minimization with maximum distance to closet points of the training set which is called support vectors [15].

5.2 SVM Problems

The SVM is based on Structural Risk Minimization theory. For a set of labelled patterns x, y where x is the observation and y is its interpretation y, we find the optimal approximation

$$f(\mathbf{x}, \alpha) = \mathbf{w} \cdot \mathbf{\Phi}(\mathbf{x}) + b \tag{4}$$

where α represents the parameters of the decision functions, $\mathbf{\Phi}$ is a map from the original data space of $\mathbf{x}$ to a high-dimensional feature space and b is the bias. If the interpretation y only takes values -1 and +1, the learning problem is referred to as Support Vector Classification (SVC) [15].

SVM can be extended to non-linear decision surfaces by using a kernel $K(\cdot, \cdot)$ transformation in case the data is not linearly separable in the input space.

The kernel $K(\mathbf{x}_i, \mathbf{x}_j)$ defines a dot product between the projections of two inputs $\mathbf{x}_i, \mathbf{x}_j$, in a feature space. Therefore the choice of the kernel is very much related to the choice of the "effective" image representation. So we can study different representations of the images through the study of different kernels for SVM.

The mapping $\Phi(\cdot)$ is represented by a kernel function $K(\cdot, \cdot)$ which defines an inner product in Φ. The decision function of the SVM has the form

$$f(\mathbf{x}) = \sum_{i=1}^{l} a_i y_i K(\mathbf{x}_i, \mathbf{x}) \tag{5}$$

where l is the number of data points, and $y_i \in \{-1, 1\}$ is the class label of training point x_j. Coefficients a_i can be found by solving a quadratic programming problem with linear constraints.

The kernel functions used in the experiments are linear, RBF and polynomial defined as

$$K(\mathbf{x}, \mathbf{y}) = \mathbf{x} \cdot \mathbf{y} \tag{6}$$

$$K(\mathbf{x}, \mathbf{y}) = exp(- \parallel \mathbf{x} - \mathbf{y} \parallel /2\sigma^2) \tag{7}$$

$$K(\mathbf{x}, \mathbf{y}) = (1 + \mathbf{x} \cdot \mathbf{y})^d \tag{8}$$

with σ the variance of the RBF and d degree of the polynomial which use the user-controlled parameters.

5.3 Classifier Evaluation

To evaluate the performance of the classifier, one desires to know how well it classifies "unseen" data, i.e., data not used to design the classifier. One approach is to divide all data in a design set used for designing the classifier and a test set used for performance evaluation. This is the hold-out method. The major drawback of this technique is that it reduces the size for both the training and the testing data.

Another problem is to decide how many of the N available data will be allocated to the training set and how many to the test. As an alternative, we have employed the leave-one-out method, which sequentially picks each available data sample and classifiers it (by the SVM) using the remaining samples.

The leave-one-out method can be considered as an extension of the cross-validation method [16]. The basic idea is to split the given samples into $(N - 1)$ samples that serve as training part and into only 1 sample as the holdout part; this process is repeated N times so that all N samples are used as holdout sample. If this is misclassified an error is counted. The total number of errors leads to the estimation of the classification error probability. Thus, training is achieved using, basically, all samples, and at the same time independence between training and test sets is maintained.

The possible advantage of this approach is that all N samples are used both for the training part and the holdout part thus an efficient exploitation of the given N samples is achieved. In particular, for each of the N observed events, the effect of not being observed is simulated by the leave-one-out method.

Suppose that there are c possible classes with N_i feature vectors from the ith class. Each available sample is thus employed once as a test sample. Classifier performance is measured using the error counting approach. The class error rate $\hat{\epsilon}_i$ is defined as:

$$\hat{\epsilon}_i = \frac{\text{number of falsely classified test samples from class i}}{N_i} \tag{9}$$

and the mean error rate $\hat{\epsilon}_i$ as

$$\hat{\epsilon} = \frac{1}{c} \sum_{i=1}^{c} \hat{\epsilon}_i = \frac{\text{total number of falsely classified test samples}}{N} \tag{10}$$

where $N = \Sigma_{i=1}^{i} N_i$ is the total number of samples. This number estimates the percentage of test samples classified correctly and is used as a measure for the performance of the classifier. Whenever we mention "classification performance" we refer to the mean error rate.

6   Experimental Results

6.1   Experimental Environments

Eye images were acquired through CCD camera with LED (Light-Emitting Diode) lamp around lens under indoor light. The size of images is 240 × 320 pixels with 256 grey intensity values, and is composed of 1831 eye data acquired from 120 individuals (left and right eye).

The images of the left and right eye were treated differently from the same person, because they have different patterns. Both males and females were among the data. The ages of all ranges from the early twenties to mid-thirties. In case of individuals with glasses, images are captured both removing their glasses and having their glasses; however, contact lenses remained place.

Table 1. Experimental data configuration.

Gender	Naked Eye	Glasses	Contact Lenses	Total
Male	66	19	0	85
Female	25	5	5	35
Total	91	24	5	120

6.2   SVM-Based Pattern Matching

In identification, there is a gallery $\{g_j\}$ of m known individuals. The algorithm is presented with a unknown identity p to be identified. The first step of the identification algorithm computes a similarity score between the unknown and each of the gallery images. The similar score between p and g_i is

$$\sigma_j = \sum_{i=1}^{N_s} \alpha_i y_i K(\mathbf{s}_i, \mathbf{g}_j - \mathbf{p}) + b. \tag{11}$$

In the second step, the unknown identity is identified as person j that has maximum similarity score σ_j.

In verification, there is a gallery $\{g_j\}$ of m known individuals. The algorithm is presented with a unknown identity p to be identified and a claim to be person j in the gallery. The first step of the verification algorithm computes a similarity score.

$$\sigma = \sum_{i=1}^{N_s} \alpha_i y_i K(\mathbf{s}_i, \mathbf{g}_j - \mathbf{p}) + b. \tag{12}$$

The second step accepts the claim if $\sigma \leq \triangle$. Otherwise, the claim rejected. The value of $\triangle$ is set to meet the desired tradeoff between FAR and FRR.

A set of experiments was performed using SVMs with different kernels(linear, RBF, polynomial) and parameters associated to kernel function were tuned manually. Fig. 8 shows the recognition rates of the four aforementioned methods for the combination of feature vectors, using SVMs with various kernel functions.

The best recognition rate is obtained by combining mean and standard deviation value from local windows of intermediate subbands as feature vectors (number of feature vectors: 46) using SVMs with RBF kernel function. The recognition rate for RBF kernel is 99.1%, polynomial kernel is 98.6%, and for linear kernel is 96.8%.

To compare SVMs with the other similarity measures in terms of the performance, Euclidean Distance, Normalized Euclidean Distance, and Cosine Distance applied [17]. First, the SVMs gives the best performance, the Normalized Euclidean distance the second, the Euclidean distance the third, and the Cosine distance the worst.

As can be seen in Fig. 8, the best recognition rate is obtained by combining mean and standard deviation value from local windows of intermediate subbands as feature vector.

7 Conclusions

In this paper, iris recognition system using wavelet packet and support vector machines is presented. The proposed algorithms are translation, rotation, and scale invariant. It is also insensitive to variations in the lighting conditions and noise levels.

It specifically uses the multiresolution decomposition of 2-D discrete wavelet packet transform for extracting the unique features from the iris acquired iris image. This method of feature extraction is well suited to describe the shape of the iris while allowing the algorithm to be translation and rotation invariant. The SVM approach for comparing the similarity between the similar and different irises can be assessed to have the feature's discriminative power.

We have showed that the proposed method for human iris recognition gave a way of representing iris patterns in an efficient manner and thus had advantages

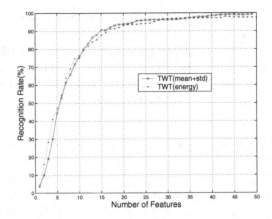

Fig. 7. Comparison of recognition performance as different feature vectors of pyramid-structured wavelet transform.

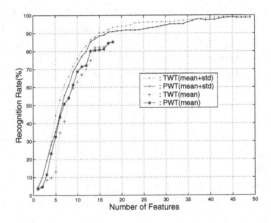

Fig. 8. Comparison of recognition performance as different feature vectors of pyramid-structured and tree-structured wavelet transform.

of saving both time and space. Thanks to the efficiency of the proposed method, it can be easily applied to the real problems. For future works, it is necessary to conduct experiments on a large number of data so as to verify the efficiency and robustness of our approach. Other techniques for feature extraction and identification or verification can be handled from this point of view so as to propose the efficient methods for a reliable human iris recognition system in real problems.

Acknowledgements. This work was supported in part by BERC/KOSEF and in part by Brain Neuroinformatics Program sponsored by KMST.

References

1. John G. Daugman, "High Confidence Visual Recognition of Persons by a Test of Statistical Independence", *IEEE Trans. on Pattern Analysis and Machine Intelligence*, 15(11), pp. 1148–1161, 1993.
2. Wildes, R.P., "Iris Recognition : An Emerging Biometric Technology", *Proc. of the IEEE*, 85(9), pp. 1348–1363, 1997.
3. Boles, W.W., Boashash, B., "A Human Identification Technique Using Images of the Iris and Wavelet Transform", *IEEE Trans. on Signal Processing*, 46(4), pp. 1185–1188, 1998.
4. Williams, G.O., "Iris Recognition Technology", *IEEE Aerospace and Electronics Systems Magazine*, 12(4), pp. 23–29, 1997.
5. Dimitrios, I., Walter, H., and Andrew, F.L., "Circle recognition through a 2D Hough Transform and radius histogramming", *Image and Vision Computing*, 17, pp.15–26, 1999.
6. Coifman, R.R. and Wickerhauser, M.V., "Entropy based algorithms for best base selection," *IEEE Transactions on Information Theory*, vol. 38, pp. 713–718, 1992.
7. Mallat, S.G., "A Theory for Multiresolution Signal Decomposition: The Wavelet Representation", *IEEE Trans. Pattern Recognition and Machine Intelligence*, 11(4), pp.674–693, 1989.
8. Learned, R.E., Karl, W.C., and Willsky, A.S., "Wavelet packet based transient signal classification," *Proceedings of IEEE Conference Time Scale and Time Frequency Analysis*, pp. 109–112, 1992.
9. Jain, A.K., Duin, P.W., and Mao, J., "Statistical pattern reognition: a review," *Proceedings of Internationsl Conference on Image Analysis and Processing*, pp. 376–381, 1999.
10. Chang, T. and Kuo, C.C.J., "Texture analysis and classification with tree structured wavelet transform," *IEEE Transactions on Image Processing*, vol. 2, pp. 429–440, 1993.
11. Pudil, P., Ferri, F.J., Novovicova, J., and Kittler, J., "Floating search methods for feature selection with nonmonotonic criterion functions," *Proceedings of the 12th IAPR International Conference on Computer Vision and Image Processing*, vol. 2, pp. 279–283, 1994.
12. Krim, H., Willinger, W., Juditski, A., and Tse, D., "Introduction To The Special Issue On Multiscale Statistical Signal Analysis And Its Applications." *IEEE Transactions on Information Theory*, vol. 45, pp. 825–827, 1999.
13. Tefas, A., Kotropoulos, C., and Pitas, I., "Using support vector machines to enhance the performance of elastic graph matching for frontal face authentication," *IEEE Transactions on Pattern Analysis and Machine Intelligence*, vol. 23, no. 7, 2001.
14. Yao, Y., Frasconi, P., and Pontil, M., "Fingerprint classification with combinations of support vector machines," *In Proceedings of the third International Conference on Audio- and Video-Based Biometric Person Authentication*, ISSN 0302-9743, pp. 253–258, 2001.
15. Vapnik, V., *Statistical learning theory*, John Wiley Sons, New York, 1998.
16. Ney, H., Essen, U., and Kneser, R., "On the estimation of 'small' probabilities by leaving-one-out," *IEEE Transactions on Pattern Analysis and Machine Intelligence*, Vol. 17, pp. 1202–1212, 1995.
17. Wilson, D.R., and Martinez, T.R., "Improved heterogeneous distance functions", *Journal of Artificial Intelligence Research*, vol. 6, pp.1–34, 1997.

Biometrics Identification and Verification Using Projection-Based Face Recognition System

Hyeonjoon Moon* and Jaihie Kim

Biometrics Engineering Research Center (BERC)
School of Electrical & Electronic Engineering,
Yonsei University, Seoul, 120-749, Korea
hmoon@yonsei.ac.kr

Abstract. Over the last several years, numerous biometrics algorithms have been investigated for face, fingerprints, iris, and voice reocognition applications. For face recognition research, projection-based face recognition system form the basis of numerous algorithms and studies [3]. For biometrics identification and verification scenarios, we explicitly state the design decisions by introducing a generic modular face recognition system. We explored different implementations of preprocessing, feature extraction, and recognition module, and evaluate the different implementations using the FERET evaluation protocol. Our experiment includes changing the illumination normalization procedure, studying effects on algorithm performance of compressing images using JPEG and wavelet compression algorithms, and varying the number of eigenvectors in the representation. We perform series of experiments based on the standard FERET database and report results for identification and verification scenarios.

1 Introduction

In face recognition research, projection-based algorithms has been major interest because of its capability to reduce the dimensionality of a data set while retaining most of the variation present in the data set [1]. Their popularity is due to ease of implementation and their reasonable performance levels. Principal component analysis (PCA) serves as the basis for new face recognition algorithms, benchmark for comparison with new algorithms, and a computational model in psycho-physics. The PCA-based algorithms has been applied in broad spectrum of studies including face detection, face recognition and gender classification.

However, the details of the basic algorithm require a number of design decisions [2].Each of these design decisions has an impact on the overall performance of the algorithm [7]. Some of these design decisions have been explicitly stated in the literature; for example, the similarity measure for comparing two faces. However, a large number of decisions are not mentioned and are passed from

---

* *This work was supported by Korea Science and Engineering Foundation (KOSEF) through Biometrics Engineering Research Center (BERC) at Yonsei University.*

K. Chae and M. Yung (Eds.): WISA 2003, LNCS 2908, pp. 380–394, 2004.

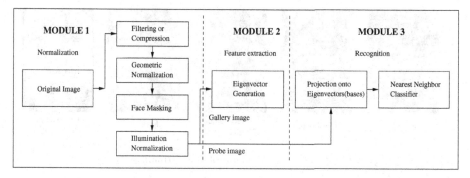

Fig. 1. Block Diagram of PCA-based Face Recognition System

researcher to researcher by word of mouth. For example, illumination normalization and number of eigenfeatures included in the representation [15,9]. Because the design details are not explicitly stated, a reader cannot assess the merits of a particular implementation and the associated claims. Knowledge of the basic strengths and weaknesses of different implementations can provide insight and guidance in developing algorithms that build on PCA [8].

In this paper, we present a generic modular projection-based face recognition system (see Figure 1). Our projection-based face recognition system consists of normalization, PCA feature extraction, and recognition modules. Each module consists of a series of basic steps, where the purpose of each step is fixed. However, we systematically vary the algorithm in each step. The selection of which algorithm is in each step is a design decision. Based on the generic model for PCA-based algorithms, we evaluate different implementations. Because we use a generic model, we can change the implementation in an orderly manner and assess the impact on performance of each modification. We report identification and verification performance scores for each category of probes. We report performance results using top rank score for identification and equal error rate (EER) for verification. The algorithms are evaluated with the FERET evaluation procedure [10,12].

In our experiment, we performed a detailed evaluation of variations in the implementation. By testing on standard galleries and probe sets, the reader can compare the performance of our PCA implementations with the algorithms tested under the FERET program [13]. In this experiment, we vary the illumination normalization procedure and the number of eigenvectors in the representation; and we study the effects of compressing facial images on algorithm performance. The effects of image compression on recognition is of interest in applications where image storage space or image transmission time are critical parameters.

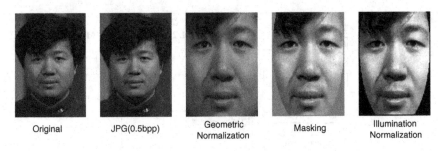

Original   JPG(0.5bpp)   Geometric   Masking   Illumination
                                    Normalization   Normalization

Fig. 2. Input and output images of the normalization module.

2   Projection-Based Face Recognition System

2.1   System Modules

Our face recognition system consists of three modules and each module is composed of a sequence of steps (see Figure 1). The first module normalizes the input image. The goal of normalization is to transform facial images into a standard format that removes variations that can affect recognition performance. This module consists of four steps. Figure 2 shows the input and output of some of the steps in the normalization module. The first step filters or compresses the original image. The image is filtered to remove high frequency noise in the image. An image is compressed to save storage space and reduce transmission time. The second step places the face in a standard geometric position by rotating, scaling, and translating the center of eyes to standard locations. The goal of this step is to remove variations in size, orientation, and location of the face. The third step masks out background pixels, hair, and clothes to remove unnecessary variations which can interfere identification process. The fourth module removes some of the variations in illumination between images. Changes in illumination are critical factors in algorithm performance.

The second module performs the PCA decomposition on the training set. This produces the eigenvectors (eigenfaces) and eigenvalues. We did not vary this module because we use the training set which was used for FERET program for the generation of eigenvectors [11].

The third module identifies the face from a normalized image, and consists of two steps. The first step projects the image onto the eigen representation. The critical parameter in this step is the subset of eigenvectors that represent the face. The second step recognizes faces using a nearest neighbor classifier. The critical design decision in this step is the similarity measure in the classifier. We have explored different algorithms using L1 distance, L2 distance, angle between feature vectors, Mahalanobis distance. Additionally, Mahalanobis distance was combined with L1, L2, and angle between feature vectors mentioned above.

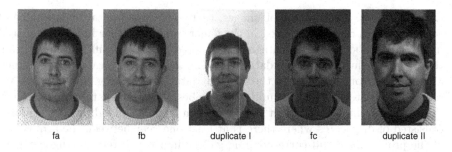

fa   fb   duplicate I   fc   duplicate II

Fig. 3. Category of images (example of variations).

Table 1. Size of galleries and probe sets for different probe categories.

Probe category	duplicate I	duplicate II	**FB**	fc
Gallery size	1196	864	1196	1196
Probe set size	722	234	1195	194

3 Test Design

3.1 Test Sets, Galleries, and Probe Sets

In the FERET database, images of individual were acquired in sets of 5 to 11 images. Each set includes two frontal views (**fa** and **fb**); a different facial expression was requested for the second frontal image. For 200 sets of images, a third frontal image was taken with a different camera and different lighting (**fc**)(see figure 3). The remaining images were collected at six head aspects: right and left profile, right and left quarter profile, and right and left half profile.(The non-frontal images were not used in this study.) One emphasis of the database collection was obtaining images of individuals on different days (duplicate sets). A *duplicate* is defined as an image of a person whose corresponding gallery image was taken on a different date. The database contains 365 duplicate sets of images. For 91 duplicate sets, the time between the first and last sittings was at least 18 months.

The target and query sets are the same for each version. The target set contained 3323 images and the query set 3816 images. All the images in the target set were frontal images. The query set consisted of all the images in the target set plus rotated images and digitally modified images. We designed the digitally modified images to test the effects of illumination and scale. For each query image q_i, an algorithm outputs the similarity measure $s_i(k)$ for all images t_k in the target set. The output for each query image q_i is sorted by the similarity scores $s_i(\cdot)$. Since the target set is a subset of the query set, the test output contains the similarity score between all images in the target set.

To allow for a robust and detailed analysis, we report identification and verification scores for four categories of probes. The first probe category was the **FB** probes. For each set of images, there were two frontal images. One of the images was randomly placed in the gallery, and the other image was placed in the **FB** probe set. (This category is denoted by **FB** to differentiate it from the **fb** images in the FERET database.) The second probe category contained all duplicate frontal images in the FERET database for the gallery images. We refer to this category as the duplicate I probes. The third category was the **fc** (images taken the same day, but with a different camera and lighting). The fourth consisted of duplicates where there is at least one year between the acquisition of the probe image and corresponding gallery image. We refer to this category as the duplicate II probes. The size of the galleries and probe sets for the four probe categories are presented in Table 1. The **FB**, **fc**, and duplicate I galleries are the same. The duplicate II gallery is a subset of the other galleries. None of the faces in the gallery images wore glasses.

3.2   Identification Model

The FERET evaluation protocol was designed to assess the state of the art, advance the state of the art, and point to future directions of research. To succeed at this, the test design must solve the *three bears problem*; the test cannot be too hard or too easy, but has to be just right. If the test is too easy, the testing process becomes an exercise in "tuning" existing algorithms. If the test is too hard, the test is beyond the ability of existing algorithmic techniques. The result from the test are poor and does not allow for an accurate assessment of algorithmic capabilities.

The solution to the three bears problem is through the selection of images in the test set and the testing protocol. Tests are administered using a testing protocol, which states the mechanics of the tests and the manner in which the test will be scored. In face recognition, for example, the protocol states the number of images of each person in the test, how the output from the algorithm is recorded, and how the performance results are reported.

The characteristics and quality of the images are major factors in determining the difficulty of the problem being evaluated. For example, if the faces are in a predetermined position in the images, the problem is different from that for images in which the faces can be located anywhere in the image. In the FERET database, variability was introduced by the inclusion of images taken at different dates and locations. This resulted in changes in lighting, scale, and background.

The testing protocol is based on a set of design principles. Stating the design principle allows one to assess how appropriate the FERET test is for a particular face recognition algorithm. Also, the design principles help in determining if an evaluation methodology for testing algorithm(s) for a particular application is appropriate. Before discussing the design principles, we state the evaluation protocol.

The second design principle is that training is completed prior to the start of the test. This forces each algorithm to have a general representation for faces, not a representation tuned to a specific gallery. Without this condition, virtual galleries would not be possible.

For algorithms to have a general representation for faces, they must be gallery (class) insensitive. Examples are algorithms based on normalized correlation or principal component analysis (PCA). An algorithm is class sensitive if the representation is tuned to a specific gallery. Examples are straight forward implementation of Fisher discriminant analysis [5,14]. Fisher discriminant analysis technique was adapted to class insensitive testing methodologies by Zhao et $al.$ [16,17] with performance results of these extensions being reported in this paper.

The third design rule is that all algorithms tested compute a similarity measure between two facial images; this similarity measure was computed for all pairs of images in the test set. Knowing the similarity score between all pairs of images from the target and query sets allows for the construction of virtual galleries and probe sets.

3.3   Verification Model

In our verification model, a person in image p claims to be the person in image g. The system either accepts or rejects the claim. (If p and g are images of the same person then we write $p \sim g$, otherwise, $p \nsim g$.) Performance of the system is characterized by two performance statistics. The first is the probability of accepting a correct identity; formally, the probability of the algorithm reporting $p \sim g$ when $p \sim g$ is correct. This is referred to as the verification probability, denoted by P_V (also referred to as the hit rate in the signal detection literature). The second is the probability of incorrectly verifying a claim formally, the probability of the algorithm reporting $p \sim g$ when $p \nsim g$. This is called the false-alarm rate and is denoted by P_F.

Verifying the identity of a single person is equivalent to a detection problem where the gallery $G = \{g\}$. The detection problem consists of finding the probes in $p \in P$ such that $p \sim g$.

For a given gallery image g_i and probe p_k, the decision of whether an identity was confirmed or denied was generated from $s_i(k)$. The decisions were made by a $Neyman\text{-}Pearson$ observer. A Neyman-Pearson observer confirms a claim if $s_i(k) \leq c$ and rejects it if $s_i(k) > c$. By the Neyman-Pearson theorem [6], this decision rule maximized the verification rate for a given false alarm rate α. Changing c generated a new P_V and P_F. By varying c from it's minimum to maximum value, we obtained all combinations of P_V and P_F. A plot of all combinations of P_V and P_F is a receiver operating characteristic (ROC) (also known as the relative operating characteristic) [4,6]. The input to the scoring algorithm was $s_i(k)$; thresholding similarity scores, and computing P_V, P_F, and the ROCs was performed by the scoring algorithm.

The above method computed a ROC for an individual. However, we need performance over a population of people. To calculate a ROC over a population, we performed a round robin evaluation procedure for a gallery G. The gallery contained one image per person.

The first step generated a set of partitions of the probe set. For a given $g_i \in G$, the probe set P is divided into two disjoint sets D_i and F_i. The set D_i

consisted of all probes p such that $p \sim g_i$ and F_i consisted of all probes such that $p \not\sim g_i$.

The second step computed the verification and false alarm rates for each gallery image g_i for a given cut-off value c, denoted by $P_V^{c,i}$ and $P_F^{c,i}$, respectively. The verification rate was computed by

$$
P_V^{c,i} = \begin{cases} 0 & \text{if } |D_i| = 0 \\ \frac{|s_i(k) \le c \text{ given } p_k \in D_i|}{|D_i|} & \text{otherwise}, \end{cases}
$$

where $|s_i(k) \le c \text{ given } p \in D_i|$ was the number of probes in D_i such that $s_i(k) \le c$. The false alarm rate is computed by

$$
P_F^{c,i} = \begin{cases} 0 & \text{if } |F_i| = 0 \\ \frac{|s_i(k) \le c \text{ given } p_k \in F_i|}{|F_i|} & \text{otherwise}. \end{cases}
$$

The third step computed the overall verification and false alarm rates, which was a weighted average of $P_V^{c,i}$ and $P_F^{c,i}$. The overall verification and false-alarm rates are denoted by P_V^c and P_F^c, and was computed by

$$
P_V^c = \frac{1}{|G|} \sum_{i=1}^{|G|} \frac{|D_i|}{\frac{1}{|G|} \sum_i |D_i|} P_V^{c,i} = \frac{1}{\sum_i |D_i|} \sum_{i=1}^{|G|} |s_i(k) \le c \text{ given } p_k \in D_i| \cdot P_V^{c,i}
$$

and

$$
P_F^c = \frac{1}{|G|} \sum_{i=1}^{|G|} \frac{|F_i|}{\frac{1}{|G|} \sum_i |F_i|} P_F^{c,i} = \frac{1}{\sum_i |F_i|} \sum_{i=1}^{|G|} |s_i(k) \le c \text{ given } p_k \in F_i| \cdot P_F^{c,i}.
$$

The verification ROC was computed by varying c from $-\infty$ to $+\infty$.

In reporting verification scores, we state the size of the gallery G which was the number of images in the gallery set G and the number of images in the probe set P. All galleries contained one image per person, and probe sets could contain more than one image per person. Probe sets did not necessarily contain an image of everyone in the associated gallery. For each probe p, there existed a gallery image g such that $p \sim g$.

For a given algorithm, the choice of a suitable hit and false alarm rate pair depends on a particular application. However, for performance evaluation and comparison among algorithms, the *equal error rate* (EER) is often quoted. The equal error rate occurs at the threshold c where the incorrect rejection and false alarm rates are equal; that is $1 - P_V^c = P_F^c$ (incorrect rejection rate is one minus the verification rate.) In verification scenario, the lower EER value means better performance result.

4   Experiment

The purpose of our experiment is to examine the effects of changing the steps in our projection-based face recognition system. We do this by establishing a

Table 2. Identification performance results for illumination normalization methods. Performance score are the top rank match.

| | Probe category | | | |
Illumination normalization	duplicate I	duplicate II	**FB** probe	**fc** probe
Baseline	0.35	0.13	0.77	0.26
Original image	0.32	0.11	0.75	0.21
Histogram Eq. only	0.34	0.12	0.77	0.24
$\mu = 0.0$, $\sigma = 1.0$ only	0.33	0.14	0.76	0.25

Table 3. Verification performance results for illumination normalization methods. Performance score are equal error rate (EER).

| | Probe category | | | |
Illumination normalization	duplicate I	duplicate II	**FB** probe	**fc** probe
Baseline	0.24	0.30	0.07	0.13
Original image	0.25	0.31	0.07	0.14
Histogram Eq. only	0.25	0.30	0.07	0.13
$\mu = 0.0$, $\sigma = 1.0$ only	0.25	0.29	0.07	0.14

baseline algorithm and then varying the implementation of selected steps one at a time. Ideally, we would test all possible combination of variations. However, because of the number of combinations, this is not practical and we vary the steps individually.

The baseline algorithm has the following configuration: The images are not filtered or compressed. Geometric normalization consists of rotating, translating, and scaling the images so the center of the eyes are on standard pixels. This is followed by masking the hair and background from the images. In the illumination normalization step, the non-masked facial pixels were normalized by a histogram equalization algorithm. Then, the non-masked facial pixels were transformed so that the mean is equal to 0.0 and standard deviation is equal to 1.0. The geometric normalization and masking steps are not varied in the experiment.

The training set for the PCA consists of 501 images (one image per person), which produces 500 eigenvectors. The training set is not varied in this experiment. In the recognition module, faces are represented by their projection onto the first 200 eigenvectors and the classifier uses the L_1 norm [10].

4.1   Variations in the Normalization Module

Illumination Normalization. We investigated three variations to the illumination normalization step. For the baseline algorithm, the non-masked facial pixels were transformed so that the mean was equal to 0.0 and standard deviation was equal to 1.0 followed by a histogram equalization algorithm. First

Table 4. Identification performance score for low pass filter, JPEG, and wavelet compressed images (0.5 bits/pixel compression). Performance scores are the top rank match.

	Probe category			
Normalization	duplicate I	duplicate II	**FB** probe	**fc** probe
Baseline	0.35	0.13	0.77	0.26
JPEG	0.35	0.13	0.78	0.25
Wavelet	0.36	0.15	0.79	0.25
LPF	0.36	0.15	0.79	0.24

Table 5. Verification performance score for low pass filter, JPEG, and wavelet compressed images (0.5 bits/pixel compression). Performance scores are equal error rate (EER).

	Probe category			
Normalization	duplicate I	duplicate II	**FB** probe	**fc** probe
Baseline	0.24	0.30	0.07	0.13
JPEG	0.24	0.29	0.06	0.13
Wavelet	0.23	0.29	0.07	0.13
LPF	0.23	0.28	0.07	0.13

variation,the non-masked pixels were not normalized (original image). Second variation, the non-masked facial pixels were normalized with a histogram equalization algorithm. Third variation, the non-masked facial pixels were transformed so that the mean was equal to 0.0 and variance equal to 1.0. The identification and verification performance results from the illumination normalization methods are presented in Table 2 and 3.

Image Compression and Filtering. We examined the effects of JPEG and wavelet compression, and low pass filtering (LPF) on recognition. For this experiment, the original images were compressed and then uncompress prior to being feed into the geometric normalization step of the normalization module. For both compression methods, the images were compressed approximately 16:1 (0.5 bits per pixel). We examined other compression ratios and found that performance was comparable. The results are for eigenvectors generated from noncompressed images. We found that performance in this case was slightly better than on eigenvectors trained from compressed images. Because compression algorithms usually low pass filter the images, we decided to examine the effects on performance of low pass filtering the original image. The filter was a 3x3 spatial filter with a center value of 0.2 and the remaining values equal to 0.1. Table 4 and 5 report identification and verification performances for the baseline algorithm, JPEG and wavelet compression, and low pass filtering.

Table 6. Identification performance score with low order eigenvectors removed. Performance scores are the top rank match.

Number of low order	Probe category			
eigenvectors removed	duplicate I	duplicate II	**FB** probe	**fc** probe
0 (Baseline)	0.35	0.13	0.77	0.26
1	0.35	0.15	0.75	0.38
2	0.34	0.14	0.74	0.36
3	0.31	0.14	0.72	0.37

Table 7. Verification performance score with low order eigenvectors removed. Performance scores are equal error rate (EER).

Number of low order	Probe category			
eigenvectors removed	duplicate I	duplicate II	**FB** probe	**fc** probe
0 (Baseline)	0.24	0.30	0.07	0.13
1	0.21	0.23	0.08	0.15
2	0.23	0.25	0.10	0.14
3	0.22	0.23	0.11	0.13

4.2   Variations in the Recognition Module

Number of Low Order Eigenvectors. The higher order eigenvectors which are associated with smaller eigenvalues encode small variations and noise among the images in the training set. One would expect from the exponentially decreasing eigenvalues that the higher order eigenvectors would not contribute to recognition. We examined this hypothesis by computing performance as a function of the number of low order eigenvectors in the representation.

Removing Low Order Eigenvectors. The low-order eigenvectors encode gross differences among the training set. If the low-order eigenvectors encode variations such as lighting changes, then performance may improve by removing the low-order eigenvectors from the representation. We looked at this hypothesis by removing the 1, 2 and 3rd eigenvector from the representation; i.e., the representation consisted of $e_i, \ldots, e_{200}$, $i = 1, 2, 3, 4$. The identification and verification performance results from these variations are given in Tables 6 and 7. Table 7 shows that removing the first three eigenvector resulted in an overall increase in verification performance of duplicate I and duplicate II probes. (b). Because there was a noticeable variation in performance for **fc** probes among different category of probes, we report cumulative match score and ROC for **fc** probes.

4.3   Discussion

We conducted experiments that systematically varied the steps in each module based on our PCA-based face recognition system. The goal belongs to understand the effects on performance scores from these variations. In the normalization module, we varied the illumination normalization and compression steps. The results show that performing an illumination normalization step improves identification performance (see Table 2) but which implementation that is selected is not critical (see Table 3). The results also show that compressing or filtering the images does not significantly effect performance (see Table 4, 5).

In the recognition module, we explored three classes of variations. First, we varied the number of low order eigenvectors in the representation from 50 to 500 by steps of 50. We have learned from our experiment that the performance increases until approximately 150–200 eigenvectors are in the representation and then performance decreases slightly. Representing faces by the first 30–40% of the eigenvectors is consistent with results on other facial image sets that the authors have seen. Second, low order eigenvectors were removed. Table 6 shows that removing the first eigenvector resulted in an overall increase in identification performance. For the identification performance, the largest increase was observed with the **fc** probes. (a). The low order eigenvectors encode the greatest variations among the training set. The most significant difference between the **fc** probes and the gallery images was a change in lighting. If the low order eigenvectors encode lighting differences, then this would explain the substantial increase in performance by removing the first eigenvector. Third, the similarity measure in the nearest neighbor classifier was changed. This variation showed the largest range of identification and verification performance. For duplicate I, duplicate II and **FB** probes, the angle+Mahalanobis distance performed the best. For the **fc** probes, the L_1+Mahalanobis distance performed the best for identification and the angle+Mahalanobis distance performed the best for verification [10]. Because of the range of performance, it is clear that selecting the similarity measure for the classifier is the critical decision in designing a PCA-based face recognition system. However, decision of selecting similarity measure is dependent on the type of images in the galleries and probe sets that the system will process.

For **FB** probes, there is not as sharp a division among classifiers. One possible explanation is that the top match scores for the **FB** probes did not vary as much as the duplicate I scores. There is consistency among the best scores (L_1, L_2+Mahalanobis, and angle+Mahalanobis). The remaining classifiers' performances can be grouped together. The performance scores of these classifiers are within each other's error margins. We defined *error margins* as a robust range of performance scores. This suggests that either the L_1, L_2+Mahalanobis, or angle+Mahalanobis distance should be used.

5   Conclusion

The main goal of our experiment is to point out the directions for optimal configuration of PCA-based face recognition system. We introduced a modular

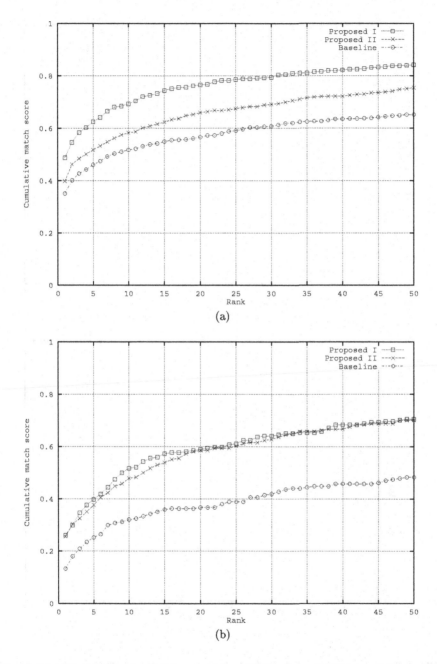

Fig. 4. Identification performance comparison of Baseline and Proposed I ($\mu = 0.0$ and $\sigma = 1.0$, LPF, first low order eigenvector removed, angle+Mahalanobis distance), and Proposed II ($\mu = 0.0$ and $\sigma = 1.0$, Wavelet [0.5bpp], first low order eigenvector removed, L1+Mahalanobis distance) algorithms. (a) duplicate I probes and (b) duplicate II probes.

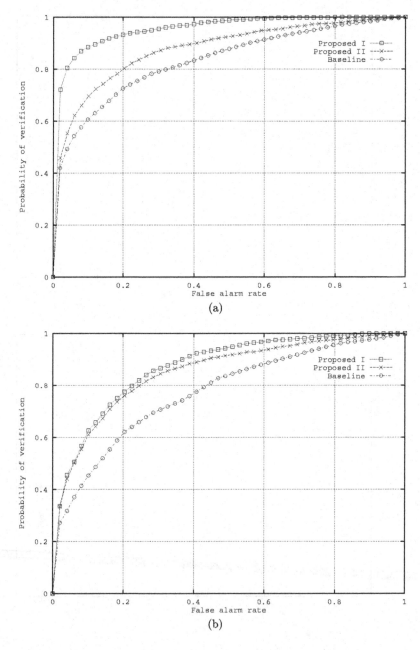

Fig. 5. Verification performance comparison of Baseline and Proposed I ($\mu = 0.0$ and $\sigma = 1.0$, LPF, first low order eigenvector removed, angle+Mahalanobis distance), and Proposed II ($\mu = 0.0$ and $\sigma = 1.0$, Wavelet [0.5bpp], first low order eigenvector removed, L1+Mahalanobis distance) algorithms. (a) duplicate I probes and (b) duplicate II probes.

design for PCA-based face recognition systems. This allowed us to systematically vary the components and measure the impact of these variations on performance. From the results throughout the series of experiments, we present two models for PCA-based face recognition system. In proposed models, our design decision includes processing steps with better performance in each module.

The choice of steps used in Proposed I system includes: (1) illumination normalization ($\mu = 0.0$ and $\sigma = 1.0$), (2) Low-pass filtering (LPF), (3) remove first low order eigenvector, and (4) angle+Mahalanobis distance. The choice of steps used in Proposed II system includes: (1) illumination normalization ($\mu = 0.0$ and $\sigma = 1.0$), (2) wavelet compression [0.5 bpp], (3) remove first low order eigenvector, and (4) L_1+Mahalanobis distance. Proposed I system addresses the effects of LPF with angle+Mahalanobis distance while Proposed II system represents wavelet compression with L_1+Mahalanobis distance.

In Figure 4, the identification results are reported for duplicate I and duplicate II probes. The identification performance score for duplicate I probe is increased from 0.35 to 0.49 for Proposed I method, and duplicate II probe from 0.13 to 0.26 for both Proposed I and II method (top rank score). The identification performance score for **FB** probe is slightly increased from 0.77 to 0.78 for both Proposed I and II methods, and **fc** probe from 0.26 to 0.33 for Proposed II method (top rank score). In Figure 5, the verification performances are reported for duplicate I and duplicate II probes. The verification performance for duplicate I probe is improved from 0.24 to 0.11 for Proposed I method, and duplicate II probe improved from 0.30 to 0.21 for Proposed I method (equal error rate). The verification performance score for **FB** probe shows same results for all three methods, and **fc** probe improved from 0.13 to 0.10 for Proposed II method (equal error rate). Based on these results, the proposed algorithms show reasonably better performance for duplicate I, duplicate II (for Proposed I method) and **fc** probes (for Proposed II method) than the baseline algorithm in both identification and verification scenarios. For **FB** probes, both identification and verification results show almost identical performance scores for each method used.

From the series of experiments with optimal configuration of projection-based face recognition system, we have come to three major conclusions. First, JPEG and wavelet compression algorithms do not degrade performance. This is important because it indicates that compressing images to save transmission time and storage costs will not reduce algorithm performance. Second, selection of the nearest neighbor classifier is the critical design decision in designing a PCA-based algorithm. The proper selection of nearest neighbor classifier is essential to improve performance scores. Furthermore, our experiments shows similarity measures that achieve the best performance are not generally considered in the literature. Third, the performance scores vary among the probe categories, and that the design of an algorithm need to consider the type of images that the algorithm will process. The **FB** and duplicate I probes are least sensitive to system design decisions, while **fc** and duplicate II probes are the most sensitive.

We introduced a modular design for PCA-based face recognition systems. This allowed us to systematically vary the steps and measure the impact of these variations on performance. Like PCA, the majority of the face recognition algorithms in the literature are projection-based and have the same basic architecture as our PCA-based system. By following the evaluation procedure presented in this paper, an algorithm designers can determine the optimal configuration of their face recognition system.

References

1. R. Brunelli and T. Poggio. Face recognition: Features versus templates. *IEEE Trans. PAMI*, 15(10), 1993.
2. R. Chellappa, C. L. Wilson, and S. Sirohey. Human and machine recognition of face: A survey. *Proceedings of the IEEE*, 83:704–740, 1995.
3. J. Daugman. High confidence visual recognition of persons by a test of statistical independence. *IEEE Trans. PAMI*, 15(11):1148–1161, 1993.
4. J. P. Egan. *Signal Detection Theory and ROC Analysis*. Academic Press, 1975.
5. K. Etemad and R. Chellappa. Discriminant analysis for recognition of human face images. *J. Opt. Soc. Am. A*, 14:1724–1733, August 1997.
6. D. Green and J. Swets. *Signal Detection Theory and Psychophysics*. John Wiley & Sons Ltd., 1966.
7. S. Gutta, J. Huang, D. Singh, I. Shah, B. Takacs, and H. Wechsler. Benchmark studies on face recognition. In M. Bichsel, editor, *International Workshop on Automatic Face and Gesture Recognition*, pages 227–231, 1995.
8. I. T. Jolliffe. *Principal Component Analysis*. Springer-Verlag, 1986.
9. M. Kirby and L. Sirovich. Application of the karhunen-loeve procedure for the characterization of human faces. *IEEE Trans. PAMI*, 12(1), 1990.
10. H. Moon and P. J. Phillips. Analysis of PCA-based face recognition algorithms. In K. W. Bowyer and P. J. Phillips, editors, *Empirical Evaluation Techniques in Computer Vision*. IEEE Computer Society Press, Los Alamitos, CA, 1998.
11. P. J. Phillips, H. Moon, P. Rauss, and S. Rizvi. The FERET evaluation methodology for face-recognition algorithms. In *Proceedings Computer Vision and Pattern Recognition 97*, pages 137–143, 1997.
12. P. J. Phillips, H. Moon, S. Rizvi, and P. Rauss. The FERET evaluation. In P. J. Phillips, V. Bruce, F. Fogelman Soulie, and T. S. Huang, editors, *Face Recognition: From Theory to Applications*. Springer-Verlag, Berlin, 1998.
13. P. J. Phillips, P. Rauss, and S. Der. FERET (face recognition technology) recognition algorithm development and test report. Technical Report ARL-TR-995, U.S. Army Research Laboratory, 1996.
14. D. Swets and J. Weng. Using discriminant eigenfeatures for image retrieval. *IEEE Trans. PAMI*, 18(8):831–836, 1996.
15. M. Turk and A. Pentland. Eigenfaces for recognition. *J. Cognitive Neuroscience*, 3(1):71–86, 1991.
16. W. Zhao, R. Chellappa, and A. Krishnaswamy. Discriminant analysis of principal components for face recognition. In *3rd International Conference on Automatic Face and Gesture Recognition*, pages 336–341, 1998.
17. W. Zhao, A. Krishnaswamy, R. Chellappa, D. Swets, and J. Weng. Discriminant analysis of principal components for face recognition. In P. J. Phillips, V. Bruce, F. Fogelman Soulie, and T. S. Huang, editors, *Face Recognition: From Theory to Applications*. Springer-Verlag, Berlin, 1998.

Visualization of Dynamic Characteristics in Two-Dimensional Time Series Patterns: An Application to Online Signature Verification

Suyoung Chi[1], Jaeyeon Lee[1], Jung Soh[1], Dohyung Kim[1],
Weongeun Oh[1], and Changhun Kim[2]

[1] Computer & Software Technology Laboratory, ETRI
161 Gajeong-dong, Yuseong-gu, Daejeon, 305-350, KOREA
{chisy,leejy,soh,dhkim008,owg}@etri.re.kr
http://www.etri.re.kr
[2] Korea University, 5-Ka, Anam-dong Sungbuk-ku, Seoul,136-701, Korea
{chkim}@korea.ac.kr

Abstract. An analysis model for the dynamics information of two-dimensional time-series patterns is described. In the proposed model, two novel transforms that visualize the dynamic characteristics are proposed. The first transform, referred to as speed equalization, reproduces a time-series pattern assuming a constant linear velocity to effectively model the temporal characteristics of the signing process. The second transform, referred to as velocity transform, maps the signal onto a horizontal vs. vertical velocity plane where the variation of the velocities over time is represented as a visible shape. With the transforms, the dynamic characteristics in the original signing process are reflected in the shape of the transformed patterns. An analysis in the context of these shapes then naturally results in an effective analysis of the dynamic characteristics. The proposed transform technique is applied to an online signature verification problem for evaluation. Experimenting on a large signature database, the performance evaluated in EER(Equal Error Rate) was improved to 1.17% compared to 1.93% of the traditional signature verification algorithm in which no transformed patterns are utilized. In the case of skilled forgery experiments, the improvement was more outstanding; it was demonstrated that the parameter set extracted from the transformed patterns was more discriminative in rejecting forgeries

1 Introduction

In analyzing two-dimensional time series patterns such as gestures, handwritten characters or signatures, dynamic characteristics often play an important role. Especially in signature verification problems, dynamics information is considered integral in providing security against skilled forgery [1,2]. First, in the context of shape, a sample generated by a skilled forger is almost indistinguishable from an authentic source. Furthermore, the signature patterns are often exposed to the public giving ideas to the

K. Chae and M. Yung (Eds.): WISA 2003, LNCS 2908, pp. 395–409, 2004.

potential forgers, while the signing process itself, thus the dynamics information of the signatures is generally out of their reach.

However, in the reported literatures, often the emphasis is on the analysis of the finalized shapes, referring to the dynamic properties only in the form of simple parameters such as average velocity, average acceleration, etc [2,3]. Of course, this is partially due to the importance of shape in recognizing signature patterns, but a lack of effective analysis models for the dynamic characteristics is also responsible. The signature is one of the oldest authentication means in human history. Unlike fingerprints, another traditional authentication means, signatures are free from the nuance of criminality. Furthermore, signatures are a widely accepted form of authentication in social, cultural and legal aspects [7]. With these advantages, the signature is one of the most promising biometric features and many researches have focused on this subject [8,9,10].

The signature is classified as a behavioral biometric feature compared to physiological features such as face, fingerprints and/or iris [7,11,12]. This means the risk of intentional imitation should be considered seriously in the development of practical systems. In signature verification, forgeries are often classified into the following three types [13].

1.   random forgery: where the forger uses his/her own signature instead of the signature supposed to be tested.
2.   simple forgery: where the forger does not make any effort to simulate a genuine signature but has access to the name of the author.
3.   skilled forgery: where the forger tries to simulate a genuine signature as closely as possible to the original.

On the contrary, forgers generally have difficulty in imitating the dynamic characteristics at the same time; thus dynamics information still preserves its discriminative ability [1]. Signature dynamics has been considered as a biometric feature for its dynamics information arising from the involuntary behavior of the author. Even in an offline case where no dynamics information is available, it is known that the key to discriminate an individual is peculiarities caused by involuntary motions rather than overall shape characteristics [16].

In signal analysis or the pattern recognition arena, it is a common practice to transform the original signal to another form to investigate a certain property more effectively. For instance, the well-known FFT transforms the signal into the frequency domain revealing many useful characteristics in respect of signal frequency that were ambiguous in the original signal [4]. Likewise, a proper transform can be an effective tool for the analysis of dynamic characteristics in time series patterns. In this paper, two novel transforms that visualize the dynamic characteristics of two-dimensional time-series patterns are proposed. With the transforms, dynamic characteristics of the original signal are reflected to the transformed patterns; thus analyzing them with traditional shape analysis tools naturally results in the analysis of dynamic characteristics. These transforms are applied to an online signature verification problem to evaluate the effectiveness of the approach.

The first transform, which we refer to as speed equalization, is a reproduction of the pattern assuming a constant linear velocity. That is, the transformed pattern shows how the pattern would look like if the signer wrote it with constant velocity. Naturally, the pattern is distorted reflecting the dynamic characteristics of the signing process. The sections where original linear velocities were high shorten, while those with low linear velocities lengthen. After the transform, two patterns with similar shapes may result in completely different patterns in the transformed domain if their dynamic properties were different, providing an excellent basis for discriminating them.

The second transform, referred to as velocity transform, is more straightforward. At each sample point, the first derivative of the point sequence is calculated and is drawn on the v_x versus v_y plane, where v_x and v_y are the horizontal and vertical velocities respectively. Naturally, the transformed pattern shows how the signing process changes as time evolves.

The virtue of the proposed transforms is that the transformed results are represented by completely the same format as the original pattern. Thus virtually every analysis techniques developed to analyze the original pattern can be applied, providing an effective analysis model for dynamic characteristics of two dimensional time series patterns.

2 Speed Equalization

Humans tend to adjust their signatures to given forms, resulting in a large variance in size and aspect ratio. These variances create many differences in the resulting patterns. Many relevant features such as velocity, length of the loci and relative directions are influenced. Most algorithms suggest normalization to compensate for these variances [1,2,5].

However, in spite of the variances, the signing process is not so variable in the temporal domain. Fig. 1 shows an example of signature patterns. In the figure, thick lines represent the loci when an electronic pen was in contact with the tablet, while thin lines represent the loci when the pen was in the air. The dots in the figure are drawn every 0.5 seconds along the signing process. The width and height of the signature shown in Fig. 1(a) are about 2.2 times larger than those of Fig. 1(b). However, as indicated in the figure, the signing time is almost identical. Furthermore, in spite of the huge difference in size, the dotted positions are similar relative to the whole pattern. The observations imply that the involuntary ballistic motion of human muscles that generates a signature pattern is more consistent in the temporal domain than in the spatial domain.

Signing Time	2.670 seconds
Width	1,036 pixels
Height	544 pixels

Signing Time	2.607 seconds
Width	455pixels
Height	256 pixels

Fig. 1. (a) A Signature on a Large Form. (b) A Signature on a Small Form

Speed equalization is a transform to reflect the temporal characteristics of the signing process to the pattern. Speed equalization is a reproduction of the signing process assuming constant linear velocity. By assuming constant linear velocity, the length of the loci corresponds to the time taken to draw that pattern, thus effectively modeling temporal information.

A two-dimensional time series pattern C is generally represented by a series of points whose attributes are x, y coordinates and sampled time. Here, time attributes can be omitted without losing generality by assuming a constant sampling interval, resulting in the following representation of the curve C.

$$C = \{ \mathbf{p}_1, \mathbf{p}_2, ..., \mathbf{p}_N \} \tag{1}$$

where $\mathbf{p}_i$ is a two-dimensional vector of x, y coordinates that are denoted as $p_i(x)$ and $p_i(y)$, respectively.

For obtaining velocity at each point, the first derivative of the sequence is calculated by the following equation for horizontal and vertical directions [6].

$$v_x = (- p_{i+2}(x) + 8 \bullet p_{i+1}(x) - 8 \bullet p_{i-1}(x) + p_{i-2}(x)) / 12 \tag{2}$$

$$v_y = (- p_{i+2}(y) + 8 \bullet p_{i+1}(y) - 8 \bullet p_{i-1}(y) + p_{i-2}(y)) / 12 \tag{3}$$

Then the direction of loci at the point is defined as follows.

$$\theta = \arctan(\frac{v_y}{v_x}) \tag{4}$$

With the above notations, speed equalization is defined as a transform from a two-dimensional point sequence C=$\{ \mathbf{p}_1, \mathbf{p}_2, ..., \mathbf{p}_N \}$ to another two-dimensional point sequence S=$\{ \mathbf{s}_1, \mathbf{s}_2, ..., \mathbf{s}_N \}$ of the following.

$$\begin{cases} s_i = \mathbf{p}_i & i = 1,2 \\ s_i = s_{i-1} + (\mathbf{p}_i - \mathbf{p}_{i-1}) & i = N-1, N \\ s_i = s_{i-1} + v \bullet \Delta t \bullet \Theta & otherwise \end{cases} \tag{5}$$

where, v: constant velocity
Δt: time interval between points
Θ: Unit Vector in direction θ of eq. 4)

The first two equations of the above are for handling the exceptional cases at the head and the tail of the sequence for which the derivative cannot be calculated by equations (2) and (3). The remaining points are sequentially transformed by the third equation to generate a speed equalized pattern. In the formula, v and Δt are constants as it is assumed that each point is determined by the previous point and Θ.

Fig. 2 shows speed equalized patterns of Fig. 1. Though the sizes of the original patterns were remarkably different, they are very similar to each other in the transformed domain even in the context of size. On the other hand, Fig. 3 shows two patterns created by a skilled forger, which are very similar to the genuine ones in terms of shapes. But in the transformed domain (Fig. 4), the patterns are completely different from those of Fig. 2. Even Fig. 4(a) and Fig. 4(b) are quite different from each other, indicating they have different dynamic characteristics.

Width	297 pixels
Height	280 pixels

Width	256pixels
Height	240 pixels

Fig. 2. Speed Equalization: (a) Transformed Pattern of Fig. 1 (a), (b) Transformed Pattern of Fig. 1(b)

Fig. 3. Skilled Forgery Samples

All these examples demonstrate that the difference in dynamic characteristics is mapped to the difference in shape in the transformed domain. In the context of a signature verification problem in which the authenticity of the test pattern is determined by the dynamic characteristics to a large extent, the transformed patterns provide an excellent basis to distinguish a skilled forgery (with very similar shapes, but generally with different dynamic characteristics) from an authentic sample.

(a)   (b)

Fig. 4. Speed Equalization on the Skilled Forgery Samples. (a) Transformed Pattern of Fig. 3 (a), (b) Transformed Pattern of Fig. 3(b)

3 Velocity Transform

Velocity transform is another transform that visualizes the dynamic characteristics of the signing process by transforming the point series at the spatial domain to the velocity domain. Given a point sequence $C=\{\mathbf{p_1}, \mathbf{p_2},..., \mathbf{p_N}\}$, the velocities at each point then constitute another two-dimensional vector list $V=\{\mathbf{v_1}, \mathbf{v_2},..., \mathbf{v_N}\}$, where $\mathbf{v_i}$ is a two-dimensional vector whose components are horizontal and vertical velocities v_x and v_y of equations (2) and (3) at the point $\mathbf{p_i}$. At the head and tail of the sequence where equations (2) and (3) cannot be applied, the nearest available value is assigned. That is, $\mathbf{v_1}=\mathbf{v_2}=\mathbf{v_3}$ and $\mathbf{v_N}=\mathbf{v_{N-1}}=\mathbf{v_{N-2}}$, where $\mathbf{v_3}$ and $\mathbf{v_{N-2}}$ can be calculated by the equations.

Unlike speed equalization, the velocity transform is influenced by scale. To compensate for this factor, the original pattern is normalized so that the height of the resulting pattern is equal to a predetermined constant before the transform is applied. Also, for the elimination of noisy factors, a low pass filter applied after the transform.

The transformed sequence V represents dynamics information of the signing process in its shape. For instance, the width of the sequence V shows how much the horizontal velocity changes, the center of gravity for the pattern corresponds to the average velocity, and so on.

Fig. 5 shows velocity transformed patterns for the patterns of Fig. 1 while Fig. 6 shows those transformed from Fig. 3. Comparing Fig. 5 to Fig. 6 the size and the overall characteristics of the patterns are quite different though their original patterns were very similar. These differences in the transformed domain make the task of discrimination far easier.

(a)   (b)

Fig. 5. Velocity Transform : (a)Transformed Pattern of Fig. 1(a), (b)Transformed Pattern of Fig. 1(a)

(a)   (b)

Fig. 6. Velocity Transform on the Skilled Forgery Samples: (a)Transformed Pattern of Fig. 3(a), (b)Transformed Pattern of Fig. 3(a)

4   Application to Signature Verification Problem

4.1   Signature Verification Algorithm

Signature verification algorithms are typically classified into two types [8]. The first, often called the global parametric approach, represents a signature pattern by a set of parameters and compares the parameter sets to determine whether the test pattern is genuine. On the contrary, the functional approach represents a signature as a function of time and compares the functions to make a decision regarding the veracity of the signature.

Though each approach has strengths and drawbacks in the respects of stability and discriminative ability, we adopted the global parametric algorithm as an evaluation model. The reason for this selection is chiefly simplicity of implementation. But more importantly, the clear distinction of static and dynamic parameters in this model is essential for a proper evaluation of effectiveness in the context of dynamic characteristics analysis. Through this evaluation, we should verify if better performance is achieved compared to the traditional methods that use only the original pattern. Evaluation of security against skilled forgery is another important checkpoint.

When a signature pattern is given, the feature extraction module extracts a predetermined feature vector $\mathbf{F}_T$, and this is compared with the enrolled template $\mathbf{F}_E$ to generate the difference vector $\mathbf{F}_D$. The classifier then decides whether $\mathbf{F}_D$ belongs to the genuine class.

In designing an algorithm for this model, two decisions should be made. One is the selection of parameters and the other is the decision strategy based on the evaluated similarity or difference of the parameters [2]. The latter problem is a two-class classification of the difference vector $\mathbf{F}_D$. Here, a neural network of a back error propagation model is adopted for its simplicity in implementation and with consideration of its reputation as a good classifier for problems of this nature [17].

The former problem requires more careful attention. The selection of the feature determines the nature of the verification algorithm. For instance, if we select static parameters only, the algorithm may not reflect the dynamic characteristics properly though it may be sensitive in context of shapes, and vice versa. Here, the purpose of this paper is to evaluate the effectiveness of the proposed transform techniques rather than to develop a good signature verification algorithm. In this respect, we constructed several verification models with different combination of parameter sets.

Thus far, the global parametric approach has been investigated with great enthusiasm and hundreds of parameters of static and dynamic nature have been proposed and claimed to be effective [18]. From the huge candidate list found in the literatures, the parameter pool listed in Table 1 is selected considering a balance between static and dynamic parameters.

In the literatures [2,3,19]. most of the listed parameters are described in detail, but the final parameter 'radial histogram' is new and as such requires a brief explanation. The radial histogram is a radial distribution of the sampling points. The origin of the Cartesian coordinates is the center of gravity of the pattern, and the space is divided as shown in the figure. The sampling points belonging to each region are counted to construct the radial histogram, which is then normalized by the total number of sampling points in the whole pattern.

Once the feature set is determined, the next step is the calculation of the difference vector $\mathbf{F_D}$. Most elements of the difference vector are the absolute difference between the corresponding elements of the reference and test feature vectors as shown in the following equation.

$$F_{Di} = | F_{Ti} - F_{Ei} | \qquad (6)$$

where F_{Di} is an i-th element of $\mathbf{F_D}$, F_{Ti} is an i-th element of $\mathbf{F_T}$ and F_{Ei} is i-th element of $\mathbf{F_E}$.

Two exceptions are the direction and radial histograms. Instead of considering differences of each bin, only the sum of the differences of the following equation is inserted to the difference vector, reducing the dimension to 22 from 44 of the feature vectors.

$$D = \sum_{i=1}^{N} | H_r(i) - H_t(i) | \qquad (7)$$

where, D is a histogram difference, N is the number of bins, H(i) is the value of the histogram for the i-th bin represented in ratio to the total number of sampling points, and the subscript r and t of H represent the reference and test pattern, respectively.

The parameters in the pool are classified into the following three classes.

1. Transform Invariant Parameters: Values that are not altered by the proposed transforms
2. Static Parameters: Represents static shape characteristics of the pattern
3. Dynamic Parameters: Represents dynamic characteristics of the signing process

Feature vectors for each class are denoted as $\mathbf{I}$, $\mathbf{S}$, $\mathbf{D}$, respectively. As mentioned earlier, the original pattern and the transformed patterns are represented by completely the same format, thus the same feature extraction module can be applied to all the patterns. The feature vectors are extracted from the original, speed equalized and velocity transformed patterns, which are denoted as $\{\mathbf{I}, \mathbf{S_O}, \mathbf{D_O}\}$, $\{\mathbf{I}, \mathbf{S_S}, \mathbf{D_S}\}$ and $\{\mathbf{I}, \mathbf{S_V}, \mathbf{D_V}\}$ respectively. Here, parameters extracted from the original pattern are also affected by scale. Hence the same normalization with the case of velocity transform (refer to Section III) is conducted before it is fed to the feature extraction module.

For the evaluation of the proposed transform techniques, 12 verification models with different combinations of the above parameter sets are constructed. At first, as a representative of the traditional approach where no transformed patterns are utilized, a verification model of the feature vector $\mathbf{T_O} = \mathbf{I} \oplus \mathbf{S_O} \oplus \mathbf{D_O}$ is constructed (Here $\oplus$ is the vector concatenation operator that concatenates two vectors to form a new vector whose elements are the sum of the original two vectors. That is, if vector $\mathbf{A} = \{a_1, a_2, ..., a_N\}$ and vector $\mathbf{B} = \{b_1, b_2, ..., b_M\}$ are given, then $\mathbf{A} \oplus \mathbf{B} = \{a_1, a_2, ..., a_N, b_1, b_2, ..., b_M\}$.) Similarly, the same feature vectors are extracted from the transformed patterns to form $T_S=I\oplus S_S\oplus D_S$ for the speed equalized pattern and $T_V=I\oplus S_V\oplus D_V$ for the velocity transformed pattern, respectively. These models are referred to as T-O, T-S and T-V, respectively. The 'T' in the name indicates that all the parameters in the pool are utilized and the concatenated character 'O', 'S' and 'V' stand for the source pattern; 'O' for the original, 'S' for the speed equalized pattern and 'V' for the velocity transformed pattern. By further combining these parameters, T-OS, T-OV and T-OSV models can be constructed.

Similar models using only static parameters are constructed, which are referred to as S-* models. For the original pattern, only S_O is used as a feature vector to construct an S-O model and S_S and S_V are used to form the S-S and S-V models respectively. Same combinatorial models S-OS, S-OV and S-OSV are also constructed. These 12 verification models are summarized in Table 1.

Table 1. Verification Models

Name	Parameters	Source Pattern	Feature Vector
T-O	All	Original	$I\oplus D_O\oplus S_O$
T-S		Speed Equalized	$I\oplus D_S\oplus S_S$
T-V		Velocity Transformed	$I\oplus D_V\oplus S_V$
T-OS		Original + Speed Equalized	$I\oplus D_O\oplus S_O\oplus D_S\oplus S_S$
T-OV		Original + Velocity Transformed	$I\oplus D_O\oplus S_O\oplus D_V\oplus S_V$
T-OSV		Original + Speed Equalized + Velocity Transformed	$I\oplus D_O\oplus S_O\oplus D_S\oplus S_S\oplus D_V\oplus S_V$
S-O	Static Parameter	Original	S_O
S-S		Speed Equalized	S_S
S-V		Velocity Transformed	S_V
S-OS		Original + Speed Equalized	$S_O\oplus S_S$
S-OV		Original + Velocity Transformed	$S_O\oplus S_V$
S-OSV		Original + Speed Equalized + Velocity Transformed	$S_O\oplus S_S\oplus S_V$

4.2 Experimental System Model

The system consists of two main parts, enrollment and verification. In the enrollment stage, a new user registers his/her signature pattern to the system to make a template. Generally, several specimens of the user signature are submitted to the system so that a reliable template can be created. In the implemented systems, every user is required to present 5 samples first. And the validation module evaluates the reliability of the samples by conducting verification between the samples. That is, if 5 samples C_1 to C_5 are given to the system, the feature extractor extracts the feature vectors F_1 to F_5 for each pattern. And for every possible pairing (F_1+F_2, F_1+F_3, ... , F_4+F_5), verification is conducted to generate $10(=_5C_2)$ matching scores. If all of them exceed the predetermined threshold, the enrollment is declared as a success and the template F_T is generated by averaging the 5 vectors as follows.

$$F_T = \frac{\sum_{i=1}^{5} F_i}{5} \qquad (8)$$

If this is not the case, matching scores for each pattern (each pattern is related to 4 matching operations) are summed up, and the pattern whose score summation is smallest is discarded. Another pattern is then summoned to repeat the above procedures.

In practical systems, it is a common practice to deny enrollment itself if the evaluation fails even after a certain number of retrials as shown in the figure. This seems to be a reasonable policy as the risk is too high to lower the thresholds for accommodating such unstable patterns.

Here however, for fair performance evaluation, enrollment failure is not allowed. In the implemented systems, two more trials are allowed to make 7 samples in total. If the case still fails to clear the criterion, the best template is created based on available samples.

The feature extraction module extracts the feature vector from the input pattern while the reference feature vector is retrieved from the template database based on the given ID. The difference vector between two feature vectors is calculated and is fed to the classifier for a final decision.

As a classifier, the neural network is utilized. The input to the network is the difference vector and the network consists of a hidden layer and an output layer with 2 neurons. The network is trained so that the two-dimensional output vector is like the following equation and the final matching score S is given as O_1-O_2.

$$O = \begin{cases} (1,0) & \text{for a genuine pair} \\ (0,1) & \text{for a forgery pair} \end{cases} \qquad (9)$$

That is, if $S=O_1$-O_2 is greater than a given threshold, the given pair is declared genuine; otherwise it is classified as a forgery. In training the neural network, samples reserved from the experimental database are utilized..

5   Experiments and Discussion

5.1   Experimental Data

The signature database used in the experiment is provided by the University of Kent. Fairhust, et al. described the characteristics of the database as follows [3]: "The signatures are collected from a wide cross-section of the general public at a typical retail outlet providing a genuine and real-world environment within which to investigate the signing process. The database therefore provides a much more realistic test for signature verification experimentation than the many smaller and laboratory-based databases often encountered."

The captured data is re-sampled so that the time interval is the same using quadratic interpolation, which is followed by a Gaussian low-pass filtering that is characterized before being added to the database.

The original database consists of 7,428 samples from 359 persons. The number of samples per person varies from 2 to 79 depending on the times they visited the site. In this paper, a subset of the original database that consists of only the persons whose sample count is greater than 10 is used, resulting in 6,790 samples from 271 persons. In the experiment, 3 samples from each person are reserved to train the neural networks, 7 samples are utilized for enrollments, and the remaining samples are used for evaluation.

5.2 Experimental Results in Context of Random Forgery

For the experiment, 271 persons are enrolled to the implemented 12 systems using the reserved 7 samples. Excluding the first 10 samples (for enrollment and training), the remaining 4,080 samples are fed to each system for performance evaluation. Each test sample is compared against all the enrolled persons generating 4,080 trials

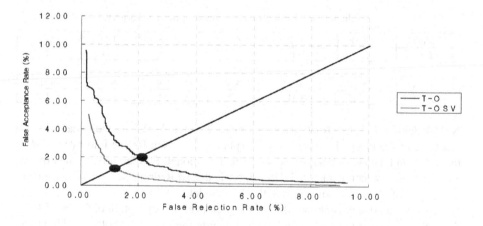

Fig. 7. Error Trade-off Curve for the T-O and T-OSV models

for genuine pairs and 1,101,600 trials for random forgery.

Fig. 7 shows the error trade-off curve for the T-O and T-OSV models. As shown in the figure, FAR (false acceptance rate) and FRR (false rejection rate) changes as the threshold changes, where the threshold is determined by the requirements of each application. That is, for applications with strict security requirements, a higher threshold is adopted to lower the FAR, but inevitably results in a higher FRR, and vice versa. Typically, the performance of the algorithm is evaluated by EER (equal error rate), the error rate when FAR and FRR become equal as indicated by dots in the figure.

Table 2 shows the EER of the 9 models in the context of random forgery. The first model, which is the traditional approach without using transformed patterns, shows an EER of 1.93 %, while that of the T-S and T-V models is 2.11% and 3.00% respectively. Though the EER for the original pattern is better than those of the transformed patterns, this is to be expected because users intentionally try to be consistent in shape more so than the signing process itself. It is not rare even for someone to pause for a moment during signing, causing large intra-personal variability (the variation observed within a class of genuine signature specimens of one individual)[8] in dynamic characteristics.

Table 2. Equal Error Rates in context of Random Forgery

Model	T-O	T-S	T-V	T-OS	T-OV	T-OSV
EER(%)	1.93	2.11	3.00	1.40	1.61	1.17

Model	S-O	S-S	S-V	S-OS	S-OV	S-OSV
EER(%)	3.11	2.57	4.97	1.66	2.14	1.37

Table 3. Equal Error Rates in context of Skilled Forgery

Model	T-O	T-S	T-V	T-OS	T-OV	T-OSV
EER(%)	3.03	2.00	2.11	2.80	2.43	2.34

Model	S-O	S-S	S-V	S-OS	S-OV	S-OSV
EER(%)	13.15	3.41	4.25	3.99	5.75	3.17

Nonetheless, the transformed patterns obviously include information that was not available in the original pattern, which explains the reason for the improved EER of the T-OS and T-OV models over that of the T-O model. Furthermore, by incorporating all the information in the T-OSV model, the EER dropped to 1.17 %, an improvement of about 39% over that of the T-O model.

The same tendency is observed in S-* models with the exception of better EER for the S-S model over the S-O model. By combining the parameters of the original and transformed patterns, far better results could be obtained. In the case of the S-OSV model, an EER of 1.37 % is obtained, which is almost a 56% improvement over the S-O model.

Here, it is important to compare the T-O model with the S-OSV model. The T-O model is the traditional approach where the dynamic characteristics are considered as a form of parameters, while the S-OSV model uses only static parameters but considers the dynamic characteristics via the transformed patterns. As the table shows, the EER of the S-OSV model is 1.37 % compared to 1.93% of the T-O model, an improvement of about 29%. Considering the fact that the S-* model utilizes only a small portion of the parameter pool, the 29% improvement is quite a promising result, indicating that utilizing transformed patterns provides a more effective model for the analysis of dynamic characteristics as compared to traditional techniques.

5.3 Experimental Results in Context of Skilled Forgery

Although the Kent database is an excellent dataset, it does not include skilled forgery samples, which are important in evaluating signature verification algorithms.
For the experiments, 5 volunteers were requested to imitate the enrolled signatures
as closely as possible.

Due to the large size of the Kent database, it was difficult for each volunteer to generate all the forgery examples of 271 persons. Hence they were requested to select
the signatures that appeared easier to imitate. During a period of 3 months, 2,000
skilled forgery samples were collected.

Table 3 shows the EER of the 12 models. As expected, the S-O model in which only
static parameters are considered on the original pattern shows the worst result,
13.15%. This result demonstrates that a skilled forgery cannot be rejected in context
of shape only. Furthermore, it is important to notice the higher performance of the *-
S and *-V models over *-O model, which is contrary to the results of the random
forgery experiment. As mentioned earlier, users intentionally try to be consistent in
the finalized shape of their signature. In other words, typically smaller intra-personal
variability is observed in static parameters than in the dynamic ones. Furthermore,
inter-personal variability in static parameters is typically very large in the case of
random forgery, which makes static characteristics ideal as a discriminating feature.
This is the reason for the higher performance of the *-O model in the random forgery
experiment.   However, in skilled forgery, the forgers also try to imitate the shape as
closely as possible and they certainly succeeded in doing so to a large extent. As a
result, inter-personal variability for static parameters becomes very small, decreasing
the ability to discriminate forgery samples. Naturally, the importance of dynamic
parameters increases in this case.

The traditional approach (T-O model) also considers the dynamic characteristics.
Parameters such as total signing time, average velocity and other parameters of dynamic nature play an important role in rejecting a skilled forgery, which is evidenced
by the large improvement from 13.15% of the S-O model to 3.03%. However, by
applying transforms, far better results, 2.00% for the T-S model and 2.11% for the T-
V model, were achieved, demonstrating the effectiveness of the transform techniques
in analyzing dynamic characteristics. These results are even better than the combinatorial models such as T-OS, T-OV or T-OSV.

For the S-* model, the same tendency is observed. As in the cases of the T-* models, the S-S and S-V models are far superior to the S-O model. The 13.15% EER of
the S-O model drops to 3.41% when the same parameter set was extracted from the
speed equalized pattern. For the S-V model, the EER was 4.25%, also a large improvement over the S-O model. In the case of combinatorial models, it seems that the
results were strongly influenced by the poor result of the S-O model; the EERs for the
S-OS and S-OV models were worse than that of the S-S model. Only the S-OSV
model showed a slightly improved result of 3.17% compared to the 3.41% of the S-S
model

6 Conclusion

Dynamic characteristics are important information in the analysis of two-dimensional time-series patterns such as signatures captured by a tablet digitizer. Especially in the context of skilled forgery where inter-personal variability in static characteristics becomes negligible, an effective analysis of dynamic characteristics is indispensable for the achievement of a proper performance. In the reported works, however, dynamics information has been considered mainly in the form of simple parameters such as average velocity, average acceleration, etc, which although efficient, could achieve only limited success in performance.

In this paper, two novel transforms, speed equalization and velocity transform, are proposed as a means to visualize the dynamic characteristics of the signing process. With the visualized dynamics information in the transformed domain, an analysis in the context of shapes naturally results in an analysis of dynamic characteristics.

The proposed analysis model is applied to the online signature verification problem. For comparison, 12 systems are implemented with various combinations of parameters and tested on a large signature database of 6,790 samples from 271 persons. In the context of random forgery, the EER for the T-O model (only the parameters from original pattern were used) was 1.93%. However, if the information from the original pattern and transformed patterns are utilized fully as in the T-OSV model, the EER drops to 1.17%. Even the model that adopted only the parameters of static nature but considers dynamic characteristics purely through the transformed patterns (S-OSV model) scored 1.37 %, an impressive improvement over the T-O model.

In the case of skilled forgery, the effectiveness of the transforms is more apparent. The T-S and T-V models, where the parameters are extracted from the transformed patterns, showed 2.00% and 2.11% EERs respectively, while the EER of the T-O model was 3.03%. In the case of skilled forgery, inter-personal variability in shapes is very small. Thus the performance is mainly influenced by the effectiveness of the dynamic characteristics analysis. These experimental results show that the analysis of the dynamic characteristics by using transformed patterns delivers superior performance to the traditional approach.

In this paper, the proposed transform technique is applied only to the global parametric algorithm. However, with the completely identical format of the original and the transformed patterns, virtually any signature verification algorithm can be applied to the transformed patterns to improve performance, especially in the context of skilled forgery where the proper analysis of dynamic characteristics is essential.

References

1. R. Kashi, J. Hu, W.L. Nelson, W. Turin.: A Hidden Markov Model Approach to online handwritten signature verification. International Journal on Document Analysis & Recognition, vol. 1, no. 2, (1998)102–109
2. W. S. Wijesoma, M. Mingming, E. Sung.:Selecting Optimal Personalized Features for Online Signature Verification Using GA. in Proc. SMC 2000, vol. 4, (2000)2740–2745

3. M.C. Fairhust, S. Ng,.: Management of access through biometric control: A case study based on automatic signature verification. Universal Access in the Information Society, vol. 1, no. 1, 2001(31–39)
4. R. C. Gonzalez, P. Wintz. :Digital Image Processing. Addison-Wesley Publishing Company, Inc., (1977)78–87
5. T. Wessels and C.W.Omlin,.: A Hybrid System for Signature Verification. in Proc. IJCNN 2000, vol. 5, (2000)509–514
6. R.L. Burden, J. D. Faires. :Numerical Analysis. 5th ed., International Thomson Publishing, (1993)57–168
7. M.C.Fairhust.: Signature Verification Revisited: promoting practical exploitation of biometric technology. Electronics & Communication Engineering Journal, vol. 9, no. 6, (1997) 273–280
8. R. Plamondon and G. Lorette. :Automatic Signature Verification and Writer Identification – The State of the Art. Pattern Recognition, Vol. 22, No. 2, (1989) 107–131
9. F. Leclerc, R. Plamondon.: Automatic Signature Verification: The State of the Art – 1989-1993. International Journal of Pattern Recognition & Artificial Intelligence, vol. 8, no. 3, (1994)634–660
10. R. Plamondon, S. Srihari. :On-Line and Off-Line Handwriting Recognition: A Comprehensive Survey. IEEE Trans. Pattern Analysis & Matchine Intelligence, vol. 22, no. 1, (2000) 63–84
11. K. Huang and H. Yan. :Off-Line Signature Verification based on Geometric Feature Extraction and Neural Network Classification. Pattern Recognition, vol. 30, no. 1, (1997) 9–17
12. R. Martens, L. Classen.: Incorporating local consistency information into the online signature verification process. International Journal on Document Analysis & Recognition, vol. 1, no. 2, (1998) 110–115
13. J. Ribeiro and G. Vasconcelos.: Off-Line Signature Verification Using an Auto-associator Cascade-Correlation Architecture. in Proc. International Joint Conference on Neural Networks, vol. 4, (1999) 2882–2886
14. A. El-Yacoubi, E. J. R. Justino, R. Sabourin, F. Bortolizzi.: Off-Line Signature Verification Using HMMs and Cross-Validation. Proc. Signal Processing Society Workshop 2000, vol. 2. (2000)859–868
15. E. J. R. Justino, F. Bortolozzi, R. Babourin.: Off-line Signature Verification Using HMM for Random, Simple and Skilled Forgeries. Proc. 6th International Conf. on Document Analysis and Recognition, (2001)1031–1034
16. R. Sabourin, G. Genest and F. J. Preteux.: Off-Line Signature Verification by Local Granulometric Size Distributions. IEEE Trans. Pattern Analysis & Machine Intelligence, vol. 19, No. 9. (1997) 976–988
17. V. Kecman.: Learning and Soft Computing. The MIT Press. (2001)255-312
18. K. Zhang, I. Pratikakis, J. Cornelis and E. Nyssen.: Using Landmarks to Establish a Point-to-Point Correspondence between Signatures. Pattern Analysis & Applications, vol. 3, no. 1, (2000) 69–74
19. G. V. Kiran, R. S. Kunte, S. Samuel.: On-Line Signature Verification System Using Probablistic Feature Modeling. Proc. 6th International Symposium on Signal Processing and its Applications, vol. 1. (2001) 355–358

E-MHT. An Efficient Protocol for Certificate Status Checking

Jose L. Muñoz, Jordi Forné, Oscar Esparza, and Miguel Soriano

Technical University of Catalonia (Telematics Engineering Department)*
1-3 Jordi Girona, C3 08034 Barcelona (Spain)
{jose.munoz,jordi.forne,oscar.esparza,soriano}@entel.upc.es

Abstract. Public-key cryptography is widely used as the underlying mechanism for securing many protocols and applications in the Internet. A Public Key Infrastructure (PKI) is required to securely deliver public-keys to widely-distributed users or systems. The public key is usually made public by way of a digital document called a certificate. Certificates are valid during a certain period of time, however, there are circumstances under which the validity of a certificate must be terminated sooner than assigned and thus, the certificate needs to be revoked. The revocation of certificates implies one of the major costs of the whole PKI. The goal of this paper is to present an efficient offline revocation system based on the Merkle Hash Tree (MHT) named Enhanced-MHT (E-MHT). The authors propose several mechanisms that allow the E-MHT to provide a response size that is close to (or even better than) online systems. These mechanisms include the optimization of the MHT $\mathcal{P}$aths for non-revoked certificates, the division of the status data among multiple MHTs and a low cost mechanism for re-utilization of MHT digests and E-MHT responses. Furthermore, an ASN.1 protocol for the E-MHT is introduced and discussed. Finally, a performance evaluation of the E-MHT using this protocol is presented.

1 Introduction

Many protocols and applications which use the Internet employ public-key technology for security purposes. In public key cryptography a couple of keys are used: one is "public" (i.e. known by everybody) and the other is "private" (i.e. secret). The public-key is usually made public by way of a digital document called a certificate. Certificates are signed digitally by a *Trusted Third Party* (TTP) called the "issuer", this allows a user who trusts issuer "X" to trust the contents of any certificate issued by "X". There are several kinds of certificates but the most widely used are the Identity Certificates (ICs), whose main function is to bind a public-key with an identity. An IC states an association between a name called a "Distinguished Name" (DN) and the user's public-key. Therefore, the authentication of the certificate relies on each user possessing a unique DN. DNs

---

* This work has been supported by the Spanish Research Council under the project DISQET (TIC2002-00818).

K. Chae and M. Yung (Eds.): WISA 2003, LNCS 2908, pp. 410–424, 2004.

use the X.500 standard [14] and are intended to be unique across the Internet. All X.509 certificates have the following data, in addition to the signature:

- *Version.* This field identifies which version of the X.509 standard applies to this certificate, which affects what information can be specified in it.
- *Serial Number.* The entity that created the certificate is responsible for assigning it a serial number to distinguish it from other certificates it issues.
- *Signature Algorithm Identifier.* Identifies the asymmetric algorithm used by the issuer to sign the certificate.
- *Issuer Name.* The DN of the issuer.
- *Validity Period.* Each certificate is valid only for a limited amount of time. It is not valid prior to the activation date and it is not valid beyond the expiration date.
- *Subject Name.* The DN of the entity whose public-key the certificate identifies.
- *Subject Public Key Information.* This is the public-key of the entity being named, together with an algorithm identifier which specifies which public-key crypto system this key belongs to and any associated key parameters.

On the other hand, the X.509 standard [6] defines what information can go into a certificate and its data format. The TTP that issues the ICs is called the Certification Authority (CA). However, to securely deliver ICs to widely-distributed users or systems, not only the CA is necessary, but also an infrastructure that ensures the validity of electronic transactions using digital certificates. In this sense, the Public Key Infrastructure (PKI) is responsible for the certificates not only at the issuing time but also during the whole life-time of the certificate. Typically, the validity period of a certificate ranges from several months to several years. Revocation is the mechanism under which an issuer can invalidate a certificate before its expiration and hence users must assure that the certificates involved in a certain transaction are valid (not revoked). If a certificate has been revoked, any results in which this certificate has been involved must be rejected because the trust of the underlying certificates is a fundamental requirement of the applications or the protocols built over public-key technology.

A certificate may be revoked, according to [4], because of the loss or compromise of the associated private key, in response to a change in the owner's access rights, a change in the relationship with the issuer, or as a precaution against cryptanalysis. The revocation implies one of the major costs of the whole PKI and it is commonly associated with two constrains: bandwidth and processing capacity. Hence any revocation system has to be concerned about these aspects that highly affect scalability.

This paper introduces the Enhanced-MHT (E-MHT), a new proposal for offline revocation. E-MHT is an efficient revocation system based on the Merkle Hash Tree (MHT) [8]. The authors propose several mechanisms that allow the E-MHT to provide a response size that is close to (or even better than) typical online systems such as OCSP. These mechanisms include the optimization of the MHT $\mathcal{P}$aths for non-revoked certificates, the division of revocation status data among multiple MHTs and a low cost mechanism for re-utilization of MHT digests and E-MHT responses. The rest of the paper is organized as follows: in Section 2 we provide the background necessary to understand the revocation paradigm and its main approaches, including the MHT-based systems. In Section 3 E-MHT is presented as a system that provides offline responses with a reduced size. In Section 4 the authors propose a request/response protocol for status data retrieval from the E-MHT and present its ASN.1 definition. In Section 5 E-MHT is evaluated regarding OCSP [12] and AD-MHT [10]. Finally, we conclude in Section 6.

2   Background

The owner of the certificate to be revoked, an authorized representative or the issuer CA, can initiate the revocation process for this certificate. To revoke the certificate, any of the authorized entities generates a revocation request and sends it to the Revocation Data Issuer (RDI). RDI[1] is the term that we use to define the TTP that has the master database of revoked certificates. The RDI is also responsible for transforming its database revocation records into "status data". The status data ($\mathcal{SD}$ from here on) has the appropriate format in order to be distributed to the End Entities and includes at least the following data:

- *Certificate Issuer*. This is the DN of the CA that issued the target certificate or certificates.
- *Validity Period*. This period of time bounds the $\mathcal{SD}$ life-time (obviously this validity period is much smaller than the validity period of the certificate).
- *Issuer Name*. This is the DN of the TTP that issued the $\mathcal{SD}$.
- *Cryptographic Proof*. This proof must demonstrate that the $\mathcal{SD}$ was issued by a TTP.
- *Serial Number*. This is the serial number of the target certificate or certificates.
- *Revocation Date*. This is the date when the target certificate was revoked.
- *Revocation Reason*. Optionally, a revocation reason for guidance can be specified.

In the vast majority of the revocation systems, End Entities do not have a straight connection to the RDI. Instead, $\mathcal{SD}$ is published by the RDI in "repositories" or "responders". The main function of both repositories and responders is to answer the End Entities requests concerning the status of certificates (status checking). However, repositories are non TTPs that store $\mathcal{SD}$ pre-computed by the RDI (**also called offline scheme**) while responders are TTPs that can provide a cryptographic proof for $\mathcal{SD}$ in each response (**also called online scheme**).

---

[1] The CA that issued the certificate is often the one who performs the RDI functions for the certificate, but these functions can be delegated to an independent TTP.

It is worth mentioning that the status checking is the mechanism that has the greatest impact in the overall performance of a certificate revocation system. Therefore, a status checking needs to be fast, efficient, timely and it must scale well too. Figure 1 summarizes the certificate revocation paradigm.

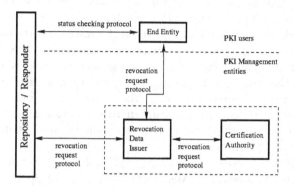

Fig. 1. Reference Model

The Certificate Management Protocol (CMP) [1] defines the mechanisms to request, renewal, reissue and revoke a certificate. In particular, CMP defines the revocation request protocol and a protocol to publish the status data.

On the other hand, there are many status checking approaches that define different formats of $\mathcal{SD}$ to be exchanged with the End Entities. The simplest of them is traditional *Certificate Revocation List* (CRL) [6]. CRL is the most mature approach and it has been part of X.509 since its first version. CRL has also been profiled for the Internet in [5]. A CRL is a digitally signed list of revoked certificates in which for each entry within the list the following information is stored: the certificate serial number, the revocation reason and the revocation date. The CRL has also a header that includes information about the version, the CRL serial number, the issuer, the algorithm used to sign, the signature, the issuing date, the expiration date and some optional fields called extensions. The CA that issued the certificate acts as RDI and repositories can be used to distribute the CRLs. Since CRLs may have a large size, they are usually cached by the client during their validity period. *Delta-CRL* (D-CRL) [6] is an attempt to reduce the size of the CRLs. A Delta-CRL is a small CRL that provides information about the certificates whose status have changed since the issuance of a complete list called Base-CRL. *CRL-Distribution Points* (CRL-DP) was introduced in the version 3 of X.509 [6]. In CRL-DP, each CRL contains the status information of a certain subgroup of certificates. Each subgroup is associated with a CRL distribution point, which can be located on the same or different repositories. Each certificate has a pointer to the location of its CRL distribution point, so there is no need to either search through distribution points or have a priori knowledge of the revocation information locations. The criteria for creating these subgroups can be geographic, by their level of importance, scope of use, etc.

Micali proposed the *Certificate Revocation System* (CRS) [9]. In CRS the RDI periodically sends to each repository the list of all issued certificates, each tagged with the signed time-stamped value of a hash chain (see the Even et al. algorithm [3]) that indicates if this certificate has been revoked or not.

The *Online Certificate Status Protocol* (OCSP) [12] has been proposed by the PKIX workgroup of the IETF. In OCSP the status of certificates is available in responders through a request/response mechanism. An OCSP client issues a status request for a particular certificate and sends it to an OCSP responder. The acceptance of the certificate in question is suspended until the responder provides a response. Upon receipt of a request, the responder determines whether the request is correct, searches the status information in its local database (which can be a CRL), creates a response with the corresponding data, signs this response and sends it back to the client.

The *Certificate Revocation Tree* (CRT) [7] and the *Authenticated Dictionary* (AD) [13] are both based on the Merkle Hash Tree (MHT) [8]. The Authenticated Search Tree (AST) [2] from Buldas et al. also uses the MHT to increase the accountability of certificate revocation by making it intractable for the CA to create contradictory statements about the validity of a certificate.

The MHT relies on the properties of the OWHF (One Way Hash Functions). It exploits the fact that a OWHF is at least 10,000 times faster to compute than a digital signature, so the majority of the cryptographic operations performed in the revocation system are hash functions instead of digital signatures. A sample MHT is depicted in Figure 2.

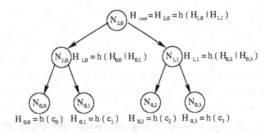

Fig. 2. Sample MHT.

We denote by $N_{i,j}$ the nodes within the MHT where i and j represent respectively the i-th level and the j-th node. We denote by $H_{i,j}$ the cryptographic value stored by node $N_{i,j}$. Nodes at level 0 are called "leaves" and they represent the data stored in the tree. In the case of revocation, leaves represent the set Φ of certificates that have been revoked,

$$\Phi = \{c_0, c_1, \ldots, c_j, \ldots, c_n\}. \tag{1}$$

Where c_j is the data stored by leaf $N_{0,j}$. Then, $H_{0,j}$ is computed as (2), where h is an OWHF.

$$H_{0,j} = h(c_j).\tag{2}$$

To build the MHT, a set of t adjacent nodes at a given level i; $N_{i,j}$, $N_{i,j+1}$, ...,$N_{i,j+t-1}$, are combined into one node in the upper level, which we denote by $N_{i+1,k}$. Then, $H_{i+1,k}$ is obtained by applying h to the concatenation of the t cryptographic variables (3)

$$H_{i+1,k} = h(H_{i,j}|H_{i,j+1}|\ldots|H_{i,j+t-1}).\tag{3}$$

At the top level there is only one node called the "root" and H_{root} is a digest for all the stored data in the MHT. The sample MHT of Figure 2 is a binary tree because adjacent nodes are combined in pairs to form a node in the next level ($t = 2$) and $H_{root} = H_{2,0}$.

Definition 1. *The Digest is defined as* $\{DN_{RDI}, H_{root}, Validity\ Period\}_{SIG_{RDI}}$

Definition 2. $Path_{c_j}$ *is defined as the set of cryptographic values necessary to compute* H_{root} *from the leaf* c_j.

Notice that the Digest is trusted data because it is signed by the RDI and it is unique within the tree, while the Path is different for each leaf.

Claim. An End Entity can verify if $c_j \in \Phi$ if the MHT provides a response with the Digest and the proper $Path_{c_j}$.

Example 1. Let us suppose that a certain user wants to find out whether c_1 belongs to the sample MHT of Figure 2. Then $Path_{c1} = \{N_{0,0}, N_{1,1}\}$ and the response verification consists in checking that the $H_{2,0}$ computed from the $Path_{c1}$ matches $H_{2,0}$ included in the $Digest = \{DN_{RDI}, H_{2,0}, Validity\ Period\}_{SIG_{RDI}}$,

$$H_{root} = H_{2,0} = h(h(h(c_1)|H_{0,0})|H_{1,1}).\tag{4}$$

Remark 1. The MHT can be pre-computed by a TTP and distributed to a repository because a leaf cannot be added or deleted to Φ without modifying H_{root}[2] which is included in the Digest and as the Digest is signed it cannot be forged by a non-TTP.

The CRT is a binary MHT. The main drawback of CRT is the management of the dynamism of the binary tree. That is, searching, adding and removing a leaf might be performed in the worst case in $o(n)$ where n is the number of leaves. This is an important problem taking into account that the freshness requirements of the revocation may lead the MHT to be updated frequently.

On the other hand, the AD is a 2-3 MHT. In a 2-3 tree, each internal node can have two or three children ($t \in \{2, 3\}$). The main advantage of this type of

---

[2] To do such a thing, an attacker needs to find a pre-image of a OWHF which is computationally infeasible by definition.

tree over the binary one is that searching, adding and removing a leaf can be performed in $o(log(n))$. Each leaf within the AD tree represents a certificate; certificates are distinguished by their serial number and, leaves are ordered by serial number. The order of the leaves is essential to prove that a certain certificate, identified by serial number c_{target}, is not revoked ($c_{target} \notin \Phi$). To do so, it is enough to demonstrate the existence of two **adjacent leaves**: a minor adjacent leaf and a major adjacent leaf which fulfill that $c_{minor} \in \Phi$, $c_{major} \in \Phi$ and $c_{minor} < c_{target} < c_{major}$. In [11] it is proposed an algorithm to efficiently choose the adjacent leaves and in [10] it is proposed an algorithm that given a certain couple of leaves verifies whether they are "authentic" adjacent leaves.

3   The Enhanced-MHT Basics

In this Section, the authors propose E-MHT which arises from a performance analysis of an AD implementation named AD-MHT [10]. Remember that MHT-based systems are offline because the MHT can be pre-computed by the RDI and distributed to repositories. Offline systems are more robust than online systems in the sense that it is more complex to maintain the level of security of a responder than of a repository: a responder has to be online, but at the same time, it has to protect its private key against intruders. Regardless, AD-MHT repositories share the following characteristics with online responders:

- A MHT provides status data for particular certificates rather than data of a whole set of certificates.
- The repository computes part of the cryptographic proof for each response (i.e. the $\mathcal{P}$ath or $\mathcal{P}$aths).

Taking into account the previous features, it is easy to understand why the size of an AD-MHT response is usually some orders of magnitude smaller than a classical CRL. However, the size of an AD-MHT response is larger than an OCSP one because of the cryptographic values. For instance, we have observed in our tests with AD-MHT that for a population of 1,000 revoked certificates, the AD-MHT response doubles the size of an OCSP response. E-MHT agglutinates several mechanisms for enhancing the efficiency of traditional MHT-based systems. These mechanisms, which are explained below, include the optimization of the MHT $\mathcal{P}$aths for non-revoked certificates, the division of the revoked certificates among multiple MHTs, the re-utilization of the tree $\mathcal{D}$igest and the cached responses updating at a low cost.

3.1   Optimization of $\mathcal{P}$aths

As discussed in the previous section, the response for non-revoked certificates in the AD must include the $\mathcal{P}$ath$_{c_{minor}}$ and the $\mathcal{P}$ath$_{c_{major}}$. Taking into account that only a small percentage of the certificates are revoked (usually a 10% are considered in similar studies), the majority of the requests will be performed over non-revoked certificates. Therefore, a size reduction over this kind of response will have a great impact over the AD performance. With this idea in mind, the authors propose below a way of reducing the number of cryptographic values for non-revoked certificates.

The repository builds the responses for non-revoked certificates as follows:

– It provides the complete $\mathcal{P}$ath for c_{minor}.
– To build the $\mathcal{P}$ath$_{c_{major}}$, the repository omits the cryptographic values that fulfil that $H_{i,j} \in \mathcal{P}$ath$_{c_{minor}}$ (i.e. redundant values that were already included in the $\mathcal{P}$ath$_{c_{minor}}$).

To verify an optimized response:

– The client verifies the $\mathcal{P}$ath$_{c_{minor}}$. To do so, the client computes H_{root} and checks that it matches the one included in the MHT $\mathcal{D}$igest.
– To check the $\mathcal{P}$ath$_{c_{major}}$, it is enough to reach a cryptographic value already computed in the verification of the $\mathcal{P}$ath$_{c_{minor}}$ (in the worst case H_{root} might be the only common cryptographic value between the two adjacent leaves).

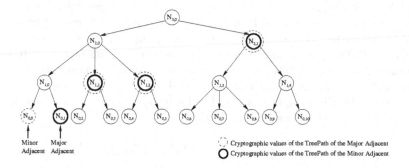

Fig. 3. $\mathcal{P}$ath's optimization

Example 2. Figure 3 shows an example where $H_{1,0}$ was already computed for the minor adjacent, therefore the repository omits $H_{1,1}$, $H_{1,2}$ and $H_{2,1}$ in the $\mathcal{P}$ath$_{c_{major}}$. In this example, the number of values necessary to verify the response is reduced from 8 to 5, within a bigger MHT the saving can be considerable.

3.2   Multi-MHT

We borrow the philosophy of the X.509 CRL-DP as another way of reducing the response size: the group of revoked certificates Φ is divided into k subgroups and each subgroup is used to build a smaller MHT. Similarly to CRL-DP, the criteria for creating these subgroups can be geographic, by their level of importance, scope of use, etc. or the certificate population can also be uniformly divided into subgroups just for reducing the AD-MHT response size.

A priori, the MHT division is not as beneficial as the CRL division. Notice that with k Distribution Points, the CRL size is divided by k while the number of cryptographic values per $\mathcal{P}ath$ in the MHT is only divided by $o(log(k))$. Moreover, the resources needed for the revocation publication are increased since now the RDI has to update k $\mathcal{D}igests$ every validity period instead of just one. Even so, the division might be worth taking into account that scalability problems are usually related to the status checking.

3.3 $\mathcal{D}igest$ Re-utilization

Dividing the MHT on its own is not a spectacular breakthrough, but combined with $\mathcal{D}igest$ re-utilization and caching, the overall performance can be considerably improved as we will show in Section 5.

Because AD-MHT is composed by a single MHT, a new root value has to be computed for any revocation or expiration during the validity period. On the contrary, data is fragmented among multiple MHTs in E-MHT. This circumstance favours that many MHTs stay unchanged after a validity period[3]. Although a tree does not change its shape, the RDI must sign its $\mathcal{D}igest$ with a new validity period due to the revocation freshness requirements. $\mathcal{D}igest$ re-utilization offers an alternative to signature in case we need to setup a new validity period of an unchanged $\mathcal{D}igest$. The point of the re-utilization mechanism is that resources consumed to update a $\mathcal{D}igest$ are drastically reduced in comparison with conventional signature. A hash chain using the Even et al. algorithm [3] is used to implement the $\mathcal{D}igest$ re-utilization. The hash chain results from applying $d+1$ times a OWHF h over a secret nonce (5)

$$R \xrightarrow{h} R_d \xrightarrow{h} R_{d-1} \xrightarrow{h} \cdots \xrightarrow{h} R_i \xrightarrow{h} \cdots R_2 \xrightarrow{h} R_1 \xrightarrow{h} R_0 \qquad (5)$$

From now on, the validity period included in the $\mathcal{D}igest$ will be denoted as the "documented" validity period and `nextUpdate` will denote the end of this period. Let's see the parameters involved in the process:

`primaryUpdateValue` (R) is the secret nonce. R is only known by the RDI and it is generated each time a MHT is created or its root has changed.

`maximumUpdateIndex` (d) is the maximum number of periods that a $\mathcal{D}igest$ can be re-utilized.

`baseUpdateValue` (R_0) is the last value of the hash chain and it is included in the signature computation of the $\mathcal{D}igest$. R_0 is computed by applying $d+1$ times h over R: $R_0 = h^{d+1}(R)$.

`currentUpdateValue` (R_i) is computed by applying $d+1-i$ times h over R: $R_i = h^{d+1-i}(R)$. Where i will denote the number of periods "Δ" elapsed from the documented one.

---

[3] Actually, the probability that a MHT does not change during a validity period gets multiplied by k.

A relying party can verify the validity of a $\mathcal{D}$igest that it is living beyond its documented life-time, say, at time t, where t is included within the period $[\texttt{nextUpdate} + (i-1)\Delta, \texttt{nextUpdate} + i\Delta]$, by checking the equality of equation (6)

$$R_0 = h^i(R_i) \quad with \ i \leq d \tag{6}$$

It must be stressed that to forge a `currentUpdateValue` with the information provided by a previous update value an attacker needs to find a pre-image of a OWHF which is computationally infeasible by definition. Notice also that the resources increase in the revocation publication due to the division can be compensated with $\mathcal{D}$igest re-utilization because to update an unchanged MHT, the RDI just needs to send the appropriate `currentUpdateValue` instead of a new $\mathcal{D}$igest[4].

3.4 E-MHT Responses Update

An E-MHT response can also be updated beyond its documented life-time with a `currentUpdateValue` if the $\mathcal{D}$igest included in it has not changed. In this sense, previous E-MHT responses can be cached by clients, so that if the client needs to check the status of the same certificate later, the client can ask for a `currentUpdateValue` instead of downloading a complete E-MHT response which is larger[5]. Moreover, if a client usually requests for a given set of certificates, then, the responses of these certificates will be likely cached and they might be updated by means of a `currentUpdateValue` parameter. On the other hand, response re-utilization permits the relying parties to retrieve more timely status data from the system without perceptibly affecting the scalability, due to the following reasons:

- A small validity period makes less probable that a MHT changes during this period of time.
- With small validity periods, the responses need to be updated more often but this can be performed at a very low cost (using response re-utilization) if the corresponding MHT has not changed.

4   E-MHT Status Checking Protocol

At the moment, most of the protocols and data structures used in computer security are defined in ASN.1. ASN.1 (Abstract Syntax Notation number One) is an international standard [15] which aims to provide a means to formally specify data structures independent of machine or transfer syntax. This is the reason

---

[4] A $\mathcal{D}$igest is about 10 times larger than a `currentUpdateValue` (using our implementation).

[5] A E-MHT response is about 20 times larger than a `currentUpdateValue` (using our implementation).

why ASN.1 is commonly used to define the Protocol Data Units (PDUs) to be exchanged between heterogeneous systems. The ASN.1 PDUs are encoded with one of several standardized encoding rules to produce an efficient bit-pattern representation which can be later transmitted. Security protocols are normally encoded using the Distinguished Encoding Rules (DER) [16] because DER is intended for applications in which given an ASN.1 value, a unique bit-pattern encoding is possible, as is the case when a digital signature is computed on an ASN.1 value. DER encoded PDUs can be placed over many transport mechanisms such as raw-sockets, HTTP, SMTP, LDAP, etc.

Taking into account the previous discussion, the request-response protocol for the E-MHT status checking has been designed and implemented by the authors in ASN.1. Figure 4 shows the ASN.1 description for an E-MHT request.

```
EMHTRequest ::=      SEQUENCE {
 tbsRequest               EMHTTBSRequest,
 optionalSignature [0] EXPLICIT OCTET STRING OPTIONAL }
EMHTTBSRequest ::=   SEQUENCE {
 version             [0] EXPLICIT Version OPTIONAL,
 requestList             SEQUENCE OF EMHTCertRequest }
EMHTCertRequest::=   SEQUENCE {
 reqCert                 CertID,
 baseUpdateValue   [0] EXPLICIT OCTET STRING OPTIONAL }
CertID ::= SEQUENCE {
 issuerName        [0] EXPLICIT OCTET STRING OPTIONAL,--Issuer DN hash
 issuerKeyHash [1] EXPLICIT OCTET STRING OPTIONAL,--Issuer pub key hash
 serialNumber      CertificateSerialNumber }
```

Fig. 4. E-MHT Request ASN.1 code

Each `EMHTRequest` contains:

- The protocol version.
- An unique identifier for each target certificate.
- The request signature that is optional.
- The `baseUpdateValue` is also optional and it is included in the request if the client has an entry in its cache for the target certificate and the response re-utilization has not overflow ($i \leq d$), i.e. the inclusion of `baseUpdateValue` means that client wants a re-utilization of its cache entry if possible.

The response syntax is presented in Figure 5. Upon receipt of a request, the repository determines whether the message is well formed, whether it is configured to provide the requested service and whether the request contains the compulsory information. If any one of the prior conditions are not met, the repository produces a response with an error message that it is indicated in `MHTResponseStatus`. Otherwise, it returns a response with the corresponding status.

```
EMHTResponse    ::=    SEQUENCE {
 responseStatus        ResponseStatus,
 basicResponse    [0] EXPLICIT BasicEMHTResponse OPTIONAL }
BasicEMHTResponse    ::=    SEQUENCE { singleResponse SingleEMHTResponse }
SingleEMHTResponse ::= SEQUENCE {
 currentUpdateValue [0] EXPLICIT OCTET STRING OPTIONAL,
 emhtResponseData    [1] EXPLICIT EMHTResponseData OPTIONAL }

ResponseStatus ::= ENUMERATED {
 successful         (0), --Response has valid confirmations
 malformedRequest   (1), --Illegal confirmation request
 internalError      (2), --Internal error in issuer
 tryLater           (3), --Try again later
                        --(4) and (5) are not used
 unauthorized       (6) }--Request unauthorized

EMHTResponseData ::= SEQUENCE {
 signedTreeDigest      SignedTreeDigest,
 minorAdjacent         TreePath,
 majorAdjacent    [0] EXPLICIT TreePath OPTIONAL } --Only for not revoked
SignedTreeDigest ::= SEQUENCE {
 tbsTreeDigest         TBSTreeDigest,
 signature             OCTET STRING }
TBSTreeDigest ::= SEQUENCE {
 issuer                Name,
 validity              Validity, --Validity Period
 numberOfTrees         INTEGER,
 baseUpdateValue       OCTET STRING,
 maxUpdates            INTEGER,
 rootHash         [0] EXPLICIT OCTET STRING OPTIONAL}
TreePath ::= SEQUENCE {
 adjacentID            CertID,
 status                RevokedInfo,
 firstPathStep         PathStep }
PathStep ::= SEQUENCE {
 leftNode         [0] EXPLICIT OCTET STRING OPTIONAL,
 mediumNode       [1] EXPLICIT OCTET STRING OPTIONAL,
 rightNode        [2] EXPLICIT OCTET STRING OPTIONAL,
 nextPathStep     [3] EXPLICIT PathStep OPTIONAL }
RevokedInfo ::= SEQUENCE {
 revocationTime        GeneralizedTime,
 revocationReason [0] EXPLICIT CRLReason OPTIONAL }
```

Fig. 5. E-MHT Response ASN.1 code

The `BasicEMHTResponse` contains a `SingleEMHTResponse` for each target certificate included in the request and the `SingleEMHTResponse` is formed by two optional fields:

- The `emhtResponseData` which contains all the information necessary to check the status of a certain target certificate during the documented validity period.
- The `currentUpdateValue` is necessary to check the status of a target certificate whose $Digest$ has been signed prior to the current period (i.e. it is necessary to verify a re-utilization).

If the client has a cached `emhtResponseData` that can be updated with a re-utilization only the `currentUpdateValue` is included in the response, if not, an `emhtResponseData` and perhaps a `currentUpdateValue` are sent to the client. The `emhtResponseData` is formed by:

- The `signedTreeDigest` which includes the `issuer`, the `validityPeriod`, the `numberOfTrees`, the `baseUpdateValue` and the `maxUpdates`.
- The `minorAdjacent`, actually, represents the target certificate if it has been revoked.
- The `majorAdjacent` is optional and it is included only when the target certificate has not been revoked.

Each `TreePath` is formed by:

- The `adjacentID` which is an unique identifier of a certain certificate.
- The `status` that contains the revocation date and reason.
- The `PathStep`(s) that allow to compute the H_{root} recursively.

5   Evaluation: E-MHT versus OCSP and AD-MHT

In this section the authors present an evaluation of E-MHT versus AD-MHT and OCSP in terms of down-link bandwidth utilization (repository-to-clients) for the status checking and we show what benefits E-MHT may provide. The experimental results have been obtained under the following conditions:

- Certificates are randomly expired and revoked.
- The revocation and expiration rates are both one per hour.
- The clients generate status checking requests following an exponential probability density function and the target certificates are randomly chosen.
- There are 10,000 clients and each client has one certificate and a 10% of certificates are revoked before their expiration.
- Each user has a set of 50 frequently asked certificates that take the 50% of the status checking requests.
- E-MHT is configured with 8 MHTs and 100 `maxUpdates`.

It can be observed from Figure 6 that the AD-MHT is the system that requires the highest downlink bandwidth. On the other hand, the bandwidth used by E-MHT is measured after 2 hours and after 24 hours. Notice that after 2h the bandwidth reduction is mainly due to the division mechanism and

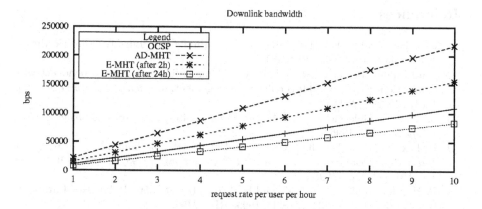

Fig. 6. Downlink utilization for OCSP, AD-MHT and E-MHT status checking.

the optimization of the MHT $\mathcal{P}$aths for non-revoked certificates (with this little time elapsed, the response re-utilization is practically not working). In this case, obviously the bandwidth required is higher than in OCSP, because without response re-utilization, MHT-based systems require always a higher bandwidth than OCSP. However, after 24h, the combination of the previous mechanisms and the response updating makes the E-MHT performance even better than OCSP.

6   Conclusions

This paper introduces a new MHT-based revocation system named E-MHT. E-MHT agglutinates several mechanisms to enhance the efficiency of traditional MHT-based systems, such as CRT or AD. These mechanisms include the optimization of the MHT $\mathcal{P}$aths for non-revoked certificates, the division of the revoked certificates among multiple MHTs, the re-utilization of the tree $\mathcal{D}$igest and the cached responses updating at a low cost.

E-MHT is not only a set of theoretical mechanisms but it is also a practical revocation system that has been implemented by the authors. As real revocation system, E-MHT requires additional elements beyond the merely definition of the data structures and mechanisms involved in. An important element to take into account is the protocol for status data retrieval. In this sense, a request/response protocol for the status checking has been defined in ASN.1. The main goal of E-MHT was to design an enhanced MHT-based system with laxer bandwidth requirements than the AD without deteriorating other aspects of the system. As shown in Figure 6 this goal has been by far achieved. Furthermore, under certain circumstances, E-MHT has proven to be even more efficient than OCSP due to the combined effect of the proposed mechanisms.

References

1. C. Adams and S. Farrell. Internet X.509 Public Key Infrastructure Certificate Management Protocols, 1999. RFC 2510.
2. Ahto Buldas, Peeter Laud, and Helger Lipmaa. Eliminating counterevidence with applications to accountable certificate management. *Journal of Computer Security*, 10(3):273–296, 2002.
3. S. Even, O. Goldreich, and S. Micali. Online/offline signatures. *Journal of Criptology*, 9:35–67, 1996.
4. B. Fox and B. LaMacchia. Certificate Revocation: Mechanics and Meaning. In *International Conference on Financial Cryptography (FC98)*, number 1465, pages 158–164, February 1998.
5. R. Housley, W. Ford, W. Polk, and D. Solo. Internet X.509 Public Key Infrastructure Certificate and CRL Profile, 1999. RFC 2459.
6. ITU/ISO Recommendation. X.509 Information Technology Open Systems Interconnection - The Directory: Autentication Frameworks, 2000. Technical Corrigendum.
7. P.C. Kocher. On certificate revocation and validation. In *International Conference on Financial Cryptography (FC98). Lecture Notes in Computer Science*, number 1465, pages 172–177, February 1998.
8. R.C. Merkle. A certified digital signature. In *Advances in Cryptology (CRYPTO89). Lecture Notes in Computer Science*, number 435, pages 234–246. Springer-Verlag, 1989.
9. S. Micali. Efficient certificate revocation. Technical Report TM-542b, MIT Laboratory for Computer Science, 1996.
10. J.L. Muñoz, J. Forné, O. Esparza, and M. Soriano. A Certificate Status Checking Protocol for the Authenticated Dictionary. In *Computer Network Security*, volume 2776 of *LNCS*, pages 255–266. Springer-Verlag, 2003.
11. J.L. Muñoz, J. Forné, Oscar Esparza, and Miguel Soriano. Implementation of an Efficient Authenticated Dictionary for Certificate Revocation. In *The Eighth IEEE Symposium on Computers and Communications (ISCC'2003)*, volume 1, pages 238–243. IEEE Computer Society, June 2003.
12. M. Myers, R. Ankney, A. Malpani, S. Galperin, and C. Adams. X.509 Internet Public Key Infrastructure Online Certificate Status Protocol - OCSP, 1999. RFC 2560.
13. M. Naor and K. Nissim. Certificate Revocation and Certificate Update. *IEEE Journal on Selected Areas in Communications*, 18(4):561–560, 2000.
14. CCITT Recommendation X.500. The directory overview of concepts, models and services, 1988.
15. ITU-T Recommendation X.680. Abstract syntax notation one (asn.1): Specification of basic notation, 1995.
16. ITU-T Recommendation X.690. ASN.1 Encoding Rules: Specification of Basic Encoding Rules (BER), Canonical Encoding Rules (CER) and Distinguished Encoding Rules (DER), 1995.

A Comment on Group Independent
Threshold Sharing

Brian King

Indiana University Purdue University Indianapolis
briking@iupui.edu

Abstract. Secret sharing is important in the cases where a secret needs to be distributed over a set of n devices so that only authorized subsets of devices can recover the secret. Some secret sharing schemes can be used with only certain algebraic structures (for example fields). Group independent linear threshold sharing refers to a t out of n linear threshold secret sharing scheme that can be used with any finite abelian group. Group independent secret sharing schemes were introduced in [16] and a formal definition was given in [25] and [10]. Here we describe additional properties of group independent sharing schemes. In particular, we discuss how to construct the dual from the shareholder reconstruction matrix, new bounds on the computational requirements of group independent sharing and new necessary and sufficient conditions to test if a matrix will provide a group independent sharing scheme.

Keywords: secret sharing, threshold cryptography, monotone span programs, integer span programs, group independent threshold schemes, black-box sharing.

1 Introduction

Secret sharing is important in the cases where a secret needs to be distributed over a set of n devices so that only authorized subsets of devices can recover the secret. Secret sharing is typically used in situations where it is not possible for the secret to reside on a single device. A setting where the authorized sets consists of all subsets of t or more is called a t out of n threshold secret sharing scheme. The importance of threshold cryptography, especially in the context of threshold signature sharing, was noted in [9,14].

Threshold cryptography is closely tied to public-key cryptography. Many applications of threshold sharing revolve around the use of digital signatures which use public-key primitives. Within a threshold signature scheme, the participants are not recovering the secret but a function of the secret (i.e. a signature). Shamir's scheme [28] provides an efficient way to construct t out of n threshold sharing over a field. However if the algebraic setting of the signature scheme is not a field then one cannot use Shamir's scheme. In such cases, one must use the algebraic setting for which the secret space resides. RSA is an example of a public-key primitive whose secret space is not a field. When developing RSA threshold signature schemes an alternative to Shamir's scheme must be used.

K. Chae and M. Yung (Eds.): WISA 2003, LNCS 2908, pp. 425–441, 2004.
© Springer-Verlag Berlin Heidelberg 2004

Some of these alternatives rely on tailoring the scheme to this algebraic setting, some examples of this approach include [19,20,22]. Other alternatives introduced the concept of developing threshold schemes which can be used over any finite abelian group, see [13,16]. A very efficient threshold RSA signature scheme was developed in [29]. Thus there are a number of ways to achieve threshold RSA signatures and many of them are "efficient". However, if one is interested in developing zero-knowledge threshold schemes (see [16]), then one cannot tailor the scheme to the algebraic setting, and so the only alternative is to use threshold sharing schemes that can be used over any finite abelian group. Known methods to construct group independent sharing schemes have succeeded at an expense of share expansion (for example [16]). However a recent result at Crypto 2002 [10] has established that the share expansion is not as costly as previously thought.

Further, there is increase in activity to develop public-key primitives based on new number-theoretic problems[1]. Some of these primitives will fall to the wayside, while others, perhaps because of some efficiency property may become popular. Many of these primitives are based in a finite abelian group and not in a field. Once a new primitive becomes popular, threshold applications will soon follow. The specter of developing threshold cryptography for an arbitrary finite abelian group does loom. So it is important to discuss group independent threshold sharing schemes, the computational requirements for group independent threshold sharing schemes, properties of group independent threshold sharing schemes, and methods to construct group independent threshold sharing schemes.

Group independent threshold sharing schemes were first introduced in [16]. A formal definition of group independent threshold sharing schemes called *GILTS* was given [25]. In [10], an equivalent but distinct definition of group independent threshold sharing schemes called *Black-box sharing* was given. Our goal here is to discuss additional properties of group independent threshold sharing schemes. In particular we provide an *illustration on how to construct the dual of a group independent threshold sharing scheme from the shareholder reconstruction matrix*. We also provide new computational requirements concerning the generation of group independent sharing schemes, in particular on the amount of randomness required. Lastly we provide new necessary and sufficient conditions which will allow us to test if a reconstruction matrix truly describes a group independent threshold sharing scheme (i.e. will the reconstruction matrix provide the needed security requirements.) We point out that the **redistribution matrix** is a more natural way to view a secret sharing scheme, since this represents how the participants must act. Whereas an **integer span program** represents how the distributor will construct the shares. However the integer span program provides much more algebraic structure to derive properties of group independent sharing schemes.

The outline of the paper is as follows: Sections 2 and 3 provide definitions and some mathematical background. Section 4 describes the two definitions of

---

[1] New in the sense that such problems had not been considered in the past as problems to base a public-key cryptosystem on.

group independent threshold sharing, GILTS and Black-box sharing. Section 5 describes group independent sharing schemes and their relation to integer span programs. Section 6 describes the dual of group independent threshold sharing. Section 7 provides some observations about group independent sharing, Section 8 describes new bounds on randomness required in a group independent threshold sharing scheme and Section 9 describes new necessary and sufficient conditions for group independent sharing schemes.

2   Definitions and Notation

If A is some subset of a universal set $\mathcal{U}$ then we will use $\tilde{A}$ to denote the complement of A. Let $\mathbf{Z}^{m,n}$ represent the set of all m by n matrices with integer entries. If A is a matrix, it's transpose will be denoted by A^T. A row (column) operation of type I is a row (column) interchange. A row (column) operation of type II is a row (column) multiplied by a nonzero constant. A row (column) operation of type III is a row (column) multiplied by a nonzero constant added to another row (column) leaving this result in the second row (column). The rank of a matrix is the number of linearly independent rows within the matrix. We will denote a row matrix by x and a column matrix by $\bar{y}$. If $x_1 \ldots x_n$ are vectors then a linear combination is $\sum_{i=1}^{n} \lambda_i x_i$ where $\lambda_i \in \mathbf{Z}$. $GL(n, \mathbf{Z})$ will denote the group with respect to matrix multiplication of all $n \times n$ nonsingular integer matrices. All row vectors will be denoted as x. If A is a matrix where A is partitioned by $A = [A_1|A_2|\cdots|A_n]$ and x is a row of A, then we can partition x as $x = (x_1, x_2, \ldots, x_n)$. Column vectors will be denoted by $\bar{x}$. The exponent of a group G is the smallest positive integer a such that $a \cdot g$ is the identity for all elements $g \in G$.[2] The set Γ of all sets of t or more participants is called the access structure. Because every set of t or more participants contains a set of precisely t participants, we will use Γ_0 to represent those sets which contain exactly t participants. Let μ and τ be positive integers, $M \in \mathbf{Z}^{\mu,\tau}$ and suppose that there exists a function ρ which labels each column of M with an element of $\{1, 2, \ldots, n\}$. Now if $B \subset \{1, 2, \ldots, n\}$ then M_B is the matrix which consists of all columns in M which are labeled to an element in B by ρ. (A simple example of a labeling function ρ is a partition of $M = [M_1|\cdots|M_n]$.)

3   Background Mathematics

Most of the mathematics in this section can be derived using simple tools from linear algebra. We do provide some of their proofs in the appendix as an aid to the reader. Let $A \in \mathbf{Z}^{\mu,\tau}$. Then the null space of A is defined as $ker(A) = \{\bar{x} \in \mathbf{Z}^\tau : A\bar{x} = \bar{0}\}$. We define the column space of A as $im(A^T) = \{\bar{y} \in \mathbf{Z}^\tau : y = A^T\bar{z} \text{ for some } \bar{z}\}$.

Lemma 1. *For all $\bar{x} \in ker(A)$ and $\bar{y} \in im(A^T)$, $\bar{y}^T\bar{x} = \bar{x}^T\bar{y} = 0$.*

___
[2] If G is an additive group then the exponent is the smallest positive integer a such that $ag = e$ for all $g \in G$ (here e denotes the identity of G).

Let $\mathcal{B} = \{\bar{b}_1, \bar{b}_2, \ldots, \bar{b}_\beta\}$ be a basis for $ker(A)$ and let $\mathcal{C} = \{\bar{c}_1, \bar{c}_2, \ldots, \bar{c}_\gamma\}$ be a basis for $im(A^T)$. Then the $span(\mathcal{B} \cup \mathcal{C})$ is the group generated by $\mathcal{B} \cup \mathcal{C}$. Consequently for each $z \in span(\mathcal{B} \cup \mathcal{C})$, there exists integers $u_1, \ldots u_\beta, v_1, \ldots, v_\gamma$ such that $z = \sum_{i=1}^{\beta} u_i \bar{b}_i + \sum_{i=1}^{\gamma} v_i \bar{c}_i$.

Lemma 2. *Let $\bar{z} \in span(\mathcal{B} \cup \mathcal{C})$ and suppose that for all $\bar{x} \in ker(A)$ we have $\bar{z}^T \bar{x} = 0$ then $\bar{z} \in im(A^T)$.*

Lemma 3. *Let $\bar{z} \in span(\mathcal{B} \cup \mathcal{C})$ and suppose that for all $\bar{x} \in im(A^T)$ we have $\bar{z}^T \bar{x} = 0$ then $\bar{z} \in ker(A)$.*

3.1 Smith-Normal Form

An important tool will be the reducing a matrix to Smith-normal form (for more information see [1,24]).

Let $A \in \mathbf{Z}^{\mu, \mathcal{T}}$. Suppose we reduce A to Smith-normal form, then there exists $U \in GL(\mu, \mathbf{Z})$ and $V \in GL(\mathcal{T}, \mathbf{Z})$ such that $U A V = D$ with $D = \begin{bmatrix} D_l & 0 \\ 0 & 0 \end{bmatrix}$, where D_l is a diagonal $l \times l$ matrix with nonzero integer entries d_i along the diagonal, called invariant factors, and satisfy $d_i | d_{i+1}$. U and V are nonsingular matrices which have integer entries. Let l denote the rank of A. Observe that U can be interpreted as a series of row operations of types I and/or III, and V can be interpreted as a series of column operations of type I and/or III that are performed on A to reduce it to D. Since the ring $\mathbf{Z}$ is a principal ideal domain, the invariant factors of A are unique, up to sign, we assume without loss of generality that all invariant factors are positive.

Note that $ker(D) = \{(0, 0, \ldots, 0, x_{l+1}, x_{l+2}, \ldots, x_\mathcal{T})^T : x_i \in \mathbf{Z}\}$ and that $im(D^T) = \{(d_1 x_1, d_2 x_2, \ldots d_l x_l, 0, 0, \ldots, 0)^T : x_i \in \mathbf{Z}\}$.

We now observe that $ker(A)$ and $im(A^T)$ can be computed by using the Smith-normal form of A. Reduce A to Smith-normal form. Thus $UAV = D$. It follows then that $U^{-1}DV^{-1} = A$. Now consider $\bar{x}$ such that $A\bar{x} = \bar{0}$. Then $UAVV^{-1}\bar{x} = \bar{0}$. Thus $DV^{-1}\bar{x} = \bar{0}$. Consequently $ker(D) = V^{-1} \cdot ker(A)$ and so $ker(A) = V \cdot ker(D)$. Now consider $\bar{y} \in im(A^T)$, then there exists $\bar{x}$ such that $\bar{y} = A^T\bar{x}$. Observe then that $V^T\bar{y} = V^T A^T U^T (U^T)^{-1}\bar{x}$. Hence $V^T\bar{y} = D^T (U^T)^{-1}\bar{x}$. Thus $V^T \cdot im(A^T) = im(D^T)$, which implies that $im(A^T) = (V^{-1})^T \cdot im(D^T)$.

Lemma 4. *Consider the equation $A\bar{x} = \bar{b}$ for fixed matrix $A \in \mathbf{Z}^{\mu, \mathcal{T}}$ and fixed column matrix $\bar{b} \in \mathbf{Z}^\mu$. Suppose $UAV = D$ reduces A to Smith-normal form, and that $d_1, \ldots, d_l$ represents the invariant factors of A. Then $A\bar{x} = \bar{b}$ has a solution iff for $i = 1, \ldots, l$, the invariant factor d_i divides $\sum_{j=1}^{\mathcal{T}} u_{ij} b_i$ and for all $i = l+1, \ldots, \mu$ we have $\sum_{j=1}^{\mathcal{T}} u_{ij} b_i = 0$, where u_{ij} is the ij term of the matrix U.*

Due to limited space we omit the proof.

Suppose we have reduced $A \in \mathbf{Z}^{\mu, \mathcal{T}}$ to Smith-normal form and we have derived

$$DV^{-1}\bar{x} = U\bar{b}. \tag{1}$$

In light of Lemma 4, we make the following observations. Observe that $l \leq min(\mu, \mathcal{T})$, and that $U \in \mathbf{Z}^{\mu,\mu}$ and $V \in \mathbf{Z}^{\mathcal{T},\mathcal{T}}$. Also note that $D \in \mathbf{Z}^{\mu,\mathcal{T}}$ and $U\bar{b} \in \mathbf{Z}^{\mu}$, where the $l + 1^{st}$ through the μth rows of D and $U\bar{b}$ consists of zeros. Therefore we can delete a suitable number of zero rows (or add zero rows if appropriate) of D and $U\bar{b}$, respectively, without altering the equality of the left and right hand sides of equation (1) until we form matrices with $\mathcal{T}$ rows. We will denote these two matrices by D_{del} and $(U\bar{b})_{del}$, respectively (now note that $D_{del} \in \mathbf{Z}^{\mathcal{T},\mathcal{T}}$ and $(U\bar{b})_{del} \in \mathbf{Z}^{\mathcal{T}}$). Also note that we will still have $D_{del}V^{-1}\bar{x} = (U\bar{b})_{del}$.

Let U' denote the product of elementary matrices which will normalize the nonzero diagonal entries of D_{del} (i.e. divide the diagonal entries by the invariant factors). Then $U' \in \mathbf{Q}^{\mathcal{T},\mathcal{T}}$, where $\mathbf{Q}$ denotes the set of rational numbers. Note that $(U')^{-1} \in \mathbf{Z}^{\mathcal{T},\mathcal{T}}$ and that

$$U'D_{del}V^{-1}\bar{x} = U'(U\bar{b})_{del} \text{ where } U'(U\bar{b})_{del} \in \mathbf{Z}^{\mathcal{T}}.$$

Lastly note that since U' does not modify rows $l + 1$ through $\mathcal{T}$, and that the $l + 1^{st}$ row through the $\mathcal{T}^{th}$ row of $U'(U\bar{b})_{del}$ will still consist of zeros. Let $X' = U'(U\bar{b})_{del}$.

Lemma 5. $\bar{x}$ *is a solution to the equation* $A\bar{x} = \bar{b}$ *(provided a solution exists) iff there exist integers* $z_{l+1}, \ldots, z_{\mathcal{T}}$ *such that* $\bar{x} = V\left(X' + [0, \ldots, 0, z_{l+1}, \ldots, z_{\mathcal{T}}]^T\right)$

Again, due to limited space we omit the proof.

We define $||\cdot||$ to be a function $||\cdot|| : \mathbf{Z}^{\mathcal{T}} \longrightarrow \mathbf{Z}$, such that $||\cdot||$ is additive, that is, $||\bar{x} + \bar{y}|| = ||\bar{x}|| + ||\bar{y}||$. [3] Then for all integers a, $||a\bar{x}|| = a||\bar{x}||$. Throughout this paper we will use $||\bar{x}|| = \sum_{i=1}^{\mathcal{T}} x_i$ where $\bar{x} = [x_1, \ldots, x_{\mathcal{T}}]^T$. However one could make several different choices for $||\cdot||$ (the choice of $||\cdot||$ will be dependent on the target vector used in the integer span program).

4   GILTS and Black-Box Secret Sharing

4.1   Definition of a t out of n Group Independent Linear Threshold Sharing Scheme

As introduced in [25], a group independent linear threshold sharing scheme is defined as:

Definition 1. *[25] Let* $\mathbf{K} = \{\mathcal{K} | \mathcal{K} \text{ is a finite abelian group}\}$. *A group independent t out of n linear threshold scheme or GILTS is an ordered pair* $(\Psi, \mathcal{S})$ *such that:*

(1) For each $\mathcal{K} \in \mathbf{K}$ *and for each* $i = 1, \ldots, n$ *there corresponds a sharespace* $S_{i,\mathcal{K}}$. *We write* $\mathcal{S}_i = \{S_{i,\mathcal{K}} : \mathcal{K} \in \mathbf{K}\}$ *and* $\mathcal{S} = (\mathcal{S}_1, \mathcal{S}_2, \ldots, \mathcal{S}_n)$.
(2) For all $B \in \Gamma_0$ *and for all* i *there exists a function* $\psi_{B,i}$ *such that for all* $\mathcal{K} \in \mathbf{K}$, $\psi_{B,i} : S_{i,\mathcal{K}} \longrightarrow \mathcal{K}$ *is a homomorphism. Further, for all* $k \in \mathcal{K}$,

---

[3] We are abusing the traditional use of $||\cdot||$ notation since norms are nonnegative, whereas in our definition there will be $\bar{x}$ such that $||\bar{x}|| < 0$.

shares $\bar{s}_i$ belonging to $S_{i,\mathcal{K}}$ are distributed to participant P_i such that $\forall B \in \Gamma_0$,
$k = \sum_{i \in B} \psi_{B,i}(\bar{s}_i)$ (here k is the secret that would be shared out),

(i) (privacy) $Prob(\mathbf{k} = k|\bar{s}_{i_1} = \bar{s}_{i_1}, \ldots, \bar{s}_{i_{t-1}} = \bar{s}_{i_{t-1}}) = Prob(\mathbf{k} = k)$, and

(ii) (completeness) $Prob(\mathbf{k} = k|\bar{s}_{i_1} = \bar{s}_{i_1}, \ldots, \bar{s}_{i_t} = \bar{s}_{i_t}) = 1$.

Thus in a GILTS $(\Psi, \mathcal{S})$, the Ψ refers to a collections of group independent functions which map sharespaces to the secret space (group), and $\mathcal{S}$ refers to a collection of sharespaces. We now make a series of assumptions. The same assumptions were made in [25], they are:

- We assume that $S_{i,\mathcal{K}}$ is the direct product $\mathcal{K}^{a_i}$ (since this is the only method known to achieve group independent sharing). Here $S_{i,\mathcal{K}}$ denotes participant P_i's share space, $\mathcal{K}$ is the keyspace (group), and a_i is some positive integer which will denote the number of subshares given to participant P_i.

- It is assumed that $\psi_{B,i}$ is a row matrix (with a_i columns) of integers (i.e. P_i possesses subshares which belong to the keyspace), such that $\psi_{B,i}(\bar{s}_i) = \psi_{B,i} \cdot \bar{s}_i$ where the latter is the scalar dot product between an integer vector and a vector containing group entries.

- When we use Ψ to describe a group independent t out of n threshold scheme, then Ψ will denote an integer matrix, i.e. $\Psi \in \mathbf{Z}^{\mu,\mathcal{T}}$ where $\mathcal{T} = \sum_{i=1}^{n} a_i$ (where a_i is described above and μ represents the cardinality of the access structure Γ [4]). We assume that Ψ has a partition into n submatrices. i.e. $\Psi = [A_1| \cdots |A_n]$ (here each row of A_i represents a $\psi_{B,i}$ described above). Shares are distributed to the n participants (which we collectively represent by $\bar{s}$) such that

$$\Psi \bar{s} = \bar{k} \text{ where } \bar{k} = [k, k, \ldots, k]^T. \tag{2}$$

Suppose that Ψ is reduced to Smith-normal form. Then there exists $U \in GL(\mu, \mathbf{Z})$ and $V \in GL(\mathcal{T}, \mathbf{Z})$ such that $U\Psi V = D$. Let l denote the rank of Ψ. Then $U\Psi V V^{-1}\bar{s} = U\bar{k}$. Hence $DV^{-1}\bar{s} = U\Psi V V^{-1}\bar{s} = U\bar{k}$. Consider the first l rows of the column matrix $U\bar{k}$. Each row can be interpreted as an integer $\sum_j \alpha_j u_{ij}$ applied to k. It follows then that $d_i|(\sum_j \alpha_j u_{ij})$. Since $d_i|\sum_{j=1}^{\mu} \alpha_j u_{ij}$ (for $i = 1, \ldots, l$), we can divide each of the first l rows by the corresponding d_i and still retain the form of an integer matrix. It follows then that we have

$$\begin{bmatrix} I_{l \times l} & 0_{l \times (\mathcal{T}-l)} \\ 0_{(\mu-l) \times l} & 0_{(\mu-l) \times (\mathcal{T}-l)} \end{bmatrix} V^{-1}\bar{s} = [k\frac{\sum_{i=1}^{\mu} \alpha_i u_{1i}}{d_1}, \ldots, k\frac{\sum_{i=1}^{\mu} \alpha_i u_{li}}{d_l}, 0, \ldots, 0]^T.$$

Let $R = \mathcal{T} - l$, and let $r_1, \ldots, r_R$ be chosen uniformly at *random* from $\mathcal{K}$. Then $V^{-1}\bar{s} = [k\frac{\sum_{i=1}^{\mu} \alpha_i u_{1i}}{d_1}, \ldots, k\frac{\sum_{i=1}^{\mu} \alpha_i u_{li}}{d_l}, r_1, \ldots, r_R]^T$. Therefore

$$\bar{s} = V[\frac{\sum_{i=1}^{\mu} \alpha_i u_{1i}}{d_1}k, \ldots \frac{\sum_{i=1}^{\mu} \alpha_i u_{li}}{d_l}k, r_1, \ldots, r_R]^T. \tag{3}$$

---

[4] At a later point in the paper, we will remark that Ψ does not need to have μ rows, but Ψ does need to have a basis for the row span for Ψ.

Represent V as $V = [X|Y]$, where X is a $\mathcal{T} \times l$ matrix (which is formed by using the first l columns of V). Then $\bar{s}$ can be represented as

$$\bar{s} = C[k, r_1, \ldots, r_R]^T, \tag{4}$$

where $C = \left[X \cdot [\frac{\sum_{i=1}^{\mu} \alpha_i u_{1i}}{d_1}, \ldots, \frac{\sum_{i=1}^{\mu} \alpha_i u_{li}}{d_l}]^T | Y\right]$. Consequently the application of Smith-normal form on the integer matrix Ψ that describes how the shareholders reconstruct the secret will provide the distributor's matrix C, which describes how to construct the shares. Further, the total number of subshares $\mathcal{T} = \sum a_i$ can be expressed as $R + l$. R is the number of random elements required, and l is the rank of Ψ.

In [17] the following necessary privacy condition was established.

Theorem 1. *[17,26] For all $B \subset \{P_1, \ldots, P_n\}$ with $B \notin \Gamma$, there exist matrices $Y_B \in \mathbf{Z}^{\mathcal{T}_B,R}$ and $Z_B \in \mathbf{Z}^R$ such that $\bar{s}_B = Y_B(Z_B k + \bar{r})$ where $\mathcal{T}_B = \sum_{i \in B} a_i$ and $\bar{r} = [r_1, \ldots r_R]^T$.*

Remark: Because one only needs to use a basis for the row span of Ψ, we will assume from now on that Ψ consists of l rows where l is the rank of Ψ and that $\Psi\bar{s} = [k, k, \ldots, k]^T$. If Ψ did not conform to this assumption one could perform row operations on Ψ to zero out the unneeded rows and drop these zeroed rows to form a new Ψ' which does conform to this assumption. Second, note that $\Psi \cdot C = [\bar{1}, \bar{0}, \ldots, \bar{0}]$ where $\bar{1} = [1, 1, \ldots, 1]^T$ and $\bar{0} = [0, 0, \ldots, 0]^T$.

4.2   Black-Box Secret Sharing and Integer Span Programs

At Crypto 2002 Cramer and Fehr [10] introduced what they called Black-box secret sharing. An important tool that was utilized in the development of black-box secret sharing scheme was their generalization of the Karchmer and Widgerson monotone span program [23]. Monotone span programs have been shown to be equivalent to linear secret sharing [2,21,23,31]. Here Cramer and Fehr generalized the monotone span program over arbitrary rings. Of particular interest to group independent threshold sharing schemes would be span programs over the set of integers, i.e. integer span programs.

Let S denotes a (not necessarily finite) commutative ring with 1. Let Γ be a monotone access structure on $\{1, \ldots, n\}$, and let $M \in S^{d,e}$ be a matrix whose d rows are labelled by a surjective function $\rho : \{1, \ldots, d\} \to \{1, \ldots, n\}$.

Definition 2. *[10] $\epsilon = (1, 0, \ldots, 0)^T \in S^e$ is called the target vector. $\mathcal{M} = (S, M, \rho, \epsilon)$ is called a monotone span program (over the ring S). If $S = \mathbf{Z}$, it is called an integer span program, or ISP, for short. The size of the ISP is defined as $size(M) = d$, where d is the number of rows of M.*

Definition 3. *[10] Let Γ be a monotone access structure and let $\mathcal{M} = (S, M, \rho, \epsilon)$ be a monotone span program over S. Then M is a monotone span program for Γ, if for all $A \subset \{1, \ldots, n\}$ the following holds.*

(i) (completeness) If $A \in \Gamma$, then $\epsilon \in im(M_A^T)$.

(ii) (privacy) If $A \notin \Gamma$, then there exists $\kappa = (\kappa_1, ..., \kappa_e)^T \in ker(M_A)$ with $\kappa_1 = 1$.

One says that M computes Γ.

Definition 4. *[10] Let Γ be a monotone access structure on $\{1, ..., n\}$, let $M = \mathbf{Z}^{d,e}$ matrix, ρ be a surjective labeling of the rows of M to $\{1, ..., n\}$. For each $A \in \Gamma$ let $\lambda(A) \in \mathbf{Z}^{d_A}$. Let E be the collection of all $\lambda(A)$. Then (M, ρ, E) is called an integer Γ scheme*

Formally the definition of Blackbox secret sharing is:

Definition 5. *[10] Let Γ be a monotone access structure on $\{1, ..., n\}$ and let $\mathcal{B} = (M, \rho, E)$ be an integer Γ scheme. Then $\mathcal{B}$ is a black-box secret sharing scheme for Γ if the following holds. Let G be an arbitrary finite Abelian group G, and let $A \subset \{1, ..., n\}$ be an arbitrary non-empty set. For arbitrarily distributed $s \in G$, let $\overline{g} = (g_1, ..., g_e)^T \in G^e$ be drawn uniformly at random, subject to $g_1 = s$. Define $\overline{s} = M\overline{g}$. Then:*

(Completeness) If $A \in \Gamma$, then $\overline{s}_A^T \lambda(A) = s$ with probability 1, where $\lambda(A) \in E$ is the reconstruction vector for A.

(Privacy) If $A \notin \Gamma$, then $\overline{s}_A$ contains no Shannon information on s.

Theorem 2. *[10] Let Γ be a monotone access structure on $\{1, ..., n\}$, and let $\mathcal{B} = (M, \rho, E)$ be an integer Γ scheme. Then $\mathcal{B}$ is a black-box secret sharing scheme for Γ if and only if $\mathcal{M} = (S, M, \rho, \epsilon)$ is an ISP for Γ and for all $A \in \Gamma$, its reconstruction vector $\lambda(A) \in E$ satisfies $M_A^T \lambda(A) = \epsilon$.*

5   Some Observations Concerning a GILTS and an ISP

We modify the definition of integer span program (ISP), this definition will be equivalent to the definition of an ISP as given in [10], but we use the target vector $\overline{1} = [1, 1, ..., 1]^T$ rather than ϵ. Due to this choice, we need to make other modifications to the definition of an ISP using a different completeness and privacy condition. As a side remark, we note that there are numerous equivalent versions of ISP using different target vectors. Our choice of this target vector is strategic in that the target vector $\overline{1}$ is a target vector that best illustrates the construction of the reconstruction matrix for the dual scheme.

Definition 6. *We say that $(M, \Gamma, \rho, \overline{1})$ is an integer span program over Γ provided*

(i)(completeness) for all $A \in \Gamma$ there exists $\overline{1} \in im(M_A^T)$ i.e. there exists $\overline{x}$ such that $\overline{1} = M_A^T \overline{x}$

(ii) (privacy) for all $A \notin \Gamma$, there exists a $\overline{x}$ with $\sum x_i = 1$ such that $\overline{x} \in ker(M_A)$.

Here ρ is the labeling of the rows of M (we will assume that M^T is an n-partitioned matrix). If $(M, \Gamma, \rho, \overline{1})$ is an ISP over Γ where Γ is the collection of all sets of participants that contain t or more members, then we will say that $(M, \Gamma, \rho, \overline{1})$ computes T_t^n (so T_t^n implies an ISP which computes a t out of n

threshold). If $(M, \Gamma, \rho, \bar{1})$ is an ISP that computes T_t^n, then we will say that M is an ISP that computes T_t^n with target vector $\bar{1}$. This definition is equivalent to Cramer and Fehr's.

Suppose Ψ is a t out of n GILTS, we construct a integer span program M in the following way. Recall that the representation of $\bar{s}$ given by (4), $\bar{s} = C[k, r_1, \ldots, r_R]^T$. We define the $\mathcal{T} \times (R+1)$ matrix M by $M = C \cdot F$ where F and F^{-1} are respectively

$$
F = \begin{bmatrix} 1 & 1 & 1 & \cdots & 1 \\ 0 & 1 & 0 & \cdots & 0 \\ 0 & 0 & 1 & \cdots & 0 \\ \vdots & & & & \\ 0 & 0 & 0 & \cdots & 1 \end{bmatrix} \quad F^{-1} = \begin{bmatrix} 1 & -1 & -1 & \cdots & -1 \\ 0 & 1 & 0 & \cdots & 0 \\ 0 & 0 & 1 & \cdots & 0 \\ \vdots & & & & \\ 0 & 0 & 0 & \cdots & 1 \end{bmatrix}. \tag{5}
$$

For $i = 1, .., R+1$, let $e_i \in \mathbf{Z}^{1,R+1}$ be the row vector with a 1 in the ith column and zeros elsewhere. Then $e_1 \cdot F = [1, 1, \ldots, 1]$ and for $2 \le i \le R+1$, $e_i \cdot F = e_i$. Observe that if $\bar{x}$ is such that $\sum x_i = 1$ then the first coordinate of $F \cdot \bar{x}$ is 1. Now note that $\bar{s}$, which is defined by equation (4), can be expressed as

$$
\bar{s} = M \cdot F^{-1} \cdot [k, r_1, \cdots, r_R]^T \tag{6}
$$

In [10], the following result was established using the target vector ϵ. We establish this result for the target vector $\bar{1}$ and our definition of an ISP. This result demonstrates that our use of the target vector $\bar{1}$ in the definition is appropriate. In addition, this proof will merge several ideas from [10] with [25] and [16]. However due to space consideration we have moved the proof to the appendix.

Theorem 3. *[10] M is an integer span program which computes T_t^n with target vector $\bar{1} = [1, 1, \ldots, 1]$ iff Ψ is a t out of n GILTS.*

Thus we see the connection between the ISP M and the distributor's sharing matrix C, since $M = C\dot{F}$. Because we have already established the relationship between Ψ and C, using Smith-normal form, we have implicitly developed a relationship between GILTS Ψ and ISP M.

6   The Dual

If Γ is an access structure for a secret sharing scheme, then the dual of this secret sharing scheme is a secret sharing scheme whose access structure is $\{B \subset \{P_1, \ldots, P_n\} : B \notin \tilde{\Gamma}\}$. The dual of the t out of n threshold sharing scheme is a $n - t + 1$ out of n threshold sharing scheme (and vice versa). The dual of t out of n threshold scheme has been discussed thoroughly in literature [2,21,18,31], however all of these have been limited to sharing over finite fields. At Crypto 2002, Cramer and Fehr [10] established that for each ISP which computes T_t^n there exists an ISP, of equal size, which computes T_{n-t+1}^n. Their proof was a constructive proof in that they constructed the T_{n-t+1}^n ISP from the ISP which computed T_t^n. Our contribution here shows how to construct the dual from a t out of n GILTS. It will become apparent how to construct a $n - t + 1$ out of n GILTS from a t out of n GILTS. Again recall that we are using an target vector different than the one use in [10]. Our construction of the dual will demonstrate why we choose to use the target vector equal to $\overline{1}$.

Suppose Ψ is a t out of n GILTS, such that shares $\overline{s}$ are distributed to participants so that $\Psi \overline{s} = \overline{k}$ where $\overline{k}^T = [k, k, \ldots, k]$. Let M represent the integer span program derived from Ψ which computes T_t^n. Thus $\Psi \cdot M = [\overline{1}, \ldots, \overline{1}]$. Let $M_{dual} = \Psi^T$ and let $\Psi_{dual} = M^T$. We claim that M_{dual} is a an integer span program which can compute T_{n-t+1}^n, and that Ψ_{dual} is a $n - t + 1$ out of n GILTS.

Theorem 4. *[10] M_{dual} is a an integer span program which computes T_{n-t+1}^n.*

We attribute this theorem to Cramer and Fehr. Because we are using a slightly different definition of an ISP, a proof is provided in the pre-proceedings version of this paper [27].

Corollary 1. *Ψ_{dual} is a $n - t + 1$ out of n GILTS.*

If Ψ is a t out of n GILTS, then we will use an $*$ to refer to the corresponding dual GILTS. Thus $\Psi^* = M^T$, $M^* = \Psi^T$ and $C^* = M^* \cdot F^{-1}$ (where F^{-1} represents the $l \times l$ matrix described by (5)). That is the transpose of the ISP is the reconstruction matrix of the dual. Let R^* denote the number of random elements needed to generate the GILTS Ψ^*, and let l^* denote the rank of Ψ^*. Then $R^* = l - 1$ and $l^* = R + 1$. These results are very ironic. For example, the shareholders reconstruction matrix can be used to develop the distributor sharing matrix for the dual.

Example 1. Consider the following 2 out of 3 GILTS. Suppose k is the secret and two random elements r_1, r_2 are selected uniformly random from the group. Now suppose that the dealer deals the following shares to the 3 participants: $\overline{s}_1 = (k - r_1, r_2)$, $\overline{s}_2 = k - r_2$ and $\overline{s}_3 = (r_1, r_2)$. Then

$$\Psi = \begin{bmatrix} 1 & 0 & 0 & 1 & 0 \\ 0 & 1 & 1 & 0 & 0 \\ 0 & 0 & 1 & 0 & 1 \end{bmatrix}.$$

It can be shown that

$$C = \begin{bmatrix} 1 & -1 & 0 \\ 0 & 0 & 1 \\ 1 & 0 & -1 \\ 0 & 1 & 0 \\ 0 & 0 & 1 \end{bmatrix} \quad \text{where } \overline{s} = \begin{bmatrix} s_{11} \\ s_{12} \\ s_{21} \\ s_{31} \\ s_{32} \end{bmatrix} = C \begin{bmatrix} k \\ r_1 \\ r_2 \end{bmatrix} \quad \text{and where } M = \begin{bmatrix} 1 & 0 & 1 \\ 0 & 0 & 1 \\ 1 & 1 & 0 \\ 0 & 1 & 0 \\ 0 & 0 & 1 \end{bmatrix}$$

(here $M = C \cdot F$ where F is a 3×3 matrix). Observe that $\overline{s} = [\overline{s}_1, \overline{s}_2, \overline{s}_3]^T = C \cdot [k, r_1, r_2]^T$. Now $\Psi^* = M^T$ describes a $3 - 2 + 1 = 2$ out of 3 GILTS.

We now summarize how to construct the dual. The algorithm is based on equation (3) and equation (4).

Algorithm 1 *(Input = Ψ; Output = Ψ^*)*
Let Ψ be a t out of n GILTS. Assume that $\Psi \in \mathbf{Z}^{l,\mathcal{T}}$ where $l=$ rank of Ψ. Observe that to determine $\bar{s}$ such that $\Psi \bar{s} = \bar{k}$ is comparable to solving $\Psi \bar{x} = \bar{1}$.

(i) Reduce Ψ to Smith-normal form. i.e. $U\Psi V = D$. (Then $U\Psi V V^{-1}\bar{x} = U\bar{1}$.)

(ii) Let $U'\bar{1}$ denote the column matrix generated by dividing each row of $U\bar{1}$ by the invariant factor d_i of D.

(iii) Represent V by $V = [X|Y]$ where X denoted the first l columns of V and Y denotes the remaining R columns of V.

(iv) Let

$$C = \left[X \cdot U'\bar{1} \,|\, Y \right]$$

(iv) Set $M = C * F$ where F is given by equation (5).
(v) Lastly, let $\Psi^* = M^T$.

Observe that this algorithm can be used as well to output the ISP M, since $M = (\Psi^*)^T$. Further this algorithm can be used to determine C, since C is computed in step (iv) of the algorithm. If the reader is interested in an algorithm which can compute a Ψ, there are several in literature including [15,16]. Some of the methods defined to compute secret sharing schemes over fields can be modified to generate group independent sharing schemes. For example one can modify the monotone circuit construction algorithm in [30] to generate a group independent sharing scheme.

7   An ISP M Implies the Reconstruction Matrix Ψ

In [10], the authors constructed a ISP of size $O(n \log_2 n)$ which computed T_t^n with a target vector $\epsilon = [1, 0, \dots, 0]$. The authors then suggested that the corresponding Blackbox secret sharing could be generated using techniques in [16]. We point out that by utilizing the Smith-normal form technique on the dual, we can generate the reconstruction matrix Ψ. Let us denote the ISP developed [10] which computes T_t^n and has target vector ϵ by W. Then set $M = W \cdot F$ where F is given by (5). It follows that M is an ISP which computes T_t^n with target vector $\bar{1}$. Given M, we know that $\Psi^* = M^T$ is a $n-t+1$ out of n GILTS. Using the Smith-normal form derivation method, given Ψ^* we can compute C^* by using equation (4). We then can compute $M^* = C^* \cdot F$. Now set $\Psi = (M^*)^T$. Thus we have constructed the reconstruction function Ψ for the secret sharing scheme implied by the ISP W.

From the above remark we see that by starting with an ISP M, we can construct Ψ, by utilizing the dual. We now ask if we go in a complete circle will we derive M. That is, will M^{**} always be equivalent to M? We can ask the analogous question will Ψ^{**} always be equivalent to Ψ?[5] The answer to both of these questions is no, the proof is by example.

Theorem 5. *There exists a Ψ, a t out of n GILTS, such that $im(\Psi^{**}) \neq im(\Psi)$. Similarly there exists an ISP M which computes T_t^n such that $im((M^{**})^T) \neq im(M^T)$.*

The proof is given by Example 2 in the appendix.

8   Randomness Required to Generate a GILTS

Because one needs to seed a sharing scheme with truly random elements, it is important for the distributor to know the randomness requirement needed to generate a secret sharing scheme. Considerable amount of work has been done on generating bounds on randomness in secret sharing schemes, see [5,6,7,8,11, 12]. In the cases of [6,11] it was to develop randomness bounds for secret sharing schemes, that were not necessarily threshold sharing schemes. In [7,8], bounds were developed for multisecret sharing scheme and/or dynamic threshold scheme. Bounds on the amount of randomness in group independent sharing schemes have been discussed in [25].

Theorem 6. *[25] For a t out of n GILTS, the number R of random elements needed to generate a GILTS satisfies $R + 1 \geq \sqrt{1 + \log_2 \binom{n}{t-1}}$.*

The bound $R + 1 \geq 1 + \log_2 \binom{n}{t-1}$ can be established under certain conditions[6]. We now find that we can improve upon all the bounds as a consequence of the following result and Theorem 4.
From [26] the following was established.

Theorem 7. *[26] If Ψ is a t out of n GILTS then the rank l of Ψ is bounded by $l \geq 1 + \log_2 \binom{n}{t}$.*

We now observe that the rank l^* of a $n - t + 1$ out of n GILTS Ψ^* must satisfy $l^* \geq 1 + \log_2 \binom{n}{n-t+1}$. Since $l^* = R + 1$, we find that the following is true.

Theorem 8. *If Ψ is a t out of n GILTS then the number R of random elements needed to generate a GILTS is bounded by $R \geq \log_2 \binom{n}{n-t+1}$.*

Since the bound in Theorem 7 is tight in the case $n - t + 1 = n - 1$, it immediately follows that the bound Theorem 8 is tight when $t = 2$. Observe that $\binom{n}{t-1} = \binom{n}{n-t+1}$ and so this new randomness bound has improved upon Theorem 6, no longer requiring the square root.
The following result was established in [10]. We restate it using our notation.

---

[5] By equivalent we are referring to the condition that the row spans of each matrix are equal to each other. For example, $im(\Psi^{**}) = im(\Psi)$.

[6] If any set of t participants can not only compute k but possess enough information that they can compute all shares distributed to the n participants.

Theorem 9. *[10] Let Ψ denote a t out of n GILTS then the size of Ψ, denoted by $\mathcal{T} = \sum_{i=1}^{n} a_i$ is bounded by $\Omega(n \log n)$.*

Using the above bound, the bounds on rank and randomness can be improved upon. First we need to state a result from [25].

Theorem 10. *[25] For each $i = 1, \ldots, n$, either the rank of A_i equals the size of $\bar{s}_i$ or participant P_i can reduce his share size to the rank of A_i. Thus one can assume that the rank of A_i is equal to a_i (the number of columns of A_i).*

Theorem 11. *Let Ψ be a t out of n GILTS and l the rank of Ψ, then $l \geq 1 + \log_2(n \cdot (n-1) \cdots (t+1))$.*

Proof. We provide a sketch of the proof. Recall $\Psi = [A_1 | \cdots | A_n]$ where A_i is a $l \times a_i$ matrix. Since the size of a ISP which computes T_t^n is $\Omega(n \log_2 n)$, we have $\sum_{i=1}^{n} a_i \geq n \log_2 n$. Therefore there exists an i such that $a_i \geq \log_2 n$. We will assume without loss of generality that $i = 1$ (otherwise we would interchange submatrices until we have interchanged A_i with A_1). By Theorem 10, each A_i has rank a_i. To establish the lower bound on rank we reduce Ψ to a triangular form (we do not require the leading entry to be a one) and make an argument about the number of rows remaining in the triangularized Ψ. Since A_1 has rank $a_1 \geq \log_2 n$, if U_1 is the product of elementary row operations that triangularize the first a_1 columns, then $U_1\Psi$ will have at least a_1 nonzero rows. Now consider the GILTS where we remove participant P_1, this is a t out of $n-1$ scheme. By Theorem 9 this requires $\Omega((n-1) \log_2(n-1))$ shares, so there exists a submatrix for which has at least $\log_2(n-1)$ column entries in the rows where participant P_1 does not participate that were not affected by row operations U_1. We assume without loss of generality that this is submatrix A_2. We continue the process of triangularizing, however we now use $U_1\Psi$. Now U_1 has not modified at least $\log_2(n-1)$ columns of A_2, so if we let U_2 be the product of elementary row operations that triangularize the columns $a_1 + 1$ through a_2, then $U_2U_1\Psi$ has at least $\log_2 n + \log_2(n-1)$ nonzero rows. So far we see that $l \geq \log_2 n + \log_2(n-1)$. We continue this process. At the $n - t - 1$ stage we have triangularized the first $\sum_{i=1}^{n-t-1} a_i$ columns od Ψ, we have computed $U_{n-t-1} \cdots U_2U_1\Psi$ and we have established $l \geq \log_2 n + \log_2(n-1) + \cdots + \log_2(n - (n-t-1) + 1)$. At this stage we can see that by removing participants $P_1, \ldots, P_{n-t-1}$ we still have a t out of $t+1$ scheme. By Theorem 9 we see that the number of shares is $\Omega((t+1) \log_2(t+1))$. Thus there exists a submatrix for which at least $\log_2(t+1)$ columns entries in the rows for which participants $P_1, \ldots, P_{n-t-1}$ do not participate that were not affected by $U_{n-t-1} \cdots U_2U_1$. We assume without loss of generality this is submatrix A_{n-t}. We now continue the triangularization process focusing on columns $\sum_{i=1}^{n-t-1} a_i + 1$ though $\sum_{i=1}^{n-t} a_i$. Again $U_{n-t-1} \cdots U_2U_1$ has not modified at least $\log_2(t+1)$ of these columns. Let U_{n-t} be the product of elementary row matrices which triangularize these columns, then $l \geq \log_2 n + \log_2(n-1) + \cdots + \log_2(t+2) + \log_2(t+1)$. Now consider the removal of participant $P_1, \ldots, P_{n-t}$, what remains is a t out of t scheme, thus each participant must be given at least one subshare. As we continue to triangularize we see that in columns $\sum_{i=1}^{n-t} a_i + 1$ though $\sum_{i=1}^{n-t+1} a_i$ there must be at least one column entry in the rows for which participants $P_1, \ldots, P_{n-t}$ do not participate which has not been modified by the product $U_{n-t} \cdots U_2 U_1$. Hence $l \geq 1 + \log_2 n + \log_2(n-1) + \cdots + \log_2(t+2) + \log_2(t+1)$ Thus $l \geq 1 + \log_2(n \cdot (n-1) \cdots (t+2) \cdot (t+1))$, and so the proof is complete.

Theorem 12. *If Ψ is a t out of n GILTS then the number R of random elements needed to generate the GILTS is bounded by $R \geq \log_2(n \cdot (n-1) \cdots (n-t+3) \cdot (n-t+2))$.*

Proof. Let Ψ be a t out of n GILTS. Let M denote the ISP which computes T_t^n. Then $\Psi^* = M^T$ is a $n-t+1$ out of n GILTS. Therefore by Theorem 11, $l^* \geq 1 + \log_2(n \cdot (n-1) \cdots (n-t+1+1))$. Since $1 + R = l^*$, we have $R \geq \log_2(n \cdot (n-1) \cdots (n-t+2))$.

This bound on randomness, as well as the bound on the rank of Ψ, is a significant improvement on all previous bounds on rank and randomness of group independent threshold sharing schemes. These bounds most definitely reflect (not necessarily tightly in all cases) known values for rank and randomness of GILTS and ISP that have been constructed with minimal number of subshares. For example we know of a 7 out of 8 GILTS which requires the minimal number of subshares 24 and has minimal rank of 4 hence $R = 20$. Previous randomness bounds did not explain why R needed to be so close to 24. The randomness bound described in Theorem 12 clearly demonstrates that if $n-t$ is small then R will be asymptotically close to $\log_2 n!$. Lastly, Cramer and Fehr have established that $\mathcal{T} = \sum_{i=1}^{n} a_i$ has an asymptotic bound of $\Omega(n \log n)$. Notice that $\mathcal{T} = l + R \geq 1 + \log_2(n \cdot (n-1) \cdots (t+2) \cdot (t+1)) + \log_2(n \cdot (n-1) \cdots (n-t+3) \cdot (n-t+2)) \geq \log_2(n!)$. Asymptotically $O(\log_2(n!)) = O(n \log_2 n)$, and so it does not appear that one could make any improvements on these bounds from an asymptotic sense.

9   Necessary and Sufficient Conditions for a GILTS

Let $\Psi \in \mathbf{Z}^{l,\mathcal{T}}$ be a $l \times \mathcal{T}$ integer matrix. Suppose that there exists a function ρ which assigns to each column of Ψ a member of $\{1, 2, \ldots, n\}$. To this end, by rearranging columns we can just assume that ρ implies a partition of Ψ such that $\Psi = [A_1 | A_2 | \cdots | A_n]$. We will assume that the column rank of A_i is equal to the number of columns of A_i. And lastly we will assume that the rank of Ψ is l.

We now ask what are the necessary conditions for Ψ to define a t out of n GILTS. That is, what are the formal requirements for Ψ to satisfy Definition 1? The necessary and sufficient conditions for Ψ to be a t out of n GILTS can be summarized as follows (i) The integer matrix equation $\Psi \overline{x} = [1, 1, \ldots 1]^T$ must be solvable. Thus Ψ must satisfy Lemma 4. (ii) For each $B \in \Gamma$ there exists integers $x_1, \ldots x_\mu$ where $\sum x_i = 1$ such that the linear combination $\sum_{i=1}^{\mu} x_i \psi_i$

reduces to a row vector whose column entries that correspond to participants in $\tilde{B}$ are zero. (iii) Theorem 1 must be satisfied for all $B \subset \{P_1, ..., P_n\}$ with $B \notin \Gamma$.

In light of recent work in [10] and our observations we can revise the necessary and sufficient conditions to a set of criteria that only Ψ needs to satisfy. That is, we have the following.

Theorem 13. *The necessary and sufficient conditions for Ψ to be a t out of n GILTS is:*

(i) for all $B \subset \{P_1, \ldots, P_n\}$ with $|B| \geq n - t + 1$ there exists $\bar{x}$ such that $\bar{1} = \Psi_B \bar{x}$, and

(ii) for all $B \subset \{P_1, \ldots, P_n\}$ with $|B| \leq n - t$ there exists $\bar{x}$ with $||x|| = \sum x_i = 1$ such that $\bar{0} = \Psi_B^T \bar{x}$.

The proof is provided in the pre-proceedings version of this paper [27].

10   Conclusion

This work has merged several works. Our contributions include: we have demonstrated how to construct the dual of a t out of n GILTS from the shareholders reconstruction matrix Ψ. In the appendix we have provided an example. As we have stated earlier the shareholders reconstruction matrix is a more natural way to view a threshold sharing scheme than by the distributor's share construction matrix. The shareholders reconstruction matrix is what a GILTS represents and an ISP implies the distributor's share construction matrix. Further we have demonstrated how to use Smith-normal form to derive the distributor's share construction matrix from a GILTS Ψ. Using results by Cramer and Fehr, we have developed new bounds on the rank of the reconstruction matrix and the amount of randomness needed to generate a t out of n GILTS. These bounds are significant improvements to any other existing bounds for group independent sharing and their asymptotic sum equals the minimal size GILTS (Block-box sharing scheme). Thus these bounds cannot be improved upon asymptotically. Since one requires truly random elements to be generated to develop a group independent scheme, the amount of randomness required does place a computational burden on the distributor. Consequently these bounds are important. Bounds on rank are important due to the nature that the dual of a t out of n GILTS is a $n - t + 1$ out of n GILTS. Lastly we have developed a new set of criteria to determine if a n-partitioned integer matrix is a t out of n GILTS. Let the term *optimal GILTS* refer to a GILTS which uses a minimal number of subshares. We do raise a few questions. In our attempt to describe group independent linear sharing we assumed that each homomorphism $\psi_{B,i}$ was a row of integers. All known group independent schemes are of this form. Does there exist a group independent scheme not of this form? Do all optimal group independent t out of n threshold scheme have invariant factors equal to 1? All optimal schemes discussed in previous works are such that the integer entries of Ψ is 0,1, or -1. Is this true in general for all optimal schemes? That is, is it a requirement? (Here we are not referring to schemes that are asymptotically optimal.)

References

1. W. Adkins and S. Weintrab. *Algebra, an approach via module theory.* Springer-Verlag, NY, 1992.
2. A. Beimel. "Secure schemes for secret sharing and key distribution". Ph.D.-thesis, Technion, Haifa, June 1996.
3. J. Benaloh and J. Leichter. "Generalized secret sharing and monotone functions". In *Proc. CRYPTO '88*, Springer LNCS, vol. 765, pp. 274–285, 1988.
4. S. Blackburn, M. Burmester, Y. Desmedt, and P. Wild. "Efficient Multiplicative Sharing schemes". In *Advances in Cryptology - Eurocrypt '96, LNCS 1070*, pp. 107–118, Springer-Verlag, 1996.
5. C. Blundo, A. De Santis, and U. Vaccaro. "Randomness in Distribution Protocols". *Inform. Comput.* pp. 111–139, 1996.
6. C. Blundo, A.G. Gaggia, and D. R. Stinson. "On the Dealer's randomness Required in Secret Sharing Schemes". In *Design, Codes and Cryptography*, 11, pp. 235–259, 1997.
7. C. Blundo and B. Masucci. "Randomness in Multi-Secret Sharing Schemes". In *Journal of Universal Computer Science*, Vol. 5, No. 7, 1999, pp. 367–389.
8. C. Blundo and B. Masucci. "A note on the Randomness in Dynamic Threshold Scheme". In *Journal of Computer Security*, Vol. 7, No. 1, 1999, pp. 73–85.
9. C. Boyd. "Digital Multisignatures", *Cryptography and coding*, Clarendon Press, 1989, pp 241–246.
10. R. Cramer and S. Fehr. "Optimal Black-box secret sharing over arbitrary abelian groups". In *CRYPTO 2002*.
11. L. Csirmaz. "The dealer's random bits in perfect sharing schemes" In *Studia Sci. Math. Hungar.* 32(1996) pp.429–437.
12. A. De Santis, and B. Masucucci. "Multiple Ramp Schemes". In *IEEE Transns. on Inform. Theory*, 45, no. 5, pp. 1720–1728, 1999.
13. A. De Santis, Y. Desmedt, Y. Frankel, and M. Yung. "How to share a function". In *Proceedings of the twenty-sixth annual ACM Symp. Theory of Computing (STOC)*, pp. 522–533, 1994.
14. Y. Desmedt. Society and group oriented cryptography: a new concept. In *Advances of Cryptology- Crypto '87*
15. Y. Desmedt, G. Di Crescenzo, and M. Burmester. "Multiplicative non-Abelian sharing schemes and their application to threshold cryptography". In *Advances in Cryptology - Asiacrypt '94, LNCS 917.* pp. 21–32, Springer-Verlag, 1995.
16. Y. Desmedt and Y. Frankel. "Homomorphic zero-knowledge threshold schemes over any finite Abelian group". In *Siam J. Disc. Math. vol 7, no. 4* pp. 667–679, SIAM, 1994.
17. Y. Desmedt and S. Jajodia. "Redistributing secret shares to new access structures and its applications". Tech. Report ISSE-TR-97-01, George Mason University, July 1997 ftp://isse.gmu.edu/pub/techrep/97.01.jajodia.ps.gz
18. S. Fehr. "Efficient Construction of the Dual Span Program". May 1999, Manuscript, ETH Zurich.
19. Y. Frankel, P. Gemmel, P. Mackenzie, and M. Yung. "Proactive RSA". In *Advances of Cryptology-Crypto '97*, 1997, LNCS 1294, Springer Verlag, 1997, p. 440–454.
20. Y. Frankel, P. Gemmel, P. Mackenzie, and M. Yung. "Optimal-Resilience Proactive Public-key Cryptosystems". In *Proc. 38th FOCS*, IEEE, 1997, p. 384–393.
21. A. Gal. "Combinatorial methods in boolean function complexity". Ph.D.-thesis, University of Chicago, 1995.

22. R. Gennaro, S. Jarecki, H. Krawczyk, and T. Rabin. "Robust and efficient sharing of RSA functions". In *Advances of Cryptology-Crypto '96*, LNCS 1109, Springer Verlag, 1996, p. 157–172.
23. M. Karchmer and A. Wigderson. "On span programs" In *Proc. of 8th annual Complexity Theory Conference*, pp 102–111, 1993.
24. H.L. Keng. *Introduction to Number Theory*. Springer Verlag, NY 1982
25. B. King. "Randomness Required for Linear Threshold Sharing Schemes Defined over Any Finite Abelian Group". In *ACISP 2001*. pp. 376–391.
26. B. King. "Some results in linear secret sharing". Ph.D. thesis, University of Wisconsin Milwaukee, 2001.
27. B. King. "A comment on group independent threshold sharing". *Pre-Proceedings of WISA 2003*, Aug. 25-27, 2003. pg. 471–488.
28. A. Shamir. "How to share a secret", *Comm. ACM*, 22(1979), pp 612–613.
29. V. Shoup. "Practical Threshold Signatures". In *Advances in Cryptology - EU-ROCRYPT 2000*, LNCS 1807, Springer Verlag 2000, p. 207–220.
30. D. Stinson. *Cryptography, Theory and Practice*. CRC Press, NY, 1995
31. M. van Dijk. "A Linear Construction of Secret Sharing Schemes". In *Design, Codes and Cryptography* 12, pp. 161–201, 1997.

Appendix

Example 2. The following 2 out of 4 GILTS example illustrates that Ψ^{**} does not necessarily equal Ψ. Consider the following 2 out of 4 GILTS satisfying $\Psi \overline{s} = \overline{k}$ where Ψ is 6×8 matrix (partitioning is described below). The last row of Ψ implicitly describes a relation between s_{22} and s_{32}, the relation is that $2s_{22} + 2s_{32} = 0$. The invariant factors of Ψ are: $d_1 = \cdots d_5 = 1$ and $d_6 = 2$. By applying the techniques that we have described (i.e. reducing Ψ to Smith-normal form) we derive the matrix M (see below). As we have illustrated earlier $\Psi^* = M^T$, where Ψ^* will be a $4 - 2 + 1$ out of 4 GILTS, i.e. 3 out of 4 GILTS. We apply that same techniques (reduce Ψ^* to Smith-normal form) to derive M^*. The result is illustrated below.

$$\Psi = \begin{bmatrix} 1 & 0 & 0 & 0 & 0 & 0 & 1 & 0 \\ 1 & 0 & 0 & 0 & 1 & 0 & 0 & 0 \\ 0 & 0 & 1 & 0 & 1 & 0 & 0 & 0 \\ 0 & 1 & 0 & 1 & 0 & 0 & 0 & 0 \\ 0 & 0 & 0 & 0 & 0 & 1 & 0 & 1 \\ 0 & 1 & 0 & 3 & 0 & 2 & 0 & 0 \end{bmatrix}$$

$$M = \begin{bmatrix} 0 & -1 & 0 \\ 1 & 1 & 2 \\ 0 & -1 & 0 \\ 0 & 0 & -1 \\ 1 & 2 & 1 \\ 0 & 0 & 1 \\ 1 & 2 & 1 \\ 1 & 1 & 0 \end{bmatrix}$$

$$M^* = \begin{bmatrix} 0 & -2 & -1 & 0 & -1 & 1 \\ 0 & 1 & 0 & 0 & 0 & -1 \\ 1 & 1 & 2 & 1 & 3 & 1 \\ 0 & 0 & 0 & 1 & 1 & 0 \\ 1 & 1 & 1 & 1 & 2 & 1 \\ 0 & 0 & 0 & 1 & 0 & 1 \\ 0 & -2 & 0 & 0 & 0 & 1 \\ 0 & 1 & 0 & 0 & -1 & 0 \end{bmatrix}$$

Now $\Psi^{**} = (M^*)^T$, we claim that $\Psi^{**} \neq \Psi$. This can be seen by the fact that $[0,0,0,1,0,1,0,0]^T \notin im(\Psi^T)$. (Although it is true that $[0,0,0,2,0,2,0,0]^T \in im(\Psi^T)$.) Now observe that $[0,0,0,1,0,1,0,0]^T = (\Psi^{**})^T \cdot [-1,0,0,1,0,0]^T$

Automation-Considered Logic of Authentication and Key Distribution

Taekyoung Kwon[1]* and Seongan Lim[2]

[1] Sejong University, Seoul 143-747, Korea
[2] Korea Information Security Agency, Seoul 138-803, Korea

Abstract. This paper presents an automation-considered logic of authentication for reasoning about principals' belief on authentication and key distribution protocols. The so-called ASVO logic is based upon the famous SVO logic but designed in the slightly different way that minimizes the protocol idealization needs. For the purpose, message receiving and message recognition are reformulated in the similar semantic model. As an experimental study, we implemented the proposed logic to a semi-automated formal verification tool, and analyzed several protocols.

Keywords: Authentication protocols, formal methods in security.

1   Introduction

Authentication and key distribution protocols are typical forms of security protocols which should not be designed without careful construction and verification processes. These are composed of a set of messages having a specific form for authentication of principals and key distribution among them using cryptographic algorithms. Authentication is essentially assurance of who the principal is talking to, while key distribution is represented as key transport or key exchange among the principals. In that sense, a formal method is necessary for verifying formally if the principal is talking to the correct counterpart and they share the correct session key via protocols [23]. There has been a great amount of work related to the formal verification of such protocols. We can classify them simply into *inference construction* and *attack construction* methods [12]. The former schemes are based on modal logics in order to infer the belief or knowledge of principals as logical formulae, while the latter methods are focused on the automation-based model checking that relies on building a finite model of a system and checking that a desired property holds in that model [21]. In spite that both approaches are equally important, our main concerns are simply automation-considered logic methods, so that this paper will describe the method related to the former only. Readers are assumed to be familiar with notations and schemes of [6,11,22]

* This work was supported in part by R&D project 2002-S-073 of Korea Information Security Agency.

K. Chae and M. Yung (Eds.): WISA 2003, LNCS 2908, pp. 442–457, 2004.
© Springer-Verlag Berlin Heidelberg 2004

The rest of this paper is organized as follows: Section 2 describes backgrounds and problems, while Section 3 summarizes the ASVO (Automation-considered SVO) logic designed for automation-considered reasoning about principals' belief. Section 4 shows experimental results and Section 5 concludes this paper.

2   Preliminaries

2.1   Logics of Authentication

In 1989, Burrows, Abadi, and Needham presented the first logic of authentication, BAN logic [6], for the analysis of authentication protocols. The BAN logic is a logic of belief, so that its inference system uses formulae which express belief of principals. This logic is quite simple and useful in uncovering some flaws in authentication protocols but has intrinsic weaknesses and limitations specifically related to its semantics. The lack of semantics has produced confusion and controversy about the logic [1,3,18]. In the sequel, a lot of successors have followed the BAN logic. For example, Abadi and Tuttle defined the semantics for BAN in their extension, AT logic [1]. Gong, Needham, and Yahalom reformulated BAN for better reasoning about belief of principals in their extension, GNY logic [11]. Van Oorschot defined additional rules for reasoning about key agreement protocols in his extension, VO logic [20]. More recently, Syverson and Van Oorschot devised SVO logic in order to unify the previous BAN family of authentication logics [22]. Note that the SVO logic provided a model-theoretic semantics along with the desirable features of its predecessors. As for automated reasoning, Brackin extended GNY to BGNY logic in implementing his AAPA system [5], while Dekker fragmented SVO to SVD logic in his C3PO system [7].

2.2   Protocol Idealization

There are several steps to a protocol analysis using BAN-family logics [1,6,11, 22,20]. We can generalize them as follows. For a given protocol:

1. State goals to achieve.
2. Write assumptions about initial state.
3. Idealize (or annotate) the protocol.
4. Annotate (or idealize) the protocol.
5. Apply the logic to derive principals' beliefs.

Notice that step 3 and step 4 are interchangeable. For example, BAN and AT make idealization precede annotation while GNY and SVO reverse it. Readers are referred to [1,6,11,22,20] for more details.

The *idealization* is an important step in BAN-family logics, which transforms some protocol messages into logical formulae in order to apply the given logics. In other words, the idealization step presents a message *interpretation* to the logic because a protocol message is interpreted into a truth value. BAN-family logics have respective idealization methods, for example, BAN injects implicit terms or formulae into protocol messages for transformation, while GNY labels *recognizable* messages and postfixes BAN ideal formulae onto the message as a meaning conveyed from the message [6,11]. Wedel and Kessler intended that formulae do not occur in messages but the received messages still need to be interpreted manually [24]. SVO divided the idealization step into message comprehension and message interpretation. On message comprehension, messages which cannot be comprehended by principals are substituted by $*_i$. Subsequently the BAN ideal formulae are injected to protocol messages on message interpretation [22]. For example, when a principal, A, received from S a message, $\{N_A, B, K_{AB}, \{K_{AB}, A\}_{K_{BS}}\}_{K_{AS}}$, the message comprehension step should produce a formula in SVO, such as A believes A received $\{N_A, B, *_1, *_2\}_{K_{AS}}$. In the sequel, message interpretation should yield the following logical inference.

A believes A received $\{N_A, B, *_1, *_2\}_{K_{AS}} \Rightarrow$

A believes A received $\{N_A, B, A \xleftrightarrow{K_{AB}} B, \mathsf{fresh}(K_{AB}), *_2\}_{K_{AS}}$

Also $*_2$ must be re-transformed to $\{(K_{AB}, A)^S\}_{K_{BS}}$ on applying the rules or axioms in the protocol analysis. The superscript S is added to indicate that the message is from S but it is informal. $A \xleftrightarrow{K_{AB}} B$ and $\mathsf{fresh}(K_{AB})$ are BAN formulae that must be attained as implicit interpretation of messages. As we can see, the so-called idealization is informal and far from automation-considered reasoning in all BAN-families [23]. For instance, the previous automated reasoning systems such as AAPA and C3PO still needed manual interpretation of messages for accommodating automated reasoning processes [5,7,16]. Note that it is not easy to demonstrate the correctness of idealization results. Hence, the informal idealization is greatly error-prone and its formal handling is not simple. Mao showed a method to idealize a given protocol by rule-based techniques which are context-sensitive [15]. Such a method must be less error-prone but need an analyzer to understand the protocol in more depths for applying the rules.

2.3   Contribution

In this paper, we present ASVO logic that is intended to simplify the idealization process by removing the message comprehension and interpretation steps from the predecessor, SVO logic. In ASVO, we express and manipulate those error-prone steps by logic itself. Hence, we designed more concrete language and axioms for better reasoning about principal's belief on the framework of SVO. This work must be advantageous to automation-considered analysis of authentication and key distribution protocols. Also a human user could analyze a given protocol more easily and correctly in BAN-family style. As an experiment, we implement the ASVO logic by using the Isabelle/Isar, semi-automated reasoning system [19], and describe its experimental results. Interestingly we are able to find some known flaws that were neglected in the predecessor.

3   ASVO Logic

The ASVO logic is typically composed of formal language, formal logic, and formal goals by asserting its syntax and semantics. All predecessors (BAN, GNY,

AT and SVO) have intended to use competent cryptographic techniques. In that sense, they could not provide any guarantee to debug design flaws resulting from the misuse of cryptographic algorithms [15]. However, ASVO does not basically assume those techniques, so as to provide more concrete analysis.

3.1   Formal Language

Following the SVO logic, we define the symbolic language for messages and formulae. They are expressed and distinguished by distinct types in a functional language. We assume the existence of a set of primitive terms, T, containing a number of sets of constant symbols representing principals, shared keys, public keys, private keys, numerical constants, etc. Messages and formulae of the language are built from T by mutual induction. Only formulae can express a truth condition and have a principal's belief attributed to them.

Messages.   The language of messages, M_T, is the smallest language over T satisfying:

- X is a message if $X \in T$,
- $F(X_1, ..., X_n)$ is a message if $X_1, ..., X_n$ are messages and F is any function,
- $H(X_1, ..., X_n)$ is a message if $X_1, ..., X_n$ are messages and H is a one-way function,
- φ is a message if φ is a formula.

Note that $F \supset H$ since F is meta-notation for any function computable by principals while H is that of a one-way function. Specifically, $H(K, X)$ denotes a message authentication code (MAC). For type conversion from a formulae to a message, it is assumed to have a type casting mechanism.

Formulae.   The language of formulae, M_F, is the smallest language over T satisfying:

- p is a formula if p is a primitive proposition,
- $\neg\varphi$ and $\varphi\wedge\psi$ are formulae if φ and ψ are formulae,
- the followings are formulae if P is a principal and φ is a formula,
    - P believes φ,
    - P controls φ,
- the followings are formulae if P is a principal and X is a message,
    - P has X,
    - P received X,
    - P received2 X,
    - X from P,
    - P said X,
    - P says X,
    - P understands X,
- the followings are formulae if X is a message,

- fresh(X),
- vague(X),
- the followings are formulae if P and Q are principals and K is a key,
  - $P \overset{K}{\leftrightarrow} Q$ (or share P, Q, K),
  - $PK(P, K)$.

Notice that **believes** is a modal operator for expressing principal's belief while the other predicates represent principal's behaviors in a protocol. The meaning of each predicate will be discussed in Section 3.2. We rather use a form like "has P X" and "share(P, Q, K)" when we implement the logic in a functional language.

Keys. Cryptographic keys are represented as K while $\{X\}_K$ means encryption of X under K. Also K^- implies an inverse of K, so that $K = K^-$ in a symmetric key system. K^{-1} means a private key when K is a public key in an asymmetric key system. Let us define possible public keys:

- $PK_e(P, K)$ for encryption,
- $PK_s(P, K)$ for signature verification,
- $PK_d(P, K)$ for key agreement.

In addition, we define possible instances of cryptographic keys as follows:

- K_{PQ} where $P \overset{K}{\leftrightarrow} Q$,
- K_P where $PK_e(P, K)$ or $PK_s(P, K)$,
- K_p where $PK_d(P, K)$.

When we define a Diffie-Hellman key derivation function as $F_0()$, we could have $K_{pq} = F_0(K_p, K_q)$. Upper and lower cases are respectively used in that manner.

3.2   Formal Logic

The logic is represented by the language defined above. We denote logical implication by $\Rightarrow$. Also we use $\vdash$ as a metalinguistic symbol. $\Gamma \vdash \varphi$ implies that φ is derivable from the set of formulae Γ, while $\vdash \varphi$ means that φ is a theorem.

Inference Rules. ASVO has two inference rules as a modal logic:

Modus Ponens: From φ and $\varphi \Rightarrow \psi$ infer ψ.
Necessitation: From $\vdash \varphi$ infer $\vdash P$ **believes** φ.

Modus Ponens (MP) is required for basic deduction, while necessitation (Nec) corresponds to generalization in the logic. These are applied with axioms.

Axioms. Axioms are all instances of tautologies of classical propositional calculus and all instances of the axiom schemata. Axioms A6, A8, A11, A13, A14, A18, A19, A20, A21, and A22 are derived from SVO. Readers are referred to [22].

▷ **Believing.** For any principal P and formulae φ and ψ,

A1) P believes $\varphi \wedge P$ believes $(\varphi \to \psi) \Rightarrow P$ believes ψ
A2) P believes $\varphi \Rightarrow \varphi$
A3) P believes $\varphi \Rightarrow P$ believes $(P$ believes $\varphi)$
A4) $\neg(P$ believes $\varphi) \Rightarrow P$ believes $(\neg P$ believes $\varphi)$

These are derived from traditional axioms of modal logic for reasoning about principal's belief. A principal believes all that logically follows from his beliefs in A1 and expresses the fact that he believes or not in A3 and A4. $\to$ is used for expressing the fact of implication. Note that A2 is applicable when φ is true [23].

▷ **Source Association.** When a received message is recognizable and implies its source, the identity of a sender can be deduced. Also a principal receives the message contained in any received signed message.

A5) P understands $X \wedge P$ received2 $(X$ from $Q) \Rightarrow Q$ said $(X, P \overset{K}{\leftrightarrow} Q)$

A5a1) $\mathsf{PK}_s(Q, K) \wedge P$ received $\{X\}_{K^{-1}} \Rightarrow Q$ said $X \wedge P$ received X

We have A5 since competent cryptographic techniques are not assumed. Note that received2 is distinguished from received because the latter means explicit receiving only. In other words, received2 does not imply that a principal could obtain the message explicitly. A5a1 means that a signature, $\{X\}_{K^{-1}}$, is verifiable only with its corresponding public key which is assumed universally available.

▷ **Key Agreement.** Session keys resulting from good key agreement keys are good, while good key agreement needs explicit source association.

A6) $\mathsf{PK}_d(P, K_p) \wedge \mathsf{PK}_d(Q, K_q) \Rightarrow P \overset{K_{pq}}{\longleftrightarrow} Q$
A6a1) P says $K_p \wedge \neg \mathsf{PK}_d(R, K_p) \Rightarrow \mathsf{PK}_d(P, K_p)$
A7) $\varphi(F_0(K_p, K_q)) \equiv \varphi(K_{pq})$
A7a1) $\mathsf{PK}_d(P, K_p) \wedge P$ has $K_q \Rightarrow P$ has $F_0(K_p, K_q)$

A6 represents a typical form of good key agreement along with A6a1 and A7. Notice that A7 is composed of meta formulae to indicate that $F_0(K_p, K_q)$ and K_{pq} are substitutable in any formulae. A6a1 is asserted by source association axioms, in order to express good key agreement. A7a1 is proposed to distinguish good key agreement from weak one. In the sequel, '$P \overset{K_{pq}}{\longleftrightarrow} Q$' and

'P has K_{pq}' are explicitly distinguishable when we assert a principal's belief in a protocol analysis.

▷ **Receiving.** A principal receives the concatenates of received messages and decryptions with available keys if the message is recognizable.

A8) P received $(X_1, ..., X_n) \Rightarrow P$ received X_i
A9) P received $\{X\}_K \land P$ has $K^- \Rightarrow P$ received vague(X)
A9a1) P understands $X \land P$ received vague$(X) \Rightarrow P$ received X
A9a2) P received vague$(\{X\}_K) \Rightarrow P$ received $\{$vague(X)$\}_K$
A10) P received $H(X) \land P$ has $X \Rightarrow P$ received2 X

In A9 and its addendum, vague implies that a message is not recognizable. A10 indicates that the fact of receiving a function of a message is confirmed. Also A10 could express SVO's comprehending axiom on a hash function H. If a principal comprehends[1] a messages and receives a function of it, then the fact is confirmed.

▷ **Possession.** A principal obtains anything (s)he receives. A principal has what (s)he said or says. Also a principal obtains all components of every message (s)he has and a function of them.

A11) P received $X \Rightarrow P$ has X
A12) P said $X \Rightarrow P$ has X
A12a1) P says $X \Rightarrow P$ has X
A13) P has $(X_1, ..., X_n) \Rightarrow P$ has X_i
A14) P has $X_1 \land ... \land P$ has $X_n \Rightarrow P$ has $F(X_1, ..., X_n)$

▷ **Key Ownership.** A principal has a cryptographic key if (s)he is the owner of it. The language can express it.

A15) P said $P \overset{K}{\leftrightarrow} Q \Rightarrow P$ has K
A16) $\mathsf{PK}_e(P, K) \Rightarrow P$ has K^{-1}
A16a1) $\mathsf{PK}_s(P, K) \Rightarrow P$ has K^{-1}

▷ **Saying.** A principal who has said a concatenated message has also said the concatenates of that message. A principal who has recently said a message has said it.

A17) P said $(X_1, ..., X_n) \Rightarrow P$ said X_i
A17a1) P says $(X_1, ..., X_n) \Rightarrow P$ says $X_i \land P$ said $(X_1, ..., X_n)$

▷ **Freshness.** A concatenated message is fresh if one of its concatenates is fresh. A function of a fresh message is also fresh.

---

[1] In our axiom A25, we could deduce message comprehension.

A18) $\mathsf{fresh}(X_i) \Rightarrow \mathsf{fresh}(X_1, ..., X_n)$

A19) $\mathsf{fresh}(X_1, ..., X_n) \Rightarrow \mathsf{fresh}(F(X_1, ..., X_n))$

▷ **Jurisdiction.** If a principal controls something, then what (s)he tells about it is law for it in question.

A20) P controls $\varphi \wedge P$ says $\varphi \Rightarrow \varphi$

A20a1) P controls $\varphi(K) \wedge P$ says $K \Rightarrow \varphi(K)$

For example, when a principal controls $P \overset{K}{\leftrightarrow} Q$, the fact of saying K implies that (s)he says $P \overset{K}{\leftrightarrow} Q$.

▷ **Nonce Verification.** If a principal said a fresh message, then (s)he has said it during the current epoch.

A21) $\mathsf{fresh}(X) \wedge P$ said $X \Rightarrow P$ says X

▷ **Symmetric Goodness.** A shared key or an agreed key is good for P and Q if and only if it is good for Q and P.

A22) $P \overset{K}{\leftrightarrow} Q \equiv Q \overset{K}{\leftrightarrow} P$

▷ **Interpretation.** If a principal received encryption or keyed hash of a message, then implicitly (s)he received the message from a principal who shares the corresponding key.

A23) $P \overset{K}{\leftrightarrow} Q \wedge P$ received $\{X\}_K \Rightarrow P$ received2 X from Q

A23a1) $P \overset{K}{\leftrightarrow} Q \wedge P$ received $H(K, X) \Rightarrow P$ received2 X from Q

A24) $P \overset{K}{\leftrightarrow} Q \wedge \mathsf{fresh}(K) \Rightarrow \mathsf{fresh}(P \overset{K}{\leftrightarrow} Q)$

A23 and A23a1 are only about implicit receiving. They do not indicate explicit receiving (of X from Q). A24 implies the freshness of a shared key. These axioms are all about principal's interpretation.

▷ **Recognition.** A principal recognizes what (s)he has. A concatenated message is recognizable if one of its concatenates is recognizable. A principal recognizes an encryption or signature message block if a corresponding key is available.

A25) P has $X \Rightarrow P$ understands X

A26) P understands $X_i \Rightarrow P$ understands $(X_1, ..., X_n)$

A27) P understands $X \wedge P$ has $K^- \Rightarrow P$ understands $\{X\}_K$

A27a1) P understands $X \wedge \mathsf{PK}_s(Q, K) \Rightarrow P$ understands $\{X\}_{K^{-1}}$

Note that the meaning of a predicate, understands, is far from that of SVD logic [7]. For example, ASVO does not allow a reverse form of A25 while SVD puts an equivalence to has and understands.

Semantics. The semantic soundness of ASVO can be examined on the framework of SVO in Kripke's possible world semantics. The main difference is that semantic message sets are extended. As we have learned from SVO and its model of computation, there are *seen messages* comprised of *received messages*, *newly generated messages*, and *initially available messages* for a principal at a world, (r, t) [22]. In ASVO, message sets are extensively divided into the seen messages and the external messages that are mapped to specific parts of the received messages. The received messages are comprised of *explicitly received messages*, *implicitly received messages*, and *vaguely received messages*. The explicitly received messages are specified explicitly in a protocol, while the latters are presented by ASVO analysis. The *external messages* include *virtually received messages* and *vague messages*. Those external messages are mapped to the received messages. For example, a vague message, X, is a message not yet understood and is mapped to a vaguely received message, vague(X). In a possible world, X will replace vague(X) in the received message set if a given truth condition satisfies. Those message sets are minutely defined and truth conditions are set out under which a formula is assigned to be true. Then the soundness theorem is not difficult to prove. In spite that we have done it, this paper does not handle the soundness issue in more detail due to the strict page restriction.

3.3 Formal Goals

We define formal goals related in part to those of elegant VO logic [20]. The main difference is that the goals of ASVO avoid obscure formulae needing extra axioms. Protocols are poorly designed or verified if it is unclear what are the goals intended to achieve in the protocol [4]. ASVO has seven goals in five categories.

Activeness. We define two formulae for achieving activeness in a protocol. These are related to the *far-end operative* goal of VO but different in focusing more on the status of the subject for the case that the partner's identity is not yet assured contextually. For example, *identity protection* can be handled concretely before the identity is confirmed in the midst of the protocol run. If A received some message expected contextually in the protocol, it must simply be assured that A was running the protocol with some party, by not assuring an exact identity.

ASVO1: A believes A received X

Similarly, if A received some message expected contextually in the protocol and the message is fresh, A has been running the protocol with some party.

ASVO2: A believes A received $X \wedge A$ believes fresh(X)

Notice that ASVO1 does not guarantee to check typical replays while ASVO2 does it. In order to check reflection or deflection, aliveness must be achieved.

Aliveness. Aliveness means that if A runs a protocol apparently with B, then B has been running the protocol.

ASVO3: A believes B says X

This is closely related to the *far-end operative* goal of VO. It could be confirmed by the fact that B sends a message contextually-expected from B in the protocol.

Authentication. We define two formulae for achieving authentication in a protocol. These are of course related to that of VO but different in requiring the concrete and granulated formulae for the same goal. If B apparently replied to a specific challenge in the current protocol run, A could authenticate B.

ASVO4: A believes B says $F(X) \wedge A$ believes A has X

If B explicitly says A and B share a good key while A also believes the good key, then A could authenticate B. Note that ASVO is different from its predecessors in that the formulae and axioms are applied by the rules on the belief of the principals only. In that sense, B must say $A \overset{K}{\leftrightarrow} B$ when (s)he believes it, and logically A must believe B says it when (s)he can believe B believes it. The ASVO logic can infer such a fact by A5 and its related axioms. The *key confirmation* and *mutual belief* goals of VO are manipulated in that different manner.

ASVO5: A believes B says $A \overset{K}{\leftrightarrow} B \wedge A$ believes $A \overset{K}{\leftrightarrow} B$

Both formulae are equally reasonable because they assert not only freshness but also possession. Note that A15 infers 'A has K' from '$A \overset{K}{\leftrightarrow} B$'.

Naive key distribution. Like unauthenticated Diffie-Hellman key agreement, A could have a fresh key but without authentication. In this case, it is a misconception to assume that the key is good for communication with a specific partner. Say, the *key establishment* goal of VO is differently manipulated.

ASVO6: A believes A has $K \wedge A$ believes fresh(K)

In that sense, its expression is a little bit different from that of VO [20].

Key distribution. A believes K is good for communication with B, saying that the key is authenticated, even if B does not participate in any manner in the current protocol run. This goal manipulates the key distribution regardless of key confirmation, such as a simple exchange of signed Diffie-Hellman public keys. Note that ASVO handles the key confirmation in the realm of authentication.

ASVO7: A believes $A \overset{K}{\leftrightarrow} B \wedge A$ believes fresh(K)

Note that key distribution is stronger than naive key distribution in their meaning, due to axiom A15.

4   Protocol Analysis

4.1   Summary of Experiments

We implemented the ASVO logic and built it in the Isabelle/Isar, semi-automated reasoning system [19]. For the purpose, we had to translate ASVO in

Isar language and define types and their conversion carefully. Due to the property of semi-automation, we were able to analyze many protocols more easily though it was necessary to define external tactics. A current state of the implementation is premature, for example, a specification language is not defined and automation tactics are not perfect. So, a user must understand the language of Isar. However, it was possible to analyze various protocols more conveniently and correctly than manual work due to the semi-automation. Exact *subgoals* were presented by the so-called Isabelle/ASVO system[2] and subsequently resolved by ASVO when we analyzed the protocols including NSSK [17,8], NSSK7, NSPK [17,13], NSPK2, NSPK3, DH [9], STS [14], and STS2. Those protocols could be good examples for describing the analysis of the proposed logic. We were able to confirm it experimetally by ASVO, that NSSK, NSPK, DH, and STS protocols are insecure. So, NSSK7, NSPK2, NSPK3 and STS2 were reformulated throughout the weaknesses found by ASVO. We summarize those results briefly in this section.

4.2   Procedures

The first step is to set out the goals that are expected in a given protocol. Those goals are formulated from the ASVO goals described in Section 3.3. Subsequently we should define *initial state assumptions* and *received message assumptions* in order to apply ASVO. These will serve as premises, which we will use together with ASVO axioms and rules to derive goals above. The initial state assumptions are basic premises that are needed to run the protocol, while the received message assumptions are derived from the protocol specification. Those assumptions must be able to declare principals' beliefs. For example, the received message assumptions express principals' beliefs on messages that are expected in the protocol run. Then we can use the Isabelle/ASVO for semi-automated reasoning.

In the Isabelle/ASVO system, we should declare each theorem for achieving the stated goals. Then Isabelle/ASVO assists to prove it by backward proof. Theorems are made in the following form where each formula is constructed with modal operator, for example, P believes φ.

$\vdash Assumption_1; \cdots; Assumption_n \Rightarrow Goal_i$

Following the Gödel's second theorem, we could analyze the protocol in a way that P believes $(\varphi \Rightarrow \psi)$ for asserting that P believes $\varphi \Rightarrow P$ believes ψ in ASVO. The former will need A2 and Nec (necessitation) while the second will require A1 and Nec. The Isabelle/ASVO backward-proves the theorem in the former way while we could prove it manually in the latter way as we did in SVO.

4.3   Experimental Results

Secret Key Protocols. NSSK stands for Needham-Schroeder Shared Key and is a typical protocol for authentication and key distribution between two principals, A and B, under postulating a trusted server, S [17]. The NSSK protocol is a standard example for protocol analysis because it had been understood secure

---

[2] Figure 1 shows a screen shot in Appendix A.

before Denning and Sacco found its critical flaw [8]. When we expect authentication and key distribution between two principals, the goals need to be derived from ASVO5 and ASVO7 as described in Section 3.3. Those goals should have been achieved in NSSK under presented premises. Theorem 1 is one of them. Note that $\hookrightarrow$ implies transition with some of or without {A1, A2, Nec, MP}.

Theorem 1 (NSSK-G1). $\vdash P12; P1; P7; P6; P3 \Rightarrow A$ *believes* $A \overset{K_{AB}}{\longleftrightarrow} B$

(proof) P12 $\hookrightarrow$ P1 $\hookrightarrow$ A23 $\hookrightarrow$ P7 $\hookrightarrow$ A25 $\hookrightarrow$ A26 $\hookrightarrow$ A5 $\hookrightarrow$ A17 $\hookrightarrow$ P6 $\hookrightarrow$ A18 $\hookrightarrow$ A21 $\hookrightarrow$ A17a1 $\hookrightarrow$ P3 $\hookrightarrow$ A20a1 $\hookrightarrow$ A20   □
However, we couldn't prove the following theorem within the given premises.

Theorem 2 (NSSK-G3). $\vdash P13; P2; P91; P9; P8; P4 \Rightarrow B$ *believes* $A \overset{K_{AB}}{\longleftrightarrow} B$

The abnormal assumptions were necessary for some subgoals[3].

P92: B believes fresh(K_{AB})
P93: A believes A understands N_B

Note that P92 and P93 shows the weak points of NSSK. An adversary E could exploit P92 in step 3 for the famous Denning-Sacco attack [8], while (s)he could exploit P93 in step 4 for a dumb-authentication attack in which A could not authenticate B. So we need modifications for removing P92 and P93 from NSSK. In order to remove P92, a nonce must be included for B in the corresponding message. Likewise, a recognizable value must be included for A in the message so as to remove P93. Hence, we could formulate the following NSSK7 Protocol:

1. $A \to B$: A
2. $B \to A$: B, N_{B1}
3. $A \to S$: A, B, N_A, N_{B1}
4. $S \to A$: $\{N_A, B, K_{AB}, \{N_{B1}, K_{AB}, A\}_{K_{BS}}\}_{K_{AS}}$
5. $A \to B$: $\{N_{B1}, K_{AB}, A\}_{K_{BS}}$
6. $B \to A$: $\{A, B, N_{B2}\}_{K_{AB}}$
7. $A \to B$: $\{N_{B2} - 1\}_{K_{AB}}$

NSSK7 was proved by ASVO without P92 and P93 in the similar way of GNY [11].

Public Key Protocols. NSPK is another protocol devised by Needham and Schroeder, in which public key system and challenge-response are typically used for authentication [17]. Hence, goal ASVO4 must be achieved in this protocol. However, we had to add the following assumptions for given subgoals.

P121: A believes A received2 (N_A, N_B) from B
P131: B believes B received2 N_B from A

---

[3] See Figure 1 in order to find the subgoal that needs P92, in Appendix A.

In other words, the source association was not asserted in the original protocol. So, we declared carefully a contextual axiom, A23a2, in order to express the source association to a public-key-encrypted message. In the encrypted message, $\{Q, X\}_K$, Q implies a sender of the message very contextually.

A23a2) $\mathsf{PK}_e(P, K) \wedge P$ received $\{Q, X\}_K \Rightarrow P$ received2 X from Q

Then we could formulate the following protocol, NSPK2, and prove that the goals are achieved by ASVO without P121 and P131.

1. $A \rightarrow B$: $\{A, N_A\}_{K_B}$
2. $B \rightarrow A$: $\{B, N_A, N_B\}_{K_A}$
3. $A \rightarrow B$: $\{A, N_B\}_{K_B}$

In the sequel, we could say that P121 and P131 are the weak points against Lowe's attack on NSPK [13]. However, the contextual axiom, A23a2, is strong postulation for the logic. Without A23a2, we could formulate the following protocol, NSPK3, and prove it easily by ASVO. Readers are referred to A5a1.

1. $A \rightarrow B$: $\{N_A, B\}_{K_A^{-1}}$
2. $B \rightarrow A$: $\{N_A - 1, N_B\}_{K_B^{-1}}$
3. $A \rightarrow B$: $\{N_B - 1\}_{K_A^{-1}}$

Key Agreement Protocols. A basic constituent of key agreement protocols is a Diffie-Hellman method [9]. However, as we described already, the Diffie-Hellman protocol can be proved for ASVO6 only. ASVO7 is not achievable without adding the following assumption, for instance, for A.

P111: A believes $A \xleftrightarrow{K_{ab}} B$

So, we need authentication for achieving ASVO7. In other words, ASVO4 or ASVO5 must be achieved for purporting ASVO7. STS protocol is one of the most famous and influential authenticated Diffie-Helman key agreement protocols. We analyzed if STS achieves ASVO5 as well as ASVO7. However, we found that ASVO5 does not satisfy for A if the following assumptions are not defined for B. We assert that these are the well-known weak points against STS [2,14].

P112: B believes A says K_a
P132: B believes A says $A \xleftrightarrow{K_{ab}} B$

Finally we were able to reformulate it to remove those assumptions, and prove the new protocol, STS2, though a contextual axiom was needed.

1. $A \to B$: $A, \{K_a\}_{K_A^{-1}}$
2. $B \to A$: $B, \{K_b\}_{K_B^{-1}}, H(K_{ab}, A, B, K_a)$
3. $A \to B$: $H(K_{ab}, A, B, K_b)$

Note that it was able to replace symmetric encryption with MACs due to A23a1.

5 Conclusion

We presented the automation-considered logic of authentication and key distribution. The so-called ASVO logic was based upon the SVO logic but designed in a different way of minimizing the protocol idealization needs. Also message recognition was considered in a very different manner within a similar semantic model. The proposed logic was implemented as a semi-automated formal verification tool, and its experimental results were discussed. A current state of the implementation is premature, for example, a specification language is not defined and automation tactics are not perfect. So, a user must understand the language of Isar. Otherwise, a human user could analyze a protocol more easily and correctly in BAN-style by ASVO. It was possible to analyze and refine various protocols correctly by Isabelle/ASVO. This work must be advantageous to automation-considered analysis of authentication and key distribution protocols. For example, in the future C3PO [7] can be updated with ASVO and an elegant specification language can be applied for more convenient interactions.

Acknowledgement. We thank anonymous referees for kind comments, and Sookhyun Yang and Donghyun Kim for helpful discussions on the Isabelle/Isar system.

References

1. M. Abadi and M. Tuttle, "A semantics for a logic of authentication," In Proc. of the ACM Symposium on Principles of Distributed Computing, pp. 201–216, August 1991.
2. S. Blake-Wilson and A. Menezes, "Unknown key-share attacks on the station-to-station (STS) protocol," Proceedings of PKC '99, Lecture Notes in Computer Science, vol. 1560, Springer-Verlag, pp. 154–170, 1999.
3. C. Boyd and W. Mao, "On a limitation of BAN logic," Lecture Notes in Computer Science, vol. 765, Springer-Verlag, pp. 240–247, 1993.
4. C. Boyd, "Towards extensional goals in authentication protocols," In Proc. of DIMACS Workshop on Cryptographic Protocol Design and Verification, 1997.
5. S. Brackin, "A HOL extension of GNY for automatically analyzing cryptographic protocols," In Proc. of the IEEE Computer Security Foundation Workshop, June 1996.

6. M. Burrows, M. Abadi, and R. Needham, "A logic of authentication," Technical Report SRC RR 39, Digital Equipment Corporation, Systems Research Center, February 1990.
7. A. Dekker, "C3PO: a tool for automatic sound cryptographic protocol analysis," In Proc. of the IEEE Computer Security Foundation Workshop, June 2000.
8. D. Denning and G. Sacco, "Timestamps in key distribution protocols," Communications of the ACM, vol. 24, no. 8, pp. 533–536, August 1981.
9. W. Diffie and M. Hellman, "New directions in cryptography," IEEE Transactions on Information Theory, vol.22, no.6, pp.644–654, November 1976.
10. R. Goldblatt, "Mathematical modal logic: a view of its evolution," http://www.mcs.vuw.ac.nz/ rob, February 2002.
11. L. Gong, R. Needham, and R. Yahalom, "Reasoning about belief in cryptographic protocols," In Proc. of the IEEE Symposium on Research in Security and Privacy, pp. 234–248, 1990.
12. S. Gritzalis, D. Spinellis, and P. Georgiadis, "Security protocols over open networks and distributed systems: formal methods for their analysis, design, and verification," Computer Communications, vol. 22, no. 8, pp. 695–707, May 1999.
13. G. Lowe, "Breaking and fixing the Needham-Schroeder public-key protocol using FDR," Software - Concepts and Tools, vol. 17, pp. 93–102, 1996.
14. G. Lowe, "Some new attacks upon security protocols," IEEE Computer Security Foundations Workshop, pp.162–169, 1996.
15. W. Mao, "An augmentation of BAN-like logics," IEEE Computer Security Foundations Workshop, pp.44–56, 1995.
16. A. Mathuria, R. Safavi-Naini, and P. Nickolas, "On the automation of GNY logic," Austrialian Computer Science Communications, vol. 17, no. 1, pp. 370–379, 1995
17. R. Needham and M. Schroeder, "Using encryption for authentication in large networks of computers," Communications of the ACM, vol. 21, no. 12, pp. 993–999, 1978.
18. D. Nessett, "A critique of the BAN logic," ACM Operating Systems Review, vol. 24, no. 2, pp.35–38, 1990.
19. T. Nipkow, L. Paulson, and M. Wenzel, "Isabelle/HOL", Lecture Notes in Computer Science, Vol. 2283, Springer- Verlag, 2002.
20. P. van Oorschot, "Extending cryptographic logics of belief to key agreement protocols," In Proc. of the ACM Conference on Computer Communications Security, pp.232–243, 1993.
21. D. Song, "Athena: a new efficient automatic checker for security protocol analysis," In Proc. of the IEEE Computer Security Foundation Workshop, pp.192–202, 1999.
22. P. Syverson and P. van Oorschot, "A unified cryptographic protocol logic," NRL Publication 5540–227, Naval Research Lab, 1996.
23. P. Syverson and Iliano Cervesato, "The logic of authentication protocols," Lecture Notes in Computer Science, Vol. 2171, Springer- Verlag, 2002.
24. G. Wedel and V. Kessler, "Formal semantics for authentication logics," In Compueter Security - ESORICS 96, pp. 219–241, Springer-Verlag, LNCS 1146, September 1996

A   Figure of Isabelle/ASVO

Readers are referred to Figure 1. Note that the following formula is clearly marked in the figure.

```
ASvo.Trueprop(Fresh{|Key(Principal A)(Principal B),Principal A
|})
```

It means that a message $(K_{AB},\ A)$ is fresh. However, A is not fresh, so that K_{AB} must be fresh for obtaining the truth value from the formula.

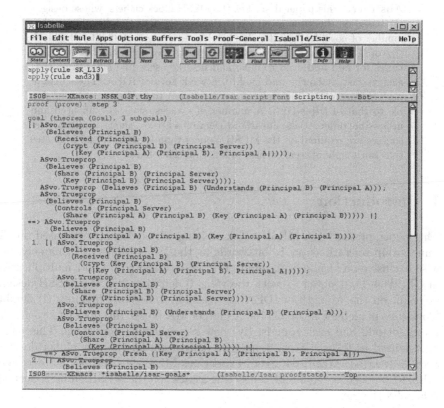

Fig. 1. Isabelle/ASVO

The MESH Block Ciphers

Jorge Nakahara Jr*,, Vincent Rijmen, Bart Preneel, and Joos Vandewalle

[1] Katholieke Universiteit Leuven, Dept. ESAT/SCD-COSIC, Belgium
{jorge.nakahara,bart.preneel,joos.vandewalle}@esat.kuleuven.ac.be
[2] Cryptomathic, Belgium & Graz University of Technology, Austria
vincent.rijmen@cryptomathic.com

Abstract. This paper describes the MESH block ciphers, whose designs are based on the same group operations as the IDEA cipher, but with a number of novel features: flexible block sizes in steps of 32 bits (the block size of IDEA is fixed at 64 bits); larger MA-boxes; distinct key-mixing layers for odd and even rounds; and new key schedule algorithms that achieve fast avalanche and avoid the weak keys of IDEA. The software performance of MESH ciphers are estimated to be better or comparable to that of triple-DES. A number of attacks, such as truncated and impossible differentials, linear and Demirci's attack, shows that more resources are required on the MESH ciphers than for IDEA, and indicates that both ciphers seem to have a large margin of security.

1 Introduction

This paper presents the MESH block ciphers, whose designs are based on the same group operations on 16-bit words as the IDEA cipher [11], namely, bitwise exclusive-or, denoted $\oplus$, addition in $\mathbb{Z}_{2^{16}}$, denoted $\boxplus$, and multiplication in $GF(2^{16}+1)$, denoted $\odot$, with the value 0 denoting 2^{16}. The MESH designs are built on the strength of IDEA, but include some novel features: (i) flexible block sizes in increments of 32 bits; (ii) larger MA-boxes; (iii) distinct key-mixing layers for odd and even rounds; (iv) new key schedule algorithms. This paper is organized as follows: Sect. 2 provides motivation for the new cipher designs; Sect. 3 describes MESH-64; Sect. 4 describes MESH-96, and Sect. 5 describes MESH-128. Sect. 6, 7, 8 and 9 describe attacks on the MESH ciphers. Sect. 10 concludes the paper.

2 Design Rationale and Motivations

Since the publication of IDEA in [11], no extended IDEA variant has being proposed with block sizes larger than 64 bits (or word sizes larger than 16 bits). Maybe such attempts were jeopardized due to the fact that $2^{32}+1$ is not a prime

---

* Sponsored by a grant from the Katholieke Universiteit Leuven, and partially by GOA project Mefisto 2000/06 of the Flemish Government.

K. Chae and M. Yung (Eds.): WISA 2003, LNCS 2908, pp. 458–473, 2004.

number,[1] and thus, $\mathbb{Z}^*_{2^{32}+1}$ is not a finite field [12, p. 77, Fact 2.184]. The MESH designs provide an alternative approach that does not rely on the need for larger word sizes. This motivates the design of larger MA-boxes. All MA-boxes in the MESH ciphers involve at least three interleaved layers of multiplication and addition operations in a zig-zag pattern, in comparison to two layers in IDEA. The MA-boxes of some MESH ciphers have the property that not all multiplications involve subkeys directly as an operand, but rather depend upon internal data values. These designs effectively avoid many one-round linear relations and one-round characteristics (to be discussed further). All the new MA-boxes are bijective mappings (permutations), in order to avoid non-surjective attacks [14]).

Another feature of the MESH ciphers is the key schedule algorithm. Note that in IDEA all multiplications involve a subkey as an operand. Since the modular multiplication is the main non-linear operator in the cipher, the key schedule needs to be designed to avoid weak subkeys for any choice of the user key, otherwise, all multiplications could, in principle, be manipulated (Daemen [5]). The following design principles were used in the key schedule of MESH ciphers to avoid weak keys:

- fast key avalanche: each subkey generated from the user key quickly depends, non-linearly, upon all user key words. This dependence is expressed by the exponents of a primitive polynomial (one polynomial for each MESH cipher). All key schedule algorithms interleave addition with exclusive-or operations. There is additionally a fixed bit-rotation operation, because in both $\boxplus$ and $\oplus$ the relative position of the subkey bits is preserved and otherwise, two related keys with subkeys differing only in the most significant bit could propagate this difference to several other subkeys.
- use of fixed constants to avoid patterns in subkeys. For instance, without the constants the user-defined key with all-zero words would result in all subkeys being zero (independent of the non-linear mixing or the bit rotation) for any number of rounds.

Common properties to IDEA and MESH ciphers include: (i) complete diffusion is achieved in one round; (ii) no operation is used twice in succession in any part of these ciphers; (iii) neither cipher uses explicit S-boxes, nor depend on particular properties of Boolean functions such as in Camellia [1] or AES [8].

Three designs will be described: MESH-64, MESH-96 and MESH-128, where the suffix denotes the block size.

3   The MESH-64 Block Cipher

MESH-64 is a 64-bit block cipher with a 128-bit key and 8.5 rounds (Fig. 1 and Table 1). The last 0.5 round is the output transformation (OT). The key schedule for MESH-64 is defined as follows:

---

[1] $2^{32} + 1 = 4294967297 = 641 \cdot 6700417$.

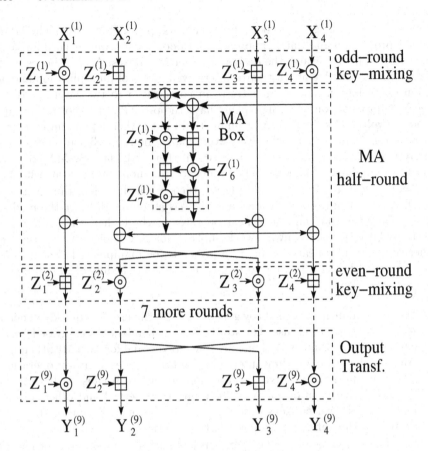

Fig. 1. Computational graph of the MESH-64 cipher.

- First, 16-bit constants c_i are defined as: $c_0 = 1$, and $c_i = 3 \cdot c_{i-1}$, $i \geq 1$ with multiplication in $GF(2)[x]/p(x)$, under the primitive polynomial $p(x) = x^{16} + x^5 + x^3 + x^2 + 1$. The constant '3' is represented by the polynomial $x + 1$ in $GF(2)$.
- The 128-bit user key is partitioned into eight 16-bit words K_i, $0 \leq i \leq 7$, and assigned to $Z_{j+1}^{(1)} = K_j \oplus c_j$, $0 \leq j \leq 6$, and $Z_1^{(2)} = K_7 \oplus c_7$.
- Finally, each subsequent 16-bit subkey is defined as follows:

$$Z_{l(i)}^{(h(i))} = (((((Z_{l(i-8)}^{(h(i-8))} \boxplus Z_{l(i-7)}^{(h(i-7))}) \oplus Z_{l(i-6)}^{(h(i-6))}) \boxplus \qquad (1)$$
$$Z_{l(i-3)}^{(h(i-3))}) \oplus Z_{l(i-2)}^{(h(i-2))}) \boxplus Z_{l(i-1)}^{(h(i-1))}) \lll 7 \oplus c_i,$$

for $8 \leq i \leq 59$; '$\lll 7$' is left rotation by 7 bits; $h(i) = i$ div $7 + 1$, and $l(i) = i$ mod $7 + 1$.

The key schedules of MESH-64 is designed to achieve fast key avalanche, due to (1) being based on the primitive polynomial $q(x) = x^8 + x^7 + x^6 + x^5 +$

$x^2 + x + 1$ in GF(2), and the interleaving of $\oplus$ and $\boxplus$ operations. For instance, $Z_4^{(2)}$ and all subsequent subkeys already depend upon all eight user key words. The dependence of (1) on $q(x)$ can be made clear by ignoring the left rotation for a while, changing the $\boxplus$ to $\oplus$, and denoting $Z_{l(i)}^{(h(i))}$ simply as $Z^{(i)}$. Then (1) becomes $Z^{(i)} = Z^{(i-8)} \oplus Z^{(i-7)} \oplus Z^{(i-6)} \oplus Z^{(i-3)} \oplus Z^{(i-2)} \oplus Z^{(i-1)} \oplus c_i$. A similar reasoning applies to the other MESH ciphers. Notice that both $\boxplus$ and $\oplus$ preserve the relative bit position of its operands. The left-rotation destroys that property, so that changes only at the most significant bit of some subkeys (in a differential related-key attack) would not propagate to other subkeys with probability one. Without the constants, the all-zero user key would result in all subkeys being zero (for any number of rounds), independent of the mixing of addition and exclusive-or. Decryption in MESH-64 uses the same framework in Fig. 1 as encryption, but with transformed round subkeys. Formally, let the r-th round encryption subkeys be denoted $(Z_1^{(r)}, \ldots, Z_7^{(r)})$, for $1 \leq r \leq 8$, and $(Z_1^{(9)}, \ldots, Z_4^{(9)})$, for the OT. The decryption round subkeys are:

- $((Z_1^{(9)})^{-1}, -Z_2^{(9)}, -Z_3^{(9)}, (Z_4^{(9)})^{-1}, Z_5^{(8)}, Z_6^{(8)}, Z_7^{(8)})$, for the first round.
- $(-Z_1^{(10-r)}, (Z_3^{(10-r)})^{-1}, (Z_2^{(10-r)})^{-1}, -Z_4^{(10-r)}, Z_5^{(9-r)}, Z_6^{(9-r)}, Z_7^{(9-r)})$, for the r-th even round, $r \in \{2, 4, 6, 8\}$.
- $((Z_1^{(9-r)})^{-1}, -Z_3^{(9-r)}, -Z_2^{(9-r)}, (Z_4^{(9-r)})^{-1}, Z_5^{(8-r)}, Z_6^{(8-r)}, Z_7^{(8-r)})$, for the r-th odd round, $r \in \{3, 5, 7\}$.
- $((Z_1^{(1)})^{-1}, -Z_2^{(1)}, -Z_3^{(1)}, (Z_4^{(1)})^{-1})$, for the OT.

A similar procedure applies to the decryption subkeys of the other MESH ciphers.

4   The MESH-96 Block Cipher

MESH-96 is a 96-bit block cipher, with a 192-bit key, and 10.5 rounds (Fig. 2 and Table 1). The last 0.5 round is the output transformation (OT).

The key schedule for MESH-96 is defined as follows:

- The 16-bit constants c_i are the same as defined for MESH-64.
- The 192-bit user key is partitioned into twelve 16-bit words K_i, for $0 \leq i \leq 11$, that are assigned to: $Z_{j+1}^{(1)} = K_j \oplus c_j$, for $0 \leq j \leq 8$, $Z_1^{(2)} = K_9 \oplus c_9$, $Z_2^{(2)} = K_{10} \oplus c_{10}$, and $Z_3^{(2)} = K_{11} \oplus c_{11}$.
- Finally, each subsequent 16-bit subkey is defined as follows:

$$Z_{l(i)}^{(h(i))} = (((((Z_{l(i-12)}^{(h(i-12))} \boxplus Z_{l(i-8)}^{(h(i-8))}) \oplus Z_{l(i-6)}^{(h(i-6))}) \boxplus$$
$$Z_{l(i-4)}^{(h(i-4))}) \oplus Z_{l(i-2)}^{(h(i-2))}) \boxplus Z_{l(i-1)}^{(h(i-1))}) \lll 9 \oplus c_i, \qquad (2)$$

for $12 \leq i \leq 95$, '$\lll 9$' is left rotation by 9 bits, $h(i) = i$ div $9 + 1$, and $l(i) = i \bmod 9 + 1$.

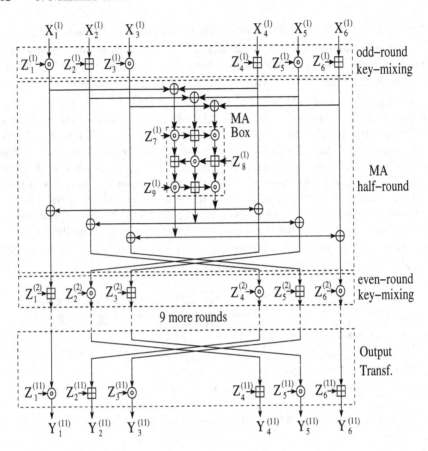

Fig. 2. Computational graph of the MESH-96 cipher.

The key schedule of MESH-96 is designed to achieve fast key avalanche due to the use of the primitive polynomial $x^{12}+x^{11}+x^{10}+x^8+x^6+x^4+1$ in GF(2), and the mixing of $\boxplus$ and $\oplus$ operations. All subkeys starting with $Z_7^{(2)}$, already depend (non-linearly) on all user key words. Decryption uses the same computational framework as in Fig. 2 for encryption, but with transformed subkeys.

5   The MESH-128 Block Cipher

MESH-128 is a 128-bit block cipher, with a 256-bit key, and 12.5 rounds (Fig. 3 and Table 1). The last 0.5 round is the output transformation (OT). The key schedule for MESH-128 is defined as follows:

- First, 16-bit constants c_i are defined as in MESH-64.
- Next, the 256-bit user key is partitioned into sixteen 16-bit words K_i, $0 \leq i \leq 15$, and are assigned to $Z_{j+1}^{(1)} = K_j \oplus c_j$, $0 \leq j \leq 11$, and $Z_{t\,\mathrm{mod}\,12+1}^{(2)} = K_t \oplus c_t$, $12 \leq t \leq 15$.

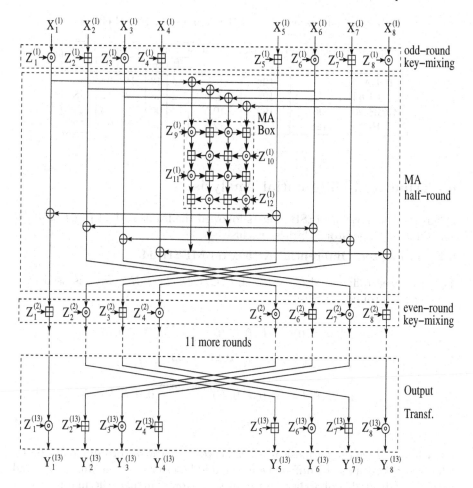

Fig. 3. Computational graph of the MESH-128 block cipher.

– Finally, each subsequent 16-bit subkey is generated as follows:

$$Z_{l(i)}^{(h(i))} = (((((Z_{l(i-16)}^{(h(i-16))} \boxplus Z_{l(i-13)}^{(h(i-13))}) \oplus Z_{l(i-12)}^{(h(i-12))}) \boxplus \qquad (3)$$

$$Z_{l(i-8)}^{(h(i-8))}) \oplus Z_{l(i-2)}^{(h(i-2))}) \boxplus Z_{l(i-1)}^{(h(i-1))}) \lll 11 \oplus c_i,$$

for $16 \leq i \leq 151$; '$\lll 11$' is left rotation by 11 bits; $h(i) = i \operatorname{div} 12 + 1$, and $l(i) = i \operatorname{mod} 12 + 1$.

The key schedule of MESH-128 achieves fast key avalanche due to the use of the primitive polynomial $r(x) = x^{16} + x^{15} + x^{14} + x^8 + x^4 + x^3 + 1$, and the mixing of $\boxplus$ and $\oplus$ operations. All subkeys starting with $Z_{10}^{(2)}$, already depend upon all sixteen user key words. Decryption in MESH-128 uses the same framework as in Fig. 3, but with transformed subkeys.

Table 1. Main parameters for IDEA and some MESH ciphers.

Cipher	Block Size	Key Size	#Rounds	#Operations				#Subkeys
				$\boxplus$	$\oplus$	$\odot$	$\odot$	$\boxplus$
IDEA	64	128	8.5	34	48	34	34	18
MESH-64	64	128	8.5	42	48	42	42	18
MESH-96	96	192	10.5	73	90	83	53	43
MESH-128	128	256	12.5	148	144	148	100	52

6   Truncated Differential Analysis

Differential analysis of MESH ciphers followed the framework of Borst *et al.* [4]. The difference operator is bitwise exclusive-or.

6.1   Truncated Differential Attack on MESH-64

The truncated differential (4), with $A, B, C, D, E, F, G, H \in \mathbb{Z}_2^{16}$, is used in an attack on 3.5-round MESH-64.

$$(A, 0, B, 0) \overset{2^{-16}}{\to} (C, 0, C, 0) \overset{(0,0) \overset{1}{\to} (0,0)}{} (C, C, 0, 0)$$

$$(C, C, 0, 0) \overset{1}{\to} (D, E, 0, 0) \overset{(D,E) \overset{2^{-32}}{\to} (E,D)}{} (0, D, 0, E)$$

$$(0, D, 0, E) \overset{2^{-16}}{\to} (0, F, 0, F) \overset{(0,0) \overset{1}{\to} (0,0)}{} (0, 0, F, F)$$

$$(0, 0, F, F) \overset{1}{\to} (0, 0, G, H) . \tag{4}$$

In each line of (4) the leftmost arrow indicates that the 4-word difference on the left-hand side causes the difference in the middle after a key-mixing half-round, with the indicated probability on top of the arrow. Further, the middle 4-word difference causes the round output difference (on the right-hand side) across an MA-box, with the indicated probability. The truncated differential (4) has average probability 2^{-64} over all keys.

From (4), the attack recovers subkeys $Z_1^{(1)}$, $Z_3^{(1)}$, $Z_3^{(4)}$, and $Z_4^{(4)}$ that satisfy equations $(P_1 \odot Z_1^{(1)}) \oplus (P_1^* \odot Z_1^{(1)}) = (P_3 \boxplus Z_3^{(1)}) \oplus (P_3^* \boxplus Z_3^{(1)})$, and $(C_3 \odot (Z_3^{(4)})^{-1}) \oplus (C_3^* \odot (Z_3^{(4)})^{-1}) = (C_4 \boxminus Z_4^{(4)}) \oplus (C_4^* \boxminus Z_4^{(4)})$. Estimates for the complexity of truncated differential attacks on MESH-64, using (4) are based on experimental results on mini-MESH variants, following [4], and give[2] $2^{32} \cdot 2^{31} \cdot 2 \cdot 2^{16} \cdot 2^{-3} \approx 2^{77}$ 3.5-round MESH-64 encryptions, 2^{64} chosen plaintexts, and 2^{32} 64-bit blocks (memory). Note that the new key schedule does not allow key bit overlap. Therefore, there is no reduction in complexity for a key-recovery attack. The mirror image of the differential (4), in [13], allows to recover $Z_2^{(1)}$, $Z_4^{(1)}$, $Z_1^{(4)}$, and $Z_2^{(4)}$, with the same complexities.

---

[2] (#structures)×(#surviving pairs per structure)×(#equations)×(#key pairs to find per equation)×(#operations).

6.2 Truncated Differential Attack on MESH-96

A truncated differential attack on 3.5-round MESH-96 can use the following differential, where $A, B, C, D, E, F, G, H, I, J, K, L \in \mathbb{Z}_2^{16}$:

$$(A,B,0,C,D,0)\overset{2^{-32}}{\to}(E,F,0,E,F,0)\overset{(0,0,0)\overset{1}{\to}(0,0,0)}{}(E,E,F,F,0,0)$$

$$(E,E,F,F,0,0)\overset{2^{-16}}{\to}(G,H,I,G,0,0)\overset{(0,H,I)^2\overset{2^{-48}}{\to}(I,H,G)}{}(0,0,H,0,0,I)$$

$$(0,0,H,0,0,I)\overset{2^{-16}}{\to}(0,0,J,0,0,J)\overset{(0,0,0)\overset{1}{\to}(0,0,0)}{}(0,0,0,0,J,J)$$

$$(0,0,0,0,J,J)\overset{1}{\to}(0,0,0,0,K,L)\,,\tag{5}$$

that has average probability 2^{-112}, and allows recovery of $Z_1^{(1)}$, $Z_2^{(1)}$, $Z_4^{(1)}$, $Z_5^{(1)}$, $Z_5^{(4)}$, and $Z_6^{(4)}$. A differential attack on MESH-96 using (5) works similarly to the attack on MESH-64, and has estimated complexity, based on experimental results following [4], as follows: $2^{32} \cdot 2^{63} \cdot 3 \cdot 2^{16} \cdot \frac{1}{13} \approx 2^{109}$ 3.5-round MESH-96 encryptions, 2^{96} chosen plaintexts, and 2^{64} 96-bit blocks of memory. There are two additional truncated differentials with the same probability [13] that allows to recover $Z_3^{(1)}$, $Z_6^{(1)}$, $Z_3^{(4)}$, $Z_4^{(4)}$, $Z_1^{(4)}$, and $Z_2^{(4)}$.

An attack on 4-round MESH-96 can guess subkeys $Z_7^{(4)}$, $Z_8^{(4)}$, $Z_9^{(4)}$, and apply the previous attack on 3.5 rounds, with time complexity $2^{109+48} = 2^{157}$ 4-round computations.

6.3 Truncated Differential Attack on MESH-128

A differential attack on 3.5-round MESH-128 can use the following differential, with average probability 2^{-128}, and with $A, B, C, D, E, F, G, H, I, J, K, L, M, N, O, P \in \mathbb{Z}_2^{16}$:

$$(A,0,0,B,C,0,0,D)\overset{2^{-32}}{\to}(E,0,0,F,E,0,0,F)\overset{(0,0,0,0)\overset{1}{\to}(0,0,0,0)}{}(E,E,0,0,0,0,F,F)$$

$$(E,E,0,0,0,0,F,F)\overset{1}{\to}(G,H,0,0,0,0,I,J)\overset{(G,H,I,J)^2\overset{2^{-64}}{\to}(J,I,H,G)}{}(0,G,H,0,0,I,J,0)$$

$$(0,G,H,0,0,I,J,0)\overset{2^{-32}}{\to}(0,K,L,0,0,K,L,0)\overset{(0,0,0,0)\overset{1}{\to}(0,0,0,0)}{}(0,0,K,L,K,L,0,0)$$

$$(0,0,K,L,K,L,0,0)\overset{1}{\to}(0,0,M,N,O,P,0,0)\,.\tag{6}$$

Conservative complexity estimates, based on experimental results following [4], for a truncated differential attack on 3.5-round MESH-128 using (6) are as follows: $2^{64} \cdot 2^{63} \cdot 4 \cdot 2^{16} \cdot \frac{6}{116} \approx 2^{141}$ 3.5-round MESH-128 encryptions, 2^{128} chosen plaintexts, and 2^{64} 128-bit blocks of memory, to recover $Z_1^{(1)}$, $Z_4^{(1)}$, $Z_5^{(1)}$, $Z_8^{(1)}$, $Z_3^{(4)}$, $Z_4^{(4)}$, $Z_5^{(4)}$, $Z_6^{(4)}$. An additional truncated differential [13], can be used to recover $Z_2^{(1)}$, $Z_3^{(1)}$, $Z_6^{(1)}$, $Z_7^{(1)}$, $Z_1^{(4)}$, $Z_2^{(4)}$, $Z_7^{(4)}$, $Z_8^{(4)}$. In total, using both differentials, 128-bit user keys are recovered. The remaining 128 key bits can be found by exhaustive search.

An attack on 4-round MESH-128 can guess $Z_9^{(4)}$, $Z_{10}^{(4)}$, $Z_{11}^{(4)}$, $Z_{12}^{(4)}$, and apply the previous attack on 3.5 rounds, with time complexity $2^{142+64} = 2^{206}$ 4-round computations.

7   Linear Attack

Our linear analysis on MESH ciphers followed the framework of Daemen *et al.* [6]. Initially, all one-round linear relations under weak-key assumptions were exhaustively obtained for MESH-64, MESH-96, and MESH-128.

7.1   Linear Attack on MESH-64

For MESH-64, an example of a one-round relation under weak-key assumptions is $(0,0,0,1) \rightarrow (0,0,1,0)$, with $Z_4^{(1)}$, $Z_6^{(1)}$, $Z_7^{(1)} \in \{0,1\}$ (an odd-numbered round). According to the key schedule, the user key words are xored to fixed constants c_i, $0 \le i \le 7$, and are used as the first eight subkey words. It means that the subkey restrictions $Z_4^{(1)}$, $Z_6^{(1)}$, $Z_7^{(1)} \in \{0,1\}$ can be satisfied if the most significant 15 bits of the key words match the corresponding bits of the associated constants. Multiple-round linear relations are obtained by concatenating one-round linear relations, and deriving the corresponding fraction of keys from the key space from which the relation holds. This fraction of keys can be derived from the restrictions on subkeys in the one-round linear relations. Nonetheless, the key schedule of MESH-64 does not have a simple mapping of subkey bits to user key bits such as in IDEA. The fraction of keys for the linear relations in MESH-64 was estimated from the weak-key class sizes obtained by exhaustive key search in a mini-version of MESH-64 with[3] 16-bit blocks, denoted MESH-64(16), where the key size is 32 bits. Analysis of MESH-64(16) indicated that each subkey restriction (most significant three bits equal to zero) is satisfied for a fraction of 2^{-3} or less per subkey. This observation allowed to estimate the fraction of keys (and the weak-key class size) that satisfy a linear relation for MESH-64 as 2^{-15} per subkey.

The longest linear relations obtained (starting from the first round) are as follows:

. $(0,1,0,1) \overset{1r}{\rightarrow} (0,0,1,1) \overset{1r}{\rightarrow} (1,0,1,0) \overset{1r}{\rightarrow} (1,1,0,0) \overset{1r}{\rightarrow} (0,1,0,1) \overset{1r}{\rightarrow} (0,0,1,1)$,   provided $Z_4^{(1)}$, $Z_3^{(2)}$, $Z_5^{(2)}$, $Z_6^{(2)}$, $Z_1^{(3)}$, $Z_2^{(4)}$, $Z_5^{(4)}$, $Z_6^{(4)}$, $Z_4^{(5)} \in \{0,1\}$. For MESH-64(16) this relation holds for a weak-key class of size 4, which corresponds to a fraction of $4 \cdot 2^{-32} = 2^{-30}$ of its key space. This fraction is less than $2^{-3*9} = 2^{-27}$, that is to be expected if each subkey restriction held independently. For MESH-64, the weak-key class size is estimated as $2^{128-15*8} = 2^8$ for 4 rounds at most;

---

[3] With left rotation by 3 bits per word in the key schedule.

. $(1,0,1,0) \overset{1r}{\rightarrow} (1,1,0,0) \overset{1r}{\rightarrow} (0,1,0,1) \overset{1r}{\rightarrow} (0,0,1,1) \overset{1r}{\rightarrow} (1,0,1,0) \overset{1r}{\rightarrow} (1,1,0,0)$, provided $Z_1^{(1)}$, $Z_2^{(2)}$, $Z_5^{(2)}$, $Z_6^{(2)}$, $Z_4^{(3)}$, $Z_4^{(4)}$, $Z_5^{(4)}$, $Z_6^{(4)}$, $Z_1^{(5)} \in \{0,1\}$. For
MESH-64(16) this relation holds for a weak-key class of size 5, which is
a fraction of $5 \cdot 2^{-32} \approx 2^{-30}$ of its key space. This fraction is less than
$2^{-3*9} = 2^{-27}$, that is to be expected if each subkey restriction held independently. For MESH-64, the weak-key class size is estimated as $2^{128-15*8} = 2^8$
for 4 rounds.

These linear relations can distinguish the first four rounds of MESH-64 from
a random permutation, under weak-key assumptions, or can be used in a 0.5R
attack on 4.5-round MESH-64 to recover at least one of the subkeys $Z_i^{(5)}$, $1 \le i \le 4$, using $N \approx 8 \cdot (2^{-1})^{-2} = 32$ known plaintexts and about $32 \cdot 2^{16} = 2^{21}$
parity computations.

7.2 Linear Attack on MESH-96

The MA-box of MESH-96 effectively avoids many one-round linear relations,
because it contains multiplications in which subkeys are not directly involved
as operands. The approach to a linear attack on MESH-96 is similar to that
on MESH-64. Exhaustive key search was applied to a mini-version MESH-96
with 4-bit words, denoted MESH-96(24), in order to estimate the weak-key class
size from the fraction of the key space satisfying the weak-key restrictions. The
longest linear relation (starting from the first round) uses the one-round iter-
ative relation: $(1,1,1,1,1,1) \overset{1r}{\rightarrow} (1,1,1,1,1,1)$, repeated for 3.5 rounds, provided
$Z_1^{(1)}$, $Z_1^{(1)}$, $Z_5^{(1)}$, $Z_2^{(2)}$, $Z_4^{(2)}$, $Z_6^{(2)}$, $Z_1^{(3)}$, $Z_3^{(3)}$, $Z_5^{(3)}$, $Z_2^{(4)}$, $Z_4^{(4)}$, $Z_6^{(4)} \in \{0,1\}$, for
MESH-96(24) the weak-key class size is 620, which corresponds to a fraction of
$2^{9.27-48} \approx 2^{-38.72}$ of its key space. This fraction is smaller than $2^{-3*12} = 2^{-36}$
that would be expected if each subkey restriction held independently. For MESH-
96, the weak-key class size is estimated as at most $2^{192-15*12} \approx 2^{12}$. This linear
relation can distinguish the first 3.5-round MESH-96 from a random permutation, or can be used in a key-recovery attack on 4-round MESH-96, to find $Z_7^{(4)}$,
$Z_8^{(4)}$, $Z_9^{(4)}$, with $N \approx 8 \cdot (2^{-1})^{-2} = 32$ chosen plaintexts, and $32 \cdot 2^{48} = 2^{53}$ parity
computations. Attacking 4.5 rounds requires guessing six subkeys of the fifth
key-mixing layer, leading to a complexity of $2^{96+53} = 2^{149}$ parity computations.

7.3 Linear Attack on MESH-128

The MA-box of MESH-128, similar to that of MESH-96, also avoids, for the
same reasons, many one-round relations. Estimates for the weak-key class size
of MESH-128 are derived similarly to that of MESH-64 and MESH-96, namely,
assuming a fraction of 2^{-15} of the key space satisfies each subkey restriction.
The longest linear relation (starting from the first round), uses the one-round iterative relation: $(1,1,1,1,1,1,1,1) \overset{1r}{\rightarrow} (1,1,1,1,1,1,1,1)$, repeated for 3.5 rounds,
provided $Z_1^{(1)}$, $Z_3^{(1)}$, $Z_6^{(1)}$, $Z_8^{(1)}$, $Z_2^{(2)}$, $Z_4^{(2)}$, $Z_5^{(2)}$, $Z_7^{(2)}$, $Z_1^{(3)}$, $Z_3^{(3)}$, $Z_6^{(3)}$, $Z_8^{(3)}$, $Z_2^{(4)}$,

$Z_4^{(4)}$, $Z_5^{(4)}$, $Z_7^{(4)} \in \{0, 1\}$, this relation implies a weak-key class of estimated size $2^{256-15*16} = 2^{16}$.

This linear relation can distinguish the first 3.5 rounds of MESH-128 from a random permutation, or can be used in a 0.5R attack on 4-round MESH-128, to recover subkeys $Z_9^{(4)}$, $Z_{10}^{(4)}$, $Z_{11}^{(4)}$, $Z_{12}^{(4)}$, with about $N \approx 8 \cdot (2^{-1})^{-2} = 32$ chosen plaintexts and $32 \cdot 2^{64} = 2^{69}$ parity computations. Attacking 4.5 rounds involves guessing eight subkeys of the fifth key-mixing layer, leading to a complexity of $2^{69+128} = 2^{197}$ parity computations.

8   Impossible Differential Attacks

Impossible differential (ID) attacks on MESH ciphers follow a similar setting of Biham *et al.* [2].

8.1   Impossible Differential Attack of MESH-64

A key-recovery ID attack on 3.5-round MESH-64 uses the 2.5-round impossible differential $(a, 0, a, 0) \nrightarrow (b, b, 0, 0)$, with $a, b \neq 0$, starting after the first key mixing until the end of the third round. Let $(X_1^1, X_2^1, X_3^1, X_4^1)$ be a plaintext block, and $(Y_1^4, Y_2^4, Y_3^4, Y_4^4)$ the corresponding ciphertext block. The attack chooses a structure of 2^{32} plaintexts with fixed X_2^1 and X_4^1, and all possible values for X_1^1 and X_3^1. There are about $2^{32} \cdot (2^{32} - 1)/2 \approx 2^{63}$ plaintext pairs with xor difference $(X_1^{1'}, 0, X_3^{1'}, 0)$. Collect about 2^{31} pairs from the structure whose ciphertext difference after 3.5 rounds satisfies $Y_3^{4'} = 0$ and $Y_4^{4'} = 0$. For each such pair try all 2^{32} subkeys $(Z_1^{(1)}, Z_3^{(1)})$ and partially encrypt (X_1^1, X_3^1) in each of the two plaintexts of the pair. Collect about 2^{16} subkeys $(Z_1^{(1)}, Z_3^{(1)})$ satisfying $(X_1^1 \odot Z_1^{(1)}) \oplus (X_1^{1*} \odot Z_1^{(1)}) = (X_3^1 \boxplus Z_3^{(1)}) \oplus (X_3^{1*} \boxplus Z_3^{(1)})$. This step takes 2^{17} time, and 2^{16} memory. Next, try all 2^{32} subkeys $(Z_1^{(4)}, Z_2^{(4)})$ to partially decrypt (Y_1^4, Y_2^4) in each of the two ciphertexts of the pair. Collect about 2^{16} subkeys $(Z_1^{(4)}, Z_2^{(4)})$ such that $(Y_1^4 \boxminus Z_1^{(4)}) \oplus (Y_1^{4*} \boxminus Z_1^{(4)}) = (Y_2^4 \odot (Z_2^{(4)})^{-1}) \oplus (Y_2^{4*} \odot (Z_2^{(4)})^{-1})$. This step takes 2^{17} time and 2^{16} memory. Make a list of all 2^{32} 64-bit subkeys $(Z_1^{(1)}, Z_3^{(1)}, Z_1^{(4)}, Z_2^{(4)})$, combining the two previous steps. Those subkeys cannot be the correct values, because they lead to a pair of the impossible differential. Each pair defines a list of about 2^{32} 64-bit wrong subkey values. It is expected that after 90 structures, the number of remaining wrong subkeys is: $2^{64} \cdot (1 - \frac{2^{32}}{2^{64}})^{2^{31} \cdot 90} \approx \frac{2^{64}}{e^{45}} \approx 2^{-0.92}$. Therefore, the correct subkey can be uniquely identified. The attack requires $90 \cdot 2^{32} \approx 2^{38.5}$ chosen plaintexts. The memory complexity is 2^{61} bytes, dominated by the sieving of the correct 64-bit subkey. The time complexity is $2^{31} \cdot 90 \cdot (2^{17} + 2^{17}) \approx 2^{56}$ steps. The 2.5-round impossible differential $(0, a, 0, a) \nrightarrow (0, 0, b, b)$, with $a, b \neq 0$, can be used to discover $(Z_2^{(1)}, Z_4^{(1)}, Z_3^{(4)}, Z_4^{(4)})$. The joint time complexity is about 2^{57} steps. If a step consists of a modular multiplication and there are 17 multiplications in 3.5 rounds then the latter corresponds to $2^{57} \cdot 1/17 \approx 2^{53}$ 3.5-round computations.

Data complexity amounts to $2^{39.5}$ chosen plaintexts, and 2^{61} bytes of memory. In total, the first 64 user key bits are recovered, and the remaining 64 key bits can be obtained by exhaustive search, and the final time complexity becomes 2^{64} 3.5-round computations. To attack 4-round MESH-64, the subkeys $Z_5^{(4)}$, $Z_6^{(4)}$, $Z_7^{(4)}$ are guessed, and the previous attack on 3.5 rounds is performed. The time complexity increases to $2^{64+48} = 2^{112}$ steps.

8.2   Impossible Differential Attack of MESH-96

An ID attack on MESH-96 can use the 2.5-round distinguishers $(a, 0, 0, a, 0, 0)$ $\not\to$ $(b, b, c, c, 0, 0)$, $(0, a, 0, 0, a, 0)$ $\not\to$ $(0, 0, b, b, c, c)$, and $(0, 0, a, 0, 0, a)$ $\not\to$ $(b, b, 0, 0, c, c)$, with $a, b, c \neq 0$, each one starting after the first key-mixing half-round, until the end of the third round. The attack discovers $(Z_i^{(1)}, Z_i^{(4)})$, $1 \leq i \leq 6$, and is analogous to the attack on MESH-64. Data complexity is about 2^{57} chosen plaintexts, 2^{93} bytes of memory, and time equivalent to $2^{73.5}$ steps. In total, the first 96 user key bits were directly recovered, and the remaining 96 key bits can be found by exhaustive search, which leads to a final time complexity of 2^{96} 3.5-round computations.

An attack on 4 rounds can guess $Z_7^{(4)}$, $Z_8^{(4)}$, $Z_9^{(4)}$, and apply the previous attack on 3.5 rounds. The time complexity becomes $2^{96+48} = 2^{144}$ 4-round computations.

8.3   Impossible Differential Attack of MESH-128

The best trade-off ID attack uses the following 2.5-round distinguishers: $(a, b, 0, 0, a, b, 0, 0)$ $\not\to$ $(c, c, d, e, d, e, 0, 0)$, $(0, 0, a, b, 0, 0, a, b)$ $\not\to$ $(c, c, 0, d, 0, d, e, e)$ with $a, b, c, d, e \neq 0$. The attack proceeds similar to the one on MESH-96, and recovers $(Z_i^{(1)}, Z_i^{(4)})$ for $1 \leq i \leq 8$. Data complexity is 2^{65} chosen plaintexts, 2^{157} bytes of memory and time equivalent to 2^{107} 3.5-round computations. In total, the first 128 user key bits are effectively recovered, and from the key schedule, $Z_i^{(4)}$, $1 \leq i \leq 8$ do not provide enough information to deduce the remaining 128 user key bits, which are then recovered by exhaustive search, leading to a final time complexity of 2^{128} 3.5-round MESH-128 computations. An attack 4 rounds can guess $(Z_9^{(4)}, Z_{10}^{(4)}, Z_{11}^{(4)}, Z_{12}^{(4)})$, and apply the attack on 3.5 rounds. Time complexity increases to $2^{128+64} = 2^{192}$ steps.

9   Demirci's Attack

This section follows the work of Demirci in [9].

9.1   Demirci's Attack on MESH-64

Demirci's attack using 1st-order integrals [10,7] can be adapted to MESH-64 starting from the 2nd round, or any other even round. The integral operator is exclusive-or. Consider a multiset of the form $(P\ P\ P\ A)$, namely, with the first three words constant (passive) and the 4th word active. Let $C^{(i)} = (C_1^{(i)}, C_2^{(i)}, C_3^{(i)}, C_4^{(i)})$ denote the ciphertext after i rounds. After 1-round MESH-64, the output multiset has the form $(?\ ?\ A\ *)$, that is, the first two words are garbled, the 3rd word is active and the 4th is balanced. The multiset after 1.5-round becomes $(?\ ?\ A\ ?)$ but the least significant bit of $C_2^{(1.5)}$ is constant because it is a combination of only active words from the MA-box of the initial round. This property is used as a distinguisher for Demirci's attack on 2-round MESH-64:

$$\text{LSB}(C_2^{(2)} \oplus C_3^{(2)} \oplus Z_6^{(3)} \odot ((C_1^{(2)} \oplus C_2^{(2)}) \odot Z_5^{(3)} \boxplus (C_3^{(2)} \oplus C_4^{(2)}))) = 0, \quad (7)$$

where LSB denotes the least significant bit function. Therefore, over a multiset, equation (7) can be used to find $(Z_5^{(3)}, Z_6^{(3)})$. It provides a one-bit condition, thus, this search over 32 key bits requires $32 \cdot 2^{16} = 2^{21}$ chosen plaintexts, and an effort of $2^{32} \cdot 2^{16} + 2^{31} \cdot 2^{16} + \ldots 2^1 \cdot 2^{16} \approx 2^{49}$ half-round computations or about 2^{47} 2-round computations. An attack on 2.5 rounds can guess $(Z_1^{(4)}, Z_2^{(4)}, Z_3^{(4)}, Z_4^{(4)})$ and apply the previous attack, at the cost of $2^{47} \cdot 2^{64} = 2^{111}$ 2.5-round MESH-64 computations.

9.2   Demirci's Attack on MESH-96

For MESH-96, Demirci's attack on 2 rounds can use 1st-order multisets of the form $(P\ P\ P\ P\ P\ A)$ with only the 8th input word active, and the distinguisher:

$$\begin{aligned} \text{LSB } (C_3^{(2)} \oplus C_5^{(2)} \oplus (Z_7^{(2)} \odot (C_1^{(2)} \oplus C_2^{(2)}) \boxplus (C_4^{(2)} \oplus C_3^{(2)})) \odot \quad &(8) \\ (Z_8^{(2)} \boxplus (C_1^{(2)} \oplus C_2^{(2)}) \odot Z_7^{(2)} \boxplus (C_4^{(2)} \oplus C_3^{(2)}) \odot (C_5^{(2)} \oplus C_6^{(2)}))) = 0, \end{aligned}$$

where $(C_1^{(i)}, C_2^{(i)}, C_3^{(i)}, C_4^{(i)}, C_5^{(i)}, C_6^{(i)})$ is the ciphertext after i rounds. The attack is analogous to that on MESH-64. Equation (9) allows to recover $(Z_7^{(2)}, Z_8^{(2)})$ using $32 \cdot 2^{16} = 2^{21}$ chosen plaintexts and time about 2^{49} 2-round MESH-96 computations. To attack 2.5 rounds guess $(Z_1^{(3)}, Z_2^{(3)}, Z_3^{(3)}, Z_4^{(3)}, Z_5^{(3)}, Z_6^{(3)})$ and apply the previous attack, leading to $2^{49} \cdot 2^{96} = 2^{145}$ 2.5-round MESH-96 computations.

9.3   Demirci's Attack on MESH-128

For MESH-128, Demirci's attack with 1st-order integrals does not apply, because the four layers in its MA-box do not allow any balanced output word, not even their LSBs, which is a necessary condition for the attack. Nonetheless, there are alternative attacks using higher-order integrals [9,10] that can cross the 4-layer MA-box. A 2nd-order Demirci's attack on 2-round MESH-128 can use, for instance, multisets in which the first and fourth input words are jointly active, and all the other six words are passive. Such multiset requires 2^{32} chosen plaintexts. The multiset after 1.5 rounds contains only balanced words. In particular, the integral of the inputs to the MA-box of the second round all sum to zero. Some terminology for the attack description follows: let $(C_1^{(i)}, C_2^{(i)}, C_3^{(i)}, C_4^{(i)}, C_5^{(i)},$ $C_6^{(i)}, C_7^{(i)}, C_8^{(i)})$ be the ciphertext multiset after i rounds, and $p = C_1^{(2)} \oplus C_2^{(2)}$, $q = C_3^{(2)} \oplus C_5^{(2)}$, $r = C_4^{(2)} \oplus C_6^{(2)}$, and $s = C_7^{(2)} \oplus C_8^{(2)}$. The distinguisher for the higher-order Demirci's attack is obtained by exploring the least significant bit of the leftmost two output words of the MA-box of the second round:

$$\text{LSB } (C_4^{(2)} \oplus C_7^{(2)} \oplus C_4^{(1)} \odot Z_4^{(2)} \oplus C_7^{(1)} \odot Z_7^{(2)}) =$$
$$\text{LSB } (Z_{11}^{(2)} \odot (p \odot Z_9^{(2)} \boxplus (p \odot Z_9^{(2)} \boxplus q) \odot$$
$$(r \odot (p \odot Z_9^{(2)} \boxplus q) \boxplus (r \odot (p \odot Z_9^{(2)} \boxplus q) \boxplus s) \odot Z_{10}^{(2)}))). \tag{9}$$

Over the given plaintext multiset, the integral of $\text{LSB}(C_4^{(2)} \oplus C_7^{(2)} \oplus C_4^{(1)} \odot Z_4^{(2)} \oplus C_7^{(1)} \odot Z_7^{(2)})$ is zero, because the subkeys are fixed, and the corresponding intermediate values are balanced. Therefore, (9) provides a one-bit condition to recover $Z_9^{(2)}$, $Z_{10}^{(2)}$ and $Z_{11}^{(2)}$. The data requirements are $48 \cdot 2^{32} = 2^{37.6}$ chosen plaintexts, and time equivalent to $2^{48} \cdot 2^{32} + 2^{47} \cdot 2^{32} + \ldots 2 \cdot 2^{32} = 2^{32} \cdot 2 \cdot (2^{48} - 1) \approx 2^{81}$ half-round computations, or about 2^{79} 2-round computations.

10 Conclusions

This paper described the MESH block ciphers, which are based on the same group operations of IDEA, but with a number of novel features:

. flexible block sizes in steps of 32 bits. For more than ten years since the publication of IDEA [11], no IDEA variant has been proposed with block sizes larger than 64 bits or word sizes larger than 16 bits. Maybe such attempts were hindered by the fact that $2^{32} + 1$ is not a prime number, and thus, $\mathbb{Z}_{2^{32}+1}^{*}$ is not a field. The MESH ciphers provide an alternative approach that do not depend on the need for larger word sizes or finite fields.
. new key schedule algorithms with fast key avalanche. Each subkey of IDEA depends (linearly) on exactly 16 user key bits, while in MESH all subkeys after the second round depend (non-linearly) on all user key words. Moreover, the new key schedules avoid (differential and linear) weak keys as existing in IDEA. Software simulations[4] of the key schedule give about 1888 cycles/key-setup for IDEA, 2054 cycles/key-setup for MESH-64, 3869 cycles/key-setup for MESH-96, and 5536 cycles/key-setup for MESH-128.
. larger MA-boxes designed to better resist differential and linear attacks.
. distinct key-mixing layers, originally designed to counter slide attacks [3], but also proved useful against Demirci's attack [9]. The design of the MESH ciphers incorporates measures to counter a number of modern cryptanalytic attacks developed along the past 12 years [2,3,4,6,9,10,11,14]. The security margin of MESH ciphers, as well as of IDEA, against the described attacks seems relatively high. Table 2 in Appendix A details the attack complexity figures for IDEA and MESH ciphers, where linear attacks are restricted to a weak-key class; 'KP' means Known Plaintext and 'CP', Chosen Plaintext.

---

[4] On a Pentium III 667 MHz under Linux.

Acknowledgements. We would like to thank Alex Biryukov for the many explanations concerning the impossible differential technique. We are also grateful to the anonymous referees, whose comments helped improve the presentation of this paper.

References

1. Aoki,K., Ichikawa,T., Kanda,M., Matsui,M., Moriai,S., Nakajima,J., Tokita,T.: Camellia: a 128-bit Block Cipher Suitable for Multiple Platforms, 1st NESSIE Workshop, Heverlee, Belgium, Nov. 2000.
2. Biham, E., Biryukov, A., Shamir, A., Miss-in-the-Middle Attacks on IDEA, Khufu and Khafre, In: Knudsen, L.R. (ed.): 6th Fast Software Encryption Workshop, LNCS, Vol. 1636. Springer-Verlag (1999), 124–138.
3. Biryukov,A., Wagner,D.: Slide Attacks, In: Knudsen,L.R. (ed): 6th Fast Software Encryption Workshop, LNCS, Vol. 1636. Springer-Verlag (1999), 245–259.
4. Borst,J., Knudsen,L.R., Rijmen,V.: Two Attacks on Reduced IDEA, In: Fumy, W. (ed.): Advances in Cryptology, Eurocrypt'97, LNCS, Vol. 1233. Springer-Verlag (1997), 1–13.
5. Daemen, J.: Cipher and Hash Function Design – Strategies based on Linear and Differential Cryptanalysis," PhD Dissertation, Dept. Elektrotechniek, Katholieke Universiteit Leuven, Belgium, Mar. 1995.
6. Daemen, J., Govaerts, R., Vandewalle, J.: Weak Keys for IDEA, In: Stinson, D.R. (ed.): Advances in Cryptology, Crypto'93, LNCS, Vol. 773. Springer-Verlag (1994), 224–231.
7. Daemen, J., Knudsen,L.R., Rijmen, V.: The Block Cipher SQUARE, In: Biham,E. (ed.): 4th Fast Software Encryption Workshop, LNCS, Vol. 1267. Springer-Verlag (1997), 149–165.
8. Daemen,J., Rijmen, V.: The Design of Rijndael – AES – The Advanced Encryption Standard, Springer-Verlag, 2002.
9. Demirci,H.: Square-like Attacks on Reduced Rounds of IDEA, In: Nyberg,K., Heys,H. (eds.): 9th Selected Areas in Cryptography Workshop, SAC'02, LNCS, Vol. 2595. Springer-Verlag (2002), 147–159.
10. Knudsen,L.R., Wagner,D.: Integral Cryptanalysis, In: Daemen, J., Rijmen,V. (eds): 9th Fast Software Encryption Workshop, LNCS, Vol. 2365. Springer-Verlag (2002), 112–127.
11. Lai,X., Massey, J.L., Murphy,S.: Markov Ciphers and Differential Cryptanalysis, In: Davies, D.W. (ed.): Advances in Cryptology, Eurocrypt'91, LNCS, Vol. 547. Springer-Verlag (1991), 17–38.
12. Menezes, A.J., van Oorschot, P.C., Vanstone, S., Handbook of Applied Cryptography, CRC Press, 1997.
13. Nakahara Jr, J.: Cryptanalysis and Design of Block Ciphers," PhD Dissertation, Dept. Elektrotechniek, Katholieke Universiteit Leuven, Belgium, Jun. 2003.
14. Rijmen, V., Preneel, B., De Win, E.: On Weaknesses of Non-Surjective Round Functions, In: Design, Codes and Cryptography, Vol. 12, number 3, Nov. 1997, 253–266.

A   Attack Summary

This appendix lists the attack complexities on MESH ciphers and compares them with previous attacks on IDEA.

Table 2. Summary of attack complexities on IDEA and MESH ciphers.

Cipher	Block Size	Key Size	Attack	#Rounds	Data	Memory	Time
IDEA	64	128	Demirci	2	23 CP	23	2^{64}
			Demirci	2.5	55 CP	55	2^{81}
(8.5 rounds)			Demirci	3	71 CP	71	2^{71}
			Demirci	3	2^{33} CP	2^{33}	2^{82}
			Demirci	3.5	103 CP	103	2^{103}
			Trunc. Diff.	3.5	2^{56} CP	2^{32}	2^{67}
			Imp. Diff.	3.5	$2^{38.5}$ CP	2^{37}	2^{53}
			Demirci	4	2^{34} CP	2^{34}	2^{114}
			Imp. Diff.	4	$2^{38.5}$ CP	2^{37}	2^{70}
			Imp. Diff.	4.5	2^{64} CP	2^{32}	2^{112}
MESH-64	64	128	Demirci	2	2^{21} CP	2^{16}	2^{47}
			Demirci	2.5	2^{21} CP	2^{16}	2^{111}
(8.5 rounds)			Imp. Diff.	3.5	$2^{39.5}$ CP	2^{61}	2^{64}
			Trunc. Diff.	3.5	2^{64} CP	2^{32}	2^{78}
			Imp. Diff.	4	$2^{39.5}$ CP	2^{61}	2^{112}
			Trunc. Diff.	4	2^{64} CP	2^{32}	2^{126}
			Linear	4.5	32 KP	32	2^{21}
MESH-96	96	192	Demirci	2	2^{21} CP	2^{16}	2^{47}
			Demirci	2.5	2^{21} CP	2^{16}	2^{143}
(10.5 rounds)			Imp. Diff.	3.5	2^{56} CP	2^{93}	2^{96}
			Trunc. Diff.	3.5	2^{96} CP	2^{64}	2^{109}
			Linear	4	32 KP	32	2^{53}
			Imp. Diff.	4	2^{56} CP	2^{93}	2^{144}
			Trunc. Diff.	4	2^{96} CP	2^{64}	2^{157}
			Linear	4.5	32 KP	32	2^{149}
MESH-128	128	256	Demirci	2	$2^{37.6}$ CP	$2^{37.6}$	2^{79}
			Demirci	2.5	$2^{37.6}$ CP	$2^{37.6}$	2^{143}
(12.5 rounds)			Imp. Diff.	3.5	2^{65} CP	2^{157}	2^{128}
			Trunc. Diff.	3.5	2^{128} CP	2^{64}	2^{142}
			Linear	4	32 KP	32	2^{69}
			Imp. Diff.	4	2^{65} CP	2^{157}	2^{192}
			Trunc. Diff.	4	2^{128} CP	2^{64}	2^{206}
			Linear	4.5	32 KP	32	2^{197}

Fast Scalar Multiplication Method Using Change-of-Basis Matrix to Prevent Power Analysis Attacks on Koblitz Curves

Dong Jin Park, Sang Gyoo Sim, and Pil Joong Lee

Department of Electronic and Electrical Engineering,
Pohang University of Science & Technology (POSTECH),
Hyoja-dong, Nam-gu, Pohang, Kyoungbuk, Korea
{djpark, sim}@oberon.postech.ac.kr, pjl@postech.ac.kr

Abstract. We propose a fast scalar multiplication method using a change-of-basis matrix to prevent power analysis attacks on Koblitz curves. Our method assures the fastest execution time without offline computation compared with previous countermeasures against power analysis attacks. Using the change-of-basis matrix, the Frobenius endomorphism of Koblitz curves is executed in the normal basis representation, whereas point addition is executed in the polynomial basis. In addition, we restrict the range of the number of additions. Even though we do not conceal the number perfectly, the algorithm remains secure with a security parameter chosen carefully. These techniques enable our method to prevent SPA with little computational overhead. For DPA prevention, we introduce randomness with negligible overhead. Timings results show that the proposed method is as efficient as a sliding window method.

Keywords: SPA, DPA, scalar multiplication, sliding window methods, basis conversion, Koblitz curve cryptosystems

1 Introduction

Elliptic curve cryptosystems (ECC) are based on the difficulty of the discrete logarithm problem (DLP) over elliptic curves. Compared to multiplicative groups with a prime modulus, the DLP over elliptic curves appears to be much more difficult. Additionally, no subexponential-time algorithm is known for DLP in the class of non-supersingular elliptic curves. Therefore, keys can be much smaller in ECC than in other public-key cryptosystems. The smaller key size makes the ECC appropriate for implementations of cryptographic algorithms on low computing-powered devices, such as smart cards, mobile phones, and PDAs.

Unfortunately, these devices are highly vulnerable to power analysis attacks [10]. The attacks are so practical and powerful that attackers can obtain secret information even from physically shielded devices by observation(s) of power consumption. Therefore, power analysis attacks [1,14,18] and their countermeasures [1,6,7,8,12,16,17,19] have attracted much attention from researchers. According

K. Chae and M. Yung (Eds.): WISA 2003, LNCS 2908, pp. 474–488, 2004.

to the techniques employed thus far, power analysis has two categories: simple power analysis (SPA) and differential power analyses (DPA).

SPA exploits the differences between group operations. If one implements scalar multiplication using a double-and-add method, SPA can discover the entire secret exponent with a simple classification. Therefore, SPA is the first threat to all implementations of cryptographc algorithms on mobile devices. In order to prevent SPA, the instructions performed during a cryptographic algorithm should be independent of the data being processed [1,8,12,17,19].

On the other hand, DPA uses statistical analysis to extract minute differences in power consumption traces. A classic DPA entails averaging and subtraction. After measuring a sufficient number of power traces, DPA divides them into two groups by a selection function. The power traces of each group are averaged, and then subtracted. A correct guess of the secret key provides a peak in subtraction. Because averaging can improve the signal to noise ratio, DPA can distinguish between smaller differences than SPA. Introducing randomness to the computation can prevent DPA [1,6,16].

Recently, Coron *et al.* proposed a method to increase the speed of scalar multiplication on Koblitz curves [2]. Their algorithm combines normal and polynomial basis operations to achieve optimal performance. We found that the basis conversion technique in [2] is also useful for making an SPA resistant algorithm.

We propose a fast scalar multiplication method using the change-of-basis matrix to prevent power analysis attacks on Koblitz curves. Based on a sliding window method, we applied SPA countermeasure and DPA countermeasures. For SPA prevention, we use the basis conversion technique, which enables τ-operations to be executed in normal basis. In addition, we restrict the range of the number of additions. Even though we do not conceal the number perfectly, the algorithm remains secure with a security parameter chosen carefully. Also, we proposed highly efficient DPA countermeasures, which are to randomize computational order and precomputed points. Implementation results are included, which show that the proposed algorithm is as efficient as a sliding window method.

This paper is organized as follows: In section 2, we present some preliminaries. Proposed algorithm is presented in section 3. In section 4, security analysis is presented. Section 5 is for timing results. This paper concludes in section 6.

2   Preliminaries

2.1   Koblitz Curves

Koblitz curves are elliptic curves, E_0 and E_1, of the form:

$$E_a : y^2 + xy = x^3 + ax^2 + 1, \text{defined over } GF(2^m). \tag{1}$$

Since E_a is defined over $GF(2^m)$, the Frobenius map $\tau : E_a(GF(2^m)) \mapsto E_a(GF(2^m))$ defined by $\tau(\mathcal{O}) = \mathcal{O}$ and $\tau((x,y)) = (x^2, y^2)$, is well-defined.

It is known that all points $P = (x, y) \in E_a(GF(2^m))$ satisfy

$$(\tau^2 + 2)P = \mu\tau P \Leftrightarrow (x^4, y^4) + 2(x, y) = \mu(x^2, y^2) \text{ with } \mu := (-1)^{1-a}. \quad (2)$$

Hence the Frobenius map can be regarded as the complex number satisfying $\tau^2 + 2 = \mu\tau$, i.e., $\tau = (\mu + \sqrt{-7})/2$. It now makes sense to multiply points by elements of the ring $Z[\tau]$. To compute the scalar multiplication kP, we need to transform an integer k into a τ-adic expansion $k_{l-1}\tau^{l-1} + k_{l-2}\tau^{l-2} + \cdots + k_1\tau^1 + k_0 \in Z[\tau]$.

The strategy for developing an efficient scalar multiplication algorithm is to find a 'nice' expression for k as a τ-adic expansion form. Here 'nice' means that the length l is relatively small, and that the nonzero coefficients k_i are sparse. If no consecutive powers of τ are nonzero in a τ-adic expansion, we say the expansion is in τ-adic non-adjacent form (TNAF).

To reduce the length of TNAF, note that if $\rho = k \bmod \delta$, then $\rho P = kP$ for all points P of order n because $\delta P = \mathcal{O}$, where $\delta = \frac{\tau^m - 1}{\tau - 1}$ and $n = \frac{\#E_a(GF(2^m))}{\#E_a(GF(2))}$. The length of TNAF($\rho$) is approximately $log_2 N(\rho) \simeq log_2 n \simeq m$ for $\rho = k \bmod \delta$, while the length of TNAF(k) is approximately $log_2 N(k) \simeq 2m$. This suggests that TNAF(ρ) should be used instead of TNAF(k) for computing kP. Here, $N(\alpha)$ means the norm of $\alpha \in Z[\tau]$. Since $\tau^2 = \mu\tau - 2$, every element $\alpha \in Z[\tau]$ can be expressed in the canonical form $\alpha = a_0 + a_1\tau$, where $a_0, a_1 \in Z$. The ring $Z[\tau]$ is a Euclidean domain, and hence also a unique factorization domain, with respect to the norm function $N(a_0 + a_1\tau) = a_0^2 + \mu a_0 a_1 + a_1^2$. The norm function is multiplicative. We have $N(\tau) = 2, N(\tau - 1) = \#E_a(GF(2)), N(\tau^m - 1) = \#E_a(GF(2^m))$, and $N(\delta) = n$.

To make a TNAF sparse, we consider a width-w TNAF analogue to the sliding window algorithm. Let $t_w := 2U_{w-1}U_w^{-1} \pmod{2^w}$, where $\{U_k\}$ is the Lucas sequence defined by $U_0 = 0, U_1 = 1$, and $U_{k+1} = U_k - 2U_{k-1}$ for $k \geq 1$. Then, the map $\varphi_w : Z[\tau] \mapsto Z/2^w Z$ induced by $\tau \mapsto t_w$ is a surjective ring homomorphism with kernel $\{\alpha \in Z[\tau] : \tau^w | \alpha\}$. It follows that a set of distinct representatives of the congruence classes $\pmod{\tau^w}$ whose elements are not divisible by τ is $\{\pm 1, \pm 3, \ldots, \pm(2^{w-1} - 1)\}$. Define $\alpha_i = i \bmod \tau^w$ for $i \in \{1, 3, \ldots, 2^{w-1} - 1\}$. A width-$w$ TNAF of k, denoted by TNAF$_w(k)$, is an expression $k_{l-1}\tau^{l-1} + k_{l-2}\tau^{l-2} + \cdots + k_1\tau^1 + k_0$, where $k_i \in \{0, \pm 1, \pm 3, \ldots, \pm(2^{w-1} - 1)\}$, and at most one of any w consecutive coefficients is nonzero.

The input c_0 and c_1 are given from k via

$$c_0 + c_1\tau = k \bmod \frac{\tau^m - 1}{\tau - 1}. \quad (3)$$

The average density of nonzero coefficients among all TNAF$_w$'s is approximately $\frac{1}{w+1}$. Since the length of TNAF$_w(\rho)$ is about the length of TNAF(ρ), the number of nonzero coefficients in TNAF$_w(\rho)$ is approximately $\frac{m}{w+1}$ on average. From TNAF$_w(\rho)$ for $\rho = k \bmod \delta$, we can compute scalar multiplication kP.

Algorithm 1. Construction of TNAF_w

PREPARAMETER: $w, t_w, \alpha_u = \beta_u + \gamma_u \tau$ for $u = 1, 3, \ldots, 2^{w-1} - 1$
INPUT: integers c_0, c_1
OUTPUT: $S \leftarrow \text{TNAF}_w(c_0 + c_1 \tau)$
  1. $i \leftarrow 0$
  2. While $c_0 \neq 0$ or $c_1 \neq 0$ do
      2.1 If c_0 is odd then
          2.1.1 $u \leftarrow c_0 + c_1 t_w \mod 2^w$
          2.1.2 If $u > 0$ then $\xi \leftarrow 1$
          2.1.3 Else $\xi \leftarrow -1; u \leftarrow -u$
          2.1.4 $c_0 \leftarrow c_0 - \xi \beta_u; c_1 \leftarrow c_1 - \xi \gamma_u$
          2.1.5 $s_i \leftarrow \xi u; i \leftarrow i + 1$
      2.2 Else
          2.2.1 $s_i \leftarrow 0; i \leftarrow i + 1$
      2.3 $(c_0, c_1) \leftarrow (c_1 + \mu c_0/2, -c_0/2)$
  3. Return $S = (s_{i-1}, \ldots, s_1, s_0)$

Algorithm 2. Scalar Multiplication using TNAF_w

PREPARAMETER: $\alpha_u = \beta_u + \gamma_u \tau$
INPUT: $S = (s_{n-1}, \ldots, s_1, s_0), P$
OUTPUT: kP
  1. Compute $P_u = \alpha_u P$ for $u = 1, 3, \ldots, 2^{w-1} - 1$
  2. $Q \leftarrow \mathcal{O}$
  3. For i from $n - 1$ downto 0 do
      3.1 $Q \leftarrow \tau Q$
      3.2 $u \leftarrow s_i$
      3.3 If $u > 0$ then $Q \leftarrow Q + P_u$
      3.4 If $u < 0$ then $Q \leftarrow Q - P_{-u}$
  4. Return Q

The precomputation P_u involves computing and storing $2^{w-2} - 1$ points, which requires $2^{w-2} - 1$ elliptic curve additions. The main loop executes an addition for each nonzero s_i. It follows, therefore, that a scalar multiplication requires about $(2^{w-2} - 1 + \frac{m}{w+1})$ elliptic curve additions on average.

For more information on Koblitz curves, see [22].

2.2 Power Analysis Attacks

The goal of power analysis attacks in ECC is to acquire information on the secret exponents in victim scalar multiplications. To discover secret information, the attacks exploit correlations between an exponent and sampled power traces. According to the techniques employed, power analysis has two categories, SPA and DPA. Countermeasures have attempted to reduce the correlations.

SPA is based on the common belief that different group operations have different power trace shapes.[1] Differences exist between addition and doubling in

---

[1] In cases of Jacobi form and Hessian form, SPA could not distinguish group operations.

random curves, and between addition and τ-operation in Koblitz curves. If one implements a scalar multiplication using a double-and-add method, SPA can discover the entire secret exponent. For the case of TNAF in Koblitz curves, $2m/3$ bits of a secret exponent are revealed because the attacker can verify the positions of τ-operations. SPA does not require complex power analysis techniques. In addition, SPA can extract some information, which may help to break the cryptosystem even from DPA resistant algorithms that cannot prevent SPA. Therefore, all implementations of cryptographic algorithms on the embedded systems should resist SPA.

In order to prevent SPA, the sequence of instructions performed during a cryptographic algorithm should not depend on the secret data being processed. There are two approaches in preventing SPA. One approach eliminates the branch instructions conditioned by data. This approach, however, is generally less efficient because it repeats many dummy operations, such as additions. Coron's simple countermeasure [1] is an example. Another approach employs non-standard elliptic curves, such as those in Jacobi form [12], Hessian form [8], and Montgomery form over finite fields with odd characteristics [17]. However, these are impractical because elliptic curves of non-standard forms are not widely used.

DPA is based on the same underlying principle of an SPA attack, but it uses statistical analysis to extract minute differences in power consumption signals. A classic DPA entails averaging and subtraction. After measuring a sufficient number of power traces, DPA divides them into two groups by a selection function. The power traces of each group are averaged, and then subtracted. A correct estimation of the secret key provides a peak in subtraction. Because averaging can improve the signal to noise ratio (SNR), DPA is sensitive to smaller differences below the noise level.

We can prevent DPA by introducing randomness to the execution. In random curves, the following countermeasures can be considered: randomizing the secret exponent, blinding the point, randomizing the projective coordinate representation, and randomizing the algorithm itself. In Koblitz curves, Hasan [7] proposed three DPA countermeasures: key making with localized operations (KMLO), random rotation of key (RRK), and random insertion of redundant symbols (RIRS). However, KMLO and RIRS are inapplicable to efficient scalar multiplications like TNAF$_w$.

2.3   Basis Conversion Technique

There are two common families of basis representation: polynomial basis representation and normal basis representation.

In a polynomial basis representation, each element of $GF(2^m)$ is represented by a different binary polynomial where the degree is less than m. More explicitly, the bit string $(a_{m-1}, \ldots, a_2, a_1, a_0)$ is taken to represent the binary polynomial $a_{m-1}t^{m-1} + \ldots + a_2t^2 + a_1t^1 + a_0$. The polynomial basis is the set $B_p = \{t^{m-1}, \ldots, t^2, t^1, 1\}$. Polynomial basis representation has a computational advantage in software implementation.

A normal basis for $GF(2^m)$ is a set of the form $B_n = \{\theta, \theta^2, \theta^{2^2}, \ldots, \theta^{2^{m-1}}\}$. Normal bases for $GF(2^m)$ exist for every positive integer m. The representation of $GF(2^m)$ via the normal basis B_n is carried out by interpreting the bit string $(a_0, a_1, a_2, \ldots, a_{m-1})$ as the element $a_0\theta + a_1\theta^2 + a_2\theta^{2^2} + \cdots + a_{m-1}\theta^{2^{m-1}}$. All of the elements of a normal basis B_n satisfy the same irreducible binary polynomial $p(t)$. This polynomial is called a field polynomial for the basis. An irreducible binary polynomial is called a normal polynomial if it is the field polynomial for a normal basis. Normal basis representations have the computational advantage that squaring an element can be performed very efficiently.

It is possible to convert between two bases. The general method employs a change-of-basis matrix, which involves a matrix operation. Suppose that Γ is the change-of-basis matrix from B_0 to B_1, and $\underline{u}$ is the bit string representing $\alpha \in GF(2^m)$ in term of B_0. Then $\underline{v} = \underline{u}\Gamma$ is the bit string representing α in term of B_1. This matrix requires the storage of m^2 bits, and the conversion time is approximately equivalent to one field multiplication. If Γ is the change-of-basis matrix from B_0 to B_1, then the inverse Γ^{-1} of the matrix over $GF(2)$ is the change-of-basis matrix from B_1 to B_0.

Explicit algorithms for basis conversion are presented in [21].

3   Proposed Algorithm

We chose Algorithm 1 and 2 as base algorithms to construct the power analysis resistant algorithm, because the scalar multiplication using TNAF_w is a highly efficient algorithm without offline computation. SPA countermeasure and DPA countermeasures are applied to Algorithm 2, which produce the proposed algorithm.

Recall that $\text{TNAF}_w(k)$ is an expression $k_{l-1}\tau^{l-1} + k_{l-2}\tau^{l-2} + \cdots + k_1\tau^1 + k_0$, where $k_i \in \{\pm 1, \pm 3, \ldots, \pm(2^{w-1}-1)\}$. If we consider nonzero coefficient k_i's only, the expression can be rewritten as $k_{e_{n-1}}\tau^{e_{n-1}} + k_{e_{n-2}}\tau^{e_{n-2}} + \cdots + k_{e_1}\tau^{e_1} + k_{e_0}\tau^{e_0}$, where n is the number of nonzero coefficients. This expression can be stored as a sequence $((s_{n-1}, e_{n-1}), (s_{n-2}, e_{n-2}), \ldots, (s_1, e_1), (s_0, e_0))$, where s_i means k_{e_i}. In the sequence, information is embedded in s_i's, e_i's, and n. Information of e_i's and s_i's is concealed by proposed SPA and DPA countermeasures, respectively. Instead of fixing n perfectly, we restrict the range of n; we will show that this technique does not decrease the security level of the proposed algorithm.

3.1   SPA Countermeasure

Restricting the range of n. We will define $I'(m, w, n)$ as the number of candidates having n nonzero coefficients in TNAF_w of length m. Since a nonzero coefficient in TNAF_w means an addition in a scalar multiplication, $I'(m, w, n)$ is the number of all cases depending on what value is added and where the addition occurs. The added values and their positions are independent of each other, hence, $I'(m, w, n)$ equals to the product of $I'_v(m, w, n)$ and $I'_p(m, w, n)$; $I'_v(m, w, n)$ denotes the number of candidates if the added positions are fixed, and $I_p'(m, w, n)$ denotes the number of candidates if the added values are fixed. Since, for a randomly given k, the nonzero coefficients are elements in $\{\pm 1, \pm 3, \pm 5, \ldots, \pm(2^{w-1} - 1)\}$ and mutually independent, we can obtain

$$I_v'(m, w, n) = 2^{(w-1)n}.$$

In TNAF_w, an added position is apart from the neighboring added position by more than $w - 1$ bits, and an addition occupies the successive w bit positions. Thus, $I_p'(m, w, n)$ is the number of cases selecting unorderly n positions from the sum of $m - wn$ empty positions and n added positions, that is

$$I_p'(m, w, n) = \binom{m - wn + n}{n},$$

where $\binom{m}{k}$ means the number of ways of picking k unordered outcomes from m possibilities, which is equivalent to $\frac{m!}{k!(m-k)!}$.

Now, we will define $I(m, w, n)$ as the number of candidates for m-bit positive integer k having n nonzero coefficients in $\text{TNAF}_w(k \bmod \delta)$. The only differences between $I(m, w, n)$ and $I'(m, w, n)$ are that, in the most significant nonzero coefficient (s_{n-1}, e_{n-1}) in the former, s_{n-1} should be positive and e_{n-1} can be larger than $m - w$. Thus, $I(m, w, n)$ can be obtained by summation of the number of the cases which are categorized by the position e_{n-1}.

$$
\begin{aligned}
I(m, w, n) = \ & 2^{-1} I'(m + 1, w, n) \\
& + \ 2^{(w-2)-1} I'(m - (w - 2), w, n - 1) \\
& + \ 2^{(w-3)-1} I'(m - (w - 3), w, n - 1) \\
& \qquad \vdots \\
& + \ 2^0 I'(m - 1, w, n - 1) \\
& + \ 2^{-1} I'(m, w, n - 1).
\end{aligned}
$$

We introduce security parameters L, n_{min}, and n_{max}. The parameters should be chosen so that 2^L is the minimum number of candidates for k when the number of additions is known. The security level of our algorithms depends on the parameter L. In Section 4.1, we will suggest an appropriate value. Parameters n_{min} and n_{max} are determined by selecting L.

First, we chose a parameter n_{min} as the minimum value of n satisfying an inequality $I(m, w, n) > 2^L$ and n_{max} as the maximum value. For example, if L is chosen to 153 in $m=163$ and $w=5$, then $n_{min}=23$ and $n_{max}=31$. Thus, if n is between n_{min} and n_{max}, it gurantees that $I(m, w, n)$ is larger than 2^L.

If n is out of the range between n_{min} and n_{max}, the sequence $((s_{n-1}, e_{n-1}), (s_{n-2}, e_{n-2}), \ldots, (s_1, e_1), (s_0, e_0))$ should be extended so that the length of the extended sequence becomes to $\lceil m/w \rceil$ by two extending methods:[2] adding

---

[2] If k is a nonce employed in signature schemes, it can be a more efficient solution to regenerate k whose length n is in the range between n_{min} and n_{max}.

dummy pairs and spliting a coefficient. A dummy pair is $((s, e), (-s, e))$ where s and e are random values selected from $\{1, 3, \ldots, 2^{w-1} - 1\}$ and $\{0, 1, \ldots, m - 1\}$, respectively. Adding a dummy pair increases the length by two. Spliting method devide a coefficient (s_i, e_i) into two coefficients (s_u, e_u), (s_v, e_v) where $s_i \tau^{e_i} = s_u \tau^{e_u} + s_v \tau^{e_v}$. If s_i is not 1, any coefficient can be splited. This method increases the length by one. Thus, the length of any sequence can be $\lceil m/w \rceil$. We will denote the extended sequence as $\text{STNAF}_w(k)$, whose length is in $\{n_{min}, n_{min} + 1, \ldots, n_{max} - 1, n_{max}\}$ or $\lceil m/w \rceil$. Unfortunately, if the length of an integer is $\lceil m/w \rceil$ in STNAF_w, the number of candidates for the integer is generally smaller than 2^L, which violates the initial selecting criterion of L. Thus, we adjust n_{min} and n_{max}: If $I(m, w, n_{min}) \leq I(m, w, n_{max})$, we increase n_{min} by one; otherwise, we decrease n_{max} by one.

Our algorithms use $\text{STNAF}_w(k)$ as an input. This sequence can be generated by a slight modification of Algorithm 1. Remark that the modified algorithm itself should be SPA resistant. Because one can easily obtain the SPA immunity by introducing dummy operations, we will not describe the algorithm to make STNAF_w.

Hiding the positions where additions occur. We propose Algorithm 3 to hide the positions where additions occur.

Algorithm 3. (SPA resistant) Scalar Multiplication using STNAF_w

PREPARAMETER: $\alpha_u = \beta_u + \gamma_u \tau$
INPUT: $S = ((s_{n-1}, e_{n-1}), \ldots, (s_1, e_1), (s_0, e_0)) \leftarrow \text{STANF}_w(k \bmod \delta), P$
OUTPUT: kP

1. Compute $P_u = \alpha_u P$ for $u = 1, 3, \ldots, 2^{w-1} - 1$ in polynomial basis
2. Convert P_u into normal basis
3. $Q \leftarrow \mathcal{O}$
4. For i from $n - 1$ downto 0 do
   4.1 If $s_i > 0$ then $R \leftarrow P_{s_i}$
   4.2 Else $R \leftarrow -P_{-s_i}$
   4.3 $R \leftarrow \tau^{e_i} R$
   4.4 Convert R into polynomial basis securely
   4.5 $Q \leftarrow Q + R$
5. Return Q

In Algorithm 3, the computational sequence is invariant to an input sequence S. Also, τ-operations are executed in normal basis, in which the operation is implemented as a circular shift. With a careful implementation, the circular shift is executed in a static manner. Therefore, it is reasonable to assume the impracticality of SPA in detecting e_i from the operation in Step 7.

Two types of basis conversion occur in the above algorithm: from polynomial basis to normal basis in step 2, and from normal basis to polynomial basis in step 8. Since the first conversion is not dependant on an input k and precomputed values P_u's are not secret data, we employed a regular method in step 2. It is possible that the regular method may leak information on the hamming weight of an element. However, R in step 8 is secret data; if the information on R is leaked, the information on k is. Therefore, we employed an SPA immune basis conversion technique in step 8. This conversion method can be obtained by inserting dummy operations to a regular method, which doubles the conversion time.

Thus, Algorithm 3 does not leak the positions where additions occur.

3.2   DPA Countermeasures

To prevent DPA, we propose two countermeasures that introduce randomness in computation with negligible computational overhead.

The first method is to permute a sequence $STNAF_w$. Since the length of the sequence is n, there are $n!$ permutations. The length n is approximately $m/(w+1)$. Thus introduced randomness is approximately $(m/(w+1))!$. Because the randomly permuted computational order does not change the result of scalar multiplication, this method does not need a compensation step. And permutation is a very simple operation.

The second method is to randomize precomputation points. The computation kP is equivalent to the computation $(\tau^{m-r}k)\tau^r P$, where r is a random integer less than dimension m. For this method, we insert two steps. The first step is to replace all precomputed points P_u with $\tau^r P_u$. The other is to replace the result Q with $\tau^{m-r}Q$. Introduced randomness is m. This method is similar to randomization of projective coordinate representation, which is one of the Coron's DPA countermeasures. However, our method uses a simpler operation; that is, a circular shift. In addition, our method enables precomputation to be computed in affine coordinates. Since Coron's method constrains precomputation to be computed in projective coordinates, it is impossible to use the efficient mixed coordinates technique in [5].

Permutation occurs in step 1. And step 5 and 14 randomize the precomputed point P_u. Embedded randomness is approximately $((m/(w+1))!) \cdot m$.

Note that Algorithm 4 still does not increase the number of additions.

4   Security Analysis

4.1   Simple Power Analysis: *Selecting Security Parameter L*

The computational order of the proposed method is independent of an exponent k. The only leaked information is the number of additions, which is bounded in the range of $\{n_{min}, n_{min}+1, \ldots, n_{max}-1, n_{max}, \lceil m/w \rceil\}$. Thus SPA reduces the number of candidates for an m-bits integer from 2^m to $I(m, w, n)$, which is larger than 2^L. We will investigate the security level according a security parameter L, and suggest a suitable value.

Pollard's rho method is the most efficient method to solve ECDLP. The method has time complexity $O(2^{m/2})$ with only negligible space requirements. In Koblitz curves, search space can be reduced by a factor $\sqrt{2m}$ [4,23]. Pollard's rho method requires an appropriate iteration function f, which has the same domain and range (i.e., $f : S \to S$) and behaves like a random mapping [20]. To break the proposed algorithm with Pollard's rho method, the domain and range should be integers of which the length in $STNAF_w$ is n. The size of S is $I(m, w, n)$.

Algorithm 4. (SPA & DPA resistant) Scalar Multiplication using $STNAF_w$

PREPARAMETER: $\alpha_u = \beta_u + \gamma_u \tau$
INPUT: $S = ((s_{n-1}, e_{n-1}), \ldots, (s_1, e_1), (s_0, e_0)) \leftarrow STANF_w(k \bmod \delta), P$
OUTPUT: kP

1. *Permute the sequence S at random*
2. *Compute $P_u = \alpha_u P$ for $u = 1, 3, \ldots, 2^{w-1} - 1$ in polynomial basis*
3. *Convert P_u into normal basis*
4. *Choose random integer r less than m*
5. *$P_u \leftarrow \tau^r P_u$ for $u = 1, 3, \ldots, 2^{w-1} - 1$*
6. *$Q \leftarrow \mathcal{O}$*
7. *For i from $n - 1$ downto 0 do*
    7.1 *If $s_i > 0$ then $R \leftarrow P_{s_i}$*
    7.2 *Else $R \leftarrow -P_{-s_i}$*
    7.3 *$R \leftarrow \tau^{e_i} R$*
    7.4 *Convert R into polynomial basis securely*
    7.5 *$Q \leftarrow Q + R$*
8. *Convert Q into normal basis*
9. *$Q \leftarrow \tau^{m-r} Q$*
10. *Convert Q into polynomial basis*
11. *Return Q*

Thus, if we can find an iteration function defined on this domain and range, a variant of Pollard's rho method can break our algorithm with time complexity $O(I(m, w, n)^{1/2})$. However, we could not find any such function. In other words, the information of the number of additions may not reduce the search space for Pollard's rho method. For this reason, we did not consider Pollard's rho method, when selecting the security parameter L.

Compared with Pollard's rho method, an exhaustive search method traverses all candidates, that is, $I(m, w, n)$. The minimum size of $I(m, w, n)$ is 2^L. The value of L is approximately $m/2$, where the exhaustive search method is as efficient as Pollard's rho method. Therefore, L should be larger than $m/2$, which is not a difficult constraint.

With a time-space tradeoff, the exhaustive search method can be modified to a method having time complexity $O(I(m, w, n)^{1/2})$ and space complexity $O(I(m, w, n)^{1/2})$. We will denote the method as mBSGS (modified baby-step giant-step) method. Because the minimum size of $I(m, w, n)$ is 2^L, the minimum requirements of mBSGS method are time complexity $O(2^{L/2})$ and space complexity $O(2^{L/2})$. Unlike the exhaustive search method, it is difficult to determine the value of L where mBSGS method is as efficient as Pollard's rho method. The value may be smaller than $(m - log_2 m - 1)$, but much larger than $m/2$, which is the constraint for the exhaustive search method.

By intuition, we choose L as m-10. In case of $m = 163$ and $w = 5$, then $L = 153$. Thus mBSGS requires 2^{76} elliptic operations and 2^{76} storage ($\simeq 2^{76} \times 163 \times 2$ bits $= 2.80 \times 10^{12}$ Tbytes) to solve ECDLP. Pollard's rho method requires 2^{77} elliptic operations, which is believed to be infeasible [13]. Thus, we can conjecture that the requirements of mBSGS are also infeasible. For a larger m, the same argument is possible.

Thus we can assume that the proposed algorithm is secure under SPA, if L is selected as m-10.

4.2 Differential Power Analysis

Our DPA countermeasures introduced randomness in the computation. Permuting STNAF$_w$ randomizes the computational sequence, which significantly diminishes DPA attacks such as SEMD, MESD, and ZESD [14]. Also, randomizing computational sequence can prevent second-order DPA attacks and Goubin's refined power analysis attack [3]. Randomizing precomputation points provides additional defense, since it is difficult for the attacker to predict any specific bit of the binary representation of P.

5   Timing Analysis

Execution time for Algorithm 4 consists of time for additions, τ-operations and basis conversions. Algorithm 4 does not increase the number of additions over Algorithm 2.[3] Thus, the number of additions are $(2^{w-2} - 1 + m/(w + 1))$ on average. And, τ-operations occur $(2^{w-2}+m/(w+1))$ times on average: $(2^{w-2}-1)$ times in the precomputation, $m/(w + 1)$ times in the main computation, and 1 time in the final compensation. Basis conversions are divided into two parts: a regular conversion and a SPA resistant conversion. The regular conversion occurs $(2^{w-2}+1)$ times: $(2^{w-2}-1)$ times in the precomputation and 2 times in the final compensation. And the SPA resistant conversion occurs $m/(w + 1)$ times in the main computation. Execution time for random number generation is ignored. As a result, the execution time for Algorithm 4 is approximately

$$(2^{w-2} - 1 + \frac{m}{w + 1}) \times T_{addition} + (2^{w-2} + \frac{m}{w + 1}) \times T_{\tau(NB)}$$

$$+(2^{w-2} + 1) \times T_{conv} + \frac{m}{w + 1} \times T_{sconv}, \qquad (4)$$

where $T_{addition}$, $T_{\tau(NB)}$, T_{conv}, and T_{sconv} are execution times for an elliptic addition, a τ-operation in normal basis, a regular basis conversion, and a SPA resistant basis conversion, respectively. Here, execution time for Algorithm 2 is approximately

$$(2^{w-2} - 1 + \frac{m}{w + 1}) \times T_{addition} + (m - 1) \times T_{\tau(PB)}, \qquad (5)$$

where $T_{\tau(PB)}$ is execution time for a τ-operation in polynomial basis.

---

[3] Since we chose L as m-10, the exceptional cases arise with a probability approximately $1/2^{10}$. Therefore the cases are ignored.

Therefore, the computational overhead is approximately

$$(2^{w-2} + \frac{m}{w+1}) \times T_{\tau(NB)} + (2^{w-2} + 1) \times T_{conv}$$
$$+ \frac{m}{w+1} \times T_{sconv} - (m-1) \times T_{\tau(PB)}. \qquad (6)$$

Equation (6) does not include the execution time for an elliptic addition which is the most time comsuming operation. Included operations are very fast operations. With Equation (6) and Tables 1, 2, and 3, one can verify that the computational overhead is very low.

Tables present timing results for field operations, point operations, and scalar multiplications in a 163-bit Koblitz curve. Operations were implemented in C and timings obtained on ARM7TDMI 10MHz using ADS 1.1.

Table 1. Timings (in ms) for field operations in $GF(2^{163})$ on ARM7TDMI 10MHz

Field operation	Time (ms)
Multiplication (polynomial basis)	0.467
Squaring (polynomial basis)	0.070
Circular shift (normal basis)	0.014
Regular basis conversion	0.320
SPA resistant basis conversion	0.640

Table 2. Timings (in ms) for point operations in a 163-bit Koblitz curve on ARM7TDMI 10MHz

Point operation	Coordinate	Time(ms)
τ-operation	Affine	0.028
(normal basis)	Projective	0.042
τ-operation	Affine	0.140
(polynomial basis)	Projective	0.210
Addition	Affine + Affine → Affine	5.480
(polynomial basis)	Projective + Affine → Projective	5.014

Precomputations of algorithms in Table 3 are executed in affine coordinates, and main computations in projective coordinates. The modified 2^{w-1}-ary method in Table 3 is an analogue of the method in [15] for Koblitz curves. The method requires 2^{w-2} precomputation points and $\lceil \frac{m}{w} \rceil$ elliptic additions. Note that Algorithm 2 and 4 require $2^{w-2} - 1$ precomputation points.

Table 3 shows that the speed of the proposed algorithm (Algorithm 4) lies between Algorithm 2 and the modified 2^{w-1}-ary method. the execution time

Table 3. Timings (in ms) for scalar multiplication in a 163-bit Koblitz curve on ARM7TDMI 10MHz

w	Algorithm 2	Algorithm 4	Modified 2^{w-1}-ary
2	332.8	357.3	928.3
3	264.2	277.8	487.7
4	230.7	238.7	349.9
5	223.8	229.6	298.2
6	247.2	254.9	298.2

for the proposed algorithm is similar to the time for Algorithm 2. Note that Algorithm 4 resists SPA and DPA, but Algorithm 2 does not. Also the proposed algorithm is much faster than the modified 2^{w-1}-ary method that is vulnerable to DPA.

6   Conclusion

We proposed a fast scalar multiplication method using the change-of-basis matrix to prevent power analysis attacks on Koblitz curves. We designed the algorithm to execute in an order of τ-operation in the normal basis and addition in the polynomial basis. The computational order is invariant to integer k. Even though our algorithm does not conceal the number of additions perfectly, the algorithm remains secure with a proper security parameter L. In addition, we proposed two DPA countermeasures. They introduce $((m/(w+1))!) \cdot m$ randomness with negligible computational overhead. Timing results show that the (SPA and DPA resistant) proposed algorithm is as fast as a (power analysis vulnerable) sliding window method using TNAF_w.

Therefore, if the change-of-basis matrix is supported, the proposed method is a good candidate for power analysis resistant scalar multiplication. In environments supporting efficient normal basis arithmetic, the proposed method can be modified not to use the change-of-basis matrix. Also, the technique to restrict the range of the number of additions can be utilized as a countermeasure to prevent timing attack against sliding window methods.

Acknowledgement. The authors would like to thank anonymous refrees for their comments, which are helpful to improve the presentation of this paper.

This research was supported by University IT Research Center Project, the Brain Korea 21 Project, and Com2MaC-KOSEF.

References

1. J. S. Coron, "Resistance against Differential Power Analysis for Elliptic Curve Cryptosystems," *Cryptographic Hardware and Embedded Systems - CHES'99*, LNCS 1717, pp. 292–302, 1999.

2. J. S. Coron, D. M'Raihi and C. Tymen, "Fast Generation of Pairs $(k, [k]P)$ for Koblitz Elliptic Curves," *Selected Areas in Cryptography - SAC 2001,* LNCS 2259, pp. 151–164, 2001.

3. L. Goubin, "A Refined Power-Analysis Attack on Elliptic Curve Cryptosystems," *International Workshop on Practice and Theory in Public Key Cryptosystems - PKC 2003,* LNCS 2567, pp. 199–211, 2003.

4. R. Gallant, R. Lambert and S. A. Vanstone, "Improving the parallelized Pollard lambda search on anomalous binary curves," *Mathematics of Computation ,* 69, pp. 1699–1705, 2000.

5. D. Hankerson, J. L. Hernandez and A. Menezes, "Software Implementation of Elliptic Curve Cryptography over Binary Fields," *Cryptographic Hardware and Embedded Systems - CHES 2000,* LNCS 1965, pp. 1–24, 2000.

6. J. Ha and S. Moon, "Randomized signed-scalar multiplication of ECC to resist power attacks," *Cryptographic Hardware and Embedded Systems - CHES 2002,* LNCS 2523, pp. 551–563, 2002.

7. M. A. Hasan, "Power Analysis Attacks and Algorithmic Approaches to Their Countermeasures for Koblitz Curve Cryptosystems," *IEEE Transactions on Computers,* vol. 50, no. 10, pp. 1071–1083, 2001.

8. M. Joye and J.-J. Quisquater, "Hessian Elliptic Curves and Side-Channel Attacks," *Cryptographic Hardware and Embedded Systems - CHES 2001,* LNCS 2162, pp. 402–410, 2001.

9. N. Koblitz, "CM-curves with good cryptographic properties," *Advanced in Cryptography - CRYPTO '91,* LNCS 576, pp. 279–287, 1991.

10. P. Kocher, J. Jaffe and B. Jun, "Differential power analysis," *Advances in Cryptography - CRYPTO '99,* LNCS 1666, pp. 388–397, 1999.

11. B. S. Kaliski Jr. and Y. L. Yin, "Storage-Efficient Finite Field Basis Conversion," *Selected Areas in Cryptography - SAC'98,* LNCS 1556, pp. 81–93, 1998.

12. P.-Y. Liardet and N. P. Smart, "Preventing SPA/DPA in ECC Systems Using the Jacobi Form," *Cryptographic Hardware and Embedded Systems - CHES 2001,* LNCS 2162, pp. 391–401, 2001.

13. A. K. Lenstra and E. R. Verheul, "Selecting Cryptographic Key Sizes," *Journal of Cryptology,* 14(4), pp. 144–157, 1999.

14. T. S. Messerges, E. A. Dabbish and R. H. Sloan, "Power Analysis Attacks of Modular Exponentiation in Smartcards," *Cryptographic Hardware and Embedded Systems - CHES '99,* LNCS 1717, pp. 144–157, 1999.

15. B. Möller, "Securing Elliptic Curve Multiplication against Side-Channel Attacks," *Information Security Conference - ISC 2001,* LNCS 2200, pp. 324–334, 2001.

16. E. Oswald and M. Aigner, "Randomized Addition-Subtraction Chains as a Countermeasure against Power Attacks," *Cryptographic Hardware and Embedded Systems - CHES 2001,* LNCS 2162, pp. 39–50, 2001.

17. K. Okeya, K. Miyazaki and K. Sakurai, "A Fast Scalar Multiplication Method with Randomized Projective Coordinates on a Montgomery-Form Elliptic Curve Secure against Side Channel Attacks," *International Conference on Information Security and Cryptology - ICICS 2001,* LNCS 2288, pp. 428–439. 2001.

18. K. Okeya and K. Sakurai, "Power Analysis Breaks Elliptic Curve Cryptosystems Even Secure against the Timing Attack," *Progress in Cryptology - INDOCRYPT 2000,* LNCS 1977, pp. 178–190 2000.

19. K. Okeya and T. Takagi, "The Width-w NAF Method Provides Small Memory and Fast Elliptic Scalar Multiplications Secure against Side Channel Attacks," *Topics in Cryptology - CT-RSA 2003,* LNCS 2612, pp. 328–343, 2003.

20. P. C. van Oorschot and M. Wiener, "Parallel Collision Search with Cryptanalytic Applications," *Journal of Cryptology,* 12(12), pp. 1–28, 1999.
21. IEEE P1363-2000: Standard Specifications for Public Key Cryptography, IEEE, 2000.
22. J. Solinas, "Efficient arithmetic on Koblitz curve," *Designs, Codes and Cryptography,* vol. 19, pp. 195–249, 2000.
23. M. J. Wiener and R. J. Zuccherato, "Faster Attacks on Elliptic Curve Cryptosystems," *Selected Areas in Cryptography - SAC'98,* LNCS 1556, pp. 190–200, 1998.

Constructing and Cryptanalysis of a 16×16 Binary Matrix as a Diffusion Layer[*]

Bon Wook Koo, Hwan Seok Jang, and Jung Hwan Song

CAMP Lab., Hanyang University
17 Haengdang-dong, Seongdong-gu, Seoul, 133-791, Korea
{kidkoo,jhs1003}@ihanyang.ac.kr, camp123@hanyang.ac.kr
http://math.hanyang.ac.kr/camp/

Abstract. In this paper, we construct a 16×16 involution binary matrix of branch number 8 and estimate security of an 128-bit SPN(a substitution and permutation encrpion network) block cipher which uses the matrix as a diffusion layer in a round function. We show how to construct such an involution binary matrix of branch number 8, and use some mathematical techniques to find a form in product of matrices, which is for increasing efficiency in software implementations. We also show that the cryptanalytic properties such as the resistance to differential, linear, impossible differential, and truncated differential cryptanalysis.

1 Introduction

Confusion and diffusion effects are two major cryptographic properties which should be considered for designing a round function in a block cipher [1]. A substitution and permutation encryption network(SPN) is a secret key block cipher and constitutes with iterative rounds where each round has a confusion layer followed by a diffusion layer. A diffusion layer is one of cryptographic function, which prevents in preserving some characteristics that result from a substitution layer.

An SPN block cipher has advantage of simple structure which is possible to show cryptographic properties such as resistance to differential and linear cryptanalysis [2] and to be implemented in increasing efficiency. In an SPN, decrypting procedure is executed by running the data backwards through the inverse network. In a Fiestel cipher, the inverse s-boxes and inverse permutation are not required. Hence, a practical disadvantage of the basic SPN structure compared with Fiestel structure is that both the s-boxes and their inverses must be located in the same encryption hardware or software. The resulting extra memory or power consumption requirements may render this solution less attractive in some situations especially for hardware implementations. For the both the inverse confusion layer and the inverse diffusion layer being located in the same

---

[*] This research is supported by Hanyang University and National Security Research Institute(NSRI), Korea

K. Chae and M. Yung (Eds.): WISA 2003, LNCS 2908, pp. 489–503, 2004.
© Springer-Verlag Berlin Heidelberg 2004

encryption hardware or software, one has to design an involution structure of SPN.

Most of diffusion layers that have been introduced by now are linear transformations on the vector space $GF(2^m)^n$ for mn-bit SPN block cipher, which means that they have matrix representations over $GF(2^m)$. Throughout this paper we use a diffusion layer which is represented by an $n \times n$ matrix $A = (a_{ij})_{n \times n}$, where $a_{ij} \in GF(2^m) \cap \{0, 1\}$. We construct a matrix A for a diffusion layer and cryptanalyze when it applied to an SPN block cipher.

The maximum branch number of 16×16 binary matrix is known to be 8 [3]. In this paper, we construct a 16×16 involution binary matrix A with branch number 8, which is efficient in speed and memory space for hardware implementations such as smartcards which have 8-bit processors. We also estimate its security level in respect to differential, linear, truncated differential, and impossible differential cryptanalysis when it is used as a diffusion layer. Finally we also show how to construct A that can be implemented efficiently for 32-bit processors.

2   Notations and Definitions

We consider an SPN structure where mn is the input and output bit length consisting of m-bit s-boxes.

We assume that round keys, which are xored with the input data in each round, are independent and uniformly random. Round keys that xored with data bits before each round are derived from a master key by a key schedule algorithm which is not considered in this paper. By assumption on round keys, xoring key layer does not effect on the number of active m-bit s-boxes.

For measuring diffusion effects, we define the branch number which is related to the number of active s-boxes [4, 5].

Definition 1. *An s-box S_i is an active s-box if input difference or output mask value of S_i is nonzero for $i = 1, 2, \cdots, n$.*

Definition 2. *Let all s-boxes be bijective. The minimum number of active s-boxes n_d, n_l in consecutive 2-round SPN for DC and LC are defined*

$$n_d = \min_{\Delta x \neq 0} [w_H(\Delta x) + w_H(A(\Delta x))]$$

$$n_l = \min_{\Gamma A(x) \neq 0} [w_H(\Gamma x) + w_H(A(\Gamma x))],$$

where A is a diffusion layer and $w_H(x)$ is the hamming weight of x which is the number of nonzero subblocks over $GF(2^m)$ of x; i.e. $w_H(x) = \#\{i | 0 \leq i < n, x_i \neq 0\}$.

In this paper, we consider A as a $n \times n$ binary nonsingular matrix.

We define the following definition for the use of Lemma 6 in the next section.

Definition 3. *Two $n \times n$ binary matrices A, B are permutation homomorphic to each other if there exists a row permutation ρ and a column permutation γ satisfying*

$$\rho(\gamma(A)) = \gamma(\rho(A)) = B.$$

3   Constructing of a Diffusion Layer

A round function is supposed to be designed to satisfy both strong security and high efficiency as possible. We construct a diffusion layer with large diffusion effect to meet security, and with simple operations to meet efficiency.

Let a round function be a composition of three layers(functions), a key addition, a confusion, and a diffusion layer.

Most of confusion layers are consisting of nonlinear bijective functions and described as pre-calculated tables in a certain size of input and output word, which is 8-bit in most of block ciphers. Designing a round function with provable security and in a simple form, a diffusion layer can be selected from linear transformations. Notice that a linear transformation should be selected to maximize diffusion effect such as the input/output correlation of individual s-boxes.

Let L be a diffusion layer of AES and A be a diffusion layer which we will construct. Then

$$L \in GF(2^8)^{16 \times 16} \quad \text{and} \quad A \in (GF(2^8) \cap \{0,1\})^{16 \times 16}.$$

Multiplication and addition operations over $GF(2^8)$ should be implemented for L, but only byte XOR operations are implemented for A. In 8-bit processor, multiplication and addition operations over $GF(2^8)$ can be changed to byte XOR operations by a technique as described in [10], where the total number of operations is increased. Therefore, the total number of XOR operations for implementing A can be less than the total number of XOR operations for implementing L. The following matrix L in (1) is represented 16×16 matrix over $GF(2^8)$ as a diffusion layer of AES.

$$
L = \begin{pmatrix}
02 & 00 & 00 & 00 & 00 & 00 & 00 & 03 & 00 & 00 & 01 & 00 & 00 & 00 & 01 & 00 \\
00 & 02 & 00 & 00 & 03 & 00 & 00 & 00 & 00 & 00 & 00 & 01 & 00 & 00 & 00 & 01 \\
00 & 00 & 02 & 00 & 00 & 03 & 00 & 00 & 01 & 00 & 00 & 00 & 00 & 01 & 00 & 00 \\
00 & 00 & 00 & 02 & 00 & 00 & 03 & 00 & 00 & 01 & 00 & 00 & 01 & 00 & 00 & 00 \\
01 & 00 & 00 & 00 & 00 & 00 & 00 & 02 & 00 & 00 & 03 & 00 & 00 & 00 & 01 & 00 \\
00 & 01 & 00 & 00 & 02 & 00 & 00 & 00 & 00 & 00 & 00 & 03 & 00 & 00 & 00 & 01 \\
00 & 00 & 01 & 00 & 00 & 02 & 00 & 00 & 03 & 00 & 00 & 00 & 00 & 01 & 00 & 00 \\
00 & 00 & 00 & 01 & 00 & 00 & 02 & 00 & 00 & 03 & 00 & 00 & 01 & 00 & 00 & 00 \\
01 & 00 & 00 & 00 & 00 & 00 & 00 & 01 & 00 & 00 & 02 & 00 & 00 & 00 & 03 & 00 \\
00 & 01 & 00 & 00 & 01 & 00 & 00 & 00 & 00 & 00 & 00 & 02 & 00 & 00 & 00 & 03 \\
00 & 00 & 01 & 00 & 00 & 01 & 00 & 00 & 02 & 00 & 00 & 00 & 00 & 03 & 00 & 00 \\
00 & 00 & 00 & 01 & 00 & 00 & 01 & 00 & 00 & 02 & 00 & 00 & 03 & 00 & 00 & 00 \\
03 & 00 & 00 & 00 & 00 & 00 & 00 & 01 & 00 & 00 & 01 & 00 & 00 & 00 & 02 & 00 \\
00 & 03 & 00 & 00 & 01 & 00 & 00 & 00 & 00 & 00 & 00 & 01 & 00 & 00 & 00 & 02 \\
00 & 00 & 03 & 00 & 00 & 01 & 00 & 00 & 01 & 00 & 00 & 00 & 00 & 02 & 00 & 00 \\
00 & 00 & 00 & 03 & 00 & 00 & 01 & 00 & 00 & 01 & 00 & 00 & 02 & 00 & 00 & 00
\end{pmatrix}
\tag{1}
$$

So, we consider two properties and four criteria for finding a matrix $A \in (GF(2^8) \cap \{0,1\})^{16 \times 16}$ as a diffusion layer.

Property 1. The matrix is binary involution matrix.

Property 2. The binary matrix is of branch number 8 and a cipher with the matrix is resisting against truncated and impossible differential cryptanalysis in reasonable rounds.

3.1 Criterion 1: Binary Matrix with Branch Number 8

Let we have an 128-bit SPN block cipher and $P = (a_1, a_2, \cdots, a_{16})$ be a input block of s-box layer where $a_i \in GF(2^8)$ for $i = 1, 2, \cdots, 16$. An s-box S_i is a function where

$$S_i : GF(2^8) \to GF(2^8) \tag{2}$$

and an s-box layer S is a function where

$$S : GF(2^8)^{16} \to GF(2^8)^{16}$$
$$(a_1, a_2, \cdots, a_{16}) \mapsto (S_1(a_1), S_2(a_2), \cdots, S_{16}(a_{16})).$$

We consider the following steps [6], which are L-type and M-type linear transformations as follows.

Let $S(P)$ be a 4×4 matrix with $S_i(a_i) \in GF(2^8)$ and

$$S(P) = \begin{pmatrix} S_1(a_1) & S_2(a_2) & S_3(a_3) & S_4(a_4) \\ S_5(a_5) & S_6(a_6) & S_7(a_7) & S_8(a_8) \\ S_9(a_9) & S_{10}(a_{10}) & S_{11}(a_{11}) & S_{12}(a_{12}) \\ S_{13}(a_{13}) & S_{14}(a_{14}) & S_{15}(a_{15}) & S_{16}(a_{16}) \end{pmatrix} = (C_1 \, C_2 \, C_3 \, C_4),$$

where $C_j = (S_j(a_j), S_{j+4}(a_{j+4}), S_{j+8}(a_{j+8}), S_{j+12}(a_{j+12}))^T \in GF(2^8)^4$, $j = 1, 2, 3, 4$.

Let $T = (S_1(a_1), S_2(a_2), \cdots, S_{16}(a_{16}))^T \in GF(2^8)^{16}$, and let $H = \{H_l | H_l = (h_{ij})_{4 \times 4}$ is a binary nonsingular matrix which has hamming weight 3 in each row and column, $l \in N, i, j = 1, 2, 3, 4\}$

1. Define a linear transformation L_l as

$$L_l = \begin{pmatrix} B_{11} & B_{12} & B_{13} & B_{14} \\ B_{21} & B_{22} & B_{23} & B_{24} \\ B_{31} & B_{32} & B_{33} & B_{34} \\ B_{41} & B_{42} & B_{43} & B_{44} \end{pmatrix}, \text{ where } B_{ij} = \begin{cases} I_{4 \times 4} & \text{if } h_{ij} = 1 \\ O_{4 \times 4} & \text{if } h_{ij} = 0 \end{cases},$$

h_{ij} is the (i, j)-component of H_l, $I_{4 \times 4}$ is a 4×4 identity matrix and $O_{4 \times 4}$ is an 4×4 zero matrix. We call L_l the L-type linear transformation. Notice that $L_l \cdot T$ is represented as

$$L_l \cdot T = \begin{pmatrix} H_l & 0 & 0 & 0 \\ 0 & H_l & 0 & 0 \\ 0 & 0 & H_l & 0 \\ 0 & 0 & 0 & H_l \end{pmatrix} \begin{pmatrix} C_1 \\ C_2 \\ C_3 \\ C_4 \end{pmatrix}, \text{ where } H_i \in H.$$

2. Define a linear transformation M_m as

$$M_m = \begin{pmatrix} H_{m_1} & 0 & 0 & 0 \\ 0 & H_{m_2} & 0 & 0 \\ 0 & 0 & H_{m_3} & 0 \\ 0 & 0 & 0 & H_{m_4} \end{pmatrix} \quad \text{where} \quad H_{m_k} \in H, \quad k = 1, 2, 3, 4.$$

We call M_m the M-type linear transformation.
3. Composition by multiplications as $A = L_l \cdot M_m \cdot L_{l'}$.

Notice that such a binary matrix A satisfies $A^T = A^{-1}$.

Remark 4. If $A = L_1 \cdot L_2 \cdots L_l$ for some $l \geq 1$, or $A = M_1 \cdot M_2 \cdots M_m$ for some $m \geq 1$, then the branch number of A is at most 4.

Two L and M-types linear transformations are multiplied for A to be the branch number greater than 4.

Remark 5. If $A = L_l \cdot M_m$ or $A = M_m \cdot L_l$, for some l, m, then the branch number of A is smaller than 8. Thus A is a multiple of at least 3 matrices as the following Form 1,2,3, and 4.

Form 1. $A = L_l \cdot M_m \cdot L_{l'}$.
  There exist l, m, l' such that A is a matrix of branch number 8 which we will find in this section.
Form 2. A is one of $L_l \cdot L_{l'} \cdot M_m$, $M_m \cdot L_l \cdot L_{l'}$, $M_m \cdot M_{m'} \cdot L_l$, $L_l \cdot M_m \cdot M_{m'}$.
  Since $L_l \cdot L_{l'}$ or $M_m \cdot M_{m'}$ is a permutation matrix, the branch number of A is at most 4.
Form 3. $A = M_m \cdot L_l \cdot M_{m'}$.
  If the branch number of A is 8, there is some disadvantage for 32-bit word implementation by comparing the Form 1 because M_m and $M_{m'}$ need extra operations to be implemented into 32-bit word operation.
Form 4. A is a multiple of more than 3 matrices.
  There are more operations to be applied for implementing A compared with the Form 1 and consider its cryptographic characteristics.

So we set a first criterion as follow.

Criterion 1. A binary matrix of branch number 8 is generated by $A = L_l \cdot M_m \cdot L_{l'}$.

The following Lemma follows from Definition 3.

Lemma 6. If two matrices A, B are permutation homomorphic to each other, then A, B are of the same branch number.

  Proof. Let ρ, γ be row and column permutations and $A \cdot x = y$ $(x, y \in Z_2^n)$, then $\rho(A)x = \rho(Ax) = \rho(y)$, $Ax = \gamma(A)(\gamma(x^T))^T = y$.
Since $w_H(x) = w_H(\gamma(x^T))$, $w_H(y) = w_H(\rho(x))$, A and $\gamma(\rho(A)) = \rho(\gamma(A)) = B$ are of the same branch number.

By the Lemma 6, the branch number is the same for any row or column permutation, thus there are many matrices of branch number 8, which have different forms and characteristics. Therefore, we will find a binary matrix of the form 1.

3.2   Criterion 2: Involution Binary Matrix

Key addition K, an s-box S, the inverse of the s-box S^{-1}, a matrix A and the inverse of the matrix A^{-1} are components of an involution SPN block cipher. In hardware application, only 4 components K, S, S^{-1} and A are required if A is involution.

From the method that has been discussed in Section 3.1, the binary matrix A represents a multiple of binary matrices as

$$L_l \cdot M_m \cdot L_{l'}. \tag{3}$$

If A is involution, then

$$A \cdot A = L_l \cdot M_m \cdot L_{l'} \cdot L_l \cdot M_m \cdot L_{l'} = I. \tag{4}$$

By the equation (4), we consider the following steps to find an involution binary matrix A.

Step 1. Find a symmetric L_l.
Step 2. Set $l = l'$.
Step 3. Find a symmetric M_m.

Note that L_l, M_m and $L_{l'}$ are involution binary matrices. So we set a second criterion as follow.

Criterion 2. An involution matrix A is the following form

$$A = L_l \cdot M_m \cdot L_l. \tag{5}$$

3.3   Criterion 3: Resistance against TDC

Truncated differential is a differential where only a part of the difference in the ciphertexts is predicted [7]. We measure the resistance against TDC attack [8] in considering hamming weights of byte patterns of input differences.

We assume that each s-box S_i in the substitution layer is arbitrary and the output differences of each S_i are considered as uniformly distributed which is

$$p(S_i(\Delta x_i) \oplus S_j(\Delta x_2) = 0) = \frac{1}{2^8 - 1} \approx \frac{1}{2^8}, \tag{6}$$

where S_i, S_j are two s-boxes and Δx_1, Δx_2 are input differences.

Setting a criterion for a TDC, let $\Delta x = (\Delta x_1, \Delta x_2, \cdots, \Delta x_{16})$ and $\Delta x_i = x_i \oplus x_i' \in GF(2^8)$ be the input differences of s-box S_i and let $\Delta \widetilde{x} = (\Delta \widetilde{x_1}, \Delta \widetilde{x_2}, \cdots, \Delta \widetilde{x_{16}})$ be the byte pattern of input differences of s-box where

$$\Delta \widetilde{x_i} = \begin{cases} 1 & \text{if } \Delta x_i \neq 0 \\ 0 & \text{otherwise} \end{cases} \tag{7}$$

From the assumption, we obtain 2^{16}-1 input byte patterns $\Delta \widetilde{x}$ of A and its output byte patterns $A(\Delta \widetilde{x})$. The probability of a given input and output difference of a round function is depending on the hamming weight of the byte patterns of input differences of s-box. And we need to find pairs of patterns of input and output differences of a round function which lead to a possible TDC attack. Let a "byte characteristic" be a pair of byte patterns of input and output differences of a round function. Thus we only investigate iterate differences for each round. Since A is involution, we know that $A^2(\Delta \widetilde{x}) = \Delta \widetilde{x}$. If 1-round iterate differences are ruled out for consideration, then there is no 3 or more rounds iterate difference. So we set a third criterion as follow.

Criterion 3. 1-round iterate byte characteristic needs to have as large hamming weights as possible.

Notice that let κ be the complexity of finding a 16×16 binary matrix with $A(\Delta \widetilde{x}) = \Delta \widetilde{x}$ where, $\Delta \widetilde{x} \in Z_2^{16}$, then the complexity of finding a 16×16 binary matrix with $A(\Delta \widetilde{y}) = \Delta \widetilde{y}$ where $\Delta \widetilde{y} \in Z_3^{16}$ is $O(\kappa^3)$.

3.4   Criterion 4: Resistance against IDC

Impossible differential attack uses differentials with probability 0, which are called impossible differentials [9].

Remark 7. *Let $X_i = (x_{i,1}, x_{i,2}, \cdots, x_{i,16})$ be input difference and $X_{i+1} = (x_{i+1,1}, x_{i+1,2}, \cdots, x_{i+1,16})$ be output difference of i-th round of an SPN where each $x_{i,j}$ represents "state" such as zero, nonzero, or unknown. unknown state is derived from two or more nonzero states and does not indicate useful information where impossible differentials are located.*

1. *If $x_{i,j}$ is unknown state for some j, then $x_{i+1,j'}$ is unknown state, where j' is related with j by a diffusion layer.*
2. *If $x_{i+k,j}$ is unknown states for each $j = 1, 2, \cdots, 16$ and for some i, then there is no impossible differential for more than $2k$-round.*

By the above Remark 7, we have the following criterion for finding a binary matrix which has no 4 or more rounds impossible differential characteristic.

Criterion 4. For any input difference $X_i = (x_{i,1}, x_{i,2}, \cdots, x_{i,16})$, there exist $k \leq 2$ such that $x_{i+k,j}$ is unknown state for each $j = 1, 2, \cdots, 16$.

3.5   The Results

Using the above Criteria 1, 2, 3, and 4, we find matrices L_l and M_m as follows.
Let

$$H_l = \begin{pmatrix} 1 & 1 & 1 & 0 \\ 1 & 0 & 1 & 1 \\ 1 & 1 & 0 & 1 \\ 0 & 1 & 1 & 1 \end{pmatrix} \quad \text{and}$$

$$H_{m1} = \begin{pmatrix} 0 & 1 & 1 & 1 \\ 1 & 0 & 1 & 1 \\ 1 & 1 & 0 & 1 \\ 1 & 1 & 1 & 0 \end{pmatrix}, H_{m2} = \begin{pmatrix} 1 & 0 & 1 & 1 \\ 0 & 1 & 1 & 1 \\ 1 & 1 & 1 & 0 \\ 1 & 1 & 0 & 1 \end{pmatrix}, H_{m3} = \begin{pmatrix} 1 & 1 & 0 & 1 \\ 1 & 1 & 1 & 0 \\ 0 & 1 & 1 & 1 \\ 1 & 0 & 1 & 1 \end{pmatrix}, H_{m4} = \begin{pmatrix} 1 & 1 & 1 & 0 \\ 1 & 1 & 0 & 1 \\ 1 & 0 & 1 & 1 \\ 0 & 1 & 1 & 1 \end{pmatrix}.$$

By the definition of L and M-type linear transformations, L_l and M_m are represented as follows;

$$L_l = \begin{pmatrix}
1 & 0 & 0 & 0 & 1 & 0 & 0 & 0 & 1 & 0 & 0 & 0 & 0 & 0 & 0 & 0 \\
0 & 1 & 0 & 0 & 0 & 1 & 0 & 0 & 0 & 1 & 0 & 0 & 0 & 0 & 0 & 0 \\
0 & 0 & 1 & 0 & 0 & 0 & 1 & 0 & 0 & 0 & 1 & 0 & 0 & 0 & 0 & 0 \\
0 & 0 & 0 & 1 & 0 & 0 & 0 & 1 & 0 & 0 & 0 & 1 & 0 & 0 & 0 & 0 \\
1 & 0 & 0 & 0 & 0 & 0 & 0 & 1 & 0 & 0 & 0 & 1 & 0 & 0 & 0 & 0 \\
0 & 1 & 0 & 0 & 0 & 0 & 0 & 0 & 1 & 0 & 0 & 0 & 1 & 0 & 0 \\
0 & 0 & 1 & 0 & 0 & 0 & 0 & 0 & 0 & 1 & 0 & 0 & 0 & 1 & 0 \\
0 & 0 & 0 & 1 & 0 & 0 & 0 & 0 & 0 & 0 & 1 & 0 & 0 & 0 & 1 \\
1 & 0 & 0 & 0 & 1 & 0 & 0 & 0 & 0 & 0 & 0 & 1 & 0 & 0 & 0 \\
0 & 1 & 0 & 0 & 0 & 1 & 0 & 0 & 0 & 0 & 0 & 0 & 1 & 0 & 0 \\
0 & 0 & 1 & 0 & 0 & 0 & 1 & 0 & 0 & 0 & 0 & 0 & 0 & 1 & 0 \\
0 & 0 & 0 & 1 & 0 & 0 & 0 & 1 & 0 & 0 & 0 & 0 & 0 & 0 & 1 \\
0 & 0 & 0 & 0 & 1 & 0 & 0 & 0 & 1 & 0 & 0 & 0 & 1 & 0 & 0 & 0 \\
0 & 0 & 0 & 0 & 0 & 1 & 0 & 0 & 0 & 1 & 0 & 0 & 0 & 1 & 0 & 0 \\
0 & 0 & 0 & 0 & 0 & 0 & 1 & 0 & 0 & 0 & 1 & 0 & 0 & 0 & 1 & 0 \\
0 & 0 & 0 & 0 & 0 & 0 & 0 & 1 & 0 & 0 & 0 & 1 & 0 & 0 & 0 & 1
\end{pmatrix}, M_m = \begin{pmatrix}
0 & 1 & 1 & 1 & 0 & 0 & 0 & 0 & 0 & 0 & 0 & 0 & 0 & 0 & 0 & 0 \\
1 & 0 & 1 & 1 & 0 & 0 & 0 & 0 & 0 & 0 & 0 & 0 & 0 & 0 & 0 & 0 \\
1 & 1 & 0 & 1 & 0 & 0 & 0 & 0 & 0 & 0 & 0 & 0 & 0 & 0 & 0 & 0 \\
1 & 1 & 1 & 0 & 0 & 0 & 0 & 0 & 0 & 0 & 0 & 0 & 0 & 0 & 0 & 0 \\
0 & 0 & 0 & 0 & 1 & 0 & 1 & 1 & 0 & 0 & 0 & 0 & 0 & 0 & 0 & 0 \\
0 & 0 & 0 & 0 & 0 & 1 & 1 & 1 & 0 & 0 & 0 & 0 & 0 & 0 & 0 & 0 \\
0 & 0 & 0 & 0 & 1 & 1 & 1 & 0 & 0 & 0 & 0 & 0 & 0 & 0 & 0 & 0 \\
0 & 0 & 0 & 0 & 1 & 1 & 0 & 1 & 0 & 0 & 0 & 0 & 0 & 0 & 0 & 0 \\
0 & 0 & 0 & 0 & 0 & 0 & 0 & 0 & 1 & 1 & 0 & 1 & 0 & 0 & 0 & 0 \\
0 & 0 & 0 & 0 & 0 & 0 & 0 & 0 & 1 & 1 & 1 & 0 & 0 & 0 & 0 & 0 \\
0 & 0 & 0 & 0 & 0 & 0 & 0 & 0 & 0 & 1 & 1 & 1 & 0 & 0 & 0 & 0 \\
0 & 0 & 0 & 0 & 0 & 0 & 0 & 0 & 1 & 0 & 1 & 1 & 0 & 0 & 0 & 0 \\
0 & 0 & 0 & 0 & 0 & 0 & 0 & 0 & 0 & 0 & 0 & 0 & 1 & 1 & 1 & 0 \\
0 & 0 & 0 & 0 & 0 & 0 & 0 & 0 & 0 & 0 & 0 & 0 & 1 & 1 & 0 & 1 \\
0 & 0 & 0 & 0 & 0 & 0 & 0 & 0 & 0 & 0 & 0 & 0 & 1 & 0 & 1 & 1 \\
0 & 0 & 0 & 0 & 0 & 0 & 0 & 0 & 0 & 0 & 0 & 0 & 0 & 1 & 1 & 1
\end{pmatrix}$$

By the criterion 1, we choose a matrix A as the followingg form.

$$A = L_l \cdot M_m \cdot L_l = \begin{pmatrix}
0 & 0 & 0 & 1 & 1 & 0 & 1 & 0 & 1 & 1 & 0 & 0 & 0 & 1 & 1 & 0 \\
0 & 0 & 1 & 0 & 0 & 1 & 0 & 1 & 1 & 1 & 0 & 0 & 1 & 0 & 0 & 1 \\
0 & 1 & 0 & 0 & 1 & 0 & 1 & 0 & 0 & 0 & 1 & 1 & 1 & 0 & 0 & 1 \\
1 & 0 & 0 & 0 & 0 & 1 & 0 & 1 & 0 & 0 & 1 & 1 & 0 & 1 & 1 & 0 \\
1 & 0 & 1 & 0 & 0 & 1 & 0 & 0 & 1 & 0 & 0 & 1 & 0 & 0 & 1 & 1 \\
0 & 1 & 0 & 1 & 1 & 0 & 0 & 0 & 0 & 1 & 1 & 0 & 0 & 0 & 1 & 1 \\
1 & 0 & 1 & 0 & 0 & 0 & 0 & 1 & 0 & 1 & 1 & 0 & 1 & 1 & 0 & 0 \\
0 & 1 & 0 & 1 & 0 & 0 & 1 & 0 & 1 & 0 & 0 & 1 & 1 & 1 & 0 & 0 \\
1 & 1 & 0 & 0 & 1 & 0 & 0 & 1 & 0 & 0 & 1 & 0 & 0 & 1 & 0 & 1 \\
1 & 1 & 0 & 0 & 0 & 1 & 1 & 0 & 0 & 0 & 0 & 1 & 1 & 0 & 1 & 0 \\
0 & 0 & 1 & 1 & 0 & 1 & 1 & 0 & 1 & 0 & 0 & 0 & 0 & 1 & 0 & 1 \\
0 & 0 & 1 & 1 & 1 & 0 & 0 & 1 & 0 & 1 & 0 & 0 & 1 & 0 & 1 & 0 \\
0 & 1 & 1 & 0 & 0 & 0 & 1 & 1 & 0 & 1 & 0 & 1 & 1 & 0 & 0 & 0 \\
1 & 0 & 0 & 1 & 0 & 0 & 1 & 1 & 1 & 0 & 1 & 0 & 0 & 1 & 0 & 0 \\
1 & 0 & 0 & 1 & 1 & 1 & 0 & 0 & 0 & 1 & 0 & 1 & 0 & 0 & 1 & 0 \\
0 & 1 & 1 & 0 & 1 & 1 & 0 & 0 & 1 & 0 & 1 & 0 & 0 & 0 & 0 & 1
\end{pmatrix} \tag{8}$$

The following Fig. 1 is an example of a round function of an SPN with the matrix A in (8) as a diffusion layer.

In the next section, we explain how to implement A into an 8-bit processor and give some techniques to reduce the number of operations for implementing A in (8) into 32-bit processor.

4   Implementation

4.1   8-Bit Processor

If the matrix A in (8) is implemented into 8-bit processor, then A is represented by byte XORs of binary vectors as follows ;

$$A \cdot x = y,$$

where $x = (x_1, x_2, \cdots, x_{16})^T$, $y = (y_1, y_2, \cdots, y_{16})^T$ with x_i, $y_i \in GF(2^8)$, $i = 1, 2, \cdots, 16$. Then,

$$
\begin{aligned}
y_1 &= x_4 \oplus x_5 \oplus x_7 \oplus x_9 \ \oplus x_{10} \oplus x_{14} \oplus x_{15} \\
y_2 &= x_3 \oplus x_6 \oplus x_8 \oplus x_9 \ \oplus x_{10} \oplus x_{13} \oplus x_{16} \\
y_3 &= x_2 \oplus x_5 \oplus x_7 \oplus x_{11} \oplus x_{12} \oplus x_{13} \oplus x_{16} \\
y_4 &= x_1 \oplus x_6 \oplus x_8 \oplus x_{11} \oplus x_{12} \oplus x_{14} \oplus x_{15} \\
y_5 &= x_1 \oplus x_3 \oplus x_6 \oplus x_9 \ \oplus x_{12} \oplus x_{15} \oplus x_{16} \\
y_6 &= x_2 \oplus x_4 \oplus x_5 \oplus x_{10} \oplus x_{11} \oplus x_{15} \oplus x_{16} \\
y_7 &= x_1 \oplus x_3 \oplus x_8 \oplus x_{10} \oplus x_{11} \oplus x_{13} \oplus x_{14} \\
y_8 &= x_2 \oplus x_4 \oplus x_7 \oplus x_9 \ \oplus x_{12} \oplus x_{13} \oplus x_{14} \\
y_9 &= x_1 \oplus x_2 \oplus x_5 \oplus x_8 \ \oplus x_{11} \oplus x_{14} \oplus x_{16} \\
y_{10} &= x_1 \oplus x_2 \oplus x_6 \oplus x_7 \ \oplus x_{12} \oplus x_{13} \oplus x_{15} \\
y_{11} &= x_3 \oplus x_4 \oplus x_6 \oplus x_7 \ \oplus x_9 \ \oplus x_{14} \oplus x_{16} \\
y_{12} &= x_3 \oplus x_4 \oplus x_5 \oplus x_8 \ \oplus x_{10} \oplus x_{13} \oplus x_{15} \\
y_{13} &= x_2 \oplus x_3 \oplus x_7 \oplus x_8 \ \oplus x_{10} \oplus x_{12} \oplus x_{13}
\end{aligned}
$$

$$
\begin{aligned}
y_{14} &= x_1 \oplus x_4 \oplus x_7 \oplus x_8 \oplus x_9 \ \oplus x_{11} \oplus x_{14} \\
y_{15} &= x_1 \oplus x_4 \oplus x_5 \oplus x_6 \oplus x_{10} \oplus x_{12} \oplus x_{15} \\
y_{16} &= x_2 \oplus x_3 \oplus x_5 \oplus x_6 \oplus x_9 \ \oplus x_{11} \oplus x_{16} \quad .
\end{aligned}
$$

Note that the total number of byte XOR operations can be reduced to 60 in each diffusion layer by a simple algebraic technique.

4.2   32-Bit Processor

For implementing into a 32-bit processor, AES is encoded by tables which are combined s-box layer with the diffusion layer [10]. So we apply this method to our diffusion layer.

As we explained by the equation in (5), A is represented as $A = L_l \cdot M_m \cdot L_l$. The s-box layer S is implemented into 16 times table-lookups. There are two cases for implementing $L_l \cdot M_m \cdot L_l$ as follows.

If we implement L-type linear transformation into 32-bit word operations, then we need to implement M-type linear transformation into table-lookups. If we implement M-type linear transformation into 32-bit word operations, then we need to implement L-type linear transformation into table-lookups.

The following table shows that the different number of operations are needed for implementing the above two cases.

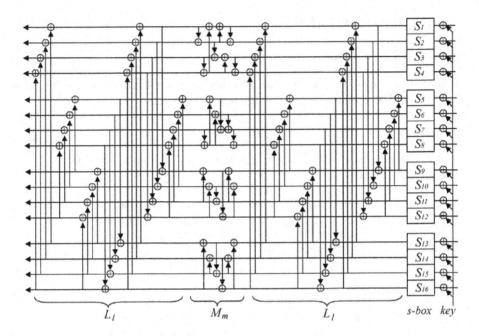

Fig. 1. An example of a round function with the matrix A as a diffusion layer

Table 1. Number of operations for $L_l \cdot M_m \cdot L_l$

$L_l M_m L_l$		Number of XORs	Number of table-lookups
Case 1.	L_l : Word XOR	8	16
	M_m : Table		
Case2.	L_l : Table	4	32
	M_m : Word XOR		

As described in the Table1, the Case 1. which is implementing L into word XOR's and M into table-lookups is more efficient than the Case 2.

By equation (5), we decide to implement M_m into 16 table-lookups. So, there are at least 32 table-lookups for 5 tables to implement $A \cdot S = L_l \cdot M_m \cdot L_l \cdot S$.

If we find a matrix E such that

$$M_m \cdot L_l \cdot S = E \cdot M_{m'} \cdot S, \tag{9}$$

where $M_{m'}$ is a M-type linear transformation which has the same blocks in the diagonal.

Then $M_{m'}$ and S can be combined into 16 table-lookups with 4 tables as described in [10].

Since $M_{m'}$ is a M-type linear transformation, there is a permutation matrix Q such that

$$M_{m'} = Q \cdot M_m.$$

Because of the algebraic structures of L and M-type linear transformations, there exists a permutation matrix P satisfying $M_m \cdot L_l = P \cdot L_l \cdot Q \cdot M_m$.

Therefore, the number of tables and lookups can be reduced by using permutation matrices P and Q such as

$$L_l \cdot M_m \cdot L_l \cdot S = L_l \cdot P \cdot L_l \cdot Q \cdot M_m \cdot S. \tag{10}$$

If P and Q are chosen as in (11), then just 4 tables and 16 table-lookups are needed by using $Q \cdot M_m \cdot S$ to implement A in (8).

$$P = \begin{pmatrix}
1 & 0 & 0 & 0 & 0 & 0 & 0 & 0 & 0 & 0 & 0 & 0 & 0 & 0 & 0 & 0 \\
0 & 1 & 0 & 0 & 0 & 0 & 0 & 0 & 0 & 0 & 0 & 0 & 0 & 0 & 0 & 0 \\
0 & 0 & 1 & 0 & 0 & 0 & 0 & 0 & 0 & 0 & 0 & 0 & 0 & 0 & 0 & 0 \\
0 & 0 & 0 & 1 & 0 & 0 & 0 & 0 & 0 & 0 & 0 & 0 & 0 & 0 & 0 & 0 \\
0 & 0 & 0 & 0 & 0 & 1 & 0 & 0 & 0 & 0 & 0 & 0 & 0 & 0 & 0 & 0 \\
0 & 0 & 0 & 0 & 1 & 0 & 0 & 0 & 0 & 0 & 0 & 0 & 0 & 0 & 0 & 0 \\
0 & 0 & 0 & 0 & 0 & 0 & 1 & 0 & 0 & 0 & 0 & 0 & 0 & 0 & 0 & 0 \\
0 & 0 & 0 & 0 & 0 & 0 & 0 & 1 & 0 & 0 & 0 & 0 & 0 & 0 & 0 & 0 \\
0 & 0 & 0 & 0 & 0 & 0 & 0 & 0 & 0 & 0 & 1 & 0 & 0 & 0 & 0 & 0 \\
0 & 0 & 0 & 0 & 0 & 0 & 0 & 0 & 0 & 0 & 0 & 1 & 0 & 0 & 0 & 0 \\
0 & 0 & 0 & 0 & 0 & 0 & 0 & 0 & 1 & 0 & 0 & 0 & 0 & 0 & 0 & 0 \\
0 & 0 & 0 & 0 & 0 & 0 & 0 & 0 & 0 & 1 & 0 & 0 & 0 & 0 & 0 & 0 \\
0 & 0 & 0 & 0 & 0 & 0 & 0 & 0 & 0 & 0 & 0 & 0 & 0 & 0 & 0 & 1 \\
0 & 0 & 0 & 0 & 0 & 0 & 0 & 0 & 0 & 0 & 0 & 0 & 0 & 0 & 1 & 0 \\
0 & 0 & 0 & 0 & 0 & 0 & 0 & 0 & 0 & 0 & 0 & 0 & 0 & 1 & 0 & 0 \\
0 & 0 & 0 & 0 & 0 & 0 & 0 & 0 & 0 & 0 & 0 & 0 & 1 & 0 & 0 & 0
\end{pmatrix}, Q = \begin{pmatrix}
1 & 0 & 0 & 0 & 0 & 0 & 0 & 0 & 0 & 0 & 0 & 0 & 0 & 0 & 0 & 0 \\
0 & 1 & 0 & 0 & 0 & 0 & 0 & 0 & 0 & 0 & 0 & 0 & 0 & 0 & 0 & 0 \\
0 & 0 & 1 & 0 & 0 & 0 & 0 & 0 & 0 & 0 & 0 & 0 & 0 & 0 & 0 & 0 \\
0 & 0 & 0 & 1 & 0 & 0 & 0 & 0 & 0 & 0 & 0 & 0 & 0 & 0 & 0 & 0 \\
0 & 0 & 0 & 0 & 0 & 1 & 0 & 0 & 0 & 0 & 0 & 0 & 0 & 0 & 0 & 0 \\
0 & 0 & 0 & 0 & 1 & 0 & 0 & 0 & 0 & 0 & 0 & 0 & 0 & 0 & 0 & 0 \\
0 & 0 & 0 & 0 & 0 & 0 & 1 & 0 & 0 & 0 & 0 & 0 & 0 & 0 & 0 & 0 \\
0 & 0 & 0 & 0 & 0 & 1 & 0 & 0 & 0 & 1 & 0 & 0 & 0 & 0 & 0 & 0 \\
0 & 0 & 0 & 0 & 0 & 0 & 0 & 0 & 0 & 0 & 1 & 0 & 0 & 0 & 0 & 0 \\
0 & 0 & 0 & 0 & 0 & 0 & 0 & 0 & 1 & 0 & 0 & 0 & 0 & 0 & 0 & 0 \\
0 & 0 & 0 & 0 & 0 & 0 & 0 & 0 & 0 & 1 & 0 & 0 & 0 & 0 & 0 & 0 \\
0 & 0 & 0 & 0 & 0 & 0 & 0 & 0 & 0 & 0 & 0 & 0 & 0 & 0 & 0 & 1 \\
0 & 0 & 0 & 0 & 0 & 0 & 0 & 0 & 0 & 0 & 0 & 0 & 0 & 0 & 1 & 0 \\
0 & 0 & 0 & 0 & 0 & 0 & 0 & 0 & 0 & 0 & 0 & 0 & 0 & 1 & 0 & 0 \\
0 & 0 & 0 & 0 & 0 & 0 & 0 & 0 & 0 & 0 & 0 & 0 & 1 & 0 & 0 & 0
\end{pmatrix} \tag{11}$$

$$Q \cdot M_m = \begin{pmatrix}
0 & 1 & 1 & 1 & 0 & 0 & 0 & 0 & 0 & 0 & 0 & 0 & 0 & 0 & 0 & 0 \\
1 & 0 & 1 & 1 & 0 & 0 & 0 & 0 & 0 & 0 & 0 & 0 & 0 & 0 & 0 & 0 \\
1 & 1 & 0 & 1 & 0 & 0 & 0 & 0 & 0 & 0 & 0 & 0 & 0 & 0 & 0 & 0 \\
1 & 1 & 1 & 0 & 0 & 0 & 0 & 0 & 0 & 0 & 0 & 0 & 0 & 0 & 0 & 0 \\
0 & 0 & 0 & 0 & 0 & 1 & 1 & 1 & 0 & 0 & 0 & 0 & 0 & 0 & 0 & 0 \\
0 & 0 & 0 & 0 & 1 & 0 & 1 & 1 & 0 & 0 & 0 & 0 & 0 & 0 & 0 & 0 \\
0 & 0 & 0 & 0 & 1 & 1 & 0 & 1 & 0 & 0 & 0 & 0 & 0 & 0 & 0 & 0 \\
0 & 0 & 0 & 0 & 1 & 1 & 1 & 0 & 0 & 0 & 0 & 0 & 0 & 0 & 0 & 0 \\
0 & 0 & 0 & 0 & 0 & 0 & 0 & 0 & 0 & 1 & 1 & 1 & 0 & 0 & 0 & 0 \\
0 & 0 & 0 & 0 & 0 & 0 & 0 & 0 & 1 & 0 & 1 & 1 & 0 & 0 & 0 & 0 \\
0 & 0 & 0 & 0 & 0 & 0 & 0 & 0 & 1 & 1 & 0 & 1 & 0 & 0 & 0 & 0 \\
0 & 0 & 0 & 0 & 0 & 0 & 0 & 0 & 1 & 1 & 1 & 0 & 0 & 0 & 0 & 0 \\
0 & 0 & 0 & 0 & 0 & 0 & 0 & 0 & 0 & 0 & 0 & 0 & 0 & 1 & 1 & 1 \\
0 & 0 & 0 & 0 & 0 & 0 & 0 & 0 & 0 & 0 & 0 & 0 & 1 & 0 & 1 & 1 \\
0 & 0 & 0 & 0 & 0 & 0 & 0 & 0 & 0 & 0 & 0 & 0 & 1 & 1 & 0 & 1 \\
0 & 0 & 0 & 0 & 0 & 0 & 0 & 0 & 0 & 0 & 0 & 0 & 1 & 1 & 1 & 0
\end{pmatrix}$$

Notice that the form of $Q \cdot M_m \cdot S$ is implemented into 16 table-lookups and matrices L_l, P are implemented into simple forms such as 32-bit word XOR operations. Using the equation in (10), the number of table-lookups are reduced to 16 with 4 tables.

5 Cryptanalysis for an SPN Block Cipher with the Matrix A as a Diffusion Layer

We find a binary matrix A which satisfies Property 1 and 2 as we have discussed in Section 3. We analyze an SPN block cipher with the matrix A that we have found as a diffusion layer as follows.

5.1   Resistance against Differential and Linear Cryptanalysis

We consider a $2r$-round SPN with the 16×16 binary matrix of branch number 8 as a diffusion layer. If the maximum probability for a differential characteristic and a linear approximation of s-box is 2^{-6}, then the maximum probabilities [5] for a differential characteristic and a linear approximation of a $2r$-round SPN block cipher are

$$P_D^{2r} \le (2^{-6})^{(r \times 8)}, \qquad P_L^{2r} \le (2^{-6})^{(r \times 8)}.$$

And if 128-bit key is used, then the minimum number of rounds to be secure against differential and linear cryptanalysis is at least 6. The TABLE 2 shows a lower bound on the number of active s-boxes in each round. Also, we obtain upper bounds of probabilities for differential characteristics and linear approximations as follows where the maximum probability for a differential characteristic and a linear approximation of an active s-box is 2^{-6}.

Table 2. A lower bound on the number of active S-boxes, probabilities for a differential characteristic and bias for a linear approximation.

Rounds	A lower bound on the number of active s-boxes	Probability for a differential characteristic	Bias for a linear approximation
2	8	2^{-48}	2^{-48}
3	9	2^{-54}	2^{-54}
4	16	2^{-96}	2^{-96}
5	17	2^{-102}	2^{-102}
6	24	2^{-144}	2^{-144}
7	25	2^{-150}	2^{-150}
8	32	2^{-192}	2^{-192}
9	33	2^{-198}	2^{-198}
10	40	2^{-240}	2^{-240}

5.2   Cryptanalysis against Truncated Differential Attack

As defined $\Delta \tilde{x}$ in (7), we consider $\Delta \tilde{x}$ is an input of the diffusion layer A. By the assumption (6) in the Section 3.3, the probability p_r of an iterate difference can be estimated for r-round as the following [8].

$$p_r \approx (2^{-8})^{w_H(\Delta \tilde{x}^1)-1} \times \cdots \times (2^{-8})^{w_H(\Delta \tilde{x}^r)-1}$$
$$= (2^{-8})^{w_H(\Delta \tilde{x}^1)+\cdots+w_H(\Delta \tilde{x}^r)-r}, \tag{12}$$

where $\Delta \tilde{x}^1$ is the byte pattern of an input difference and $\Delta \tilde{x}^{i+1} = A(\Delta \tilde{x}^i)$ is the byte pattern of the output difference.

By investigating all byte pattern $\Delta \tilde{x}$ of input differences with the matrix A in (8), we summarize the cases of iterate differences and estimated probabilities as follows.

- The minimum hamming weight of byte patterns of input differences in 1-round iterate byte characteristics is 4 and those estimated probability is 2^{-24}.
- A byte characteristic is a 2-round byte characteristic because A is involution. Since the branch number of A is 8, an upper bound of estimated probability for 2-round byte characteristic is 2^{-48}.
- There is no 3 or more rounds iterate byte characteristic because the matrix A is involution.

In the above summary, the probabilities are estimated under the assumption that output differences of each s-box are random. Notice that the probability can be changed according to the s-box layer.

5.3 Cryptanalysis against Impossible Differential Attack

Resisting against impossible differential attack, we need to consider patterns of "state" of 2-round for any input state that zero state is denoted by "0" and nonzero state is denoted by "1". In our simulations, for all input states, every byte of 2-round output state is unknown state. Thus, an SPN block cipher with the matrix A has no 4 or more rounds impossible differential characteristic. The number in each byte position as in Table 3 is the number of previous nonzero byte position affecting the current byte position.

6   Conclusion

In this paper, we construct a 16×16 involution binary matrix A of branch number 8 which is known to be the maximum branch number and estimat cryptographic strength of an SPN cipher which uses A as a diffusion layer. We compare the number of operations with the other diffusion layer such as AES.

6.1   Comparison with Round Functions of Other Ciphers

To compare with AES, we consider a round function as we described in Fig.2. In Section 5, we showed that the minimum number of rounds to be secure against DC and LC is 6. We set the total number of rounds 8, which is the minimum number of rounds derived from [11]. We call the SPN-A is an SPN block cipher as described in Section 3.5. We give some basic theoretic numbers for measuring computational complexities of two SPN block ciphers. The followings are the comparison with results of the number of operations for 8-bit and 32-bit processors.

Table 3. The byte pattern of 2-rounds for 16 input byte differences which are hamming weight 1.

Input	(1000 0000 0000 0000)	(0100 0000 0000 0000)	(0010 0000 0000 0000)
1-round result	(0001 1010 1100 0110)	(0010 0101 1100 1001)	(0100 1010 0011 1001)
2-round result	(7222 2424 2244 2442)	(2722 4242 2244 4224)	(2272 2424 4422 4224)
Input	(0001 0000 0000 0000)	(0000 1000 0000 0000)	(0000 0100 0000 0000)
1-round result	(1000 0101 0011 0110)	(1010 0100 1001 0011)	(0101 1000 0110 0011)
2-round result	(2227 4242 4422 2442)	(2424 7222 2442 2244)	(4242 2722 4224 2244)
Input	(0000 0010 0000 0000)	(0000 0001 0000 0000)	(0000 0000 1000 0000)
1-round result	(1010 0001 0110 1100)	(0101 0010 1001 1100)	(1100 1001 0010 0101)
2-round result	(2424 2272 4224 4422)	(4242 2227 2442 4422)	(2244 2442 7222 2424)
Input	(0000 0000 0100 0000)	(0000 0000 0010 0000)	(0000 0000 0001 0000)
1-round result	(1100 0110 0001 1010)	(0011 0110 1000 0101)	(0011 1001 0100 1010)
2-round result	(2244 4224 2722 4242)	(4422 4224 2272 2424)	(4422 2442 2227 4242)
Input	(0000 0000 0000 1000)	(0000 0000 0000 0100)	(0000 0000 0000 0010)
1-round result	(0110 0011 0101 1000)	(1001 0011 1010 0100)	(1001 1100 0101 0010)
2-round result	(2442 2244 2424 7222)	(4224 2244 4242 2722)	(4224 4422 2424 2272)
Input	(0000 0000 0000 0001)		
1-round result	(0110 1100 1010 0001)		
2-round result	(2442 4422 4242 2227)		

Table 4. 8-bit processor

Cipher name	Input size of round function	Number of XOR per round	Number of table-lookups per round
AES-128	128-bit	140	16
SPN-A	128-bit	76	16

Table 5. 32-bit processor

Cipher name	Input size of round function	Number of XORs per round	Number of table-lookups per round	Number of shift operation
AES-128	128-bit	16	16	12
SPN-A	128-bit	23	16	20

In 8-bit processor, as described in Table 3, the total number of operations in the SPN-A is less than the AES. In 32-bit processor, as described in Table 4, the total number of operations in the AES-128 is less than the SPN-A.

As described in Table 4 and 5, the SPN -A is more efficient in 8-bit processor applications and the AES-128 is more efficient in 32-bit processor applications.

6.2   Future Works

Authors are working on designing an involution SPN block cipher with the A as a diffusion layer. In addition, we need to find various types of truncated differential characteristics and cryptanalyze with those characteristics for the future work.

References

1. C.E. Shannon 'Communication theory of secrecy systems'. Bell Systems Technical Journal, Vol.28, pp. 656–715, 1949.
2. H.M. Heys and S.E. Tavares. *'Avalanche characteristics of substitution-permutation encryption networks'*. IEEE Trans. Comp., Vol. 44, pp.1131–1139, Sept. 1995.
3. Simon Litsyn, E. M. Rains, N. J. A. Sloane. available at http://www.math.unl.edu/ djaffe/codes/webcodes/codeform.html
4. Kanda, M., Takashima, Y., Matsumoto, T., Aoki, K., and Ohta, K. *'A strategy for construction fast round functions with practical security against differential and linear cryptanalysis'*. Selected Areas in Cryptography-SAC'98, LNCS 1556, (Springer-Verlag, 1999), pp.264–279.
5. Kanda, *'Practical Security Evaluation against Differential and Linear Cryptanalysis for Feistel Ciphers with SPN Round Function'*, Selected Areas in Cryptography 2000: 324–338
6. Bonwook Koo, Junghwan Song. *'Construction a diffusion layer in SPN structure against differential and linear cryptanalysis'*, Proceedings of KIISC conference Region Chung-Cheong, 2002, pp. 23–39.
7. Lars.R.Knudsen, *'Truncated and Higher Order Differentials'*, Fast Software Encryption Second International Workshop, Lecture Notes in Computer Science 1008, pp.196–211, Springer-Verlag, 1995.
8. NTT Laboratories. *'Security of E2 against Truncated Differential Cryptanalysis(in progress)'*. 1999, available at http://info.isl.ntt.co.jp/e2/RelDocs/
9. Kazumaro Aoki, Masayuki Kanda. *'Search for impossible Differential of E2'*. 1999, available at http://csrc.nist.gov/CryptoToolkit/aes/round1/pubcmnts.htm
10. J.Daemen, V.Rijmen. *'AES proposal:Rijndael(Version 2)'*. Available at NIST AES website http://csrc.nist.gov/encryption/aes, 1999.
11. Lars.R.Knudsen, *'The Number of Rounds in Block Ciphers'*, NESSIE public reports, NES/DOC/UIB/WP3/003/a, Available at http://www.cosic.esat.kuleuven.ac.be/nessie/reports/, 2000.

Author Index

Lecture Notes in Computer Science

For information about Vols. 1–2844
please contact your bookseller or Springer-Verlag

Vol. 2845: B. Christianson, B. Crispo, J.A. Malcolm, M. Roe (Eds.), Security Protocols. Proceedings, 2002. VIII, 243 pages. 2004.

Vol. 2847: R. de Lemos, T.S. Weber, J.B. Camargo Jr. (Eds.), Dependable Computing. Proceedings, 2003. XIV, 371 pages. 2003.

Vol. 2848: F.E. Fich (Ed.), Distributed Computing. Proceedings, 2003. X, 367 pages. 2003.

Vol. 2849: N. García, J.M. Martínez, L. Salgado (Eds.), Visual Content Processing and Representation. Proceedings, 2003. XII, 352 pages. 2003.

Vol. 2850: M.Y. Vardi, A. Voronkov (Eds.), Logic for Programming, Artificial Intelligence, and Reasoning. Proceedings, 2003. XIII, 437 pages. 2003. (Subseries LNAI)

Vol. 2851: C. Boyd, W. Mao (Eds.), Information Security. Proceedings, 2003. XI, 443 pages. 2003.

Vol. 2852: F.S. de Boer, M.M. Bonsangue, S. Graf, W.-P. de Roever (Eds.), Formal Methods for Components and Objects. Proceedings, 2003. VIII, 509 pages. 2003.

Vol. 2853: M. Jeckle, L.-J. Zhang (Eds.), Web Services – ICWS-Europe 2003. Proceedings, 2003. VIII, 227 pages. 2003.

Vol. 2854: J. Hoffmann, Utilizing Problem Structure in Planning. XIII, 251 pages. 2003. (Subseries LNAI)

Vol. 2855: R. Alur, I. Lee (Eds.), Embedded Software. Proceedings, 2003. X, 373 pages. 2003.

Vol. 2856: M. Smirnov, E. Biersack, C. Blondia, O. Bonaventure, O. Casals, G. Karlsson, George Pavlou, B. Quoitin, J. Roberts, I. Stavrakakis, B. Stiller, P. Trimintzios, P. Van Mieghem (Eds.), Quality of Future Internet Services. IX, 293 pages. 2003.

Vol. 2857: M.A. Nascimento, E.S. de Moura, A.L. Oliveira (Eds.), String Processing and Information Retrieval. Proceedings, 2003. XI, 379 pages. 2003.

Vol. 2858: A. Veidenbaum, K. Joe, H. Amano, H. Aiso (Eds.), High Performance Computing. Proceedings, 2003. XV, 566 pages. 2003.

Vol. 2859: B. Apolloni, M. Marinaro, R. Tagliaferri (Eds.), Neural Nets. Proceedings, 2003. X, 376 pages. 2003.

Vol. 2860: D. Geist, E. Tronci (Eds.), Correct Hardware Design and Verification Methods. Proceedings, 2003. XII, 426 pages. 2003.

Vol. 2861: C. Bliek, C. Jermann, A. Neumaier (Eds.), Global Optimization and Constraint Satisfaction. Proceedings, 2002. XII, 239 pages. 2003.

Vol. 2862: D. Feitelson, L. Rudolph, U. Schwiegelshohn (Eds.), Job Scheduling Strategies for Parallel Processing. Proceedings, 2003. VII, 269 pages. 2003.

Vol. 2863: P. Stevens, J. Whittle, G. Booch (Eds.), «UML» 2003 – The Unified Modeling Language. Proceedings, 2003. XIV, 415 pages. 2003.

Vol. 2864: A.K. Dey, A. Schmidt, J.F. McCarthy (Eds.), UbiComp 2003: Ubiquitous Computing. Proceedings, 2003. XVII, 368 pages. 2003.

Vol. 2865: S. Pierre, M. Barbeau, E. Kranakis (Eds.), Ad-Hoc, Mobile, and Wireless Networks. Proceedings, 2003. X, 293 pages. 2003.

Vol. 2866: J. Akiyama, M. Kano (Eds.), Discrete and Computational Geometry. Proceedings, 2002. VIII, 285 pages. 2003.

Vol. 2867: M. Brunner, A. Keller (Eds.), Self-Managing Distributed Systems. Proceedings, 2003. XIII, 274 pages. 2003.

Vol. 2868: P. Perner, R. Brause, H.-G. Holzhütter (Eds.), Medical Data Analysis. Proceedings, 2003. VIII, 127 pages. 2003.

Vol. 2869: A. Yazici, C. Şener (Eds.), Computer and Information Sciences – ISCIS 2003. Proceedings, 2003. XIX, 1110 pages. 2003.

Vol. 2870: D. Fensel, K. Sycara, J. Mylopoulos (Eds.), The Semantic Web - ISWC 2003. Proceedings, 2003. XV, 931 pages. 2003.

Vol. 2871: N. Zhong, Z.W. Raś, S. Tsumoto, E. Suzuki (Eds.), Foundations of Intelligent Systems. Proceedings, 2003. XV, 697 pages. 2003. (Subseries LNAI)

Vol. 2873: J. Lawry, J. Shanahan, A. Ralescu (Eds.), Modelling with Words. XIII, 229 pages. 2003. (Subseries LNAI)

Vol. 2874: C. Priami (Ed.), Global Computing. Proceedings, 2003. XIX, 255 pages. 2003.

Vol. 2875: E. Aarts, R. Collier, E. van Loenen, B. de Ruyter (Eds.), Ambient Intelligence. Proceedings, 2003. XI, 432 pages. 2003.

Vol. 2876: M. Schroeder, G. Wagner (Eds.), Rules and Rule Markup Languages for the Semantic Web. Proceedings, 2003. VII, 173 pages. 2003.

Vol. 2877: T. Böhme, G. Heyer, H. Unger (Eds.), Innovative Internet Community Systems. Proceedings, 2003. VIII, 263 pages. 2003.

Vol. 2878: R.E. Ellis, T.M. Peters (Eds.), Medical Image Computing and Computer-Assisted Intervention - MICCAI 2003. Part I. Proceedings, 2003. XXXIII, 819 pages. 2003.

Vol. 2879: R.E. Ellis, T.M. Peters (Eds.), Medical Image Computing and Computer-Assisted Intervention - MICCAI 2003. Part II. Proceedings, 2003. XXXIV, 1003 pages. 2003.

Vol. 2880: H.L. Bodlaender (Ed.), Graph-Theoretic Concepts in Computer Science. Proceedings, 2003. XI, 386 pages. 2003.

Vol. 2881: E. Horlait, T. Magedanz, R.H. Glitho (Eds.), Mobile Agents for Telecommunication Applications. Proceedings, 2003. IX, 297 pages. 2003.

Vol. 2882: D. Veit, Matchmaking in Electronic Markets. XV, 180 pages. 2003. (Subseries LNAI)

Vol. 2883: J. Schaeffer, M. Müller, Y. Björnsson (Eds.), Computers and Games. Proceedings, 2002. XI, 431 pages. 2003.